Reading Problems: Assessment and Teaching Strategies

FOURTH EDITION

Reading Problems: Assessment and Teaching Strategies

Margaret Ann Richek

Northeastern Illinois University

JoAnne Schudt Caldwell

Cardinal Stritch University

Joyce Holt Jennings

Northeastern Illinois University

Janet W. Lerner

Northeastern Illinois University

Allyn and Bacon

Boston ▪ London ▪ Toronto ▪ Sydney ▪ Tokyo ▪ Singapore

This book is dedicated to our parents and teachers who shared their love of reading with us and to our students who inspire us to keep sharing that love with them.

Series Editor: Aurora Martinez
Editor-in-Chief: Paul Smith
Editorial Assistant: Beth Slater
Marketing Manager: Brad Park
Editorial-Production Coordinator: Mary Beth Finch
Editorial-Production Service: Modern Graphics, Inc.
Composition and Prepress Buyer: Linda Cox
Electronic Composition: Modern Graphics, Inc.
Manufacturing Buyer: Julie McNeill

Copyright © 2002, 1996, 1989, 1983: by Allyn & Bacon
A Pearson Education Company
75 Arlington St.
Boston, Massachusetts 02116

Internet: www.ablongman.com

Library of Congress Cataloging-in-Publication Data

Reading problems : assessment and teaching strategies / Margaret Ann Richek . . . [et al.].--4th ed.
    p. cm.
Includes bibliographical references and indexes.
ISBN 0-205-33022-3
1. Reading disability. 2. Reading--Remedial teaching. I. Richek, Margaret Ann.

LB1050.5 .R53 2001
372.43--dc21

                                                       00-050799

Printed in the United States of America

10 9 8 7 6 5 4 3 2 1   05 04 03 02 01 00

CONTENTS

List of Snapshot Strategies

PREFACE

This book is concerned with helping the many children, adolescents, and adults who encounter difficulty with reading. Designed as a text for both undergraduate and graduate students, *Reading Problems: Assessment and Teaching Strategies* guides prospective and present teachers in assessing and teaching students with reading problems.

Reading Problems is a comprehensive survey of teaching strategies, formal and informal assessment, theory, and research. The reader will find information both from the field of reading and from allied fields, such as special education, bilingual education, medical science, and policy studies. Together, these areas provide a coherent framework for helping students with reading problems.

The fourth edition of *Reading Problems* combines new approaches with time-tested ones to provide teachers a wide variety of approaches from which to choose. Recent research has clarified the reading process and substantiated effective instructional strategies. New insights provide a rich source of innovative diagnostic and teaching methods.

Most of all, we want *Reading Problems* to be a valuable resource for teachers. Hundreds of instructional strategies are presented for immediate use by teachers. Many of the strategies are illustrated by "Strategy Snapshots" depicting examples of actual classroom use. These snapshots are from our own experiences in working with students in the Reading Centers at our universities and with teachers and students in schools.

Chapters 1 through 4 present general information about the reading process and students with reading problems, the use of interviews to obtain information about correlates of reading disabilities, and an overview of assessment, including informal assessment with an emphasis on the vast amount of information gained through an informal reading inventory.

Chapters 5 through 11 provide in-depth information about language processes, including emergent literacy, listening comprehension, word recognition, meaning vocabulary, and writing. Each chapter includes specific tools for assessment in these areas followed by principles of teaching and extensive practical instructional strategies.

Chapter 12, new to the fourth edition, discusses successful reading intervention programs, including Reading Recovery™ and Success for All. Teachers can use this information to choose a program or to think about developing their own intervention plans.

Chapter 13 presents guidelines, strategies, and materials that have proven effective for teaching in multicultural, multilingual, and multiage instructional settings. Chapter 14 discusses the correlates of reading disabilities, including recent research in these areas. Chapter 15 provides ideas for instructional options for severely disabled readers. Chapter 16 is an in-depth look at available resources for assessing reading performance and potential.

The appendices provide many resources. Appendix A presents instructional materials useful in building a positive, rich literacy environment. Appendix B provides an extensive annotated list of available tests. Appendix C includes information for contacting prominent publishers of instructional and diagnostic materials. Appendix D presents the *Jennings Informal Reading Assessment*, an informal reading inventory developed specifically for this text. Field-testing has shown that the natural-sounding text and topics appeal to children of various ages. Please feel free to duplicate any components of the test to use with your students.

Many people have contributed to this book. We wish to thank the reading professionals who deepened and extended our understanding of issues and strategies by taking the time to answer personal inquiries. We thank the graduate students, undergraduate students, and children we have worked with for giving us feedback on instructional strategies. The indispensible Sandy Weiss worked tirelessly to ensure accuracy and consistency. The staff at Allyn and Bacon, including Patrice Mailloux, Mary Beth Finch, Aurora Martinez, and Arnis Burvikovs, provided invaluable assistance in developing this manuscript.

Margaret Ann Richek
JoAnne Schudt Caldwell
Joyce Holt Jennings
Janet W. Lerner

1 Reading Ability and Disability

Introduction

Who has a reading problem? To help answer this question, we describe five students who were brought to our Reading Center:

- **Jason's** mother began to suspect that her son was not developing normally during his early years. He was later than other children in sitting by himself, crawling, and walking. He was slow in talking, and his speech was difficult to understand. Jason's concerned parents took several measures to help him, including obtaining speech therapy, participating in a motor training program, and delaying his entrance to school by enrolling him in preschool for an extra year. These steps did not eliminate Jason's problems. At the age of 11, when he was in the fifth grade, Jason entered our Reading Center. By this time, he was falling behind his classmates, both socially and academically. While the rest of his class read from a literature series, Jason was struggling with the easy-to-read book *Curious George*.
- **Diane** was born to a substance-addicted mother. At age eight, she was brought to our Reading Center by her grandmother. Identified as a special education student, Diane had extreme difficulty reading even the simplest material. Her teachers were confounded and frustrated with her poor achievement and lack of self-discipline. They had given up even attempting to teach her to read.
- **Ilya** was a child in a family of struggling Russian immigrants. He did not go to kindergarten because his parents could not make the necessary arrangements. Ilya seemed to be intelligent and able, but he was not proficient in English. By the time he entered our Reading Center at the end of first grade, he was half a year behind his classmates.
- **Gail's** mother became concerned when her daughter's once-excellent grades began to fall in fourth grade. She was having difficulty in science and social studies. Gail was confused by the difficult words, sentences, and concepts in her textbooks.
- **Roy**, an adolescent classified as a special education student, had many learning problems. Despite his teachers' best efforts, he had entered high school with a second-grade reading level. He came to our Reading Center when he was unable to pass the written examination for a driver's license.

For Roy, coming for assistance was a desperate cry for help before he completed high school.

This book is dedicated to these five youngsters and to the many other students who have attended our Reading Center. Although reading problems are a national concern, each child (or adult) faces the failure to read individually. For many, the results are heartbreaking. Reading problems can devastate students and their families. In school, these children are forced to face their inadequacies day after day and are often rejected by teachers and peers. Students with reading problems may be fed a daily diet of textbooks they cannot read and homework they cannot do. In response, they may turn to misbehavior or simply give up, displaying what is called *learned helplessness*. Not surprisingly, poor readers often suffer from low self-esteem. As these children mature, they often find that the doors to personal enrichment and career opportunities are closed to them.

Educators, parents, physicians, and psychologists as well as society in general share a concern about individuals who do not learn to read. However, the primary responsibility for reading instruction belongs to teaching professionals. The teacher is the coordinator and deliverer of instructional services, the person most able to help youngsters with reading problems. Throughout our nation, hundreds of thousands of classroom teachers, reading teachers, and special education teachers help these students read better and enjoy reading.

This book helps teachers to instruct children like Jason, Diane, Ilya, Gail, and Roy. It contains many instructional strategies and diagnostic tools that teachers may use to understand and aid students in their struggles to read. To do something well, people must enjoy doing it. Hence, inspiring a love of reading is important. For this reason, our book also refers to children's literature and materials that help students realize the wealth of information and enjoyment that reading can provide. The strategies and materials we present in this book have helped these five youngsters and countless others. We hope that the students you teach will also benefit from them.

Reading Problems: A National Dilemma

Although teaching is a personal activity, professionals need to understand the overall situation of reading problems. For this reason, having focused on students as individuals in the previous section, we now need to consider reading problems from a national perspective.

Society suffers when citizens cannot read adequately. People with low reading levels comprise many of the unemployed, high school dropouts, the poor, and those convicted of crimes. The problems of our schools, the growth of poverty, and the loss of family values all show some association with poor reading.

Illiteracy is debilitating. If children in a modern society do not learn to read, they cannot succeed in life. A few generations ago, people managed to get along reasonably well in the business and social worlds without literacy skills, a situation no longer possible in today's world. Students face more mandatory tests required by federal, state, and local laws than ever before. Periods of compulsory education are longer, and students need diplomas and degrees to obtain jobs. These hurdles, as well as the necessity of filling out application forms and taking licensing examinations, make life for the poor reader uncomfortable and, indeed, full of impassable barriers.

Teachers often hear that "children must learn to read so that later they can read to learn." In fact, because reading is the basic requirement for all academic subjects, failure in school can often be traced to inadequate reading skills. Poor reading leads to many problems. Opportunities for gainful employment decrease for poor readers. Youth who drop out of high school have twice the unemployment rate, few opportunities for continued training, and inadequate qualifications for postsecondary school or college (Gerber, 1997).

National Reading Levels

How serious is the problem of illiteracy in the United States? National longitudinal studies show that more than 17.5 percent of the nation's schoolchildren—about one million children—will encounter reading problems in the crucial first three years of their schooling (National Reading Panel, 1999). Accumulating evidence shows that many of America's schoolchildren are not mastering essential reading skills. The National Assessment of Education Progress (NAEP), national tests that follow student learning, show that more than 40 percent of fourth-grade students performed below basic reading levels. More than 10 percent of fourth-grade children could not even participate in the NAEP test because of their severe reading difficulties. Further, these problems persisted even in upper grades: 26 percent of eighth graders and 23 percent of eleventh graders read below basic levels. Among 17 year olds, only 33 percent were able to understand complex information, and only 3 percent were reading at the highest level of understanding (Donahue, P. L., Voelkl, K. E., Campbell, J. R., & Mazzeo, J., 1999; National Assessment of Educational Progress, 1999; National Reading Panel, 1999; National Institute of Child Health and Human Development, 1999).

Overall, the statistics about illiteracy are dismal. The National Audit Literacy Survey (U.S. Department of Education, 1994) and the National Longitudinal Transition Study (Blackorby & Wagner, 1997) report that:

- 85 percent of delinquent children and 75 percent of adult prison inmates are illiterate.
- 90 million adults are, at best, functionally literate.
- The cost to taxpayers of adult illiteracy is $224 billion a year in welfare payments, crime, job incompetence, lost taxes, and remedial education.
- U.S. companies lose nearly $40 billion annually because of illiteracy.
- Adults on the lowest level of the literacy scale comprise 44 percent of the

population and are more likely to live in poverty than adults at higher levels of literacy.

Reading Needs in Today's World

In today's world, high technology and automation have spurred a demand for highly trained people. Because jobs rapidly become obsolete, the process of retraining is a necessity. Workers in every occupation will have to retrain themselves to prepare for new jobs many times during their work careers. The ability to read efficiently is a key tool for retraining and maintaining employment.

Because fewer jobs will be available for unskilled and semiskilled workers, they are likely to end up being chronically unemployed. Moreover, the lack of reading skills among large numbers of young adults threatens to divide society deeply between the highly literate and a low-income, low-achieving underclass unequipped for educational and professional advancement.

Need for Early Identification and Instruction

Current research shows the importance of identifying young children with reading problems and providing early reading instruction. Seventy-four percent of children who are unsuccessful at reading in third grade are still unsuccessful in ninth grade (Lerner, 2000; National Institute of Child Health and Human Development, 1999). Moreover, many of the reading problems faced by today's adolescents and adults were not resolved during their early childhood years (National Research Council, 1998).

Unfortunately, many young children with reading problems are not identified early and thus are not given appropriate instruction. For example, most children with reading and learning disabilities are unidentified until ages 9 to 14, after they have actually failed (U.S. Department of Education, 1998). This approach is sometimes called the *wait-and-fail* approach to identification.

The National Institute of Child Health and Human Development, a division within the National Institute of Health, is currently engaged in a wide-scale research program in reading development, reading disorders, and reading instruction. Some of their major findings (National Institute for Child Health and Human Development, 1999) are that:

- Reading is so critical to success in our society that reading failure not only constitutes an educational problem but also rises to the level of a major public health problem.
- Children most at risk for reading failure are those who enter school with limited exposure to the English language and who have little prior understanding of concepts related to phonemic sensitivity, letter knowledge, print awareness, the purposes of reading, and oral language and verbal skills, including vocabulary.
- Early identification of young children with precursors of reading problems

and timely intervention are essential to maximizing treatment success in children who are at risk for reading failure.

Reading Assistance

Most children with reading problems need help in reading and other language-related areas. What kinds of reading assistance are these students receiving? Some students with reading problems are in general education classes and receive no special assistance. Other students are served by school- or state-sponsored programs. Some students are served through Title I programs, federal programs that fund the teaching of basic skills education for students in low-income areas. Some children are identified as having disabilities. About five million children with disabilities receive special education services through the 1997 Individuals with Disabilities Act (IDEA). Most students with learning disabilities are placed in the regular education class (42 percents); but some are in resource rooms (39 percent), some are in special classes (17 percent), and a small percentage are in other settings (1 percent) (Lerner, 2000).

Despite all of these sources for help, a substantial number of students with reading problems receive no help other than regular classroom instruction. Available funding and human resources simply are not great enough to cover the needs of all students with reading problems.

Factors Associated with Reading Problems

Reading problems are rooted in factors within the individual; factors within the home, social, and cultural environments; and factors in the school environment. At times, all of these factors may play a role in any one student's reading problem.

Factors within the Individual

Many reading problems are due to intrinsic factors; that is, they stem from factors within the individual. Every teacher has known students such as Jason, the first child described in this chapter. Despite a dedicated family, a nurturing school environment, and many economic advantages, Jason continued to struggle with reading.

For more than 100 years, medical researchers have tried to determine those factors within the individual that are related to reading problems. As early as 1896, P. Morgan, a physician, reported on "word blindness" in an otherwise normal teenage boy who could not learn to read (Hinshelwood, 1917). Other medical researchers reported on similar cases (Orton, 1937; Critchley, 1970; Rabinovitch, 1989; Shaywitz & Shaywitz, 1998). The researchers suspected that these reading problems were related to a neurological condition. Although the research is not yet conclusive, neurological studies have strengthened this suspicion. For example, using a new technology to study the brain as the individual reads, the fMRI

(functional magnetic resonance imaging), Shaywitz and Shaywitz (1998) found evidence of brain function differences in poor readers.

Psychologists and educators also have looked at factors within the individual by investigating cognitive factors such as phonemic awareness, visual processing, auditory processing, memory abilities, and language factors (Stanovich, 1982b; Stanovich & Siegal, 1994; Lyon, 1997).

However, identifying the causes of reading problems has proven to be a complex process. Some studies show that even within one individual, reading problems have many causes. Several types of factors, including physical, emotional, and language factors, contribute to individual reading problems (Kibby, 1995).

Reading problems may vary in severity. The term *dyslexia* is sometimes used to describe individuals with severe disabilities, that is, individuals who acquire each word with extreme difficulty. Fortunately, such individuals make up only a small fraction of individuals with reading problems. The condition of dyslexia is addressed in Chapter 15.

Factors in the Home, Social, and Cultural Environments

The home, social, and cultural environments in which children grow can also influence their ability to read. One child whose story we have told, Diane, grew up in an environment that could not nurture school achievement. Homes that are plagued with poverty and family instability and neighborhoods where violence is commonplace produce children who are at risk for school failure. Sadly, many social and economic indicators show that the number of such children has risen:

- The child poverty rate rose by more than 11 percent during the 1980s and was almost 18 percent in 1989 (Kameenui, 1993). Since 1987, 25 percent of all preschool children in the United States have been born into poverty (Hodgkinson, 1991).
- Every year, about 350,000 children are born to cocaine-addicted mothers. Those who survive have many learning and behavioral problems. The cost of preschool therapy for these children and for those suffering from fetal alcohol syndrome is estimated at $40,000 per child (Hodgkinson, 1991).
- On any given night, the number of homeless children is estimated to be at least 500,000 (Hodgkinson, 1991).

At times, even a well-meaning, stable family may not be able to prepare a child for the school situation. Such was the case with Ilya, whose family was not able to enroll him in kindergarten or prepare him for reading instruction in English.

Problems within the individual, such as health and emotional problems, tend to increase when students live in difficult environments. Poorer mothers are less likely than more affluent ones to seek prenatal care. Alcohol addiction in parents may affect a child in two ways simultaneously: the child may be born with fetal alcohol syndrome, and the parent may not have the energy to nurture the child's education. Thus, individual and environmental causes combine to produce an increased risk for reading problems.

Children who are hungry or homeless have little energy to focus on school. Their overburdened, often undereducated parents and guardians may lack the time and skills to nurture literacy by sharing books with them, encouraging them to do homework, or communicating with their teachers. Some families are able to rise above their problems and provide warm, nurturing places that support education, but the sad fact remains that children born into poor or unstable families are at risk for educational failure.

The home environment has increasingly become a factor in the reading problems of children. Even in affluent neighborhoods, teachers are noticing an increase in family breakups. School problems are multiplied in less fortunate settings. As family instability becomes commonplace, teachers in *all* schools are instructing at-risk children.

Factors in the School Environment

Surprisingly, research indicates that some school practices can contribute to reading problems. Is it possible that teachers, whose job is to help, can actually be doing some things that are harmful? Think back to Diane, whom we introduced at the beginning of this chapter. Diane's teachers had entirely given up teaching her to read; instead they simply read everything to her. When other children had reading time, Diane was expected to sit quietly and do nothing.

Although such dramatic lack of reading instruction is rare, school instruction often does little to help children with reading problems. In an intensive study of one school, Juel (1994) found that a child who is a poor reader in first grade has an 88 percent chance of being a poor reader in fourth grade.

Why is school instruction often ineffective in helping to solve reading problems? One important reason is that students with reading problems do not read much in school. In an extensive line of research, Allington (1977, 1983, 1984, 1986), Walmsley and Allington (1995), and Stanovich (1986, 1993–4) compared the time spent and amount of reading in low-achieving and average students. They found that unskilled readers spent less time reading than did average students and that low-achieving students read only a third as many words as average students. These findings mean that students with reading problems are not practicing enough to improve their reading abilities.

Students with reading problems are a challenge to teach, but they still must be provided with the best instruction possible. This book is filled with suggestions that aid youngsters in breaking the cycle of reading failure and help them to love reading. Because students with reading problems are already lagging behind, we do not have a moment to waste!

What Is Reading?

A physician trying to heal a sick patient must have an understanding of the healthy human body. In the same way, a teacher trying to help a student who has reading problems must understand what good readers do. Many studies have examined the reading process. The findings of these studies have enabled us to improve our understanding of reading and thus to improve our ability to teach it.

When people read, they actually construct their own meaning of a text (Rosenblatt, 1983; Anderson & Pearson, 1984). In other words, people create their own mental version of what they read. The *reader*, the *material*, and the *reading situation* all contribute to the meaning that is constructed (Rumelhart, 1985; Wixson, Peters, Wever, & Roeber, 1987).

Constructing Meaning

Imagine that you are reading a novel. Rather than simply acquiring information, you are actively creating, in your mind, your own personal version of the material you are reading. The version you make is not exactly like what you read on paper. Instead, you, the reader, contribute to the construction of meaning. You visualize the characters and the scenery in a story. In fact, your mind probably even supplies details that are not in the book.

Compare your mental image of a character in the novel with that made by a friend. You will find that no two people's images are ever exactly alike. Most people have had the rude shock of seeing a movie made from a favorite book and realizing that the actors look nothing like the image they created when they read.

To prove to yourself that reading is actually constructing meaning in your own mind, read this short selection:

> The minute she saw the weight register on the scale, she realized she was the winner. She knew exactly how she would spend the prize money.

What meaning do you construct from this passage? Perhaps you "see" a dieter involved in a contest to lose weight and looking forward to buying new clothes. Or you might imagine a farmer getting an award for the largest livestock or pumpkin and planning to spend it on a new tractor or a family vacation. You might imagine a person who caught a large fish, and the money might be reinvested in expensive fishing equipment. Perhaps you thought of even another interpretation. Isn't it true that the meaning you constructed reflected your background and life experiences?

Sadly, students with reading problems are often reluctant to construct their own meaning and interpretation of the text. Instead, the terror that they might get something "wrong" prevents them from interpreting the text in an imaginative way. This fear is reinforced when teachers ask large numbers of factual questions, thus giving a perception that reading is a "right" and "wrong" act. Chapter 8 of this book provides several suggestions for fostering personal responses in students when they read. These personal responses help students to create their own meaning in the text, and the result is better and deeper comprehension.

Contribution of the Reader

The *reader* forms the cornerstone of reading, for meaning is actually constructed in the reader's mind. The reader activates and controls the reading process. The reader's *background, interest, attitude, purpose,* and *ability* dramatically influence the reading process.

Reading builds on the reader's *background knowledge*; and the richer or more detailed this background is, the richer the reading experience will be (Hirsch,

1987; Daneman, 1991). All of us have an easier time reading about familiar topics. A child who has ridden horses is able to understand the terms about horseback riding in the children's book *Black Beauty* (by Sewell). This child will have pleasant associations with the book and will find it relatively easy to identify with the problems of the characters. In contrast, a child who brings little background knowledge to *Black Beauty* is likely to have a less rewarding reading experience.

The background information a reader has is often called *schema*. Researchers have learned much about reading using schema theory, the study of how people store knowledge in their minds and use it to assimilate new information (Spiro, Bruce, & Brewer, 1980; Anderson, 1984).

Helping low-achieving students to build up their background information is important for two reasons: First, research has shown that these students have less background information than their average-achieving peers. Second, because students with reading problems often have difficulty recognizing words, they need clues to help them. A good grasp of background information enables the student to use the clue of meaning (or context) when a word cannot be immediately recognized.

The effects of improving background knowledge can be shown through the third-grade reading instruction that we planned for a school with many at-risk children. One reading selection "Through Grandpa's Eyes" (by MacLachlan) dealt with the concept of blindness and how blind people can cope through their other senses. Before the children worked with the story, teachers read an encyclopedia article about blindness to them. Next, teachers listed story words that could be identified through other senses, such as *marigold* and *cello*; and the children determined how each could be identified, whether by taste, touch, hearing, or smell. After these background knowledge activities, the children's new understanding of blindness and the five senses helped them to comprehend subtle ideas and to recognize words in the story.

Interest is another important way that the reader influences the reading process. Have you ever noticed that many people don't read the sports section of a newspaper until a hometown champion sparks their interest? Interests seem to be particularly important during childhood, as children pursue dozens of series books, such as *Baby-Sitter's Club* (by Martin), or read intensively about a favorite topic, such as dinosaurs.

Interest can be a critical factor in helping students with reading problems. Engagement in a subject can keep a struggling reader both absorbed in a book and wanting to read other books. Ten-year-old Georg, a child in our Reading Center, refused to read until his tutor discovered his passion for snakes. Suddenly, he was devouring fact books on snakes, snake stories, and snake poems. Throughout this instruction, Georg was gaining critical practice in reading. He was delighted when his father bought him *Snakes* (by Wexo) and *Amazing Poisonous Animals* (by Parsons) for Christmas.

Of course, interest and background are related. People who are interested in a topic will read about it and, as they read, increase their background information. Therefore, when teachers build their students' interests in what they are reading, they also strengthen their students' reading processes.

The *attitude* of the reader is also an important factor in constructing meaning (Beach & Hynds, 1991). Because of an unfriendly teacher long ago in a high school physics class, one adult finds any article about physics almost impossible to understand. However, warm memories of a chemistry teacher make this subject more readable. Many students with reading problems are literally afraid of books. Nine-year-old Kenisha experienced a magical feeling of achievement after she overcame her fear of books and read and enjoyed her first hardcover book. For those who teach students with problems, developing positive attitudes toward reading is an extremely important and sometimes challenging task. Many suggestions are given in Chapter 4.

A reader's *purpose* also affects the reading process. Good readers use strategies that fulfill their purposes for reading. Most people use a phone book, for example, simply to locate the number they want. They turn as quickly as possible to the right page, locate the number, and close the book. Unfortunately, many students with reading problems are not this efficient. We still remember, with horror, a reading-disabled teenager who was trying to locate the name "Weiss" by starting from page one of a telephone book. When we read to fulfill our purposes, we are doing *strategic* reading (Paris, Wasik, & Turner, 1991). Strategic reading is difficult for students with reading problems.

The reader's *ability* plays a part in meaning construction. Students with reading problems must often struggle to recognize words and comprehend text. Therefore, they have less energy to pay attention to the meaning of what they are reading.

Contribution of the Material

The *material*, or *text*, read is a second contribution to the construction of meaning. Without the text, no reading can occur, for the reader uses the material as the input from which to construct meaning. The material sets limits on the construction of meaning that the reader may make. A person reading a manual about health care may decide that some of the author's points are more important than others or may even disagree with some things. However, the reader would probably not think the manual was about using a computer.

Finding the right materials is particularly important for a student who experiences reading difficulties. As we showed in the case of Georg, interesting materials (in his case, about snakes) can be a key factor in the success of instruction. Finding books that are interesting yet not too difficult may be a particular challenge. This point is addressed in several chapters of this book, and a list of easy but interesting reading is given in Appendix A.

Students must also learn how to handle many different types of materials. Good readers can often teach themselves to read science texts, computer manuals, and novels strategically. In contrast, readers with problems need direct instruction in the strategies appropriate for different types of reading.

Contribution of the Reading Situation

The *reading situation* forms a third contribution to meaning construction. One element of the reading situation is the *task the reader must accomplish*. Imagine that you are leisurely reading, and enjoying, Ernest Hemingway's novel *The Old Man and the Sea*. In fact, you are enjoying this novel *despite* the fact that it was assigned for an English class. Suddenly, you realize that you have a test on the book tomorrow. The reading situation changes dramatically. You read hurriedly, focusing on getting through the book and trying to understand what it *means*. In later years, your memory of this novel (or put another way, your construction of meaning) will probably include unpleasant associations of rapid reading and tension.

Students with reading problems often find themselves studying difficult material at a rapid pace to meet classroom demands. They rarely have time to enjoy true leisure reading. Teachers must structure their activities so that these students *can* read for enjoyment.

The *environment* in which we read is another element of the reading situation. We relax by reading magazines or novels on a couch or in a bed (these situations often result in an even more relaxing nap). Teachers should do all they can to make the environment inviting for students with reading problems. A well-organized, colorful room with beanbag chairs and pillows to curl up with helps them experience reading as pleasurable. Chapter 4 gives many suggestions for creating a pleasant reading situation and environment.

Components of the Reading Process

Accomplished readers are able to construct meaning from reading without conscious effort and to combine many abilities into the single act of reading. However, teachers who work with low-achieving students need to be aware of the different components involved in learning to read so that they know when students need assistance in using them.

In this book we have addressed these topics separately, providing distinct chapters to help you teach each one. However, remember that our ultimate goal is for the student to experience the act of reading as a pleasurable and informative whole. Some of the components of good reading are:

- Knowing what reading is and how to deal with books (Chapter 5)
- Recognizing words accurately (Chapter 6)
- Recognizing words with ease and fluency (Chapter 7)
- Understanding and being able to study and learn what is read (Chapters 8 and 9)
- Understanding language structures and word meanings (Chapter 10)
- Responding actively to reading (Chapter 11)
- Enjoying and appreciating reading (Chapter 4)

To illustrate the components of reading, read this excerpt from the *Miami Herald* newspaper (Phillips, 1990). After you have read the excerpt, let's consider each component of the reading process:

> ### *Ephemeral Ixia Plant Kept Off Federal Endangered List*
>
> In 1791, writing of his travels through the wilds of Florida, naturalist William Bartram admired the "azure fields of cerulian ixia" gracing what is now greater Jacksonville.
>
> What Bartram witnessed was one of the most ephemeral delights in Nature's bouquet: a violet-blue wildflower that blooms for as little as a few hours every two decades.
>
> The plant, now called Bartram's ixia, is so reclusive that the U.S. Fish and Wildlife Service proposed listing the species as endangered. But the agency reversed that decision last month after timber companies produced evidence that *** plant is hiding out on thousands of privately owned pine lands in several northeastern Florida counties.
>
> The companies, through the Florida Forestry Association, argued that timber harvesting actually helps the plant. Ixia bulbs are drawn into bloom by fires, bulldozers, and other soil disturbances.

"Ephemeral Ixia Plant Kept Off Federal Endangered List," by Michael Phillips, 1990, *Miami Herald.* Reprinted with permission.

Emergent Literacy

As an adult, you realize that newspapers supply information about the world. You also know how to identify the title of an article and that reading, in English, is done from left to right. Such knowledge is usually learned in the preschool and kindergarten years, but students with reading problems may still be mastering emergent literacy skills long after these ages. Emergent literacy is discussed in detail in Chapter 5.

Word Recognition: Accuracy and Fluency

To read the text, we need to recognize the words *accurately*. But word recognition is partly a product of our comprehension. In the newspaper article, one word has been replaced by asterisks. You probably guessed that the missing word is *the*. In fact, fluent readers don't even bother to fix their eyes on some of the small words in text such as *the* and *is*, because this type of word can often be predicted from our general comprehension of the material. In this way, our comprehension of material actually contributes to the words we recognize.

However, we can only use our comprehension abilities to guess a small proportion of the words in our reading; we must learn to read most of them accurately. Accurate word recognition is often difficult for disabled readers. One study found that 77 percent of students with reading problems believed that the difficulties they experienced were due to difficulty in recognizing words (Miller & Yochum, 1991). Word recognition accuracy is discussed in Chapter 6 of this book.

In addition to recognizing words accurately, we need to read them quickly and *fluently*. Otherwise our reading will be labored and unenjoyable, and we will lose meaning. Reading fluency is recognized as "the missing ingredient" (Anderson, 1981) in the instruction for problem readers. Fluency is discussed in Chapter 7.

Comprehension and Studying

Comprehension is the essence of the reading act. The many levels of comprehending include drawing on background experiences (or schema), literal comprehension, higher-level comprehension, and the ability to study and learn from text. These different levels of comprehension are strongly related.

To comprehend material effectively, readers require some background knowledge. In fact, in these days of environmental concerns, most readers are aware of the efforts to save rare plant and animal species that are addressed in the ixia article. You may also be conscious of the growing concerns of businesses that use natural resources (such as lumber, water) as they find their activities affected by efforts to save wildlife. You probably know that Jacksonville is a city in the state of Florida, which is located in the southeastern United States. The background that you already have enables you to build bridges to your experiences and connect what you read to what you know.

Literal comprehension, or understanding the information stated directly in the text, is another part of comprehension. Yet even here, the good reader picks and chooses, remembering the most important facts. You may remember that the plant mentioned in the article was named after a man who lived a long time ago. You are less likely to remember that his name was William Bartram or that he described the plant in 1791.

Perhaps the thing you are most likely to remember is your construction of the central thought of the article. Formulating this thought is part of higher-level comprehension. The main thought we construct is a little different for each of us. For us, the central thought was that a pretty, but rarely blooming Florida plant was taken off a federal endangered species list. In this way, we actively participate in the reading process by constructing meaning.

Another form of higher-level thinking consists of the *inferences*, or implied information, we draw from the text. The experienced reader will draw many inferences. For example, in the first paragraph, the reader will infer that two hundred years ago the metropolitan area of Jacksonville was not developed. In the second paragraph, we could infer that the plant was put on the endangered species list because it is hard to find. In the fourth paragraph, we might infer (although it is not stated) that the forestry industry does *not* want the plant on the endangered list. We might further draw the conclusion that the forestry industry wants to harvest timber on lands that they were forbidden to lumber because of this plant.

Critical or evaluative thinking is also a part of higher-level comprehension. As you read, you are probably developing a point of view about whether the ixia plant should be kept on the endangered species list. You are evaluating the information in the light of your thinking and experiences. What might motivate lumber companies to ask that the ixia be taken off the endangered species list? Perhaps you feel that the lands will not be maintained as lumber sites, thus helping the flowers, but will eventually be developed as housing or commercial sites. In this case, you would probably oppose taking the ixia off of the endangered list.

Although your task was not to study this article, the accomplished reader can easily understand how to gain information from it. In school, students are often called on to study (gain information) from their textbooks. Using books, manuals, directions, and many other materials continues throughout adult life. The ability to study is important in school and daily life.

Students with reading problems need work in many areas of comprehension and studying. As mentioned earlier, they do not construct meaning effectively in their minds the way we did when we constructed a central thought for this article.

In addition, low-level readers are particularly at risk in content-area subjects, such as science, social studies, and health. In these areas, the reading is *expository*, or focuses on giving information rather than telling a story. This book deals with the comprehension of *narratives* (or stories and novels) in Chapter 8 and the comprehension and study of *expository* text (informational materials, such as textbooks) in Chapter 9.

Language and Meaning Vocabulary

To read a text effectively, you must understand its sentence structures and word meanings. Yet you can certainly read something without understanding every word in it. In fact, using your comprehension processes, you are able to increase your vocabulary as you read. When you started, the word *ephemeral* may have been unfamiliar to you. From the clue in the text, "blooms for as little as a few hours every two decades," you probably figured out that *ephemeral* means "lasting for a short time." If you did know the word before you read the passage, your knowledge has been reinforced with another example. In a similar way, *azure* and *cerulean*, which also may have been unknown to you, are now somewhat more familiar. You may realize that both are adjectives (in fact, they describe shades of blue).

In addition to knowing vocabulary, you need a knowledge of difficult language structures to read this article. It contains a quote from 1791 that is rather formal by today's standards. It also contains many long and complicated sentences. For example, the second sentence ("What Bartram witnessed . . .") has 30 words and many complex structures.

So, to read this article, you need a knowledge of word meanings and language. Yet, as you read it, you also acquired new word meanings and gained experience with language. The more students read, the more word meanings and language they acquire (Stanovich & Cunningham, 1993; West, Stanovich, & Mitchell, 1993). Thus, teachers need to encourage students with reading problems to read as much as possible.

The language we understand is the natural limit of our reading ability. Meaning vocabulary is an extremely important factor in reading, particularly in the intermediate and upper grades (Davis, 1968; Stanovich, 1986). Students with reading problems lag behind their average-achieving peers in both language development and meaning vocabulary. Chapter 10 contains many motivating ideas to help build the language and vocabulary of low-achieving readers.

Reading-Writing Connection

Perhaps including writing as a part of reading seems strange. Yet we have already pointed out that as we read the article, we mentally constructed its central thought. In other words, we composed, or wrote, in our minds. As we are constructing our own meaning, we are always composing, so reading actually involves "writing."

Reading the ixia article involves composing in our minds. However, when students actually take pencil in hand and write down their thoughts, they learn even more about reading. Trying to spell gives them insights into sound-symbol relationships, or *phonics*. Creating their own writing shows them that somebody actually *writes* what is read and that they can write too. Thus, students acquire a sense of control over reading. In this book, the reading-writing connection is addressed in Chapter 11.

Enjoyment and Appreciation

The newspaper article we have been referring to is on a controversial topic of current importance. The editors of the *Miami Herald* decided that it would interest you; that is why they printed it. In addition, the writer (Michael Phillips) tried to write it in an engaging way. He reminded you of a time long past; he conjured up images of wild blue flowers in a forgotten wilderness. People do what they enjoy and appreciate. For the reading act to be complete, the reader's interest must be engaged.

Suggestions for helping students with reading problems enjoy reading are found throughout this book but are particularly concentrated in Chapter 4. We give many different strategies and materials that you can use to motivate your students.

As you can see, the reader is an active participant in the many components of reading. Although these components can be analyzed separately, fluent readers are not aware of most of them. In accomplished reading, these components interact with one another and take place simultaneously. Our goal as teachers is to foster this interaction; yet, when instructing students with reading problems, we must be aware of the components of reading so that we know how to develop each one.

When the Process Breaks Down

What is the reading process like for students with problems? In one study (Liebert, 1970–1), professors asked university students to read text written in a mirror (or backwards) form.

The text looked like this.

Instantly, the backwards text transformed excellent readers into individuals with reading problems. Here is how they reacted:

- I resorted to finger pointing to keep my place in a maze of unfamiliar print . . . . I guessed words, repeated words and phrases continually.
- I guessed, repeated, reversed, inverted, and giggled. To be specific, I became entirely frustrated.
- What was most frustrating to me after correctly identifying . . . the word, was the awkward inability to recognize the identical symbol in other locations . . . . Such words as *and, the, as,* or *but* were particularly troublesome.

Although the print was normal in size, the readers felt it was too small:

- . . . all of the words were so close to each other that they were hard to recognize . . . . *O*'s looked like *a*'s, *f*'s like *t*'s, *b*'s like *h*'s, etc.
- It would have been a help to have the print considerably enlarged.

As readers struggled, their fluency disappeared and comprehension was lost. In less than 10 minutes, they developed negative attitudes, lowered self-esteem, and undesirable behaviors:

- I laughed, looked around to see the reaction of other people, became fidgety.
- I gave up quite easily. After the test I was quite weary and felt headachey.
- This nervousness, insecurity, or frustration was shown by pointing with my pen and glancing up to see if I were being closely observed by the teacher.

If skilled adults reacted this way after 10 minutes, what must be the feelings of schoolchildren who face reading problems year after year? Is it any wonder that they lose their places, complain about small print, fidget, and suffer from lack of self-esteem? As one adult in the experiment stated:

- I now can really feel strong sympathy toward children who are faced with a similar situation 180 days a year.

Overview of This Book

This book provides teachers and prospective teachers with techniques for assessing and helping students who are experiencing reading problems.

In this first chapter, we discuss the widespread nature of reading problems and some of the factors that contribute to them. We define the many components of the reading process of skilled readers.

In Chapter 2, Obtaining Background Information, we discuss background factors, both within the individual and in the environment, that may contribute to a reading problem. We also provide interviews and related tools to help you assess these factors.

Chapter 3, Assessing Reading Achievement: Overview and Informal Measures, first provides a framework for diagnosis and assessment and then thoroughly discusses informal measures you can use to identify a student's reading level and determine patterns of strengths and weaknesses. One important instrument, the Informal Reading Inventory, is discussed in detail.

Chapter 4, An Overview of Instruction, deals with overall principles of providing motivation and effective instruction for students who experience reading difficulties.

Chapters 5 through 11 discuss the component parts of reading. In each chapter, we give the abilities involved in the particular area of reading, specific strategies for assessment, and instructional strategies. The chapters include:

Chapter 5 – Emergent Literacy

Chapter 6 – Improving Word Recognition Accuracy

Chapter 7 – Improving Word Recognition Fluency

Chapter 8 – Improving Comprehension of Narrative Text

Chapter 9 – Improving Comprehension of Expository Text

Chapter 10 – Improving Language Abilities: Listening Comprehension and Meaning Vocabulary

Chapter 11 – Reading and Writing

Chapter 12, Reading Intervention Programs, reviews a number of structured intervention programs that are effective and widely used. The chapter then details the common elements of structured intervention programs and gives guidelines for constructing such a program.

Chapter 13, Literacy in a Diverse Society, presents the special considerations needed when teaching students who speak English as a second language and the strategies for teaching in today's multicultural society. In addition, resources are given for working with parents. Finally, the special needs of adolescents and adults are presented.

Chapter 14, Correlates of Reading Disabilities, gives a detailed, theoretical description of the factors associated with reading problems. We discuss factors both within the individual and in the environment and present relevant research and in-depth assessment tools.

Chapter 15, Severe Reading Disabilities, addresses the needs of severely disabled readers. We address the characteristics of these students and the programs designed to serve them. We give new research insights into severe reading disabilities, and we present several instructional options for addressing the needs of these students.

Chapter 16, Assessing Reading Achievement: Formal Measures, discusses formal tests. It describes the types of tests, considerations in using tests, interpretation of standardized tests, and an overview of many specific, widely used instruments.

Appendix A gives selected resources for students with reading problems. Appendix B describes tests that are widely used in reading diagnosis. Appendix C gives publisher addresses, telephone numbers, and web sites. In Appendix D, we present the *Jennings Informal Reading Assessment* (Jennings, 2001), an informal reading inventory (IRI) that you may administer to your students. The book concludes with a list of references.

Summary

Teachers bear the primary responsibility for instructing students who have reading problems. Reading problems are associated with difficulties in life, including poverty, unemployment, and problems with the law. Because they lack skills, individuals with reading problems are often unable to train for jobs in an increasingly technological society.

A substantial portion of our school population has learning problems, and most of these problems are related to reading. Such students may receive help through Title I programs, the special education Individuals with Disabilities Act (IDEA), or through state or locally funded programs. However, many students with reading problems receive no special help. If help is given, students may be placed in self-contained, resource, or regular classroom settings.

Factors associated with reading problems include those within the individual and those in the environment. Factors within the individual include physical factors (neurological ones), language factors, and emotional factors. Although neurological problems were the first to receive intense study, the causes of reading problems are quite complex.

Environmental factors include the home, social setting, culture, and school. In today's society, increasing numbers of students come from homes that cannot support literacy. Also, the school environment has not proven entirely effective in eliminating reading problems. A key problem is that students with reading problems often do not read enough to develop the ability to read effectively.

Reading is the construction of meaning from text. The reader constructs meaning in his or her own mind; and each reader constructs this meaning a bit differently. The reader contributes to meaning construction through background, interest, attitude, purpose, and ability. The text that is read also contributes to the meaning that is constructed. Finally, the reading situation—the reader's purpose and the reading environment—contributes to meaning construction.

We are often not conscious of the components of the reading process as we read because good readers use these components unconsciously and automatically. However, to help students with reading problems, teachers must be able to identify these components. They include emergent literacy, word recognition accuracy and fluency, comprehension and studying, the understanding of language structures and word meanings, an active response to reading (the reading-writing connection), and the enjoyment and appreciation of reading.

2 Obtaining Background Information

Introduction

Accurate assessment helps teachers plan the best possible instruction for students. Chapters 2 and 3 provide information on gathering and analyzing data about students and their reading. Chapter 2 discusses background information. Chapter 3 concentrates on the assessment of reading abilities. Both kinds of information are essential to good teaching.

This chapter examines ways to obtain a broad understanding of a student's background. Background information is divided into two parts: (1) the student's environments, including home, school, social, and cultural, and (2) background factors within the individual, including emotional, potential (intelligence), physical, and language development. Then specific methods of gathering information are provided.

Background factors can profoundly affect a student's reading. Chapter 1 gave several examples. Some were of students whose *environmental backgrounds* did not foster reading development—Diane's family could not provide a stable home life; Ilya missed a year of important preparation when he did not attend kindergarten. For other students, problems in reading seem to come from *within the individual*—Jason's reading problems were related to his physical development.

At times, identified problems can be corrected. For example, a student with visual difficulties may be referred to an eye doctor, receive corrective lenses, and show immediate reading gains.

However, students face problems that cannot be resolved easily. For example, a teacher has little ability to affect a difficult home situation. But even in that instance a teacher can make a difference. During a time of family turmoil, a student may need a compassionate, understanding adult. Knowing background information enables the teacher to deal sympathetically with a fragile human being and to adjust instruction to special needs.

The discussion of background factors in this chapter is oriented to the immediate, practical needs of teachers. More theoretical, research-oriented information is presented in Chapter 14, Correlates of Reading Disabilities, and in Chapter 15, Severe Reading Disabilities.

When dealing with background factors, teachers must remember that these factors have a complex relationship to reading problems. A factor may coexist with a reading problem but not actually cause that reading problem. For example, some students manage to achieve well in school despite difficult home lives. For other students, however, problems at home may impede learning. Thus interpreting background information judiciously is important.

Information about the Environment

Students live in several environments: the home, the school, the social, and the cultural environment. Each of these influences how students think about reading, the desire to learn, and access to reading materials. In addition, these environments interact. For example, a difficult situation at home may contribute to difficulty making friends in the social realm and to trouble in cooperating with teachers at school.

Home Environment

The home exerts a powerful influence on the development of reading and writing. Parents play an important role in modeling the value of literacy and bringing children to books, and the general home situation can influence a student's academic achievement. Events such as divorce or a move to a new neighborhood can affect a student's ability to profit from school reading instruction.

Parents as Models for Literacy.   Parents are a child's earliest and most important literacy role models. If parents read for both recreation and information and provide many reading materials at home, the child learns to value literacy. Parents also stimulate a love of books by reading to their children, taking them to the library, and buying books as gifts. A home environment that is rich in books and in literacy activities fosters success in reading.

A reading teacher can determine whether the home supports and values literacy by interviewing the parents or by asking them to fill out a questionnaire. What information is helpful? Some of the questions to ask parents about their own reading habits are the following: Do they read regularly? Do they subscribe to newspapers and magazines? Do they buy books? Next, parents should be asked about literacy interactions with their child. Do they regularly read to their child? Do they encourage their child to read? Do they take their child to the library or buy books for the child? Do they subscribe to any children's magazines? Do they limit television viewing? Responses to such questions indicate how parents and other family members, including grandparents and older siblings, foster literacy at home.

Information obtained directly from a student can also give insights into how literacy is modeled at home. As you gather information from interviewing and working with your students, you learn whether they have books at home and if reading is done regularly.

What can a reading teacher do if the home does not nurture literacy? We have found that many parents are grateful for teacher suggestions about improving literacy in their homes. Often, the parents of students with reading problems are worried about their child's future and have misgivings about their own parenting skills. A few suggestions often help foster a sense of family security and enhance literacy. For some families, these suggestions reinforce the good things they are doing already:

- Provide a good reading-studying environment. Advise parents to provide a quiet, stable, well-lighted place in which their child will study. Supplies (paper and pencils) and reference materials (dictionaries, maps) should be located near this area. Make sure that the television is off during homework or reading time.

- Share literacy with the child. When parents read to young children, they promote an interest in reading, foster language development, and share close family experiences. If the child is older, parent and child can share reading time as they each read silently. Students of all ages enjoy reading material that they have mastered to a parent who listens enthusiastically. Encourage parents to take children to a local library and to look for a helpful children's librarian, who will aid them in locating suitable books.

- Accept the child as he or she is. Admitting that one's own child has a problem is often difficult. Some parents deny that difficulties exist or hold unrealistic expectations for their child. Children are sensitive to their parents' disappointments. To prevent a reading problem from becoming a family problem, children must know that parents accept and love them as they are.

- Help the child to feel secure and confident. Encourage activities that a child does successfully. Playing baseball or basketball, taking cooking lessons, or just being dad's special helper may acquire a special meaning for a child with reading problems.

When parents are unable to provide literacy experiences at home, teachers must nurture a love of literacy during instruction. Classrooms filled with different types of books and magazines, invitingly displayed, show students that literacy is important. Give students time to browse through and share these materials. Teachers can also read to students on a regular basis and ask them to share their own thoughts and feelings about the selections. More suggestions for teachers are given in Chapter 4.

General Home Situation. Children are profoundly affected by what happens to their families. They are often dramatically touched by a move to a new location, divorce or separation of parents, the death of relatives, or older siblings leaving home. A child may not be able to pay attention to reading instruction when the father has just moved out or the mother has taken a new job and will no longer be at home after school.

A parent interview is often the means of collecting helpful information about a family. This information includes the names, ages, and occupations of the parents; the number and ages of siblings; names of other family members living in the home; and the members of the nuclear family (parents, siblings) who are not living at home. During this interview, ask parents to share any other information that might help to explain their child's difficulties. Often parental insights give valuable ideas for cooperation between a reading teacher and the family.

Occasionally, the parent interview reveals that a family situation is causing stress for the student and contributing to difficulty in school. Although teachers cannot intervene in a divorce or prevent an impending move to a new neighborhood, they can be sensitive to a student's feelings and emotional needs. At such critical times, the reactions and guidance of an understanding teacher may be more important for the child than direct instruction in reading. Our work with Shannon at our Reading Center illustrates this point. When Shannon's parents separated, she reacted with fits of crying and withdrawal from other children. We realized that certain topics would upset her, so we allowed her to select her own materials for instruction. Shannon avoided books about families. Instead she chose nonsense books such as *Chicken Soup with Rice* (by Sendak) and books featuring brave young children, such as *Hatupatu and the Birdwoman* (by Cowley) and *Where the Wild Things Are* (by Sendak). These selections proved to be key elements in improving her reading.

Teachers can help students cope with difficult home situations by:

- Being sensitive. Sensitivity in talking to students and allowing them to express their feelings is extremely important.
- Reducing demands. Teachers may want to "go easy" on students for a while by reducing both academic and behavioral demands.
- Being aware of the student's living situation. Teachers should be knowledgeable and understanding about the student's living and legal custody arrangements. If parents do not live together, make sure the appropriate parent receives communications. With permission from the custodial parent, both parents may be informed.

School Environment

Many factors in the school environment can influence reading achievement. Information about educational history, school attendance, and instructional methods helps us understand the student's problem and forms a basis for cooperation among *all* the professionals who are helping a student.

Educational History.   By gathering information about a student's educational history, teachers learn what the youngster has already experienced and are able to select new options for instruction. Students differ widely in their educational histories. For some, first grade is the initial instructional experience; others enter first grade with a rich history of preschool and kindergarten. Some students are barely six years old when they first encounter formal reading instruction; others are almost seven. Some students have repeated a grade or have received an extra year of kindergarten instruction. Some children have received private tutoring; some have been placed in special school programs.

Educational history may offer some hints about the seriousness of a student's problem. For example, a student who has had many enriching experiences, such as preschool education and previous tutoring, and still has difficulty in reading probably has a serious problem. In contrast, a student who comes with no preschool education or history of special reading help may simply have lacked the opportunities needed for learning to read.

Educational history is gathered from many sources: interviews with parents or guardians and students, teacher interviews and questionnaires, cumulative school records (which follow the student from year to year), portfolios, and report cards. If you are not a staff member at the student's school, you must obtain written permission from parents before contacting school personnel.

A complete history of schooling covers several areas.

- Ask about preschool experiences, including the length of nursery or preschool education and kindergarten attendance.
- Ask about the student's early reading and writing instruction and the age and grade at which such instruction began. Children's early literacy instruction must be considered in conjunction with their age and development (Galda, Cullinan, & Strickland, 1997).
- Ask if the student has ever repeated a grade; if so, try to determine the cause of retention.
- Ask if the student is currently in, or has ever been in, a special school program. Placement in such programs as special education, special reading, or Chapter I/Title I can influence the type of instruction and attention a student receives. If the student is in a special program, is the placement full-time or part-time? Does the student receive supportive help in a "resource room" setting or in the regular classroom?
- If previous diagnostic work has been done for the student through the school or a private agency, ask the parents to bring in a copy of the findings. You must have written consent from parents or guardians to contact these professionals.

School Attendance.   Absence from school and frequent transfers can be harmful to a student's progress. Some children are absent from school for weeks at a time, missing critical instruction. Other students change schools several times during the year, resulting in abrupt changes in instructional approaches and materials.

Information about school attendance can be obtained from parents, teachers, and cumulative school records. Try to determine how many times the student has been absent in the current school year and in earlier years. Instruction missed in first and second grade seems to have a particularly damaging effect on reading progress. Extended absences are also harmful. Try to determine how long the student has been in a particular school, and how many different schools the student has attended. Ask about the reasons for frequent absences or transfers.

School Instruction.   The type of reading instruction that students receive dramatically affects their ability to read. Often students with reading problems have received instruction that does not match their unique needs. Some have not received enough direct instruction in critical concepts. Although the typical student often learns word recognition and comprehension strategies through extensive reading, low-achieving students may need direct, sequenced lessons. Biemiller (1994) found that direct and prescribed practice in reading was more beneficial to some students than a less controlled literature approach to reading.

At other times, low-achieving students are given books that are too hard for them. The basal reading series of the 1990s and 2000s contain more difficult words, complex concepts, and longer selections than earlier series (Hoffman, et al., 1994). If the whole class is using one textbook series or novel, poorer readers may not be able to read it successfully. Even teachers who group their students for reading are likely to have one or two very low readers who cannot handle the easy books that are comfortable for the rest of the reading group. As a consequence, these poor readers have no material at their level and little opportunity to read.

Information about a student's first experiences with reading instruction may provide insights into how a problem developed. Was the initial method suited to the student's needs and level of development? Did the reading problem start in first grade, or were the student's early experiences successful? Reading problems that begin in first and second grade often involve word recognition abilities; problems that develop in the intermediate grades (or later) tend to focus on comprehension and language abilities.

Information about school instruction can be obtained from school personnel, parents, and students. The school is a particularly valuable source. Teacher interviews and questionnaires, school records, and information about schoolbooks and assignments all provide insight into instruction. In gathering information from the school, the reading teacher should try to get a full picture of instruction and progress. Is the student receiving specific reading instruction, or is reading addressed only as a part of other subjects (such as social studies and science)? If reading is taught as a subject, is a reading textbook series used? If so, which one, and at what level is the student placed? If novels and trade books are used, which ones has the student read? Is the class organized into reading groups, or is the whole class instructed together? Are word recognition and comprehension strategies taught directly? Are students given strategies for reading in social studies, health, and science books? Does the class have time to do recreational reading? If so, are books provided at the student's level? Is writing encouraged? How is the student performing in areas such as math, science, social studies, art, and physical education?

The student's own perceptions about reading instruction can also offer valuable insights. Interviews and informal conversations provide information about whether a student likes reading class (or instruction) and whether the books and stories are easy and interesting to read. Ask the student what activities take place during reading instruction. Are stories and novels read orally or silently? We have found that students with reading problems often would like to change something about their instruction. For this reason, we often ask them, "If you could change one thing about reading class, what would it be?" A student's perceptions of reading can also be revealing. You might ask the student what reading is or what makes a good reader.

Parents' perceptions of the school environment come from their child's comments, homework examples, report cards, and teacher conferences. During an interview, ask the parents to describe the type and amount of homework their child is given. Ask parents if the student brings books home from school to read. Parents often have strong feelings about instructional factors that may have contributed to their child's reading problems. Obtaining this information from parents is important in fostering a cooperative spirit between the school and home.

Sometimes, the information suggests that school factors may have indeed contributed to the reading problem. What can you, as a reading teacher, do? You cannot change the past. Furthermore, assigning blame to a particular school or teacher is not helpful. A classroom teacher may have difficulty responding to the special needs of one individual when coping with a group of 25 to 35 students. A reading teacher *can* make helpful suggestions to the school and can foster cooperation among all of the professionals who are trying to help the student. For example, one reading teacher suggested the titles of easy books for a low-achieving student to read during recreational reading time in his class. Another reading teacher worked with the classroom teacher to adjust difficult homework assignments for a special-needs student.

In some cases, information about past instruction is helpful in planning an effective current reading program. Ten-year-old Gregg loudly stated that he hated school reading class and "all those hard worksheets." Gregg defined reading as "saying the words right," which explained his lack of interest and enthusiasm for it. To help him overcome negative past experiences, his reading teacher avoided any tasks that resembled rote instruction and emphasized comprehension rather than accurate word pronunciation. Gregg selected the stories that he and his teacher read together. They paused periodically to discuss and predict what might happen next. Because Gregg enjoyed art, the tutor encouraged him to illustrate parts of the story and vocabulary words. At the end of the semester, Gregg proclaimed that these lessons "weren't real reading classes, but I learned to read better."

Social and Cultural Environments

Reading is a social process because during reading, an author communicates his (or her) ideas to the reader. Because of the social nature of reading, a student's relationships with parents, teachers, and peers can affect reading achievement. Social interactions occur through specific personal relationships and through the student's general cultural environment (Gillet & Temple, 2000).

Successful social interactions can provide the student with feelings of high self-esteem and confidence that encourage reading achievement. Unfortunately, for many poor readers, the social sphere is yet another area of personal failure. Students with reading problems are often rejected by their classmates and viewed with disfavor by their teachers. They may be a source of concern to their parents. As a result, poor readers often have difficulty relating to others.

In today's schools, reading instruction tends to be a social experience. Students often read orally in pairs or groups, sharing thoughts and feelings about a novel, or working in cooperative groups. These activities can be burdensome to a student who lacks ability in social interactions. Students who are poor readers may withdraw in shame when they have to share their reading.

The student's cultural environment may also affect reading progress. Some students are surrounded by peers who do not value literacy. In addition, the student's cultural background may make asking a teacher for help a difficult and uncomfortable experience. When a student's culture does not value academic achievement, instruction can be made relevant by having the student read and write about interesting topics, such as popular TV programs and movies, video games, and favorite musicians or comedians.

Reading teachers should gather background information about both the student's social and cultural environments. Often the parents' description of their child's social interactions is informative. Ask the parents to describe their child's relationships with them and with siblings. Does the student have many friends? Do these friends value education? What is the student's relationship with the teacher and classmates? Does the student willingly join in group activities or prefer to work alone? Is the student shy and withdrawn or outgoing?

Interviewing the student about friends and interests can also be useful. Does the student see reading as something that friends and family value? Does the student spend time with friends? What are the student's interests? Such information provides hints about how to make reading a motivating experience.

At times, the investigation of a student's social relationships indicates cause for concern. However, we often find that these relationships improve when academic problems are alleviated. When the student reads better, feelings of success provide more confidence in social interactions. Thus, by offering good instruction, reading teachers can often affect both a student's achievement and her or his social relationships.

At other times, a teacher's use of a student's interests may draw him or her more comfortably into social interactions. Eamon, the poorest reader in his third-grade class, seldom interacted with his peers. During recess, he stood in the corner of the playground; at lunch, he usually sat and ate alone. To help him, the reading teacher made a point of talking to Eamon alone whenever possible. Discovering that Eamon was passionately interested in snakes and had two pet reptiles at home, she gave him several books about snakes and asked him to bring his pets to school. The eager fascination of the other children motivated Eamon to talk about the care of his pets and how they should be handled. The teacher also read several books about snakes to the class and encouraged Eamon to critique them. Were the facts accurate? Had Eamon ever seen a snake do that? As Eamon became the class "snake expert," he gradually increased his willingness to participate in class activities and to seek out the company of his peers.

Carefully planned reading with peers can promote social and reading competence. Jennifer, a sixth-grade student in our Reading Center, was reading at the third-grade level and had a history of negative social interactions. To improve reading and social skills, Jennifer was paired with Samantha, a fifth-grade student. The two girls read *Charlotte's Web* (by White) at home and returned to the Reading Center to discuss difficult words, the characters in the book, and the plot. Sharing the reading experience helped Jennifer overcome her shyness. Jennifer and Samantha became good friends as they enjoyed the positive social experience of reacting to good children's literature.

Information about the Individual

Many of the factors that contribute to reading problems are found within the individual student. This section discusses information about emotional status, potential (intelligence), physical health, and language development.

Emotional Information

Poor readers often display emotional problems that impede learning. Not surprisingly, many students who have problems in their social environments (discussed in the previous section) also display emotional problems.

For some students, problems with learning to read may result in emotional problems. For example, some children withdraw and refuse even to attempt to read or write. Seven-year-old Carlos eagerly participated in classroom activities that did not involve reading or writing. However, when the teacher asked students to take out their books, Carlos would either put his head down on the desk or turn his chair away from the teacher. To avoid repeated failure, Carlos had decided not to read anymore.

If learning has been a painful experience, some students develop a block against all school activities. Others react by becoming hostile or aggressive. Still others develop self-images of poor readers; because these students believe that they are "dumb," they give up trying to learn. Other students become overcome with anxiety, and may start to shake or stutter when asked to read.

For another group of students, the reading problem may be a result of an underlying emotional problem. For example, some of the students in our Reading Center first developed problems with literacy just as their parents were separating or going through a divorce.

Teachers, parents, and students themselves can all offer insights about emotional factors that may affect reading achievement. The teacher, who sees the child in class, can note reactions to instructional activities. The parents can describe the child at home and with peers. Finally, the perceptions of the student are perhaps the most revealing.

What types of school information are useful in determining a student's emotional state? Knowing whether the student works independently in class is helpful. Does the student cooperate well with others? Does the student pay attention and follow directions? Does the teacher see evidence of emotional outbursts, inappropriate behavior, or depression? Does the student willingly participate in reading activities? How does the student interact with others?

From interviewing a parent, the reading teacher can also gain insight into a student's interactions, behavior, and attitudes within the family and with friends. For example, can the child take enough responsibility to do chores and complete work? Does the youngster often withdraw from peer groups? Does the child seem unhappy?

Of course, simply observing and interacting with a student also gives much information. Observation of a student's behaviors and attitudes during reading class can make you aware of that student's emotional state. Finally, as you interact with a student, you will be able to judge the appropriateness of responses.

At times, you may suspect that emotional factors may be affecting reading. However, because a reading teacher is not a psychologist or psychiatrist, directly addressing emotional problems is not appropriate. Rather, a reading teacher may best address these problems by planning sensitive instruction.

Donny, one student in a group of five, was quite hostile during reading instruction. He accused the teacher of liking the other children better and of thinking that he was "dumb." He deliberately dropped books and pencils, loudly complained of a stomachache, and refused to answer questions or read orally. In fact, his behavior totally disrupted group activities. To help Donny, his reading teacher made a special effort to spend some time with him alone. She read orally with Donny, praising him when he was successful and gently helping him when he had difficulties. Donny enjoyed this private attention, away from the possibly negative reactions of others. Slowly, Donny's trust in his teacher developed into an improved self-concept, and he became more cooperative during group reading activities.

Information about Potential (Intelligence)

A student's potential for learning affects his or her ability to read. Potential for learning is often measured by tests of intelligence; however, an individual's total potential cannot be fully captured in a test. This issue is discussed further in Chapter 14.

Physical Information

Many physical factors, including hearing problems, vision problems, general health problems, and neurological dysfunction, affect a student's ability to read. This section provides a brief overview of these factors.

Hearing Problems.   A hearing loss, even if it is moderate or temporary, can greatly impede reading instruction. A student who cannot hear the teacher or who cannot differentiate the sounds needed for phonics instruction will often develop reading problems. However, the most serious effect of hearing loss is that it impedes normal language development, which is the basis of reading.

When students cannot hear adequately, all of their communication skills are impaired. The result can be problems with vocabulary, grammar, and verbal thinking skills. Hearing loss is most devastating if it occurs during the language acquisition years (between the ages of two and four).

Because of the importance of adequate hearing, students need to be screened for possible hearing impairment. Often schools do this testing, or preliminary screening may be done by a reading teacher (see Chapter 14).

Additional information can also help pinpoint a hearing problem. The reading teacher can ask the parents if they have observed any speech problems, such as slurred speech or difficulty in making sounds. Has the student suffered frequent ear infections? Does the student turn her or his head to one side while listening? Does the student seem inattentive or ask for information to be repeated? Does the student fail to respond immediately when called? Of course, if you observe such behaviors during your own work with a student, you should immediately request a screening for hearing loss.

What should be done if a teacher suspects a hearing problem? As we have mentioned, many schools and reading clinics have devices for screening students. However, because the testing of hearing is complex and the results may vary from time to time in children, a reading teacher cannot make a definitive diagnosis. Rather, if screening devices or symptoms suggest a hearing loss, the parents or school should be referred to a professional in the field, such as an audiologist.

Reading teachers can also adjust their instruction to meet the needs of a student with a hearing loss or a suspected hearing loss. Remember to sit close to and face the student directly when speaking. If the student does not respond directly to questions or comments, try to repeat them in a cheerful fashion. Let the student watch you pronounce the words.

Vision Problems.   The ability to see clearly is critical to the reading process. Vision problems may be quite complex, involving difficulties in seeing close up or far away or in focusing both eyes together. In addition, certain students may have difficulties with glare, fluorescent lights, and distinguishing colors. Because vision changes rapidly for children, it should be tested often.

As with possible hearing loss, a reading teacher should try to determine whether the student has a vision problem. School records or parents can provide the results of recent vision screenings. Reading teachers can also administer vision-screening tests (see Chapter 14).

Visual behaviors that indicate problems include:

- Avoidance of reading and writing
- Holding a page very close or at an unusual angle
- Losing one's place while reading
- Frowning, squinting, or scowling during reading
- Headaches, rubbing the eyes, or covering one eye

What can a teacher do to help a student with a suspected vision problem? If a screening test or student behaviors indicate a vision problem, the youngster should be referred to a vision professional (optometrist or ophthalmologist) for further testing.

If a reading teacher is dealing with an uncorrected vision problem, certain accommodations will make the student more comfortable. Use books with larger type if they are available. Some computer software allows the teacher to adjust the size of the print. In addition, the teacher may record some of the student's books on audiotape.

General Health Problems.   Because learning is an active process, it requires that a student be alert, energetic, and able to concentrate for long periods. Poor physical health can impair the ability to concentrate. Through parent interviews and questionnaires, reading teachers can determine whether the child has any medical conditions that may affect learning or if the child suffers from conditions or takes medications that affect the ability to concentrate.

What can a teacher do when a student suffers from health problems? Sensitivity to the needs of the student is often crucial. Meghan suffered from severe allergies, and the strong medication that she took during certain times of the year tended to make her lethargic. Knowing this situation, her reading teacher praised Meghan for the work she completed and never suggested that Meghan was not trying her best.

Neurological Problems.   All learning, including the ability to learn to read, is neurologically based. The reading process demands an intact and well-functioning nervous system; a neurological dysfunction can destroy reading ability.

Children with damaged neurological systems are often "hard-core" disabled readers, who have extreme difficulty learning to read (Vellutino, et al., 1996) or are labeled *dyslexic* (see Chapter 15). Thus, if assessment of a student's reading (as we describe in the next chapter) suggests a serious reading problem, a teacher might consider the possibility of a neurological examination.

To probe further, ask the parents if any other member of the family has experienced a serious reading problem. A history of a difficult pregnancy and delivery may also point to neurological damage. Certain studies suggest that approximately half of reading disabilities may be hereditary (Torgeson, 1998). Other signs of possible neurological dysfunction are: a history of clumsiness, slow physical development, and accidents that have involved damage to the brain.

Evidence indicates that attention deficit disorder (ADD), a problem that affects the ability to concentrate, is caused by neurological problems (Lerner, Lowenthal, & Lerner, 1995). Students who suffer from ADD are often prescribed medications, such as Ritilan™, to help control their behavior.

Finally, many practitioners believe that children with learning disabilities may also have subtle problems in their neurological functioning. Students with learning disabilities are entitled to special services under the provision of the Individuals with Disabilities Education Act (IDEA) of 1997.

Information on possible neurological problems can be gathered from the parents, school records, and specialists (such as physicians) who have been consulted by the child's parents. If students with suspected neurological problems have been diagnosed as having ADD or a learning disability, the school will have already gathered much information about these students. For example, thorough testing is required for every special education student to comply with IDEA regulations (see Chapter 15). With parental consent, these records can be released to a reading teacher.

What can be done if a teacher suspects that a student may have a neurological dysfunction? If students need further testing, they should be referred to physicians specializing in pediatrics and neurology or to appropriate professionals in their schools.

However, the teacher is still responsible for teaching these students to read. Can we help them? The answer is a resounding *yes*. At one time, educators believed that very specialized methods were required to teach students with neurological difficulties to read. More recent studies suggest that the same methods that are effective with all students who have reading problems will also work with those who have a neurological dysfunction (Cunningham & Allington, 1999). A reading teacher who concentrates on effective and motivating methods will often help these students make substantial gains. Be aware, however, that students with neurological problems (or suspected neurological problems) may improve at a slower rate and may need longer and more intense instruction than most reading-disabled students.

Information about Language Development

Because reading is language expressed in written form, a student's language development forms the basis for all reading. The ability to express and receive thoughts through language is fundamental to being able to read. A student who is confused about oral language sounds will have difficulty pronouncing written words. A student who does not know many word meanings will gain little information from reading, even if he or she can pronounce all of the words.

In other instances, a student's language patterns may be mature but may differ from the language used in school. Many students come to school speaking languages other than English. They need rich experiences in learning English, plus experiences reading in their native languages, to develop high-level comprehension. Students who speak nonstandard dialects may lack both exposure to more standard English language patterns and a feeling of pride and proficiency in their own dialect.

A reading teacher can easily obtain background information about the student's language. Simply listening to or conversing with a student gives many valuable insights. A student who speaks in long sentences, provides full answers to questions, and is able to use many words probably has an excellent language base for reading. Unfortunately, many students with reading problems speak haltingly in short sentences and use just a few words.

Joey, for example, was in kindergarten, yet his language patterns resembled those of a three- or four-year-old. He often used his name instead of a pronoun or used pronouns incorrectly. "Joey needs crayons" or "Me need crayons" were typical utterances. Similarly, eight-year-old Paul had difficulty dictating even a single sentence to his reading teacher.

In addition to observation, interview questions can reveal much about a student's language. Ask the parents whether their child's language development was slower than that of other children or was within a normal range. Did their child experience any speech difficulties? Has the child had any language or speech therapy? To obtain information about language differences, ask parents what languages are spoken in the home and whether the child knew English when entering school. A history of class placements, including bilingual services or ESL (English as a Second Language), often gives much information about a student's proficiency in English.

What can be done if a teacher suspects that language problems are affecting a student's reading? At times, evaluation by a language professional (speech therapist or language specialist) may be needed to pinpoint the precise source of the difficulty. However, in many other instances, a reading teacher can foster the development of rich language by employing enjoyable instructional strategies, such as reading language-rich storybooks to the student, encouraging conversation, and developing knowledge of abstract concepts (see Chapter 10).

Twelve-year-old José, a student in our Reading Center, could speak and understand basic English, but he lacked the English skills to read more sophisticated material. His tutor began by reading selections from the daily newspaper that focused on news about Mexico, his homeland. José enjoyed helping his tutor with the pronunciation of Spanish names. They then discussed what was happening in Mexico and read portions of the articles together several times. Finally José attempted to read articles alone. At one point, he joyfully exclaimed, "That's what NAFTA looks like!" José and his tutor continued this process, moving gradually into other familiar topics such as television and sports. As he did this, José began to locate cognates—words that are the same in Spanish and English—to help his tutor learn Spanish.

Methods of Collecting Information

As we have shown, a wealth of important background information may be collected about a student with reading difficulties. This information helps us understand the factors that contribute to a reading problem. It also aids us in planning effective and motivating instruction.

Generally, background information is collected at the beginning of our work with a student. The assessment tools most frequently used are (1) interviews and questionnaires, (2) informal talks with the student, parents, and professionals, (3) records of previous testing, school achievement, or report cards, and (4) observation.

Interview and Questionnaire

Interviews and questionnaires with informed and concerned people yield information about the student that cannot be obtained in any other way. In these two formats, those concerned with a student's reading problem are able to state important information frankly and fully.

Interview. In an interview, a reading teacher follows a prescribed set of questions, asking them orally of the person who is being interviewed. A teacher can interview parents, the student, or the classroom teacher. The personal and informal atmosphere of an interview encourages the sharing of valuable information in a sympathetic setting. We generally interview the parents separately from the student and use different interview forms. A reading teacher who works outside the student's school may get valuable information from interviewing the classroom teachers and other professionals in the school. However, *written permission* must be obtained from the parents before a student's school may be contacted. Some important procedures ensure a successful interview:

- Begin by telling the parents, student, or classroom teacher that this information will be kept confidential.
- Strive for an amiable, open atmosphere. Briefly discussing a neutral topic, such as the weather or sports, can reduce initial fears or discomfort about the interview process.
- Avoid indicating disapproval of responses.
- Follow a directed plan. You should know what questions to ask before the interview begins. These questions should be in front you so they will not be forgotten.
- Take notes, because remembering everything that was said is difficult. Explain why you are taking notes. If the person being interviewed asks about what he or she said, cheerfully read the notes back aloud.
- Because of important legal and moral considerations involved in the interview, it must be kept confidential. If you wish to tape-record the interview, you must obtain written consent from parents, guardians, or the professionals involved. The presence of another individual during the interview also requires consent. Finally, information shared during an interview or any other part of the assessment procedure cannot be released to another agency without parental permission.

Questionnaire. Like an interview, a questionnaire consists of a group of questions to which parents, a student, or another professional respond. However, the list of questions is responded to in writing. A questionnaire may simply be mailed to the respondent, filled out, and mailed back. Alternatively, it may be filled out in the presence of the reading teacher.

Questionnaires are valuable when a face-to-face interview is not feasible. In our Reading Center, we often mail questionnaires to the classroom teachers of the students we serve because they have difficulties coming in for interviews. In addition, because questions are responded to independently, the use of a questionnaire enables parents, students, and classroom teachers to formulate thoughtful responses and take the time to gather valuable information about developmental history, school attendance, and grades. However, questionnaires may be unproductive with parents and children who find writing difficult.

Parent Background Information Form. Figure 2.1 (at the end of this chapter) presents a sample form for gathering background information from parents. We suggest that, if possible, this form be used as an interview, rather than as a questionnaire.

Student Background Information Form. Figure 2.2 (at the end of this chapter) presents a student information form for younger students that can be used either in an interview or as a questionnaire. Figure 2.3 (also at the end of this chapter) provides a parallel form for older students. Questions about student interests help to establish rapport with a student and give the teacher information to motivate and personalize reading instruction. Questions may be modified to suit your locality (for example, adding skiing or surfing).

A final section gives information on how the student thinks about reading (Johnston, 1997). Often, low-achieving students think that reading is just saying words; and not surprisingly, they do not focus on meaning. These questions also explore the student's reading strategies. Many students with reading problems will just "sound it out" as the only strategy they use to cope with an unknown word; they do not realize that meaning can also be used. Other low-achieving students have unrealistic pictures of good readers and believe that such readers know all the words and never make mistakes.

School Information Form. Figure 2.4 (at the end of this chapter) presents a form useful for collecting information from the student's school. Remember that written permission from parents or guardians is needed whenever you contact a student's school.

Informal Talks

In addition to interviews and questionnaires, informal conversations throughout the year can keep providing valuable insights. Twelve-year-old Adam continued to share his frustrations with homework assignments through the school year, thus enabling us to help his classroom teacher modify them.

The parents of another child revealed, over an informal cup of coffee, that he had had extensive difficulties immediately after birth. This information, which was not given in an initial interview, was shared only as the parents became more comfortable with us. The reading teacher should be alert to opportunities to gather information through these continuing, informal means.

We have found that keeping in touch with parents as instruction continues is important. Continued contact with parents provides teachers with valuable information about how students are reacting to instruction, whether they are improving, and if their attitudes toward reading are becoming more positive. Finally, contact helps families to encourage children to read at home.

School Records and Materials

School records, previous diagnostic reports, report cards, and student portfolios (organized collections of student's work kept in school) are all valuable sources of information. In addition, cumulative records, which detail a student's progress over a number of years, provide information about the history of a reading problem. Reports, such as an individualized educational program (IEP) prepared for special education students under the provisions of the IDEA, are also valuable sources of information. Encourage parents to allow you access to school information, for it enables you to gain a more thorough and balanced view of a child's reading problem.

Observation during Reading Lessons

In our discussion of background information, we presented many types of information that could be gathered through direct observation of your student. Direct observation provides insight into students' social interactions and language development. As a reading teacher, you can make observations as you work with a student. However, if possible, observe the student in many different settings. Student reactions and behaviors often vary according to the environment in which we observe them. A student who is quiet and cooperative in individual instruction may be noisy and defiant in a large class. In fact, sometimes a description of one student in these two settings is so different that we wonder if the same individual is being observed. To gain a realistic picture of students, observe them in natural settings (at parties, on the playground, in their classes) as well as in special reading classes.

As you make observations, be sure to note them in writing for future reference. Further information about observations is given in Chapter 14.

Summary

This chapter discusses collecting background information on students with reading problems, including information about the environment and the individual. Background factors interact with reading problems in complex ways; a background factor can coexist with a reading problem and yet not cause that problem.

Environmental factors include the home, school, social, and cultural environments. The home influences a child as parents serve as role models for literacy and provide a general environment that nurtures the child. The child's school history, attendance, and school instruction also affect a reading problem. Often, students who have reading problems are not receiving instruction that meets their needs. Students with reading problems also tend to have social difficulties. They may also come from a culture that does not support literacy.

Individual factors include emotional status, potential or intelligence, physical health, and language development. Students with reading problems may have emotional difficulties. Sometimes these emotional problems are alleviated as reading improves. Physical factors include hearing problems, visual problems, general health problems, and neurological problems. Students with ADD and learning disabilities may have subtle neurological problems. Students with reading problems may also have difficulties with language development.

Information may be collected through interviews, written questionnaires, informal talks, school records and materials, and observation.

FIGURE 2.1 Parent Information Form

PARENT INFORMATION

Student's Name _____   Age ____   Grade ____   Birth Date ____

Person Being Interviewed _____   Relationship to Student _____

Person Conducting Interview _____   Date of Interview _____

Can you tell me three positive things about your child?

1. _____

2. _____

3. _____

Environmental Information

Home Environment

Family Members Present in Home:

Name	Relationship to Student	Age	Birthplace	Occupation

Family Members Not Living in Home:

Name	Relationship to Student	Age	Birthplace	Occupation

(continued)

FIGURE 2.1   Parent Information Form, continued

Describe any reading or learning problems experienced by family members. _____

_____

_____

What reading activities, including reading to or with your child, are done at home? _____

_____

Describe your child's TV viewing. _____

_____

What are your child's responsibilities at home? _____

_____

What are the attitudes of family members toward reading? _____

_____

School Environment

Describe your child's preschool and kindergarten experiences. _____

_____

At what age did your child enter first grade? _____

_____

Describe your child's reading experiences in first grade. _____

_____

Has your child repeated any grade? If so, why? _____

_____

Describe your child's current school and classes, including any special placements such as special
education or bilingual instruction. _____

_____

Describe the homework your child gets. _____

_____

How does your child do in areas other than reading, such as math, spelling, handwriting, social
studies, and science? _____

_____

FIGURE 2.1   Parent Information Form, continued

Has your child's school attendance been regular? _____

_____

Describe any extended absences from school. _____

_____

Describe your child's reading instruction, including grouping within the class if any. _____

_____

_____

Does your child receive any special help in school? If so, please describe. _____

_____

Please describe any testing your child has experienced. _____

_____

Please describe any help your child has received outside of school, such as summer school or outside tutoring. _____

_____

When did you first become concerned about your child's reading? _____

_____

Can you think of anything that might have contributed to your child's reading problem? _____

_____

_____

Social and Cultural Environment

Describe your child's relationship with other family members. _____

_____

What are your child's interests and leisure activities? _____

_____

Describe your child's friends and social group. _____

_____

(continued)

FIGURE 2.1 Parent Information Form, continued

INFORMATION ABOUT THE INDIVIDUAL

Physical Information

How would you compare your child's physical development with that of other children of the same age?

_____

Please describe pregnancy, delivery, and early history of your child. _____

_____

Please describe your child's general health. _____

Please describe any specific illnesses, allergies, or accidents. _____

_____

Is your child taking any medications? If so, please list and describe. _____

_____

Has your child ever been unconscious? If so, please describe the circumstances. _____

_____

Does your child seem to have difficulty maintaining attention? _____

When is the last time your child's hearing was tested? _____

Who tested his/her hearing, and what were the recommendations? _____

_____

Has your child ever experienced a hearing loss? _____

When is the last time your child's vision was tested? _____

Who tested his/her vision, and what were the results? _____

_____

Emotional Information

Does your child seem to be happy? _____

_____

Does your child exhibit any signs of emotional tension or lack of self-confidence? If so, please describe. _____

_____

FIGURE 2.1   Parent Information Form, continued

What is your child's attitude toward reading? _____

_____

Language Development

What languages are spoken in your home? _____

_____

What languages does your child speak? _____

How did your child's early language development compare with that of others? _____

_____

Has your child received any bilingual or ESL services? _____

Has your child received any speech or language therapy? _____

Comments and Suggestions

Can you think of anything else we should know about in working with your child? Does he or she have any special needs that we should take into consideration? _____

_____

_____

_____

_____

FIGURE 2.2   Student Information Form for Younger Students

ALL ABOUT ME

_____   _____   _____   _____
Your Name   Age   Grade   Date

Who lives at home with you?_____

_____

What are some things that you and your family do together? _____

_____

What are some of your favorite books? _____

_____

Do you read at home?_____

Do you get book from the library or store? _____

What are some of your favorite TV shows?_____

_____

What are some of your favorite movies and videos? _____

_____

FIGURE 2.2 Student Information Form for Younger Students, continued

What kinds of music do you like? _____

What are some of your favorite songs? _____

_____

Who are your favorite actors? _____

Singers? _____

Do you like sports? _____

If yes:

What is your favorite sport? _____

What is your favorite team? _____

Who is your favorite sports star? _____

What sports do you play? _____

Do you have any pets? What kinds? _____

Do you have any chores to do at home? _____

What is your favorite subject in school? _____

What are some subjects you don't like? _____

(continued)

FIGURE 2.2   Student Information Form for Younger Students, continued

Do you have reading groups, or does the whole class read together? _____

_____

What are the names of some books you are reading in school? _____

_____

What happens in your class during reading time? _____

_____

Do you like learning to read? _____

If you could change one thing about your reading class, what would it be? _____

_____

What kind of homework do you get? _____

_____

Who are your best friends? _____

Who are your friends in school? _____

What do you like to do with your friends? _____

Do you ever have trouble hearing things? _____

FIGURE 2.2   Student Information Form for Younger Students, continued

Do your eyes ever hurt? _____

Do you ever have trouble seeing the board in school? _____

Do you ever have trouble seeing the print in books? _____

What clubs do you belong to? _____

What lessons do you take? _____

What are you interested in? _____

What do you want to do when you grow up and finish school? _____

_____

Why do people read? _____

What do you do when you come to something you don't know while you are reading?

_____

Who is the best reader you know? _____

What makes this person such a good reader? _____

_____

FIGURE 2.3 Student Information for Older Students

INTEREST/ATTITUDE INTERVIEW FOR ADOLESCENTS

Student Name _____   Age _____   Grade in School _____

Person Conducting Interview _____   Date of Interview _____

Home Life

How many people are in your family? _____

Names _____   Relationship to You _____

_____   _____

_____   _____

_____   _____

_____   _____

_____   _____

Do you have your own room, or do you share a room? _____

Do your parent(s) work? _____

   What kinds of jobs do they have? _____

Do you have jobs around the house? What are they? _____

What do you usually do after school? _____

Do you have a TV in your room? _____

How much time would you say you spend watching TV a day? _____

Do you have a certain time to go to bed during the week? What time do you usually go to bed on a school night? _____

Do you belong to any clubs at school or outside school? What are they? _____

_____

What are some things you like to do with your family? _____

_____

FIGURE 2.3   Student Information Form for Older Students, continued

School Environment

Do you like school? _____

What is your favorite class? _____

What classes do you not like? _____

How much homework do you usually have on a school night? _____

What kinds of homework do you usually have? _____

Do you have a special place to study at home? _____

Does anyone help you with your homework? Who? _____

What kind of reader do you consider yourself? [*Good, not so good*] _____

If good: What do you think has helped you most to become a good reader? _____

_____

If not so good: What do you think causes someone to not be a good reader? _____

_____

Is there anything you can think of that would help you get better at reading? _____

_____

Do you like to write? _____

What kinds of writing do you like to do? _____

Do you do much writing at school? _____

What kinds of writing do you do at school? _____

What kinds of writing assignments do you like? _____

What kinds do you dislike? _____

If you went to a new school, what is one thing you would like the teachers to know about you?____

_____

If you were helping someone learn to read, what would be the most important thing you could do
to help that person? _____

_____

How does knowing how to read help people? _____

_____

_____

(continued)

FIGURE 2.3   Student Information Form for Older Students, continued

Social Life

What do you like to do after school and on weekends? _____

Who are your best friends? _____

   Does your best friend go to your school? _____

What do you like to do with your friends? _____

Do you like music? _____

   What kinds: _____

   Who are your favorite performers? _____

What are your favorite TV shows? _____

   Who are your favorite TV stars? _____

Do you like movies or videos? _____

   What kinds of movies do you like? _____

   Who are your favorite stars? _____

Do you like sports? _____

   What kinds of sports do you play? _____

   What kinds of sports do you like to watch? _____

   What is your favorite team? _____

   Who are your favorite athletes? _____

If you could read a book about anything, what would you choose? _____

_____

   What is the best book you've ever read? _____

Do you have any favorite magazines? _____

Do you ever read the newspaper? _____

   What parts do you usually read? _____

FIGURE 2.4 School Information Form

SCHOOL INFORMATION FORM

_____   _____   _____
Student's Name   Grade   Date

_____   _____
School or Organization Name   Tutor Requesting Information

_____   _____
Person Providing Information   Position or Title

School Attendance

How long has this student attended this school? _____

Describe regularity of attendance. _____

_____

Reading Performance

Is this student having problems in reading? _____

_____

Please describe these problems. _____

_____

When were these problems first noticed? _____

_____

Describe this student's areas of strength in reading. _____

_____

Describe this student's areas of weakness in reading. _____

_____

Please describe the reading instruction provided, including whether reading is taught as a separate subject, whether students are grouped and which group this student is in, whether students change classes for reading, whether a reading series or separate reading book is used for instruction, and what supplementary materials are used. _____

_____

_____

(continued)

FIGURE 2.4   School Information Form, continued

List some books this student is reading. _____

_____

_____

Describe this student's progress in other areas, such as spelling, writing, math, science, social studies, and gym. _____

_____

_____

Describe any help this student receives in addition to regular classroom instruction. _____

_____

Describe the student's independence, ability to complete tasks, follow directions, and pay attention. _____

_____

_____

What kinds of homework is this student given? Is it usually completed? _____

_____

_____

Does this student read for pleasure? _____

_____

Does this student seem tired at school? _____

Does this student seem to have any vision or hearing problems? _____

How does this student's physical development compare with that of others? _____

_____

How does this student's oral language compare with that of other students? _____

_____

Has any testing been done at school? If so, please provide a summary below or attach information with returned form. _____

_____

_____

CHAPTER

3 Assessing Reading Achievement: Overview and Informal Measures

Introduction

This chapter describes the process of assessing a student's reading performance. It begins by presenting two general questions that form an overview of diagnosis. Next, it discusses both formal and informal assessment. A major portion of the chapter is devoted to informal measures and in particular the informal reading inventory, a fundamental tool that gives many insights into a student's reading.

Other tools for informal assessment are discussed in Chapters 5 through 11. In addition, Chapter 16 presents an in-depth discussion of formal tests.

General Diagnostic Questions: An Overview

The process of assessing reading involves more than giving tests. In fact, a good reading teacher uses tests, background information, and observation to formulate answers to diagnostic questions. A reading diagnosis is thus a thoughtful synthesis and interpretation of all the information that is collected about a student.

What questions need to be answered about the student? Assessing a student's reading achievement involves answering two general questions: (1) How severe is the reading problem? and (2) What is the general area of the reading problem? You can answer these questions by observing and working with a student and by administering assessment tools. Often a single assessment tool, such as an informal reading inventory, can answer both questions as well as provide much specific information about a student.

How Severe Is the Reading Problem?

Because resources for special reading help are scarce, we must allocate them to the students who need them most. In fact, some of the students who are referred for help actually do not need it. Sometimes recognizing that a student has a reading problem is easy. For example, a child who has finished second grade and still cannot read a first-grade text is clearly having difficulty. At times, however, students have been referred to our Reading Center simply because they were not selected for a gifted program.

To determine the severity of a reading problem, we need to determine at what level a student is reading and to compare this level with the level at which that student should be reading. Thus, we compare

- The student's current reading level to
- The student's appropriate reading level

By appropriate level, we mean the books and stories that are used in the student's classroom, both for reading and for content area instruction (math, social studies, science). Usually, appropriate materials mean those at a student's grade level. However, if the student's class is reading at a higher level, then appropriate materials are at that higher level.

However, the opposite is not true. Children who are experiencing problems in school are often placed in special classes where they read materials well below their grade level. For example, a fourth grader might be in a special class that is reading second-grade material. In this case, second-grade text is *not* an appropriate level; the appropriate level for this student would be the fourth-grade level, the actual grade placement.

A student who can read at an appropriate level with acceptable word recognition and comprehension does not have a reading problem. However, a student who cannot read appropriate materials has a reading problem, and our next step is to determine the severity of that problem. The difference between the student's grade placement and the grade placement of the texts he or she can read shows us how severe the reading problem is.

How do we know whether a student's problem can be classified as severe? Guidelines provided by Spache (1981), presented in Table 3.1, compare a student's current grade placement to the student's reading level. As you can see, the younger the student, the less difference is needed to define a reading problem as severe.

Using these criteria, a student who is placed in fourth grade but is reading at the second-grade level would have a reading problem that is severe. A fourth-grade student reading at the third-grade level would have a reading problem, but not a severe one. A fourth-grade student reading at the fourth-grade level would not have a reading problem.

The severity of the student's reading problem helps us determine what type of special instruction is most effective. Students with severe reading problems may require long and intensive intervention in daily classes with individual instruction. In contrast, students with less severe problems may blossom in small group settings that meet once or twice a week.

TABLE 3.1   Criteria for Determining a Severe Reading Problem

Student's Grade Placement	Difference between Grade Placement and Reading Level
Grades 1, 2, 3	One year or more
Grades 4, 5, 6	Two years or more
Grades 7 and above	Three years or more

Source: Spache (1981).

What Is the General Area of the Reading Problem?

As we discussed in Chapter 1, reading consists of many different components, or areas. Problems with reading fall into several general areas:

- Emergent literacy
- Word recognition accuracy
- Word recognition fluency
- Comprehension
- Language and meaning vocabulary

Some students may have problems in only one of these general areas. Other students may have problems in a combination of areas. Deciding the general area of a student's reading problem is important, for this information helps you, as a reading teacher, deliver the most effective instruction.

Problems with Emergent Literacy.   Emergent literacy refers to the understandings and skills that underlie reading. These skills include the knowledge that print stands for meaning, the recognition of alphabet letters, and the ability to recognize letter sounds. Although most students have acquired emergent literacy skills by the time they enter first grade, some students with reading problems continue to lack them long after formal reading instruction has begun.

Problems with Word Recognition Accuracy.   Many students with reading problems cannot recognize words accurately. They lack strategies for identifying unfamiliar words. For example, trying to read a passage about farms, nine-year-old Carlos pronounced the word *farm* as *from, form*, and *for*.

Without accurate word identification, a student cannot comprehend a passage. For example, Carlos's summary of the farm passage was "They—the kids—were going someplace."

Problems with Word Recognition Fluency.   In addition to recognizing words accurately, readers need to identify them quickly. Words that we recognize instantly, without any need for analysis, are often called *sight vocabulary*. When we read fluently, we read text without stopping to analyze words. Fluency is important because human beings have limited memories. If we direct all our attention to figuring out the words, we will have difficulties understanding what the author is saying because we will have no resources to devote to comprehension (LaBerge & Samuels, 1974). Only if we recognize words quickly can we devote attention to comprehension. One of our students, Sofia, did a flawless oral reading of a story about Johnny Appleseed. However, because she labored over many words, she read slowly and without fluency. As a result, she could answer only 3 of 10 comprehension questions.

Problems with Comprehension.   Many students have problems comprehending what they read. At times, youngsters do not actively construct meaning but simply read to pronounce words or answer questions. Thus, they are not reading to comprehend. Comprehension occurs at different levels. Literal comprehension includes applying background knowledge to what is being read. Higher-level comprehension includes organizing what is read, drawing inferences, and thinking critically.

However, at times, poor understanding of text may be rooted in causes other than comprehension. For example, a student who lacks adequate word recognition may not be able to comprehend material. Sofia, whom we mentioned previously, could not comprehend material because she lacked word recognition fluency. Similarly, apparent problems in reading comprehension may actually be caused by underlying problems in understanding language and word meanings.

Students need comprehension strategies when they read storylike or narrative text. Learning from expository text, or studying, is also part of comprehension; many students with reading problems do not know how to summarize, take notes, or prepare for multiple-choice and essay examinations.

Problems with Language and Meaning Vocabulary.   Because reading is a language process, our ability to read cannot exceed the language we can understand and the word meanings we already know. Students who can pronounce words as they read but cannot understand them are not really reading. Aushabell, a second-grade student in our Reading Center, had recently arrived from Turkey. She could read orally with amazing accuracy. However, she had little idea of what she was reading, for she lacked an understanding of such common English words as *mother, school, run*, and *night*. Many other students in our Reading Center do speak English fluently but lack the rich language patterns and meaning vocabulary needed to read more sophisticated stories, novels, and textbooks. In fact, problems with underlying language and word meaning have been recognized as an extremely important factor in reading disabilities for intermediate and upper-grade students beyond third grade (Stanovich, 1986).

Overview of Formal Assessment Measures

In reading diagnosis, we use both formal and informal tests. By formal tests, we mean commercially and formally prepared instruments. Many formal tests are *norm-referenced*, or *standardized*. Using norm-referenced tests, we can compare a student's score with those of the sample of students who were used to standardize the test (the *norm sample*). To ensure that we can compare student scores to the norm sample, we must strictly follow the procedures for test administration, scoring, and interpretation. Unlike informal assessment measures, the teacher cannot adapt or change formal testing procedures.

Other formal instruments are called *criterion-referenced* tests. These tests are constructed from a different theoretical view. Instead of comparing a student's score with those of the norm group, a criterion-referenced test determines whether a student has mastered certain competencies, such as specific reading skills. The student's score is compared to a cutoff score (or criterion) set by the authors of the test.

Each type of formal reading test offers a different kind of information. Formal tests that assess general reading abilities usually give a student's reading level and suggest general areas of reading strengths and weaknesses. Other formal tests are used for more specific or diagnostic reading assessment and assess strengths or weaknesses within a certain area (such as word recognition). A thorough discussion of formal measures is presented in Chapter 16.

Overview of Informal Assessment Measures

Informal measures refer to tools, other than published instruments with prescribed procedures, that can be used to collect information about a student's reading. We can modify informal measures to suit the needs of our students and the information we want to gather. This chapter describes the informal reading inventory. Chapters 5 through 11 describe various informal measures for evaluating various components of the reading process.

The three key differences between formal and informal measures are:

- Informal measures have not been normed, or standardized, on large populations of students, as have many formal tests. Therefore, we cannot use informal measures to compare one student's performance to that of others. To make such comparisons, we must use formal tests that have been normed.
- Informal measures are flexible. Because informal measures have not been standardized, teachers are free to make modifications in test procedures, adapting them to serve the specific needs of the diagnostic situation. In contrast, formal measures must be administered in the same way to all students. Because of their flexibility, many reading teachers consider informal measures to be the cornerstone of reading assessment.

    Informal tests allow teachers to personalize assessment to the needs of the student and tailor testing to account for the different backgrounds, interests, and attitudes of students. For example, fifth-grade Jon was interested and active in sports. Jon insisted that although he wasn't doing well in schoolwork, he could read sports material "like a champ." When we carefully chose different selections, we found that, indeed, he comprehended a fifth-grade narrative about the soccer star, Pele, very well but could read at only a third-grade level when the subject was plants or frontier life. This informal assessment told the reading teacher that Jon's background and interest had a marked effect on his reading.
- Informal measures often give a more *authentic assessment* than formal ones. Authentic assessments are measures that are similar to the actual reading tasks a student does in school. In such measures, students read longer selec-

tions, summarize them, and answer questions, just as they would in a typical classroom or when reading for their own information or enjoyment.

For example, to get a picture of why 11-year-old Duane was failing in social studies, his reading teacher asked him to read a selection from a textbook and take notes as if he were preparing for a test. His difficulties with this task enabled his teacher to precisely pinpoint his instructional needs.

In contrast to this use of authentic materials, many formal tests measure the student's ability to read short passages and answer multiple-choice questions. These tasks do not represent what real readers do on a daily basis.

To summarize, informal measures allow teachers the flexibility to adapt assessment so that it gives maximum information about how students, materials, and classroom situations interact to affect a reading problem. In this way, teachers can best determine how students can meet the demands of school reading.

Informal Reading Inventory

The informal reading inventory (IRI) is one informal assessment instrument that is widely used in reading diagnosis. The IRI is one of the best tools for observing and analyzing reading performance and for gathering information about how a student uses a wide range of reading strategies.

The IRI is administered to students individually. In an IRI, a student reads graded passages orally and silently and answers questions about them. As a student reads, the teacher records performance in word recognition and comprehension. Generally, passages are given at the preprimer, primer, first-grade, and all other grade levels through the eighth grade. However, inventories vary in the levels they present. In addition, many inventories contain graded word lists, which are used to help select appropriate passage levels for students to read.

Passages in IRIs are representative of textbooks at different grade levels. Thus, a teacher can see how a student functions with classroom-like materials (Johnson, Kress, & Pikulski, 1987). Because it is classroom-based, the information gained from an IRI is often more useful and realistic than the results of a standardized test. An IRI is also effective for assessing both short-term and long-term growth (Caldwell, Fromm, & O'Connor, 1997–1998; Leslie & Allen, 1999).

A teacher can use an IRI to assess student reading achievement at different times during the school year. After a student has participated in an intervention program, an IRI can be used to measure the student's reading growth.

There are many different types of IRIs. Some are published as separate tests (Appendix B), and others are available with reading textbook series. Teachers may also construct their own IRIs. We include an IRI in Appendix D. Whatever IRI you choose, remember that it is an informal measure you can adapt for different purposes and needs.

Obtaining Answers to General Diagnostic Questions

The IRI helps us obtain information on the two general assessment questions presented in the beginning of this chapter: (1) What is the severity of the student's reading problem? and (2) What is the general area of the student's reading problem?

To answer the first question, the reading teacher determines an *instructional* reading level for the student. This is the level of material that the student can read with instructional support, such as that provided in a typical classroom. The reading teacher then compares the instructional level on the IRI to the level of reading appropriate for the student. This comparison shows the severity of the reading problem. For example, a student who has an instructional level of fifth grade on the IRI and is in fifth grade does not have a reading problem. On the other hand, a fifth-grade student who has an instructional level of first grade has a severe reading problem.

The IRI can also help to reveal the general area of the reading problem. Through listening to a student read orally, the teacher can determine whether word recognition accuracy or fluency is the student's problem. By asking questions and having students retell passages that have been read, the teacher can assess comprehension. By having the student listen to a passage and respond to questions, the teacher can determine whether the areas of language and meaning vocabulary are problems.

Finally, because the IRI is an individual test, a teacher has opportunities during its administration to make diagnostic observations that answer many different questions. Does the student read better orally or silently? Become easily frustrated? Point to each word or regularly lose the place in reading? Does the student have particular difficulty with drawing conclusions in material? The IRI is a rich source of these and many other insights.

However, like all other assessment tools, IRIs have some limitations. For example, examiners, especially untrained ones, can miss some problems with oral reading (Pikulski & Shanahan, 1982). In addition, a student's performance on a passage may be affected by the amount of personal interest in the subject, background knowledge, and text organization (Caldwell, 1985; Leslie & Caldwell, 2001; Lipson, Cox, Iwankowski, & Simon, 1984). Finally, the shortness of IRI selections (often a few hundred words) may not allow teachers to determine how well a student reads a multipage selection.

To obtain the greatest assessment value, teachers need to prepare carefully for administering an IRI. They need to use professional observation and judgment in effectively translating IRI results into instructional decisions. In short, the IRI is only a tool to be used in gathering diagnostic information.

Administering and Scoring the Informal Reading Inventory

Each published IRI comes with directions for administration that may vary in detail from other IRIs. All IRIs have some common features, however, and the directions given in this chapter are based on these similarities.

The informal reading inventory consists of a series of graded reading selections followed by questions. Some IRIs, such as one provided in Appendix D, also contain graded word lists. The teacher can use these lists to decide which passage to administer first. The student reads passages (orally or silently) at different grade levels and stops when the material becomes too difficult. After the student reads each passage, the teacher asks comprehension questions. For passages read orally, the teacher records reading errors, or *miscues*, which are deviations from what is written. The teacher also records the time needed to read the passage and student responses to the questions. For passages read silently, the teacher records the time needed for reading and the responses to questions. In addition, the teacher may wish to ask students to retell a selection in their own words.

The percentage of reading miscues determines word recognition accuracy. The time needed for reading, which determines word recognition fluency, may also be used to judge passages, if you wish. The responses to questions determine the comprehension score. In turn, word recognition and comprehension scores determine three reading levels for the student:

- An *independent* level, at which a student can read without teacher guidance. Use this level for recreational reading.
- An *instructional* level, at which a student can read with teacher support. Use this level for reading instruction.
- A *frustrational* level, which is too hard for the student. Avoid this level.

Each level is expressed as a grade level (from preprimer through eighth grade). Teachers can use these three levels to determine the severity of a reading problem as well as to select reading materials for various purposes. Thus, a unique and valuable assessment feature of the IRI is that it gives guidelines for selecting classroom materials.

Materials and General Preparation.   To give an IRI, select a period of about an hour to work with an individual student. For younger students and students who are extremely nervous, you may want to divide the testing into two periods.

Materials you will need usually include:

- Student copy of the IRI for word lists and passages
- Protocol (or teacher copy) for word lists and passages
- Stopwatch or watch with a second hand
- Tape recorder and audiotape
- Clipboard

Seat the student across from you and hand him or her the student copy of the passage to read. The student copy contains only the passage, without the questions. Record oral reading miscues and responses to questions on a teacher copy, referred to as a *protocol*. The protocol also contains questions to ask the student. Place the protocol on a clipboard for ease in handling.

Even experienced examiners find that taping the entire session is helpful so that they can refer to it later. Explain to the student that you are taping because you can't remember everything. Then place the tape recorder off to one side to reduce its intrusion into your testing situation. Because using the tape recorder often makes students nervous, you might ask your student to state his or her name and the date and then play these back to test the tape recorder.

If you wish to record the speed of your student's reading, you will need a stopwatch. Again, explain what you are doing, allow your student to handle the stopwatch for a short time, and then place it off to one side.

To help prepare a student for the IRI, explain that he or she will read passages both orally and silently and answer questions after each passage. Finally, tell the student that the material will become progressively more difficult.

Administering Word Lists.   Many IRIs provide a set of graded word lists. A student's performance on reading these word lists provides a quick way to determine which passage in the IRI the student should read first. Word lists generally start at the preprimer level and continue up through the sixth-grade level. Each level has 25 words.

Students usually begin by reading the easiest list. As your youngster reads from the student's copy, record the responses on your teacher's copy. If the student recognizes a word instantly, mark a "+" in the timed column. If the student must analyze the word, mark a "+" in the untimed column. Administer the graded word lists until the student scores below 60% on any list (for example, misses 11 or more words out of 25 on the timed words). Begin the oral reading passages at the highest level on which the student scores at least 90% (no more than two miscues) on the timed column. If students score low on the word lists, begin by testing at the preprimer level or eliminate the IRI and use emergent literacy assessments (see Chapter 5).

For example, fourth-grade Reyna's scores on the IRI word lists follow:

Preprimer: 90%   Grade 2: 80%
Primer: 100%   Grade 3: 55%
Grade 1: 80%

The primer level is the highest level at which Reyna scored 90% or above. Therefore, the teacher should begin testing Reyna at the primer level.

In addition to determining which passage to administer first, a student's performance on word lists can provide important diagnostic information about word recognition abilities. By looking at incorrect responses on a word list, you can gain insights about how a student analyzes words. You can see, for example, whether students are matching letters and sounds (phonics). You can also determine if they use structural analysis, such as examining prefixes and suffixes. Figure 3.1 shows Reyna's responses to the second-grade word list. If you look at Reyna's incorrect responses, you can see that she is able to use sounds (such as *t, dr, wh*) at the beginnings of words but does not always use correct vowels and ending sounds.

FIGURE 3.1 Reyna's Scored IRI Word List, Level 2

| | Target Word | Student's Attempt | | Knew in Context (in oral passage) + or − |
		Timed Presentation	Untimed Presentation	
Oral	camp	+		
	year	+		
	spend	+		
	whole	what	when	
	week	will	+	
	packed	pick	+	
	clothes	clap	+	
	dressed	dr...	drossed	
	brushed	+		
	teeth	test	tooth	
	kitchen	+		
	eggs	+		
	toast	test	+	
	seemed	s...	+	
	forever	+		
	hundreds	+		
	shorts	+		
	shirts	shark	shirk	
	tent	+		
	knew	k...	know	
Silent	teacher	+		
	world	work	+	
	playground	+		
	classroom	+		
	card	+		
Results		# Correct	Multiplied by 4	% Correct
Timed Presentation		14	x 4	56
Untimed Presentation		6	x 4	24
Total		20	x 4	80

This information provides the reading teacher with suggestions of phonics strategies that need to be taught.

Some children score much lower on word lists than they do when reading a selection. This situation suggests that the student is using the context of the passage as an aid to word recognition. Although this strategy is normal for beginning readers, older and skilled readers do not use context for word pronunciation, and poor readers often overuse it (Stanovich, 1993–4; 1991).

Administering Reading Passages.   If you have given a word list, you will know the passage level to administer first. If not, start at a level that you think will be easy for the student. Sometimes information from other testing or classroom performance can suggest a beginning passage level. Remember that beginning too low is better than beginning too high. Students who have difficulty on the first IRI passage they read often become nervous. If you find that the first passage you have chosen is too challenging, stop the reading and immediately move down to an easier level.

Most IRIs provide passages for both oral and silent reading. Administer all of the oral passages first and obtain independent, instructional, and frustrational levels for oral reading. Then administer the silent passages and obtain reading levels for this mode. (For an alternative plan, see the section in this chapter on Special Issues and Options in Using IRIs.)

The following steps are appropriate for administering passages for the IRI in Appendix D as well as for many other published IRIs:

1. Before reading, orally give the student a brief introduction to the topic: For example, say "this story is about a girl who wanted to become a champion skater."
2. Ask a background question to determine how familiar the student is with the topic: "What do you know about championship skating?" Answers to such questions allow you to determine whether problems with reading might be due to lack of background knowledge. (The IRI in Appendix D provides instructions and background questions.)
3. Hand the student copy to the student to read. State that you will ask questions after reading is completed. Have the student read orally (for oral passages) or silently (for silent passages). If the passage is to be read orally, tell the student that you will not be able to help with words and that he or she can say "pass" if a word cannot be figured out. (See Special Issues and Options in Using IRIs later in this chapter for a discussion of teacher aid.) If the passage is to be read silently, ask your student to look up immediately when finished so that you can record the time correctly.
4. For oral reading, record any differences between the text and the student's reading on your protocol. If you want to record reading speed, time the student with a stopwatch.

5. After the student finishes, take away the passage and ask the comprehension questions. If you want additional information, you may also ask the student to retell the passage in his or her own words.
6. Continue testing until you have determined the independent, instructional, and frustrational levels for your student. For example, if a student scores at an independent level for third grade, have the student read the fourth-grade passage. Continue moving up until you reach the student's frustrational level. If a student scores at a frustrational level on the first passage read, move down until you reach the independent level. The next section explains how to determine these levels.

Reading Levels Obtained from the IRI. Using an IRI, a reading teacher can determine the student's independent, instructional, and frustrational reading levels. The instructional level is particularly critical because the severity of a student's reading problem is determined by *comparing the instructional level with the level at which the student should be reading* (usually the student's grade placement). For example, if a student's IRI instructional level is third grade but he is in a sixth-grade class, he would have a severe reading problem.

How do we calculate reading levels? As stated earlier, reading levels on an IRI are determined by performance on the passages, not scores on the word lists.

The level of an orally read passage is based on (1) the word recognition accuracy score for the passage and (2) the comprehension score. The level of a silently read passage is based on the comprehension score.

The word recognition score comes from the number of miscues, or errors, that the student makes while orally reading a passage. The comprehension score comes from the number of correct responses on the comprehension questions. Table 3.2 lists the criteria suggested for the different IRI levels.

Scoring Word Recognition Accuracy. A word recognition score is obtained from the student's oral reading of passages. To obtain this score, you must code and score this oral reading.

TABLE 3.2 IRI Passage Criteria for Three Reading Levels

Reading Level	Word Recognition Accuracy (%)		Comprehension (%)
Independent	98–100	and	90–100
Instructional	95–98	and	70–89
Frustrational	Less than 95	or	Less than 70

Your first step is to code the oral reading. As the student reads, you need to mark all miscues, using a standard system, so that you can later determine exactly what the student said. Commercial IRIs generally provide their own coding systems. Teachers who construct their own IRIs or use the one in Appendix D should use the coding system presented in Figure 3.2.

Omissions, additions, substitutions, and reversals usually count as word recognition errors. You might, in addition, want to *record* repetitions, hesitations, omissions of punctuation, and spontaneous corrections of errors. Because these four things do not usually alter the meaning of text, we do not recommend counting them as errors (McKenna, 1983). However, they can provide additional information about a student's word recognition strategies.

After coding the oral reading, you need to score it. The easiest and most reliable way to score the oral reading is to assign one point to each omission, addition, substitution, and reversal (Leslie & Caldwell, 2001). Two sets of extensive field testing (Leslie & Caldwell, 2001; Jennings, 2001) indicate that this scoring sys-

---

FIGURE 3.2   Coding System for Scoring IRI Passage Miscues

1. *Omissions:* Circle.
   □ on ⟨the⟩ table

2. *Insertions:* Insert the added word above a caret.
   □ on the ^big^ table

3. *Substitutions, mispronunciations:* Underline the word in the text and write the word that the student said above the word in text.
   □ on the <u>table</u> (tablet)

4. *Reversals:* Same as substitutions.

5. *Repetitions:* Draw a line with an arrow below the words.
   □ on the table ←┘

6. *Words pronounced correctly but with hesitations:* Write an *H* over the word.
   □ on the ^H^ table

7. *Lack of punctuation:* Circle ignored punctuation.
   □ I saw Mary⟨.⟩ She was happy.

8. *Student corrections:* Cross out any previous responses and mark with *SC*.
   □ on the ~~table~~ (tablet) ^SC^

---

tem places students at appropriate instructional levels. However, some alternatives for scoring miscues are discussed in the section Special Issues and Options in Using IRIs.

Certain scoring problems may arise during an IRI. We propose solutions to some of these based on field testing by Leslie & Caldwell (2001) and Jennings (2001):

- If a student repeatedly mispronounces the same word, count it as incorrect each time. If a student were reading an assignment in school, each mispronunciation would affect comprehension.
- If a student omits an entire line or phrase, count it as one miscue. In this situation, the student simply lost his or her place.
- Proper names are difficult for students because they often do not follow regular phonics patterns. Do not count a mispronunciation of a proper name as incorrect unless it changes the sex of the character. For example, do not count the substitution of *Mary* for *Maria*. However, do count the substitution of *Mark* for *Maria*. Sometimes students use a nonword to pronounce a proper name such as *Manee* for *Maria*. If the student says this consistently throughout the passage, do not count it as an error. If, however, the student pronounces it differently on other occasions, count it as incorrect each time. Follow these guidelines for names of places.
- Miscues that reflect a student's speech patterns should never count as errors. In other words, mispronunciations resulting from dialect differences, speaking English as a second language, immature speech patterns, or speech impediments do not count as errors. For example, a student who speaks a dialect other than Standard English might pronounce the word *tests* as *tes*, both in speaking and in reading an IRI passage. In such miscues, readers are simply recoding the written word into their own pronunciation. Pupils should never be penalized for such recoding.

After you have counted all of the errors on an individual passage, total them. Then compute the percentage of words read correctly in the passage. In the coded and scored passage in Figure 3.3, the student had 4 errors, and 92 correct words in the total 96 words. The percentage correct is 96%, an instructional level.

$$\frac{92 \text{ Words Correct}}{96 \text{ Total Words}} \times 100 = 96\%$$

To make this process easier, use Table 3.3. Simply find the intersection between the number of words in the passage and the error count. For example, if the passage contains 103 words and the error count is 9, then the percentage correct is 91.

After you have determined a percentage of words read correctly, translate this percentage score into a level (independent, instructional, or frustrational) by using Table 3.2.

FIGURE 3.3 Student's Coded Oral Reading of a Primer-Level IRI Passage

Nick's Trip to the Lake

Once
Nick and his dad like animals. One (day) Nick and his dad went to the lake. They

went to see the animals. They sat next to the lake. They were very still.

out   Then
Then Nick saw a big duck. He saw the duck swim to ∧ a big rock in the lake ∧ Some-

thing made the duck fly away fast.

Nick asked his dad, "Why did the duck fly away?"

Nick's dad said, "Look over there." He showed Nick something in the lake. Nick
H
thought he would see something big.

SC
What a surprise to see a little green ~~frog~~!

Scoring System

Omissions: ◯		Repetitions: ⟵⏌
Insertions: ∧		Hesitations: H
Substitutions: Write the word and underline		Student corrections: SC

Words in passage	96
Errors	4
Oral Reading Accuracy Score	96%

Grading Comprehension.   After the student reads each passage, the teacher asks
questions to check comprehension. If the student's answer is incorrect, the teacher
writes the exact student response; if the response is correct, simply mark a "+".
The teacher obtains a percentage score: for example, if the student answers three
of four comprehension questions correctly, the comprehension score would be 75
percent on that selection. Table 3.4 provides the percentage of correct scores for
different numbers of comprehension questions. Translate the percentage score on
comprehension into a level (independent, instructional, or frustrational).

TABLE 3.3 Percentages for Word Recognition Accuracy Scores
(Each Number Indicates Percentage Correct)

Number of Words in Passage

Number of Errors

	1	2	3	4	5	6	7	8	9	10	11	12	13	14	15	16	17	18	19	20	21	22	23	24	25	26
28–32	97	93	90	87	83	80	77	73	70	67	63	60	57	53	50	47	43	40	37	33	30	27	23	20	17	13
33–37	97	94	92	89	86	83	80	77	74	72	69	66	63	60	57	54	52	49	46	43	40	37	34	32	29	26
38–42	98	95	93	90	88	85	82	80	78	75	72	70	68	65	62	60	58	55	52	50	48	45	42	40	38	35
43–47	98	96	93	91	89	87	84	82	80	78	76	73	71	69	67	64	62	60	58	56	53	51	49	47	44	42
48–52	98	96	94	92	90	88	86	84	82	80	78	76	74	72	70	68	66	64	62	60	58	56	54	52	50	48
53–57	98	96	95	93	91	89	87	86	84	82	80	78	77	76	73	71	69	67	66	64	62	60	58	56	55	53
58–62	98	97	95	93	92	90	88	87	85	83	82	80	78	77	75	73	72	70	68	67	65	63	62	60	58	57
63–67	98	97	95	94	92	91	89	88	86	85	83	82	80	78	77	75	74	72	71	69	68	66	65	63	62	60
68–72	99	97	95	94	93	92	90	89	87	86	84	83	82	80	79	77	76	74	73	72	70	69	67	66	64	63
73–77	99	97	96	94	93	92	91	89	87	86	85	84	83	81	80	79	77	76	75	73	72	71	69	68	67	65
78–82	99	98	96	95	94	92	91	90	89	88	86	85	84	82	81	80	79	78	76	75	74	72	71	70	69	68
83–87	99	98	96	95	94	93	92	91	89	88	87	86	85	84	82	81	80	79	78	76	75	74	73	72	71	69
88–92	99	98	97	96	94	93	92	91	90	89	88	87	86	84	83	82	81	80	79	78	77	76	74	73	72	71
93–97	99	98	97	96	95	94	93	92	91	89	88	87	86	85	84	83	82	81	80	79	78	77	76	75	74	73
98–102	99	98	97	96	95	94	93	92	91	90	89	88	87	86	85	84	83	82	81	80	79	78	77	76	75	74
103–107	99	98	97	96	95	94	93	92	91	90	90	89	88	87	86	85	84	83	82	81	80	79	78	77	76	75
108–112	99	98	97	96	95	94	93	92	91	91	90	89	88	87	86	85	85	84	83	82	81	80	79	78	77	76
113–117	99	98	97	97	96	95	94	93	92	91	90	90	89	88	87	86	85	84	84	83	82	81	80	79	78	77
118–122	99	98	98	97	96	95	94	93	92	92	91	90	89	88	88	87	86	85	84	83	82	82	81	80	79	79
123–127	99	98	98	97	96	95	94	94	93	92	91	90	90	89	88	87	86	86	85	84	83	82	82	81	80	79
128–132	99	98	98	97	96	95	95	94	93	92	92	91	90	89	88	88	87	86	85	85	84	83	82	82	81	80
133–137	99	99	98	97	96	96	95	94	93	93	92	91	90	90	89	88	87	87	86	85	84	84	83	82	81	81
138–142	99	99	98	97	96	96	95	94	94	93	92	91	91	90	89	89	88	87	86	85	85	84	84	83	82	81
143–147	99	99	98	97	97	96	95	95	94	93	92	92	91	90	90	89	88	88	87	86	86	85	84	83	83	82
148–152	99	99	98	97	97	96	95	95	94	93	92	92	91	91	90	89	89	88	87	87	86	86	85	84	83	83
153–157	99	99	98	97	97	96	95	95	94	94	93	92	92	91	90	90	89	88	88	87	86	86	85	85	84	83
158–162	99	99	98	98	97	96	96	95	94	94	93	92	92	91	91	90	89	89	88	88	87	86	86	85	84	84
163–167	99	99	98	98	97	96	96	95	95	94	93	93	92	92	91	90	90	89	88	88	87	87	86	85	85	84
168–172	99	99	98	98	97	96	96	95	95	94	94	93	93	92	91	91	90	89	89	88	88	87	87	86	86	85
173–177	99	99	98	98	97	97	96	95	95	94	94	93	93	92	91	91	90	90	89	89	88	87	87	86	86	85
178–182	99	99	98	98	97	97	96	96	95	95	94	94	93	93	92	92	91	91	90	89	89	88	88	87	87	86
183–187	99	99	98	98	97	97	96	96	95	95	94	94	93	93	92	92	91	91	90	90	89	89	88	88	87	87
188–192	99	99	98	98	97	97	96	96	95	95	94	94	93	93	92	92	91	91	90	89	89	88	88	87	87	86
193–197	99	99	98	98	97	97	96	96	95	95	94	94	93	93	92	92	91	91	90	90	89	89	88	88	87	87
198–202	100	99	98	98	98	97	96	96	96	95	94	94	93	93	92	92	91	91	90	90	89	89	88	88	87	87
203–207	100	99	99	98	98	97	97	96	96	95	95	94	94	93	93	92	92	91	91	90	90	89	89	88	88	87
208–212	100	99	99	98	98	97	97	96	96	95	95	94	94	93	93	92	92	91	91	90	90	90	89	89	88	88
213–217	100	99	99	98	98	97	97	96	96	95	95	94	94	93	93	92	92	91	91	90	90	89	89	88	88	88
218–222	100	99	99	98	98	97	97	96	96	96	95	95	94	94	93	93	92	92	91	91	90	90	90	89	89	88
223–227	100	99	99	98	98	97	97	96	96	96	95	95	94	94	93	93	92	92	92	91	91	90	90	89	89	88
228–232	100	99	99	98	98	97	97	97	96	96	95	95	94	94	94	93	93	92	92	91	91	90	90	90	89	89
233–237	100	99	99	98	98	98	97	97	96	96	95	95	95	94	94	93	93	92	92	92	91	91	90	90	89	89
238–242	100	99	99	98	98	98	97	97	96	96	96	95	95	94	94	94	93	93	92	92	92	91	91	90	90	89

TABLE 3.4   Percentages for Comprehension Scores
(Each Number Indicates a Percentage-Correct Score)

Number of Correct Responses

		1	2	3	4	5	6	7	8	9	10	11	12
	1	100											
	2	50	100										
	3	33	67	100									
	4	25	50	75	100								
Number of Questions	5	20	40	60	80	100							
	6	17	33	50	67	83	100						
	7	14	26	43	57	71	86	100					
	8	12	25	38	50	62	75	88	100				
	9	11	22	33	44	56	67	78	89	100			
	10	10	20	30	40	50	60	70	80	90	100		
	11	9	18	27	36	45	55	64	73	82	91	100	
	12	8	17	25	33	42	50	58	67	75	83	92	100

Determining Passage Levels.   Once you have scored both word recognition accuracy and comprehension, you are ready to determine a *total level for that passage*. For a silent passage, a student has only one score that determines passage level; the comprehension score. Leslie, for example, read a fourth-grade passage silently and achieved at an instructional level for comprehension. Therefore, her level for that passage was instructional.

However, if a student has read a passage orally, the teacher has both a word recognition accuracy score and a comprehension score to determine whether the passage is at a student's independent, instructional, or frustrational level. If a student achieves the same level for both word recognition accuracy and comprehension, determining the level is easy. For example, on a second-grade passage, Leslie achieved at an independent level for both word recognition and comprehension. Therefore, the second-grade passage was at an independent level.

However, students sometimes have different levels for word recognition accuracy and comprehension. In this case, use the lower level to determine passage level. For example, on a third-grade passage, Leslie achieved an instructional level for word recognition accuracy but an independent level for comprehension. Therefore, the third-grade passage was at an instructional level. Table 3.5 helps you to assign levels to oral passages.

At times, a student may achieve at the independent or instructional levels on two (or even more) passages. For example, a student reading oral passages might achieve an instructional score on the primer, first-grade, and second-grade passages. If this situation happens, the *highest* level is the instructional level. In this case, the instructional level is second grade.

Combining Oral and Silent Levels into One Overall Level.   Determine the levels for oral reading and then determine the levels for silent reading. Students often

TABLE 3.5 Criteria for Assigning Levels to Oral Reading Passages		
Comprehension	**Word Recognition**	**Passage Level**
Independent	Independent	Independent
Independent	Instructional	Instructional
Independent	Frustrational	Frustrational
Instructional	Instructional	Instructional
Instructional	Independent	Instructional
Instructional	Frustrational	Frustrational
Frustrational	Frustrational	Frustrational
Frustrational	Independent	Frustrational
Frustrational	Instructional	Frustrational

perform differently on oral and silent reading and so may achieve different levels for each one. However, to make instructional decisions, you should combine your results for both modes of reading.

To combine oral and silent levels, first put the level of each oral and silent passage side by side according to grade level. Then, if the two levels are different, choose the *lower* level for the total reading level.

For example, Leslie, who is in the fifth grade, achieved these levels on *orally* read passages:

Grade 2 – Independent
Grade 3 – Instructional
Grade 4 – Frustrational

In this case, Leslie's *oral reading levels*, which are quite easy to determine, are:

Grade 2 – Oral Independent Reading Level
Grade 3 – Oral Instructional Reading Level
Grade 4 – Oral Frustrational Reading Level

On *silently* read passages, Leslie received these levels:

Grade 2 – Independent
Grade 3 – Independent
Grade 4 – Instructional
Grade 5 – Frustrational

Based on these passages, Leslie's *silent reading* levels are:

Grade 3 – Silent Independent Level
Grade 4 – Silent Instructional Level
Grade 5 – Silent Frustrational Level

To determine Leslie's *combined* reading levels, place the results from each silent and oral passage side by side and then choose the lower level.

Oral Reading Passages	Silent Reading Passages	Combined Level
2 Independent	2 Independent	2 Independent
3 Instructional	3 Instructional	3 Instructional
4 Frustrational	4 Frustrational	4 Frustrational
5 (not given)	5 Frustrational	

Based on this information, Leslie's total reading levels are:

Grade 2 – Combined Independent Reading Level
Grade 3 – Combined Instructional Reading Level
Grade 4 – Combined Frustrational Reading Level

Assigning a combined reading level is helpful in situations where you need a general level for assigning school materials. For example, because Leslie's combined reading is instructional at the third-grade level, she should be reading a third-grade book. However, if you know that the text will be read orally, she can use a fourth-grade book.

Interpreting the Scores of the IRI

The IRI is a rich source of information about a student's reading, and it can provide detailed answers to the two diagnostic questions asked earlier in this chapter: (1) How severe is the reading problem? and (2) What is the general area of the reading problem? Answering these two questions requires adding some procedures to ones already given. These procedures provide options for enriching the information obtained from an IRI.

How Severe Is the Student's Reading Problem?   To estimate the severity of a reading problem, the teacher should examine the gap between a student's highest instructional level on the IRI and the level of text that would be appropriate for that student.

Let's consider the case of Subash, a sixth grader whose IRI summary is presented in Table 3.6. His teacher reported that Subash's class is reading sixth-grade material. On the IRI, Subash's combined independent level is 2. Because he scored at an instructional level on both grades 3 and 4, his instructional level is 4. His frustrational level is 5. The gap between Subash's appropriate reading level (6) and his highest instructional level on the IRI (4) indicates that he has a severe reading problem, according to the criteria by Spache (1981) mentioned earlier in this chapter (Table 3.1).

We now move to the second diagnostic question: determining the general area(s) of the reading problem. To answer this question, we will consider the areas one by one.

TABLE 3.6   IRI Summary for Subash

Level	Oral Passages			Silent Passages	Combined Reading	Listening
	Word Recognition Accuracy Level	Comp Level	Passage Level	Comp & Passage Level	Passage Level	Passage Level
Pre-P	—	—	—	—	—	—
Primer	—	—	—	—	—	—
1	—	—	—	—	—	—
2	Ind	Ind	Ind	Ind	Ind	—
3	Ind	Ins	Ins	Ins	Ins	—
4	Ind	Ins	Ins	Ins	Ins	—
5	Ind	Frus	Frus	Frus	Frus	Ind
6	—	—	—	—	—	Ins
7	—	—	—	—	—	Frus
8	—	—	—	—	—	—

What Is the Nature of Word Recognition Accuracy?   How accurate is word recognition? The student's word recognition accuracy score is generally based on passages because reading a passage is a more authentic task than reading a word list. However, the teacher should be aware that certain things, such as context of the passage, the familiarity of the topic, and the presence of pictures, may inflate a student's score (Leslie & Caldwell, 2001). Rhyme or repetition of phrases in the passage can also aid word recognition. If time permits, the teacher should verify the word recognition level with another passage at the same level. A word recognition accuracy below the third-grade level on IRI passages is one sign that the primary nature of the reading difficulty is word recognition.

Judging a student's word recognition accuracy also involves determining the strategies the student uses to recognize words. Only by knowing the tools that students use to identify words can the teacher help them develop missing skills. Miscues, which are mismatches between the text and what the student says, provide opportunities to analyze these strategies.

Some miscues show that the student is using meaning or context clues. A student using context might substitute a word that makes sense in the context, for example, *Kleenex*® for *handkerchief*. Readers bring a vast store of knowledge and competence to the reading act. When students use context clues, they are using this store of information to bring meaning to reading. The use of context clues shows a positive effort to preserve comprehension (K. S. Goodman, 1965; Goodman & Gollasch, 1980–1981; Y. M. Goodman, 1976).

Other miscues show that the student is using phonics clues to recognize words. A student who uses phonics clues makes miscues that contain many of the same sounds as the words that are in the passage. However, the miscues will often not make sense in context. In fact, sometimes they are not even real words.

An exact recording of oral reading can be analyzed to see which strategies a student tends to use. We call this *miscue analysis* (Goodman, 1969). Some forms of miscue analysis are complex; others are simple. However, they all share a common purpose: to determine the reader's strategies for identifying words. Almost all try to determine whether the reader pays primary attention to letter-sound matching, to meaning, or to both as skilled readers do.

To help you analyze a reader's strategies, look at a form of miscue analysis adapted from Leslie (1993) and Leslie and Caldwell (2001). Table 3.7 presents the miscue analysis worksheet.

Ask three sets of questions about each miscue:

- Is the miscue similar in sounds to the original word?
  a. Does it begin with the same sound?
  b. Does it end with the same sound?
     If the answers are yes, the student is paying attention to phonics when reading. Beginning and ending similarity is sufficient to determine whether the student is paying attention to letter-sound matching. We do not ask about middle sounds because these are often vowels, which have highly variable sounds.
- Does the miscue retain the author's meaning?
     If the answer is yes, the reader is paying attention to meaning and using it to help recognize words.
- Did the reader correct the miscue?
     Self-correction can indicate two things. The self-correction of an acceptable miscue, which is one that does not change meaning, suggests that the reader is paying attention to letter-sound matching. Self-correction of a miscue that changes text meaning suggests that the reader is not paying attention to meaning during the reading process.

To examine reading patterns, choose about 25 miscues from the instructional-level text. Analyze them and record them on the sheet provided by Table 3.7. Now you can look for patterns. Several patterns typical of students with reading problems follow:

- If the student has a large number of miscues that do not change the author's meaning, the student is using the meaning (or context) of a passage as a clue to recognizing words. Another indication that the student is using the meaning of the passage as a clue is the self-correction of miscues that do not make sense.
- If the student has a high number of miscues that are similar in sound and a small number of miscues that retain the author's meaning, the reader may

TABLE 3.7   Miscue Analysis Work Sheet

Word in Text	Miscue	Sounds Alike		Meaning Is Retained	Corrected
		Begin	*End*		
Column Total					

be paying more attention to phonics clues than to the meaning. Some readers show a large number of miscues that are similar in sound to the beginning of the text word and a small number that are similar at the end. Examples are pronouncing *when* for *wanted*; *dog* for *don't*; *live* for *liked*; and *truck* for *teach*. In this case, instruction should focus on guiding the reader to look at all the letters in a word.

■ If the worksheet shows a pattern of miscues that do not contain the same sounds as the text words, as well as a small number of acceptable miscues or self-corrections, the reader may be a wild guesser, one who is not using either phonics or context effectively.

In the examples presented in Figure 3.4, the first student is using meaning clues and the second is using phonics.

What Is the Nature of Word Recognition Fluency?   To assess word recognition fluency, calculate the reading rate, or the number of words per minute, for oral and silent passages. To determine the reading rate, take the number of words in the passage, multiply by 60, and divide by the number of seconds required by the student to read the selection. This calculation yields a word-per-minute score.

$$\frac{\text{Number of words} \times 60}{\text{Number of seconds to read}} = \text{Words per minute}$$

For example, Tammie read a second-grade passage that contained 249 words in two minutes and fifteen seconds (or 135 seconds). Two hundred and forty-nine

---

FIGURE 3.4   Examples of Oral Reading Patterns

Example 1.   Use of Context Clues

---

                                                   sea   *lots of*

Kim lives on an island far out in the <u>ocean</u>. You may think that it would be ∧ fun to live

                        unhappy

on an island. But Kim is <u>miserable</u>. Kim hasn't seen her friends in a year. There is no

one to play with or talk to. There isn't even a school!

Example 2.   Use of Phonics Clues

---

    likes   *open*

Kim <u>lives</u> on an island far out in the <u>ocean</u>. You may think that it would be fun to live

                          mysterious   *family*   *Then*

on an island. But Kim is <u>miserable</u>. Kim hasn't seen her <u>friends</u> in a year. <u>There</u> is no

                  Then

one to play with or talk to. <u>There</u> isn't even a school!

multiplied by 60 equals 14,940. Divide this number by 135 seconds. Tammie's reading rate for that passage is 110 words per minute.

What is a normal rate for different levels of passages? Guidelines for reading rates, based on normal students at their instructional level, are given in Table 3.8 (Leslie & Caldwell, 2001). Notice that the ranges for reading rate at each grade level are quite wide because individuals tend to have very different rates of reading (Carver, 1990).

When you have determined a student's reading rate at a certain grade level of the IRI, use Table 3.8 to compare your student's rate with the acceptable range provided. For example, Arliss read a third-grade oral passage at 135 words per minute. This rate is within the normal range of the third-grade level: 85–139 words per minute. However, the guidelines in Table 3.8 are only advisory. Reading rate must always be interpreted in relation to comprehension.

A student who reads below the lowest reading rate given for a passage level probably needs work in word recognition fluency, especially if comprehension is poor. A slow reader who cannot comprehend adequately is probably concentrating all of his or her attention on recognizing the words. This situation strongly suggests a need for fluency instruction. However, fluency instruction may be less important for a student who reads slowly but comprehends well.

At times, the teacher may only need to listen to a student to determine that the need is word recognition fluency. Slow, hesitant, expressionless reading that is filled with pauses suggests that a student is working hard to identify words and lacks the fluency essential for making sense of the author's message (Wilson, 1988).

What Is the Nature of Comprehension? If both word recognition and comprehension levels are at the frustrational level on a passage, the comprehension problems are probably due to poor word recognition. Because of this relation-

TABLE 3.8 **Reading Rates at Instructional Levels**

Level	Oral Reading Words per Minute	Silent Reading Words per Minute
Preprimer	13–35	—
Primer	28–68	—
First	31–87	—
Second	52–102	58–122
Third	85–139	96–168
Fourth/Fifth	78–124	107–175
Sixth/Seventh/Eighth	113–165	135–231
High School	—	93–334

ship, the student needs to concentrate on improving word recognition accuracy or fluency.

However, if word recognition accuracy and fluency are good but comprehension is poor, the student probably has a comprehension problem and needs to focus on comprehension strategies. If the problem is comprehension, careful analysis of an IRI can provide some important instructional hints.

Some students have problems in comprehension because they believe that reading is "getting all the words right." These readers are often extremely accurate and tend to self-correct miscues that do not change meaning. As a result, they do not actively construct meaning as they read. For example, Susan was asked to read an IRI passage containing the following sentences: "Bill's mom saw the dog. Bill asked, 'May I keep it?'" She read, "Bill's mother saw the dog. Bill asked, 'Can I have it?'" Then she paused and went back, carefully correcting each miscue. Susan's comprehension of the total passage was poor, probably the result of her concern with accuracy. For a reader like Susan, the teacher should emphasize that reading is meaning, not just saying words.

An analysis of IRI questions may also provide insight into comprehension patterns. In the IRI presented in Appendix D of this book, for example, questions are divided into literal and inferential categories. Comparing the percentages correct on these two types of questions helps determine whether the reader is focused on factual information or able to draw inferences. You might also note whether a student appears to get the central focus of the passage or is more observant of details.

If you ask a student to retell a passage after reading it, you can see exactly how he or she constructs meaning. In judging a retelling, use these questions as guidelines for a narrative or story:

- Does the retelling contain the central events of the passage?
- Does the student remember the most important facts?
- Is the student able to retell the events in sequence?

More detailed guidelines for judging retellings are provided in Chapter 8.

The IRI can also give insights into the adequacy of the student's background information. If you begin each selection by asking the student questions to assess background, you have a good idea of the richness of a student's prior knowledge. If you find that the student has problems with the background for several passages, your comprehension instruction may concentrate on enriching background information and applying it to reading.

Finally, when students read both oral and silent passages, you can determine whether they comprehend better after oral or silent reading. Young or very disabled students are usually able to comprehend better after they have read orally. These students need practice to increase their comfort in silent reading. Other, more mature readers comprehend better after silent reading than after oral reading.

Most IRIs are based on narrative passages, that is, passages that tell stories. Although these passages allow you to assess comprehension, it is more appropriate to judge study strategies from expository, or informational, passages. In the section that follows, we address the use of IRIs that contain expository passages.

Extending the IRI to Examine the Nature of Studying Expository Text. Students who have problems studying can often comprehend narrative (storylike) text but have problems with expository (informational) text. Typically, IRIs focus on narrative passages. However some, like the *Qualitative Reading Inventory III* (Leslie & Caldwell, 2001), offer both narrative and expository passages at all levels.

If the IRI you are using does not have both types of passages, use the narrative passages, which all IRIs have, to determine an instructional level for your student. Then, have your student read expository material at the instructional level to see how he or she handles material commonly used for content area instruction.

Modifying the typical IRI procedure can often answer important questions about a student's ability to study. One extension of the IRI procedure can determine whether students can locate information to answer questions. Give the student an IRI passage that was previously read so that he or she can look at it. Then ask the questions that were missed during the original administration and see whether the student can use the passage to locate the answers to these questions.

Other modifications allow a teacher to assess the student's ability to locate main ideas and take notes. To evaluate the ability to determine main ideas, give the student an instructional-level expository passage along with a pencil. Then ask him or her to underline the most important parts of the selection. To investigate study strategies, ask the student to take notes on the passage as if he or she were studying for a test. A teacher can use these procedures with any text, not just an IRI.

What Is the Nature of Language and Meaning Vocabulary? Because reading is a language process, people read only as well as they can understand language and word meanings. An IRI enables a teacher to determine a student's language level by finding a student's listening level.

To do this, the teacher reads IRI passages aloud to the student, starting at the reading frustrational level, and asks the comprehension questions about the passage. The highest level at which the student gets 70 percent or more of the answers correct is the listening level.

The listening level provides an estimate of the student's listening, or language, comprehension level. If a student's listening level is lower than his or her grade level, that student needs to develop better language skills. Instruction should then focus on developing rich language and learning more word meanings.

In contrast, the example of Subash, the sixth-grader whose IRI summary sheet is presented in Table 3.6, shows a student who has a good language base.

Subash's high listening level (6) but lower instructional reading level (4) indicate a two-year gap between his current reading level and his language level. The fact that his listening level is equal to his grade level indicates that his language base is sufficient for reading at grade level. No language development is needed for him; instead, he needs to work on reading.

You can also use the IRI to directly assess knowledge of meaning vocabulary. After the student has read and answered the questions in a passage, ask the student to define (or use in a sentence) key vocabulary words in the passage. Remember that you may have to pronounce words that the student has not read correctly in the passage. A student who knows the meanings of difficult words in a grade-level passage has a strong vocabulary base. A student who cannot define these words or use them in a sentence needs more development of meaning vocabulary. If a student cannot define a word in isolation, you might ask him or her to reread the sentence in the passage to see if context helps the student with word meaning.

Special Issues and Options in Using IRIs

The informal nature of an IRI allows many options for administration and adaptation to the special needs of students. At times, you may face some difficult decisions. This section discusses some of these issues and, in addition, presents some alternatives for administering and interpreting the IRI.

Pronouncing Words for Students.   When reading IRI selections orally, a student may sometimes become "stuck" on a word. The teacher may be tempted to supply this word to make the student more comfortable and able to continue. However, pronouncing words for the student may inflate the student's comprehension score, because understanding the passage depends on reading the words accurately. To obtain the most accurate assessment, teachers are strongly discouraged from supplying words. Tell students to say "pass" for unknown words, and score these passes as omission errors. Also encourage students to try pronouncing a word before they give up. However, some guidelines for IRI administration permit teachers to aid students.

Alternative Administration of Oral and Silent Passages.   We suggest that you administer all the oral passages first to determine the oral reading levels before administering the silent passages. Then combine oral and silent reading levels into a total reading level. Some clinicians prefer a different administrative procedure. They alternate oral and silent passages at each grade level to determine the student's reading levels.

Unclear IRI Results.   When administering an IRI, you may sometimes have difficulty determining a stable level. What are some of the things that can happen? A student may score just slightly below the criteria for a specific level, for example, scoring 94% for word recognition accuracy on one passage, only slightly below the frustrational cutoff of 95%. At other times, a student may not do well on a certain topic. Should the teacher count these passages as frustrational and simply discontinue testing? If you are unsure of the correct decision, you should continue to gather information by testing at higher levels or administering another passage at the same level.

At times, however, you will be not be able to come to a perfectly clear-cut decision and may have to make exceptions to some of the scoring criteria. Because the IRI is an informal instrument, you should feel free to modify criteria by using your own judgment. You should, however, note that you have made an exception to the scoring criteria and explain the reason for this exception.

Alternative Ways to Score Miscues. As stated earlier, scoring each miscue as one error is the best and most reliable way to reach an appropriate reading level for your student. This recommendation has been verified with extensive field testing.

However, miscues that do not change the author's meaning suggest that the student is comprehending the passage. For example, consider the following sentence: "The teachers divided the children into four groups." A substitution of "put" for "divided" would not affect meaning. On the other hand, the substitution of "from" for "four" does distort meaning. Some reading teachers prefer to count miscues that retain meaning ("put" for "divided") less severely than miscues that change meaning ("from" for "for"). If you wish to do this, count a miscue that retains the original meaning as one-half error. If a miscue changes the meaning, however, count it as one full error.

Which option should you use? Since the IRI is an informal instrument, you are free to choose the scoring system that makes you most comfortable. However, once you choose the scoring system that best fits your needs, you should use it consistently.

Alternative Norms. As with many informal measures, alternative criteria for determining reading levels have been suggested by others. Based on our own field testing, the criteria suggested in this chapter for word recognition accuracy and comprehension place students at appropriate reading levels. These criteria reflect the authors' experiences in developing an informal inventory with students who have reading difficulties. More information on norms for informal reading inventories is summarized by Johns (1993).

Allowing Students to Look for Answers. Another option in administering an IRI is to use "look-backs." After scoring the questions and determining the comprehension level, you can ask the student to look back in the text to locate or correct answers. This procedure allows you to note the difference between comprehension during reading and memory after reading. A student may read a passage and understand it fully. However, when asked questions following reading, the student may forget certain parts. Hasn't this happened to you? If a student can locate or correct answers, you can assume that he or she understood the passage. If a student is unable to successfully use the look-back strategy, perhaps the problem is one of basic comprehension during reading.

Leslie and Caldwell (2001) found that students reading at the third-grade level and above could effectively use look-backs to raise their comprehension score. This was most evident in upper middle school and high school passages. Students who scored at the frustrational level for comprehension often raised their scores to an instructional or independent level following look-backs. In fact, Leslie and Caldwell (2001) recommend that comprehension levels for upper level text (sixth grade and above) be determined following look-backs. Actually, the look-back strategy parallels what students are asked to do in school. Rarely are they expected to answer questions without the support of the text.

If you wish to use look-backs, first ask and score the questions to arrive at a comprehension level without look-backs. Then ask the student to look back and score the results of his or her efforts. A comprehension score with look-backs represents the total of all questions answered correctly for both procedures.

Using an IRI to Assess a Student's Comprehension Strategies. The teacher can ask a student to stop at various points during reading and *think out loud,* that is, explain what is in his or her mind at that point. The think-aloud process has been examined by a variety of researchers (Pressley & Afflerbach, 1995) who agree that it offers an interesting opportunity to gather observations about the thinking that occurs during reading. Think-alouds can be divided into two categories: those that signal understanding and those that suggest the reader does not understand what he or she is reading.

Leslie and Caldwell (2001) identified several types of think-aloud comments that suggest understanding on the part of the reader. Most students offer a variety of comments as they read. Some students paraphrase or summarize the text. Others make new meaning by drawing inferences, reaching conclusions, or engaging in reasoning. Students ask questions about character motivation or events that might logically follow what they are reading. They also comment on their own understanding and tie the reading to their prior knowledge. They identify personally with a character or event. However, students may indicate that they do not understand what they are reading by asking questions about words or concepts. They may state that what they are reading does not make sense. Leslie and Caldwell (2001) found that think-aloud comments indicating understanding were positively and strongly related to comprehension after reading.

If you wish to use think-alouds, first show students how to do it and interact with them in thinking aloud during reading. Then ask students to demonstrate their understanding of the procedure. Although a think-aloud can be a time-consuming process, it does provide an interesting window to the comprehension process.

Using an IRI to Measure a Student's Growth. If you are measuring classroom growth or growth following an intervention program, decide when you wish to assess the student. Every three or four months is a realistic interval for a classroom. Intervention program intervals can be of short or long duration. Choose an IRI passage to administer prior to instruction. Obtain a score for both word recognition and comprehension. If the student scores at an independent level, continue at higher levels until you reach the student's frustrational level. Then, when the classroom interval is over or the intervention is completed, administer the same passage as a posttest measure.

You have another option. You can administer a different IRI passage for the pretest and the posttest. This option is preferable if the duration between pretest and posttest is short and you think that memory for the initial passage may inflate the results. Of course, the two passages should be as alike as possible. They should be at the same level and have the same structure: narrative or expository. They should both be relatively familiar to the student.

Summary

Assessing reading achievement involves answering two questions: How severe is the student's reading problem? and What is the general area of the reading problem?

Reading assessment measures may be divided into formal and informal. Formal reading tests are commercially prepared instruments. Formal, norm-referenced tests compare students with a representative sample of other students. Formal criterion-referenced tests measure mastery of specific skills.

Informal measures have not been normed on large populations as have standardized formal measures. Therefore, they may be used more flexibly and may be adapted to the needs of the student and the demands of the diagnostic situation.

The informal reading inventory (IRI) consists of a series of graded reading selections. The student reads increasingly difficult material until a frustrational level is reached. IRIs measure both oral and silent reading. Three levels of reading are obtained: the independent level, the instructional level, and the frustrational level. These levels are based on the student's word recognition accuracy and ability to comprehend the passages. Generally, separate passages are provided for oral and silent reading.

The IRI provides information about both the severity of a reading problem and its general area(s). Careful analysis of the IRI can suggest whether a student is having problems with word recognition accuracy, word recognition fluency, comprehension, language base and meaning vocabulary, or studying. Miscue analysis, the analysis of a student's oral reading deviations, allows the reading teacher to examine the strategies that a student uses to recognize words.

Special issues and options in using IRIs involve pronouncing words for students, alternating oral and silent passages, finding unclear results, using alternative miscue scoring procedures or norms, allowing students to look back for answers, assessing comprehension strategies, and using an IRI to assess student growth.

4 Overview of Instruction

Introduction

How can teachers best help students with reading problems? This chapter presents an overview of instruction. Topics include the components of effective instruction, general principles of instruction, guidelines for building rapport, considerations in delivering instruction, creating a community of readers and writers, and using computers to help students read.

Components of Effective Reading Instruction

Because students with reading problems are already behind their peers, instructional time is precious. This section describes the components of reading instruction that enable students to make the most effective progress.

A balanced approach to instruction includes four components essential to effective reading development: *guided reading, work in word knowledge, writing,* and *independent reading* (Cunningham & Allington, 1999). Each lesson should include guided reading and some form of word knowledge instruction. Writing instruction is usually based on the text read during the guided reading component. However, writing can also be used as a tool to help reinforce strategies learned in word knowledge. Independent reading occurs both as part of instructional time and as an at-home activity. Through independent reading, students have opportunities to enjoy reading outside of instructional time and to share reading experiences with teachers and family. Finally, because the learning of students with reading problems is often inconsistent, every program should include frequent review and opportunities for practice.

Guided Reading

The guided reading component is the core of the reading lesson. It provides opportunities for students to engage in *reading experiences* and to learn effective *strategies* for understanding text.

Reading Experiences.   Readers "learn by doing." In fact, many students who are reading at grade level have acquired good reading skills simply by doing lots of reading (Anderson, Wilson, & Fielding, 1988). Thus, *students with reading problems* *need to read at every lesson.* Typically, during lessons, students read material at their *instructional reading level* (see Chapter 3).

Reading experiences are particularly critical for low-achieving readers, because these students actually read *less* than their average-achieving peers. After an extensive review of the research on time spent in reading, Johnston and Allington (1991) concluded:

> Currently we find a major characteristic of remediation is that participation rarely involves the reading of stories, magazines, or books; in fact, that students served by remedial programs typically spend less time reading any text and read less text during instruction than do non-participating peers. (p. 993)

This unfortunate fact of limited reading has been documented in many different settings, some of them quite surprising. Low-achieving students who are served by supplementary classes, Title I (formerly called Chapter I) or special education, in *addition* to reading instruction in regular classrooms, actually read *less* than classmates who receive no special services (Allington & McGill-Frazen, 1989; Allington & Walmsley, 1995; Birman, et al., 1987). One study found that special education services for students with learning disabilities often *reduced* the time devoted to reading instruction (Zigmond, Vallecorsa, & Leinhardt, 1980). Allington (1977) found that reading-disabled students in grades two through eight read an average of only 43 words per reading session.

What are students doing if they are not reading? Much instructional time is spent on "skills and drills" and worksheets. Students seem to know this. When Johnston, Allington, and Afflerbach (1985) asked students in Title I classes to name their most frequent activity, they overwhelmingly cited filling out worksheets.

However, students must actually read if they are to learn to read well. Compare learning to read with learning to drive, skateboard, or swim. Some of you have taken swimming lessons that required you to sit at the side of a pool doing exercises for breathing, kicking, and arm strokes. Yet learning these isolated skills did not make you swimmers. You became swimmers only after you learned to apply these skills *as you were swimming.* In the same way, students can learn to read only by applying what they learn about reading as they are actually reading a story or book. To ensure that students become actively involved in their own learning from the beginning, teachers must establish expectations and foster active learning even in kindergarten and first grade (Askew & Fountas, 1998).

Getting students with problems to do extensive reading is a challenging task. Stanovich (1986) describes a negative cycle called the *Matthew effect.* The cycle begins when students who are not skilled readers avoid reading. Then, because they have not practiced reading, they become less skilled. In turn, because they are less skilled, they tend to further avoid reading, and so on. This pattern continues until, tragically, the students are doing almost no reading. Baker (1993) presents a familiar portrait of what low-achieving readers do when other class members are reading independently:

> In each class a few low-progress readers spent much of their reading time wandering: getting a Kleenex, picking another book, dropping something on the floor and retrieving it, gazing around or at a page for several minutes.

Teachers need to prevent the Matthew effect. Their most important job is fostering the desire to read so that students will, ultimately, make learning to read a self-sustaining process. There are many ways to encourage students with problems to read:

- *Give students books that are easy for them.* If students have to struggle, they are likely to abandon reading.
- *Have students share their reading experiences.* When students feel that others take an interest in their responses, they are more likely to read (Baker, 1993). Thus, students read more if they form small groups and read the same books. The groups meet to share responses to the book (Richek, 1999; Spiegel, 1998; Eldridge, 1998).
- *Explore many different types of reading materials.* Help students find books that match their interests. They can read scary books (a favorite of many children), books about snakes, joke books, bubble gum jokes, stories about other children, series books, comics, sports pages, and "News for Kids" in a local adult paper.
- *Encourage students to read books several times.* Repeated readings of a story or chapter improve both word recognition and comprehension (Stahl & Heubach, 1993; Samuels, 1997; Dowhower, 1994). Reading a favorite picture book again helps beginning readers feel comfortable (Gillet & Temple, 2000). Students also enjoy rehearsing material for choral reading and performing plays.

Strategy Instruction.   In addition to student reading, each lesson should include *strategy instruction.* In guided reading, the teacher combines *reading* with *strategy instruction* that teaches students *how* to read. In a reading strategy, students learn *how* to read as they are actively reading. Acquiring strategies allows students to consciously monitor and control their own reading processes. Two essential characteristics of reading strategies are that they (1) occur within the context of a reading situation and (2) teach students how to think about reading.

Strategy instruction is important because students with disabilities have difficulty approaching learning situations strategically or systematically. Although they may have learned basic skills, such as phonics principles or isolated facts from content areas, they may not be able to generalize these skills or use this information efficiently or effectively in new contexts. They often focus their attention and effort on avoidance rather than facing the task at hand (Larkin & Ellis, 1995).

A large body of research has focused on the most effective means of teaching students with disabilities. Repeatedly, explicit instruction has proved to be the most effective means of supporting achievement. However, Ellis (1998) points out that students with learning disabilities need instruction that explicitly explains both the specific behavioral processes (the *steps*) of a strategy as well as the underlying thought processes (the *why*) of a strategy. Students who have difficulty learning to read and write require more explicit instruction in applying the skills and strategies learned in reading instruction to specific contexts (Idol & Rutledge, 1993; Gaskins, et al., 1994). Such instruction helps students understand *how* to implement a strategy as well as *when* it will be applicable. Helping students understand when a given strategy is useful fosters their self-reliance and academic independence (Ellis, 1998).

Sadly, instruction for low-achievers rarely includes teaching strategies. In a wide-reaching study of Title I programs, Birman, et al. (1987) found little emphasis on high-level thinking and almost no instances of teaching reading strategies. However, research shows that low-achieving readers are capable of mastering the demands of reading strategy instruction (Larkin & Ellis, 1998). Reading strategy application should be included in every lesson (Gaskins, 1998).

Teaching a reading strategy is different from teaching a reading skill. Having a student fill out worksheets to identify the main ideas of short paragraphs is skills instruction. Because this activity is not connected to other reading that the student does, the student probably will not apply this gained knowledge when reading other materials. In contrast, strategy instruction teaches a student to think in a certain way and to apply this thinking to a variety of reading materials.

All phases of learning a strategy include talking about thinking. In a strategy, thinking is "made public" through discussion, teacher modeling, and practice (Ellis, 1998). Examples of reading strategies include teaching students to use background knowledge, to predict, to find main ideas, and to use known words to figure out unknown ones. Strategy instruction can also help students with simpler tasks, such as how to choose and read a book independently. Teaching a strategy involves four key steps:

1. *The teacher should tell students why the strategy is important.* Like most people, low-achieving readers do only what they consider to be helpful. Students want to know how a strategy makes reading easier for them.
2. *The teacher should model the strategy.* When teachers demonstrate a strategy and explain why each component is helpful, they help students connect activities with goals.
3. *Students should demonstrate the strategy.* By verbalizing or writing about the strategy, students demonstrate their understanding.

4. *Students should practice using the strategy*. Students should practice, first under the direction of a teacher, until they gradually develop independence.

Trina, a second-grade student in the Reading Center, was unable to answer any questions about the books she took home. Through probing, her teacher discovered that Trina did not know the appropriate conditions for reading, such as turning off the TV and finding a comfortable seat. Trina also did not know how to choose books she could read or how to keep her place while reading. In fact, Trina was not even aware that the sequence of pages was important. On one occasion, she told us that she had started on pages 9 and 10 of her book, and then had gone back to the beginning.

To help Trina master the strategies of choosing and reading books, the teacher discussed why these things were important. Then she modeled finding a comfortable, quiet place. She showed Trina's class why reading a storybook in correct sequence is important. Next, students were asked to demonstrate their understanding by preparing *think cards* (Caldwell, 1990). In this activity, students write their own understandings of a strategy on an index card, which they keep with them when they practice the strategy. The card enables students to record the features of a strategy that are most useful for them. Because a think card is the student's own creation, it is an important step in transferring control of strategic reading from the teacher to the student. In making a think card, students demonstrate how they use a strategy. Think cards are useful in many types of strategy instruction. Chapter 6 discusses using them for word recognition strategies.

A sample of Trina's think card for independent reading is shown in Figure 4.1. After Trina prepared her think card, she referred to it whenever she chose a book or read one independently. At first, this practice took place under the direction of a teacher. Later, however, Trina was able to practice her strategies independently, using her think card to guide her.

Work in Word Knowledge

Word knowledge includes both meaning vocabulary development and word recognition. Students whose areas of instructional need are related to comprehension often need extensive instruction in vocabulary development to understand text (see Chapter 10). Other students need help in word recognition, including both fluency and accuracy. Students whose diagnoses indicate a need to improve fluency should develop stronger sight word vocabularies (see Chapter 6). Those who have problems accurately identifying unfamiliar words need to develop effective strategies for analyzing words (see Chapter 7).

Writing

By becoming authors themselves, low-achieving students gain dramatically in their sense of power over reading. Students who write regularly come to feel a

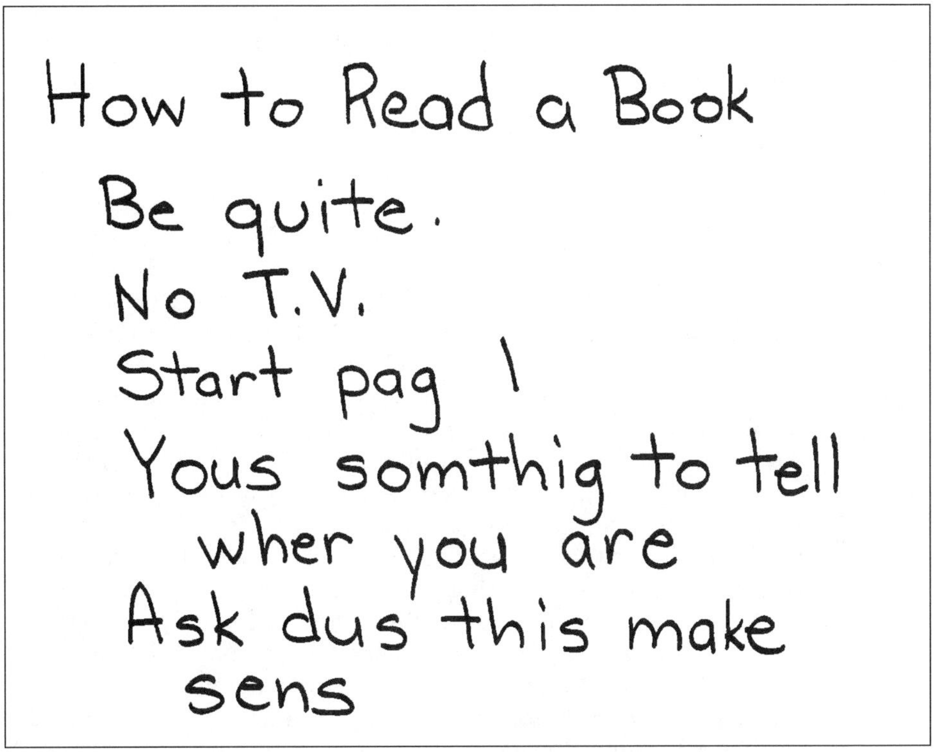

How to Read a Book
Be quite.
No T.V.
Start pag 1
Yous somthig to tell
wher you are
Ask dus this make
sens

FIGURE 4.1 Example of Trina's Think Card Strategy

sense of control over both reading and writing and to approach literacy with more interest. Students also enjoy expressing their opinions and showing their creativity through writing. Finally, through frequent writing experiences, students practice phonics by trying to spell words.

Students write in a wide variety of forms at the Reading Center:

- Seven-year-old Luis, who was at the beginning stages of reading, wrote "love notes" to his teacher. He usually wrote something like U AR PTE ("You are pretty"). These elaborately folded notes were given with instructions "For your eyes only."
- Heather, a sixth-grader, wrote a variation on *How Much Is a Million?* (by Schwartz) entitled "How Much Is My Allowance?"
- Alfonso, a seventh-grader, composed an elaborate, multipage biography of his best friend.

The student-authored books that fill the library in the Reading Center motivate new students to make their own contributions. Writing is further addressed in Chapter 11.

Independent Reading

To establish permanent reading habits, students need to read when they are not under direct supervision. Many schools and classrooms reserve 15 to 20 minutes per day when everyone in the school reads: the principal, teachers, students, and lunchroom staff. These reading times are often called SSR (sustained silent reading) or DEAR (drop everything and read). The model of adults "practicing what they preach" about reading is a powerful one.

In addition to reading in school, students need to form the habit of reading at home. Students may read a chapter in a book under teacher supervision and then read a chapter at home, or they can choose books specifically for home reading.

When helping students choose books for independent reading, the teacher should guide them to select materials at their *independent level*, which is an easier level than the *instructional level* often used for lessons. Children, like adults, like to curl up with an easy, amusing book or magazine. They can also reread favorite books. Independent reading should be fun, not work. Research shows that students make important gains when they read material that is easy for them. Extensive easy reading provides the practice students need to maintain the gains they have made in lessons (Anderson, Wilson, & Fielding, 1988; Berliner, 1981; Guthrie & Greaney, 1991).

Students can also read material they bring from home. Valuable reading and study strategies can be learned from *TV Guide*, newspapers, baseball and football programs, popular magazines, and manuals. Using these materials demonstrates to students that reading is directly connected to their lives. One teacher asked primary students to each bring in something their parents read. The resulting display of college texts, telephone books, memos, and the Bible was a highly motivating experience.

Students with reading problems often have difficulty choosing appropriate books. When choosing a book, the teacher should have students look at the cover, the length, and the size of the print. They can read the summaries on the back cover and ask opinions of friends who have read the book. Teachers can give short *book talks* that describe the book briefly. In a book talk, the teacher holds up a book and describes it in an enticing way. Next, the teacher chooses an exciting part and reads it to the students. The reading should take no more than five minutes, and the excerpt should be from the first third of the book. Try to choose a reading that will keep your students in suspense so they will want to read the book. The teacher should have copies of the book available after the book talk so that students can read the book for themselves. After hearing several book talks, students may want to give their own.

Readers who have enjoyed one book in a series, such as *Curious George* (by Rey), are likely to enjoy a sequel, such as *Curious George Gets a Medal*. Finally students can learn the *five finger rule*. Students read one page of a book and use one finger to count each unfamiliar word. If they count past five before the end of the page, they should choose another book.

Review of Material Learned

Students with a history of low achievement must work hard to learn new concepts, and they need extensive review to remember those concepts. Review is especially important for beginning learners, who are still becoming familiar with the act of reading.

What should your students review? Older students can profit from review of difficult vocabulary words or important facts. Some keep a personal collection of words they have learned on cards and review these cards periodically. Beginning readers can benefit from reading a story again, reviewing words containing a certain phonics pattern, or reviewing word cards. Review can also emphasize *strategies*. Because strategies involve a change in thinking, they are mastered slowly and require much review before they can be thoroughly understood and used.

Principles of Teaching Students with Reading Problems

The most important principle of teaching low-achieving students is to *provide extensive opportunities to read,* as discussed earlier in this chapter. This section discusses other principles to help you plan effective instruction.

Begin Instruction at an Appropriate Level

Choose materials at the student's instructional level for teaching lessons. Materials above this level will frustrate students; materials that are too easy will not provide sufficient challenge. Seventh-grader Robert had a fourth-grade instructional level. Because all of the materials in his regular classroom were at the seventh-grade level, the work was frustrating for him. On the other hand, in his Title I class, Robert was reading a book written on the second-grade level, which was too easy and wasted valuable instructional time. His Reading Center teacher located materials at his fourth-grade instructional level, and Robert's reading level improved rapidly.

However, instructional level is not an absolute guide. Readers' backgrounds or interests can often motivate them to handle difficult material. Joshua, a star high-school athlete, was able to read only fifth-grade materials, except when the subject was basketball. On this topic, he could read advanced newspaper and magazine articles with greater understanding than his teacher.

Support Instruction in the Regular Classroom

An important goal of supplementary reading instruction is to help students function better in regular classes. To accomplish this goal, special reading teachers need to be familiar with the curriculum of the student's classroom. The classroom teacher and reading resource teacher must jointly decide how best to help the student through collaborative planning and teaching (Walmsley & Allington, 1995). If teachers do not communicate with one another and coordinate their programs, the student suffers greatly.

For example, a first-grade student was confused by three conflicting forms of reading instruction. In his regular classroom, he received instruction in a traditional reading textbook series. In his Title I class, he was taught using the DISTAR system (see Chapter 15), which uses a special alphabet. In his learning disabilities resource room, he used the Orton-Gillingham method (see Chapter 15). Each teacher was unaware of what the others were doing. The student, who could barely master one method of learning to read, was bombarded with three different methods every day.

Resource teachers should teach strategies that help students to succeed in the regular classroom. Instruction in implementing strategies is especially important for students who are performing near the level of their regular classroom (Walmsley & Allington, 1995).

Richek and Glick (1991) developed a model for supporting students in their regular classroom work. Before students read a story in their regular reading book, the resource teacher read background information to them. For example, to prepare students to read a story featuring fireflies, the teacher read a children's encyclopedia article on fireflies. Then the story in the textbook was processed three times: (1) the resource teacher read the story to the students and stopped periodically to ask for predictions; (2) each student reread the story with a partner; and (3) the students dramatized the story as they read it. When the students then read the story (again) in their regular classroom, they were highly proficient. Cooperative efforts between the two teachers resulted in dramatic improvement in coping with regular classroom tasks, in reading scores, and in interest in reading (L. Glick, personal communication, 1990; Richek & Glick, 1991).

In preparing students to function independently in their classrooms, the teacher should be aware of opportunities to give students progressively more difficult tasks and materials, for example, moving them from a second- to a third-grade book. In addition, the teacher should try to gradually increase the length of materials that students read. Teachers must ensure that students with reading problems do not get caught in the "rut" of simply proceeding through a workbook until they finish it.

Use Time Effectively

Because students with reading problems are already behind their peers, time is precious and must be used wisely. Much time in a school day is spent *off task*, that is, on activities such as taking students to and from class and passing out papers (Fisher, et al., 1978a, b; Allington, 1980; McGill-Franzen & Allington, 1991). Time off task is a particular problem for low-achieving readers. Because many low achievers have problems controlling their behavior, teachers must spend important instructional time on discipline and management (Gaskins, 1988). Even calling on students to read orally can become a complex negotiation when low-achieving readers are involved. McDermott (1978) found that students in a top reading group spent three times as much time on task as did students in the bottom group. Stanovich (1986) describes this phenomenon as "the rich" (the top readers) getting "richer" as they read 30 to 90 times as much as "the poor" (the low-achieving readers).

How can teachers use instructional time effectively?

- Streamline noninstructional activities by establishing routines for coming to class and settling down to work.
- Call on specific students to increase their attention. Often teachers avoid calling on low-achieving or inattentive students even though these students are precisely the ones who tend to be off task.
- Do not allow supplemental reading instruction to replace reading in the regular classroom. Supplemental instruction should be given in addition to classroom reading, as specified in current federal Title I guidelines.

Use Silent and Oral Reading Appropriately

Reading instruction should include both oral and silent reading. At different times, both of these modes are appropriate.

Silent Reading. Through silent reading, students gain control of the reading process and can pace themselves, review material, and deepen personal reactions to literature. Unfortunately, research shows that students with reading problems do little silent reading. Allington (1984) found that good readers read three times as much material silently as poor readers. Low-achieving first graders read only five words silently per day. In a study of compensatory classes, Quirk, Tristman, Nailn, and Weinberg (1975) found that only 2 percent of time was spent on reading silently. Chapter 7 contains many ideas for encouraging silent reading.

Oral Reading. Although silent reading is the more desirable mode, some oral reading activities are useful for increasing fluency and comfort, as well as providing an avenue for sharing text (McCormick, 1999). Beginning readers in particular are most comfortable reading orally. Many strategies for encouraging appropriate oral reading are given in Chapter 7.

Teachers of low-achieving students need to monitor oral reading wisely. Studies show that teachers tend to overinterrupt low-achieving readers who make miscues when they read orally. Allington (1980) studied what happened when two groups of primary grade students, reading comfortable materials, came across words they did not know. When students could not figure out words immediately, teachers interrupted the students in a high-reading group 31 percent of the time, but they interrupted students in a low group 74 percent of the time.

Further, when high-achieving students missed a word, they were encouraged to figure it out for themselves. In contrast, low-achieving readers were often immediately supplied with the word by the teacher (Allington, 1980). Unfortunately, supplying words to students (called *terminal clues*) results in the least gain in reading performance (Hoffman, et al., 1984).

Allington (1994) also found that low-achieving readers were often interrupted even when their miscues made sense. Thus, when high-group students made a miscue such as substituting *a* for *the*, the teacher stopped them only 10 percent of the time. When low-group students made such a misreading, teachers stopped them 56 percent of the time. Thus, teachers were unintentionally conveying to less able students that reading is *word-perfect performance*.

To encourage independence, teachers should limit interruptions for all students. If mistakes do not affect meaning, you should not stop students. When you do interrupt, encourage students to monitor meaning and figure out words for themselves. In addition, insist that other group members not interrupt readers by calling out words. The student who is reading needs time to figure out words independently. If the student wants assistance, he or she may hold up a finger, indicating "help me."

Of course, these guidelines for oral reading must be used sensibly. The teacher should assist students when they can read no further or have lost the meaning of the material.

Building Rapport

The value of a successful teacher-pupil relationship cannot be overestimated; it is more important than the methods or materials used for instruction. Several suggestions for building rapport are discussed in this section.

Acceptance

Students with reading problems need to feel that teachers accept them as individuals. Too often, by the time students are identified for special attention, behavioral problems have developed that invite rejection by teachers. Low-achieving students often suffer from low self-esteem, nervousness, and defeatism (Bryan, Sullivan-Burnstein, & Mathur, 1998).

One simple way of fostering a positive self-image in students is to show a genuine enthusiasm for your students' interests, be they wrestling, motorcycles, baseball cards, cosmetics, or ballet. Teachers' verbal comments set the tone for instruction.

Another way is to foster intrinsic motivation, which makes students feel that learning is its own reward. Praise for work well done is an important component in fostering intrinsic motivation. Praise given to a student should be specific and related to what has actually been done well. For example, if a student has demonstrated understanding of a story, you might say, "You really understood that story." This *specific* praise is much more powerful than nondescriptive comments, such as "good." Praise should also be contingent, that is, given only when students do something well. Giving praise for things that have been done badly confuses students. An "I know you can do it if you try" attitude on the part of the teacher is also motivational for students. Finally, teachers should avoid making negative comments, which are powerful disincentives to learning.

Security

Students with reading problems also need to feel secure in the instructional setting. One way to instill this feeling is to start each instructional session in the same way so that students have a sense of routine.

Security may also involve a sense of personal space. Eleven-year-old Janet resisted coming to her special reading lesson. However, when the teacher made a "place" for her by covering the top of her desk with specially patterned paper, Janet felt she had a "home" and started to come willingly to class. If desks are shared with students who come at other times, movable name cards can be used.

Emotional security is crucial for allowing students to take such risks as reading difficult material. They need to feel confident skimming material for information without having to read every word. If teachers assure students that making some mistakes is all right and that nobody is perfect, learners will take the kinds of instructional risks that are needed to become good readers.

Success

Students with reading problems are in desperate need of experiencing success. Too often, their lives have been filled with unrelenting failure. If you plan lessons so that tasks can be accomplished successfully, you will have taken an important step in building a solid relationship with your student.

Your own belief in the capabilities of your students is also important. In classic studies, Rosenthal and Jacobson (1968) and Cooper (1979) demonstrated that if teachers expect a student to succeed, that student's performance will improve.

Finally, your students need to believe in the power of their own efforts. Low achievers often suffer from feelings of "learned helplessness," believing that their efforts cannot affect success and that success (or failure) is due to "luck"

(Abramson, Garber, & Seligman, 1980; Diener & Dweck, 1978). Your students need to know that *their own efforts* will lead to improvement in reading and writing.

Charting progress (discussed later in this chapter) is one effective way to demonstrate student success. In another strategy, you can keep tape recordings of students orally reading the same passage at intervals of a few months. When students listen to their own improved reading, they gain a substantial sense of accomplishment.

Delivering Instruction

How should instruction be implemented? This section examines the setting for instruction, materials for instruction, and the use of individual, group, or cooperative instruction.

Setting for Instruction

At one time, most supplementary instruction, both in special education and reading, was given to small groups of students in resource rooms by "pulling out" students from their regular classrooms. Although such resource instruction continues in many schools, some problems have been associated with it. Often the instruction of regular classes and resource rooms is not coordinated (Walmsley & Allington, 1995). In addition, students who attend resource rooms may miss instruction in the regular classroom. Researchers have also found that the labels that students receive (e.g., reading disabled, learning disabled, dyslexic) often are somewhat arbitrary and that, in reality, students bearing different labels have few differences (Garcia, Pearson, & Jiménez, 1994; Jenkins, Pious, & Peterson, 1988; Kamhi, 1992; Walmsley & Allington, 1995).

For these reasons, recent trends have provided more instruction in regular classrooms. In special education, *inclusion* or the *regular education initiative*, provides that all students, regardless of the type or extent of disability, be taught in the regular classroom in the students' neighborhood schools. Title I regulations have also been changed to enable instruction for school populations as a whole rather than being limited to specifically designated students who are taken out of their classrooms for instruction.

Today, many alternative models are being used. In some schools, the resource room arrangement, or "pull out," continues. In other schools, the resource teacher goes into the regular classroom to assist students. This arrangement is referred to as an inclusion, in-class, or "push-in" model.

Is one model of instructional placement more effective than another? Although professionals have debated this issue hotly, some studies indicate that the placement of the student for delivery of services may make little difference in student achievement. Rowan and Guthrie (1989) found that for Chapter I programs (now called Title I), pull-out and in-class models made no difference in achievement. In fact, later studies suggest that such programs may actually contribute to students' lower levels of achievement because they restrict students' access to the kinds of instruction that foster comprehension and achievement (McGill-Franzen & Allington, 1991; Allington, 1994).

Federal authorities have responded to these findings in their more recent reauthorizations of Title I (U.S. Department of Education, 1999) and in the funding of federal programs. In recent years, classification has received less emphasis, and greater emphasis has been placed on programs that help whole schools meet the needs of low-achieving students (Walmsley & Allington, 1995). Three models for delivery of instruction have emerged as the most common instructional support models: in-class instructional support, extended schooling, and schoolwide restructuring (Allington, 1993).

For the teacher, the model adopted can have a major impact. In a resource room, teachers can arrange their own classrooms and allow students greater freedom of movement and noise level. However, resource room teachers may feel isolated and often find it burdensome to assume the responsibilities of getting students from one room to another. In an in-class model, supplementary teachers find it easier to communicate with the classroom teacher and to support the students' regular curriculum. However, some supplementary teachers report that they lose autonomy and are hesitant to plan instruction that is too exciting or different. In fact, classroom teachers may assign them tasks, such as helping students to complete worksheets, that do not allow them to make instructional decisions. In both resource and in-class models, teachers need to plan instruction jointly.

Materials Used for Instruction

A wealth of materials can be used to entice students to read and improve their achievement. Major types of materials are listed in this section. Materials designated specifically for reading instruction are found in Appendix A.

Trade Books. Trade books are published for students' reading pleasure. Because they are geared for enjoyment and often provide extended reading, trade books are invaluable for low-achieving students.

Fiction books and novels get children "into" reading. Some favorite children's titles for easy books include *The Napping House* (by Wood), *Brown Bear, Brown Bear, What Do You See?* (by Martin), and *In a Dark, Dark Room* (by Schwartz). Intermediate choices include *Charlotte's Web* (by White), *Superfudge* (by Bloom), *James and the Giant Peach* (by Dahl), and *Scary Stories to Tell in the Dark* (by Schwartz). More advanced favorites include *The Indian in the Cupboard* (Banks) and *Where the Red Fern Grows* (by Rawls).

Series books, which repeat the same characters and story lines, help students with reading problems feel secure and accomplished. Favorite easy book series include *The Berenstain Bears* (by Berenstain), *Clifford the Big Red Dog* (by Bridwell), and *Curious George* (by Rey). Students take an important step when they begin to read chapter books. Table 4.1 (at end of chapter) lists favorite series of books that are divided into chapters. These books encourage students with reading problems to experience more extended reading.

Nonfiction books with factual information open up worlds of experience. Students enjoy such books as *Mummies Made in Egypt* (by Aliki) and *The Popcorn Book* (by de Paola).

Children's favorite fairy tales include *Cinderella*, *Goldilocks*, and *Snow White*. Children list Dr. Seuss, Judy Blume, Roald Dahl, Maurice Sendak, and the poet Shel Silverstein among their favorite authors.

Many popular easy trade books have been enlarged into big books (about 21 inches by 24 inches), enabling them to be shared easily with large groups. Other popular books have been recorded into audiocassette and video formats. Children enjoy hearing and seeing these stories presented in different ways.

An increasing number of trade books are written in a language other than English or in English and a second language. These provide motivating reading experiences for students who do not speak English as a native language (see Chapter 13).

Remedial Reading Series Books.   These series of graded books are designed to be used as instructional materials for students achieving below grade level. They contain stories or articles that are sometimes accompanied by comprehension questions and practice exercises. An example of a popular series is *Reading for Concepts* and *Sprint Plus*. Generally, these books contain selections of only one or two pages.

Easy Reading Books.   Often called *high-interest/low-vocabulary books*, these books are designed to provide enjoyable reading experiences. They contain longer stories and do not concentrate on skill development. Some, such as the *Dolch First Reading Books*, provide reading practice using a total vocabulary of 200 to 500 words in 75 to 100 pages. Such books enable very disabled students to practice sight words several times. Others are controlled for reading level but do not contain specific word lists, nor do they repeat a limited number of words. These books may be used with more advanced students, and they often incorporate such topics as sports, rock stars, and teenage problems. Still others contain classic stories rewritten in easier language. Examples of these are *Jamestown Classics*.

Basal Readers, Literature Anthologies, Literature Textbook Series.   These series of books are often used in schools for reading instruction, and many low-achieving readers use them in regular classrooms. To help ensure a student's success, supplementary reading instruction should be aimed at providing success in reading the classroom series.

Most classroom series include suggested learning experiences for students who are struggling with grade-level materials. In addition, most publishing companies recommend an extensive classroom library of trade books written in a wider range of reading levels than those presented in the basal reading program.

In an effort to match materials to students' reading levels, teachers sometimes use reading series intended for younger students with older students who are struggling with grade-level materials. Although some of these materials may be useful, they should be selected judiciously so that older students are not insulted by content or illustrations that are too childish. One way to avoid this problem is to use informational books written at lower levels but illustrated with photographs rather than childish drawings or paintings.

Some materials have been specially developed for use with students reading below grade level. A limited number of series have been developed for this purpose. For example, *Early Success* is an early intervention program developed by Houghton Mifflin for use with struggling readers in primary grades. *Soar to Success* is a companion program for intermediate grades. However, teachers in supplementary programs most often rely on alternative materials and ensure consistent, logically sequenced instruction through their own careful planning.

Content Area Texts. These books are used in students' social studies, health, and science classes. Reading teachers may help students cope better in school by teaching them to use effective comprehension and study strategies with these informational texts.

Real-Life Materials. These abundant reading materials include newspaper articles, captions of pictures, magazines, manuals, advertisements, and travel brochures. Because such real-life materials interest students, vocabulary control becomes a matter of secondary interest.

Children's Magazines. Children's magazines make excellent reading material. Currently, the Reading Center subscribes to many, including *Sports Illustrated for Kids*, *World* (published by National Geographic), *Ranger Rick* (published by the National Wildlife Federation), and *Cobblestone* (a history magazine for intermediate students).

Plays. Plays written for students help them foster their sense of drama and engage them in motivated, expressive oral reading. Some plays have been written specifically to be read rather than performed from memory. Examples of series of these plays for reading include *Theatre Workshop Playbooks* (Scholastic) and *Readers Theatre for Children* (Teacher Ideas Press). This series includes plays written in content areas as well.

The younger children in the Reading Center enjoy the *Sunshine Books*, a series of plays published by the Wright Group. Our older students like *Just a Minute*, a book containing 10 short plays published by Pembroke Publishers, Limited. These plays are based on stories and legends from around the world.

Individual, Group, and Cooperative Instruction

Students with reading problems may be instructed individually or in groups. For students with severe difficulties in reading, individual instruction is often preferable because it allows the teacher to monitor and respond to instructional needs. In addition, at times highly distractable students need an environment that protects them from irrelevant stimuli. Finally, in individual instruction, students can avoid the embarrassment of peer pressure. According to McCormick (1999) students who received individual instruction have consistently outperformed those receiving group instruction.

However, because individual instruction is not always possible, teaching is often done in groups. Group instruction often has benefits for students past the beginning stages of reading. Group instruction enables students to learn from each other. As students listen to the reactions others have to a story, their own comprehension deepens. Sometimes students can explain concepts to peers more effectively than the teacher can. Students can also share background knowledge.

Group instruction also helps students to become more active. They may ask each other questions about material, share and discuss predictions about what will happen in their reading, and study with one another. They have opportunities to interact and to share literacy experiences by taking parts in plays and writing to one another. Finally, group instruction enables students to develop close personal ties to someone who is like them. Friendships often develop between students in groups.

Peer tutoring is a special type of group work in which students teach each other directly. Generally, one student is assigned to another as a tutor. Older students are often used to teach younger ones (cross-age tutoring), or the tutor and learner may be the same age. A noteworthy finding is that students who act as tutors often gain more in reading skills than do the students they are teaching (Fuch, Fuch, Mathes, & Simmons, 1997). With careful teacher supervision, peer tutoring has proven to be worthwhile for both tutor and learner (Mathes, Grek, Howard, Babyak, & Allen, 1999; Krueger & Braun, 1998–1999).

There are many other creative ways to group students. Teachers in one school had lower-achieving readers in sixth and third grades go into kindergarten rooms to read to children. This option fostered practice and a sense of accomplishment in the older students and delighted the kindergarteners.

In another grouping method, low-achieving students are put into pairs and asked to reread a story. Students take turns, alternating the reading by paragraphs or pages or taking parts. Richek and Glick (1991) and Stahl, Heubach, and Cramond (1997) have reported excellent results using this strategy with primary children. Stahl, Heubach, and Cramond (1997) reported that it worked best when students chose their own partners.

However, working in pairs often challenges the social skills of low-progress students. To ensure that they will have a successful experience, they should first concentrate on something that is purely social. Often students are asked to form pairs and complete these statements together:

- A food we both like is _____.
- A TV program we both like is _____.
- A color we both like is _____.
- An animal we both like is _____.
- A book we both like is _____.
- A type of pizza we both like is _____.

The teacher needs to emphasize that students should formulate *group* answers and not answer as individuals.

More advanced students who are comfortable sharing may read books independently and then share their responses in a reading conference (Galda, Cullinan, & Strickland, 1997; E. Costa, personal communication, 1990). Some questions that students might ask each other include:

- Does the author make you want to read on? How?
- What was the most exciting thing that happened?
- Was the book (or story) easy to read? Why?
- Would you recommend this book (or story) to a friend?

Working with groups of students is, of course, not limited to pairs. In *cooperative learning*, students form small groups, and each group is responsible for the joint learning of its members. Cooperative learning fosters a sense of solidarity among students and often increases the enthusiasm as well as the mastery of all students. This organization pattern is effective with low-achieving students even if they are grouped with higher achievers (Galda, Cullinan, & Strickland, 1997; Slavin, 1984).

Creating a Community of Readers and Writers

Because reading and writing are used to communicate to other people, the more students talk, write, and communicate about their reading, the deeper and more motivating their literacy will be. This section describes methods to build a self-sustaining community of readers and writers. Using these strategies, our students come to look forward to their reading lessons and read willingly at home (Jennings, Richek, Chenault, & Ali, 1993).

Filling the Environment with Literacy Materials

When your room, school, and home are filled with motivating, colorful literacy materials, children are hard pressed *not* to read and write. Classrooms should contain many books, displayed at students' eye level, with covers facing forward. This arrangement is far more inviting than seeing rows of book spines. Books are separated by genre, putting adventure books, scary books, joke books, and sports books in their own separate, labeled baskets. Popular series have their own baskets.

Reading materials should be varied in levels and interests. Big books, audiocasette and book sets, and videos of favorite books are also motivating. Picture books motivate all types of students with reading problems, including those in secondary school.

Students' own work can be included in displays. Books written by students, favorite jokes, and book jackets should be placed around the room. Teachers can also display student comments about books or illustrations of stories they have read.

Special corners can develop interests. In poetry corners, poems, including those written by students, are displayed on the wall, and poetry books are put on slanted shelves. A writing corner can include space to compose, different types of paper (notes, scented paper, neon paper), crayons, magic markers, pens, pencils, scissors, a word processor, and other materials that encourage written responses.

An area with a tape recorder and head phones can house audiotape and book sets. In working with three middle-school students on American history, we constructed an American history corner in the Reading Center. This corner featured books about the topic, a map of America, flags of the original colonies, and student writing.

Color and good design are important in creating an attractive environment. The Reading Center has painted secondhand bookshelves red, yellow, and blue. The slanted shelf book displays used by bookstores to feature new books are quite useful. Because these display stands are often thrown out after use, bookstores have been happy to donate them.

Physical arrangement should provide a space for students to read. Beanbag chairs, pillows, and carpets or carpet squares provide an environment that welcomes students to sit or lie down and look at books. You may provide a special class library area or distribute books and reading places throughout the room.

A classroom library should be comfortable, attractive, and inviting. Books and magazines should be displayed in a manner that invites students to browse. Multiple copies of some titles will encourage small groups of students to read the same book. The area should include furniture or pillows arranged to allow for students to talk about the books they are reading (Galda, Cullinan, & Strickland, 1997). Props to encourage sharing may include flannel boards, stuffed animals, book jackets, bulletin boards, hand puppets, and posters.

An effective learning community also features pictures of the students, parents, and teachers. In the Reading Center, we take candid photos of participants. These photos are cut into different shapes, backed with bright neon-colored paper, and changed weekly. Excited students, parents, and teachers enjoy seeing themselves in action.

Sharing Literacy

Sharing and reacting to books foster literacy at all levels. Providing lots of books and sharing them can result in marked increases in reading and achievement (Elley & Mangubahi, 1983; Ingham, 1982; Morrow & Weinstein, 1986).

Teachers who read books to students encourage them to later read these books for themselves. Reading to students is important at all grade levels; in one successful program, community readers came in to read to at-risk senior high students. Favorite authors included Erma Bombeck and Harry Caray (J. Monahan, personal communication, 1990).

Students may be encouraged to continue a book for themselves if a teacher orally reads the first few pages to them. Make sure to break off your reading at a suspenseful point so that students will want to know what happens.

A book chain encourages several classrooms to share literacy. Small shopping bags, each containing one book to read to students, are distributed among classroom teachers (S. Ali, personal communication, 1994). The shopping bags are rotated every two days until each class has listened to every book. Doing this activity with seven third-grade rooms enabled at-risk students to share themed reading experiences. In one book chain, seven third-grade teachers shared the picture books *Two Bad Ants* (by Van Allsberg), *Horton Hears a Who* (by Dr. Seuss), *Amos and Boris* (by Steig), *The True Story of the Three Little Pigs* (by Sczieka), *Streganona* (by de Paola), *The Three Little Wolves and the Big Bad Pig* (by Trivizas), and *Bartholomew and the Ooblek* (by Dr. Seuss). After listening to each book, students voted for their favorite and justified their choice. The winner was *The Three Little Wolves and the Big Bad Pig*. Student comments (including those from a bilingual room, in Spanish) were displayed in the hall. The students were thrilled to read their words as they passed to gym and lunch. In another book chain, children shared seven selected poetry books. As a final project, students illustrated the poem "If You Were Only One Inch Tall" (by Silverstein) and displayed their artwork in the hall (Richek, 1994). Several classrooms have used a *Great Books* book to encourage sharing. In a large, blank artist's sketch pad, each page is reserved for one book that students have enjoyed. After they read a book, they write their comments about it. When looking for a good book, other students peruse the pages of the Great Books.

Visual displays also invite sharing. For example, after reading *The Ballad of Belle Dorcas* (by Hooks), 30 third-grade students each recorded their responses as a leaf on a tree, a central concept of the story (Y. Brown, personal communication, 1994). In another example of recording responses to different books, a class of fourth graders each read a fairy tale of their choice and then rated it with one, two, three, or four stars (E. Costa, personal communication, 1990).

Author studies provide another effective way to encourage student sharing. Many students with reading problems fail to realize that books are written by real people. When teachers share the story of an author's life and when students relate books to one another, students are able to personalize the connection to reading. When students read several books by the same author, they are encouraged to compare them. For example, Jim, a seventh grader in the Reading Center, became interested in books by Gary Paulsen. Although Jim had previously been identified as a reluctant reader, he loved reading about adventurous boys about his age and a little older who overcame difficulties and proved to be self-reliant. We gathered several copies of titles such as *The River, Hatchet, The Foxman,* and *Tiltawhirl John.* Jim convinced a couple of other middle school boys in the Reading Center to join him in reading these adventures. The teachers found information about the author in *Something About the Author: Major Authors and Illustrators for Children and Young Adults* (Hedblad, 1998). Information about Paulsen's life and his own adventures piqued the students' interest, and they concluded their study with *Woodsong,* Paulsen's account of his own adventures in the North Woods of Minnesota and his participation in Alaska's famous Iditarod Race. Other students and pairs of students have read books by Ezra Jack Keats (*The Snowy Day, Peter's Chair,* and *Whistle for Willie*) and Robert McCloskey (*Make Way for Ducklings, One Morning in Maine,* and *Time of Wonder*).

These small groups of students have especially enjoyed e-mailing one another and pen pals in other places with similar interests about their reading. Sometimes authors include their e-mail addresses in their books. When students have found these addresses and had the opportunity to contact authors directly with comments or questions about their reading, they have been thrilled and anxiously await their replies.

Displaying Literacy and Using Themes

How can students show their accomplishments? In the Reading Center, teachers choose a different theme for each semester and display books read by planning visuals based on this theme (Jennings, et al., 1993). In the fall of 1993, teachers and students "walked" an orange neon bear around the room by recording each book (or book chapter) a student read on a paw print. Finally, the bear came out the door and into the hall. In the winter of 1999, the theme was Fantasy Island, and shapes representing students' own fantasies, such as rockets, basketballs, cars, and musical notes, were hung from palm tree mobiles. As the end of one millennium and the beginning of the next approached, the theme was Treasures of the Millennium. The Reading Center was decorated with treasures from the areas of music, sports, science, history, and nature; and students wrote the titles of chapters and books they read on gold-coin shapes to hang from treasure chest mobiles. Other themes have included the sea, folktales, and people around the world.

Displays may also record words and concepts learned as well as books. Words that students have learned can be placed on charts. Eight-year-old Samantha enjoyed her personal "word worm" that the teacher displayed on the wall. Each segment of the worm represented a word she had mastered. A group of teenagers who were working to improve reading rate charted progress every day so that they could see how their rates were climbing. When charting progress, however, teachers should remember that publicly displayed charts may embarrass the student who makes few or no gains. For some students, records of progress should be kept private.

A small group of students work independently to practice newly acquired skills.

Using Computers to Help Students Read

Computers offer many instructional advantages for students with reading problems. They can dramatically expand the motivation and time spent practicing reading. However, computers cannot, and should not, take the place of books for teaching reading or supplant the teacher, but the technology of the computer can expand instructional possibilities.

The use of computers offers four advantages in helping students improve their reading:

- *Computer instruction offers the poor reader more time for learning on a one-on-one basis.* Students are given the valuable time they need to practice and strengthen newly acquired reading abilities. Computer programs have been shown to hold the attention of students with reading problems, dramatically increasing the amount of "engaged time" spent in learning (Balajthy, 1995).
- *Computers can help develop automaticity (or fluency) in word recognition.* Students with reading problems often need extended practice before they can recognize words quickly. Practice with the computer helps the poor

reader recognize words rapidly and accurately. Research has verified automaticity training on the computer for students with reading problems (Holt-Ochsner, 1992; Segalowitz & Catbonton, 1995).

- *The computer offers the student private instruction.* Because students usually work at a computer privately, potential problems with peer criticism, poor self-concept, and embarrassment are avoided.
- *The computer offers the opportunity and time to think about the reading passage.* Computer programs that provide interactive feedback actually guide the student in problem solving and metacognitive skills. Further, because the computer provides immediate feedback, the pupil does not practice an incorrect answer for a long period.

Computers in the classroom, particularly those linked to the Internet, have opened a broad avenue of opportunities for teachers to expand their students' learning experiences. However, teachers should read reviews of software carefully before investing heavily. The quality of the software varies tremendously. Often, companies will provide preview software, or the teacher can find reviews of the software on the Internet. In some cases, introductory versions of software can be downloaded so that teachers can determine whether or not it will serve the instructional purposes and meet the needs of their students.

Teachers should also check carefully to see that the school computers will support the software. Some software is available for only Macintosh systems, and some is available for only Windows systems. Teachers should also read the minimum requirements for either system before ordering. This information is provided in catalogs as well as on Web sites.

Programs for emergent literacy typically reinforce letter-sound correspondence and sight word development. Popular programs include:

- *Muppet Learning Keys,* Sunburst: Wings for Learning
- *Muppet Word Book,* Sunburst: Wings for Learning
- *Early Learning Series,* Marblesoft
- *Reading and Me,* Davidson & Associates
- *The Playroom,* Broderbund
- *Talking Classroom,* Orange Cherry Software
- *Bailey's Book House,* Edmark
- *Arthur's Reading,* Creative Wonders
- *Mia: The Search for Grandma's Remedy,* Kutoka Kids
- *Sound It Out Land Phonics Adventures,* 99V Phonics Reading and Writing
- *Roxie's Reading Fish,* Lattice Work Software. Introductory version can be downloaded from http://www.latticeworksw.com/roxread.htm.

Some companies have developed programs that span several levels of literacy development:

- *Reader Rabbit*, Learning Company
  Reader Rabbit's Interactive Reading Journey for Ages 4–6
  Reader Rabbit 1 for Grade K–1
  Reader Rabbit First Grade
  Reader Rabbit 2 for Grades 1–3
  Reader Rabbit 3 for Grades 2–4
- *JumpStart Reading*, Knowledge Adventure
- *Reading Mansion* for PreK–2, Sundance
- *First 1000 Words* for Grades PreK–2, Sundance
- *Phonics Alive* for Grades K–3, Sundance
- *The Jolly Post Office* for Grades K–3, Sundance
- *AstroWord* for Grades K–6, Sundance, includes phonics, spelling, structural analysis, and vocabulary skills
- *Kid's Media Magic*, Sundance, includes vocabulary development and support for writing through a "text-to-speech" capability

Some software is designed to provide a motivating way to develop fluency of word recognition through games and repetition:

- *Edmark Reading Program*, Edmark Corporation
- *Stickybear's Reading Room*, Weekly Reader Software
- *Paint with Words*, MECC

Programs designed to develop word recognition accuracy provide phonics practice:

- *First Letter Fun*, MECC
- *Phonics Prime Time*, MECC
- *Word Munchers*, MECC
- *Tim and the Cat*, Harley
- *Big Red Hat*, Harley
- *Reader Rabbit Series*, Learning Company
- *Word Attack 3*, Davidson & Associates
- *Zoo-Phonics*, found at http://zoo-phonics.com, which includes several additional links for teachers.
- *Kid Phonics 1* for Ages 4–7, School PC
- *Kid Phonics 2* for Ages 6–9, School PC
- *Phonics Alive* for Ages 5–8, School PC
- *Sound It Out Land* for Ages 3–5, School PC

Interactive storybooks include some children's favorites (an asterisk indicates availability in English and Spanish):

- *ABC** by Dr. Seuss, Grades PreK–3, Sundance
- *Arthur's Birthday** by Marc Brown, Grades K–4, Sundance
- *Arthur's Reading Race** by Marc Brown, Grades K–4, Sundance
- *Arthur's Teacher Trouble** by Marc Brown, Grades K–4, Sundance
- *The Berenstain Bears Get in a Fight** by Stan and Jan Berenstain, Grades PreK–3, Sundance
- *The Berenstain Bears in the Dark** by Stan and Jan Berenstain, Grades PreK–3, Sundance
- *The Cat in the Hat** by Dr. Seuss, Grades K–4, Sundance
- *Green Eggs and Ham** by Dr. Seuss, Grades PreK–3, Sundance
- *Just Grandma and Me** by Mercer Mayer, Grades PreK–3, Sundance
- *Sheila Rae, the Brave** by Kevin Henkes, Grades PreK–3, Sundance
- *Stellaluna* by Janell Canon, Grades PreK–3, Sundance
- *The Magic School Bus Series*, Broderbund
- *Reading Magic Library Series*, Tom Snyder Productions
- *Peter Pan*, EA Kids
- *K. C. Clyde in Fly Ball*, Don Johnson

Software designed to enhance vocabulary development often builds meaning vocabulary by using standard presentation and a cloze format. Programs include:

- *Words and Concepts I, II, and III*, Laureate
- *Young People's Literature*, Sunburst: Wings for Learning

Some software is designed to improve reading comprehension. These programs typically present passages followed by comprehension questions designed to elicit literal, inferential, and critical responses. These programs include:

- *Readable Stories*, Laureate Learning Systems
- *Those Amazing Reading Machines*, MECC
- *Comprehension Reading Series*, Harley Courseware
- *Twistaplot Reading Adventures*, Scholastic, Inc.
- *Read n' Roll*, Davidson and Associates
- *Stories and More*, IBM
- *Super Solvers: Midnight Rescue*, The Learning Company
- *Reading Realities*, Teacher Support Software, specifically designed to develop inferential skills

Some of this software uses popular children's literature as a basis for developing reading and writing responses:

- *Explore-a-Story Series*, William K. Bradford
- *The Ugly Duckling*, Byte Works

- *Discis Books*, Discis Knowledge Research
- *Fly Ball*, Don Johnson
- *Living Books Series*, Broderbund, individual titles presented previously
- *Reading Magic: Moonlight Madness*, Hartley Courseware
- *The Velveteen Rabbit* by Margery Williams, Grades PreK–3, Sundance
- *Mike Mulligan and His Steam Shovel* by Virginia Lee Burton, Grades PreK–3, Sundance
- *Curious George Learns the Alphabet* by H. A. Rey, Grades K–3, Sundance
- *Curious George Comes Home* by H. A. Rey, Grades PreK–2, Sundance
- *The Polar Express* by Chris Van Allsburg, Grades PreK–3, Sundance
- *The First Start Biography Series*, Grades 2–5, Sundance

Numerous Web sites designed specifically for use by teachers are available (Elish-Piper & Stahl, 1997). In addition to these instructional programs, computers can be used in writing instruction (see Chapter 11).

Summary

Essential components of effective reading instruction are guided reading; work in word knowledge, including meaning vocabulary development and word recognition; writing; and independent reading. Strategy instruction occurs in the context of these four components and teaches students to apply strategies as they read and write. Teachers should explain why strategies are important, model them, and provide opportunities for students to practice and demonstrate them. In follow-up instruction, teachers review reading and writing strategies and provide additional practice so that students can internalize strategy use.

The most important principle of teaching students with reading problems is to *provide extensive opportunities to read*. Strategy instruction and practice should occur within the context of real reading experiences. Other principles include (1) begin instruction at the student's instructional reading level; (2) provide support for the instruction in the regular classroom; (3) use time effectively by keeping transitions to a minimum and allowing students to apply the strategies they learn while they are reading real text; and (4) most reading should be done silently, with oral reading being used for specific purposes.

The most important component of instruction is the relationship between the teacher and student. Building rapport includes accepting the student; providing a safe, secure learning environment; and providing successful experiences for the student.

Supplementary reading instruction should be in addition to, and supportive of, students' regular classroom reading instruction. It may be provided in a resource room or within a student's classroom. Materials include trade books, controlled vocabulary books, content area textbooks, magazines, easy-reading books, and plays. Instruction may be individual or in groups.

Creating a literate community is important. Teachers can fill the environment with literacy materials and have special interest corners, listening centers, classroom libraries, and displays of students' literacy accomplishments.

Computer-assisted instruction is especially supportive for students with reading problems. Computers motivate students to spend more engaged learning time practicing reading, and they foster automaticity in word recognition through extended practice.

TABLE 4.1   Series of Easy Chapter Books

Primary Level

Adventures of the Bailey School Kids. Dudley and M. T. Jones, Scholastic.
   Children find adults are gremlins, witches, aliens, etc.
The Adventures of Mary-Kate and Ashley. Various Authors, Scholastic.
   The Trenchcoat Twins solve mysteries.
Aldo Books. Johanna Hurwitz, Puffin Books.
   Aldo and his sisters and friends share concerns with young readers.
Amber Brown Series. Paula Danziger, Scholastic.
   Amber shares concerns common to young children.
Baby-Sitters Little Sister Series, Ann M. Martin, Scholastic.
   Mischievous seven year-old stepsister of baby-sitter Kristy.
Ballet Slippers Series. P. R. Giff, Puffin Books.
   Rosie's dream of becoming a ballerina leads her into adventures.
Berenstain Bears–Big Chapter Books. Stan and Jan Berenstain, Random House.
   Brother and sister deal with contemporary situations as they grow up.
Cam Jansen Series. David A. Adler, Puffin Books.
   Adventurous fifth-grade girl engages her friends in solving series of mysteries.
Einstein Anderson. S. Simon, Puffin Books.
   Sixth-grade boy uses science to solve mysteries.
Henry and Mudge. Cynthia Rylant, MacMillan.
   A boy and his dog face everyday situations.
Herbie Jones Series. Suzy Kline, Puffin Books.
   Herbie and his friend Raymond encounter everyday problems.
Junie B. Jones Series. Barbara Park, Random House.
   Young girl faces situations common to young readers.
The Kids of Polk Street School. P. R. Giff, Dell Press.
   Second-grade class experiences humorous events.
Magic Tree House Series. Mary Pope Osborne, Random House.
   A collection of mysteries solved by adventurous children.
Marvin Redpost Series. Louis Sachar, Random House.
   Young boy shares concerns common to young readers.
Nate the Great. M. Sharmat, Dell Yearling.
   Nate solves many mysteries; written in easy text.

TABLE 4.1 Series of Easy Chapter Books, *continued*

New Kids of Polk Street School. P. R. Giff, Dell Press.
   Adventures of kindergarten class; written in easy chapter books.
Pet Patrol Series, Betsy Duffey, Puffin Books.
   Third-grade boys and girls striving to fit in.
Pee Wee Scouts. J. Delton, Dell.
   First- and second-grade boys and girls share scouting experiences.
Polka-Dot Private Eye. P. R. Giff, Dell.
   Student in Ms. Rooney's room solves mysteries for classmates.
Russell and Elisa Books. Johanna Hurwitz, Puffin Books.
   Brother and sister encounter everyday situations experienced by young readers.
Something Queer. L. Levy, Dell Yearling.
   Girl detectives solve mysteries; written in illustrated text.
Sweet Valley Kids. F. Pascal, Bantam.
   Second-grade girls have humorous everyday adventures.

Intermediate/Middle School Level

American Girls Collection. Various Authors, Pleasant Company.
   Stories about young girls from different generations of Americans.
Anastasia Book, Lois Lowry, Dell.
   Anastasia and her brother encounter humorous situations familiar to
      intermediate readers.
Animorphs, K. A. Applegate, Scholastic.
   Five children change into any animal they touch.
Baby-Sitters Club, Ann M. Martin, Scholastic.
   Girls form a club to share joys and problems of growing up.
Bruce Coville Books, Edited by Bruce Coville, Scholastic.
   Scary stories written by various authors.
Encyclopedia Brown Books. Donald J. Sobol, Bantam.
   Ten year-old Leroy Brown solves cases using his great brain.
Ghosts of Fear Street, R. L. Stine, Pocket Books.
   Scary stories for intermediate readers.
Give Yourself Goosebumps, R. L. Stine, Scholastic.
   Choose-your-own-ending books of scary stories.
Goosebumps, R. L. Stine, Scholastic.
   Thrillers for middle-grade readers.
Matt Christopher Sports Series, M. Christopher, Various Publishers.
   Heroic and human stories of various sports.
Matt Christopher Sports Biographies, M. Christopher, Little Brown.
   Biographies of sports heroes.
Ramona Books. Beverly Cleary, Various Publishers.
   Young readers can experience Ramona's adventures with her friends and family.

(continued)

TABLE 4.1   Series of Easy Chapter Books, continued

Spooksville. Christopher Pike, Pocket Books.
   Adam and Sally share in a variety of scary adventures.
Sweet Valley Twins. Francine Pascal, Bantam.
   Twelve-year-old Wakefield twins encounter problems in middle school.
Wayside School Books. Louis Sachar, Various Publishers.
   Middle-grade students encounter humorous situations.

CHAPTER

5 Emergent Literacy

Introduction

This chapter discusses the underlying concepts that students must develop to read. The term *emergent literacy* refers to the gradual process children go through as they develop an understanding of written language.

At one time, the field of reading focused on *reading readiness* as a set of skills students needed before they could begin reading instruction. However, research has shown that children best develop the foundation for reading as they engage in activities with print. Rather than children being "ready for reading" at one point in their lives, the basis for reading is laid gradually and involves speaking, listening, reading, and writing (Galda, Cullinan, & Strickland, 1997).

Unfortunately, many students with reading problems have not mastered these crucial concepts. If you have students who cannot comfortably read beginning-level books, you must determine whether they have developed the foundation needed for reading. Many such students, even those in intermediate grades, lack basic concepts about print. When these concepts are developed using books, stories, letters, and words, students improve dramatically. The tasks used to assess early literacy in the Reading Center are based on the Early Reading Screening Instrument (ERSI), developed by Darrell Morris (1998).

This chapter identifies critical concepts that form the basis for beginning reading, discusses how to assess them, and offers some instructional strategies to teach them. Although most disabled students progress using these techniques, some students with more severe disabilities need even more intensive measures (see Chapter 15).

Emergent Literacy Concepts

Six areas form the foundation of literacy:

- Oral language development
- Concepts about print
- Alphabet knowledge
- Phonemic awareness
- Letter-sound correspondence
- Beginning reading vocabulary

This section discusses each of these concepts and provides informal methods by which to assess them.

Oral Language Development

As described in Chapter 4, reading, writing, listening, and speaking are all aspects of language. Students whose oral language is not well developed have difficulty with literacy.

Aspects of Oral Language Important for Literacy. To read effectively, students need to be able to express and understand ideas fully. They also need to develop language skills specifically related to stories. For example, they must understand and be able to express the structure of stories. This understanding includes realizing that stories have characters and events that occur in sequence.

Questioning is also a crucial language skill. To participate fully in lessons, students must respond to teachers' questions. They also need to ask questions to clarify their own understandings or seek information. Many students with language development problems have difficulty constructing or responding to questions.

During the "get acquainted" activity in the Reading Center, it became apparent that Sean, a third grader, had language problems. When Sean's teacher asked him for a word describing himself, he could not answer. After many probes, he finally said "boy" and "brother." When he retold *Little Red Riding Hood* in his own words, he referred to the Grandmother as "Mom" and to Little Red Riding Hood as "she." Finally, despite the many problems Sean encountered, he never asked for help in reading or writing.

Assessing Oral Language Development.   One way to assess students' oral language development is through teacher observations. In informal conversations, do students talk about interests or activities? When you ask students about important events in their lives, are the responses full accounts or one-word answers? Can students tell a story in sequential order and in complete sentences? When students misunderstand directions or encounter a problem, do they ask for help?

Another method for assessing oral language development is to read a short story to students and ask them to retell it in their own words. A good retelling includes important characters and events in the story in sequential order (see Chapters 3 and 8 for further guidelines).

Concepts about Print

An understanding of how print works is critical to emergent literacy. Students must realize that print on the page is read in a certain order and that it contains individual words.

Concepts Crucial to Reading.   Students need three understandings about print:

- Print (not pictures) carries meaning.
- Reading is "tracked," or followed, from top to bottom and left to right.
- In print, words are separated by spaces.

Although these concepts are typically developed in the kindergarten years, some students with reading problems have not fully mastered them in the primary grades. Kelly, a first grader in the Reading Center, traced lines backward, from right to left, as her teacher read them. Derrick, a second-grade child, thought that every spoken syllable he heard was a printed word. These children still needed to develop fundamental concepts about print.

Assessing Concepts about Print.   In her *An Observation Survey of Early Literacy Development*, Marie Clay (1993) includes a *Concepts about Print* test using two books, *Sand* and *Stone* (see Appendix B), that are specifically designed to measure students' understanding of how print works. These books provide teachers with the opportunity to determine students' awareness of print as meaning, ability to track words and lines in text, and knowledge of what a word is. The test also measures awareness of inverted pages, transposed words, reversed letters, mismatches between pictures and text, and sentences printed out of sequence.

Many concepts about print can be measured without formal tests just by sharing a simple book with a student. Choose an 8- to 12-page book with one or two lines of text per page. The book should contain at least one multisyllabic word. To determine awareness of print as meaning, open the book and ask the student to point to "what we read." The student should identify print, not pictures. Next, to determine tracking, point to the print and ask the student to show you "where we begin to read," and "where we go next." Notice whether the student starts at the left for each line. Finally, for word awareness, ask the student to point to and repeat words after *you* have read each page. From this repetition, you can see whether the student can correctly identify a multisyllabic word as one word.

Alphabet Knowledge

Research shows that the ability to name letters is an excellent predictor of early reading achievement (Trieman, Tincoff, & Richmond-Welty, 1996; Walsh, Price, & Gillingham, 1988).

Knowledge Needed for Reading.   Alphabet knowledge consists of two parts: recognizing letters and writing letters. Students must identify letters automatically and must be able to name them when they are presented in random order. In addition, students must know both uppercase and lowercase letters.

Some reading disabled students, even in the third grade, still have problems with letter recognition. Allen, a third grader in the Reading Center, frequently asked the teacher how to make a *u* or a *j*.

Assessing Alphabet Knowledge.   A sample of an alphabet test is given in Figure 5.1. To administer the task, ask your student to say each letter, reading across the lines. Next, ask the student to write these same letters as you say them.

Phonemic Awareness

Phonemic, or phonological, awareness is the knowledge that speech is built from sounds. For example, the word *bed* consists of three speech sounds, or phonemes: *b*, *short e*, and *d*. The word *sleep* consists of four phonemes: *s*, *l*, *long e*, and *p*, even though it has five letters; the *ee* combination makes only one sound. Consonants can also combine to make one sound; the word *sheep*, which is five letters, consists of three phonemes: *sh*, *long e*, and *p*.

FIGURE 5.1   Alphabet Recognition Test

A   S   D   F   G   H   J

K   L   P   O   I   U   Y

T   R   E   W   Q   Z   X

C   V   B   N   M

a   s   d   f   g   h   j

k   l   p   o   i   u   y

t   r   e   w   q   z   x

c   v   b   n   m   a   y

g   q   t   a   g   t   q

Knowledge Needed for Reading. Phonemic awareness refers to students' knowledge of individual sounds in words and their ability to manipulate those segments (Stahl & Murray, 1994). Research shows that students' abilities to identify and manipulate these sound elements are highly related to reading achievement and spelling (Ball & Blachman, 1991; Byrne & Fielding-Barnsley, 1991; Dreher & Zenge, 1990; Muter, Hulme, & Taylor, 1998; Naslund & Schneider, 1996; Stanovich, 1988a; van Ijzendoorn & Bus, 1994).

Phonemic awareness includes a variety of abilities. Students must be able to identify and separate beginning sounds of words, identify and separate ending sounds, and substitute sounds within a basic pattern. Finally, students need to be able to manipulate sounds by putting them together (or blending them), taking them apart (or segmenting them), and deleting and substituting them. All these abilities help students to master phonics in reading.

Assessing Phonemic Awareness. Phonemic awareness is assessed by asking students to blend and segment sounds, as shown in Figure 5.2. Other tasks (Stahl

---

FIGURE 5.2   Assessing Phonological Awareness: Blending and Segmenting

Directions: I am going to say some words in a special code, and I want you to figure out the real word. If I say /s/-/a/-/t/, you say *sat*. If I say /p/-/i/-/g/, you say *pig*.

Teacher says:	Expected Response	Student's Response
/d/-/i/-/g/	dig	
/p/-/u/-/l/	pull	
/b/-/e/-/d/	bed	
/f/-/a/-/s/-/t/	fast	
/s/-/o/-/f/-/t/	soft	

Directions: Now we will change jobs. If I say *bat*, you say /b/-/a/-/t/. If I say *feet*, you say /f/-/ee/-/t/.

Teacher says:	Expected Response	Student's Response
can	/c/-/a/-/n/	
tell	/t/-/e/-/l/	
dust	/d/-/u/-/s/-/t/	
sit	/s/-/i/-/t/	
fog	/f/-/o/-/g/	

NOTE: The use of slashes (//) indicates that you should say the letter *sound*.

& Murray, 1994) include asking students to identify the first sound in a spoken word (e.g., "What is the first sound in *table*?") or to say a word without a sound (e.g., "Say *table* without the /t/.").

Letter-Sound Correspondences

To read successfully, students must be able to identify and manipulate sounds and also to associate these sounds with their corresponding letters (Ball & Blachman, 1991; Muter, Hulme, & Taylor, 1998; Busin, 1997; Trieman, Tincoff, & Richmond-Welty, 1996).

Relationship to Reading Achievement. Students' knowledge of letter-sound correspondence is highly related to later reading achievement (Dreher & Zenge, 1990; Naslund & Schneider, 1996). Most important to emergent literacy is knowledge about beginning consonants.

Assessing Knowledge of Letter-Sound Correspondence. To assess students' knowledge of beginning consonants, the teacher gives them a word and asks them to identify the beginning sound of the word and the letter that corresponds to this sound. The words in the sample task in Figure 5.3 are frequently found in beginning reading materials and all begin with single-letter initial consonant sounds. The task also includes some two-syllable words.

   Students' spelling of unfamiliar words also reveals important information about letter-sound correspondences (Gentry & Gillet, 1993; Roberts, 1996).

Beginning Reading Vocabulary

The earliest words children learn to read are from their environment. Children who recognize *MacDonald's, Cheerios,* and *Don't Walk* are reading environmental

---

FIGURE 5.3   Assessing Letter-Sound Correspondences: Beginning Letter Sounds

Practice: What is the beginning sound of *mat*? (Student should say /m/.) What letter makes that sound? (Student should say "M." If not, model and practice another word.)

Word	Beginning Sound	Beginning Letter
fish		
little		
ride		
want		
happy		

print. As books, paper, and markers become a part of children's worlds, they make a transition from recognizing logos and signs to recognizing their names or *MOM* and *DAD*.

A child's first sight words play a critical role in emergent literacy, for emergent readers gain confidence by using their beginning sight words in reading and writing. These words also form the foundation for word analysis strategies and enable students to use known words as a basis for learning about new ones.

One way to assess early reading vocabulary is to ask students to write any words they know. This activity provides students with the opportunity to show you what they know instead of what they do *not* know.

Clay (1993a) recommends that teachers assess beginning reading vocabulary by developing a word list using 15 high-frequency words drawn from the students' early reading materials and asking students to read these words. This method allows the teacher to discover both which early reading words students know and what their strategies are for coping with unknown words. Allow 10 minutes for students to repeat this activity.

Strategies to Develop Early Literacy Concepts

This section suggests activities for developing emergent literacy concepts. Although so far in this chapter separate assessment tools have been presented for different areas, in instruction these areas are integrated into a total literacy environment. Thus, one activity may foster several areas of emergent literacy (Foorman, Francis, Novy, & Liberman, 1991). As previously emphasized, emergent literacy understandings are best taught within the context of real reading and writing in literacy-rich environments. Because emerging into reading is a gradual process, the instructional activities used to support development overlap with those used for beginning reading and writing.

Oral Language Development

As stated earlier in this chapter, oral language development forms the basis for reading and writing. Three aspects of oral language development crucial to literacy are understanding and using oral language, understanding the structure of stories, and responding to and constructing questions.

Reading Aloud to Students.   Reading books aloud to children is valuable for helping them to develop language skills. Many students with reading problems have not had wide experience in sharing print with an adult. Reading to students enables them to experience the rich language of books as an adult models how reading is done. Children learn to follow a story structure and to engage in conversation about books. In the sections that follow, additional strategies are given that may be used as the teacher reads books aloud to children.

Directed Listening-Thinking Activity.   Often referred to by its initials, DL-TA, this activity is a modification of the Directed Reading-Thinking Activity (DR-TA) developed by Stauffer (1975) and discussed in Chapter 8. In DL-TA, the teacher reads the text aloud, stopping at crucial points to allow students to predict what will happen next and to confirm or revise previous predictions. These predictions and confirmations (or revisions) guide the students' understanding of the story.

After students are familiar with this strategy, the teacher can alter it by stopping before the last section of text and asking students what they think will happen in the end. Ask students to draw pictures showing what they think will happen; they may then write or dictate a sentence or two about their pictures. Next, read the author's actual ending to the story and compare it with the students' endings.

Story Structure.   The structure of stories (also presented in Chapter 8) can be used to guide the discussion of books a teacher reads to children. Focusing on story elements helps students learn that (1) stories are organized in a predictable fashion; (2) special terms, such as *characters, events*, and *setting*, are used for stories. These understandings will help children both to read and to write stories (Galda, Cullinan, & Strickland, 1997; Gillet & Temple, 2000).

After you read a story to your students, ask them, "Who is this story about?" or "Who are the main characters in this story?" Then ask the students, "Where does this story take place?" and "When does this story take place?" Next, ask students, "What is the main characters' problem?" and finally ask, "How do they solve the problem?"

In the Reading Center, questions are often placed on a chart. Students can answer the questions with pictures from the story or refer to the chart as they retell stories or construct their own. Learning about the "language of stories" provides an excellent foundation for the more complex story grammars and maps used in later comprehension instruction.

Shanahan and Shanahan (1997) have developed a related strategy called Character Perspective Charting. In this strategy, children track the main characters in stories and identify their perspectives in relation to story events. This strategy has proved quite effective in helping students understand stories.

Shared Book Experience.   In this strategy (Button & Johnson, 1997; Holdaway, 1979), teachers imitate the "bedtime story" experience of young children. You can use the shared book experience with whole classes, in small groups, or with individuals. Students are drawn into the shared book experience by the quality of the stories shared, by the teacher's enthusiasm, and by the "sharing" format. A shared book experience may be extended over several days, as children reread and engage in several different activities. Generally, the teacher uses predictable, or patterned, books, which contain repeated words or phrases and plots simple enough for students to predict outcomes. Some favorite predictable books include *Have You Seen My Duckling?* (by Tafuri), *Bears in the Night* (by Berenstain & Berenstain),

Where's Spot? (by Hill), *Have You Seen Crocodile?* (by West), *The Carrot Seed* (by Krauss), *Titch* (by Hutchins), *Ape in a Cape* (by Eichenberg), *Is Your Mama a Llama?* (by Guarino), *Green Eggs and Ham* (by Dr. Seuss), *Too Much Noise* (by McGovern), and *The Very Hungry Caterpillar* (by Carle). A list of additional suggested titles is presented in Table 7.3 (on page 168). Predictable books support students as they attempt to read on their own.

The steps in a shared book experience are:

1. *Introduce the book.* Ask students to predict what it will be about as you clarify any concepts that may be unknown. Show the pictures of the book.
2. *Read the book aloud to students.* Point to each word as you read. Read slowly but with expression rather than word by word. Position the book so that the students can see it. Then reread the book, inviting children to join you. If students do not join you in the rereading, encourage them by leaving off significant words. For example, for "I Know an Old Lady Who Swallowed a Fly," you might read:

   She swallowed a spider
   That wiggled and jiggled and tickled inside her
   She swallowed the spider to catch the fly
   But I don't know why she swallowed the fly . . .

   Who can resist joining in with "I guess she'll die"?
3. *Follow the reading with language activities.* The language-related activities developed from shared book experiences can focus on letter-sound correspondences, dramatization, learning new vocabulary, or any other aspect of literacy that the teacher chooses to develop.

   For example, if you choose to focus on letter sounds, select significant words from the story and draw pictures of them on index cards. Have students group the pictures by their beginning sounds. Next, introduce the letters that correspond to those sounds. Then, you might present a picture card and ask students to write the beginning letter.

Language Experience Activity.   The shared book experience is an excellent springboard for the language experience activity (LEA) (Stauffer, 1980; Allen, 1976; Warner, 1963). In an LEA, teachers and students compose an original story or retell a story in their own words. Generally, students dictate to a teacher, who writes down their words on a chalkboard or large piece of paper.

To try this strategy, follow these procedures:

1. *Brainstorm ideas for a story.* Topics may include shared experiences, such as field trips, science experiments, special events, or stories read aloud. Choose one topic for your story.
2. *Take dictation from students.* Ask students to tell you the words you should write. At early stages, stories should be limited to four or five sentences. Write the words in large print.
3. *Read each word as you write it.*

4. *Reread each sentence, pointing to each word as you say it.* Have students reread each sentence with you.
5. *Reread the entire story with students.*
6. *Follow up with language activities.* For example, students might select three words that they can recognize or draw pictures to go with their story. If they draw pictures, they might choose to write captions for them.

Often teachers combine the language experience activity with the shared book experience to create a cohesive lesson. One second-grade Title I teacher used this format with poetry to provide her students with rich language experiences, as seen in Strategy Snapshot 5.1.

Using Wordless Books.   Wordless books, which tell stories through pictures only and contain no text, can help students develop the skill of telling a narrative in sequence. In using a wordless book, you may wish to have students dictate a sentence for each picture. An alternative approach is to discuss the book with students, record their dictation, writing each sentence on a separate page, and have students illustrate the book. You can then bind the pages to create your own big book. Children can be encouraged to identify words that they know and to read their creation to others. Popular wordless books include *A Boy, a Dog, and a Frog*

STRATEGY SNAPSHOT **5.1**

A Shared Book Experience with an LEA

Ms. Burgess, a teacher in a second-grade Title I class, began with a favorite poem, *Honey, I Love* (by Greenfield), printed on chart paper. She pointed to the words and the students read along in a sing-song fashion.

Next, Ms. Burgess reread a favorite story, *Being Here with You* (by Nicola-Lisa, 1992), as part of a unit on friendship. Ms. Burgess introduced the LEA saying, "Today we're going to write a story like Mr. Nicola-Lisa's, except ours is going to be about our class and how nice it is that we are all so different, but alike."

The students brainstormed ways they were alike and different. As the students talked about what they liked to do together, they recalled a picnic at which they met their seventh-grade pen pals. The students created their own story, "Pen Pals in the Park."

Next, the class divided into teams. One team played a sorting game with the letters *p* and *b*. Another group used magnetic letters to write words selected from their story. The third group sorted picture cards under the headings "Alike" and "Different." The fourth group met with Ms. Burgess to read sentences they wrote about a previous story.

After several minutes, the students reassembled for Ms. Burgess to introduce a new book, *Three Friends* (by Kraus). As she read, Ms. Burgess pointed to the words in the text and stopped occasionally to ask the students how they thought the characters could solve their problems. When she came to a word that started with *b* or *p*, she asked the sorting group for help.

(by Mayer), *What?* (by Lionni), and *Apt. 3* (by Keats). Each of these authors has written additional wordless books.

Concepts about Print

The activities described in the previous sections of this chapter help to develop crucial concepts about print. This section presents some additional activities to develop these understandings.

Echo Reading/Pointing.   The echo reading procedure presented earlier to evaluate concepts about print may also be used to teach these concepts. Good assessment should have much in common with instruction (Johnston, 1997).

In echo reading, teachers help students match the spoken word with the printed word. To implement this strategy, select a predictable book with limited print. First, read the entire book to the students. Next, read one sentence, pointing to each word. To echo read, students reread what you have read as they also point to words. As students become more familiar with the process, the length students repeat may be increased. Monitor students' pointing carefully; make certain that they point to each *word* rather than to each *syllable* that is read.

Counting Words.   In this activity (Cunningham, 2000), students recognize words in speech, a skill that prepares them to recognize them later in print. To do the activity, give students objects (blocks, Popsicle sticks) to use as counters. The student listens as you say a sentence at a normal rate. Then say the sentence again, pausing after each word. Students should move a counter for each word you say. Next, have students make up their own sentences and count the words in them.

Jumbled Sentences.   In this strategy, students count words as they reorder them. Many students who develop early reading problems need this physical separation of words to develop a strong concept of word. To try this strategy, follow these procedures:

1. *Begin with a story you have read or written with your students.* Ask students to write a sentence about the story. Most students write summary sentences. For example, in a story about a hungry dog, Ramon wrote, "Duffy gobbled up all our food." Students often draw a picture about the story and write or dictate a sentence in a practice book.
2. *Write the sentence on a large sentence strip.* Have students read their sentence to you. Next, read the sentence together as you point to each word.
3. *Have students rewrite their sentence on a small sentence strip.* Use the large sentence strip as a model. Students then reread the sentence and point to each word as they read it.
4. *Cut the large sentence strip into individual words and mix them up.*
5. *Have the students reassemble the sentence, using the small sentence strip as a model.* Then students reread the sentence.

Being the Words. In this activity (Cunningham, 2000), students actually "become" one word. To start, the teacher should write the sentences from a predictable book onto sentence strips. You may, of course, need to duplicate words that are used twice in a sentence, or write some words using both lowercase and uppercase first letters. However, you need not make copies of words that reappear in different sentences. Cut the words from two sentence strips into individual words and distribute each word to a student. Make a separate card for each punctuation mark.

Now tell the students they are going to *be* the words they are holding. Display the first two sentences of the book, and read them together. Point to the words as you read them and ask students to look at their words to see if they have any matches. Students who have the words from those sentences come forward and arrange themselves in left-to-right order. Have the other students in the class read the sentences as you point to each "student word." Continue this activity until you have made all the sentences from the book.

For older students, write the sentences on smaller cards and deal a few (like a deck of playing cards) to each student. When you display the sentence, the students must cooperate to construct it.

Alphabet Knowledge

In teaching alphabet knowledge, the teacher combines letter names with letter sounds to help students progress more efficiently.

Memory Game. Sets of cards, which can be easily made or purchased, are used in this game. A set of cards is placed face down on the table. Half contain pictures (no words) of objects, and half contain the letters representing the initial consonant sounds of those objects. Students turn pairs of cards over and try to match the beginning sound of a picture card with its letter. When a match is found, students must name the object and identify the corresponding letter name.

Using Alphabet Books. A variety of beautiful alphabet books help expand children's word knowledge and appreciation of literature as they learn letters. Some of our favorites include *Alligators All Around* (by Sendak), *ABC* (by Burningham), and *I Love My Anteater with an A* (by Dahlov). Research by Stahl (personal communication, 1995) indicates that children's alphabet books that provide words starting with a letter sound (such as *dog* for *d*) also help in developing phonemic awareness. Letters in an alphabet book should be shown in both upper and lower case (e.g., *D* and *d*).

Phonemic Awareness

The phonemic awareness assessment procedures presented earlier in this chapter may also be used as activities to practice phonemic, or phonological, awareness. This section describes other procedures.

Using Nursery Rhymes and Rhyming Books.   Chanting nursery rhymes develops phonemic awareness and the ability to rhyme. Traditional poetry and songs are excellent resources to use with younger children.

Teachers can also use the many excellent books that focus on rhyming to help develop this ability. Begin by reading a rhyming book to students. Next, reread it, but this time, leave out the word that "completes the rhyme," and ask the students to provide it. For example, in the sentences "It is a nice day; I would like to play," you would omit the word *play* and ask the students to supply it. Students can also create their own rhymes.

Excellent books to model rhyming include *Sheep in a Jeep* and its sequels (by Shaw), *The Hungry Thing* and its sequels (by Slepian and Seidler), and books by Dr. Seuss, such as *One Fish, Two Fish* or *Green Eggs and Ham*. For older students, use collections of poetry, such as *The New Kid on the Block* (by Pretlutsky) or *A Light in the Attic* (by Silverstein).

Identifying Beginning Sounds.   Yopp (1992) uses well-known tunes to help reinforce the skill of identifying initial letter sounds. One song is set to the tune of "Old MacDonald Had a Farm."

> What's the sound that starts these words:
> *Basket, bug,* and *Bill*? (wait for response)
> /b/ is the sound that starts these words,
> *Basket, bug,* and *Bill,*
> With a /b/ - /b/ here and a /b/ - /b/ there
> Here a /b/, there a /b/, everywhere a /b/-/b/
> /b/ is the sound that starts these words, *basket, bug,* and *Bill.*

NOTE: The use of slashes (/ /) indicates that you should say the letter *sound.*

Rhymes and Riddles.   In the Rhymes and Riddles activity (Cunningham, 1995), teachers select two groups of words, one to rhyme with *head* and the other to rhyme with *feet*. Next, ask students a riddle so that the answer rhymes with either *head* or *feet*. The children point to the part of their bodies that rhymes with the answer to the riddle. For example, if you ask, "When you are hungry, do you want to . . . ? " students should point to their *feet*, because *eat* rhymes with *feet*. You can repeat this game with other parts of the body. For example, you can ask students to answer riddles with words that rhyme with *hand* and *knee* or *arm* and *leg*.

Counting Sounds.   In this activity, students break apart words and count their sounds. To do the activity, select 10 words that contain two to four phonemes each. The words should be regular; that is, if the word has two sounds, it should have two letters. In fact, use only words with short vowels, consonants, and consonant blends (in which each consonant says a sound). Example words would be *it, man, bent, stop.*

Students listen to you pronounce a spoken word, say it themselves, and then move one object for each sound they hear. You can use craft sticks, cubes, or counters. Try to use objects that are all the same, such as blocks of one color or similarly sized paper clips.

Begin by modeling the activity. Pronounce a word. Then pronounce each sound element of the word and move a counter for each sound that you say. Finally, move the counters back together and repeat the word as a whole.

Next, repeat the procedure with the same word, but this time ask students to try the game with you. Repeat this procedure with another word. Model the segmentation task. Then ask students to join you. Stop after the second phoneme and see if your students can complete the task. If practiced over a period of several weeks, this activity has produced substantial gains for students.

Deleting Phonemes. In this relatively advanced activity, students take a word apart, remove one sound, and pronounce the word without that sound. You might introduce this activity by removing parts of compound words. For example, pronounce a word, such as *playground*, and ask students to say it without *play*. Students should say *ground*. Next, tell students to say *applesauce* without the *sauce*.

Next, ask students to say words, omitting single sounds. Ask students to say *ball* without the /b/. (They should say *all*.) Try several of these, asking students to omit the beginning sounds; then ask students to omit ending sounds. When students successfully can omit beginning and ending sounds from words, ask them to say a word, omitting a medial sound. For example, you might say "Say *stack*, without the /t/." The student should say *sack*.

Blending. Yopp (1992) uses the familiar tune "If You're Happy and You Know It, Clap Your Hands"* to provide practice in blending phonemes together to construct words:

> If you think you know this word, shout it out
> If you think you know this word, shout it out
> If you think you know this word,
> Then tell me what you've heard,
> If you think you know this word, shout it out
> /k/ - /a/ - /t/

(Students should respond by blending the phonemes into *cat*.)

---

*Song *If You Think You Know This Word*, Included in the Article "Developing Phonemic Awareness in Young Children"; by H. K. Yopp, in the *Reading Teacher*, 45, 1992 pp 696–703. Reprinted with permission of Hallie Kay Yopp and the International Reading Association.

Letter-Sound Correspondence

As students develop stronger concepts about print and the ability to identify individual sounds in spoken words, they need to connect these spoken words with printed letters and words. Start with initial consonant sounds because they are the easiest sounds for students to hear and segment and they are therefore the easiest to associate to letters.

Acting Beginning Sounds.   Many students have difficulty breaking words down into their individual sounds and identifying these sounds. To develop this skill, Cunningham (2000) suggests that teachers start by working with individual sounds in words. Begin by showing a specific letter, such as *b*, and having all the students engage in an activity that begins with that sound as they repeat the sound. For /b/ students bounce; for /c/ they catch. Other actions might include dance, fall, gallop, hop, jump, kick, laugh, march, nod, paint, run, sit, talk, vacuum, walk, yawn, and zip.

Letter-Sound Manipulation.   In the beginning stages of reading, students look for familiar patterns and substitute sounds. Students who have experienced problems in early reading need to be taught this strategy.

In the Letter-Sound Manipulation strategy (Iversen & Tunmer, 1993), students remove letter-sound elements from words and substitute other letter-sounds. For example, a student may change the word *bat* to *cat*. Although this action seems simple, it is actually a complex task. Richek (1999) recommends using magnetic letters for this task. To try this strategy, follow this procedure:

1. *Select familiar words with simple patterns and several possible rhyming words.* Choose words students can recognize automatically. Next, create a list of words that rhyme with each word you plan to teach. An example list might be *mat, fat, bat, rat.* If possible, start with words built from the *at, in,* or *it* word families.
2. *Give each student a magnetic board with one of the words on it.* Ask students to read the word. Then ask students to remove the beginning consonant and read the resulting word.
3. *Give students a letter to replace the beginning consonant you have removed.* Ask students to read the new word.
4. *Give students three more consonants to make new rhyming words.* Ask students to read their new words.
5. *After students have made the new words with magnetic letters, ask them to write these words on paper.* When students have learned this strategy and can apply it to new words in print, they are ready for the more advanced word analysis strategies presented in Chapter 6.

Spelling.   Allowing students to spell words they have worked with provides practice in manipulating letters and sounds in print. As students gain in their understanding of letter-sound relationships, their writing will become more conventional. Encourage students to write freely and explore their own spelling. Try not to correct them, but rather let them explore their own understandings, whether or not they are completely accurate.

Beginning Reading Vocabulary

Many activities can encourage students to develop the first sight words on which reading is built. You may make a collection of logos and children's favorite words. Some teachers prepare flash cards with words that are common in the environment. They cut out pictures from newspaper and magazine advertisements and label them. Children often enjoy bringing in and identifying food labels and wrappers. In "print walks," children and adults walk through a building and identify all the times they see a certain type of print, such as the word *exit*, words about weather, or 10-letter words.

Many of the activities presented earlier, such as shared book experiences and language experience stories, help children develop a fund of sight words. However, students also need to directly learn a number of important words by sight. These words, at first, might include their names, addresses, and words that they frequently see in reading or use in writing. Students might keep personal cards for each word and form them into sentences using the jumbled-sentences activity presented earlier.

Summary

In emergent literacy, students surrounded by reading and writing gradually develop the foundation for these activities. Students with reading problems may lack some emergent literacy understandings. Six needed areas of knowledge include oral language development, concepts about print, alphabet knowledge, phonemic awareness, letter-sound correspondences, and beginning reading vocabulary.

In oral language development, students need to express and understand ideas fully, understand how stories are organized, and develop the ability to answer and formulate questions. Instruction in oral language development includes retelling stories, composing original stories, developing questions, reading to students, the Directed Listening-Thinking Activity (DR-TA), discussing story structure, shared book activities, language experience activities (LEA), and using wordless books.

Three concepts about print are crucial to reading: understanding that print carries meaning, knowing how print is organized, and understanding what words are. Instruction includes echo reading, counting words, jumbled sentences, and "being" the word.

Alphabet knowledge is strongly related to reading. Sounds can be taught with letter names. Instruction includes the memory game and the use of alphabet books.

Phonemic awareness refers to the abilities to manipulate sounds, including segmenting, blending, rhyming, sound deletion, sound addition, and sound substitution. Activities include using nursery rhymes and rhyming books, identifying beginning sounds, guessing rhymes and riddles, identifying sounds, counting sounds, deleting phonemes, and blending.

Letter-sound correspondences, identifying a letter and its sound, can be taught by acting as beginning sounds, manipulating letters and sounds, and practicing spelling as well as several strategies mentioned above.

Students' early reading vocabulary words come from their environments. As they are exposed to more print, students start to connect environmental print with specific words. Teachers and parents help the process by reading extensively to students, labeling objects in their environments, and collecting interesting words.

6 Improving Word Recognition Accuracy

Introduction

To read, readers must recognize the words that are written on the page. Poor readers have much difficulty with word recognition. Often they must exert so much energy struggling to recognize words that they are left with little energy for concentrating on comprehending the author's message (Cunningham & Stanovich, 1998; Goldman & Pelligrino, 1987). Yet this struggle often yields only inaccurate word recognition. Studies conducted by the National Institute of Child Health show that about 30 percent of the children in our schools have significant difficulties with reading and particularly with word recognition (Alexander, 1999).

Reading is not a natural process. In contrast to other developmental achievements, such as learning to talk, learning to read requires careful instruction. Learning to read is also a relatively lengthy process. It takes several years, and the learner must persevere over a long period of time. Moreover, the process of recognizing words is complex; readers must use a variety of strategies to accomplish this task (Ehri, 1995).

Word recognition strategies can be divided into those that foster reading fluency (sight words) and those that foster reading accuracy (phonics, structural analysis, and context). Sight words are words that are recognized immediately, without further analysis. Good readers identify most words easily and quickly. Right now, you are probably reading the words in this paragraph with little effort because you recognize them immediately. For fluent processing, the reader must have a large store of sight words that are recognized instantly with no analysis. Research shows that 99 percent of the words that good readers encounter are sight words (Vacca, Vacca, & Gove, 2000). Students must be helped to build an adequate sight vocabulary, and methods for building a sight-word vocabulary are presented in Chapter 7, which discusses word recognition fluency.

This chapter is aimed at helping students develop accurate word recognition. First, it presents an overview of the stages of word recognition development. Then it discusses the assessment of and teaching strategies for each of the strategies that students can use to develop word recognition accuracy:

- Phonics, matching letters with their sound equivalent
- Structural analysis, ferreting out the parts of unknown words
- Context, trying to think of a word that would fit meaningfully into the passage

Stages of Word Recognition Development

The strategies to be discussed are used at different stages of reading development, as children progress from emergent reading to fluent and accurate word recognition. Normally, readers pass through these stages with relatively little effort, but students with reading problems may become "stuck" at a stage and not develop further. Understanding the stage that comes next in the reading process helps teachers to move a student with reading problems toward more mature reading development.

The first stage is called the logographic (Ehri, 1991, 1994), or the visual cue reading stage (Spear-Swerling & Sternberg, 1996). In this stage, children identify words using only visual cues. They may use an actual logo, such as golden arches to identify *MacDonald's*, or they may use a few letter clues. A youngster once confided that he could recognize *dog* because the "barking" dog had its mouth open in the middle (the letter *o*). Of course, he confidently, but inaccurately, pronounced *got* and *from* as *dog* also. Teachers should encourage children in the logographic stage to notice phonics regularities, especially in word beginnings and endings.

Children then move into the partial alphabetic (Ehri, 1991, 1994), or phonetic cue recoding stage (Spear-Swerling & Sternberg, 1996), as they begin to match letters and sounds. In this stage, they focus on the beginnings and ends of words, pronouncing, for example, *need* as *not* and *from* as *farm*. Because decoding in this stage is slow, children depend heavily on context and picture clues. To advance, they need to think about sounds in the *whole* word and particularly vowels, which often occur in the middle of words.

Gradually children move into full, or consolidated, alphabetic reading (Ehri, 1991, 1994; Gaskins, Ehri, Cress, O'Hara, & Donnelly, 1996–1997) or controlled word reading (Spear-Swerling & Sternberg, 1996). They now pay attention to vowels and the patterns that contain them. For example, they might recognize *grape* as composed of *gr* and *ape*. Decoding becomes more accurate but is still slow. Now the child must develop automaticity, or fluency, in reading.

The next stage is sight word reading (Ehri, 1991), or automatic word recognition (Spear-Swerling & Sternberg, 1996). Children begin to recognize many words automatically, without "sounding out," and develop a large store of sight words. Word recognition becomes too rapid for context to be useful (Stanovich, 1993–1994). Because word recognition takes less attention, children begin to focus on comprehension. Teachers can help these students by fostering comprehension strategies, meaning vocabulary, and language development.

Assessing Phonics Strategies

Phonics refers to the relationship between printed letters and the sounds in language. Children must learn to decode the printed language, to translate print into sounds, and to learn about the alphabetic principle of the symbol-sound relationship.

Using phonics to decode letters into sounds can be a slow process because the reader must stop to analyze the word and match letters and letter patterns into sound. The reader can use phonics to focus on a single letter, a letter string such as *pie*, syllables, or phonograms (or rimes or word families) such as the *at* pattern in *cat* (Beck & Juel, 1995).

Much research shows that students who learn the sound-symbol system of English read better than those who have not mastered these critical skills (Alexander, 1999; Chall, 1967, 1979, 1983a; National Reading Panel, 1999; Stahl, 1992). Phonics strategies are a vital part of good reading, but poor readers usually have difficulty learning to use them. Irregularities in the English spelling system can cause problems. In addition, students with reading problems may lack phonemic awareness, which forms the basis of learning phonics (see Chapter 5). These readers are not able to identify and manipulate the sounds in spoken words. Remember that phonics instruction is only one part of a balanced reading program; poor readers need to develop a variety of strategies for recognizing words (Cunningham & Allington, 1999). Both miscue analysis and tests of phonics patterns can be used to assess phonics knowledge.

Miscue Analysis

As discussed in Chapter 3, miscue analysis can provide insight into a student's use of phonics. Analyzing miscues can tell you whether a student knows and applies phonics in reading and which particular letter-sound patterns the student can use. If a student's miscue contains the same sounds as the correct word, that student is using some phonics clues to read. For example, Chrissy read "the children were going on a trip" as "the chicken were going on a top." This shows that she knows, and uses, the sounds of *ch, short e, n, t,* and *p* but may need instruction in the sounds of *short i, l, d,* and *tr.* A teacher would need to confirm this knowledge, however, by listening to Chrissy read an entire passage.

Miscue analysis allows you to assess how students use phonics as they are actually reading, often during an informal reading inventory (IRI). In this way, you can see how their use of phonics clues interacts with their use of context and structural analysis. However, in miscue analysis, you are limited to an analysis of the words in the passage. To obtain a better overview, you can combine miscue analysis with a more systematic test of phonics patterns.

Tests of Phonics Patterns

Another way to assess knowledge of phonics principles is to construct a list of *nonsense words* (or *pseudowords*) that contain important sound-symbol relationships. Because these "words" cannot be known by sight, the student must use phonics to decode them. An informal phonics test using pseudowords is given in Table 6.1. Although this assessment provides a precise assessment of phonics knowledge, you must remember that nonsense words are not an *authentic* assessment of phonics, because such words do not appear in real-life reading. In addition, some young children may be reluctant to pronounce nonsense words and may simply make real words out of them. For these reasons, a nonsense word assessment should be used together with a miscue analysis. Finally, when analyzing

TABLE 6.1 Words for Testing Phonics Generalizations

These nonsense "words" can be used to test phonics mastery. They should be typed in a large typeface or printed neatly and presented in a list format or on individual cards. Students should be warned that they are not real words, when asked to pronounce them.

1. Single Consonants

bam	fep	dif
dup	jit	hak
sut	rez	jer

2. Consonant Digraphs

shap	chep
thip	quen
nack	

3. Consonant Blends

sput	streb	pind
crob	plut	gart
flug	grat	rupt
dreb		

4. Single Vowels: Long and Short

mab	sote	vo
mabe	lib	vom
sot	libe	

5. R-Controlled Vowels

dar	tor
set	snir

6. Vowel Combinations

toat	doil	geet
vay	roub	rood
zew		

7. Hard and Soft C and G

cit	cam	gast
cyle	ges	

8. Silent Letters

knas	wret
gnip	ghes

phonics knowledge, remember that students with reading problems are somewhat inconsistent in their knowledge. For this reason, you may need to review patterns that you thought your students had already mastered.

Teaching Phonics Strategies

Phonics refers to the relationship between printed letters and the sounds in the language. Children must learn the alphabetic principle of the symbol-sound relationship and use it to translate print into speech (Alexander, 1999; Lyon & Moats, 1997; Moats, 1998).

Unfortunately, poor instruction may actually impede the teaching of phonics. At times, children with reading problems fill out numerous phonics worksheets and are ceaselessly "skilled and drilled" at the expense of reading and enjoying meaningful text. Isolated phonics drills may rob students of precious instructional time to do the actual reading that allows them to apply their phonics. Many poor readers have spent years with phonics workbooks and still cannot use phonics to help them read.

Yet research shows that poor readers need explicit code-emphasis instruction. Because the writing system of English is alphabetic, it involves a system of mapping, or seeing, the correspondences between sounds and letters. This mapping is sometimes called *breaking the code*. Studies conducted by the National Institute of Child Health and Human Development (NICHD) show that instruction in letter-sound matching can be extremely helpful for low-achieving readers (Alexander, 1999; Lyon & Moats, 1997; Moats, 1998). The challenge is to deliver *good* phonics instruction.

Teachers have many important decisions to make about teaching phonics. Many instructional options and specific methods are available to help students with reading problems use phonics as a tool in recognizing words.

Patterns and Rules

Basic ways to organize phonics instruction for your students include teaching phonograms (often called rimes or word families) and teaching important principles or generalizations.

Phonograms (Rimes or Word Families).   You may want to organize your instruction around the teaching of phonograms, such as *pin, win, tin* or *hop, stop,* and *mop.* A phonogram is made up of a vowel and the following consonant (or consonants). The letters preceding the rime are the *onset* (such as the *d* in *day*). Children seem to learn word families easily and naturally (Adams, 1990; Fry, 1998; Moustafa, 1993; Stahl, 1992). In addition, phonogram patterns are more regular than many phonics generalizations. Table 6.2 lists common phonograms for beginning readers.

Phonograms form the basis for syllable units in multisyllabic words. Consider the word *intermittent*, which contains the following phonograms: *in, er, it,* and *ent*. In this way, knowledge of phonograms can translate into a powerful strategy for analyzing multisyllabic words.

In a word recognition strategy known as *decoding by analogy*, the reader identifies unknown words or word parts, which are often phonograms, to say the unfamiliar word. Suppose you had never seen the word *fleck*. However, you knew *flat* and *check*. You would use your knowledge of *fl* in *flat* and the *eck* in *check* to ac-

---

TABLE 6.2   Common Phonograms

ad, ag, an, ap, at, aw, ay, ack, ail, ain, air, ake, ale, all, ame, and, ang, ank, are, ash, ast, ate, ave
ed, en, et, ear (bear and dear), each, eal, eep, eet, eck, end, ent, ess, est
id, in, ip, it, ick, ide, ike, ile, ill, ine, ink, ire, ish, ight
op, ot, ow (how and blow), oy, oat, ock, oin, oil, oke, old, ole, one, ong, ook, oom, ore, oast
ug, ue, un, uck, ull, ure, use

curately pronounce *fleck*. Thus, decoding by analogy provides an efficient phonics strategy. Decoding by analogy is discussed further later in this chapter.

To decide which phonograms to teach to your students, look at their patterns of miscues. Also examine the words in books for beginning readers. Many of these words *include* common phonograms, and teaching a phonogram in combination with a book helps youngsters realize that phonics helps us gain meaning from text. Johnston (1999a) suggests teaching individual consonant sounds before phonograms and starting with phonograms that contain short vowels.

Phonics Principles.   A second option for phonics instruction is to teach important principles or generalizations. An example of a phonics principle is that a *silent e* at the end of a one-syllable word makes the preceding vowel long (as in *cane* and *stone*). Some important generalizations have been identified as extremely useful for children to learn (Clymer, 1963). Table 6.3 lists these phonics principles in approximate order of difficulty.

Choosing the Phonics Teaching Sequence

Good phonics instruction involves learning both by a *focus on words* and *application in reading*. Therefore, if you start with a phonogram or a phonics principle (focus on words), you next need to provide practice applying either in reading. However, if you start by having students read (application in reading), you next need to focus attention on phonograms or phonics principles (focus on words).

Starting with Phonograms.   If you are using *phonograms* (also called *rimes* or *word families*) as the basis of instruction, you should choose a word family and several example words (see Table 6.2). For example, if you choose the *at* family, you might use *at, fat, rat*, and *sat*. You could start by having children arrange letters to make different words. To provide manipulatives, write each letter on a card or use magnetic letters. If you are using a full set of alphabet letters, arrange them in alphabetical order so that students can find them easily.

Select your word family and then ask your students to pronounce (or make) different words containing the chosen phonogram. You might first ask the student to make *at*, then perhaps *rat*, and then *sat*. As children manipulate these patterns, they learn important vowel and consonant correspondences. Remember, however, that students need to have already acquired the emergent literacy skill of rhyming to do this (see Chapter 5).

Taking a phonogram such as *ill* and building new words, such as *hill, pill, gill, silly, miller*, and *million*, helps students extend phonics knowledge past the beginning stages and into more advanced words. Teaching with word families is the basis for using analogies, which is discussed later in this chapter. Many different word families can be used in two- and three-syllable words.

To provide application in reading and writing, you might ask children to make up sentences with these words or to write the words in a word journal.

TABLE 6.3   Useful Phonics Generalizations

Useful Phonics Generalizations

---

1. *Single Consonants:* Reading grade level 1
Generally, consonants are dependable in sound. They include *b, d, f, h, j, k, l, m, n, p, r, s, t, v, w, x, y,* and *z*. *C* and *g* have two common sounds (see item 7).

2. *Consonant Digraphs:* Reading grade level 1
These refer to two consonants that, when together, make one sound. Common digraphs are *sh, ch, ck, ph,* and *th* (as in *thy* and *thigh*). *Qu* is sometimes considered a digraph.

3. *Consonant Blends:* Reading grade level 2
These are two or three consonants blended together for pronunciation. Beginning blends include *st, gr, cl, sp, pl, tr, br, dr, bl, fr, fl, pr, cr, sl, sw, gl, str*. Ending blends include *nd, nk, nt, lk, ld, rt, nk, rm, rd, rn, mp, ft, lt, ct, pt, lm*.

4. *Single Vowels, Long and Short Vowels:* Reading grade levels 2–3
Long vowels are sometimes called *free*, or *glided*, forms. Short vowels are called *checked*, or *unglided*. Examples are:

Vowel	Short Sound	Long Sound
a	apple	pane
e	egg	teeth
i	igloo	ice
o	pot	home
u	run	use, tuba

The vowel is long when it is followed by a consonant and an *e* (the *e* is usually silent, e.g., *rate*) and when it ends a word or syllable (e.g., *be, begin*). A vowel is short when a single vowel is followed by one or more consonants (e.g., *rat*). Words like *rate* are often paired with *rat* for contrast.

5. *R-Controlled Vowels:* Reading grade levels 2–3
These include *ar* (car), *er* (her), *ir* (stir), *or* (for), *ur* (fur). Note that *er, ir,* and *ur* sound alike.

6. *Vowel Combinations:* Reading grade levels 2–3
Dependable combinations include *oa* (boat), *ai* (raise), *ee* (bee), *oi* (boil), *aw* (saw), *ay* (say), *ew* (blew), *ou* (loud). Less-dependable combinations are *ea* (seat, bear), *ow* (cloud, low), *oo* (boot, look).

7. *Hard and Soft C and G:* Reading grade level 3
Examples of hard and soft sounds are

Letter	Soft Sound	Hard Sound
c	city	cut
g	general	gold

Generally, soft sounds are followed by *e, i,* and *y*. Hard sounds occur elsewhere. These principles are more dependable for *c* than for *g*.

8. *Silent Letters:* Reading grade levels 3–4
When consonant combinations cannot be pronounced together, (e.g., *kn* or *ld*), the second is *usually* pronounced (as in *know* and *would*). However, when the second consonant is *h*, the first consonant is pronounced (as in *ghost*).

Further application in reading can be provided by easy children's books that concentrate on phonograms (see Appendix A).

Starting with Phonics Principles. If you are teaching a phonics principle, introduce the generalization, and then use several words to illustrate it. For example, to show how a *final e* changes the *short a* sound to a *long a*, use words such as *cap/cape, mad/made,* and *rat/rate.* After some work with single words, have your student read materials that contain these word patterns. A last and important step in learning a phonics principle is applying it in general reading material, such as stories, novels, and textbooks (see Appendix B and "Reading Books with Regular Phonics Patterns" later in this chapter).

Starting with Words from Reading. An excellent idea for starting phonics instruction with *reading* is to choose words that students could not pronounce in their texts (Harp, 1989). Words that children have difficulty writing are also excellent choices. Choosing words from reading and writing helps low-achieving readers connect phonics to meaning.

If, during oral reading, students come to a word they do not know, tell them the word and mark it in your book. After the story has been read and enjoyed, you can return to the problem words and use them to teach phonics clues. If children are reading silently, you can ask them to identify words that gave them trouble.

Moustafa and Maldonaldo-Colon (1999) describe a form of whole-to-part phonics instruction that begins with the teacher reading a story or presenting a song or poem to the children. Using repeated reading or shared reading (see Chapter 7), the teacher guides the students to read the selection on their own. The teacher develops the ability to match individual written words to their spoken counterparts by having students point to words as they read. Then the teacher selects words from the story, writes them on cards, and highlights common onsets and rime elements. The teacher focuses on these common elements by comparing and contrasting various words. The students then group the word cards according to common elements and place them on a word wall.

Wilson (1988) suggests using the Brain Power Word strategy for students working in groups. Either before or after reading a story, each student selects two to three words that he or she thinks are important for everyone to know. The students write these words on cards and give them to the teacher, who then pronounces and displays them. Finally, the teacher analyzes the phonics clues that could be used to pronounce these words. For example, if the word *display* were chosen, the teacher might point out the two phonograms, including the *dis* and the *ay* pattern used in *play*. "Brain Power Words" are not threatening, because the student does not have to pronounce them and each student chooses words that are important for everyone in the group.

Decoding through Analogy

Research indicates that most people (including students with reading problems) learn phonics, not by memorizing rules, but by recognizing patterns used in similar and known words (Goswami & Bryant, 1990; Goswami and Mead, 1992; Gough & Hillenger, 1980; Moustafa, 1995). In other words, people pronounce new words by using known words. This process is called *decoding by analogy*. A child learns to read *close* and *class* and thus learns how to pronounce the onset *cl*. The child learns *day* and *say* and how to pronounce *ay*. These learnings lead to the pronunciation of a new word, *clay*. Suppose you come across a word you have never seen before, such as *tergiversation*. How do you manage to pronounce it correctly? You use word elements that you know: *ter* as in *term*, the word *giver*, and *sation* as in *conversation*.

You can teach students with reading problems how to use this strategy. When they meet an unknown word, ask them to think of an analogous one. For example, if the student is unable to decode the word *bay*, you might ask, "Can you think of a word that ends like this word?" If the child can't supply an analogy, you might say, "Think of the word *day*." The use of word families helps students to recognize and use these analogies.

Combining Phonics and Meaning

Perhaps because they have had so much difficulty recognizing words, poor readers often confuse phonics with reading. Because they think that reading is simply sounding out words, they need to learn that pronouncing words is only a step toward gaining the author's meaning. As they read, students need to constantly ask themselves, "Does this make sense?" They must remember to check whether their pronunciation efforts result in sensible meaning. Of course, this strategy involves combining context clues and phonics. Two strategies to help students use these clue systems together are *cross-checking* and the *four-step procedure*.

Cross-Checking. This variation on a cloze procedure is recommended by Cunningham (2000). The teacher writes a sentence that contains one covered word. To supply this word, students "cross-check" phonics clues with context clues. Teacher and students first read the sentence, saying "blank" for the covered word. Next, the students offer suggestions as to what the missing word might be. All reasonable suggestions are written down where the students can see them. (If a student offers a suggestion that does not fit, the teacher reads the sentence, inserts this word and demonstrates how the sentence does not sound right.) The teacher then uncovers the letters, one by one. All words that do not begin with these letters are crossed out. Finally the teacher uncovers the entire word and points out that although many words might fit in the blank, the pronunciation must match the letters chosen by the author. See the example in Strategy Snapshot 6.1.

Four-Step Strategy. At a more advanced level, the four-step strategy also combines the use of several different clues to recognize words. In this sequence, students learn to use the steps that skilled readers use when they figure out unknown

STRATEGY SNAPSHOT **6.1**

Using Cross-Checking

Ms. Tate uses cross-checking with a small group of poor readers to stress that pronunciation should make sense. She presents them with the sentence. "Jane wanted to buy some _____" and asks what words would fit in the blank space. The children's suggestions, including *candy, clothes, cookies, books, raisins, flowers, toys, pets, shoes,* and *dolls,* are written on the board. When one child suggests *money* and another offers *friend,* Ms. Tate reads the sentence with those words inserted and asks if it makes sense. The children agree that it doesn't. Then Ms. Tate uncovers the first letter, which is a *c.* The choices narrow to *candy, clothes,* and *cookies.* The children agree that all three make sense; and when their teacher uncovers the entire word, they eagerly call out *candy*! Ms. Tate then gives them additional words that also start with *c* (*city, children, country, caps, cards*) and asks them if they make sense in the sentence. She reminds children that when a word is pronounced, they have to check for meaning.

words. They first use context clues, then phonics, and then structural analysis clues. This sequence is successful in showing baffled readers how to integrate and apply their word recognition skills. The steps are:

1. If you don't know a word in your reading, first reread the sentence and try to figure it out (context clues).
2. If that doesn't work, sound out the first part and reread the sentence (phonics clues).
3. If you still don't know it, look for word endings and try to figure out the base word (structural analysis clues).
4. If you still haven't figured it out, sound out the whole word. Remember you may have to change a few sounds to make the word make sense (phonics clues).

Teachers should first explain the strategy and model how to use it for several words. After that, remind students to use it whenever they read. In one fifth-grade reading class, students made a list of all the words they had figured out using the four-step strategy and determined how many steps were needed to figure out each word.

Making Students Aware of Their Strategies

Several strategies to help your students figure out unknown words in print have been presented. However, to really master a strategy, your students need to become aware of what they are doing. How can you help them?

Remember that students need to see strategies modeled many times before they can use them. You must show them, over and over again, how you use these strategies to figure out unknown words.

You can also display the strategies. Put the strategies on a poster or have each student make a bookmark containing the steps in a strategy. One teacher created a bulletin board entitled "How to Read Words" and put the children's observations on the board. Another teacher placed a large tree branch in a bucket of sand and called it the "thinking tree." As students learned strategies for identifying words, they wrote them on cards and hung them on the thinking tree.

Finally, teachers can ask students to talk about how they use strategies. Helping students periodically review steps stresses the *how* of phonics instruction. Students can write down their own strategies on think cards (see Chapter 4). When students create their own versions of strategies, they personalize what you have taught them. Figure 6.1 presents examples of some student think cards.

Dealing with Exceptions

Sooner or later, students will come across words that are exceptions to the phonics rules or patterns that you are teaching. Rather than treating such exceptions as a problem, you can use them as an opportunity to make students aware that phonics does not always work.

For example, when you ask for words that have a *silent e,* students may suggest *have* and *love,* two words that are exceptions to the rule that the first vowel in the word takes a long sound. Write down such exceptions and tell the students

---

FIGURE 6.1   Examples of Student Think Cards

(These retain original spelling)

Tiffany, grade 3

"When I read a book I use a strategie that strategie is to look at the pictures the pictures help me figure out what I an reading abot. When I use a strategie when I don't know a word frist I sond out the word if I get the word then I use my background knowlede of what I know abot the word."

Mark, grade 3

"If I come to a word in a sentence I don't know I think of a word with the same sounds as the word I don't know and see if it make sense. 1. kitchen, kitten, mitten 2. book, cook, hook, look, shook." (dictated to his teacher)

LaTonya, grade 2

"You think of a word you all redy now then you should get the word. Or tack the word in parts. Sound the word out a cople times. Think of a word you now in it. Does the word fit? grump jump"

that these words "don't play fair." Low-achieving readers often enjoy making lists of exceptions to use for sight vocabulary instruction. Exceptions also make students aware of the need to combine phonics and context clues.

You can also remind youngsters that a particularly difficult word can be skipped if they can make sense out of the rest of the reading. If all else fails, students can ask someone for help.

Ideas for Practicing Phonics

To effectively learn phonics, students need to consistently practice letter-sound patterns. Only through extended use can low-achieving students learn to apply phonics quickly and accurately. This section gives ideas for ways to practice phonics.

Making Words. Making Words (Cunningham & Cunningham, 1992; Cunningham & Hall, 1994a,b) involves students in actively thinking about letter-sound patterns as they use letters to make different words. This activity focuses on many different phonics patterns as children spell different words from a bigger word. By spelling, they practice creating phonics patterns. At the end of the activity, they can note similarities and differences among the words they have made.

To do the Making Words activity, choose a word such as *thunder* and identify *all* the words that can be made from it. Make seven cards, each containing one letter in *thunder*. Make larger squares with the same letters for your use at a chalkboard ledge. Now ask the students to make the words that you say. Begin with the shortest words, move gradually to longer words, and finally to the seven-letter word *thunder*. The sequence might look like this: *red, Ted, Ned, den, end, her, hut, herd, turn, hunt, hurt, under, hunted, turned,* and *thunder.*

Making Words can be used with an individual or with a group. If you are working in a group, have individual children or pairs form each word. Then, when they have finished, have one student come to the front of the room and arrange your large letter cards into words from memory.

As each word is made, write it on a card. When all the words have been made, you will have a list of words that you can use to sort according to phonics patterns. For example, you might have students sort all of the words (made from *thunder*) that contain *ur, er,* or *ed*. You might have students sort into piles the words that contain short vowels and long vowels. Remind students that when they meet a new word or when they need to spell an unknown word, they can use these patterns to help them (Stahl, 1992). Another word sorting activity is discussed in Chapter 7.

Using Worksheets. As you are probably aware, many different commercially produced worksheets and phonics books containing exercises for practicing phonics are available. However, many of the activities used in these materials involve youngsters in relatively passive activities, such as circling words and filling in letters.

Such practices do not lend themselves to the critical application of phonics during real reading, nor do they involve students in thoughtful problem-solving activities. In truth, we have seen low-achieving readers complete worksheets by guesswork without even referring to the directions.

If used on an occasional basis, worksheets can provide examples of a phonics pattern and give some independent practice. However, worksheets *cannot* substitute for direct, teacher-led instruction, for having children supply their own examples, or for practicing the use of phonics as students are reading.

Reading Books with Regular Phonics Patterns.   Activities for practicing phonics in isolated words are enjoyable, but they will not allow students with reading problems to master phonics principles. *To master phonics, your students must read, read, read.* Only by getting practice figuring out unknown words while they are reading will students be able to *use* phonics. For this reason, this section and the next focus on materials to help students apply phonics in reading.

Students with problems can profit from using reading materials that are not only meaningful, but also present many phonetically regular words (Anderson, Hiebert, Scott, & Wilkinson, 1985). At times, such books can sacrifice good text and an interesting story line in their efforts to include phonetically regular words. Reading "the fat cat sat on a mat" may not particularly excite children who have seen the *Indiana Jones* or *Ghostbusters* movies. Fortunately, however, some books using phonetically regular words are enjoyable for children.

Trachtenberg (1990) has identified some trade books that repeat different phonics elements:

> **Short a:** *The Fat Cat* (by Kent); *There's an Ant in Anthony* (by Most)
> **Long a:** *The Paper Crane* (by Bang); *Taste the Raindrops* (by Hines)
> **Short and long a:** *Jack and Jake* (by Aliki)
> **Short e:** *Elephant in a Well* (by Ets); *The Little Red Hen* (by Galdone)
> **Long e:** *Ten Sleepy Sheep* (by Keller); *Have You Seen Trees?* (by Oppenheim)
> **Short i:** *Willy the Wimp* (by Browne); *Small Pig* (by Lobel)
> **Long i:** *The Bike Lesson* (by Berenstain); *If Mice Could Fly* (by Cameron)
> **Short o:** *Drummer Hoff* (by Emberely); *Flossie and the Fox* (by McKissack)
> **Long o:** *The Giant's Toe* (by Cole); *The Adventures of Mole and Troll* (by Johnston)
> **Short u:** *Big Gus and Little Gus* (by Lorenz); *Thump and Plunk* (by Udry)
> **Long u:** *The Troll Music* (by Lobel); *"Excuse Me—Certainly!"* (by Slobodkin)

Other series of easy books built around phonics patterns are given in Appendix A.

Practicing Phonics in General Reading.   Phonics patterns are truly mastered only when students have had a large amount of practice using these patterns to figure out words in their general reading. General reading means stories, novels, poems, and textbooks that students read everyday and that are not controlled for phonics patterns. As they use phonics to figure out unknown words in interesting stories and selections, students with reading problems learn that phonics helps them to construct meaning. Ask them to pick out words with phonics patterns they have studied.

Because poems contain many regular words, they can serve as a rich source for phonics practice. Strategy Snapshot 6.2 shows how one poem acts as a basis for a complete phonics teaching sequence.

Teaching Multisyllabic Words

As children move beyond beginning reading levels, they face the challenge of recognizing increasing numbers of multisyllabic words (words of more than one syllable). Some are relatively easy to pronounce, such as a single-syllable word joined to a common ending (*jumping, teacher*) or a compound word (*cowboy, airplane*). However, other multisyllabic words (*lilac, assisted, autograph*) are more complex. Recognizing such words is important because they often carry much of the meaning of a text.

Students with reading problems seem to have particular difficulty with multisyllabic words for several reasons: (1) Many students are simply scared by lengthy words and refuse even to try them. Some students "freeze" in front of words that contain eight or nine letters. (2) Students forget to combine phonics and context clues when they meet a long word. Unfortunately, many poor readers who

STRATEGY SNAPSHOT **6.2**
Using Poetry to Teach Phonics

Mr. Lutz based a phonics lesson on the poem "Recipe for a Hippopotamus Sandwich" (by Silverstein). After he and his students read and discussed its silly story, he asked children for words that sounded alike. As they suggested *make, take, cake* and *ring, string,* he wrote each on the chalkboard under the headings *-ake* and *-ing.* Asked for more examples of these patterns, the children came up with and listed (in the proper place) *wake, sing,* and *rake.*

Mr. Lutz asked the children how knowing *-ake* and *-ing* would help them. He got them to verbalize the fact that they could use these sound patterns to figure out new words. To demonstrate, Mr. Lutz wrote "I will bring popcorn to the party." He asked them to pretend that they did not know "bring." How could they use the *-ing* in the word?

To apply this principle to other phonograms, Mr. Lutz picked out the words *slice* and *bread* from the poem and asked the children for other words that contain the sounds of *-ice* and *-ead.* They created two more lists of word families. When children offer *-led* as a rhyme for *bread,* Mr. Lutz pointed out that words that sound alike can be spelled differently or are exceptions.

Finally, Mr. Lutz copied the words from the board onto cards and handed some out to each child. As each child held up and read a word card (e.g., *nice*), another child supplied a word with the same phonogram (e.g., *twice*).

have learned to use context for recognizing single-syllable words revert to only matching letters and sounds when faced with long words. Using a combination of clues is important when decoding multisyllabic words, because they tend to contain irregular sound patterns; thus, students need to check what they have "sounded out" with the sense of the sentence. (3) Because students with reading problems often have limited meaning vocabularies, they may never have heard a particular long word before. If you have heard a word and know its meaning, being able to pronounce even a few parts may be enough to identify the entire word. However, if a word is not in your meaning vocabulary, you cannot check pronunciation against meaning. Several instructional strategies can help poor readers cope with long words.

Collecting Long Words. In this strategy, students are asked to collect long words that they can read. In doing this they become aware that they can pronounce many long words and can use these long words to figure out words that they do not know (Cunningham, 2000). Having a collection of big words that students know also reduces the threat that such words often pose for low-achieving readers. As they become more comfortable with long words, they become eager to learn more.

To implement this strategy, ask students to note long words that they find interesting or important as they read. Don't ask them to select unknown words, as they may feel threatened. Often, however, students with reading problems will choose words that they have found difficult. To remember the targeted word, students can check them lightly with a pencil, use page markers or Post-it™ notes, or write the words on a separate sheet of paper.

Next, put the words on a blackboard and have students discuss them. Observe which other words they bring to mind, where to divide the syllables, and the sentence in the book that contained the word. This activity enables the students to combine context and phonics. If the students cannot figure out the word, help them work through clues, even if you must pronounce the word for them. In doing this activity, do not overwhelm students or keep them from enjoying reading. Limit students to two to three very important or interesting words per story.

After discussion, have students put each word on an index card. As the pile of cards gets larger, it becomes a visible reminder that they know many long words.

As this activity proceeds, you may want to make it more complex. For example, students can search for big words that fit into categories, such as describing words (or adjectives) like *astonished* and *overbearing*. Students can also look for synonyms. One class collected *staggered, evacuated,* and *advanced* for *moved* and *requested, communicated,* and *asserted* for *said.* Students can collect words with certain prefixes or suffixes. They can collect big words that all contain the same spelling pattern (*checkered, checkerboard, rechecked, checkbook, checkroom*). Within a short time, your students will have over a hundred big words. As they list them, they will acquire comfort with multisyllabic words as well as a store of known words to use in figuring out unknown words.

Modeling Use of Analogies to Pronounce Long Words.   Good readers often use analogies to decode multisyllabic words, just as they use them to decode one-syllable words. When they meet a multisyllabic word, they match patterns in the new word to similar patterns in a known word. A student might pronounce *publisher* by using the known words *tub*, *dish*, and *her*. However, the reader must know how to break the word into parts by looking for chunks already known.

To model the use of analogies, take a long word and explain to students the strategies you would use to pronounce it. You might write "The dark clouds portended bad weather" on the board. Then read the sentence, and when you come to *portended*, say something like, "I'm not sure I have ever seen that word before. I will read on and see if the sentence gives me a clue." After finishing the sentence, say "Well, I still don't know the word but I can figure it out. I recognize parts of it. I know *or* so *por* is easy. I know the word *tend* and I can add on the *ed* ending. So this word is *portended*. Now what does it mean?" Read the entire sentence again. "I can use context here. I know about dark clouds and rain so I bet that *portended* means the same as *signaled* or *indicated*."

You will need to model the use of analogies many, many times before students become comfortable using the strategy independently. Remember to give students opportunities to pronounce big words by making analogies to words they already know. Strategy Snapshot 6.3 focuses on modeling analogies with two third graders.

Breaking Long Words into Syllables.   To use known word parts to pronounce unknown words, students must be able to break long words into syllables. Using

---

STRATEGY SNAPSHOT **6.3**

Using Analogies to Decode Multisyllabic Words

When she came to a multisyllabic word, Deneese valiantly, but vainly, attempted to match letters and sounds, and Melanie would simply stop and say "I don't know." To help both students, Ms. Katz first identified a list of one-syllable words that each girl knew. Deneese and Melanie grouped these words according to the first vowel, putting *grab, black, snail* on the *a* list; *he, scream, treat* on the *e* list; *knife, pig, will* on the *i* list; and so on for *o* and *u*. These words were used as models for long, unknown words.

First the teacher wrote a multisyllabic word, such as *republic*, on the board. The teacher then separated the syllables, forming *re/pub/lic*. Deneese and Melanie searched their word lists for model words that had matching vowel patterns and wrote the key words underneath *republic*. The match for *re* was *he*; the match for *pub* was *club*; and the match for *ic* was *tic*. The girls first pronounced the known words (*he, pub,* and *tic*) and then transferred these sounds to the new word (*re, pub, lic*). Finally, Ms. Katz presented *republic* in a sentence and the girls used context to determine its meaning. Later in the semester, Ms. Katz began to ask the girls to try to divide the word into syllables for themselves by using their model words as a guide.

analogies with a multisyllabic word will not work if you do not know how to divide that word. However, teaching complex syllabication rules is often ineffective for poor readers (Johnson & Baumann, 1984). In our experience, work with phonograms and key words is much more profitable.

Shefelbine (1991) suggests that teachers should work with *syllable transformations*. Syllable transformations illustrate the important difference between open and closed syllables. Open syllables end in a vowel, which takes the long sound (*she, go*). Closed syllables end in a consonant, and the vowel is given the short sound (*rub, grab,* and *web*). A transformation lesson demonstrates that a minor change in a word or syllable can alter its pronunciation. For example, the teacher writes *su* and guides the students to read this syllable by giving the vowel the long sound. The teacher then transforms the syllable by adding *f*. The students now say *suf* by giving the syllable the short sound. A third transformation is *uf*, which also takes the short sound. Other combinations that teachers can use include (1) *fab, fa, ab*, (2) *ho, hom, om*, (3) *wi, wim, im* (4) *nep, ne, ep*, and (5) *lu, lub, ub*.

Common syllabication patterns are given in Table 6.4 and an informal test for syllabication abilities is given in Table 6.5.

The Benchmark Program

One instructional program for teaching word analysis through analogy is of outstanding quality. The *Benchmark Word Identification/Vocabulary Development Program* (Gaskins & Downer, 1986; Gaskins, Soja, et al., 1989) was constructed for use at the Benchmark School, a facility for students with learning difficulties. The program stresses the use of context clues and decoding by analogy. It employs both mono- and multisyllabic words almost from the first lessons. The program, which can be purchased, is extremely detailed and provides scripts for daily lessons.

The Benchmark program teaches decoding by analogy through key spelling patterns. The teacher introduces key words for each common vowel pattern, and the students practice these words until they know them as sight words. Examples of key words for *o* patterns are *go, boat, job, clock,* and *long*. The students dictate language experience stories containing the key words and repeatedly read them. Students also write the key words and chant each word letter by letter. The words are displayed prominently in the classroom.

Next, the teacher shows how to use key words to identify unknown words by repeatedly modeling the process of comparing and contrasting an unknown word to a key word. For example, the teacher presents a new word in a sentence such as *Jim opened the present with joy*. Pretending not to know *joy*, the teacher thinks aloud, noting that *joy* looks like the key word *boy*. *Boy* is written below *joy*. The teacher then uses *boy* to pronounce *joy* by saying, "If b-o-y is *boy*, then j-o-y is *joy*. Does *joy* make sense in the sentence?" The teacher models by checking to see if the "unknown" word fits the context. As new key words are introduced, these same basic components are used. Other lesson activities in-

TABLE 6.4 Syllabication Guidelines

1. In a compound word, each small word is usually a syllable (e.g., *cow-boy*).
2. Structural word parts are usually syllables (e.g., *re-wind, slow-ly*).
3. Vowel combinations and *r*-controlled vowels usually retain their own sounds (e.g., *taw-her*).
4. When a single vowel occurs in a multisyllable word:
   a. It is generally given its short sound if it is followed by two consonants. This pattern may be referred to as VCC, as in *lit/tle, ap/ple, res/cue,* and *pic/nic.* Teach this rule first with words that have double consonants, as in *lit/tle* and *ap/ple.* Then teach words with different middle consonants, as *res/cue* and *pic/nic.*
   b. It may have a long or short sound if it is followed by only one consonant. This pattern is called VCV. For example, the first vowel is long in *li/lac* and *tu/ba* but short in *sev/eral, ben/efit,* and *mim/ic.* Students should try the long sound first, and then the short sound.
5. The letters *le* at the end of a word are pronounced as in *rattle.*

clude rhyme recognition, fitting words into cloze sentences, and sorting words into spelling patterns.

A revision of this program entitled *Word Detectives: Benchmark Word Identification Program for Beginning Readers* (Gaskins, Elhi, Cress, O'Hara, & Donnelly, 1996–1997) has made several research-based improvements. In the newer program, students are asked to spell and write each key word several times so that they learn each letter. In addition, the program includes more connected reading, and the pace of word introduction is slower.

The Benchmark Program can be used with students at many different reading levels, and with individuals or groups. For information write to Benchmark School, 2107 N. Providence Road, Media, PA 19063.

The Open Court Reading Program

The *Open Court Reading* program, published by SRA/McGraw-Hill, is a basal reading series which emphasizes phonics. It includes a phonemic awareness component in the early grades. *Segmenting,* the skill of recognizing sounds in words, is taught in kindergarten. Both blending and segmenting are taught in first grade. Instruction at the syllable level precedes instruction at the phoneme level. Activities are gamelike and playful and include clapping syllables for classmates' names, talking for a puppet who talks in segments rather than whole words, singing alliterative songs, and telling riddles (for example, "What rhymes with *town* but begins with *br*?" (Birsh, 1999).

TABLE 6.5   Informal Test for Syllabication Abilities

Students may be asked both to divide these nonsense words into syllables using paper and pencil and to pronounce them.

1. Compound Words	4a. Vowel Followed by One Consonant
playdog	waman
freeday	sowel
sandot	fomub
	setin

2. Structural Word Parts	4b. Vowel Followed by Consonants
stipment	mattel
gaiter	fuddot
repainly	

3. Vowel Combinations	5. Le Combinations
tainest	rettle
bayter	sontle
stirler	

In the *Open Court Reading* program, phonemic awareness is taught before phonics instruction. The phonemic awareness instruction is entirely oral. When phonics and letter-sound association are introduced in the first grade, the phonemic awareness instruction has already covered many of the sounds taught in the phonics lessons. The phonics program uses cards with letters and key word pictures (for example, *monkey* for *m*). Rhyming words are emphasized.

Foorman, Francis, Fletcher, Schat-Schneider, and Mehta (1998) conducted a research study using different reading programs with at-risk first- and second-grade children. The research showed that children taught with the *Open Court Reading* program scored significantly higher on reading achievement than children using the other two programs.

Assessing Structural Analysis Strategies

When readers use structural analysis clues, they break a word into meaningful parts and use these parts to help them both pronounce the word and understand its meaning. In contrast, low-achieving readers are unaware of how structural elements affect meaning. Thus, the teaching of structural analysis is an important element of teaching reading.

This section discusses basic structural analysis strategies, including compound words, contractions, and common word endings (inflectional suffixes), such as *s* (plural), *ed* (past tense), *er* and *est* (comparative), *'s* (possessive), and *ing* (gerunds and progressive tense). More advanced structural analysis strategies using prefixes, other suffixes, and roots are discussed in Chapter 10.

Students with reading problems tend not to use structural analysis strategies effectively. They are often unaware of how endings on words such as *talks*, *talking*, and *talked* signal time and number, and they often simply omit them during reading.

Miscue analysis provides information about a student's use of structural analysis clues. For example, students who repeatedly leave off word endings are demonstrating a need for analysis of word parts. In addition, informal discussion can provide much insight into the use of structural analysis clues.

For compound words, choose a few (*cowboy, steamboat, railroad*) and ask the students if there is anything unusual about them. Request that they tell you how each little word helps in knowing the meaning of the whole word. Asked about *cowboy*, Andy quickly stated that *cowboys* were boys that rode horses and shot guns in the movies, but he had no idea where cows fit into the picture.

To assess understanding of the meaning of contractions, write the base word on the board and then add the contraction. For example, write *can*; then under it, write *can't*. Ask the student if the two words are different in meaning. If the student seems unsure, place the contractions in two sentences: *I can write my name. I can't write my name.* If the student cannot verbalize the difference in meaning between the two sentences, target the contraction for instructional focus.

For inflectional endings, write both *bird* and *birds* on the board and ask your student to explain the difference in meaning. If the student is unsure, place the words in two sentences: *I have a bird. I have two birds.* Ask your student to explain the difference in meaning.

Teaching Structural Analysis Strategies

Many of the guidelines that are suggested for teaching phonics can also be used to teach basic structural analysis. To help students draw a connection between structural analysis elements and reading, ask students to collect words that contain certain word endings. Focus on meaning by telling students how adding endings changes the sense of a word but do not concentrate on spelling rules for adding endings or forming contractions.

One activity that we have used successfully is called Making Words Grow. Students take a one-syllable word and try to make it longer by adding inflectional endings, prefixes, or suffixes, and by forming compound words. The student first writes the base word and then, directly under this word, writes a longer word. The third word is written under the second word. The base words must be written exactly under one another, for aligning them in this way allows students to see how additional structural elements change the words. Table 6.6 presents an example of Making Words Grow.

Students enjoy trying to make lists as long as possible. They often willingly go to the dictionary to find additional words. Having students highlight the additions in color also helps to illustrate the structural analysis patterns.

One word of caution with regard to inflectional endings: They may pose a problem for speakers of nonstandard dialects and for bilingual students. Because these students may not use inflections consistently in their speech, they may have trouble reading them. When working with such students, the teacher should point out the meaning signified by the inflections but not be overly concerned about the student's pronunciation. If the student pronounces *Mary's* as *Mary* when reading orally, no corrections should be made. Rather, make sure that the student understands the meaning of the ending (Labov, 1967). Use the informal assessment procedures suggested in this chapter to determine this tendency.

Assessing Context Strategies

When readers use context strategies, they use the meaning of the passage to help them recognize a word. For example, a child might identify *elephant* because a picture of this animal appears on the page or because preceding pages were about zoo and circus animals. Thus, readers use their background knowledge and their understanding of the passage to focus on meaning. By using context clues, a student often can predict words that are left out of the text (a strategy known as *cloze*). See if you can fill in the blanks in the following story:

TABLE 6.6   Making Words Grow

jump	camp	work
jumps	camps	works
jumped	camped	worked
jumping	camping	working
jumper	camper	worker
jumpy	campsite	workbook
	campout	workbench
		workman
		workshop
		workable

We went to the zoo. We fed peanuts to the big gray _____. We watched the striped _____. The _____ was funny with its long neck. The _____ swung from tree to tree.

Answers: elephant, zebra, giraffe, monkey

Because of your experiences with zoos, you probably had little difficulty supplying the missing words. You also used your understanding of how our language works. Readers know, for example, that articles such as *the* and adjectives such as *striped* tend to come before nouns. Even beginning readers use such language cues to help them identify words (Juel, 1983).

Beginning readers and those experiencing difficulties tend to be overly dependent on context. However, as they become more skilled, readers no longer use context to recognize words for three reasons (Stanovich, 1991). First, context strategies are not dependable for identifying a word. Research shows that words can be predicted from context only 10–20 percent of the time (Alexander, 1999). Second, word recognition through sight words is so rapid and automatic that context usage does not play a meaningful part. Finally, when good readers do not recognize a word automatically, they can use well-developed phonics skills. In fact, the ability to identify words accurately and quickly *out of context* is a characteristic of good readers (Perfetti, 1983, 1988; Stanovich, 1980, 1991).

In contrast, poor readers tend to overuse context precisely because they do *not* have a large sight vocabulary and cannot decode words quickly. (Perfetti, 1985; Stanovich, 1986). However, context is not an effective clue for readers with difficulty. To use context to recognize some words, the reader needs to identify most of the other words accurately. Students with reading problems cannot recognize enough words to do this (Adams, 1990; Pflaum, Walberg, Karegianes, & Rasher, 1980). In addition, a laborious focus on matching letters and sounds often demands so much attention that they lose the sense of what they are reading.

Context strategies, or meaning clues, may be assessed by using miscue analysis, through student interview, and through comparison of words in lists and passages. Remember that students with reading difficulties have a tendency to overuse context strategies.

Miscue Analysis

As described in Chapter 3, miscue analysis, or an analysis of the errors students make during oral reading, is an excellent method for assessing the use of context clues. A student who supplies a word that makes sense in the passage is probably paying attention to context. A student whose miscue is a word that does *not* make sense in the passage is not using context clues.

Student Reading Interview

Another way of assessing the use of context is to ask the student about word recognition strategies. When asked "How do you figure out a word you don't know?" many poor readers' only response is "sound it out." However, students who say that they reread or think about the meaning of the text are aware of how context can help in word recognition.

Comparison of Words Recognized in Lists and Passages

Another way to assess the use of context is to contrast a student's ability to recognize a set of words in isolation (or list form) and in a passage. Students who can pronounce more words in a passage than a list are showing that they use context clues.

To construct this assessment, choose a passage at a student's instructional level and identify 20 words. First, ask the student to read these words in list form. Then ask the student to read the passage orally. For both readings, keep track of the number of targeted words read correctly. Students who recognize significantly more words in the passage than on the list are using context clues.

Teaching Context Strategies

As emphasized throughout this book, learning to recognize words is best done in the context of actual reading. If students with reading problems consistently read stories and books, they often naturally learn to make use of meaning clues. However, some students need further instruction with strategies that focus attention on using context.

Encouraging Students to Monitor for Meaning

Low-achieving students do not always demand meaning from reading. Often they continue reading long after the material has ceased to make sense to them. In fact, most of us have, from time to time, become aware that our eyes have been moving over the words, but we have no idea of what they mean. What do we do? As good readers, we know that the purpose of reading is to gain meaning, so we stop and reread. Students with reading problems may finish an entire selection, proud for having "got the words right," but with no understanding of what they have read.

Thus, activities that focus on the use of context clues should reinforce the idea that reading should make sense. To encourage monitoring for meaning, have students stop periodically as they read and ask themselves four questions:

- Did what I just read make sense to me?
- Can I retell it in my own words?
- Are there any words that I do not understand?
- Are any sentences confusing to me?

Students can remind themselves to consider these questions by making bookmarks that display these questions. The teacher can also place brightly colored, removable dots in the margin at regular intervals throughout a reading as reminders for students to stop and ask themselves these questions.

Using Cloze

Cloze refers to deleting words from a passage and asking students to fill in the missing words. Students can write the missing words or supply them orally. The zoo passage presented earlier in this chapter is an example of a cloze passage. In supplying words, students practice working with context clues.

In constructing a cloze exercise, simply delete words from a passage. You can retype the passage or just "blacken" the words out with a magic marker. Which words should you delete? For general practice, try deleting every 10th word. Students will not be able to supply *all* the missing words, but they will get general practice in using meaning to read. Cloze can also be used to help students focus on certain types of words. For example, you might choose to delete only adjectives or connectives (*and, but, unless*). You might even choose to delete parts of words, such as word endings.

Teachers have several options for how students can respond. You may provide choices for the deleted words or ask the students to write or say the word that they think fits. Students may work alone or cooperatively to supply the words. If students write words into the passages, accept their spellings, even if they are incorrect. After students are finished filling in a cloze, go over the exercise and have them explain the reasons for their choices. Often this discussion demonstrates how class members used context clues.

Remember that as students fill in the blanks of a cloze exercise, they are not really *guessing*. Instead, they are *hypothesizing* based on their knowledge of the world around them, the content of the passage, and their knowledge of English. Remind students that they are consciously using these clues to predict words.

Summary

The stages of reading development include the logographic, partial alphabetic, full alphabetic, and sight word reading.

Readers use a variety of word recognition strategies to recognize words fluently and accurately. The use of sight words is the word recognition strategy that promotes *fluent* reading. Mature readers recognize most words as sight words.

The word recognition strategies that promote *accurate* reading include:

- Phonics to help readers decode letters into sounds
- Structural analysis to help readers recognize compound words, word endings, contractions, and prefixes and suffixes
- Context, or meaning clues, to help readers decode words

Assessment of phonics can involve miscue analysis and using nonsense words that illustrate phonics patterns.

Poor readers need explicit emphasis on phonics. Teachers may choose to organize their teaching by using phonograms (or rimes) and analogies or, alternatively, by using phonics principles. Decoding by analogy, or recognizing unfamiliar words by using known words, is an excellent way to approach phonics instruction. The combination of phonics and meaning clues can be promoted by cross-checking and using the four-step strategy. Students should be aware both of the strategies they use and of exceptions to the phonics pattern.

Activities for providing practice in phonics include Making Words to illustrate common patterns, reading books with regular phonics patterns, and most important, extensive reading. Phonics instruction should also focus on helping students deal with long words. To learn multisyllabic words, students can collect long words, use analogy, or practice breaking words into syllables using transformations. The *Benchmark* and the *Open Court Reading* programs are both effective in teaching phonics.

Assessment of structural analysis strategies involves an informal evaluation method. Teaching methods include Making Words Grow and collecting lists of words with certain endings.

Assessment of context strategies includes analyzing miscues, interviewing students, and comparing a student's ability to read words in a list with the same words in a passage. Readers experiencing difficulties often overuse context strategies. To foster the effective use of context strategies, students should monitor for meaning as they read.

CHAPTER

7 Improving Word Recognition Fluency

Introduction

Chapter 6 discussed word recognition accuracy. This chapter continues the discussion of word recognition by focusing on fluency. *Fluency* refers to the instantaneous, automatic recognition of words in reading. Words that we read automatically are often called *sight words*. Readers who have an extensive sight vocabulary are able to read accurately, quickly, and with expression (Wilson, 1988).

This chapter first explains the importance of sight vocabulary and fluency. Next, it gives methods of assessment. Then, most of the chapter centers around instructional strategies for contextual fluency and the recognition of sight words. The chapter concludes with a description of several programs for developing word recognition.

Role of Fluency in the Reading Process

Sight words are those words that are recognized in print immediately, without any analysis. Knowing a large number of sight words enables us to read fluently in context. Fluent reading and comprehension work together as students absorb material and read it to others. Most good readers recognize almost all words automatically (LaBerge & Samuels, 1974; Samuels, 1988). Hence they can devote their energies to the meaning of what they are reading.

However, many students with reading problems have difficulty reading fluently (Rasinski & Padak, 1996). Often, because they do not possess an adequate sight vocabulary, they must labor to decode many of the words in their text. Their oral reading is filled with long pauses, constant repetitions, and monotonous expression. Little comprehension occurs because their energies are focused on recognizing words.

Students with reading problems need much reading practice if they are to achieve fluent word recognition. Unfortunately, many low-achieving readers do not enjoy reading and avoid it as much as possible. Because they do not read extensively, they cannot develop a good sight vocabulary. In turn, lack of sight vocabulary makes reading more difficult. Thus a vicious cycle develops (Stanovich, 1986). To avoid this negative cycle, teachers will find many ideas in this chapter for making reading an enjoyable, positive experience.

Assessing Word Recognition Fluency

Ways to assess fluency include listening to students read orally, determining reading rate, and timed administration of word lists. All three can be part of the administration of an informal reading inventory. However, the teacher can use these assessment procedures with any text or word list.

Listening to Students Read Orally

A teacher can determine whether or not students are fluent readers simply by listening to their oral reading. Wilson (1988) identifies three problems with fluency.

- In *choppy reading*, students stumble over words, repeat them, and pause. They treat the text as if it were a list of words.
- In *monotonous reading*, readers have little expression or variation in the rise and fall of their voices. Low-achieving readers who have finally achieved some word recognition proficiency often read in this way. Their lack of expression suggests that they still regard reading as merely pronouncing words.
- In *inappropriately hasty* reading, students race through the text, ignoring punctuation and sentence breaks. Because their goal seems to be to get through the text as quickly as possible, they make errors even on familiar words.

Many students with reading problems have a combination of these problems, because fluent reading demands that accuracy, automaticity, and expression work together.

To judge a student's fluency, simply listen to him or her read a text at an instructional or independent level. Using your own common sense and the guidelines given by Wilson (1988), you can determine whether the reading is fluent. You may want to compare audiotapes of a student's reading made at different times to assess improvement. Students are often motivated by listening to their own tapes. Josh reviewed tapes of his oral reading done at the beginning and end of the semester. He frowned and actually put his head down on the desk as he listened to his first halting and choppy rendition. When he heard himself reading the same passage several months later, he broke into smiles. In his journal, he wrote, "I sounded real real REAL good!"

Determining Reading Rate

Reading rate in passages is a good indication of fluency. Have the student read a selection at his or her instructional or independent level. As the student reads orally or silently, time the reading and then calculate words per minute (WPM). Multiply the number of words in the passage by 60 and then divide by the number of seconds it took to read the passage. Table 3.8 (page 79) gives a list of acceptable rates for students reading passages at different levels.

A student's reading rate must be interpreted with some caution. Normal readers show a wide range of acceptable reading rates, even at the same grade level (Carver, 1990). Because of this variability, do not compare the rates of individual students with one another. Reading rate also varies across different selections. Most people, for example, read movie reviews faster than they read editorials. Finally, remember that a student can read at an appropriate rate but still lack expression.

Timed Administration of Word Lists

Although the previous two strategies enable teachers to judge contextual fluency, the timed administration of word lists is used to judge automatic *sight word* recognition. Compare (1) *automatic* (or timed) recognition of isolated words with (2) *total* (or timed plus untimed) recognition of isolated words (both automatic words and those recognized after analysis).

To judge automaticity, give the student a list of words to recognize (such as the ones in the informal reading inventory (IRI) in Appendix D or in Tables 7.1 and 7.2). As the student reads, record performance on a teacher's copy. For each word in the list, three responses are possible: (1) recognized automatically, (2) recognized after hesitation or analysis, and (3) not identified correctly. A word pronounced correctly within one second is marked as an automatic word. (To judge one second, say to yourself "one thousand." If the student pronounces the word before you are finished, count the word as automatic.) A word recognized correctly, but not automatically, is an analysis word, and of course, a word recognized incorrectly is not identified correctly.

To compare a student's instantaneous word recognition, compare automatic words and total words known (automatic words plus analysis words). If a student's total number of words is much larger than the automatic words, the student needs to practice instant recognition of sight words.

Timed administration of word lists can be helpful for assessing sight words; however, remember that reading words in lists is not real reading. (In real life, we do not curl up with a good list of words!) For this reason, your assessment of a student's performance should combine word-list performance with the reading of selections.

Strategies for Developing Fluency in Context

This section describes strategies for improving the ability to read passages fluently.

Promoting Wide Reading of Easy Text

A large amount of reading is critical to developing fluent reading. As students read to enjoy a story or acquire interesting information, they are unconsciously improving their reading fluency. In addition, they become comfortable with combining all word identification strategies to read in context.

Getting students with reading problems to read is a major challenge for their teachers. To get them to read, teachers must make reading enjoyable, provide regular and daily opportunities to read, and encourage reading at home.

TABLE 7.1   Basic Sight Vocabulary Words

Preprimer	Primer	First	Second	Third
1. the	45. when	89. many	133. know	177. don't
2. of	46. who	90. before	134. while	178. does
3. and	47. will	91. must	135. last	179. got
4. to	48. more	92. through	136. might	180. united
5. a	49. no	93. back	137. us	181. left
6. in	50. if	94. years	138. great	182. number
7. that	51. out	95. where	139. old	183. course
8. is	52. so	96. much	140. year	184. war
9. was	53. said	97. your	141. off	185. until
10. he	54. what	98. may	142. come	186. always
11. for	55. up	99. well	143. since	187. away
12. it	56. its	100. down	144. against	188. something
13. with	57. about	101. should	145. go	189. fact
14. as	58. into	102. because	146. came	190. through
15. his	59. than	103. each	147. right	191. water
16. on	60. them	104. just	148. used	192. less
17. be	61. can	105. those	149. take	193. public
18. at	62. only	106. people	150. three	194. put
19. by	63. other	107. Mr.	151. states	195. thing
20. I	64. new	108. how	152. himself	196. almost
21. this	65. some	109. too	153. few	197. hand
22. had	66. could	110. little	154. house	198. enough
23. not	67. time	111. state	155. use	199. far
24. are	68. these	112. good	156. during	200. took
25. but	69. two	113. very	157. without	201. head
26. from	70. may	114. make	158. again	202. yet
27. or	71. then	115. would	159. place	203. government
28. have	72. do	116. still	160. American	204. system
29. an	73. first	117. own	161. around	205. better
30. they	74. any	118. see	162. however	206. set
31. which	75. my	119. men	163. home	207. told
32. one	76. now	120. work	164. small	208. nothing
33. you	77. such	121. long	165. found	209. night
34. were	78. like	122. get	166. Mrs.	210. end
35. her	79. our	123. here	167. thought	211. why
36. all	80. over	124. between	168. went	212. called
37. she	81. man	125. both	169. say	213. didn't
38. there	82. me	126. life	170. part	214. eyes
39. would	83. even	127. being	171. once	215. find
40. their	84. most	128. under	172. general	216. going
41. we	85. made	129. never	173. high	217. look
42. him	86. after	130. day	174. upon	218. asked
43. been	87. also	131. same	175. school	219. later
44. has	88. did	132. another	176. every	220. knew

From Dale D. Johnson, "The Dolch List Reexamined," *The Reading Teacher*, 24 (February 1971), pp. 455–456. The 220 most frequent words in the Kucera-Francis corpus. Reprinted with permission of Dale D. Johnson and the International Reading Association.

TABLE 7.2	Picture Sight Words		
1. farm	24. hat	47. garden	70. radio
2. clothes	25. window	48. hand	71. clown
3. money	26. television	49. snow	72. bread
4. water	27. car	50. rain	73. tree
5. grass	28. cookie	51. fire	74. mirror
6. fence	29. apple	52. dish	75. bag
7. stoplight	30. school	53. hair	76. pumpkin
8. bus	31. book	54. children	77. flag
9. balloon	32. chicken	55. lion	78. candle
10. cake	33. nurse	56. world	79. castle
11. duck	34. store	57. watch	80. jewel
12. barn	35. door	58. picture	81. bicycle
13. street	36. doctor	59. shoes	82. baby
14. hill	37. teacher	60. bed	83. sock
15. man	38. egg	61. chair	84. horse
16. house	39. rabbit	62. table	85. ring
17. woman	40. flower	63. spoon	
18. airplane	41. sun	64. fork	
19. train	42. cloud	65. truck	
20. boat	43. shadow	66. bird	
21. dog	44. eye	67. ear	
22. cat	45. mouth	68. skates	
23. telephone	46. nose	69. sled	

Compiled from a survey of widely used basal readers.

To build fluency, students need to read easy books filled with words they can recognize. Teachers should schedule time for reading. Begin by setting aside periods of about 10 minutes, because low-achieving students have difficulty concentrating during long sessions. Then these periods can be gradually increased to 20 or 25 minutes.

Low-achieving readers often have trouble choosing a book that will foster accurate and fluent word recognition. Students with problems generally select material that is too hard, or they flit from book to book without really reading any of them. To foster better choices, you can read easy books to students and then prominently display the books in your classroom. Students often choose these books to read on their own. You can also give the student several books and ask that he or she choose from among them, or you can allow the student to reread books or stories from past lessons.

Using Patterned Books

Patterned books, which contain refrains that are repeated over and over, are an excellent source of easy books (see Chapter 5). These books are invaluable for fostering word recognition because the repeated refrains in the books provide extensive support for word recognition. Because many patterned books are based on classic tales, their rich content interests and motivates children (Holdaway, 1979).

Some patterned books are published in the trade book market; that is, they are intended as children's literature. Table 7.3 presents a list of patterned trade books.

A second type of patterned books is designed to be used in instruction. These books are finely graded into many levels, starting with the reading of pictures. Popular series of patterned books include *The Story Box* and *Sunshine Books* (Wright Company), *Traditional Tales* and *City Kids* (Rigby Company), *Mrs. Wishy Washy*, shown in Figure 7.1, is an example of a patterned instructional book from *The Story Box*. Although most of these books tell stories (or are narratives), these

FIGURE 7.1 Mrs. Wishy Washy

Source: Mrs. Wishy Washy, by Joy Cowley, Published by The Wright Group, 19201 120th Avenue NE, Bothell, WA 98021

TABLE 7.3 Examples of Patterned Books

Level A	
At the Zoo	Carol Kloes
Ghost	Storybox Book by the Wright Group
My Home	Literacy 2000 by Rigby
The Storm	Sunshine Book by the Wright Group

Level B	
Cat on the Mat	Brian Wildsmith
Little Red Hen	Windmill-Look and Listen by the Wright Group

Level C	
Brown Bear, Brown Bear	Bill Martin, Jr.
I Went Walking	Sue Williams

Level D	
I Can Build a House	Shigeo Watanabe
Lizard Loses his Tail	PM Books by Rigby
School Bus	Donald Crews
Tails	Marcia Vaughn

Level E	
Inside, Outside, Upside Down	Stan and Jan Berenstain
All by Myself	Mercer Mayer
Big Friend, Little Friend	Eloise Greenfield
Five Little Monkeys Jumping on the Bed	Eileen Christelow

Level F	
Just Like Daddy	Frank Asch
When It Rains	Marilyn Frankford
Rosie's Walk	Pat Hutchins
Herman the Helper Lends a Hand	Robert Krauss

Level G	
More Spaghetti I Say	Rita Gelman
The Bus Stop	Nancy Hellen
Titch	Pat Hutchins
Sheep in a Jeep	Nancy Shaw
Not Me, Said the Monkey	Colin West

Level H	
Goodnight Moon	Margaret Wise Brown
A Picture for Harold's Room	Crockett Johnson
Whose Mouse Are You?	Robert Kraus
Toolbox	Anne Rockwell

Level I	
Are You My Mother?	P. D. Eastman
Hattie and the Fox	Mem Fox
Henny Penny	Paul Galdone
Goodnight Owl	Pat Hutchins
Tidy Titch	Pat Hutchins
Leo, the Late Bloomer	Robert Kraus
Noisy Nora	Rosemary Wells

Level J	
Drummer Hoff	Ed Emberley
The Doorbell Rang	Pat Hutchins
Mouse Soup	Arnold Lobel
Little Bear, Little Bear's Friend, Little Bear's Visit	Else Holmelund Minarik
Henry and Mudge Series	Cynthia Rylant
The Cat in the Hat	Dr. Seuss

Level K	
A Letter to Amy	Ezra Jack Keats
Frog and Toad Are Friends, Frog and Toad Together	Arnold Lobel
If You Give a Mouse a Cookie	Laura Joffe Numeroff

Level L	
Miss Nelson is Missing	Harry Allard
The Josefina Story Quilt	Eleanor Coerr
Over in the Meadow	Paul Galdone
The Wind Blew	Pat Hutchins
George and Martha	James Marshall

Level M	
Cloudy with a Chance of Meatballs	Judi Barrett
The Chalk Box Kid	Clyde Robert Bulla
Did You Carry the Flag Today, Charley?	Rebecca Caudill
Cherries and Cherry Pits	Vera B. Williams

Levels A–B	Kindergarten and Early Grade One
Levels C–H	Grade One
Level I	Late Grade One
Level J	Early Grade Two
Levels K–M	Grade Two

(Fountas & Pinnell, 1996; Lynch-Brown & Tomlinson, 1999)

companies also publish some excellent informational (or expository) patterned books, including *Infomazing* (Rigby). *Literacy 2000* (Rigby) contains selections of many types of patterned books.

The Reading Recovery program (Pinnell, 1989; Pinnell, Fried, & Estice, 1990), an instructional program for first graders, has done extensive work in evaluating the difficulty of patterned books. In their system, books are divided into 20 different levels, all within the first grade. Level 1 books contain one or two words on each page and a story heavily supported by pictures. In contrast, Level 20 books have several lines of text per page. Table 7.3 gives examples of patterned books that span a range of these levels.

How can teachers use patterned books most effectively? When introducing a patterned book, begin by paging through it with your students, reviewing pictures, and predicting the story line. Next, read the book to your children modeling fluent reading and perhaps invite them to join in the refrains. After reading the book once, you might invite students to join you in rereading it. Experiences with joint readings foster confidence and fluency. Then individual students may reread the book with a teacher's help at troublesome points.

A word of caution concerning patterned books: many children easily memorize the text. When they "read," they may turn pages at appropriate places and seem to look at the page, but they are actually reciting from memory. To foster real reading, you should periodically ask students to read text-only copies of patterned books (Johnston, 1998) so they focus more directly on words. You can also print the words from patterned books on word cards and use these to assess if students can recognize them.

Youngsters will probably need (and want) to review patterned books several times to foster fluency. After reading a patterned book, leave it in a conspicuous place so that students will be able to pick it up and look at it. Creating an environment rich in these books is extremely important.

In addition to their use with primary and lower intermediate-grade students, patterned books also appeal to older students who read at primary levels. To help these students, encourage them to read these books to younger children.

Assisted Reading

In assisted reading, students and a fluent reader read material together. All of the several different versions of assisted reading support the reader who is struggling with fluent word recognition. Most assisted reading strategies can be used with individuals or with a group of students.

Assisted reading is an excellent way to develop fluency for many reasons: (1) The teacher's support makes reading a nonthreatening activity. (2) Because word recognition efforts are supported by a fluent reader, students can pay attention to meaning and enjoy the selection. (3) Assisted reading gives a model of fluent reading. Students are exposed to the way that reading should sound and have a model to work toward. Too many poor readers are exposed to the halting, choppy reading of their peers. (4) Assisted reading gives much practice reading in context. It also motivates students to read more, because after joint readings, students often read the same books independently.

Because the eventual goal of assisted reading is to promote independent reading, the teacher must gradually provide less and less support. In the beginning, teachers may simply read to the students and invite them to participate and say words when they feel comfortable. Or the teacher may begin by reading an entire selection together with the students. Gradually, however, the teacher's role should be reduced so that students learn that they can read a new book on their own.

Simultaneous Assisted Reading.   In this assisted reading strategy, the teacher simply reads along with the students. The teacher sets the pace and resists the temptation to slow down to the reading rate of the student, who will always lag slightly behind. When a student meets an unfamiliar word, the teacher pronounces it, and they move on. If a group is reading with the teacher, few involved in the activity will even notice that one student did not know a word. At times, you will notice a drop in volume at a certain word. You can then mark this word as a possible problem and teach it after the reading is finished.

Simultaneous reading can be changed to meet the needs and levels of your students. Sometimes, the teacher may fade out at key words and phrases to assess whether students can identify them independently. At other times, the teacher may have several students read a page together without teacher assistance. Simultaneous assisted reading is most effective when combined with repeated reading of the same book or story. To foster independence, the teacher participates less and less in each subsequent reading.

Echo Reading.   Modeling oral reading and asking the students to imitate you is another form of assisted reading (Wilson, 1988). The teacher reads a few lines or a page of text to the students to model a fluent pace and effective voice expression. The students imitate the teacher's performance or "echo" the text (B. Anderson, 1981). Echo reading works best for short segments of text and is particularly well suited for beginning readers.

Choral Reading.   In choral reading, a group of students practices orally reading a selection together so they can perform it. The students read the entire selection together, or different groups read different parts. Because students find choral reading enjoyable, they willingly practice the word recognition that helps them to give a polished performance. Low-achieving readers enjoy this activity because it gives them the satisfaction of delivering a well-rehearsed, expressive rendition. Choral reading is particularly suited to selections, such as poetry, that contain rhythm and rhyme. We will never forget the heartfelt rendition of "Homework Oh Homework" (by Prelutsky, in *The New Kid on the Block*) delivered by three fifth-grade boys in the Reading Center.

Partner Reading.   In partner reading, students read in pairs, usually by alternating pages. This type of reading provides extensive reading practice for both students. Partner reading can be an effective way to help students with reading problems develop fluency (Stahl & Heubach, 1993). However, because you want the students to experience success, you should have them read the material alone a few times before they read as partners. This practice avoids the danger of encountering too many unknown words or becoming frustrated. Often other forms of assisted reading are used with a passage before students are asked to read with partners.

Teachers may organize students as reading partners in different ways. Sometimes students enjoy choosing their friends as reading partners. At other times, the teacher can pair students who differ in reading abilities. Low-achieving readers of similar ability work well as partners if preliminary support has been provided. Pairing two children with reading problems helps each to realize that he (or she) is not the only one who has problems with words. Student self-esteem increases through the act of helping another. Danny and Peter became fast friends as a result of consistent partner reading. At one point, Danny confided, "Peter didn't know a word, and I helped him. He helps me too. When we read together, we are pretty good readers!"

Simultaneous Listening-Reading. In this assisted strategy, students listen to tape recordings of material while following along with a book. Simultaneous listening-reading has been used successfully with different age levels (Chomsky, 1978). However, students sometimes do not follow along in the book, preferring to simply enjoy listening to the tape.

Neurological Impress Method (NIM). This read-along strategy (Heckelman, 1969), often abbreviated to NIM, involves the teacher and one student reading together. According to Heckelman, students learn by emulating a fluent reading model. The NIM technique is particularly effective with reading-disabled adolescents.

In NIM, the student and teacher read together orally. Begin by reading material at the student's independent level or material that has been read before. Tell your student not to be concerned about reading accuracy but to try to read fluently, without looking back.

At first, the teacher reads slightly louder and faster. As the student gains fluency and confidence, the teacher begins to read more softly and may even start to lag slightly behind the student. However, if the student encounters difficulty, the teacher should rescue the student in a firm manner. When beginning this procedure, teachers should follow the text with their fingers at the pace of the reading. As the student gains confidence, he or she can assume the responsibility for pointing to the words.

Use of this method may improve oral reading quickly; however, if no improvement has resulted after six sessions, you should stop. This method works for some students, but not for all. One fifth-grade student, who enjoyed NIM, improved considerably in reading fluency. Another boy, a seventh grader, had a negative reaction, and so NIM was discontinued.

Repeated Readings

In the repeated readings strategy, an individual student rereads a short selection until a certain level of word identification accuracy and fluency is attained (Samuels, 1979). As students read the same selection a number of times, they become more accurate, their reading speed increases, and their reading becomes more expressive (Dowhower, 1987; Herman, 1985; Rashotte & Torgesen, 1985).

To begin repeated readings, give the student a passage of 50 to 200 words written at his or her independent or instructional level. Have the student read the selection orally. As your student reads, record the reading speed and any deviations from the text. Next, discuss any word recognition miscues with your student. Then, over a few sessions, have the student practice the selection until he or she feels capable of reading it fluently. Then have the student read the selection orally again as you record time and accuracy. The process is repeated until a certain accuracy or rate score is reached. At this point, the student moves to another reading selection.

Repeated readings is a flexible strategy that can be adapted to different student needs. To provide more extensive assistance, a teacher can read with the student until he or she feels confident enough to read alone. Or students can be asked to listen to their own tapes to see if they chunked words into meaningful groups and read with expression.

In choosing material for repeated readings, remember that you need something that will hold a student's interest over several rereadings. If a student is passionately interested in snakes, a selection about reptiles is a good choice. Other selections might include humor, lots of action, or sports. You can also use readings from the student's content area textbooks or novels, for in addition to improving word recognition, rereading helps the student to learn the material.

Repeated readings can also be adapted for use with a group (Mossburg, 1989). Read a selection to the students while they follow along in their text. Then, before you read the selection a second time, tell the students that they must follow along carefully because you are going to stop at certain places and they must read what comes next. Read the selection a third time, asking students to take the parts of characters in the text. Then have them read the selection again in pairs.

Our experience in using repeated readings shows that students will not become bored even if they occasionally complain. Sixth-grade Gregg's tutor used repeated reading in combination with assisted reading. Gregg and his tutor worked for several months on one selection, at times reading together or taking turns on different pages. Occasionally, Gregg complained that repeated readings were "boring." But when the tutor omitted the repeated reading from the lesson one day, Gregg loudly objected. "I want to do it," he claimed, "because I like how I sound at the end!" As this story illustrates, you should pursue repeated readings on a consistent basis and not let occasional student complaints turn you away from a powerful technique for developing reading fluency.

The Language Experience Approach

In the language experience approach, students compose personal stories, which are then used for reading instruction. Generally, students dictate their stories to a teacher, who records them in writing. Stories can also be written and edited on a computer.

Because students have actually produced these stories, they are anxious to read them. In addition, students can see the direct relationship between speech and reading, for language experience stories are "talk written down." Although the language experience approach is used most widely with younger children (see Chapter 5), it is also effective with older students who are at a beginning reading level.

Many teachers make permanent records of language experience stories. For an individual student, the stories may be printed or typed and collected in a notebook. For groups, the stories may be duplicated so that each student has a copy.

To be most effective, language experience stories should be about experiences that are exciting and of personal interest. A recent firsthand experience such as an unusual event or an exciting television program provides the opportunity to develop a story.

At times, low-achieving students may have some trouble composing stories. Students who encounter this difficulty may be helped to develop stories that they enjoy. Many "wordless" picture books contain amusing stories related without words. Students can "read" and compose captions for such stories. The visual humor in comic strips can also inspire language experience stories. Teachers can eliminate the dialogue "balloons" of the strips or cut the words out of the strips and have students provide them.

Despite its motivational value, the language experience approach is not effective for some students. Because stories come directly from fluent oral language, words in a language experience story may accumulate faster than students can learn to read them. Alonzo, one severely disabled 13-year-old reader, had to give up learning to read by this approach because his inability to read his own experience stories eventually frustrated him.

Making Oral and Silent Reading Effective

To develop contextual fluency, readers need to have effective and enjoyable oral and silent reading experiences. This section discusses common problems and suggests guidelines for using oral and silent reading.

Difficulty Reading Silently. Because silent reading allows students to process and think independently, it should be used as much as possible with low-achieving students. Despite this guideline, we admit that students with reading problems often prefer to read orally. As 11-year-old Jamie often complained, "If I can't read out loud, I don't know what I am reading." Students with reading problems tend to avoid silent reading for three reasons:

- Beginning readers link reading with oral language and thus are most comfortable when can they hear what they read. Although teachers must respect the feelings of these beginning readers, they should gently and gradually move students toward silent reading.
- Many teachers are more comfortable with oral reading because they feel that both they and the students are "doing something." Oral reading also allows teachers to monitor students' word recognition skills. Although some monitoring is valuable, developing independent silent readers is even more valuable.
- Many poor readers feel that the purpose of reading is to recognize all of the words for a teacher. For these students, reading is a performance rather than an opportunity to learn information or enjoy a story. These students must be convinced that silent reading is an important adult activity. You might ask them to observe five adult readers to see whether they are reading silently or orally. Such observations generally convince students that silent reading has merit.

Students should be given direct motivation for reading silently. Stress the information or enjoyment that students will gain. If teachers follow silent reading with discussions that focus on the student's personal reactions to the text, students will start to see silent reading as meaningful.

Teachers often ask what to do when students point to words or move their lips as they read silently. Sometimes finger pointing and lip moving can act as an aid that makes halting readers more comfortable. In fact, these actions are normal for primary-grade-level readers. In addition, if the reading material is difficult, individuals of any reading level may revert to using their fingers or lips. However, because finger pointing and lip moving are often signs of frustration, you should check to make sure that the material your students are reading is not too difficult for them.

If you feel that students need to point or move their lips to feel comfortable, even on easy materials, then do not interfere with these habits. As students become more fluent readers, these actions usually disappear.

However, discourage students from moving their lips or pointing to the words if you sense they are just doing so from force of habit. First, and most effective, the student should be made aware of these habits, told how they slow readers down, and asked, respectfully, to eliminate them. This simple procedure, plus an occasional reminder, often solves the problem. Finger pointing can also be eliminated by providing a marker to replace a finger and gradually eliminating the use of the marker. For lip moving, students may be asked to consciously close their lips while reading.

Making Oral Reading Comfortable.   Although silent reading is the preferred mode of reading, oral reading can be an effective way for students to gain reading experience and for the teacher to see how students are dealing with material.

However, students, even those without reading problems, often see oral reading as a negative, performance-oriented experience. College students, telling us about their own schooling, single out oral reading as being stressful and humiliating. They remember quite vividly their feelings of anxiety and shame when they missed a word. One student rather poignantly remarked, "It was only when I did not have to read out loud that I actually began to enjoy reading. Did it have to be that way?" If successful college students have had these experiences, what must such experiences be like for children with reading problems?

Individual oral reading can be made into a more positive, meaning-focused experience in several ways:

- Students can practice a selection before being asked to read it in front of their peers.
- The amount of oral reading should be limited. It is helpful if oral reading serves only a specific purpose, such as finding information, proving a point, or reading a favorite part.
- Teachers should remember not to treat oral reading time as a chance to teach phonics. When a student attempts to pronounce an unknown word (and poor readers meet many unfamiliar words), try not to interrupt the reading by saying, "Sound it out." The student's repeated attempts to decode the word make him or her, and everyone else reading, lose the meaning of the story. Furthermore, the experience is humiliating.

What should a teacher do if a student doesn't know a word? If readers pause or stumble on an important word, the teacher should simply tell them the word and move on. Or the teacher should wait until the end of the sentence and then reread the sentence using the correct pronunciation (Wilson, 1988), at the same time marking the unknown word for later teaching.

Not all mistakes are worth correcting. If a reading mistake involves only a small "function" word (*it, the*) that does not greatly affect meaning, it should simply be forgotten. By using these guidelines, teachers emphasize that reading is an enjoyable and meaningful experience. This understanding is crucial for struggling students.

At times, if a student struggles with a word, a peer will laugh or simply call out the correct term. These unkind responses are all too common for low-achieving readers. In fact, poor readers tend to laugh at the errors of other poor readers. You can prevent this situation by taking a few simple precautions: (1) Never ask children to read alone in front of their peers without practicing first or without providing some support. (2) Teach students to signal when they meet an unfamiliar word (Wilson, 1988). They can tap the book or raise a finger (rather than looking up). If you wish, you can require that the teacher, not the other children, supply the word. (3) Stress that group members must always be respectful of one another.

Fluency Development Procedures

Several easily implemented instructional procedures have resulted in positive fluency gains. Although often designed to be incorporated into a classroom setting, they can be easily adapted for small groups or individual low-achieving readers.

Fluency Development Lesson.   Developed by Rasinski, Padak, Linek, and Sturtevant (1994), the steps in this 10- to 15-minute Fluency Development Lesson are as follows:

1. The teacher reads a short text of 50 to 150 words to the students while they follow along silently with their own copies.
2. The teacher and students discuss what the text is about. They also discuss the teacher's use of expression during the reading.
3. The teacher and class read the text chorally several times.
4. The students then practice reading the selection in pairs. Each partner takes a turn reading and receives help if needed from his or her partner. The partner also provides positive feedback.
5. Volunteers perform the text for the entire class. This performance can be done individually, in pairs, or in groups of four.

The Oral Recitation Lesson.   Developed by Hoffman (1985), this routine is similar to the Fluency Development Lesson. The teacher reads a selection to the class. The students discuss the content of the text, and they summarize it. Next, they talk about expressive oral reading and how punctuation marks signal voice changes. The students then read the text chorally. Finally, individual students select a portion of the text and practice it individually using soft or whisper reading. Students also work in pairs and read the chosen selection three times to their partners. They self-evaluate each repetition for accuracy and expression; finally they perform the selection for their peers.

The Support Reading Strategy.   Morris and Nelson (1992) designed a three-day sequence of activities to foster fluency development. On the first day, the teacher reads a selection to the students. The teacher stops during the reading to foster discussion about what is happening and what will happen next. The teacher and class then reread the story chorally. On the second day, the teacher forms pairs of readers. The pairs reread the selection with each reader reading alternate pages. Each pair is assigned a short segment to practice. On the third day individual students read their selections orally to the teacher, who carefully monitors their oral reading fluency.

Repeated Reading Using Grade-Level Text.   McCormack and Paratore (1999) developed a routine to assist below-level readers with grade-level text. They reasoned that limiting poor readers to text at their instructional reading level denies them access to the many concepts, ideas, and language patterns that they could acquire by reading grade-level text. The daily routine included the following activities:

1. The teacher introduces essential vocabulary and reviews the decoding strategies that were useful in identifying the new words. The students preview the text, make predictions, and pose questions.
2. The teacher reads the text aloud while the students follow along silently with their own copies. The teacher and students then discuss their reactions to the selection, talk about their predictions, and attempt to answer the questions they posed prior to reading.
3. The students then reread the selection with a peer using echo reading, choral reading, and buddy reading.
4. The students finally reread the selection to the teacher individually or in pairs.

Strategies for Developing Sight Words in Isolation

A *sight word* is a word recognized instantly, without analysis. How do words become sight words? Each time a reader sees the word *dog* and correctly identifies it, the next recognition of *dog* becomes a little easier and faster. Think of something you learned to do, such as knitting or driving. The early stages were difficult, time-consuming, and often frustrating. As you practiced, the action became easier and easier; and now you can do it almost automatically, even while thinking about other things. Similarly, each time you accurately identify a word, it becomes easier and easier, and eventually, the word becomes a sight word.

Students with reading problems can best learn to recognize words by reading them in context. However, they may also need additional practice with words in isolation to reinforce automaticity and give them a sense of progress. Practicing individual words is useful for readers at many different levels. A core of sight words enables beginning readers to read easy books and serves as a basis for learning phonics. Reinforcement of sight vocabulary also enables more advanced students to identify the difficult words in their classroom textbooks.

This section first discusses which words should receive additional practice in isolation. Then it suggests some guidelines and strategies for teaching these words.

Choosing Words for Instructional Focus

Lists of frequently used words can help the teacher select words for instructional focus. Table 7.1 provides high-frequency words based on a study of the Dolch Basic Sight Vocabulary, as updated by Johnson (1971). Table 7.2 lists some nouns that can be easily pictured.

Many high-frequency words are *function words*, such as *the, of,* and *to*. These words, usually articles, prepositions, and pronouns, have little meaning of their own and take on meaning only by acting as connectors for other words. Six-year-old Scott, working on the function words *when* and *then*, sighed and muttered, "These sure aren't fun words like *brontosaurus!*"

Function words are difficult to learn for several reasons: (1) As emphasized, they have abstract meanings. (2) They tend to look alike. Words such as *then, than, when, what, where,* and *were* are easily confused. (3) Because they tend to have irregular sound-spelling relationships, they often must be mastered as sight words. Because recognition of function words may be particularly troublesome for poor readers, such words deserve special attention. Function words appear so frequently that if they are not recognized instantly, reading will become uncomfortable and disfluent.

In addition to choosing high-frequency words for teaching, you might select words that are important to your students. At times, these words will appear in a novel your students are reading or be used in social studies and science texts. At other times, students may want to select words that are important in their lives. Peter, a fourth grader, insisted on learning *Pokemon, tae quon do,* and *karate*.

Guidelines for Teaching Sight Words

Several guidelines will make learning sight words more effective.

Associate Sight Words with Meaning.   This association is particularly critical for function words. When readers are simply given word cards and expected to memorize them, learning becomes a rote task that is meaningless. To make this learning more meaningful, have your students write phrases for words on their word cards. For example, they might remember *in* by thinking of the phrase *in the garbage*. Pictures can be cut out, labeled, and placed around the room to illustrate other function words: a can *of* Coke; a fish *in* water; a cat *on* the fence. The students can then be guided to think of the contents of other cans, what else can be *in* water, or *on* a fence.

Practice Sight Words Frequently.   As already emphasized, words are recognized automatically only after repeated exposures. Practice should include activities both with single words and with reading connected text. Frequent writing, reading, word games, and other word-centered activities all provide practice that develops sight word recognition. Poor readers need daily opportunities to read, write, and play with words. Recognizing quickly flashed words also seems to benefit students with reading problems (van den Bosch, van Bon, & Schreuder, 1995).

Keep Records of Progress.   Students with reading problems are motivated by their improvement. Students can keep records or journals of words they have learned. Word banks also can record progress. The one pictured in

Figure 7.2 was made from a shoe box and was used as an alphabetical file for new words. Students can refer to a word bank when they review words or when they write.

If words are prominently displayed, students will use them more often in their reading and writing. One teacher displayed words on a "word flower," a circle with petals, each one with a sight word. As the student learned more words, petals were added to the flower, and finally, new flowers were created.

Teachers can also demonstrate progress by sorting word cards into three piles: sight words, words that need to be analyzed, and unknown words. Fourth-grade Pat eagerly looked forward to going through his word cards at each lesson. His goal was to get rid of that third pile, unknown words. After each session, Pat filed his three piles separately in a shoe box and took them home for practice. Each time Pat and his teacher went through the cards, he watched the third pile get smaller, giving him visible proof of his improvement. Finally, Pat's third pile disappeared entirely.

Strategies for Focusing on Words

Several strategies provide motivating and important practice in recognizing words. These strategies include word cards, collecting words, word sorts, games, and word walls.

Word Cards. Word cards provide one way to practice sight words. Either the teacher or the student can construct the cards. Word recognition clues, such as a sentence containing the word or a picture illustrating the word, can be placed on the back of the card. Placing words on cards is motivating for students. As the number of word cards increases, they have a concrete reminder of how many words they are learning.

FIGURE 7.2   Word bank to record student progress

You can use word cards in a variety of ways. Many students enjoy forming sentences from the cards. They can also select the word card that correctly fits a missing word in a sentence. Students can collect personal cards to practice at home with a parent or friend.

Collecting Words.   Collecting words that follow certain patterns is another way to practice sight vocabulary. The patterns can emphasize the spelling of a word, its pronunciation, or its meaning. Students can collect words that contain the same letter pattern, such as *cat, bat, sat,* and so on. They can collect words about a favorite topic, such as snake words: *boa, slither, bite,* etc. The collected words are kept in a personal file.

Word Sorts.   In word sorting, students are presented with several words to sort according to different categories. The words are on cards, and the student is asked to sort the words into piles and to give reasons for placing each word in a certain pile.

The words used for word sorts can come from many sources: words collected by the students, words the students have found difficult, words from textbooks, or spelling words. Words can be sorted according to sound or spelling patterns (Bear, 1994), according to the presence of prefixes or suffixes, or according to meaning. Word sorts are enjoyable and give students with reading problems a sense of control over their language. They also offer valuable experience with letter patterns, sounds, and meanings.

Word sorts are of two different types: In a closed sort, the teacher tells the student how to sort the words. For example, you might tell students to sort the words *tree, run, sit,* and *table* by parts of speech (nouns and verbs). Closed sorts are often used to practice phonics, because teachers have patterns in mind that they want the students to notice. For example, they might ask students to sort words into *long a* and *short a* piles. In a second type of sort, an open sort, students are free to choose their own categories for sorting. Thus, they might choose long words and short words, happy words and sad words, or a phonics pattern. After sorting in one way, students may often want to repeat the sort using other categories. Strategy Snapshot 7.1 describes how a second-grade teacher used the same words for two different kinds of word sorts.

Sorting words provides many opportunities for students to look at a word and pronounce it accurately. Because low-achieving readers find this game-like activity both enjoyable and motivating, word sorts can help to increase a student's fund of sight words.

Games.   Games provide another way to practice sight words. They are easily made and can be designed for individual students. One type of game uses a "trailboard" such as that illustrated in Figure 7.3.

The game board is made from a 2′ × 3′ piece of cardboard that is laminated or coated with clear adhesive paper for durability. The words to be used are supplied by word cards that are piled on the board so that the practice cards can change easily. The student rolls dice (or one die), picks up a word from the

---

STRATEGY SNAPSHOT **7.1**

Sorting Words

To start a word sort, Ms. Lessiter gave a group of low-achieving second graders cards containing the words: *sat, mitt, rat, tin, pin, fan,* and *fin.* This sort was an open one, and the children chose to sort words by spelling patterns. They first placed the words into four piles: (1) *mitt* (2) *tin, pin, fin* (3) *fan,* and (4) *sat, rat.* This sort put the words into the word families *it, in, an, at.* Ms. Lessiter then asked the students to sort into only two piles. The children sorted on the basis of a single vowel: Group 1 had words with an *i* (*mitt, tin, pin, fin*), and Group 2 had words with an *a* (*fan, sat, rat*).

Ms. Lessiter then asked the children to sort the words by using the meaning. First, the children sorted according to what could be bought. They agreed that a *mitt,* a *pin,* a *fan,* and a *rat* could be bought, and the other words could not. Next they sorted according to what was in their houses. They first decided that all except *sat, fin,* and *rat* could be found in their homes. One of the group members then asked if pet goldfish have *fins.* The children decided they do and placed *fin* in the "home" pile. The group finally sorted according to what they actually owned. The children grouped *mitt* and *pin* together until one student informed the group that she had a *pet rat.* Word sorting was abandoned as the children discussed the joys of such an exciting pet.

---

pile, and moves the number of spaces indicated. If the word is read correctly, the card is then moved to the bottom of the pack. If the word is not read correctly, the player does not move. A few cards, such as "You have been lucky today and may move two spaces," add spice and suspense. These games can be played with a teacher and a student or several students who may wish to practice words independently.

Another game for practicing words is Bingo. Cards are prepared containing the words, and each space is covered as the word is called. If a student (rather than the teacher) calls out the words, the student must then say the word aloud as well as recognize it. Bingo is suitable for group instruction.

Word Walls. A Word Wall is an effective device (Cunningham & Allington, 1999; Cunningham, 2000) for displaying high-frequency words and making them easily accessible to the students. A Word Wall can be placed on a bulletin board or a classroom wall. It is divided into sections for each letter of the alphabet (*a, b, c* . . .). As words are selected for special emphasis, they are placed on the Word Wall according to their initial letter. These words may be suggested by the teacher or by students. Sometimes they are displayed with a picture or sentence clue; sometimes they are displayed alone. Five or so new words are added each week, and sometimes, when a space becomes full, they are taken down. To ensure that you can change words, either attach them to cards or laminate each section for individual letters (the *a* section, the *b* section) and use erasable magic marker to write the words.

FIGURE 7.3 A Trailboard for a Sight Word Game

Students can find, write, spell, and say words from their Word Wall. The teacher can devise riddles and games using the words. Students or the teacher can compose sentences from words found on the wall. If teachers dictate such a sentence, students then find the missing word. Students can also find all the words on the wall that, for example, have seven letters, are verbs, or contain an *r*-controlled vowel. In the "I'm thinking of" game, one student gives hints about a particular word on the wall, and the others try to guess it. For example, a student thinking of the word *beautiful* might give the hints that it is an adjective meaning very pretty.

To focus instruction, teachers might want to write words in different colors: for example, red could be used for social studies, blue for science, and green for health. Teachers in resource rooms might assign one color to each of the groups that they see by using, for example, green for a 9:30 group and purple for a 10:00 group. Special words, such as function words, might be written in neon marker.

An important use of Word Walls is that they serve as resources for students who have difficulty spelling words. Instead of asking a teacher or struggling for themselves, they simply find the word on the wall. This process reinforces the learning of alphabetical order.

Word Walls are an easy way to remind students of important words. A picture of a fourth-grade Word Wall is shown in Figure 7.4.

Mastering Function Words

Function words, such as *in, when,* and *there,* may be particularly troublesome for students with reading problems. The teacher needs to emphasize that context clues can help students to recognize function words. The cloze strategy described in Chapter 6 can help call attention to using context clues. In preparing a cloze passage for function words, simply delete one of every four *function* words from a passage and challenge students to provide these "little" words.

Highlighting function words in text can also help students learn them. Teachers can underline words or use highlighters to mark them. Then ask students to read the text, first silently and then aloud. Several passages should be used to give students extended practice in recognizing function words over a period of time.

An occasional student with reading problems needs intensive instruction in function words. Remember that, in this instruction, each function word should be accompanied by a phrase or sentence, because function words contain little meaning by themselves.

If a student finds a few words to be particularly difficult, use the *star word approach.* Print one word on a large star that has room for little silver stars. Then introduce this large star as the "star word" of the day. Each time your student says the word correctly, place a little silver star on the big star.

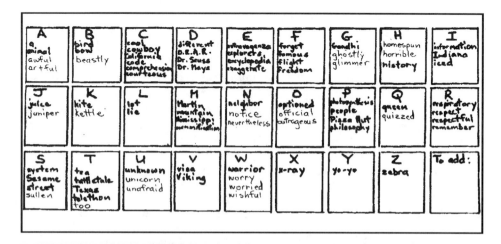

FIGURE 7.4 **Part of a Word Wall from a Fourth Grade Class**

Dealing with Reversals

Students with reading problems who are achieving on the first- and second-grade levels tend to reverse certain letters and words while reading. Commonly, they substitute *b* for *d, no* for *on,* or *saw* for *was.* In fact, emergent and beginning readers commonly produce backward "mirror writing." Reversals have sometimes been interpreted as a symptom of deep-seated reading problems or even brain dysfunction (Orton, 1937). However, in most cases, reversals simply indicate a lack of experience with literacy. They are seen often in normally achieving children reading at primary-grade levels. In fact, learning-disabled students have been found to make no more reversals than normal readers when both groups of students are reading equally comfortable material (Adams, 1991). Reversals also may occur with teenagers and adults who are just learning to read.

One reason that students make reversals is that reading and writing are the only processes in which symbols change because of their directional orientation. Thus, the only difference between the letters *b* and *d* is that one faces right and the other left. On the other hand, a real-life object, such as a *chair* or *dog,* maintains its identity regardless of its orientation in space. A student beginning to read may not yet realize that the orientation of letters and words makes a difference.

When a student with reading problems exhibits reversals, the teacher must decide whether to provide special instruction to eliminate them. If the reversal is only occasional, no special instruction is warranted. If reversals are frequent and interfere with effective reading, special instruction is needed.

To correct reversals of single letters, concentrate on one letter at a time. For example, to correct a *b-d* reversal, first concentrate on *d.* Teachers can make a large chart containing the letter *d,* a memory word (e.g., *dog*), and pictures of words that start with *d.* One teacher cut out a 2′ by 3′ felt *d* and pasted it on a board. The student reinforced the *d* concept by tracing over the letter with a finger. After the concept of *d* has been mastered thoroughly, wait a week before introducing the letter *b.* This *divide and conquer* method is effective for students with problems. Other methods are:

- Making flash cards containing confusing words and having students practice recognizing them.
- Underlining the first letter of a confusable word in a bright color, such as red.
- Having students manipulate letters on a felt or magnetic board to form words that are frequently reversed.

Reversals are discussed further in Chapter 15.

Combining Contextual Reading with a Focus on Words

This section focuses on programs that combine several clue systems to help students recognize words.

The Curious George Strategy

The interest created by a captivating book sometimes enables students to successfully read material that is above their previously determined instructional level. A technique called the Curious George strategy has helped children overcome barriers to reading. The method is most useful for small groups of students in the primary grades; it is targeted for those reading between the primer and second-grade levels. Using children's natural enthusiasm for *Curious George* (by Rey) and its sequels and employing many of the techniques described earlier (assisted reading, language experience, and focus on individual words), we have been able to achieve dramatic gains in reading level and enthusiasm.

The Curious George strategy has been used informally many times (Richek, 1999; Richek et al., 1989). A documented field study was reported by Richek and McTague (1988). At the end of an 18-day period, the experimental Curious George group had, when compared to a control group, increased comprehension by 25 percent and decreased miscues by 65 percent on passages from an IRI. These differences were statistically significant, and teachers also noticed an increase in enthusiasm for reading and in the ability to write independently. A description of the strategy in action is given in Strategy Snapshot 7.2.

In addition to using this strategy with the *Curious George* series, you can use it with the *Clifford the Big Red Dog* (by Bridwell), the *Harry the Dirty Dog* (by Zion), and other picture book series. The use of a connected series of books is critical to the strategy. A book series consists of several books that involve the same character or situation. Each book introduces new words but, more importantly, also repeats words from previous books. The repetition of words, characters, and situations provides the student with a growing sense of control over reading.

The Multiple-Exposure/ Multiple-Context Strategy

McCormick (1994) describes a method for working with a severely disabled reader involving many exposures to unknown words (Multiple-Exposure) but within a variety of different situations (Multiple-Context). As in the Curious George strategy, a series of easy books involving the same characters is used.

The teacher has the student orally read part of the first book in the series. During the reading, the teacher provides and notes the correct pronunciation of inaccurate or unknown words. These unknown words will form the target words presented through multiple exposures and in multiple contexts.

Each lesson has two parts. To extend the student's language abilities, the teacher reads literature selections to the student. In addition, the student practices target words from the book part until they can be pronounced accurately and automatically. The teacher offers a variety of activities that present the words both in isolation and in context. These activities include word cards, matching words to

STRATEGY SNAPSHOT 7.2

The Curious George Strategy

Instruction was divided into four-day segments of about 30 minutes each. On the *first* day of instruction, the teacher enthusiastically read *Curious George* to the children while holding the only copy of the book (See Figure 7.5). Next, asking the students to help in reading the book, the teacher and students read together the first 16 pages in an assisted fashion. Generally, the context enabled students to supply many words and to read with some fluency. Next, the focus was on individual words. Each child chose five words, and the teacher wrote them on pieces of construction paper. Each child was given a different color. Finally, each child was handed a paperback copy of *Curious George* to take home with his or her five cards and told to bring the cards and book back the next day.

On the *second* day of instruction, children "showed off" their cards to others and read them if they could. The teacher then continued with the assisted reading of *Curious George*, pages 17–32. Because they had had the book overnight, the children had generally gained considerable fluency. Next, the children chose five more words, and the teacher wrote them down on individual cards. They again took their personal cards and words home and were instructed to return them the next day.

On the *third* day of instruction, the procedures of the second day were repeated, but the children completed the assisted reading of the book, reading pages 32–48.

On the *fourth* day of instruction, the teacher presented a "book" made from yellow construction paper. Each page contained a picture cut out from a page of *Curious George*. Children took turns dictating the words to accompany the pictures, thus making their own Curious George book.

After completing four days of Curious George instruction, the children read sequels, including *Curious George Goes to the Hospital, Curious George Flies a Kite*, and *Curious George Takes a Job*, in the same manner. At first, the process of completing a book took four days; but as children became more confident, they took less time.

Children should be allowed to control their own reading process. For example, at a certain point, some tired of word cards and preferred to spend their time simply reading books. As children moved toward more independent reading, the teacher supplied additional books about Curious George (more than 30 are available). Children also enjoyed writing letters to Curious George or writing such personal books as "Curious George and Charita."

---

pictures, writing or tracing words, games, reading short sentences, cloze activities, making sentences, and assisted reading. As the student learns the words, the teacher visually demonstrates progress through a chart or graph.

When the target words have been learned, the student reads the first part of the book and then moves to the next part. The process is repeated as the teacher and student move on to successive books in the series.

FIGURE 7.5 The Curious George Strategy. The teacher starts instruction using the Curious George Strategy by reading the story aloud to the students.

Summary

Readers cannot take the time to analyze every word they encounter. They must develop a large store of sight vocabulary words, words that they recognize automatically. Readers who have a large sight vocabulary can read fluently. A fluent reader reads accurately, quickly, and with expression. Fluency is an important component of successful reading. Readers who can recognize words automatically and without analysis can pay attention to meaning.

Fluent reading can be assessed in three ways: listening to students read orally, determining student reading rate measured as words per minute, and timed administration of word lists.

Fluency is best developed as students read connected text. Therefore, teachers must promote wide reading of easy text. The use of predictable books and assisted reading is also effective. In assisted reading, students read material with a fluent reader, who is often the teacher. The various forms of assisted reading are simultaneous assisted reading, echo reading, choral reading, partner reading, simultaneous listening-reading, and the Neurological Impress Method.

Repeated reading is another effective technique for developing fluency. Students repeatedly read a text until a desired level of accuracy and fluency is reached.

In the language experience approach, students compose and dictate personal stories, which are then used for reading instruction. Students repeatedly read these stories and develop fluency as they do so.

Several instructional procedures can aid in fluency development. These procedures include the Fluency Development Lesson, the oral recitation lesson, the support reading strategy, and repeated reading using grade level text.

Sight vocabulary can also be developed by focusing on words in isolation. This is particularly important for helping students master high-frequency function words. Students can make word cards, collect words, engage in word sorts, play word games, and construct word walls. Reversals of letters and words are common in all beginning readers and do not signal neurological problems.

The Curious George strategy and the Multiple-Context/Multiple-Exposure strategy promote the development of fluency within contextual reading.

8 Improving Comprehension of Narrative Text

Introduction

Comprehension is the essence of reading; indeed, it is the *only* purpose for reading. Yet, many low-achieving students are unable to read effectively because they lack critical elements of comprehension. They need to develop strategies that help them become active, competent readers who demand meaning from text.

Focusing on reading comprehension is important even when a student's primary area of difficulty is word recognition. When students understand what they read, they enjoy it and are motivated to read more. This increased reading results in additional practice in recognizing words. In addition, students who are focused on meaning can use their general understanding of a story to help them recognize difficult words (Anderson, Wilkinson, & Mason, 1991).

This chapter describes the general nature of comprehension. Then the chapter discusses the comprehension of narrative (or storylike) text, including what it is, how to assess it, and strategies for instruction. The comprehension of expository (or informational) text is addressed in Chapter 9.

General Features of Effective Reading Comprehension

Good readers share subconscious knowledge and attitudes about four important aspects of comprehension:

- The purpose of reading is comprehension.
- Comprehension is an active and accurate process.
- Readers use their background knowledge to comprehend.
- Comprehension requires higher-level thinking.

The Purpose of Reading Is Comprehension

Good readers know that the purpose of reading is to understand, enjoy, and learn from material. In contrast, students with reading problems often think that reading means recognizing words. Some feel that once they have read all of the words orally, they are finished. To help students with reading problems understand that reading is comprehension, you can:

- Always ask students for a comprehension response after they read material. You can use questions, story retellings, or some of the more detailed strategies in this chapter.
- Encourage silent reading. Students who read only orally come to think of reading as a performance. Silent reading helps them to understand that reading is a personal, meaning-focused activity.

Comprehension Is an Active and Accurate Process

As discussed in Chapter 1, reading is the active construction of meaning. Good readers construct a text in their minds as they read. This text is similar to the text that the author has written, but good readers supply details and draw conclusions not stated in the text. In contrast, problem readers often focus on remembering small details rather than constructing their own meaning. As a result, low-achieving readers tend not to monitor their comprehension (Pressley, 2000; van den Broek & Kremer, 2000). That is, when they lose the meaning of the material, they do not go back in the text and try to understand. In fact, disabled readers are often unaware that something is wrong. The ability to monitor one's own comprehension and employ "fix-up" strategies is called *metacognitive awareness*.

Reading should be accurate as well as active. Sometimes, when disabled readers come across unfamiliar words, they abandon the actual text and substitute words that have little relation to the text's meaning. Some simply construct a story based on just a few words. Teachers can use several strategies to encourage active, yet accurate, reading:

- Interest students in the material before they begin. Tell them what is good or exciting about a story or topic. Discuss the author to show students that stories are written by real people. Draw parallels between the students' lives and the events in a story.
- Remind students to be aware of their own comprehension. If they are lost, they should stop and reread, look at pictures, use context clues to figure out words, or ask for help.

Comprehension Uses Background Knowledge

The ability to comprehend is highly dependent on the background knowledge, or schema, that readers bring to reading (Goldman & Rakestraw, 2000). When students understand concepts important to the story, their comprehension increases (Beck, Omanson, & McKeown, 1982).

Unfortunately, students with reading problems often lack the background knowledge that ensures comprehension. Mike, a fifth grader, read about a boy who found a skunk, which later turned out to be a mink. Unfortunately, because Mike did not know what minks were, he could not understand that most people had different attitudes toward the two animals. In short, Mike lacked the background information to understand the story.

Because print often deals with more sophisticated concepts than conversation, reading itself helps to build background information needed in school. For example, most of you learned about ancient Greece through school and leisure reading rather than at the family dinner table. However, because students with reading problems do not read much, they do not learn the many sophisticated concepts needed for success in school (Cunningham & Stanovich, 1998; Snider & Tarver, 1987).

Even when students with reading problems do have background knowledge, they may not use it effectively (Pace, et al., 1989). Some readers underuse their background knowledge and do not summon it to consciousness when they read. Other low-achieving readers overuse their background knowledge (Williams, 1993) and let their personal points of view intrude into their comprehension. To illustrate, Angel, a fourth grader, read a selection about a football game in which the star player was a girl. Unfortunately, Angel's schema that only boys played football was so strong that he overlooked the information in the text and consistently insisted that *she* was a *he*.

Research shows that increasing students' prior knowledge of a topic improves their reading (Paris, Wasik, & Turner, 1991). Many techniques help students to build and use background knowledge:

- Help students build background before they read; gently correct misperceptions.
- If you are teaching in a resource setting, discuss the background knowledge students need to comprehend their regular classroom material.
- Encourage students to modify their own ideas when the text presents new information.

Comprehension Requires Higher-Level Thinking

Higher-level thinking processes are important to story comprehension. Good readers combine their own background information with the information in the text to draw inferences. As they read, they also make predictions, which are confirmed or disproved later in the text. Unfortunately, students with reading problems are often literal readers who do not connect and reason from text in a logical manner. Teachers can foster higher-level comprehension in many ways:

- Ask students inferential and prediction questions and limit the number of factual questions asked. When teachers simply ask more inference questions, students improve in their abilities to draw inferences (Hansen, 1981; Sundbye, 1987; Wixson, 1983).

■ Model higher-level thinking skills for students. Low-achieving readers need to see the thought processes underlying skilled comprehension.

Comprehending Narrative Materials

Narrative text is one popular and common form of writing. In narratives, stories are told and plots unfold. Narratives have characters and a plot with a sequence of events. Although most stories are fiction (e.g., *Charlotte's Web* by White, the *Harry Potter* books by Rowling, *The Cat in the Hat* by Dr. Seuss, *The Three Little Pigs*) some chronicle real-life events (*My Side of the Mountain*, by George). Narrative materials inspire personal responses and are organized in certain ways.

Narratives Inspire Imaginative Personal Responses

Narratives are written to inspire personal responses (Pearson & Fielding, 1991). Through stories, children and adults leave the limits of their everyday lives and "travel" to a boarding school for wizards with *Harry Potter* (by Rowling) or to rural Wisconsin in the 1800s in *Little House on the Prairie* (by Wilder). In this way, children learn to represent people, objects, and events in their imagination (Graesser, Golding, & Long, 1991). Thus, cognitive growth is fostered by an enjoyable experience.

Good readers become involved in narratives they read. They put themselves in the character's place and ask themselves, "What would I do if I were in this situation?" Students who identify with a character comprehend better and read more (Golden & Guthrie, 1986; Thomson, 1987).

Sadly, some struggling readers have limited experience using their own imaginations and lack these responses to narratives. One group of low-achieving third graders responded negatively to all types of fiction and anything that seemed unreal. Only after several months of reading and listening to fantasies in books, poems, and stories did they begin to feel comfortable.

To foster personal responses, students must share their reactions to reading. Adults often do this naturally. Typically, if you tell a friend that you saw a movie, the first question is "Did you like it?" Most children also have strong personal responses to stories, yet teachers rarely ask for their reactions (Gambrell, 1986). When you ask students for personal reactions, you honor their opinions, focus on enjoyment, and raise their self-esteem.

To focus on students' personal responses, ask students to rate their enjoyment of a story (e.g., I disliked it. It was OK. I liked it. I loved it.). Ask them if they have anything in common with the story characters or with the situations in a story. When students share responses, they come to realize that others may have differing opinions and experiences.

Narratives Have Story Organization

Narratives are written according to a specific form, called a *story grammar*, and include different types, or genres, of materials.

Story Grammar.   A story grammar includes specific elements. If you think of a story you read recently, it had characters, a setting, events, and a conclusion. In addition, the characters probably had problems to solve. Students need to be able to:

- Identify important characters
- Identify the setting: time and place
- Recall the major events in proper sequence and separate important events from less important ones
- Identify the problem that the character(s) had to solve and explain how that problem was resolved

Shanahan and Shanahan (1997) have shown that students who use story grammar and analyze the different perspectives of the characters improve their comprehension of the story.

Many narratives also have morals and themes. Fables, for example, are short stories followed by an important moral point. As children mature, they grow in the ability to understand themes and morals.

Good readers implicitly identify story features and use them as a road map to guide their comprehension. In contrast, readers with problems are often unaware of story structure. Research shows that low-achieving students benefit from instruction in story grammar (Idol, 1987; Goldman & Rakestraw, 2000).

Genres of Narrative Text.   Different varieties of reading materials are called *genres*. Narrative genres include:

- Realistic fiction
- Fantasy, including books with talking animals, science fiction, and horror stories
- Fairy tales, folk tales, and tall tales
- Fables
- Mysteries
- Humor, language play
- Historical fiction, set in a period in the past
- Plays
- Narrative poetry: poems that tell stories
- Real-life adventures
- Biographies and autobiographies

To become good readers, students need to gain experience reading many different genres.

Assessing Abilities with Narrative Text

This section provides guidelines for measuring general comprehension abilities. These guidelines are followed by techniques to help you judge the comprehension of a specific story or book.

Measuring General Comprehension Ability

Many standardized tests of reading contain at least one subtest measuring comprehension. These tests include the *Woodcock Reading Mastery Tests–Revised*, the *Woodcock Diagnostic Reading Test*, the *Gates-MacGinitie Reading Test*, and the *Iowa Tests of Basic Skills* (see Appendix B). In interpreting these subtests, be aware that a low score on a comprehension subtest does not *always* indicate a comprehension problem. First, a low score on a comprehension subtest may be due to problems with recognizing words in the passage. Look at the student's score on a vocabulary or word recognition subtest from the same general test. If both the vocabulary (or word recognition) subtest and the comprehension subtest are low, it is likely that the student did not recognize the words on the comprehension subtest. In contrast, if the vocabulary (or word recognition) subtest is high but the comprehension subtest is low, the student's problems are probably specifically related to comprehension.

Second, the actual tasks students are asked to do on comprehension subtests may not reflect what they do in classrooms. For example, in the *Woodcock Reading Mastery Tests–Revised* Comprehension Subtest, students read a paragraph orally and fill in a missing word. In school, however, students must read long stories and answer questions after silent reading. Thus, to interpret test information correctly, you must look at the actual items on the test.

One published test, the *Test of Reading Comprehension, Third Edition* (TORC-3) is specifically designed to measure reading comprehension (see Appendix B). It contains several different subtests, which include vocabulary as well as specific comprehension measures.

Judging the Comprehension of Specific Materials

Can a student effectively comprehend a specific story? This section gives two strategies to determine how well a student has comprehended a story: retelling, and questioning. It also describes how these strategies can be used to *improve* comprehension as well as assess it.

Retelling. When students retell a story, the teacher gains insight into the text they have constructed in their minds. Retelling shows how a student has mentally organized a selection and what information the student considers important enough to remember. Thus, the teacher observes and analyzes comprehension in action.

To elicit a retelling, begin by informing the student that he or she will retell a story to you after it is read. Next, ask the student to read the story. When the student has finished, say, "Tell me about the story as if you were telling it to a person who had never read it." To avoid undue emphasis on details in a longer story, older students can be asked to summarize rather than to retell.

Do not interrupt as the story is told. When the student has finished, however, you may ask the student to tell more about certain things. This prompting is important for low-achieving readers, because they often know more about a story than they will tell in free recall (Bridge & Tierney, 1981).

Generally, retellings should include:

- The presence of the major character(s)
- The defining characteristics of the characters (good, bad, curious)
- The problem presented by the story
- The solution to that problem (or the end)
- Events presented in sequential order
- The ability to include only those events important to the story and exclude unimportant events

Teachers should be aware of some indications that a retelling may be immature:

- Referring to all characters as "him," "her," or "they"
- Giving a detailed description only of the first page or story segment

When judging retellings, remember that a student's concept of story structure may not fully mature until the teen years. Thus, young students often produce unsophisticated retellings.

Evidence suggests that students who retell stories improve their comprehension (Gambrell, Pfeiffer, & Wilson, 1985; Koskinen, Gambrell, Kapinus, & Heathington, 1988; Morrow, et al., 1986). When teachers give students feedback about their retellings, improvement in comprehension increases, especially for young students.

Asking Questions.   Although questioning is perhaps the most common way to assess comprehension, it does have two drawbacks. First, it does not demand an active response from children. Questions enable teachers to determine whether the student knows what adults consider important to the story. They do not provide information about whether students were able to construct the main events in their own minds. Second, formulating good questions is difficult.

If you are going to ask questions, remember the following guidelines:

- Don't have students spend too much time. Students should not spend more time answering questions than they spent reading a selection. When using questions from a teacher's manual, feel free to eliminate some.

- Do not provide answers to questions as you ask other questions.
- Try to avoid yes/no questions or either/or questions. Students have a 50 percent chance of a right answer just by guessing.
- Focus on some questions that require long answers. Encourage students to explain the reasons for their answers.
- Focus on asking higher-level questions, such as those calling for inferences and predictions.
- When one student gives an incorrect answer to a question, work with *that student* to correct that answer rather than redirecting the question to another student (Crawford, 1989).
- To increase comprehension, students can be encouraged to formulate their own questions (van den Broek & Kremer, 2000).

Strategies for Improving Comprehension before Reading

The remainder of this chapter focuses on strategies to develop comprehension in narrative text. These strategies are divided according to whether they are used *before, during,* or *after* reading.

This section describes strategies to use before students read. In a classic study, Durkin (1978–1979) found that the first part of a reading lesson is the most crucial and yet the most neglected. This section describes three specific activities: building background knowledge, prediction, and reading a selection to students before they read it for themselves.

Building Background Knowledge

Because background knowledge greatly influences comprehension, it is essential to build knowledge of specific concepts in a story before students read it. How can you do this?

Before students read, teachers can provide factual information about key concepts they will meet in a story (Richek & Glick, 1991). Often, teachers can simply read informational material to students. Factual books, such as *The Kids' Question and Answer Book* (edited by *Owl Magazine*), *Mammoth Book of Trivia* (by Meyers), and a children's encyclopedia are good sources for these read-aloud selections. When you read factual material to low-achieving students, you remind them of what they know about a topic and supply them with new facts. You also increase vocabulary because factual articles mention new vocabulary words that children will meet later in the story they read. Finally, you model the process of summoning up background information before reading.

In one example, before children read a story about a heroic horse, a third-grade teacher read aloud a children's encyclopedia article on horses. The article contained unfamiliar facts, and it used words, such as *mare* and *foal*, that the children later found in their story.

Objects and displays can also help children absorb background knowledge. In preparation for reading a folk tale about Russia, teachers of at-risk fourth graders brought in Russian nesting dolls, ruble currency, postcards, and books written in Russian.

Students can be actively involved in building their own background knowledge. Rather than simply supplying information, you might begin your lesson by asking them what they know about a subject or topic. Before low-achieving third graders read a story about two child detectives, they listed all of the different detectives they knew about. This activity dramatically increased their involvement in the story.

Students can also respond actively to information that the teacher presents. For example, to prepare first graders to read a story about a "sleep out," the teacher read *A New True Book: Sleeping and Dreaming* (by Milios) to them (Richek & Glick, 1991). Then the students dictated their favorite facts as the teacher listed them on the board:

- You grow when you sleep.
- Your eyelids flutter when you sleep.
- When you sleep, you dream.

Predicting and Semantic Impressions

Predicting what a story will be about before reading it gives students an active orientation toward learning and encourages them to use background knowledge. Teachers can simply use prediction or employ a prediction-related strategy called *semantic impressions*.

Predicting.   To help students predict, you might write the title of a book or selection on the board and ask students what they think it will be about or what kind of story it will be. "The Skates of Uncle Richard" will probably involve sports. "How the Duck Learned to Talk to the Pig" probably involves some fantasy.

Students can also predict what a story is about from a list of important story words. For example, after you list the words *witch, invisible,* and *wand,* students might hypothesize that the story is about magic.

Semantic Impressions.   This strategy (McGinley & Denner, 1987) enables children to create their own story by using words that they will later meet in a published story. By writing or dictating their own story, they are actively employing story grammar, using specific vocabulary, and drawing on their own background knowledge. Students may write individual stories, or a class can write a group story. In some classes, students have become so fond of their stories that they have bound them into class books.

The teacher should use the following procedure when using the Semantic Impressions strategy:

1. Before students read a story, the teacher writes important words from it on the board in the (approximate) order they appear.
2. Using their own words, students compose a story. The composed stories must use the words in the order that the teacher has given them. However, words can be reused. Students may dictate a story to the teacher or write out their own.
3. After the students' story is written, they read the published version of the story and compare the two versions. Often, intermediate and upper-grade youngsters like to write about which story they prefer.

Two excellent books to use with this strategy are *The Paper Bag Princess* (by Munsch) and, for young children, *Harriet and the Roller Coaster* (by Carlson). Strategy Snapshot 8.1 shows how semantic impressions was used with *The Paper Bag Princess*.

The semantic impressions strategy has been shown to improve comprehension across a wide variety of grade levels, and is particularly effective with low-achieving readers (McGinley & Denner, 1987; Pearson & Fielding, 1991). This valuable method, which can be used with any story or book, encourages students to think like authors and fosters comparison, a higher-level skill.

Reading a Story to Students

When a story is long or difficult, teachers can read it *to* students before the students read it for themselves. This strategy enables them to learn the story format, sequence of events, and many words in the story before they attempt to read it independently. Prereading stories to students is particularly effective if they are asked to predict what will happen next as they listen. However, prereading should be followed by opportunities for students to read the stories on their own.

Sometimes, simply reading *part* of a story to students is useful. One middle-school teacher reads the first couple of paragraphs of exciting short stories to her students. After their interest has been sparked, students continue to read these stories independently for homework.

Strategies for Improving Comprehension during Reading

Many strategies encourage understanding and enjoyment while students read. This section discusses the Directed Reading-Thinking Activity, using imagery, and Post-it™ note reactions.

The Directed Reading-Thinking Activity (DR-TA)

The Directed Reading-Thinking Activity (DR-TA) (Stauffer, 1975, 1980) is a prediction strategy that models the processes good readers use to comprehend text.

STRATEGY SNAPSHOT 8.1

Semantic Impressions

The Paper Bag Princess (by Munsch) is an excellent story to use with the semantic impressions strategy. In this "twisted" fairy tale, a princess refuses to marry a less-than-gallant prince. Begin by putting the following words from the book on the board:

> *princess*
> *prince*
> *dragon*
> *carried off*
> *chase*
> *bag*
> *forests*
> *fiery breath*
> *meatball*
> *sleep*
> *mess*
> *bum*
> *marry*

Ms. Walega's second-grade class, which included several disabled children, dictated this story:

> There once was a *princess* and a *prince*. The prince went to fight the *dragon*. The dragon got past the prince and *carried off* the princess to his cave. The prince *chased* the dragon. The dragon caught the prince in a *bag*. The dragon went into the *forest* with the prince in a bag. The dragon spit his *fiery breath* and made a fire. He ate a magic *meatball*. Then the dragon fell *asleep*. The dragon made a *mess* of his cave because he was real mad. The prince called the dragon a *bum!* The prince *married* the princess and then he killed the dragon.

After they finished, each disabled child in the class was paired with an on-level student and assigned one sentence to illustrate jointly. The resulting book, entitled "The Horrible Dragon," became part of the classroom library.

Ms. Smith's low-level fourth-grade class (Room 204) produced a somewhat more sophisticated story, which they entitled "The Fire-Breathing Dragon." After reading the published story, students wrote comparisons:

KEVIN: I like 204's story better because it had a happy ending.

CRYSTAL: I like *The Paper Bag Princess* because I hate the prince and the book has a real author.

MICHEL: I like "Fire Breathing Dragon" because it is longer, and we made it.

KATRINA: I like "Fire Breathing Dragon" because it had a lot of activities, and a dragon can't fly, and the prince saved the princess. And boys are supposed to save girls.

For maximum benefit, DR-TA should be used on a long-term basis so that students' reading processes can mature.

The DR-TA should be used with stories that students have not yet read. Before students see the story, the teacher divides it into sections varying from a few paragraphs to a few pages apiece. Generally, the story is divided into four to six parts, each ending at a natural breaking point. When possible, end sections at the bottom of pages. Teachers need not physically divide the text but just keep the sections in mind. Completing the reading of one story may take a few days.

To introduce the selection, write the title on the board before passing out the story. Then ask students to predict what will happen based on the title. For example, in one story entitled "Nate the Great and the Sticky Case" (by Sharmat), fourth-grade resource students predicted that "Something will be stolen," "It's about glue," and "Nate will be stuck somewhere."

Write the individual students' predictions on the board (Richek, 1987). Writing the names of the students next to their predictions increases a feeling of ownership. As each prediction is stated, ask the student his or her reason for making that prediction. For example, the student who predicted that "Something will be stolen" gave as his reason that "the title says 'case' and that means a crime, and that's stealing."

After several predictions are written and explained, hand out the story and have students silently read the first section. When they are finished, guide them in reviewing their earlier predictions. Which ones have actually happened in the story? Which might still happen and should be left on the board? Which need to be revised or erased? Would they like to add any new predictions?

Students then read the next section in the story, and after reading, they again revise their hypotheses. This sequence continues until they have completed the story.

The DR-TA is an extremely motivating strategy, one that often stimulates students to read longer selections and to read silently. In their predictions, students naturally combine background information with the clues in the story to anticipate the ending before they actually read it. Readers also begin to use story structure to form predictions.

Using DR-TA is no more time consuming than reading stories in a traditional manner. Almost any narrative story can be used with this strategy. Students who are reading novels can make predictions before they begin individual chapters.

However, students with reading problems do not always participate freely in a DR-TA. Some read so passively that they have trouble making predictions. In a group situation, shy students can be encouraged to participate by voting "yes" or "no" on some hypotheses. Allowing "abstentions" ensures that even the most passive students will take part. When using DR-TA in an individual situation, a teacher can model involvement by making hypotheses along with the student.

When using DR-TA, students should be told to not look ahead into a following section in the story. The occasional student who looks ahead should be pulled from a group DR-TA and asked to sit on the side without making comments. Of course, such students are unconsciously demonstrating that they see reading as "showing off" the right answer rather than thinking about the material. After using DR-TA several times, even these students will come to value the role of their own thinking in reading stories.

When low-achieving readers do their first DR-TA, their predictions are often highly implausible. Strategy Snapshot 8.2 presents a description of a teacher using DR-TA with low-achieving students. As they continue using the process, predictions will improve. In addition, as a group of students approaches the end of a story, individuals will start to agree on plausible endings. These reactions are important signs of progress in reading narrative text.

The DR-TA is a versatile strategy that can be done in many different ways. At times, you may want to write predictions on the board, and at other times, you may want students simply to give them verbally. Sometimes students who

STRATEGY SNAPSHOT 8.2
DR-TA in a Low-Achieving Fifth-Grade Class

The 31 students in this room used the DR-TA process with the stories in their fourth-grade reading series. The first story described the adventures of a misbehaving boy who interfered with a class experiment about feeding rats.

We first put the title on the board and asked for hypotheses about the story. The four hypotheses focused on a laboratory with a scientist. Then we passed out the story and asked children to read the first page silently and reformulate their hypotheses. After reading page one, students correctly refocused their predictions on the boy, Otis, and a classroom. However, the students identified the animal as a *mouse* rather than a *rat*, so they were asked to go back and reread. We finished two more sets of predictions on the first day, for pages 2–3 and 4–5 of the story.

As we proceeded, student excitement mounted. More students made predictions, and the predictions became more plausible. We ended the day by taking a vote on the weights of the rats in the story. At the conclusion of the lesson, one student, Perry, copied the predictions from the board for use the next day. In fact, three other students also copied them, just to ensure accuracy.

On the second day, Perry recopied the predictions onto the board, and the class did two more prediction segments. Students continued to increase their hypotheses, until we had so many that we were unable to call on all students who wanted to contribute. As the story progressed, students began to agree on their hypothesis for the ending. Thomas, who had been making the others wait because of his slow silent reading, started to speed up his reading rate.

On the third day, the children realized that the story would end. Keana and Ryan met us in the hall before school and asked us whether we could reveal the ending if they wouldn't tell the others. We declined to do this. In class, the ending was finally revealed, to the delight of the children. After the reading was completed, the class had an in-depth discussion of the clues the author gave about the conclusion and of other stories that had similar plots.

disagree with the author's ending for a story enjoy writing and illustrating their own endings. Other variations are using DR-TA but not giving reasons or making predictions silently.

DR-TA without Justification. In this activity (Richek, 1987), readers give predictions but are not asked to supply reasons for them. We began to use DR-TA without justification when we found that many of our students were able to predict but could not give reasons for their predictions. In fact, when asked for justification, some became quite uncomfortable. Some low-achieving students may need to use the DR-TA without justification before moving on to the more challenging step of supplying reasons.

Silent DR-TA. In this strategy, students are each given a story with pre-arranged, written stopping points. Each student reads the selection individually and silently until he or she comes to the first stopping point. Students then *write* their predictions at their desks without discussing them. Then they read until they come to another stopping point and write that prediction. In the last part of the story, the ending is, of course, revealed; and each student can see how close he or she has come to predicting the author's ending.

Silent DR-TA helps older students take responsibility for their own reading and avoids the embarrassment of public discussions (Josel, 1986; Richek, 1987). In addition, making written records of their predictions helps students to monitor their own comprehension. Silent DR-TA motivates students to read silently and respond in writing. After they have completed the story, students look back at their predictions to see how well they caught the clues given in the story.

Using Post-it™ Notes to Monitor Responses to Reading

The Post-it™ Note strategy (Caldwell, 1993a), gives students the opportunity to "talk back" to authors as they are reading silently. The Post-it™ notes, pieces of paper with one sticky edge, can be easily placed on text, removed, and reused. Using small notes helps students to pinpoint the precise part of the reading they are reacting to.

The Post-it™ notes contain three graphic messages:

- An exclamation point to indicate that a reader has been surprised by something.
- A "smiley face" to show that the reader likes something that happened in the story.
- A question mark to note a question that the reader has about something in the story.

Each reader is given three of each type per story or chapter. They can have more if needed.

As students read silently, they place a Post-it™ note wherever they meet something in the story that surprises, delights, or baffles them. In this way, they are recording their own reactions to the text. After they read, the Post-it™ notes make an excellent starting point for discussing a story. For low-achieving students, start by discussing the question-mark Post-it™ notes and then moving to surprising and well-liked parts. Students enjoy seeing that others have the same questions and appreciate the same parts as they do. Sharing responses to reading helps students to build confidence, self-esteem, and a sense of participation. Alvermann (2000) has found that middle-school students have particularly positive views toward such participation.

Making Mental Images

Developing mental imagery in response to reading is an effective way to improve comprehension and interest for students with reading problems (Gambrell & Bales, 1986; Pressley, 2000). When students form mental images as they read, they combine their background information with the text. Reading becomes more personal and relevant as students construct their unique images. In focusing on their own internal responses to text, students become more willing to read silently. Finally, mental imagery helps students to become comfortable reading text without pictures because they create pictures in their own minds.

Comparing their mental images is both enjoyable and instructive for students. When students realize that no two people see precisely the same thing, they learn to value personal response in reading (Sadowski, 1985).

Use mental imagery for students aged eight or above. To ensure maximum impact, use this strategy on a sustained basis.

Building Readiness for Mental Imagery.   To prepare students for reading activities, first develop the students' abilities to form images while *listening* by doing one of the following activities:

- Ask students to close their eyes and imagine that they are seeing their mother, father, or other adult. Each student, in turn, describes what he or she sees.
- Instruct students to imagine a hot-fudge sundae as you, verbally, build it, giving such clues as "I put in two scoops of vanilla ice cream, I slowly pour hot fudge over the top . . ." Ask students to describe the colors they see. Then, without describing the container, ask students the types of containers they imagine. By imagining something that is not directly described, students develop the ability to build a complete mental picture from partial clues, precisely what readers do when they make mental images during reading.
- Read short stories to students and ask them to describe their mental images of the characters.
- The book *Hurricane* (by Weisner) is excellent for developing imagery. In this book, a hurricane knocks over a tree. Two brothers use their imagination to

incorporate this tree into imaginary scenes, such as a safari and a space ship. After reading it, ask students to individually tell you what else they could imagine the tree to be. Responses have included a submarine, gym, airplane, raft, tank, and limousine. One fifth grader saw the tree as a castle and reported seeing dragons, a princess, and birds (because she was up high).

Mental Imagery in Reading.   After forming mental images while listening, students are ready to apply imagery to reading. Simply ask students to read something silently and then focus on their own mental images.

Imagery can be used at several points in a story. Asking for a mental image after the students have read the first few paragraphs of a story helps them to make the rest of the story more vivid. Teachers may also ask for images at places in the story where students would normally be stopped for questions. Finally, if students have read a story independently, imagery can be used as a follow-up strategy.

When working with imagery, ask students to focus on the most important or exciting part of a story and describe it. Focusing on only one image helps students to organize their thoughts and avoids confusing or conflicting responses. You might have students close their eyes immediately after reading to hold their images in their minds.

Despite the value of imagery, some students with reading problems find the strategy difficult to use at first. Teachers need to be patient with a student who reports seeing "nothing" on the first day of instruction. Within a week, such readers will often start to image. If students simply list a sequence of events in the story, special attempts should be made to focus on exciting story parts so that they will become personally involved enough to form an image. You can also focus students on imagining what a character looks like.

If students report seeing images that do not match the text, they have probably misread something. Encourage them to reread the material silently and see if their images change. If students consistently misread, break up stories into shorter segments and follow silent reading with oral reading. This strategy focuses the students' attention on the need to read more carefully.

Mental imagery was used to help Bobby, a fourth grader who had poor comprehension and found silent reading difficult. Bobby silently read the first two paragraphs in a story about a snowstorm. When he was finished, he was asked to describe his image. At first, Bobby could not report anything, but after rereading the paragraphs, Bobby said he saw snow on the lawn, children building a snowman outside, and a car up the street. This imagery activity made him interact with the text, and his comprehension of the story improved dramatically.

Strategies for Improving Comprehension after Reading

Comprehension strategies that can be used after reading include those that develop a sense of story grammar, encourage a personal response, and connect the literacy experience.

Comprehension Strategies that Develop Story Structure

As discussed earlier, narratives are usually written according to certain forms, called story grammars. Most narratives contain the elements of *characters, setting* (time and place), and *plot*. The plot is generally further broken into a *problem* that a character must solve and different *events* (or *episodes*) that take place in the story. The end of the story has a *solution* or *resolution* to the problem. When students recognize these common elements of narratives, they read with more understanding and are better able to make sense of a narrative.

Because many young children do not have a mature concept of story structure (Appleby, 1978), only a few story grammar activities are suitable for low-achieving primary children. However, these students can develop their skills by *listening* to stories and then discussing the plot, characters, and setting of the stories.

Story Maps.   Story maps are visual diagrams that show students the elements that all stories contain. When students use these maps, they learn to identify the common elements of narrative text. Story maps are suitable for both shorter stories and novels. A common story frame map contains (1) characters, (2) setting, (3) problem, and (4) solution. To illustrate, a story map has been filled out for the story "Catalog Cats" in the book *The Stories Julian Tells* (by Cameron). In "Catalog Cats," Julian tells his brother, Huey, about special kinds of cats that work in the garden.

Characters	*Setting*
Julian	In Julian and Huey's house
Huey	
Father	

Problem	*Solution*
Julian tricks Huey into believing that you can order cats from a catalog to do all the work in a garden.	Father tells Huey that catalog cats exist, but they are invisible and don't do all the work. Also, you have to request them, not order them.

A more complex story map suitable for older students contains episodes to link the problem and solution (or resolution). It also contains a goal for the character.

Teachers can introduce story maps before students read and ask them to fill in the frame either during or after reading. They can also give the map to the students after a story has been read and ask them to identify story elements. Students with reading problems often enjoy working on maps in pairs.

Shanahan and Shanahan (1977) suggest using Character Perspective Charts. Students make separate charts for the story elements as seen from the perspective of different important characters. For example, for the folk tale *The Three Little Pigs*, students make two charts: one for the three little pigs and one for the wolf. Each chart contains the setting, problem, goal, attempts to solve the problem, outcome, reaction, and theme from the point of view of the character it charts: in this case, the pigs or the wolf.

Low-achieving readers often need teacher modeling before they can successfully generalize the features of story grammar. Patient teacher demonstration followed by discussion will lead students to using story grammar independently. Remember that story structure is learned gradually and must be practiced consistently over a long period of time.

At times, you will find that students focus on only one part of the story, usually the first part or the most exciting part. To help them refocus on the story as a whole, place a story grammar frame on the board or on an overhead projector and read a short story to them. As they listen to the story, students should try to fill in the story grammar frame. Then reread the story and have them confirm or revise their story grammars.

As students become more comfortable with story grammar, they will become independent of visual maps. At that point, simply use a story grammar framework to guide comprehension by asking such questions as "Who was the main character?" and "What was the central problem in the story?" Students might also enjoy asking each other these questions.

Problem-Solution Identification. The identification of the problem and the solution to that problem in a story is a shortened form of story grammar that is useful for intermediate and secondary students. To encourage long-term learning students can make charts showing the problem of the story in one column and the solution in another.

Because the ability to identify the problem and solution is a sophisticated skill, it requires careful teacher guidance. At first, students may confuse the main problem of the story with the first event. When this situation occurs, teachers should carefully review story structure.

Story Pyramids. Students often enjoy creating their own, personal "pyramids" of stories they have read. In pyramids, students are allowed only eight lines and may only use a certain number of words per line. Each line must describe something different.

The form of a pyramid is:

- One word naming the main character
- Two words describing the main character (for students in grades three and above, encourage the use of adjectives)
- Three words describing the setting (time and place)
- Four words describing the problem (for students in primary grades who have difficulty with problem identification, ask them for four words describing the first thing that happened)

- Five words describing important events
- Six words describing more important events
- Seven words describing more important events
- Eight words describing the ending

If used in a group, the teacher should write the class pyramid on the board for all to see. If used individually, students often like to decorate and illustrate their personal constructions. Pyramids can be used by at-risk readers from kindergarten through high school.

Students with reading problems have made many creative constructions using the pyramid format. Of course, since a pyramid is a personal response, each pyramid will be a little different. Here are two pyramids from third-grade Title I classes in response to reading *Cinderella*:

Cinderella
cute   nice
palace   house   backyard
her mother was dead
stepmother made her sweep floor
She went to the palace ball.
She danced with the prince and ran.
They got married and lived happily ever after.

Cinderella
nice person
past   palace   house
had mean stepmother
had two mean stepsisters
She could not go to the ball
prince found the glass slipper for Cinderella
After they got married they lived very happily.*

*Full sentences are given capital letters and periods.

In constructing these pyramids, the children chose the characters, descriptions, and events that were most important to them. However, because a set number of words was needed, they had to manipulate words and combine them creatively. At times, they had to leave out words. This format encourages creative responses; and in fact, a group of boys in one class insisted on writing an alternative version, using the prince as the major character.

Story pyramids develop many important skills: If students work in groups, they naturally tend to discuss the story, an activity that fosters active comprehension. Pyramids give students practice with the major elements of a story (characters, setting, events). Students learn to separate important events from unimportant ones. Students develop language by manipulating and elaborating words to fit into a specified format. Students review vocabulary and concepts mentioned in the story. Building a pyramid is fun. Youngsters look forward to building and displaying their creations.

In intermediate and upper grades, pyramids make excellent alternatives to traditional book reports. Used as a response to independent reading, the pyramid activity does not require much writing, but it enables students to respond actively to their reading. Furthermore, you will always be able to tell if students have read the book.

Comprehension Strategies that Nurture Personal Response

Readers experiencing difficulties often have problems reacting fully to reading. This section describes strategies that foster creativity, engagement, and enjoyment, so that low-achieving students can see that reading belongs to them.

Drama.   Acting out a story immediately involves readers. As they experience story events from the character's point of view, students with reading problems deepen and improve comprehension (Sebesta, 1993; Wolf, 1998). Drama encourages discussion of a story and fosters cooperation and other social skills in at-risk students.

The *tableaux* strategy is one way to dramatize a story (Purves, Rogers, & Soter, 1995). We have used it effectively at elementary- and secondary-grade levels. In tableaux, students form still lifes, or tableaux, to dramatize story events. To illustrate the scenes, they assume appropriate expressions and body postures. Figure 8.1 shows one scene from the play "The Little Pine Tree" (in *Carousels*, Houghton Mifflin Company, 1989) demonstrated by two second graders in front of appreciative classmates. If possible, capture the tableaux on film.

In tableaux, students put themselves physically into the story. They discuss events as they decide which scenes they will act out. Furthermore, because tableaux involve the students "freezing" the scene, events acquire a permanence that they do not always have in the ongoing action of the story. Because these still lifes are silent, at-risk children are able to focus on the story without the distraction of movement and noise.

Tableaux can be done in many formats. In a large class, students can be divided into several groups; and after the class lists the important events, the teacher can assign one event to each group. If more students are in the group than there are story characters, some can play houses and trees. For young children, playing a noncharacter role helps establish the difference between characters and scenery. More advanced students often enjoy deciding secretly on the scene they will dramatize and asking classmates who watch the tableau to identify it. Secondary students, who are often reading longer material, should be encouraged to pick the most crucial and exciting events to dramatize.

FIGURE 8.1   Tableau of "The Little Pine Tree"

Catch a Rainbow.   Art can be used to foster personal responses to reading. In the Catch a Rainbow strategy (Richek, 1999), students are asked to represent a story or novel in an artistic form. However, because the goal is to encourage imagination, they are told that they cannot draw anything recognizable (e.g., people, trees). Instead, they must use *abstract* art, that is, colors and shapes, to represent the story. In this way, students are freed both from dependence on the illustrations in a book and differences in individual artistic abilities. Because this task requires mature abilities, it is usually limited to students in the fourth grade and above.

After having students read a story, ask them to represent it in abstract art. Give them magic markers. The easy, nonthreatening process takes less than 15 minutes for most students to complete, yet students never fail to amaze us with the originality of their personal artistic interpretations. In one fourth-grade classroom, each student produced a personal picture after reading "The Code in the Mailbox" (by Tapp), a story about a blind man, Mr. James, who is helped by young Tina. In return, Mr. James teaches Tina to read braille. In a minor incident, Tina becomes angry at her mother for making her stop dyeing a T-shirt.

Anthony used pink and yellow to honor the happiness of the story, but he drew strong lines to indicate that Tina had been annoyed at her mother. Although adults would rarely remember Tina's angry feelings, many students, like Anthony, found this incident meaningful.

Sean, a student with severe reading problems, represented braille by dots and used circular patterns to indicate "the confusion of blindness." Jagged lines registered Tina's feelings of anger at being interrupted while dyeing her T-shirt. Note how deeply Sean reacted to this story. Catch a Rainbow gives students a chance to express *their* feelings.

Students must reflect on their pictures by sharing them. Students can explain their drawing to the class or write captioned explanations for their creations and make them into a bulletin board display.

Character Webs. In this activity, the name or picture of a story character is placed in the center of a page and surrounded by the traits of that character. Then, incidents from the story that illustrate each character trait are listed. A character web done by a third grader reading the story *Clifford, the Big Red Dog* (by Bridwell) is presented in Figure 8.2.

Skinny Books. This strategy, which is most useful for primary children, combines the review of a story with a chance to create a personal version of it. To make a skinny book (Richek, 1999), the teacher needs to obtain two extra copies of the children's reading series. Illustrations are cut from a story that the children have just completed reading and pasted into a *skinny book*. (Two copies are needed because many illustrations are on the back sides of facing pages.) A front page should be left for a cover.

Now the students have an opportunity to become "authors" of the story they have just read by dictating their own text to match the story pictures. Generally, students take turns dictating pages. Individuals may want to sign each page that they have dictated.

One group of Title I third graders made a skinny book of the book *Miss Nelson Is Missing* (by Marshall). Authors Robert, Sherri, Travis, and Chris entitled their skinny book "Where Is Ms. Schultz?" Each student dictated a separate page as the teacher recorded their responses in magic marker. As they summarized the story, they changed it into their own words. These four students proudly carried their skinny book back to their regular class and read it to their peers.

Connecting the Literacy Experience

Students deepen their comprehension as they compare different texts and share their literacy experiences with one another. This section discusses two strategies that help students connect literacy experiences: conceptually connected instruction (themes) and genre studies.

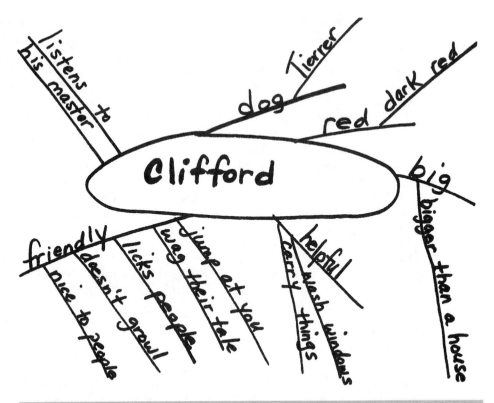

FIGURE 8.2   Character Web of *Clifford the Big Red Dog* by Norman Bridwell ©
1985, published by Scholastic, Inc.

Conceptually Connected Instruction (Themes)

In this strategy, students concentrate on one interesting topic and focus all literacy
activities around it. This strategy offers teachers an opportunity to use students'
interests for instruction, and it helps students to relate associations from known to
unknown material. Thus, a student's interest in football may lead to understanding the business concept of negotiating contracts, bringing lawsuits, and judging
profit margins.

A theme can also lead students to varied types of reading materials. Students
may explore football through stories, newspaper activities, score sheets, encyclo-
pedias, books, and manuals. They will be better able to grasp the structure of sophisticated types of text if they deal with familiar topics. The theme approach is
particularly successful with students who are quite far behind in reading and
need highly motivating instruction.

Elizabeth, a seventeen-year-old reading on a fifth-grade level, decided to research successful women who had, in her words, "made it." Role models were

·chosen from entertainment, sports, and business. Elizabeth read books, collected newspaper articles, watched TV programs, and listened to audiotapes and compact discs. Her teacher brought in technical terms from the three fields. At the end of three months, Elizabeth had dramatically improved her reading skills.

Edmund, a fifth grader reading on a second-grade level, became interested in Hawaii and volcanoes and collected many vivid pictures. For homework, his tutor asked him to find all the ways pineapples were sold in the supermarket. His results became a written essay featuring 15 different types of pineapples. Edmund also read travel brochures, maps, and social studies textbooks. At the end of instruction, he gave his tutor a fresh pineapple as a gift.

Twelve-year-old Eugene, who was reading on a third-grade level, was intrigued by the escape artist Houdini. After starting with some easy books, he read through all the books in the school and local libraries. Before another hero replaced Houdini, Eugene had made several trips to the central New York City Public Library to read about him.

Sometimes teachers must suggest a topic for a passive student. In the case of Oneka, a 14-year-old student, her tutor chose *food*. She explored the history of popcorn, the taste of egg rolls, and how to eat gyros and incidentally gathered much information about the world.

The theme approach motivates low-achieving students to read a wide variety of reading materials. At the same time, teachers can focus on specific comprehension strategies.

Studying Different Genres

Studying a genre, such as mystery stories or fairy tales, allows disabled readers to connect and compare their readings. Students should read many examples of one genre and then compare their common features. For example, Marcus, a sixth-grader who loved watching mysteries on TV, was motivated to read several with his tutor. Marcus made a chart listing how each story contained the crime, the detective, the clues to solve the mystery, and the solution.

Students with reading problems also love to explore fairy and folk tales. Students can chart the features of magic, hero, villain, beginning words (such as "once upon a time"), and ending for each tale.

Students can also compare different versions of one tale. Cinderella has been told in many versions: in *Prince Cinders* (by B. Cole), the lead is cast as a picked-on boy. The story of the three little pigs has been published as *The True Story of the Three Little Pigs* (by Szieska), a hilarious revisionist version told from the wolf's point of view, and *The Three Little Wolves and the Big Bad Pig* (by Trivizas), which reverses the usual roles. Hans Christian Andersen's tale "The Emperor's New Clothes" has been recast in a school as *The Principal's New Clothes* (by Calmenson).

Students can compare two versions of a tale using a Venn diagram, or two partially overlapping circles. The common portions contain the things that are alike about the two tales. The unique portions list things that appear in only a single tale. Figure 8.3 shows a Venn diagram that Sheila and her tutor constructed

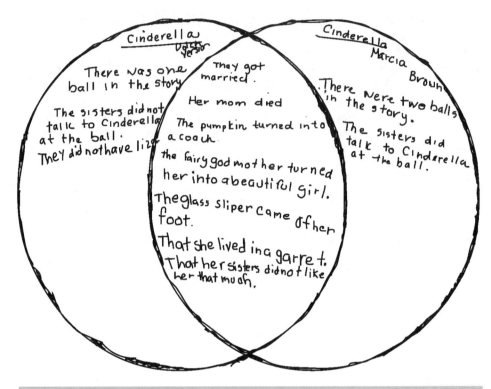

FIGURE 8.3 **Venn Diagram for** *Cinderalla*

for two versions of Cinderella. In exploring and recording differences between these different versions, students gain flexibility in thinking.

Summary

The purpose of reading is comprehension. General features of effective comprehension include (1) realizing that you read to comprehend, (2) realizing that comprehension requires the reader to actively construct a text in his or her mind, a process that accurately reflects the material that the author has written, (3) applying personal background knowledge appropriately to text, and (4) employing higher-level thinking to understand text. Too much teacher questioning discourages active responses to stories.

Narratives, or texts that tell stories, inspire imaginative personal responses. They also have certain organizational factors, including story grammars (characters, setting, plot). They include many different genres, such as adventure, fantasy, and science fiction.

To assess abilities with narrative text, you can use the comprehension tests from general standardized tests. In addition, you can judge whether a student has comprehended a specific text well by using story retelling and questioning.

Strategies for improving comprehension *before reading* include building background knowledge, predicting what will happen in a story, having students build a semantic impressions story from selected story words, and reading students the story to support comprehension.

Strategies for improving comprehension *during reading* include using the Directed Reading-Thinking Activity, a prediction strategy used while reading; using Post-it™ notes to mark pleasing, surprising, and puzzling parts of text; and responding with mental images.

Strategies for improving comprehension *after reading* can develop an understanding of story structure through story maps (using characters, settings, events), identifying the problem and solution, and building "pyramids" that retell stories in a format of eight lines that each contain one to eight words. To nurture personal response after reading, drama (including tableaux still lifes), a Catch a Rainbow response in abstract art, character webs with visual displays of traits, and skinny books that rewrite stories in students' own words can be used.

Finally, the literacy experience may be connected through the study of one theme or doing genre studies on, say, the characteristics of fairy tales.

9 Improving Comprehension of Expository Text

Introduction

As students move through the grades, the reading tasks that confront them change dramatically. Stories become less important, and work with expository, or informational, text increases.

Students are often assigned to read science and social studies textbooks independently. Thus, without any help, students are expected to read a chapter, complete a written assignment, and participate in class discussion. Not surprisingly, many low-achieving readers cannot do these tasks.

This chapter first describes the nature of expository material and discusses why it tends to be more difficult than stories and novels. Next, it describes strategies for assessing the abilities of students to read and study from expository text. Finally, it discusses three kinds of strategies for helping students with reading problems deal with expository material: using background knowledge, monitoring comprehension, and reorganizing or transforming expository text. The focus is on developing independent readers who eventually apply these strategies in the absence of a teacher.

Nature of Expository Text

Expository text conveys information, explains ideas, or presents a point of view.

Types of Expository Text

Expository material is usually organized in one of five ways (Englert & Hiebert, 1984; Horowitz, 1985; Meyer & Freedle, 1984; Taylor, 1992):

- *Sequence or time order* is often used to present events such as the French and Indian War (in history class) or cell division (in biology class).
- *Listing* (or description) is used to explain the features of an object or event. Biology textbooks list the features of reptiles, giving their body temperature, reproductive habits, eating habits, etc.
- *Compare and contrast* involves discussing similarities and differences. A social studies text might compare a congressional system of government with a parliamentary system; a science text might contrast several planets in the solar system.
- A *cause-effect* pattern outlines reasons for events. The author describes an event (such as the fall of Fort Sumter) and explains what caused the event and the effects that followed from it.
- Authors using the *problem-solution* pattern discuss a problem and then suggest possible solutions. A history author might discuss the events in a U.S. President's life in terms of the problems he faced and how he solved them.

Skilled adult readers recognize these organizational patterns and use them to facilitate comprehension (van Dijk & Kintsch, 1983). However, recognizing such patterns is not always easy. The ability to recognize and remember these patterns depends to a large degree on the reader's sensitivity to organizational patterns (Baumann, 1986).

In addition, expository materials often do not conform precisely to the patterns described. Authors may combine two patterns. For example, a listing or description of the battle of Vicksburg may be intertwined with the cause-effect pattern. Or two readers may see different patterns in the same text. An account of how trade goods in the Middle Ages were brought from Asia to Europe could be interpreted as description, problem-solution, or sequence.

Expository text also requires readers to understand main ideas and supporting details.

Difficulties Presented by Expository Text

Expository text presents difficulties for students with reading problems:

- Recognizing and using the author's organizational patterns is a complex task.
- Expository text is less personal than narrative text.
- In reading expository text, students are often required to demonstrate their understanding by taking tests.
- Expository text usually contains more difficult vocabulary and technical terms than narrative text.
- Reading expository text often requires extensive background information.
- Expository text tends to be longer than narrative text. This length may simply overwhelm students with reading problems.
- The reading level of school textbooks is often well above the frustrational level of students with reading problems.

Assessing Abilities with Expository Text

This section presents strategies for judging how well students can handle expository materials. To successfully read and remember expository text, students must do three things: use background knowledge, monitor their own comprehension, and reorganize or transform the text to remember it. The assessment and teaching of expository text is organized around these three components.

Focusing the Informal Reading Inventory on Expository Text

You can gain valuable insights into a student's ability to handle expository text by adapting the informal reading inventory (IRI) procedure to the student's own textbook.

Choose a passage of 200 to 400 words that has a clearly defined beginning, middle, and end. Duplicate the passage so you will have a copy to write on but have the student read from the book. Prepare 10 questions to ask the student that focus on important ideas in the passage. A reader cannot realistically be expected to remember insignificant details after one reading.

Have the student read the selection silently and allow him or her to reread the passage or study it for a short time before responding to the questions. When the student is ready, ask the questions. If the student scores below 70 percent, have the student look back in the text to find the answers to the missed questions. If a student can raise his or her score to an instructional level, the initial low score was probably due to memory problems rather than lack of comprehension. The ability to look back and find answers to incorrect questions also indicates that the student is monitoring his or her comprehension. If the student is unsuccessful when looking back, have the student reread the passage orally to help you determine if word recognition difficulties are interfering with comprehension.

To judge the level of the passage, use the comprehension score and, if the student reads orally, the word recognition accuracy score. The guidelines in Chapter 3, Table 3.1, can help you determine whether this passage is at an independent, instructional, or frustrational level.

If the student is at a frustrational level for word recognition, do not pursue further assessment or instruction in this textbook. If the student scores at the instructional level for word recognition but at a frustrational level for comprehension, you will need to probe further by using the procedures that follow.

Assessing the Use of Background Knowledge

Good readers use what they know about a topic to help them understand expository text. One way to determine whether a student uses prior knowledge is to compare performance on familiar and unfamiliar expository texts. Again, use the IRI procedure but choose selections that you think may be familiar to the student and ones that you believe are relatively unfamiliar. Ask the student to tell you what he or she knows about the topic of the passage. For example, if the passage is about Roosevelt's New Deal, ask the student for information on Franklin Roosevelt or the New Deal.

Next, have the student silently read a familiar passage and an unfamiliar one. You can expect that students who use their background knowledge as they read will perform better with familiar text. If a student performs equally well in both passages, you should teach the strategies for using background information that are presented later in this chapter.

Assessing Comprehension Monitoring

Skilled readers are continually aware of their own comprehension as they read expository text. In contrast, students with reading problems are often not aware of their comprehension processes and therefore do not take steps to solve problems that they may encounter in reading.

One way to assess comprehension monitoring is to use an expository passage that the student found difficult. Ask the student to go through the passage and identify "something that you found hard" or "something you didn't understand." After the student identifies these parts, try to determine whether the student actually found this section difficult or just selected something at random. You might say, "Was it a word that bothered you or a group of words?" "Is there an idea that you did not understand?" If your student tells you that *everything* was hard, reverse this procedure and ask the student to find one or two things that were easier than the rest.

Another way to assess comprehension monitoring is to ask the student to find answers to questions that were answered incorrectly. You can have the student underline the answers to literal questions. However, inferential questions demand that the reader combine background knowledge with the author's clues. For these questions, ask the student to identify anything in the selection that gives clues for answering higher-level questions. If the student cannot identify anything, provide the clue and see if he or she can use it to arrive at a correct answer. Going back into the text to correct questions requires active comprehension monitoring. In fact, you will actually be teaching as you assess comprehension.

Assessing Ability to Transform Text for Studying

Many students understand a text while they are reading but quickly forget it afterward. As a result, they perform poorly on tests. To study effectively, students must transform the text in some way so that they can remember it. For example, they must reorganize the text to identify and set apart important ideas. Students often use the tools of underlining and note-taking to help in this transformation.

To assess the student's ability to study from text, choose an expository passage and ask the student to take notes as if he or she were studying for a test. You can ask the student to underline or to choose the form of note-taking that he or she prefers. Either method enables you to identify the student who cannot pick out important main ideas, take effective notes, or reorganize the text.

Strategies for Helping Students Read Expository Text

This section focuses on strategies that can lead students to read and study expository text independently. The strategies presented are learned slowly and must be used on a long-term basis. As a teacher, you will need to model them repeatedly. You must encourage students to verbalize what they are doing, why they are doing it, and how they are proceeding. After choosing a strategy, stay with it for some length of time. Having students construct bookmarks containing the steps of a strategy also helps. They can tuck these into their content area textbooks.

When teaching students with reading difficulties to deal with expository text, try to use textbooks written at their instructional level. If you must deal with frustrational-level textbooks, you should read the text to the students in four- or five-paragraph chunks while they follow along in their books. You can also combine some form of assisted or repeated reading with the lesson. McCormack and Paratore (1999) found that teacher reading in combination with various forms of assisted and repeated reading effectively compensated for having to use a frustrational-level text.

Strategies for Combining Prior Knowledge with Expository Text

Even if you possess only a small amount of knowledge about a topic, you can use this knowledge to read more effectively. When you use your knowledge of a topic as you read, you look for familiar "landmarks," or background knowledge. For example, in reading about Theodore Roosevelt, you summon up your landmarks. You might remember when he lived and that he was a soldier, a president, and an environmentalist. You use these landmarks to organize your reading by mentally categorizing information you read in the text under these general topics.

Students with reading problems have two difficulties with background knowledge: (1) They generally have less background knowledge than good readers because they do not read as much. (2) They often do not apply the background knowledge they *do* have to their reading. In fact, they are so used to regarding themselves negatively that they often are not even aware of the knowledge and abilities they can bring to text. These problems are intensified because often content-area teachers assign chapters without preparing students for what they will be reading.

Two strategies, the expectation grid and K-W-L, are effective in teaching students to combine their prior knowledge with expository text. The expectation grid begins with general categories and moves to specific items of information. In contrast, K-W-L begins with specific bits of knowledge and moves to the general categories. With careful guidance, both can be used independently and mentally by students.

The Expectation Grid.   Constructing an expectation grid is a strategy that students can use independently to prepare for reading expository material (Caldwell, 1993b). Students first learn how to construct an expectation grid in written form. Eventually, however, the formation of the grid becomes a mental exercise that students do before reading.

As a good reader, you probably construct mental expectation grids without even being aware of them. For example, suppose you are about to read an article on a new bill before Congress. Even if you know nothing about the bill, you have certain expectations about the categories of information that you will read in the article. You expect the author to explain the purpose of the bill and describe who is supporting and opposing it. These expectations come from your knowledge of how government works. They are the landmarks that allow you to organize your reading.

Students with reading problems can be taught to approach reading with similar expectations. They may know little about the French and Indian War that they are studying, but they often know a lot about wars. Even if this knowledge comes from war movies and the Star Trek TV series, it can help them to form expectations about the categories discussed in their textbook.

To make an expectation grid, students create an organized visual representation of their knowledge before they read. A general topic (war, animals, important people, etc.) is placed in the center of the page and, around this topic, students write categories of information they expect to read about. For example, if the topic is an animal, you can expect that the author will describe the animal's appearance, behavior (movement, noise, temperament, etc.), habitat, and mating they habits. Perhaps they will learn about the animal's relationship to people. Do people use it for food or clothing? Is it dangerous? Figure 9.1 is an example of an expectation grid on the topic of *animal*.

Suppose you are reading about the *ratel*. We suspect that you do not know much about this animal. However, as a skilled reader, you expect the categories of information described, and you use them to organize your thoughts as you read and recall information.

To teach students the use of expectation grids, choose part of a chapter and help students preview it by reading headings and looking at maps, graphs, or pictures. This preview helps students choose a topic for the center of the grid. Remember that the topic must be a general one such as animal, war, country, etc. Write the topic on the grid and then model how your knowledge of this general topic allows you to form expectations for the categories of information that will be in the reading.

Let us suppose that your text is an account of the French and Indian War. Put the general topic, *war*, in the center of the grid. Next, ask the students what they know about wars, perhaps from movies, television, or stories of others. Guide

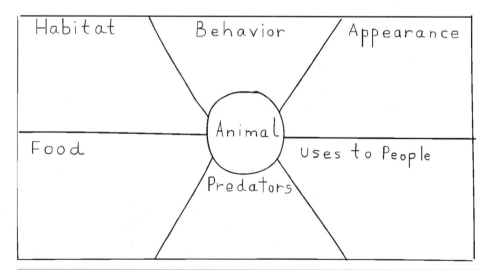

FIGURE 9.1   Expectation Grid for Animal

them to recognize such categories as who fought the war, where it was fought, causes of the war, effects of the war, who won it, and what weapons were used. Write these categories on the grid.

After you have determined your general categories of information, write *French and Indian War* under *war*. Ask the students what they know about the French and Indian War. Perhaps there are some hints in the text that they learned about during their preview. The students might have information from their own background to add to information from the preview. As students offer what they know about the French and Indian War, have them identify the proper category and write the information on the grid.

Fill in the grid as long as the students have information to offer but always have them indicate which category their information goes under. You may need to add new categories to accommodate some information.

What if a student offers something that you know is not true? Perhaps a student says that the French and Indian War was between the French and the Indians. If other students question this, put a question mark next to the item and indicate that effective learners read to answer questions. However, if no one questions it, simply let it be. You will return to the grid after reading, and at that point, erroneous information can be corrected. Students often can identify incorrect information as they read, and they are eager to correct their grid after they finish. This opportunity for correction is one of the most valuable features of an expectation grid. Students can also use the grid to take notes as they read by adding items to each category.

As you and the students construct an expectation grid, repeatedly explain that this activity is something they should do by themselves before they read. Tell students that a grid does not need to be written. In fact, the most efficient expectation grid is one that is done mentally.

Table 9.1 presents some general topics with expected categories of information. This table is merely meant as a guide, and you should feel free to modify these categories as you and your students see fit. For students in the primary and intermediate grades, use only two or three categories. Always have a category titled "other" for items of information that do not fit into your chosen categories.

Strategy Snapshot 9.1 and Figure 9.2 (p. 226) present an example of a class contructing an expectation grid.

The K-W-L Strategy.   This strategy activates prior knowledge before reading expository text and facilitates retention. Like the expectation grid, students can use K-W-L independently. The initials of K-W-L (Ogle, 1986) represent:

K - What I know
W - What I want to find out
L - What I learned

K - What I Know.   Ask students to preview part of an expository selection. Then have them think of everything that they know about the topic. List their responses on the board.

TABLE 9.1   Topics and Categories for an Expectation Grid

Animal: appearance; behavior; habitat; mating habits; life cycle; food; predators; uses to people.

Plant: type; appearance; habitat; uses; life cycle; enemies.

Important person: achievements, obstacles, personal characteristics; sequence of life; friends or associates; enemies.

Important event: causes; why important; description; people involved; countries involved; sequence; effects.

Country, city or state: location; size, geographical features; government; industry; culture; landmarks.

War: location; time; causes; effects; countries involved; significant events or battles; important people; methods of warfare.

Process: who carries it out; needed organisms; needed materials; end products; possible problems; usefulness.

Government: form of government; structure of government; when established; problems; current status.

Pupils may present some misinformation. For example, a group of low-achieving fourth graders studying the state of Washington said that "the President lives there." If they offer such misinformation, you may simply list it, as with the expectation grid, and wait for students to read and make corrections. For students who have many misperceptions, you might want to use the category "What I Think I Know" (instead of "What I Know"). This category naturally leads students to correct any misinformation after reading.

After they give information, ask students to examine their pooled information and classify it into categories. The fourth-grade class just described found this direction quite confusing at first. To begin the classification, the teacher suggested the category of mountains. The students were then able to suggest items to fit under this category. Stimulated by this hint the students were then able to add categories such as work, weather, and visiting.

W - What I Want to Find Out.   Ask each student to write down the things that he or she wants to find out or expects to learn. The W step is often difficult for low-achieving readers, as they do not have well-developed expectations of expository material. One fourth-grade boy wanted to learn, "Do nice people live in Washington?" a question he would be unlikely to learn from his text. As he experienced K-W-L over a period of several weeks, however, his expectations of text began to mature. Other children wanted to learn things that were not answered in the text but could be answered from other sources. One girl wondered how many people had been injured or killed in the eruption of Mt. St. Helens. Such questions help students realize that learning does not stop with a single textbook, and sev-

STRATEGY SNAPSHOT **9.1**

Constructing an Expectation Grid

Ms. Scanlon works with a small group of high school students who are using an expectation grid for their world history text. She helps them preview five pages on how Spanish colonies in the New World gained independence. The students decide that the topic is an important event.

She then asks them to describe some important events. Students describe a murder charge brought against a city official, an earthquake, a famine in Africa, a local train wreck, the Super Bowl, and a destructive blizzard. Ms. Scanlon asks them to imagine that they were writing about these events to someone who had never heard about them. What information would they include?

As the students offer information about their chosen event, Ms. Scanlon guides them to see how descriptions of important events are similar: they involve people, list specific places, tell why the event was important, describe causes and effects, and list events in order of time (first this happened, next this, etc.). Ms. Scanlon writes the categories: people, location, cause, effects, sequence, why important. She then writes Spanish colonies gain independence under important event and asks the students what they know about the Spanish colonies' fight for independence.

Using the headings from their book preview, students offer the expected information that the colonies had grievances, they were influenced by the American and French revolutions, Haiti gained independence early, and Father Hidalgo began Mexico's struggle. Using pictures, the students add Toussaint L'Ouverture to their grid.

When they run out of preview information, Ms. Scanlon suggests that they think of the American Revolution and leads them to offer the information that war was probably involved, people might have died, and Spain probably fought the colonies. They decide that Spain acted toward its colonies like England did toward the United States: taxing people and depriving them of rights. Finally, they suggest that colonies formed new governments when they became independent. Ms. Scanlon asks students to identify the category where each piece of information fits.

When the expectation grid is complete, Ms. Scanlon reminds the students to look for these categories as they read. One student comments that she knew more about the topic than she thought. Ms. Scanlon gives each student a blank grid and suggests using it for notes during reading. After reading, the students compare their notes and add information to the grid on the board.

Figure 9.2 shows the expectation grid that the students completed before they began reading their text.

eral learners began to bring in other resources. Often teachers use these unanswered questions as the basis for research projects to extend students' learning.

L - What I Learned. Ask students to read a section of the chapter. If the text is at their instructional level, they should read silently. If it is too difficult for them, use assisted reading or read it to them. Then, have each student write down

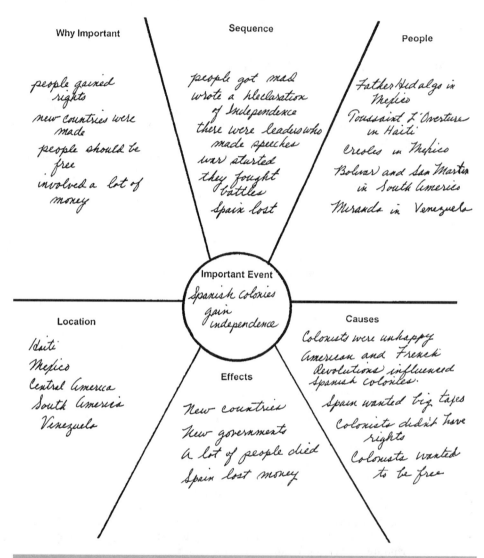

FIGURE 9.2   Expectation Grid on Spanish Colonies Gaining Their Independence

what he or she learned from reading. After recording their learning, students are usually eager to share new knowledge with others. Continue this process throughout the chapter.

Before beginning the text chapter, the fourth graders listed all that they knew or wanted to know about Washington. Then daily, as they read each of the four sections of the text, they did a K-W-L sheet for each section. To conclude the unit, the students listed all of the things that they learned about Washington and wrote a composition. Working with K-W-L, the students became more adept at understanding and remembering expository text. The K-W-L strategy can also be used to write responses that enhance comprehension (Jennings, 1991).

Strategies for Monitoring the Comprehension of Expository Text

Good readers constantly monitor their comprehension as they read. They make predictions, ask questions, and look for prior knowledge landmarks. If their comprehension falters, they stop reading and attempt to make sense of the text by rereading, identifying what confused them, and possibly using context to identify word meanings. The awareness of one's own mental activities and the ability to direct them is called *metacognition*.

Students with reading problems generally lack metacognition in reading. Because they often do not expect reading to make sense, they let their eyes move over the text and proceed on, unconcerned that they understand almost nothing. This passive orientation toward reading is one reason why low-achieving students have comprehension problems (Jenkins, Heliotis, Hayes, & Breck, 1986; Johnston, 1984). Researchers have shown that by developing an awareness of monitoring strategies, low-achieving readers can increase their learning. (Brown & Palinscar, 1982; van den Broek & Kremer, 2000). The strategies of text coding, topic/detail/main idea, think-aloud, and reciprocal teaching help students both to demand and to obtain meaning from text.

Text Coding.   Text coding (used by Caldwell, 1993c) teaches students with reading problems to recognize and remember known information, newly learned information, and remaining questions. Teaching students with reading problems to recognize these three things is an important first step in teaching them to monitor their comprehension. To make this activity short and concrete, teach them to code text, using symbols: Use a plus sign (+) to indicate something the reader already knows. Mark new information with an exclamation mark (!). Mark questions with a question mark (?). To avoid defacing books, place these symbols on small Post-it™ notes.

Teacher modeling is the best way to show students how to code text. Remember that you are teaching a *mental* process, one that you would like students eventually to do in their heads without the aid of written codes. At first, the coding symbols help to make the thinking process visible and bring it to the student's attention. Later, however, you will want the students to do this mentally.

When you teach students to use text coding, begin by getting an oral response. First, read an expository selection to them and model the coding process by stopping periodically to report information that you already knew, information you just learned, and questions you have. Invite the students to join you in talking about what they already knew or something they just learned. Do they have any questions? As you proceed, stop at specific pieces of information in the text and ask students to respond to them.

Low-achieving students tend to say they already knew an item of information when, in fact, they didn't. Refrain from criticizing them in this first stage; as the strategy proceeds, they will become more comfortable identifying new information. If students continue to say that everything was known, you might want to simplify the process by using only two categories: unknown facts, and questions. In addition, students just beginning this process will have difficulties framing questions. Again, their abilities to ask good questions will increase as you model and guide their efforts.

If some students simply echo what their peers say, you might require each student to make a personal decision about text by constructing individual coding cards. Take index cards or Post-it™ notes and print the coding symbols (+, !, ?) on each side. After giving each student one for each coding symbol, read a segment of expository text to them. Ask them to hold up one of the index cards to indicate whether they already knew this information, had just learned it, or had a question. When doing this activity, you may ask for a student's explanation.

After students have grasped the idea of identifying what they already knew, what they just learned, and what questions they have, move on to a written format. Choose a short segment of expository text and show it to the students. For a large group, you might want to code the text on an overhead. Students in a small group can sit around you and watch as you write the coding symbols on the page. As you read the text, think aloud about what you already knew, what you just learned, and what questions you have. At each item, mark the coding symbols on the text. (You can lightly pencil them in on the page or attach Post-it™ notes containing !, +, ?) The use of written symbols is an important step that makes a mental strategy visible for the students.

As a next step, students should each receive an individual copy of a short text (no more than one page) to read silently and code for themselves in the margins or above a line of print. Before students read, the teacher should decide how often they need to react. In the early stages of strategy instruction, or with easy text, you should code each sentence. However, as text gets more difficult, many different items of information can be included in a single sentence, so one sentence could have several different codes. For example, Kenneth coded one sentence by indicating already known (+) for the fact that cicada eggs hatched but just learned (!) for the fact that the animals from hatched eggs are called nymphs. He also had a question (?) because he wondered why they were called nymphs. Figure 9.3 shows Josh's coding of a paragraph about the cicada.

Coding is a flexible strategy that can be used orally or in writing to guide the understanding of any type of expository text. However, teaching this strategy requires a generous amount of teacher modeling and student response. Students need to verbalize what they are doing, why they are doing it, and how it should be done.

Twelve-year-old Tischa wrote that she used the coding strategy in this way:

1. If you already knew something put a plus and skip it when you review.

FIGURE 9.3 Josh's Text Coding

The female cicada lays $\overset{+}{}$ her eggs in tree $\overset{!}{}$ branches. She makes tiny $\overset{+}{}$ holes in the wood and $\overset{?}{}$ lays her eggs in these holes. The cicada eggs hatch $\overset{+}{}$ into nymphs. Nymphs are very $\overset{!}{}$ small and they look like $\overset{!}{}$ worms. The nymphs crawl down the trees and bury $\overset{!}{}$ themselves in the ground. They stay in the $\overset{!}{}$ ground for 17 $\overset{?}{}$ years! They feed on tree $\overset{!}{}$ roots. During the 17 years, the nymph slowly $\overset{!}{}$ turns into a cicada. It finally comes out of the ground and climbs into a tree. After it sheds its $\overset{!}{}$ skin, it can $\overset{+}{}$ fly. The cicada lives on $\overset{?}{}$ tree leaves and other plants but only lives for 6 $\overset{!}{}$ more weeks.

Josh's questions, each corresponding to a mark on the paper, were:

How many eggs does she lay?

Why do they call them nymphs?

Why don't they freeze in winter?

Do they hurt the trees?

2. If its (sic) new info and you understand it circle a key word and put an exclamation point.
3. If its (sic) confusing put a question mark and reread it or ask somebody.
4. This can help when you read new, hard, and long things.

Nine-year-old Justin explained the coding strategy by writing:

When I read I THINK
- about what I already know
- about what I will learn
- bout what questions to be ansed (sic)
I Love to think!

The Topic-Detail-Main Idea Strategy.   As they read expository text, competent readers consciously try to determine the main ideas and supporting facts. In doing this process, they effectively interrelate facts by forming a core of main ideas and a cluster of facts around those ideas. Interrelating information reduces memory load and allows more effective study.

However, constructing main ideas is a complex ability that requires many component skills (Afflerbach, 1987; Brown & Day, 1983; Goldman & Rakestraw, 2000). Because they are often not stated directly in the text, learning to identify main ideas requires careful and systematic teaching over an extended period of time. Students with reading problems tend to remember interesting, rather than important, information. Often these intriguing details obscure the more important main points (Alexander & Jetton, 2000).

In addition, low-achieving students have often formed misconceptions about main ideas, sometimes based on previous instruction. They believe that every paragraph contains a main idea, which is stated in a topic sentence. However, the reality is much more complex. An analysis of social studies texts in grades two, four, six, and eight found that only 44 percent of the paragraphs contained topic sentences. The same study discovered that only 27 percent of short passages in the social studies texts had topic sentences stating the main ideas (Baumann & Serra, 1984).

Students with reading problems also believe that the first sentence in the paragraph is the topic sentence. Asked to take notes on main ideas, Allison cheerfully underlined the first sentence in every paragraph. She then put down her pencil and announced, "I'm all done. It was real easy." In reality, finding the main idea requires hard work and careful monitoring of one's comprehension. As you read, you need to be aware of the topic of the paragraph, what you are learning about the topic, and what is the most important statement that the author has made to explain the topic (Aulls, 1986).

The Topic-Detail-Main Idea strategy is based on the strategies used by mature readers to construct main ideas and recognition of the organizational patterns of text. As with all expository text strategies, you will need to model the Topic-Detail-Main Idea strategy on a regular basis. In this strategy, students identify the topic of a paragraph, the details of a paragraph, and the main ideas of a paragraph. The main idea often must be *constructed* by the student.

The steps of the strategy are as follows:

1. Read the entire selection.
2. Reread the first paragraph and identify the topic of the paragraph. (The topic is what the paragraph is about). State the topic in one or two words. You can figure out a topic by asking yourself what each sentence is talking about.
3. Now, underline, in your paragraph, each thing that the author tells you about the topic. These ideas are the details.
4. Now that you have the topic and details, check to see if there is a main idea sentence (a topic sentence). Remember that each detail should be connected to this sentence.
5. If you don't find a main idea sentence, and you probably won't, construct one. Asking yourself these questions helps:

   - Is the author describing something: a person, a thing, a process, or an event?
   - Is the author comparing or contrasting two or more things?
   - Is the author explaining a problem or a solution?
   - Is the author explaining a cause and effect?

As students begin to construct their own main idea sentences, they often use statements such as "The author is describing the cicada's life cycle" or "The author is listing problems with the way we get rid of garbage." These main idea statements provide a good framework for clustering facts.

In modeling the Topic-Detail-Main Idea strategy, duplicate a section of the students' textbook and write directly on the page or use an overhead transparency. You might write the topic in one color and underline the details in a second color. If the paragraph contains a topic sentence, underline it in a third color or use this color to write your constructed main idea sentence. The different colors help students to visualize a strategy that, like the other strategies discussed, should eventually be done mentally.

Share with students that not every paragraph contains a main idea. Often several small paragraphs can be joined together to form one main idea unit, or long paragraphs can be split into two main idea units. A selection may also include introductory, transition, and summary paragraphs that do not really contain main ideas. Students often call these paragraphs "get going" paragraphs, "glue" paragraphs, and "bye-bye" paragraphs. Strategy Snapshot 9.2 illustrates the Topic-Detail-Main Idea procedure.

Think-Aloud Strategy. In this strategy, the teacher thinks out loud and models the way that a skilled reader makes sense of text. Pressley and Afflerbach (1995) provide an extensive summary of the cognitive behaviors that readers engage in as they read. The Think-Aloud strategy "has the potential to examine what a reader does to facilitate comprehension" (Myers & Lytle, 1996, p. 140) and the potential to be used effectively as an instructional activity (Bereiter & Bird, 1985; Davey, 1983; Nist & Kirby, 1986; Wade, 1990). Skilled readers use more and varied strategies during reading than poor readers, and those who attempt to build relationships between ideas demonstrate better comprehension than those who do not (Crain-Thoreson, Lippman, & McClendon-Magnuson, 1997; Goldman, 1997). Think-aloud procedures have been studied with readers of all ages, and with appropriate modeling, most ages can engage in think-alouds.

To use the Think-Aloud strategy, select a short passage that contains unknown words and other points of difficulty. Give the passage to each student and retain one copy for yourself. Read the passage aloud, stopping after each paragraph. Verbalize the thought processes you used in trying to make sense of the passage and ask students to do the same. Leslie and Caldwell (2000) modeled the following activities and guided students to do the same:

- Paraphrase or summarize the text in your own words. For example, say "This is all about how the war started with the assassination of the Archduke. It describes the countries on both sides."
- Create new meaning. Predict what might come next. Make an inference. Form a visual image. For example, say "I bet the Allies really wanted to hurt Germany for starting the war. A lot of times, winners really try to get back at the losers." or "I suppose the next paragraph will tell why Germany didn't want to sign the treaty."

STRATEGY SNAPSHOT **9.2**

Topic-Detail-Main Idea Strategy

Ms. Gillman and a small group of fifth-grade low-achieving readers used this selection:

> The elephant is the largest living animal and one of the most intelligent, and yet elephants are rather easily captured. They are very nearsighted, and so they cannot see anything distinctly unless it is close to them. Hunters take advantage of this to get near to elephants they wish to capture. Even if discovered, a person can escape an angry elephant by getting out of its line of vision.
>
> There are two kinds of elephants, the Asian (or Indian) elephant and the African elephant. Next time you are at the zoo, look at each kind, especially at their ears and sizes. See if you can tell the difference.
>
> Both the Asian and African elephants roam about in herds. The leader is usually an older female elephant. When grass becomes scarce in one valley, she will decide when and where to go next. The younger elephants follow her in single file to better grazing land.
>
> Members of the herd will often help one another. Once when an elephant was wounded by a hunter, others of the herd helped it to escape. Two large elephants walked on either side of the wounded animal to keep it from falling.

Excerpt from "One of the Smartest," *New Practice Readers, Book E*, 2nd ed., Phoenix Learning Resources, 1988, by permission of publishers.

Students first read the entire selection orally together and then reread the first paragraph. Ms. Gillman guided the students to see that each sentence was about elephants so this topic was written in the margin by the first paragraph. They then underlined information about the elephants and looked for a main idea sentence. When one student suggested that the first sentence was the main idea, Ms. Gillman asked if all the sentences talked about the elephant as large, intelligent, and easily captured. They agreed that none of the other sentences mentioned size or intelligence and only the third sentence talked about capture. The group decided that they had to make up their own main idea sentence. They used step 5 of the strategy and decided that the main idea sentence was "The author is describing elephants." Ms. Gillman asked if the author was describing a particular thing about the elephant. After some lively discussion, the group changed their original main idea sentence to "The author is describing the elephant's eyesight."

The second paragraph puzzled the students. Ms. Gillman suggested that they skip this paragraph and move on to the next one. She explained that not all paragraphs have main ideas.

The students reread the third paragraph and decided that the topic was elephant herds and they underlined what they learned. However, the students disagreed upon the main idea sentence. Two thought the first sentence a fine main idea sentence because each sentence talked about what the elephants did in herds. Three other students wrote: "The author is describing how the herd acts." Ms. Gillman assured them that both were fine main idea sentences.

The students chose *herd* as the topic of the last paragraph. After underlining what they learned, they all agreed that the first sentence was a good main idea sentence.

- Ask questions about the topic or events and offer probable answers. For example, say "Why didn't Britain and France think the League of Nations would work? Maybe they figured it was unrealistic to think nations would never go to war again."
- Mention that you understand what you have read. For example, say, "This makes a lot of sense to me. A new leader wouldn't want to carry on a war that he didn't believe in so I can understand why Lenin offered to make peace."
- Mention that you did not understand what you read and point out the confusing word or concept. Model a possible fix-up strategy. For example, say, "I was not sure what *stalemate* means, but I reread the sentence and if neither side is winning, then it could mean a draw or equal positions."
- Talk about your prior knowledge and indicate how the information in the text matches with what you previously knew. Explain what you have learned. For example, say, "I knew they carved up all these little countries after the war, but I didn't know that they mixed up the languages and nationalities when they did it."
- Identify personally with the text. For example, say, "I'll bet Wilson felt bad that people didn't believe in the League of Nations. It reminds me of a time when I suggested that we all go camping and no one in the family agreed. In fact, they weren't really polite in telling me so."

As you model the think-aloud process, encourage students to share their own thoughts. This process tends to be nonthreatening to poor readers, who are often asked to respond to questions for which they do not know the answers. In the think-aloud process, no answer is wrong, and students soon grasp this point. In the beginning stages, students often copy what the teacher said, saying "I thought that too" or "I didn't understand that either." As they begin to feel more comfortable with think-alouds, they offer more original thoughts. They take on more and more ownership, and the need for your modeling will diminish.

Throughout the process, you need to constantly stress that the comments made during think-alouds are what good readers do as they read. In the initial stages, when a student shares a comment, identify the type of strategy that he or she used: for example, say "Alan just tied the text to his own personal experience" or "Kelsey described what she did not understand" or "Perry made a great inference." Students should understand exactly what they are doing when they offer comments. You can also stress what they are doing by having the students make a bookmark that lists the strategies.

If you are helping poor readers prepare for their content-area classes, the think-aloud strategy has an added bonus. As students share their thoughts and listen to the thoughts of their peers, they actually learn the content of the text.

Reciprocal Teaching.   Reciprocal teaching, designed by Palincsar and Brown (1984), is similar to think-alouds. It employs teacher modeling, focuses on what good readers do as they read, and engages students in sharing their thoughts during the reading process. Reciprocal teaching stresses four reader strategies: summarizing, raising questions, clarifying vocabulary and concepts, and predicting subsequent content. Reciprocal teaching has been effectively used by Cooper (1997) in an intervention program entitled Project Success (see Chapter 12) and thus warrants discussion as an activity for poor readers. Much instruction of poor readers is in a small-group format, and reciprocal teaching lends itself to this situation.

Reciprocal teaching begins with the teacher modeling the four comprehension strategies: summarizing, questioning, clarifying, and predicting, and drawing the students into the discussion. Gradually as students begin to feel comfortable with the strategies, they take over the teaching role and model strategy use for their peers. The names of the four steps need to be used often and perhaps prominently displayed in the classroom or on a bookmark. If a student encounters difficulty, the teacher steps in to provide necessary support. The teacher then allows the student to continue.

Herrmann (1988) offers a possible sequence for a reciprocal teaching lesson:

1. Read the title, preview the pictures, and ask the students to predict possible content.
2. Read the text aloud paragraph by paragraph.
3. After each paragraph, ask questions about the content and invite students to share possible answers. Ask the students to offer additional questions.
4. At appropriate places, summarize what was read and share with students how you arrived at the summary. Did you use a topic sentence? Did the author offer any clues about important segments?
5. Discuss any words or concepts that are confusing and help the students to clarify these. As in think-alouds, the students must have names for what they are doing.

Strategies for Transforming Expository Text

In addition to understanding expository text, students must also study and remember what they read so that they can discuss it and pass tests. Effective studying requires students to do two things: recognize important information and actively process, or *transform*, it (T. H. Anderson & Armbruster, 1984). Taking notes and reconstructing the text in a visual fashion are ways of transforming the text.

One college student took a course in neuropsychology that involved remembering many details about brain structure and function. To master this difficult information, the student transformed it by creating labeled pictures of the brain and making diagrams relating the brain to body parts. She underlined the text, took notes on the underlined parts, and rewrote the notes. Finally, she mastered the course content. As this example shows, effective studying involves transforming text and changing it into a form that can be remembered.

Teachers generally expect students to study on their own, yet it is difficult to develop the self-guidance and systematic approaches necessary for this independence. Students with reading difficulties need direct instruction in transforming the text so that they can remember it.

The strategies discussed in the earlier parts of this chapter aid in understanding text and recognizing important information. This section discusses different ways of transforming text content into visual diagrams. Constructing these diagrams involves the student in actively processing the information. The diagrams can also be used as study aids.

The Main Idea Grid.   The Main Idea Grid can be used as a diagram for taking notes as students work through the Topic-Detail-Main Idea strategy (presented earlier in this chapter). After students read and analyze a paragraph, the grid is used to record the *topic, details*, and *main idea sentence*. A guide is given in Figure 9.4.

The main idea grid serves several purposes: (1) It acts as a reminder of the comprehension strategy students should be using as they read. (2) It involves students in actively transforming the text. (3) It helps students take brief notes in their own words. Because space for notes is limited, students must often shorten their writing. (4) It provides a simplified and transformed summary from which students can study. You can give the students copies of the grid to fill in or they can draw their own grids as they go along.

Idea-Mapping.   Idea-Mapping (Armbruster, 1986; Armbruster & Anderson, 1982) visually demonstrates the organizational patterns of expository text and

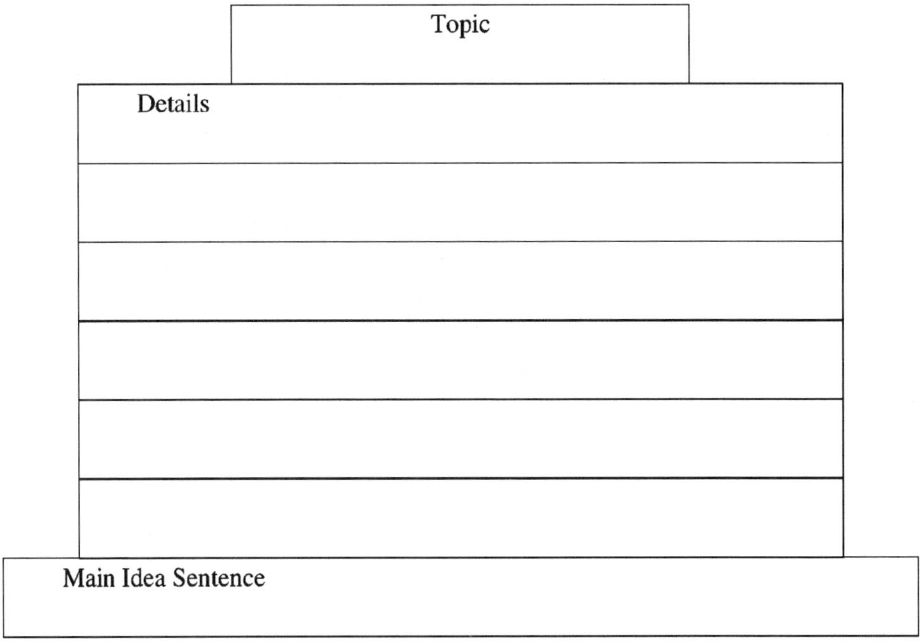

FIGURE 9.4   **Main Idea Grid**

helps students recognize how ideas in a textbook are linked together. Idea-Mapping is based on the different patterns of expository text described earlier in the chapter: sequence or time order, listing or description, comparison-contrast, cause-effect, and problem-solution. Each text structure is represented by a unique idea-map form. The students fill in the map with information from the text. We have simplified and adapted the original idea-maps of Armbruster (1986) and used them successfully with low-achieving readers. Idea-maps remind students to identify patterns of expository organization.

In the early stages of using Idea-Mapping, you should identify an organizational pattern for the students and give them the appropriate map to fill in. The next step involves giving them two idea-map choices. The students read the text and decide which organizational pattern best fits; then they fill in the map. Finally, students independently choose which idea-map to use.

The compare-contrast is an effective map to present first. The items that are to be compared are written in the top spaces. The characteristics of each are written next. If the characteristics are similar or identical, the equals symbol (=) is written between them. If the characteristics differ, the symbol is the equals sign with a line drawn through it (≠). An idea-map for comparing and contrasting deciduous and coniferous trees might look like Figure 9.5.

You can also present the idea-map for the description or listing pattern in the early stages of teaching the strategy. The item to be described is written in the top

Deciduous Trees		Coniferous Trees
Have trunk with bark	=	Have trunk with bark
Vary in size	=	Vary in size
Found throughout world	=	Found throughout world
Have leaves	≠	Have needles
Shed leaves in fall	≠	Remain green in winter
Bear fruit	≠	Bear cones

FIGURE 9.5   Compare-Contrast Idea-Map

space, and the descriptive characteristics are listed underneath. An idea-map for describing poison ivy might look like Figure 9.6.

Three other idea-maps represent the expository patterns of sequence, problem-solution and cause-effect. The first box of the sequence idea-map contains the title of the process that is being described. Numbered rectangles connected by arrows indicate that the events placed in each box occur in a set order, as in Figure 9.7.

The problem-solution idea-map has a rectangle for the problem connected by an arrow to another rectangle for the solution. Characteristics or comments about the problem or solution are written underneath each. A problem-solution idea-map might look like Figure 9.8.

The cause-effect idea-map is similar. The cause is written in one rectangle, and the effect is written in another. They are connected by an arrow indicating that the cause precedes or leads into the effect. Again, description or comments about the cause or effect can be written underneath. An example of a cause-effect idea-map is given in Figure 9.9.

Idea-maps, like most of the strategies presented in this chapter, take time for students to learn and apply independently. As mentioned earlier, these expository patterns are not always clear. Two students may choose different idea-maps to

Poison Ivy
Three leaves
Glossy or dull green leaves
Yellow-white flower
Hairy stem
Grows in woods, roadsides, fence rows
Oil causes skin inflammation
Not harmful to birds

FIGURE 9.6   Description Idea-Map

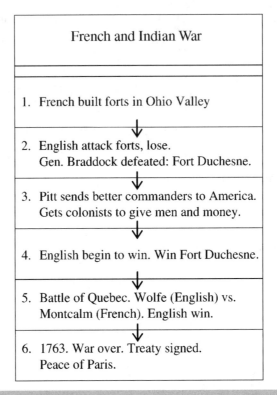

French and Indian War
1. French built forts in Ohio Valley
2. English attack forts, lose. Gen. Braddock defeated: Fort Duchesne.
3. Pitt sends better commanders to America. Gets colonists to give men and money.
4. English begin to win. Win Fort Duchesne.
5. Battle of Quebec. Wolfe (English) vs. Montcalm (French). English win.
6. 1763. War over. Treaty signed. Peace of Paris.

FIGURE 9.7   Sequence Idea-Map

represent the same text. Kelly and Amy were reading about the early years of Franklin Delano Roosevelt's presidency. Kelly chose the sequence idea-map to represent Roosevelt's actions. Amy chose the problem-solution idea-map and organized her notes around the many problems faced by Roosevelt and his attempts to solve them.

Of course, students cannot choose just any idea-map. They must choose an appropriate one that fits the text, but variation in choices will occur. Your role is to encourage the students to verbalize why they chose a particular map. Students enjoy sharing their choices with their peers, and lively discussion often occurs as students defend these decisions.

In the early stages of instruction, use short segments of text to illustrate idea-maps. Gradually increase the length of the text. As students move into longer text, they often have to use multiple idea-maps. Amy used several problem-solution maps to summarize the problems faced by Roosevelt. Kelly divided Roosevelt's early presidency into two sequence idea-maps, one for each of his first two terms.

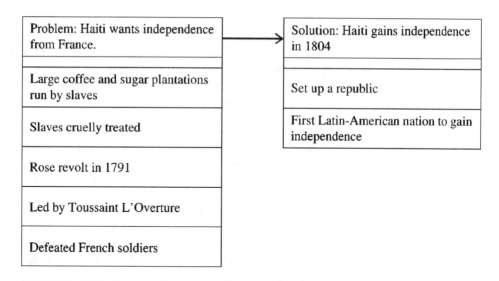

FIGURE 9.8   Problem-Solution Idea-Map

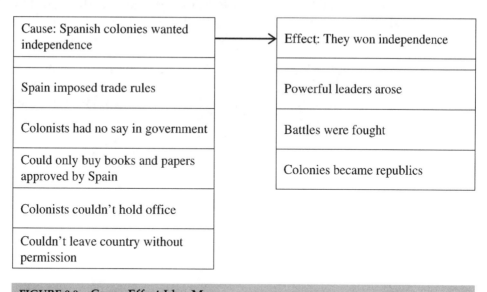

FIGURE 9.9   Cause-Effect Idea-Map

Summary

Expository material refers to informational materials such as school textbooks. Expository material is organized around five basic patterns: sequence, listing, compare-contrast, cause-effect, and problem-solution. Comprehension of the main ideas in a passage is heavily dependent on recognition of these patterns.

Expository text tends to be difficult, especially for poor readers. Text organization is often unclear. Expository text is less personal than narratives and contains more difficult vocabulary. Students must both understand and remember the content of their textbooks. Poor readers often lack the background knowledge needed to successfully comprehend expository selections.

Successful reading of expository text requires that students activate their prior knowledge before they read, monitor their own comprehension, and develop strategies for reorganizing or transforming text so they can remember it.

Several strategies can be used to assess a student's ability to read expository material. The teacher can adapt the informal reading inventory procedure for use with textbooks. The teacher can assess the use of background knowledge by comparing a student's performance on familiar and unfamiliar text. The teacher can assess comprehension monitoring by having the student identify troublesome parts of the text. Finally, the teacher can assess students' ability to reorganize text by watching them take notes.

Strategies for helping students read expository text should be student-centered; that is, they should be able to be used independently by the student. Such strategies take a long time to learn and apply. Teachers need to focus on a single strategy over a long period of time. Teachers should model the strategy and repeatedly ask students to verbalize what they are doing, why they are doing it, and the procedures they are using.

Students can activate their own knowledge of a topic by using the expectation grid and the K-W-L strategy. They can monitor their own comprehension by using Text Coding, the Topic-Detail-Main Idea strategy, the Think-Aloud strategy, or the reciprocal teaching strategy. They can transform the text to remember it by using the Main-Idea Grid and an idea-map.

10 Improving Language Abilities: Listening Comprehension and Meaning Vocabulary

Introduction

This chapter discusses two important facets of language: listening comprehension and meaning vocabulary and suggests strategies that help students with reading problems improve their language abilities. Because reading is language, students cannot read material that is above their language level. Thus, the richer a student's language is, the better he or she will read.

Importance of Language to Reading

Language abilities are critical to success in reading, particularly after the primary grades. When young children first learn to read, their greatest challenge is to recognize, in print, words that they use in everyday speech. In the third or fourth grade, high-level words and concepts start to be introduced in school reading. Those students who have a rich language background cope well with this new challenge; those who lack higher-level language do not. Many of the students in the Reading Center have developed problems as the material they have to read becomes more complex.

Researchers have found that as students mature, increasingly strong relationships develop between their reading achievement and both listening comprehension (Daneman, 1991; Dymock, 1993) and meaning vocabulary (Anderson & Freebody, 1981; Davis, 1968; Thorndike, 1973).

Causes of Problems with Language

Many low-achieving students lack a solid language base for building reading achievement. Three major causes of problems with language are language disability and delay, lack of reading, and lack of a rich language environment.

Language Disability and Delay

A problem with language may severely affect reading abilities. Dawn, an *A* pupil in first and second grades, could read words accurately and fluently. She had a highly supportive family that promoted literacy. In third grade, however, she began to fail science and social studies tests. She could not remember new terms, and her parents began to notice that she had difficulty expressing herself. At the Reading Center, Dawn's tutor orally read her social studies text to her. Not surprisingly, Dawn could not summarize, answer questions, or understand key words from the text. These responses demonstrated that Dawn's reading problem was caused by a language problem.

In some cases, language problems are severe enough to be noticed early, and they affect beginning reading skills. In other cases, like that of Dawn, problems are noticed only as children meet the complex demands of intermediate-grade material. Chall (1983b) calls this situation the "fourth-grade slump." Language disabilities and related problems, such as speech impediments, are further discussed in Chapter 14.

Lack of Reading

Of course, other students with reading problems have had problems recognizing words from the beginning of their reading instruction. Interestingly, these students also tend to have problems developing rich language. In these cases, language problems are actually caused by a lack of wide reading. How does this happen?

Many difficult words and complex syntactic structures are met only in reading. Therefore, students who read extensively have opportunities to build their meaning vocabularies and learn complex sentence structures. Unfortunately, students who have difficulties recognizing words do very little reading and, therefore, are not exposed to these rich language structures. Thus, many readers who start out with only word recognition problems also eventually develop deficiencies in language (Stanovich, 1986, 1988b).

Lack of a Rich Language Environment

Some students are not exposed to rich language structures in the home and in other everyday environments. Activities done in a nurturing home, such as reading books, listening to stories, and engaging in the free exchange of ideas, form an important basis for language skills. However, not all families can provide such advantages. Some parents lack the reading skills to foster literacy; others lack time; and others are not aware of the value of such experiences. Some parents believe a free exchange of ideas shows a lack of obedience and respect from children.

Thomas, a 10-year-old in the Reading Center, had been taught to be quiet and respectful. Before each session, his mother warned him to obey his teacher, and afterward, she asked if he had been a good boy. Thomas's mother was at first baffled by our request that she read to him, because to her, reading was the responsibility of the child. After a few months and attendance at our weekly parent program, Thomas and his mother became comfortable with the noise and excitement generated as Thomas talked freely and expressively to improve his language.

Assessing Language Abilities

Language abilities can be assessed using both formal measures and informal probes.

Formal Tests

Some formal tests are designed to measure language skills. The *Peabody Picture Vocabulary Test Third Edition (PPVT-III)* assesses listening vocabulary. In this test, an examiner reads a word, and the student chooses one of four pictures to represent that word. The examiner might say "Point to pencil," and the four picture choices might be paper, a pencil, a pen, and a crayon. No reading is involved. In addition, because the student is not required to say any words, the *PPVT-III* is a measure of understanding, or *receptive* vocabulary, rather than *expressive* vocabulary. The test covers ages 2.5 to adult, has norms enabling comparison to a reference group, and comes in two alternative forms.

The *Expressive Vocabulary Test (EVT)* is an individual, norm-referenced test used to measure expressive vocabulary using two types of items: labeling and providing synonyms. In the first portion of the test, the examiner points to a picture or part of the body and asks the student a question requiring a one-word response. In the second portion of the test, the examiner shows the student a picture and provides a stimulus word. The student responds with a one-word answer. The *EVT* was co-normed with the *PPVT-III*. By comparing the difference between a student's standard scores in receptive and expressive vocabulary, the examiner may evaluate the student's word retrieval abilities.

Informal Measures

Informal measures may also be used to assess language abilities. The teacher should determine whether (1) a student's language abilities are more advanced than reading skills or (2) language abilities and reading are at the same level. If a student's language abilities are more advanced than reading, the student needs word recognition instruction, so that the student can learn to read at the language level that he or she can understand. If a student's reading and language are at the same low level, more development of language abilities is needed to improve reading. To determine which is the case, a teacher may find whether a reading problem is due to poor word recognition (part of reading) or a low listening level (part of language).

An informal probe of a standardized test allows you to compare reading and language. First, administer a standardized reading test in the regular manner. Then, administer the same test by reading it to the student (an informal probe). If the student scores about the same on both the reading and listening versions, a need for language development is indicated. If the student scores better on the listening version than the reading version, the student needs to develop more word recognition abilities. To summarize:

Reading and listening equal: language development needed
Listening better than reading: word recognition needed

You may choose to probe only specific subtests of a test. Eric's sixth-grade teacher was interested in whether his difficulties stemmed from poor word recognition or poor language. To find out, Eric was first given the vocabulary subtest of the *Gates-MacGinitie Reading Test, Level 4.* In this subtest, he read words and chose synonyms for them. After Eric had taken the vocabulary subtest using this standard administration, the teacher orally read the same subtest to Eric and had him give his answers aloud. If Eric's ability to recognize words had been interfering with his original score, he would have improved his score when the subtest was read to him. Because Eric did not improve his score, his problem was with language rather than with recognizing words. Using the same procedure for the comprehension subtest of the *Gates-MacGinitie Reading Test,* Eric again failed to improve his score. This result further confirmed Eric's need for language development.

In another simple procedure, a teacher can determine how developed a student's language is simply by reading orally to him or her and asking comprehension questions. If a student can comprehend the material, it is within his or her language level. This procedure is recommended in Chapter 3. Using an informal reading inventory, read passages orally to a student to determine a listening (or language) level. Then compare this level with the student's reading level. Also read school materials to students. As discussed earlier in this chapter, Dawn's tutor read her school materials to her to determine if she had a language problem. When Dawn could not understand them, her tutor concluded that she needed further language development before she would be able to read school materials successfully.

Finally, conversing with a student often gives many insights into a student's level of language and comfort in expressing thoughts. Teachers may learn much from conducting student interviews, talking with students about their interests, or observing language use when students summarize stories and answer questions.

Conditions that Foster Language Learning

Language is all around, as students talk to friends, listen to a teacher, read comics, view videos, and "channel surf" using the TV remote control. From these vast opportunities for communication, how can you select the ones that best enrich the language of students with reading problems? Three principles for selection are: give wide exposure to *rich* language, actively involve students, and use both incidental exposure and direct teaching. Because everybody savors the richness of language, teaching it enables your students to enjoy themselves while building an invaluable base for reading.

Exposure to Higher-Level Language

A first priority for improving students' language is to bring high-level language to them. All children hear commands and requests in their everyday lives. However, not all have the rich experiences of listening to detailed verbal descriptions, explaining their own reasoning, or hearing a variety of uncommon words. Similarly, all children study their school texts, but not all get to listen to language-rich books, such as *Tikki Tikki Tembo* (by Mosel) or *To Think That I Saw It on Mulberry Street* (by Dr. Seuss).

The language found in books is richer than that contained in oral language, both in vocabulary (Cunningham & Stanovich, 1998) and in grammatical structures (Purcell-Gates, 1986). Books also tend to contain knowledge that is well reasoned and transcends the limits of personal information (Stanovich & Cunningham, 1993). Therefore, in working with students who have reading problems, teachers should use the *language of books*.

You will need patience to foster an appreciation of language-rich books in a student with reading problems, but you will be well rewarded. There is a special magic in seeing an at-risk child enjoy rich language for the first time. After more than a year has gone by, one class still begs to chant the refrain from *Tikki Tikki Tembo* one more time.

Active Participation

To gain full control over language, students with reading problems must be comfortable not only listening to and reading language, but also using it expressively in their own speech and writing. "Doing something" with language gives students a stake in their own learning and helps them overcome the passivity that is a problem for so many low-achieving readers. Language that has been processed deeply, through many different activities, is learned well and used often (Stahl & Fairbanks, 1986).

Incidental and Direct Instruction

Language instruction can be divided into two types: incidental and direct. In incidental instruction, students absorb meaning vocabulary, grammatical structures, and concepts simply from being exposed to rich language. In direct instruction, students are systematically taught specific words and language structures. Both types of learning improve language abilities.

Most language learning is incidental. For example, research shows that many vocabulary words are picked up through exposure during reading (Anderson & Nagy, 1991; Miller & Gildea, 1987; Nagy, Anderson, & Herman, 1987; Sternberg, 1987) and listening (Stahl, Richek, & Vandiver, 1991). We do not learn an unknown word the first time we are exposed to it. Instead we learn words gradually (Nagy & Scott, 2000) and need perhaps 20 or more exposures for full mastery. Dale (1965) found that vocabulary knowledge could be described in four stages of gradual learning:

1. Never saw or heard this word
2. Saw or heard it, but don't know it
3. Know it in a sentence; know the meaning vaguely
4. Know it well

Over time, and with maximum exposure to language, students learn many words well. Of course, the richer the language that they are exposed to, the more opportunities they will have to engage in incidental vocabulary learning.

Finally, students must learn how to learn vocabulary. Such concepts as word parts, the use of context to infer meaning, and how a definition relates to the word it defines are learned gradually and often require teacher intervention. These concepts are called the *metalinguistic awareness of vocabulary* (Nagy & Scott, 2000).

Although most language growth occurs through incidental instruction, direct instruction can also help students prepare for success in school. Students with reading problems often must master specific unknown words and concepts before they can effectively read their school assignments. Many interesting and exciting strategies are available to give these pupils the direct instruction that enables them to have successful reading and studying experiences.

Strategies for Fostering Language: Listening Comprehension

Many strategies foster students' language development through listening. These listening activities are nonthreatening, time-efficient, and pay handsome dividends in enjoyment and language growth.

Reading Books to Students

If students cannot yet read language-rich, difficult books, teachers can read these books to them. Through *listening* to reading material containing sophisticated language and structures, students acquire the language proficiency that later enables them to *read* at a high level. We highly recommend reading to low-achieving students at least a few times per week.

Listening to a teacher read is beneficial for students with reading problems for three reasons: (1) Students absorb higher-level language, build background knowledge, and learn story organization. (2) Students are motivated to learn to read as they become aware of the many interesting things that can be read. (3) Listening to a teacher read is a relaxing activity.

Materials that are above students' reading level, and on the cutting edge of their language, are most effective in fostering language growth. These materials should contain language that is challenging, but not overwhelming, for students. To build background knowledge, teachers should try to find books that are set in a different time and place or contain elements of fantasy. In addition, they should try to read both short stories and longer books. Reading full-length novels to students helps them to develop comprehension strategies for longer material.

A few suggestions for language-rich books suitable for teacher read-alouds for primary grades include *Amos and Boris* (by Steig), *Many Moons* (by Thurber), and *To Think That I Saw It on Mulberry Street* (by Dr. Seuss). For intermediate and upper grades, try *Mrs. Frisby and the Rats of NIMH* (by O'Brien), *Ben and Me* (by Lawson), *North to Freedom* (by Holm), *Sarah Plain and Tall* (by MacLachlan), *In the Year of the Boar and Jackie Robinson* (by Lord), the *Harry Potter* books (by Rowling), and *The Indian in the Cupboard* (by Banks). Short stories by Edgar Allan Poe, Jack London, Mark Twain, and Sir Arthur Conan Doyle are filled with sophisticated concepts and vocabulary. Students with reading problems also enjoy listening to expository text. One group of Title I fourth graders was kept enthralled as, using the book *Fabulous Facts about the 50 States* (by Ross), they covered one state each session. Finally, books focusing on figurative language, such as *Amelia Bedelia* (by Parish), help enrich students' language.

When reading to students, do not be alarmed if they don't know the meanings of all the words. If, however, you feel that students are uncomfortable or someone asks a question, stop and explain concepts and words. Young children often like to hear favorites reread. Such rereading enables them to get more from the story and to develop a sense of security.

Reading to students can easily be done at times when they are not at peak energy, such as after lunch or at the end of the day. Read for 10 to 15 minutes at one time. At times, however, students get "into" a book, and they may beg you to read longer. Try to stop at a meaningful point, such as the end of a chapter.

Mega-Cloze Strategy

Developed by Diane Whittier (personal communication, 1993), the Mega-Cloze strategy is a way to make listening more active as well as increase prediction skills and knowledge of story structure. In doing daily reading with her class, Ms. Whittier noticed that the attention of her low-achieving students often wandered. To focus them, she took out sentences from the chapter she was going to read and wrote them on strips of paper. She gave one strip to each student and told the children that she was going to see if they could predict when the sentence each held would appear in the text. Next, she read the chapter. When she came to a sentence that was left out, she gave a signal (such as wiggling her fingers and saying "wiggle"). The students then looked at their strips, and the person who held the right sentence read it aloud.

In preparing a mega-cloze, generally excerpt one to two sentences per page. To ensure that all students can recognize the words, have them read the sentences aloud before you start to read the story or chapter. Before you read the story, make sure to mark the sentences you have excerpted in your book; otherwise you may forget the sentences the children are responding to.

This strategy can be used with advanced books, such as *A Bridge to Terabithia* (by Patterson) and *Tuck Everlasting* (by Babbitt), or with easier, shorter materials (such as folktales like *The Three Little Pigs*). Older and more able students can predict the sentences without hearing the story beforehand. However, for younger or less able students, first read an entire story to them and do the mega-cloze activity when you reread it. Several of the groups we have worked with like to do the mega-cloze many times, changing cards each time. To avoid the embarrassment that some students feel when they get a sentence wrong, you can have two students share each card.

Paired Story Reading

Some teachers feel that their students will not be able to grasp the literary style of classic fairy and folk tales, yet recognize that these stories are valuable listening experiences. Paired story reading involves easy and hard versions of classic stories (Richek, 1989) and is particularly recommended for students with reading problems in grades one to six.

For this strategy, you need to find both an easier and a more difficult version of the same fairy or folk tale. Collections of fairy tales in easy versions are available, for example, in *Fairy Stories for Pleasure Reading* (by Dolch) and in *Fun to Read Fairy Tales* (Modern Publishing Unisystems, Inc.). More difficult versions of fairy tales can be found in Lang's *The Green Fairy Book* (and in the red, yellow, and blue books). You can use single books such as *Cinderella* (Perrault, illustrated by Brown) or *Snow White* (Grimm, illustrated by Burkert).

After you have chosen the materials, simply read an easy version of one tale to students on one day (say, *Cinderella* from the Dolch book) and discuss the story. This reading will enable them to learn and enjoy the basic plot line. On the next day, read the difficult version of the same tale (such as *Cinderella*, illustrated by Brown). Having the background of the easier tale, the students will enjoy the greater detail and richer language of the harder version. They will also want to compare the slight differences between the story lines of different versions.

Directed Listening-Thinking Activity (DL-TA)

The Directed Listening-Thinking Activity (DL-TA) parallels the Directed Reading-Thinking Activity (DR-TA) presented in Chapter 8. DL-TA is recommended for primary children who need to develop a sense of story structure and for students of any age who need to improve their language abilities.

In DL-TA, students *listen* to a story being read and predict what will happen next. When reading the story, the teacher stops at several critical points and asks students to predict (Richek, 1987). Freed from the constraints of having to recognize words, students can apply all of their energies to thinking about the story.

Formalizing the thinking process is just as important in DL-TA as in DR-TA. Thus, when using DL-TA, carefully write down all of the students' predictions on the chalkboard. This activity encourages a reading response, because students will invariably want to read their own language, as written on the board. (Adaptations of DL-TA suitable for emergent literacy are discussed in Chapter 5.)

Sentence Building

Students with reading problems often have difficulty with sentence comprehension. The Sentence Building strategy (Richek, 1999) is a creative way to give students practice in creating their own long sentences. Although best suited to a group situation, it can also be used individually.

First write a simple sentence, without punctuation or capitalization, such as

the boy walked the dog

on tag board, word cards, or sentence strips, and attach them to the board. You can also use an overhead projector and transparency sheets that have been cut into small pieces, if you prefer.

Then tell the students that you want them to add to the sentence. Each student takes a turn making the sentence longer. An important rule, however, is that a student must look at the sentence as it is printed on the board and say the sentence *plus* the addition the student wishes to add. Only then will the teacher put in that student's addition.

The first student might look at "the boy walked the dog" and say "the boy walked the dog to the park." Then the teacher will add to the sentence on the board, changing it to

the boy walked the dog to the park

The object is to create a long sentence. Because students will usually add to the end of a sentence, the teacher should also require that they make additions to the beginning and the middle. The following sentence was created by fourth-grade resource room students:

Johnny and the big muscle-bound boy, who had never seen that kind of dog, walked the dog to the park and through the alley, and a girl asked them if she could hold the dog.

This one was created by fifth- and sixth-grade learning-disabled students in a resource room:

Who was the dumb ugly boy with a holey shirt and holey pants who walked the dog all the way home and gave him a bone and gave him some food with water?

When is a sentence long enough? Ask students to stop building it when they can no longer repeat it in one breath. Because children's breaths increase with age, this rule permits older students to build longer sentences than younger ones. After a sentence has been finished, you may want to discuss appropriate capitalization and punctuation with the students. Finally, young children in a large class often enjoy each holding one word. Then, as the sentence grows, they get to move to different places.

Developing Verbal Style

Students with reading problems often fear expressing their thoughts and opinions, yet active use of language is essential to building language skills. A few principles, if practiced consistently by teachers, can make pupils feel more comfortable with expressing themselves.

- Never interrupt students who are speaking or allow others to interrupt them. Cultivate your own personal patience and *insist* on respectful behavior of students toward each other.
- Genuinely value students' points of view. This attitude is fostered when you ask students for their opinions. You can model how to express opinions by using phrases such as "I think that . . ." and "It's my opinion that . . ." Often, if you express your opinions in long sentences, students will be inspired to follow your example.
- Do not judge the *quality* of what pupils say. Instead, respond to *what* students say and try not to judge how they express themselves. This attitude gives students confidence to express themselves more fully. Students who feel that their language is being judged will be intimidated. In contrast, students who feel that their opinions are valued will be more comfortable talking.

Strategies for Fostering Language: Meaning Vocabulary

Word meanings are critical elements in instruction for students with reading problems. Meaning vocabulary is highly correlated with a student's ability to comprehend, and words themselves embody important concepts that students will meet in reading (Anderson & Freebody, 1981).

In a wide-ranging review of the literature, Blachowicz and Fisher (2000) stress the need for active, personalized, and rich vocabulary instruction. Graves (2000) states that the four components of a vocabulary program should be wide reading, teaching individual words, word consciousness, and teaching strategies for independent word learning.

This section discusses (1) direct instructional strategies for introducing and practicing words, (2) ways to encourage incidental vocabulary learning, and (3) helping students to figure out words independently. These topics address three of the four Graves' components. Suggestions to foster wide reading are found in Chapter 4.

Introducing Words before Reading

Knowing key words in a story or book helps students read more effectively. Even a short introduction of a word helps, because a large part of learning a word is simply noticing that it exists. Have you ever noticed how often you hear a word after you learn it? This phenomenon occurs because you have become conscious of the word. The strategies presented here are not meant to give students a complete mastery of words before reading, for they will understand the words better after they have read (or listened to) them in a text. Rather, these strategies focus on getting words into use so that students are comfortable enough to read.

Noticing Words.   Simply having students notice words and find them in a story often helps them to gain considerable mastery. To prepare low-achieving third-graders for reading a story, one teacher (K. Voorhees, personal communication, 1994) wrote out each new word in a story on a card. He next passed out these cards, giving one or two words to each child. Then, he read the story to the students. As he read each word, the child who had that word held up the card. In this way, the children noticed each new word *as it was read in the story*, and were able to use the sense of the text to gain information about meanings. Later, when his students read the story for themselves, they found their personal word(s) in the story.

A neighboring teacher (G. Tate, personal communication, 1994) extended this idea by having students predict, before she read the story to her class, whether each word would first appear at the beginning of the story, the middle, or the end.

Classifying.   When students classify words into categories, they are actively engaged in using higher-level skills to learn vocabulary. To ensure that students are successful, however, the teacher may have to go over some of the words with the students before they classify. To prepare third-grade children to read the story *Dragon Stew* (by McGowen), words were classified into three categories: (1) king words, (2) cook words, and (3) dragon words. The words were *stew, royal, castle, throne, palace, fellow, rare, fellow, ordinary, stirred, pork, lit, fiery breath, banquet hall, majesty, proclamations, drawbridge, roast, applesauce, sliced, bubbling, vinegar, simmer, onions, gravy-stained, assistant, fanciful*. While doing this activity, the students' lively discussions about the words helped them to deepen vocabulary learning.

Predict-o-rama.   By classifying words into story grammar categories (see Chapter 8) before they read a story, students become actively involved in learning meanings and predicting story content. To do a Predict-o-rama, list the new words in a story, and then ask students to predict whether each word will be used to describe the setting, the characters, the actions, or the ending. Next, as they read, students can see if these words are used in the way that was predicted (Blachowicz, 1986). If the words are written on Post-it™ notes, students can actually move them after reading, if the words need to be reclassified.

Knowledge Rating. The Knowledge Rating strategy fosters an awareness of words and gives students control over their own knowledge. The teacher lists the new words for a story and students think about how well they know them. Each student checks one of four categories for each word.

- I know this word.
- I know something about this word.
- I have heard or read this word.
- I don't know this word.

Students then read the selection, keeping the words in mind. After reading, the chart is reviewed again (Blachowicz, 1986). Students are delighted to find that they know many words better after they have read them in a story.

Possible Sentences. This strategy can be used to introduce new vocabulary in areas such as social studies and science texts (Moore & Arthur, 1981). First give the title of a chapter that the students are about to read. Then write the new words on the board, for example, *molecule, proton, atom, electron, neutron.* Next have students construct sentences that might possibly be true using at least two target words in each sentence. An example would be "A molecule could contain two atoms." Students develop expectations of the chapter as they go through this activity. Then have students read the chapter. After reading, students evaluate the possibly true sentences they have written to see if they are indeed true. They change sentences that are inaccurate and add other sentences reflecting their new knowledge. This simple strategy combines learning vocabulary with the learning of content material.

Practicing and Reinforcing Meaning Vocabulary

After words have been introduced, several strategies can be used to reinforce word meaning by keeping students actively engaged with words: display and vocabulary picture cards, multiple-sentence game, and automaticity.

Display and Vocabulary Picture Cards. Displaying words they have learned helps students feel a sense of accomplishment and informs others of their achievements. Placing words publicly can also help students to remember them. Eighth-grader Marvin put his words on a colorful web honoring his interest in skateboarding. Other students can use their own personal interests. (See Figure 10.1).

FIGURE 10.1   Marvin's Word Web

Caricature of skateboarder drawn by Meredith Leuck. Used with permission of artist.

Students can become "experts" on some words. In a seventh-grade learning disabilities classroom, all of the words from one book unit were placed on individual small cards, which could be flipped up. Each student was given two words and was asked to construct cards for them. On the front, the pupil wrote his or her name to establish ownership. Inside, the student wrote a definition and a sentence for the word, both of which had to be approved by the teacher. The student who had signed his or her name to the word was an "expert consultant" on that word. All word cards were put on display on the bulletin board. When students wanted to review the words, they went to the board, read the word, and flipped up the chart to check the definition.

Vocabulary cards featuring picture clues are often effective in reminding students of word meanings. Lansdown (1991) effectively combined picture clue word cards and the "expert consultant" strategies, as shown in Strategy Snapshot 10.1.

Multiple-Sentence Game. Students enjoy trying to put a number of their new words into one sentence (Richek, 1994). This difficult (but exciting) strategy is recommended for upper-elementary and secondary students. To do this activity in a

STRATEGY SNAPSHOT **10.1**

Picture Cards and Word Learning

To prepare her 20 at-risk sixth graders to read the difficult novel *Rascal* (by North), Ms. Lansdown chose 100 *difficult and important* words from the novel and assigned five to each student. The individual student became a "word expert" in these words by preparing cards for each one. The word appeared on the outside along with a picture representing it. On the inside was a definition (in the student's own language) and a sentence. The words stayed up on the bulletin board unless the students were using them. When working with the words, the students were put in pairs. For 10 minutes, each "word expert" drilled a partner on his or her five words and was drilled on the partner's words in return. Students changed partners for each drill session.

After a week, the students started to read the novel. As they went along, they noticed the words they had been studying. Ms. Lansdown began to give points, cumulative for the entire class, for finding the words either in the book, other reading materials, or nonprint sources (radio, TV, speech). In three weeks, the class had almost 1,000 points.

The excitement of learning these words was matched by the enthusiasm students felt in being able to read *Rascal* with considerable proficiency. As an ending project, Ms. Lansdown tested the students on all 100 words, and this class of low-level readers averaged 97 percent. A month later, their proficiency had not slipped. A student word card for *perpetually* is shown below.

Outside of Word Card	Inside of Word Card

group, prepare a list of target words. Next divide students into small groups and have each group select three new words. Groups now exchange words with one another. When each group gets its new list, they must put the words in the least number of sentences.

> For a sentence with 1 word, they get 1 point.
> For a sentence with 2 words, they get 3 points.
> For a sentence with 3 words, they get 6 points.

As a teacher, you need to judge the correctness and sense of a sentence before giving credit. Students are allowed to change the form of the word (for example, *slow* to *slowly*). Formerly unmotivated students have worked on this activity with unprecedented interest and have even asked to do it for homework.

Automaticity.   To fully master words, students need to recognize them quickly. Spending a few minutes a week having students say words quickly, rapidly supply definitions, or quickly compose sentences is a good way to foster automaticity. In one program, Beck, Perfetti, and McKeown (1982) had students quickly answer "yes" or "no" to statements containing vocabulary words. Examples were:

> A philanthropist steals money.
> A hermit lives by himself.
> A novice is still learning.

Fostering Incidental Vocabulary Learning

Most meaning vocabulary is learned in an incidental fashion through listening and reading. This section focuses on strategies that help students learn words from their environment. Such activities foster "word consciousness," through both knowledge and interest in words (Graves, 2000).

Modeling Difficult Words in Speech.   If teachers consciously try to use "million dollar words," students will unconsciously absorb them. Use words that challenge students to expand their vocabularies. Encourage them to ask the meanings of these words and, thus, to take control of their own learning. For example, in a noisy fourth-grade Title I class, the teacher said, "I find this noise onerous and burdensome." Fascinated by the words, the pupils immediately quieted down and requested the meaning of this intriguing statement. The teacher wrote the words on the board and discussed them. Teacher use of challenging vocabulary takes a little additional time yet exposes students to many words. One teacher (K. Voorhees, personal communication, 1994) used a million-dollar word every day for his low-achieving third-grade students. Each child had to use the word at least once during the day. Favorites included *dogmatic* and *eccentric*.

Word Collections. Collecting different types of words increases students' interest in meaning vocabulary. A class of low-achieving fifth graders collected *soft* words (*whisper, slipper*), *green* words (*grass, lime*), and *happy* words (*ecstatic, birthday*) and placed them in individual canisters. Students also collect synonyms for the overused word *say*, such as *whispered, muttered, shouted, exclaimed*, and *announced*. Other students have collected expressions. One intermediate class's collection of expressions containing the words *gold, green*, and *black*, included several figures of speech, like "golden years," "golden egg," "green-eyed," "green thumb," "black belt," and "black hole." Your students will become quite creative in thinking up categories they would like to pursue. These word collections are especially helpful in enriching students' vocabulary in their writing.

Relating Words to Students' Environments. Words become interesting when they relate to the lives of students (Richek, 1987). Students can look up the meanings of their names in How to Name Your Baby books. Car names often intrigue older students: *Chevrolet* was a famous car racer, *Cadillac* was the French explorer who founded Detroit, *Seville* and *Granada* are names of cities, and *Mustang* and *Pinto* are types of horses. Other students enjoy discussing the reasoning behind the names of common household products, such as Tide®, Wisk®, Mr. Clean®, Cheer®, and Vanish®. Common foods, such as *hamburger, frankfurter, tomato, banana*, and *tea* have origins in other languages. Students may use them to practice dictionary skills as well as to gain geographical knowledge.

The "Ears" Strategy. This strategy combines listening to books with an effort to raise children's awareness of words. First, select a story that contains several difficult words. Next, draw a picture of an ear and duplicate it several times. Each student is handed an ear with a word on it that appears in the story. To ensure that pupils recognize these words, the teacher should pronounce them before the story begins. The teacher then reads the story. Each time a child hears her or his word, the child holds it up. A group of 16 disabled third graders tried this procedure. After reading the classic story *Rapunzel*, most of the students could give substantial information about each of 18 difficult words.

Using Strategies to Figure Out Unknown Words

This section describes some strategies that students can use to figure out word meanings independently.

Using Context Clues. Instruction in context clues is an effective way to help students learn word meanings (Funnick & Glopper, 1998). Although the context will not always define a word thoroughly, it is effective in giving many clues to meaning (Gipe, 1980). However, the process of gaining meaning from context is not easy for many students with reading problems. To build vocabulary in this way, they must be encouraged to take risks and to make "intelligent hypotheses" (We often use these exact words to encourage our students).

To help students use context clues, put words in a sentence context. Ask students to read them and think about the underlined word. An example might be: "Because John *dawdled*, he arrived late." Ask students to hypothesize about what this word means. Finally, one student looks the word up in the dictionary to determine the exact meaning.

Josel (1988) dramatically demonstrated to low-achieving eighth graders that they used context clues to determine meaning. First, she gave them a list of words taken from a novel and asked them to match the words with their definitions. Because the list contained words such as *etesian* and *clamorous*, few students could match any correctly. Next, she presented sentences from the book that contained these words, such as "We are sailing before the *etesian*, which blows from the northwest," and asked students to define the words. Students found they were able to define the majority of the words. This activity demonstrated the helpfulness of context clues in determining word meanings.

After students have become comfortable with context clues, ask them to use these clues consciously as they are reading. First, list new words from a selection students are about to read. Then have students read the selection. When they finish reading, go back to the words and ask students what meanings they hypothesized from the context. The teacher should write down the location of the words in the text, so that the class can easily find the words for discussion. If questions remain, the class can consult a dictionary to clarify meanings. This procedure models the way that good readers combine context clues and dictionary skills.

Students with reading problems can also be taught that when they come to a word they don't know, they should substitute a word or phrase that makes sense. The substitution is likely to be the definition of the unknown word. For example, in the sentence "Because prices were going up, we decided to *defer* buying a car until next year," many students would substitute the phrase *put off* or the word *delay*. These words are, in fact, approximate definitions of *defer*.

Using Prefixes, Suffixes, and Roots.   The structural parts of words—prefixes, suffixes, and roots—are helpful in giving students with reading problems effective clues to meaning.

Suffixes, or word endings, are common in written English, and they provide valuable clues to recognizing long words. However, students with reading problems often ignore word endings and need to practice focusing on them. Because suffixes are relatively easy to teach, a small amount of effort can dramatically increase the ability to recognize long words. Chapter 6 gives guidelines for teaching the easiest suffixes (*s, ed*); this section gives strategies for more advanced suffixes.

Many suffixes change the part of speech of a word. Examples of this are *identify-identification* (verb becomes a noun) and *comfort-comfortable* (noun or verb becomes an adjective). Table 10.1 lists some of the most common suffixes in English and their approximate grade levels (Richek, 1969). Because almost all students have some familiarity with suffixes, you do not have to teach them one at a time. Instead, simply teach students to be aware of suffixes as they read in context.

TABLE 10.1 Graded List of Suffixes			

First Grade		*Second Grade*	
er, est*	bigger, biggest	able	serviceable
s, es (plural)*	ponies	al	seasonal
s (possessive)*	Jane's	ing	singing
s (third person)*	she dances	ly	slowly
ed (past)*	waited	ness	bigness

Third Grade		*Fourth Grade*		*Fifth Grade*	
y	cheery	ish	childish	ance	insurance
tion	relation	ive	impulsive	ity	serenity
ist	violist	ful	beautiful	ent	excellent
ic	angelic	ency	presidency	age	postage
ize	idolize	ery	slavery	an	musician
ment	contentment	ous	famous		
		ate	activate		

*Inflectional suffixes. Other suffixes are derivational.

Three activities are useful for helping students to use suffixes:

- Select a short text and ask students to underline each suffix that they find. Provide the hint that some words contain two or even three suffixes. (Words like ill*ness-es* and publish-*er-s* are found in third- and fourth-grade materials.) Once students have completed this task, review it with them. Few students catch *all* of the suffixes, and they enjoy finding out about the less obvious ones, such as *hurry-hurried.*
- In a slightly more difficult task, students listen to a text read by the teacher. Each time they hear a suffix, they tap a table. For some words, they must tap two or three times. Because this activity requires intense attention, it deepens students' understanding of suffixes. Older students often enjoy using newspaper articles.
- Select one word and see how many different words students can make from it by using suffixes. For example, from the word *sleep* they may make *sleeping, sleepily, sleepless,* etc.

Students can also increase their facility with suffixes by collecting words with suffixes and keeping notebooks of suffixed words that they meet in reading. Have students put a different suffix on the top of each page of a blank notebook. As they encounter words with this suffix, they simply enter them in the book. Figure 10.2 shows a list developed by Ramiro, a 15-year-old student reading on a sixth-grade level.

FIGURE 10.2 Ramiro's Suffix List

In addition to suffixes, difficult words include many *prefixes* (word beginnings) and *root words* (the main part of the word). Many English prefixes and roots descend from Greek and Latin. Because both prefixes and roots contribute basic meaning to the words they form, students can use them for vocabulary building. Examples of prefixes that affect word meaning are *pre* (before) and *trans* (across). Examples of roots that affect meaning are *port* (to carry) and *script* (to write). Students who know the meaning of a root such as *script* have valuable hints to the meanings of such words as *postscript, prescription, scribe,* and *inscription.* A list of useful roots and prefixes (Richek, 1969) is given in Table 10.2.

Word history adds variety to the study of word parts. For example, the word part *uni* is descended from Greek, and the many words that incorporate *uni* (*unicycle, universe, unity, unicorn*) are derived from Greek. The word *astronaut*, formed in the 1950s, is derived from the Greek elements *astro* (or star) and *naut* (or sailor).

Using the Dictionary. The dictionary gives students independence in learning word meanings; however, it should not be overused as an instructional tool.

TABLE 10.2	**Useful Prefixes and Roots**

Prefixes

ante	antedate	before
anti	antifreeze	against
aqua	aquarium	water
endo	endoderm	inner
ex	exoderm	outer
ex	ex-president	former
geo	geography	earth
im	impossible	not
non	nonparallel	not
post	posttest	after
pre	pretest	before
re	rewind	again
semi	semisweet	sort of
sub	subterranean	below
tele	television	far
trans	transistor	across
un	undo	not

Roots

aque	aqueduct	water
astro	astrology	stars, heavens
auto	automation	self
micro	microscope	small
bio	biosophere	life
dent	dentist	teeth
dict	dictate	word
equi	equivalent	equal
graph	biography	write
itis	bronchitis	illness
ling	linguistics	language
mid	amid	middle
ortho	orthodontist	straight
phobia	claustrophobia	fear
phon	phonics	sound
polit	political	politics
script	scripture	writing
sonic	resonant	sound
spec	spectator	sight
therm	thermometer	heat
viv	vivid	life

Numbers

mono, uni	1	oct	8
di, bi	2	non	9
tri	3	dec	10
quadr, tetr	4	cent	100
quint, penta	5	milli	1/1000
hex, sex	6	kilo	1000
hept, sept	7	hemi	1/2

Students with reading problems find looking up word meanings tedious, and if they can learn words through other means, they should be encouraged to do so. Interrupting the reading process to look up a word in the dictionary is disruptive to the reading. Furthermore, dictionary definitions are often more difficult than the word itself. Finally, because dictionaries do not teach correct usage, sentences using words and discussions of words should accompany dictionary study.

Research has shown that dictionary definitions, even those from children's dictionaries, are difficult to understand (McKeown, 1993). For this reason, when students ask you what a word means, you should tell them rather than requiring them to look up the meaning in a dictionary.

Even though it does not provide a complete vocabulary program, the dictionary does have many uses. It provides definitions, offers a means to distinguish among definitions, gives a key for pronunciation, and supplies the different forms of a base word. Dictionary skills, organized from less to more advanced are:

- *Alphabetizing words.* To alphabetize, teach children to use the first letter in a word and then the second letter, third letter, and so on.
- *Locating words.* Opening the dictionary to the correct half or quarter to locate a word and using key words to determine if a word is on a page.
- *Using the dictionary pronunciation key.*
- *Determining the correct dictionary entry for different word forms.* For example, the word *slowly* should be looked up under the word *slow.*
- *Determining which of several definitions should be used in a particular context.*
- *Determining the historical origin of a word.* Usually only advanced dictionaries provide this information.

Creative games help students to learn effective dictionary use:

- *Making dictionary sentences.* Students can open the dictionary to a given page and try to construct the longest sentence possible using words from that page (Moffett & Wagner, 1983). Words such as *the, and, is, if,* and *I* may have to be added.
- *Drawing pictures of words found in dictionaries.* Students can record the page where they found a word and draw a picture of it. Other pupils must then find the word in the dictionary.
- *Seeing who can locate a word in the dictionary using the fewest opening "cuts."* This exercise helps students to locate words quickly.

Remember that different dictionaries are helpful for students at different levels. Young disabled students may need a primary-level or intermediate dictionary. Older students can profit from college- or adult-level dictionaries.

Using Poetry to Develop Language

Using language in playful, imaginative ways helps students with reading problems enjoy and appreciate it. Poetry is an effective language form because in this medium, sounds and word arrangements assume a special importance. We have had enormous success using poetry to foster language and personal growth. Because poetry invites students to memorize and recite it, it is an excellent way to build expressive language skills.

Simply reading and allowing students to react to the work of outstanding children's poets helps them to explore language and ideas. Kutiper and Wilson (1993) found that narrative poetry, which tells a story, is most popular. Students like poems that contain strong rhyme, rhythm, and humor. Familiar experiences and animals are popular poetry topics. Some of the most popular children's poetry books are:

> *The New Kid on the Block*, by Prelutsky
> *Where the Sidewalk Ends*, by Silverstein
> *A Light in the Attic*, by Silverstein
> *If I Were in Charge of the World*, by Viorst

Of course, you may have your own personal choices. For example, *Hailstones and Halibut Bones* (by O'Neill), a book of nonrhyming poems that each reflect a color, became a favorite of several classes of low-achieving third graders. In reading *The Giving Tree* (by Silverstein), a short book with a poetic story, one teacher cried along with her fourth-grade students. When working with poetry, read poems that *you* enjoy.

Shapiro (1994) suggests many easy ways to encourage students to explore poetry. She urges you to make poetry books and poems readily available on a poetry shelf or in a poetry corner. Poetry is an oral medium, and it is meant to be read aloud. To set a mood, poetry can be read at a certain time, perhaps at the beginning of an instructional session. You can have a poetry reading once a week. Students can also form a group poetry circle.

Poetry can be effectively shared through the teacher's oral reading. Make sure that you practice beforehand so that you read smoothly and with interpretation. Students will often want to read the poem aloud after you finish it. As you will see, a poem takes on a different interpretation with every individual who reads it.

Students also enjoy reacting to poetry. They can share experiences that the poem reminds them of. They can discuss what they liked or disliked in the poem. They can also discuss their favorite parts, rhymes, or words.

Shapiro (1994) has invited students to copy favorite poems into a poetry journal. This is an educational experience, for as they copy poems into a journal, students realize that poets use lines and spaces for a variety of effects. They also begin to learn how poets use rhyme, rhythm, and repetition.

Students who become involved in poetry may wish to give readings of favorite poems. They can perform in choral readings, with partners, or individually. Students should always have the option of memorizing the poem or reading it. Some poetry is particularly useful for performing. For example, *Joyful Noise: Poems for Two Voices* (by Fleishman) contains parts for two voices in rhythmic, nonrhyming poetry. Of course, because fluent, expressive oral reading is the essence of reading poetry, this activity helps improve reading fluency. Remember that students with reading problems may need much practice before they become comfortable performing.

Art and writing are also effective mediums for responding to poetry. After we shared "Homework Oh Homework" (from *The New Kid on the Block*, by Prelutsky), each child in a low-achieving fourth-grade room drew a response to the unpopular topic.

Summary

Language is the basis of all reading, and you cannot read language that you cannot understand. Language development is particularly important to reading in the intermediate and upper grades. Causes of problems with language include language disability and delay, a lack of reading (because reading is the source of much language growth), and a lack of exposure to rich language in the environment.

Language abilities can be assessed through formal tests, such as the *Peabody Picture Vocabulary Test Third Edition* and the *Expressive Vocabulary Test* or through informal measures, such as comparing listening level and reading level on a standardized test or informal reading inventory.

Conditions that foster language include exposure to high-level language, active responses in learning, and direct teaching as well as incidental exposure to rich language in listening and reading.

Strategies for fostering listening comprehension include reading books to students; the Mega-Cloze strategy, in which students supply missing sentences from books read by the teacher; paired reading of easy and harder versions of one story; the Directed Listening-Thinking Activity, in which students listen to a story and predict what will happen; building sentences on the board from a short sentence; and encouraging students to employ advanced verbal styles.

Direct instructional strategies for fostering meaning vocabulary before reading include noticing words that appear in text; classifying words into categories; Predict-o-rama, or classifying how words will be used in a story; knowledge rating, or rating one's knowledge of words; and possible sentences, or composing possibly true sentences before reading. Direct instruction for reinforcing meaning vocabulary includes making word cards with pictures, fitting a multiple number of words into one sentence, and practicing responding to words quickly. Incidental vocabulary growth can be fostered by the teacher's modeling of difficult words in speech, collecting words of different types, relating words to students' environments, and holding up "ears" containing words when the teacher reads a story.

To figure out unknown words independently, students can use context clues (the sense of a sentence); structural analysis, such as prefixes, suffixes, and roots; and the dictionary. Because dictionary definitions are difficult for students, this tool should not be overused.

CHAPTER

11 Reading and Writing

Introduction

Research has consistently shown that strong ties exist between reading and writing (Tierney, 1990; Johnston, 1997). Of particular interest to those who work with students with reading problems is the support that writing provides for reading development and the influence of reading on students' writing. This chapter discusses the writing process and gives many strategies to foster its development. Some instructional strategies that help students connect reading and writing are included. Finally, suggestions are presented for teaching spelling and handwriting.

Importance of Teaching Writing

Why should a reading teacher focus on writing? The process of writing is highly related to the process of reading because readers and writers are both constructing—or composing—meaning. Readers construct meaning from the author's text; writers compose or construct meaning as they create text.

The reading-writing relationship begins in emergent literacy and continues throughout a student's literacy development (Greene, 1995). In early literacy, the relationship focuses on sound-symbol relationships and concepts about print (Castle, Riach, & Nicholson, 1994). As students mature, the relationship between reading and writing becomes more complex. As students read a wider variety of texts, the influence of those texts can be observed in their writing (Lancia, 1997; Sitler, 1995; Wollman-Bonilla & Werchadlo, 1995). As students engage in more mature writing, they begin to relate to authors' perspectives, and this relationship leads to a deeper understanding of text (Greene, 1995; Weech, 1994; White, 1995).

In emergent literacy, writing helps students understand that print progresses from left to right and from the top of the page to the bottom. In beginning reading, writing provides students with the practice they need to pay attention to individual words and helps them match letters and sounds in words (Clay, 1998).

At all levels, practice in writing increases the understanding of how authors compose text (Goodman & Goodman, 1983). Tierney (1990) interviewed students and found that those who identified themselves as authors viewed reading in a new light. These students expressed more enthusiasm for both reading and writing, and they read more critically. They viewed reading as a resource for new ideas and information for their writing.

Students also use writing to clarify their understanding of what they read. When they make written responses to reading, they increase comprehension (Jennings, 1991; Weech, 1994; Wells, 1992–1993; White, 1995; Wittrock, 1984). Writing can help students master information in science, social studies, and other subjects (Button & Welton, 1997; Mayher, Lester, & Pradl, 1983).

Using writing in instruction offers important sources of success and motivation for students with reading problems. Students just learning to read may write or dictate messages and read their *very own words*. Freed from the burden of trying to determine what another author meant, these students now have an opportunity to create, read, and display their own meanings.

For more advanced students with reading problems, writing can be used to deepen comprehension responses and to stimulate more reading. These students enjoy the permanence of responding to books they have read in writing, which can be referred to later and shared with others. In addition, students who identify a topic to write about are often motivated to use reading as a way to find information.

Writing Instruction

Many instructional strategies can be used successfully with students who have reading problems. Students learn that a person writes for different purposes and for different audiences. For example, you use lists to organize your life and letters to communicate with friends and family. You use reports to convey information; you publish books to share your thoughts with the public.

This section first describes the writing process that students may use as they develop thoughts into finished written pieces. It then explores three more specific types of personal writing: written conversations, personal correspondence, and personal journals.

Writing Process

Teachers use the writing process to help students become joyful, proficient composers of text. This process has several stages of composing, which range from a first idea to the creation of a formal product. In completing these stages, students in the Reading Center have come to write more easily and naturally. They have also become proud authors of written pieces that are now part of our library.

Selecting Topics.   Topic selection is a key feature of good writing. Students are more willing to write if they choose what to write about. In shaping their content, they also think about the audience who will listen to or read their pieces.

At first, students tend to do personal writing about their own experiences. Topics may include someone they know, a special event, or themselves. Ideally, students should select their own topics; however, low-achieving readers often have little confidence in themselves as writers. Teachers can help these students by asking them to make lists of people who are special to them. While students were creating their lists, the teacher wrote her own list on the board:

> *Special People*
> Granddaddy
> Mother
> Betty, my sister
> Dad

Next, the teacher shared her list with the students and explained briefly why she chose these people. Finally, she encouraged students to share their lists. Then, she asked students to choose one person to write about. While students wrote about their topic, she wrote about hers. When beginning the writing process, you may want to stop periodically to support students in their efforts.

Of course, some students may wish to write reports or letters rather than doing personal writing. Because topic selection is important, you should honor these choices.

Writing Drafts.   After topic selection, students begin writing drafts. Encourage your students just to write what comes to mind about their topics. Students need not worry about spelling, punctuation, or the other mechanical aspects of writing as they draft their thoughts.

You may devote several writing sessions to topic selection, drafting, and responding positively to students' writing. This procedure helps students develop the habit of writing on a regular basis and builds their confidence.

Making Revisions.   As ideas become clearer, writers revise their pieces. Mature writers do this constantly, making many insertions, deletions, and other changes. However, students with problems in reading and writing are often reluctant to revise. Sometimes, just writing a draft has required extensive effort, and making revisions seems overwhelming.

Teachers can use several strategies to encourage revision. First, teachers can model revision in dictated stories and in their own work so that students view revision as a natural part of the writing process. Share one of your unfinished pieces and ask students for suggestions. Use their responses to make changes in your own writing and share the revised version with students in the next lesson.

When students meet to share their drafts, revision is often fostered through suggestions. Writers may find that others have questions about things that are unclear or suggestions for improvement. However, sharing drafts should also be a positive experience. First have students identify something they like about the draft that is being shared. Only then should they ask questions and make suggestions.

For your most reluctant revisers, try transforming an existing text into another genre. For example, you might alter a fairy tale from its narrative version to create a play. In this process, students must revise the text to create a script. After trying this activity with well-known stories, students are usually better able to write their own stories and are more willing to make revisions.

Editing.   When students are satisfied with the content, they are ready to focus on mechanics (spelling, punctuation, and grammar), which are important so that someone else can easily read their pieces. Do not overburden students with changes. Guidelines that foster editing include:

- Focus on items that can be changed immediately.
- Limit suggestions to items that have been presented in instruction.
- Make no more than three suggestions to younger students and no more than five to older students.

Make notes about items that cannot be changed easily and save these for later instruction. Direct instruction that deals with revision or editing concerns can be given as short minilessons during writing time.

Publishing. When the editing process is complete, the writing is ready to be shared with a wider audience. Graves (1994) refers to this as "publishing." Publishing may occur as a book is bound and shared with the class or placed in a classroom library. It may consist of a presentation, a bulletin board display, or even a puppet show. As the writing process develops, students' contributions will fill your literacy environment.

Evaluation of Writing. In guiding students to improve their writing, you must be able to evaluate their pieces. The evaluation of writing should focus on several levels, including content, organization of ideas, structure, and mechanics. By evaluating each, you gain a broad overview of a student's writing capabilities. To permit organized evaluation, start with the most general level—the content—and work toward the most specific—mechanics.

First, focus on content, the ability of the student to communicate thought. Ask two questions about the student's piece: Does this student have an understanding that writing is a means of communication? Does this student use writing effectively to express his or her ideas?

Second, focus on the student's ability to organize ideas. For students in the beginning stages of writing, organization may consist of the ability to write information in sentences. Later, evaluate primary students' ability to present ideas in sequential order. For intermediate-level writers, evaluate abilities to organize related ideas into paragraphs. For more mature writers, evaluate the ability to organize paragraphs and sections of papers by related ideas.

Third, evaluate structure—the ability to use different writing forms, or genres—appropriately. For students in the beginning stages of writing, focus on sentences and grammatical structure. For intermediate students, judge paragraph structure as well. For older students, focus on the characteristics of specific formats, such as an essay or thesis.

Finally, after a selection of writing has been evaluated for content, organization, and structure, focus on the mechanics. Mechanics include spelling, punctuation, and proper use of capitalization.

From this evaluation, you can make decisions about a student's instructional needs on several different levels. For example, students may need help on aspects of writing as broad as how to write a letter or as narrow as using an apostrophe.

Evaluation leads you to two instructional decisions. First, decide what the student should correct to make his or her writing more easily read by others. This decision depends on the level of the student's reading ability. In addition, limit your corrections to ones that the student has been taught previously. The second decision is what the student needs to learn next in instruction. From the second decision, formulate instructional plans and present minilessons, short lessons focused on different aspects of writing.

Written Conversations and Personal Correspondence

In this strategy, developed by Carolyn Burke (S. Anderson, 1984), two students, or a student and a teacher, sit beside each other and communicate. The partners cannot speak; writing is the only communication allowed. If one person's message is unclear, the partner must ask for clarification in writing. Using this activity on a regular basis helps students learn to record their thoughts in writing.

This strategy is often used in our Reading Center as a way of "catching up on the news" with students. Instead of *asking* how things are going, the teacher *writes* a greeting and question to the student; the student, in turn, responds in writing. You can use different colored pens or pencils and date each page.

Some teachers like to have both partners writing at the same time. Other teachers prefer to have participants use one paper and take turns writing. Each session can include two or three exchanges.

If a teacher and a student form a partnership, the teacher can model correct spellings and grammatical structures in his or her responses. Over several weeks, you often notice significant improvements in a student's writing. Figure 11.1 presents an example of a written conversation between a teacher and her student in the Reading Center.

Of course, students also enjoy forming partnerships with one another. When two students are paired, they may form friendships and share interests and everyday experiences with their partners.

In a variation of written conversations called *personal correspondence*, students are assigned a pen pal to communicate with over a longer period of time. Partners may be in the same school, but they should not be in the same class. This activity is especially nice for establishing cross-grade partnerships. The older students' writing models the patterns the younger students need to learn, and older students become more aware of making their writing clear for their younger pen pals. Students should never be allowed to hand their correspondence to their pen pals. The teacher can serve as the "mail carrier" or a student can be assigned the job.

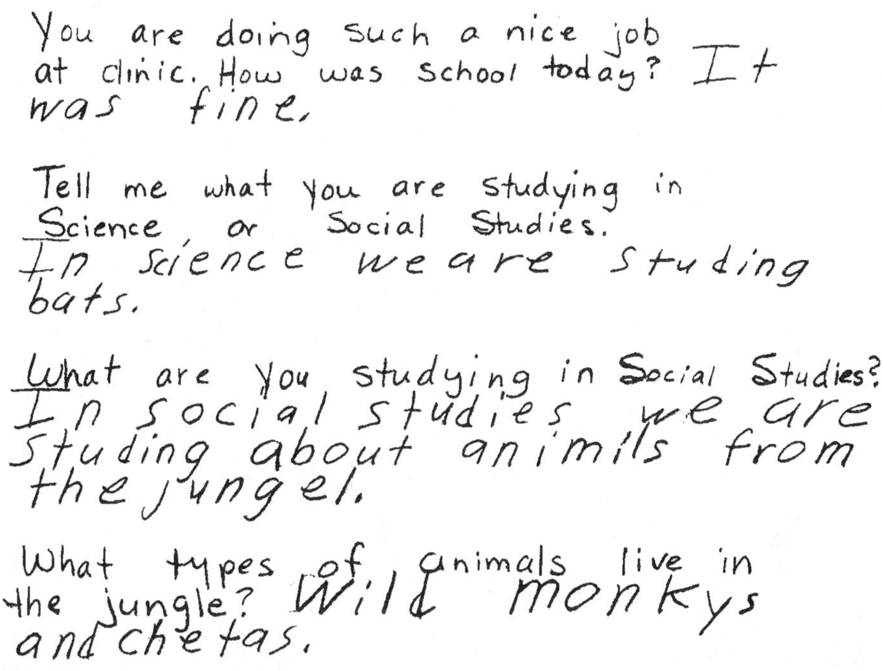

You are doing such a nice job at clinic. How was school today? It was fine.

Tell me what you are studying in Science, or Social Studies.
In science we are studing bats.

What are you studying in Social Studies?
In social studies we are studing about animils from the jungel.

What types of animals live in the jungle? Wild monkys and chetas.

FIGURE 11.1   A Written Conversation

Personal Journals

In personal journals, students reflect on events or experiences as is done in diaries: they practice recording personal experiences in writing. Usually, journals provide day-to-day records of events in their lives and how they felt about them.

When students maintain personal journals, they form a record of their own thoughts and feelings, which they can later read. To begin, each student needs a personal journal, usually a notebook of lined paper. Students may want to create titles for their journals or decorate them. Time is set aside, usually at least a few periods a week, to record personal thoughts in journals. Ask students to write only on one side of a page.

After writing, a few students may choose to read their reflections to their classmates and ask for their responses. In addition, the teacher can collect journals, read them, and write responses. However, students may not want to share all of their journal entries. To preserve privacy, students can simply fold a page in half, lengthwise, to cover it; the teacher should not read folded pages. In responding to journals, teachers should be careful not to correct grammatical and spelling errors, as this practice undermines the student's confidence and may lessen the amount of writing. Instead, try to respond personally to the content of the student's message. Try to use words the student originally misspelled in your responses so that the student can see the words spelled correctly.

Sometimes, students with reading problems have such low self-esteem that they lack the confidence to maintain journals. They often feel that their lives are not important enough to deserve recording. Teachers can help students overcome this problem by modeling journal writing about everyday issues they address.

Students with reading problems sometimes have difficulty thinking of journal topics. To help them, you can supply one category for each of the first six journal writing sessions and ask them to brainstorm a list within this category. Then, they choose one idea from their list and write about it. Topics might include favorite places, special people, favorite stories, things I like to do, things I don't like to do, things that make me angry, and things I do well. To help them keep a record of these ideas, students create an "Ideas to Write About" page, divided into six boxes, in their journals.

After you have engaged in journal writing using this technique six times, students are ready to choose their own topics without guidance. Then, if students have trouble thinking of a topic, suggest they use one of the topics from their "ideas" page.

Strategies for Integrating Reading and Writing

This section discusses ways to incorporate writing into reading instruction. Included are strategies for responding to narrative and informational text. Students need opportunities to reflect about their reading and to respond to it thoughtfully. Writing their thoughts about materials they are reading helps students to organize the ideas presented in the text and increases their comprehension (Doctorow, Wittrock, & Marks, 1978). As they formulate these responses, they also improve their writing skills.

Writing and Reading Narrative Text

Many motivating formats can be used to help students with reading problems. These formats include writing as a prereading experience, scripted stories, rewritten stories, and reader response journals.

Writing as a Prereading Experience.   Teachers often use writing prior to reading stories to provide support for students' reading. In the Story Impressions strategy (Fisher, 1998; McGinley & Denner, 1987), teachers present students with a list of words and phrases from a story and have the students construct sentences that predict the plot. Semantic Impressions, a strategy similar to Story Impressions, is presented in Chapter 8 for story comprehension. A teacher in the Reading Center presented the following list of words from *The Knight Who was Afraid of the Dark* (by Hazen) to her student:

Dark Ages
↓
Sir Fred
↓
knight
↓
afraid
↓
darkness
↓
bully
↓
Melvin the Miffed
↓
spy
↓
Lady Wendylyn
↓
love
↓
banner
↓
secret meeting

The student wrote the following possible sentences:

Long ago in the Dark Ages, there lived a knight named Sir Fred.

Sir Fred was the bravest knight in the land, but he was afraid of one thing—darkness.

One day a big bully came to the village, Melvin the Miffed.

Melvin was mad because he wanted to marry Lady Wendylyn, but she said no.

One night Melvin decided to spy on Lady Wendylyn.

He wanted to see if she was in love with someone else.

Melvin saw Lady Wendylyn making a banner for the village fair.

The banner had a picture of Sir Fred on his horse.

Melvin went to Sir Fred and told him that Lady Wendylyn wanted to meet him.

But they had to have a secret meeting at the castle at midnight.

Sir Fred was afraid, but he loved Lady Wendylyn.

Would he be brave enough to meet her?

Two other strategies that have proved successful in supporting students' understanding of narrative text include writing the story before reading and autobiographical prewriting. Using these two strategies has helped engage students in their reading and has deepened their appreciation for and understanding of text (White, 1995; Weech, 1994).

White (1995) used writing to help ninth-grade students relate to stories to be read. Students were asked to respond to questions that were designed to help them activate background knowledge and personal experiences relevant to the stories to be read. White has found this strategy to be highly effective in increasing students' engagement in the story, identification with characters, and understanding of the concepts presented.

Weech (1994) uses another kind of prereading strategy in which she has students write the story before reading it. She presents the students with scenarios, actions they must assume to have committed. These scenarios are related to events in the story to be read. For example, in preparing students to read *The Rime of the Ancient Mariner* (by Coleridge), Ms. Weech had students respond to three different situations: (1) some were friends who revealed a secret they had promised to keep, (2) some were to assume they had lost a precious family heirloom but were to pretend they hadn't, and (3) some were to assume they had accidentally killed a mother bird leaving the babies in the nest. Having students assume these roles and substantiate or defend their actions helped them relate to literature that sometimes seems irrelevant to contemporary adolescents.

Scripted Stories. Patterned, or scripted, writing is a good strategy for emergent and beginning readers. In this strategy, the teacher shares a predictable book or poem with students. Then the students write their own version, altering the author's version slightly. This activity gives them the security of a writing frame that they can use to form their own, personalized response. One good book to use is *Brown Bear, Brown Bear, What Do You See?* (by Martin). In this book, each page contains a refrain such as "Brown bear, brown bear, what do you see? I see a blue bird looking at me." Figure 11.2 illustrates the work of a first grader in the Reading Center, who used the same pattern with the words *Al* and *vet*.

Scripted writing encourages students to use their imaginations and practice words they meet in reading as they build their own confidence as writers. Good books to use for scripted writing include *Goodnight, Mr. Fly* (by Jacobs), *Polar Bear, Polar Bear* (by Martin), and *Alligator Pie* and *Jump Frog, Jump* (by Lee). Useful poems are contained in *Beneath a Blue Umbrella, Poems by A. Nonny Mouse, Zoo Doings*, and *Laughing Out Loud* (by Pretlutsky); *Honey, I Love* (by Greenfield); *The Pocketbook Book of Ogden Nash* (by Nash); *Sing a Soft Black Song* (by Giovanni); and *The Big O, The Missing Piece, Where the Sidewalk Ends*, and *A Light in the Attic* (by Silverstein).

Rewritten Stories. Having students rewrite stories is invaluable in providing a model for story structure, enhancing language development, and comprehending text. This activity can be used along with comprehension strategies, such as the Directed Reading-Thinking Activity or Story Grammar (see Chapter 8).

FIGURE 11.2 First-Graders' Scripted Story

Book cover from *Brown Bear, Brown Bear, What Do You See?* by Bill Martin, Jr., copyright 1970 by Harcourt Inc. and renewed 1998 by Bill Martin, Jr., reproduced by permission of the publisher.

After your students have read a story, you may ask them to recreate it in their own words. Young children who have difficulty with the mechanics of writing may prefer to dictate a story version to the teacher. Older students are usually able to write their own versions. In creating their own rewritten versions of stories, students need to reflect upon the structure of the story they have read. You can provide guidance for this activity in several ways:

- Use a story grammar and have students identify a character, setting, problem, and events. Then have students make sure they include these elements as they reconstruct the story. Thus, they become familiar with the story grammar elements and begin to use them as they create their own stories.
- Students can tell or write about a story they have read but take another point of view. As an example, you might use *The True Story of the Three Little Pigs* (by Sciesza), which retells the classic fairy tale from the wolf's point of view. Then students can create their own versions of classics, for example, rewriting *Snow White* from the stepmother's perspective.
- Students can rewrite by assuming a role within a story they have read. Lauren, a sixth grader in the Reading Center, read the book *If You Grew Up with George Washington* (by Fritz) and then rewrote it, casting herself as the main character. A selection from the resulting book, "If you Grew Up with Lauren Lang," is shown in Figure 11.3.

We've all read stories with disappointing or surprising endings. Students may be asked to write their own endings to such stories. After reading "The Garden Party" (by Mansfield), Karen, a high school student, wanted to change the ending. The ending she wrote is:

> I think Laura would have said, "Isn't life a learning experience?" The reason why I think Laura would have said this is because Laura has learned that life isn't always joy and happiness, but pain and sorrowful.

Karen uses her new ending to gain further insight into the story:

> I think Laura also learned about her own life. She has lived a sheltered life. Now she realizes that people don't have to dress nicely to be good. She realizes this when she apologizes for her hat.

Reader Response Journals.   A reading journal is used to write personal reactions to reading. Reading journals provide students with opportunities to connect reading to their own experiences.

These journals can also provide teachers with valuable feedback about students' understanding of ideas presented in text. When students respond to a story in writing, the teacher can tell whether or not they understood the story (Farr, et al., 1990).

To introduce reading journals, start by writing about something you and your students have read together, such as a short story. Try to connect the story to the students' own experiences. Students also like to use reading journals as opportunities to critique stories. At times, you can ask students to give "stars" in their journals to something they have read, ranging from one ("I hated it") to four ("I loved it"). Then, beneath the stars, ask them to explain why a chapter or story received this rating.

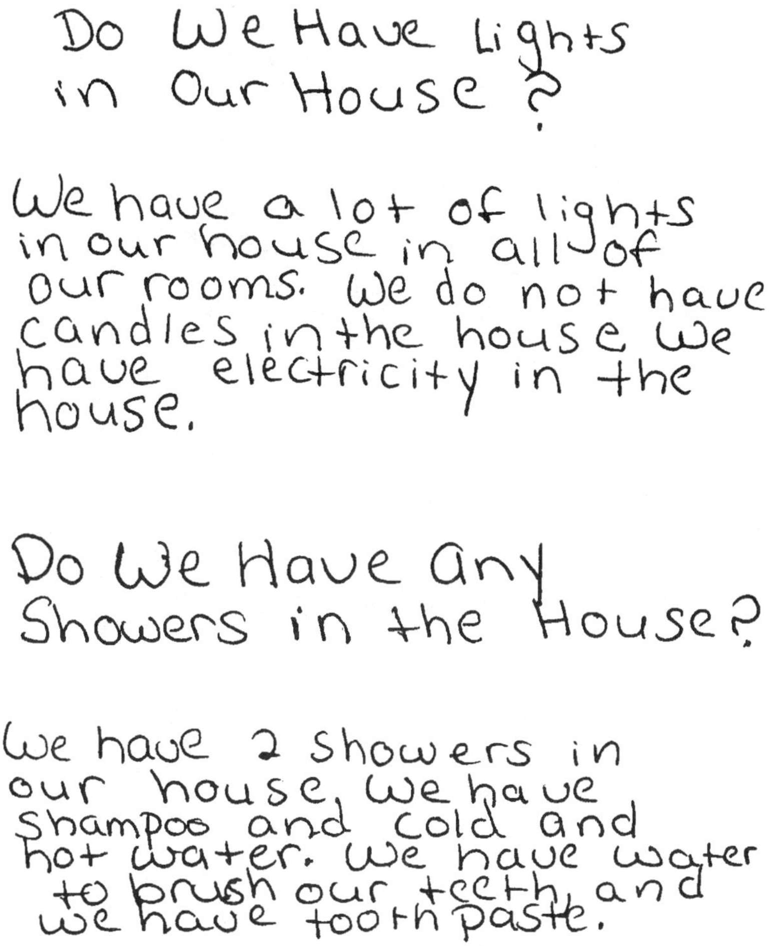

> Do We Have Lights in Our House?
>
> We have a lot of lights in our house in all of our rooms. We do not have candles in the house. We have electricity in the house.
>
> Do We Have any Showers in the House?
>
> We have 2 showers in our house. We have shampoo and cold and hot water. We have water to brush our teeth, and we have toothpaste.

FIGURE 11.3   A Rewritten Story of "If You Grew Up with Lauren Lang."

Adapted from *If You Grew Up with George Washington* by Ruth Belov and Emily Arnold McCully © 1993, published by Scholastic, Inc.

Teachers may also ask students to write about their favorite characters. Asking students to write about why they think the author had a character act in a certain way helps to make them more aware of how authors create stories. This awareness helps students when they write their own stories. Keeping a record of their own reactions to a character's development in a reading journal fosters students' literary appreciation.

Some teachers write responses to students' reading journals, thus making them into *reading dialogue journals*. Through these written responses, teachers can enhance a student's understanding, correct misunderstandings, offer a different perspective, or simply share a mutual appreciation for a story.

A special kind of response journal, the *dialogue journal*, provides an excellent opportunity for students and teachers to interact about text. In dialogue journals, students use a letter format to respond to materials read. Teachers can initiate the interaction by writing a letter to a student asking about a particular character or about the student's favorite event in the story.

When using dialogue journals, students should have opportunities to write not only to teachers but to one another as well. Students write differently to different audiences. When writing to teachers, students usually provide more thorough retellings, perhaps to show the teacher they have actually read the story. However, when writing to classmates, students usually write abstracts of the stories and focus more attention on evaluating and recommending books they have read (Wells, 1992–1993).

Writing and Reading Informational Text

This section presents strategies for responding to expository, or informational, texts that students read. In using these written responses, students are able to absorb, organize, and reflect on information more effectively and fully.

Learning Journals. In a learning journal, teachers ask students to write the most important things that they learned from a content area, such as social studies or science. Students may respond to a chapter in a textbook, an encyclopedia article, or a teacher's lecture. Students are also free to ask questions in their journals, and if a teacher notices a misunderstanding, he or she may clarify it for the student. Learning journals are especially helpful in content areas (Giacobbe, 1986). By asking students to describe what they have learned, teachers can see which concepts need reteaching. In this way, writing can help content-area teachers teach diagnostically. Figure 11.4 presents a sample of a learning journal entry by a student in the Reading Center. This entry was written in response to a science article about peccaries.

RAFT. This strategy helps students to develop imaginative responses by assuming different roles and tasks in writing (Santa, Havens, & Harrison, 1989). RAFT stands for:

> Role - who is writing
> Audience - who is being written to
> Format - the type of writing being done
> Topic - what is being written about

Each of these four parts of writing can vary. For example, a role may include any character or object that has been studied. Students may write from the point of view of a participant in a historical event or of a cell in a biological function. In addition,

THE PECCARY

Today I read about a peccary. I read that peccaries eat thorns, weeds, roots, cactus, and nuts. They live in Arizona, Texas, New Mexico, North America, South America, and Central America. The paper said they make sounds like a dog. They look like a pig and on their neck it is white and then it turns brown.

FIGURE 11.4 Robin's Learning Journal Entry

any other character or object can form an audience. A student may write to another cell or to a historical figure on the opposing side. Formats can also vary. Students can write a letter, poetry, an invitation, a television script, a telegram, or a complaint. Finally, students can choose any one of a number of topics to write about.

One middle-school teacher of at-risk students was having difficulty teaching the scientific concepts of matter. To enliven this subject, she asked each student to choose one of three roles: a solid water molecule, a liquid water molecule, or a gas molecule. Students were also free to choose their audiences, formats, and topics.

One student, for example, chose to be a liquid water molecule writing to the cloud from which he had come. His format was a letter, and the topic concerned what it felt like to be in a raindrop. The RAFT activity dramatically increased learning and enthusiasm in this science classroom.

Teachers may assign RAFT tasks or let the students choose them. The more varied the RAFT choices, the more students will develop an appreciation for other points of view and possibilities. Santa, Havens, and Harrison (1989) suggest that teachers avoid the word *write* and instead use more precise words, such as *describe, convince,* or *explain,* in assignments. These terms encourage students to be more precise in their writing and to develop the ability to write persuasively.

Figure 11.5 shows a RAFT written by a fifth-grade student during a unit on the fight for independence. In this RAFT, the student has assumed the role of an American officer. The audience was not specified because the format was a personal journal entry. However, the student indicated that he thought the officer would like to keep a journal to give to his children after the war. The topic as provided by the section of the chapter being studied: "Winning the War."

Writing with Poetry

When students write poetry, they use language actively and express themselves in imaginative ways. However, students with reading problems have difficulty writing poetry that rhymes because imposing rhyming patterns on your thoughts requires almost professional-level skill. For this reason, you should encourage students to write poetry that doesn't rhyme.

Students with reading problems often feel most comfortable creating poetry from structured formats. Character poems provide a high comfort level as well as an opportunity for getting acquainted. One of the formats the Reading Center students enjoy is presented in Table 11.1.

In Strategy Snapshot 11.1, teacher Mary Welch uses the poetic formats of haiku and rap to help Eddie, a disabled high school student, record his interests.

TABLE 11.1   The Character Poem

Format for Character Poem	Jennifer's Character Poem
First name	Jennifer
Three words describing yourself	Shopper, athlete, pretty
Sister/brother/daughter/son of ...	Sister of Steven
Who likes ...	Who likes birds and baseball
Who fears ...	Who fears the dark
Lives in ...	Lives in Chicago
Last name	Smithers

> Part 3 Winning the War/Journal of an American Officer
>
> December 19th, 1778 Valley Forge. We are having a very hard winter here in Valley Forge. While the British are in Philidespheia in people's homes, we are starving and freezing to death. Even in my cabin its cold. We are suffering heavy losses. My favorite soldier, Robert Price has died. Not only he died 2,999 others died too. We are having very hard time. But we are getting better. Baron Von Steuben of Prussia is helping us in many ways. He is turning our group of poorly trained men into a well-trained Prussian army!

FIGURE 11.5 Murray's RAFT about "Winning the War"

Recently, a third-grade class with many at-risk students read "Sarah Cynthia Sylvia Stout Would Not Take the Garbage Out," a poem by Shel Silverstein in *Where the Sidewalk Ends*, about the fate that befell a child who refused to take out garbage. Students were asked to use each of their five senses to describe what they thought garbage would be like. The class created a book consisting of five pages, one for each sense.

STRATEGY SNAPSHOT **11.1**

Eddie Writes Poetry

Mary Welch (Shapiro & Welch, 1991) used poetry to motivate and instruct Eddie, a 15-year-old boy classified as severely learning disabled and reading five years below his grade level. He wrote character poems of different forms. Eddie extended his expertise into haiku, a poem of three lines, using the following format:

> Line 1: What or who (5 syllables)
> Line 2: Feeling, action, or description (7 syllables)
> Line 3: A summative phrase (5 syllables)

Eddie wrote about his favorite motorcycle:

> Harley Davidson
> Ride into the setting sun
> Stay with their design.

Eddie also wrote raps:

> Harleys are cool, especially when they're blue
> They look so fine, all of the time
> When I go for a ride, everybody wants a ride
> If I say no, you'll say go!
> So bye-bye, it's time to fly

To help Eddie use his interest in music to improve his reading, Mary used *The Poetry of Rock* (Goldstein, 1969), which features the lyrics to popular songs. One of the best outcomes of Eddie's program was his growing sense of power as he taught Ms. Welch important facts about cars and motorcycles.

Examples of what garbage *felt* like included:

It's gooey around you
Gook
Mashed potatoes
Mud
Yuck
Nasty stuff
A soft chicken

The class book was decorated with illustrations by several students and placed in the classroom library.

Computers and Writing

Word processing, the use of the computer in writing, is one of the most effective and widely used applications of computer technology. Using a keyboard, students with reading problems can write without worrying about handwriting and revise without making a mess of the written document. Word processing also alleviates many students' concerns about spelling and grammar because they can use the spell-check and grammar-check features.

Advantages of Word Processing

Word processing, the writing tool of the contemporary classroom, has many advantages for students (MacArthur, Schwartz, & Graham, 1991):

- Students can easily produce neat, mostly error-free copies in a variety of formats.
- The visibility of a computer screen and the anonymity of printed text encourages students to write collaboratively.
- The editing power of the computer eases the physical burden of correction and revision.
- Typing is easier and neater than handwriting, especially for students with motor problems.
- Spell checkers and thesauruses facilitate writing on many computers.

Studies indicate that students with learning problems prefer using the computer to handwriting. However, teacher instruction is needed to aid inexperienced writers in using the potential of the computer to facilitate revision (MacArthur, Schwartz, & Graham, 1991).

Word Processing Programs

Many excellent word processing programs are available for students at all levels. Several programs allow students to combine graphics and text to create electronic books. The computer screen becomes equivalent to the printed page, and students have electronic tools for writing and illustrating stories. Mead (1995) and others suggest many excellent programs. *Children's Writing and Publishing Center* (Learning Company) is an easy desktop publishing software program. *Story-Maker* (Bolt, Beranek, and Newman) allows students to draw illustrations or select from a pool of prepared graphics and includes large type. *Bank Street Storybook* (Mindscape) gives a sophisticated yet easy to use illustration program. *Kidwriter's* (Gessler) choice of pictures and easy use make it excellent for primary children. To help the student, the *Co: Writer* (Don Johnson) program suggests a next word from a partial sentence the student has written. *Write: Outloud* (Don Johnson) is a talking software package that speaks words as the student writes.

For children in the intermediate grades, Ware (1995) recommends *The Amazing Writing Machine* (Broderbund) because it includes spell checking, a dictionary, quotes and jokes, page borders, and multiple fonts. In addition, this word processing program is compatible with *Kid Pix*, a well-known drawing and graphics program for children.

Keyboarding or Typing Skills

To effectively use a word processing program, students must learn to keyboard. Students need special instruction in typing on the computer keyboard, for learning the correct finger positions is better than developing the bad habit of using a hunt-and-peck method. In general, the earlier keyboarding skills can be taught, the better.

Software that supports students' learning to type includes programs recommended for both home and classroom use. The *Superkids* web site (1999) provides current reviews of education software rated for educational value, appeal to children, and ease of use. For younger children, *Disney's Adventure in Typing with Timon and Pumba* (Disney Interactive) and *Read, Write, and Type* (The Learning Company) are recommended for home use. For ages 8 to approximately 14, *UltraKey* (Bytes of Learning) and *Type to Learn* (Sunburst) are available for classroom use. For older children through adults, *Mavis Beacon Teaches Typing 5* (Mindscape), *Typing Tutor 7* (Davidson/Simon & Schuster) and *Typing Instructor Deluxe* (Individual Software) are recommended.

Developing the Ability to Spell

To make their writing more easily read by others, students need to learn to spell. Spelling is best developed by practice; daily writing experiences develop good spelling abilities. This writing should be done for genuine purposes and specific audiences rather than just being writing "exercises" (Gentry & Gillet, 1993). In addition to writing, however, many students with reading problems need more direct instruction in spelling.

Spelling is challenging for many people, even some who read well. Students who have reading problems are almost always poor spellers. Spelling is certainly more difficult than reading. The context, structural analysis, and meaning clues that help you to read a written word are not present when you want to spell it. In reading, you can sometimes substitute a word for an unfamiliar one and maintain meaning for the text. In spelling, only one pattern of letters is accepted as correct; no substitutions are allowed. Finally, the correspondence between spoken sounds and written forms in English is not always consistent.

Reading, writing, and spelling are closely related. Learning letter-sound associations in reading helps you use them in spelling. As children read, they repeatedly see words spelled correctly. As their reading and writing develop, students learn regular sound-letter patterns, which they use to read new words and to spell (Henderson, 1985; Wong, 1986).

Spelling Development

Just as children go through stages when learning to talk, they go through stages in learning to communicate in print. Much research has focused on the concept of *invented spelling*. For example, Read (1971, 1975) has documented that pre-school children use the sounds of letter names to write words before formal instruction. Children follow similar sequences as they learn to spell, although they may go through stages at different rates (Gentry & Gillet, 1993; Henderson, 1981).

Drawing and Scribbling.   Children in early stages of literacy may draw pictures to communicate ideas. As they become aware that adults communicate through lines and squiggles on paper, they begin to do so too.

Precommunicative Stage.   When children become aware that writing uses letters, they begin to make strings of letters. They may make no connection between letter sounds and names. Instead, children simply write letters they have seen in their environment, such as a cursive *K* made the way it appears on a cereal box. Adults usually cannot read what children have written at this stage. In fact, children themselves often cannot reread what they have written unless they read it immediately.

Semiphonetic Stage.   When children become aware that letters are associated with sounds, they begin to use letter names to help them in their writing. They may write only one letter (usually the first sound) to represent an entire word. Frequently, one string of letters, without spaces, represents an entire sentence or several sentences. Although children can often immediately reread what they write, teachers seldom can. Thus, it is important to have the child read the message to you so that you are aware of instructional needs.

Phonetic Stage.   Once children understand what words are, they can identify sounds within them. At the phonetic stage, students write all the sounds they hear in words. Although these "invented" spellings may not look like the English spellings, they are systematic and phonetically correct. Students at this stage still use letter names to determine which letters to write; but each sound is represented, and adults can often read them.

Transitional Stage.   As students receive reading and writing instruction, they become aware that print represents visual characteristics of words as well as sounds. For example, rather than writing the *r* that they hear for the last syllable in *letter*, they now begin to use the conventional English *er* to represent this final syllable. Frequently, students will overgeneralize patterns. After students learn the word *enough*, they may overuse the letters *gh* to represent the *f* sound in other words. Most students now separate words by spaces. Often students in the transitional stage become reluctant to take risks in writing and use only words they know how to spell.

Conventional Stage.   In this stage, students use all aspects of print to represent words. They know that letters represent specific sound patterns. They are also aware that some patterns differ from the typical English letter-sound correspondence.

Spelling Assessment

Teachers can learn a great deal about students' word knowledge by analyzing samples of their writing. However, students with reading problems often choose only familiar words in their writing. For this reason, spelling tests provide valuable tools for analyzing students' word knowledge.

To assess students' abilities to apply phonics skills, ask them to write unfamiliar words. In *Teaching Kids to Spell*, published by Heinemann, Gentry and Gillet (1993) have designed a developmental spelling test for primary children that includes 10 words:

monster	human
united	eagle
dress	closed
bottom	bumped
hiked	type

Gentry says to pronounce each word, give a sentence using that word, and repeat the word. Teachers should tell their students that the words are too difficult for most first and second graders to spell but that they are to write their best guesses. In analyzing the spellings, teachers should classify the students' responses and analyze specific patterns to determine instructional needs (Gentry & Gillet, 1993).

Gillet and Temple (2000) have more recently designed two spelling inventories to analyze students' spelling and document progress. *Developmental Spelling Inventory I* is for use with Grades K through 2. This test consists of 16 words, presented in two sessions. In the first session, teachers present eight words:

fish	learned
bend	shove
jumped	witch
yell	piece

At the second session, the teacher presents eight additional words:

late	chirped
bench	neck
drive	trained
wet	tick

The directions for administration and analysis are similar to those presented by Gentry and Gillet (1993).

Schlagal (1989) developed a more extensive spelling test. The *Qualitative Inventory of Word Knowledge* includes specific patterns students should master in Grades 1 through 6. Table 11.2 presents this test.

Begin the Schlagal one level below the student's instructional reading level and continue until the student scores below 40 percent. The highest level at which the student scores 50 percent or above is the student's spelling instructional level. Generally, the spelling level lags slightly behind the reading level. Responses of emergent spellers to the Grade 1 list will enable you to determine whether a child is at a semiphonetic, phonetic, transitional, or conventional stage.

TABLE 11.2   Schlagal Qualitative Inventory of Word Knowledge

Level 1	Level 2	Level 3	Level 4	Level 5	Level 6
1. girl	1. traded	1. send	1. force	1. lunar	1. satisfied
2. want	2. cool	2. gift	2. nature	2. population	2. abundance
3. plane	3. beaches	3. rule	3. slammed	3. bushel	3. mental
4. drop	4. center	4. trust	4. curl	4. joint	4. violence
5. when	5. short	5. soap	5. preparing	5. compare	5. impolite
6. trap	6. trapped	6. batter	6. pebble	6. explosion	6. musician
7. wish	7. thick	7. knee	7. cellar	7. delivered	7. hostility
8. cut	8. plant	8. mind	8. market	8. normal	8. illustrate
9. bike	9. dress	9. scream	9. popped	9. justice	9. acknowledge
10. trip	10. carry	10. sight	10. harvest	10. dismiss	10. prosperity
11. flat	11. stuff	11. chain	11. doctor	11. decide	11. accustom
12. ship	12. try	12. count	12. stocked	12. suffering	12. patriotic
13. drive	13. crop	13. knock	13. gunner	13. stunned	13. impossible
14. fill	14. year	14. caught	14. badge	14. lately	14. correspond
15. sister	15. chore	15. noise	15. cattle	15. peace	15. admission
16. bump	16. angry	16. careful	16. gazed	16. amusing	16. wreckage
17. plate	17. chase	17. stepping	17. cabbage	17. reduction	17. commotion
18. mud	18. queen	18. chasing	18. plastic	18. preserve	18. sensible
19. chop	19. wise	19. straw	19. maple	19. settlement	19. dredge
20. bed	20. drown	20. nerve	20. stared	20. measure	20. conceive
	21. cloud	21. thirsty	21. gravel	21. protective	21. profitable
	22. grabbed	22. baseball	22. traffic	22. regular	22. replying
	23. train	23. circus	23. honey	23. offered	23. admitted
	24. shopping	24. handle	24. cable	24. division	24. introduction
	25. float	25. sudden	25. scurry	25. needle	25. operating
			26. camel	26. expression	26. decision
			27. silent	27. complete	27. combination
			28. cozy	28. honorable	28. declaration
			29. graceful	29. baggage	29. connect
			30. checked	30. television	30. patient

For all students, an analysis of errors on the Schlagal test can help a teacher to plan spelling and phonics instruction. In analyzing the Schlagal inventory, compare your student's responses to the correct spellings of the words. Look for patterns in your student's errors to determine instructional needs. For example, if your student consistently uses initial and final consonants correctly but has problems with medial consonants, include those in your plans. If your student uses short-vowel patterns correctly, but spells all long-vowel patterns with a final *e*, plan instruction that focuses on long-vowel patterns.

Spelling Instruction

Many different formats and strategies can be used for spelling instruction.

Spelling Workshop.   Gentry and Gillet (1993) recommend a workshop approach to teaching spelling similar to that used in teaching the writing process. This approach includes several steps:

1. To foster ownership, students select their own words to study for a week. These words may be selected from their writing folders, or they may be words from stories or topics being studied. Young children should select only four or five new words. Older children may choose 10 or more. In addition, teachers may add words for study based on student needs. Sometimes, the class may decide to focus on a specific pattern, such as a word ending.
2. Students keep their own records as they progress through the week's activities. They may also monitor their progress on end-of-week tests and select missed words for another week's study. They may keep a spelling log to record their new words.
3. Students work together to learn their words. They may play games, work on common patterns, practice with one another to improve visual memory, and help provide feedback for one another.

Visual Memory.   In spelling, students need to visualize patterns in words. This visualization becomes even more important in later spelling development, as they must visualize root words to help them in spelling derivatives (e.g., *nation, nationality, nationalize*). Visual memory can be developed in many ways. Visualizing words and writing them allows students to learn words independently. It also avoids the useless step of merely having students copy words.

In tactile writing, students use their fingers to trace words cut from felt, sandpaper, or other textured paper. This technique is a good way to help very disabled students remember words and patterns. Using these aids, you can ask students to trace words within one word family (*rate, mate, skate*).

The Look-Cover-Write-Check strategy has been used successfully for years. The steps include:

1. Looking at a spelling word.
2. Covering the spelling word.
3. Visualizing the covered word in your mind.
4. Writing the spelling word from memory.
5. Checking your writing with the uncovered spelling word.

Cunningham (2000) suggests the use of Word Walls to support students' spelling and writing. Teachers can write the words being studied on word cards, order them according to their beginning letter, and attach them to the wall. Word Walls are helpful both in giving students ideas for writing and in supporting their spelling. Encourage students to visualize words and try to write them before they look at the wall. For a more complete discussion of Word Walls, see Chapter 7.

Structural Patterns. Students need to develop an awareness of root words and combining affixes to create more complex words. Compound words provide a good introduction to structural patterns.

Gentry and Gillet (1993) suggest beginning with a compound word from a story or content area lesson. For example, reading the book *Snow* (by Keats) can serve as a springboard to a lesson on such compound words as *snowfall*. Then you can brainstorm words to combine with *snow* to create other compound words (*snowbank, snowmobile*).

Students can also study root words and how prefixes and suffixes are added to create derived words. To explore such spelling patterns, students can create lists of words that end with *-tion, -ic,* or *-ence* or begin with *anti-* or *pre-*.

Gentry and Gillet (1993) describe a variation of the game *Concentration* that helps students focus on root words and derivatives. To play this game, write sets of derived words on cards. One set might include *confide, confidence, confidential, confidante*. Another set could be *remind, remember, memory, reminisce*. To play the game, students try to make words of related pairs (for example, *remind* and *reminisce*).

Handwriting

Despite the growing popularity of computers, the physical act of handwriting remains basic to many school and life activities. A student with difficulties in handwriting is greatly hampered. Many students who do not read well also suffer from problems that result in poor handwriting. These problems include poor eye-hand coordination, deficient motor development, and limited spatial judgment (Lerner, 2000). Because the writing system is adapted to right-handed students, those who are left-handed often have difficulties.

Most children begin writing in manuscript (or printing), which is relatively easy to construct and similar to the typeface in printed material. Students learn cursive writing in second or third grade. Even students without reading problems sometimes have difficulty making the transition from manuscript to cursive writing. Cursive letters are complex and require a greater variety of lines, curves, loops, and transitions.

Many teachers report easier transitions from manuscript to cursive writing if the D'Nealian method is used in beginning writing instruction. In this method, students are taught to write in manuscript, but the manuscript letters are written at a slant and the end strokes end in upward curves rather than straight lines. However, in D'Nealian, the difference between the appearance of their written words and the printed words in books is greater.

Some simple suggestions, if practiced regularly, may help improve handwriting.

- Have students practice on the chalkboard before using paper. They can make large circles, lines, geometric shapes, letters, and numbers with large, free movements using the muscles of arms, hands, and fingers.
- Some students need to trace printing and writing. Make heavy black letters on white paper and clip a sheet of onionskin (thin) paper over the letters. Have students trace letters with crayons or felt-tip pen.
- Put letters on transparencies and use an overhead projector to project the image on a chalkboard or large sheet of paper. The student can then trace over the image.
- Guide students verbally as they write. For example, say "down, up, and, around" as children form letters.
- Because writing is a matter of habit, monitor proper posture and ways to hold writing implements. Students may need lines on a desk to show them how to position paper.

Summary

Reading and writing are similar processes that involve composing. Writing strengthens reading by giving insight into spelling for emergent readers, by helping students to understand how text is organized, and by serving as a springboard to reading as students need to collect information about the pieces they compose.

Writing instruction involves the writing process: selecting topics, writing drafts, making revisions, editing, and publishing. In this process, students choose and develop their own topics and are not evaluated on mechanics until near the end of the process. To evaluate writing, focus, in this order, on content, organization, structure (the ability to use genre properly), and mechanics. Other writing strategies include written conversations (or conversing in writing), personal correspondence with another student, and journals that record personal reactions.

Teachers can help students to integrate reading and writing by using writing to support students' reading. Several ways to integrate writing and reading are using writing as a prereading activity, to organize information during reading, and in response to reading. Students can explore imaginative aspects of writing by composing poetry.

The use of computers for word processing has enabled students to experiment in writing, write more freely, and transcend the limits of handwriting.

Spelling development occurs in stages beginning with the precommunicative stage and moving through the semiphonetic, phonetic, transitional, and conventional stages. Students' writing throughout these stages should be viewed as a natural developmental process. Spelling assessment instruments can provide insight into students' abilities to apply phonics principles and enable teachers to plan for instruction as well as to monitor progress. Spelling instruction should include connections between phonics and visual memory as well as the derivational aspects of structural patterns in more complex words.

Introduction

In recent years, there have been subtle shifts in the philosophy underlying the instruction of struggling readers. These shifts have led to the development of structured intervention programs, such as Reading Recovery™ (Pinnell, Deford, & Lyons, 1988). Before these shifts, the term *remediation* was used to describe the instruction of struggling readers. This term suggested that, just like a physician, a remedy could be applied to an already existing condition.

In contrast to this perspective, a growing number of studies indicates that reading difficulties can actually be *prevented* for all but a small number of children. (Cunningham, Hall, & Defee, 1991, 1998; Hiebert, 1994; Hiebert, Colt, Catto, & Gury, 1992; Pinnell, 1989; Santa & Hoien, 1999; Slavin, Madden, Karweit, Dolan, & Wasik, 1992; Slavin, Madden, Karweit, Livermon, & Dolan, 1990; Taylor, Frye, Short, & Shearer, 1992; Taylor, Strait, & Medo, 1994). If appropriate instruction is applied early and intensively, most children will not develop reading problems. Thus, instruction for many children has shifted from *remediation* to *prevention*.

This focus on prevention, as opposed to remediation, is clearly delineated in the work of the Committee on the Prevention of Reading Difficulties in Young Children, established by the U.S. Department of Education, the U.S. Department of Health and Human Services, and the National Academy of Sciences. The committee reviewed research on intervention and instructional approaches for young children and identified "a common menu of materials, strategies and environments" to support children who are at risk for learning to read (Snow, Burns, & Griffin, 1998, p. 3). The committee concluded that most reading difficulties can be prevented with early, aggressive, and excellent instruction.

The focus on early intervention contrasts with past practices, when we often talked about waiting for the child to "catch up." Children often did not qualify for special help until they were at least two years behind their peers. Unfortunately, the evidence does not show that remedial programs past second grade are effective (Pikulski, 1994; Walmsley & Allington, 1995). Longitudinal research that follows children from first through third grade paints a similarly dismal picture. Poor readers in first grade still tend to be poor readers in third grade (Juel, Griffith, & Gough, 1986; Juel, 1988).

In the past, teachers focused on lesson planning. They attempted to find that special combination of instructional activities that would meet the child's needs. Current reading intervention programs focus on engaging the child in the process of reading as opposed to participating in and completing a set of instructional activities. Lesson activities are only tools for guiding the child to an understanding of what reading is and the strategies that children use as they progress through specific stages on their way to becoming skilled readers (Ehri, 1991; Gough & Juel, 1991; Spear-Swerling & Sternberg, 1996). Most readers move through these stages in an effortless and almost magical manner. Children who do not are at risk of becoming problem readers. Appropriate intervention can help these children move from one stage to another in a timely fashion and thus prevent reading failure.

The purpose of this chapter is to summarize reading intervention programs that have been shown to increase achievement. At first glance, the intervention programs seem to be quite different from one another. However, a closer look suggests that, in spite of the differences, they have many things in common. First and foremost, they are effective in helping children learn to read. Almost all focus on first and second graders. Most are "pull-out" programs that are not coordinated with classroom instruction. They all have a set lesson structure. However, within this structure, individualization occurs through the interaction between the teacher and child.

Many lesson activities are common across programs. For example, many intervention programs emphasize repeated oral reading of familiar text. They devote time to some form of word study. They engage the child in writing activities. As you read about representative programs, note these common elements. Many people have used them to design their own intervention programs.

First-Grade Intervention Programs

Interventions for first-grade students include Reading Recovery™, Early Steps, the Boulder Project, Early Intervention in Reading (EIR), and Book Buddies.

Reading Recovery™

Perhaps the most successful and influential program is Reading Recovery™ (Clay, 1993; Lyons & Beaver, 1995; Pinnell, 1989; Pinnell, Deford, & Lyons, 1988; Pinnell, Lyons, et al., 1994). The Reading Recovery™ program provides one-half hour per day of intensive, individual tutoring for first graders who are in the lowest 20 percent of their class. Reading Recovery™ lessons have a very structured format. Each day, the teacher and student engage in the same basic activities. The student reads both easy familiar and unfamiliar books. The student dictates a sentence or short story. The teacher reads it and guides the child to accurately write it. The teacher then copies the message onto a sentence strip, cuts it into individual words, and asks the child to reassemble it. The teacher and child also work with manipulating letters and saying letter sounds. Throughout the lesson, the teacher fosters the development of reader strategies for identifying words and comprehending text.

Students are taken through 20 levels of increasingly difficult predictable books, all within the first-grade level. The sequence of a Reading Recovery™ lesson is given in Figure 12.1 on pages 296–297.

Typically, students stay in the program for 12 to 16 weeks. At the end of this time, most can read as well as the average student in their class.

Reading Recovery™ teachers receive an intensive training program in instructional techniques and theories in which they learn how to foster the integration of clue systems in word recognition. The term *Reading Recovery* and the method are trademarks. Similar programs have been developed but with different names and slightly different instructional sequences.

Early Steps

Although Early Steps is quite similar to Reading Recovery™, it contains more explicit attention to letter-sound matching (Morris, Shaw, & Perney, 1990; Santa, Ford, Mickley, & Parker, 1997; Santa & Hoien, 1999). The lessons are 30 minutes in length. The child spends at least half of the instructional time reading books at his or her instructional level, and the teacher gradually moves the child through increasingly challenging selections. In addition, the child rereads familiar books to develop fluency. Daily writing is part of the lesson and takes the form of the sentence strip activity used in Reading Recovery™. The word study component involves word or letter sorts. The goal of this sorting activity is to foster awareness that words share common sounds and common spelling patterns. The sorts move from a focus on letters, to consonant sounds, short vowel patterns, and finally to the long vowel patterns. Throughout the lesson, the teacher helps the child to become aware of strategies for identifying words.

Early Steps shares several components with Reading Recovery™: progression through increasingly difficult text, rereading of previously read text, sentence-strip writing, and a focus on developing reader strategies for identifying unknown words. However, Early Steps provides a much more explicit emphasis on decoding that uses word patterns or phonograms. A comparison of the achievement of children who participated in Early Steps versus a control group indicated superior growth for the Early Steps children in spelling, word recognition, and passage reading (Santa & Hoien, 1999).

The Boulder Project

Reading Recovery™ and Early Steps both involve one-to-one instruction. In contrast, the Boulder Project focuses on children in groups of three (Hiebert, 1994; Hiebert, Colt, Catto, & Gury, 1992). The Boulder Project uses instructional activities that are similar to Reading Recovery™ and Early Steps. In a structured daily plan, the lesson begins with oral rereading of familiar books both individually and as a group. The teacher reviews words from the previous day's lesson and introduces a new book. The teacher and students engage in word study based on the new selection. They participate in phonemic awareness activities such as rhyming. They locate words in the text and use them in new sentences. They write the words and transform them by changing letters and letter patterns, for example, changing *stop* to *mop*. As children write on chosen topics, the teacher guides them in letter-sound matching. Like Early Steps, the Boulder Project provides explicit instruction in letter patterns as a word identification strategy. The Boulder Project also provides children with take-home book bags and emphasizes at-home reading.

Early Intervention in Reading (EIR)

Unlike the previous three programs, Early Intervention in Reading (EIR) is taught almost entirely by the classroom teacher (Taylor, Frye, Short, & Shearer, 1992; Taylor, Strait, & Medo, 1994). Each day, the classroom teacher works with five to

HI! WELCOME TO MY READING RECOVERY LESSON

Fluent Writing Practice

Before my 30 minute lesson begins, I get to write some words on the chalkboard. I'm learning to write little important words as fast as I can so I can write them in my stories. It's fun to write on the chalkboard!

Rereading Familiar Books

In every lesson every day I get to read lots of little books. I get to pick some of my favorite stories that I have read before. This is easy for me. I try to read my book like a story and make it sound like people are talking. My teacher says "That's good reading; that's how good readers read."

Taking a Running Record

Now I have to read a book all by myself! My teacher will check on me and won't help me unless I have a hard problem. If I just can't figure out a word or I get all mixed up my teacher will tell me the word or say "Try that again." I read this book yesterday. My teacher helped me work hard to figure out the tricky parts. Now I think I can read it pretty good all by myself!

Letter Identification or Word Analysis (optional)

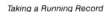

Sometimes I need to do work on learning about letters or important "chunks" of words. My teacher knows all about the things I need to learn. I like to move the magnetic letters around on the chalkboard; they help me understand what I am learning.

FIGURE 12.1   Reading Recovery Lesson

Mary D. Fried, Columbus Public Schools, The Ohio State University. Reprinted from Sandra McCormick, *Instructing Students Who Have Literacy Problems*, 2nd Ed. Merrill Press, 1995.

The Cooking Pot, I Am a Bookworm and *The Seed*, by Joy Cowley. Published by The Wright Group, 19201 120th Avenue NE, Bothell, WA 98021.

seven of the poorest readers for an additional 20 minutes of instruction. Lesson structure revolves around a three-day cycle. The students read short retellings of text after the teacher reads the actual book to the students. The children repeatedly read this retelling across the three days both as a group and individually. The teacher supports accurate word identification by suggesting and modeling contextual clues and strategies for matching letters and sounds.

On the first day, the lesson focuses on phonetically regular words from the text. The children listen for sounds and choose letters to represent sounds. On the

Writing a Story

Every day I get to think up my own story to write in my writing book. I can write lots of the little words all by myself. My teacher likes my stories and helps me work to figure out how to write some of the words. We use boxes and I say the word I want to write slowly so I can hear the sounds and then I write the letters in the boxes all by myself. I like to read my story when I'm done.

Cut-up Sentence

I read the story and my teacher writes it on a long strip of paper. My teacher cuts up my story so I can put it back together. I have to think real hard to get it all back together, then I have to check myself to see if I got it right. Most of the time I do!

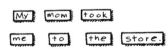

New Book Introduced

I like this part of the lesson the best! My teacher picks out a new story just for me and tells me what the story is all about. We look at the pictures and think about what the people and animals say in this book. My teacher also helps me think about some new, important words in my story. Isn't it fun to hear about the story and look at the beautiful pictures before you read it? I think it helps me read the story too!

New Book Attempted

Now it's my turn to work hard again but I like this story and I know my lesson is almost over. When I come to a hard part my teacher will ask me questions to help me think or might show me what I should try to think about or do. My teacher is trying to teach me to do all the things that good readers do. If I have to work real hard on this story we will probably read it again together so I can just think about the story but I'm not sure there is enough time.

Didn't I do lots of work in my lesson today? I hope you learned something too. Bye!

FIGURE 12.1   Reading Recovery Lesson continued

second and third days, the children, supported by the teacher, write sentences based on the story. Gradually, students shift to longer retellings, actual books, and initial reading done independently by students.

Book Buddies

This intervention is the result of a partnership between the Charlottesville, Virginia City Schools, the McGuffy Reading Center of the University of Virginia, and the Charlottesville community (Invernizzi, Juel, & Rosemary, 1996–1997; Invernizzi, Rosemary, Juel, & Richards, 1997). Tutors drawn from community volunteers work with individual at-risk first graders twice a week for 45 minutes. A reading coordinator supervises and supports the tutors, writes lesson plans, provides materials, and offers feedback on instructional techniques. The tutor follows a sequence of activities that parallel previously described interventions: rereading a familiar book, engaging in word study, writing, and reading a new book. The word study component involves word cards that are used to form a word bank of known words. Like Early Steps, word sorting is an important activity. The child first sorts picture cards by beginning sounds and then moves to sorting word cards by beginning sounds, consonant blends, and short vowels. Writing generally takes the form of dictation by the tutor. The tutor elongates the sounds in words to help children match letters to the sounds they hear. Children are also encouraged to elongate words when they read the sentence to the tutor. Yearly pretest to posttest data on this program suggest that it is effective and practical (Invernizzi, Juel, & Rosemary, 1996–1997).

Intervention beyond First-Grade

Intervention programs beyond the first-grade level include Success for All and Project Success.

Success for All

Success for All is a total school reform program for kindergarten through third grade (Slavin, Madden, Karweit, Livermon, & Dolan, 1990; Slavin, Madden, Karweit, Dolan, & Wasik, 1992). Originally implemented in low socioeconomic inner-city schools, the program has expanded to schools in suburban and rural areas. First- through third-grade students are grouped for reading instruction according to their reading levels. The groups consist of 15 to 20 students. Children who are having difficulty are individually tutored in the afternoon for about 20 minutes. This tutoring is closely coordinated with the morning lessons, and whenever possible, the classroom teacher is also the child's tutor.

The tutoring session begins with oral reading of a familiar story from previous tutoring or from class instruction. This activity is followed by a one-minute drill of the letter sounds presented in the morning session. The teacher and the student engage in shared oral reading. Phonetically controlled words are printed in large type, and all other words are printed in small type. The child reads the large type, and the teacher provides support by reading the small type. The teacher and student discuss the story, and the child rereads it, supported as necessary by the teacher. Like other intervention programs that have been described, a writing component is included.

Project Success

Project Success is an intervention program targeted for grades three and above (Cooper, 1997). A group includes up to seven students who have daily lessons of approximately 45 minutes in length. The lessons emphasize expository text. In the structured lessons, the students begin by silently reading a familiar book or orally reading it with a partner. The students then discuss the previous day's reading by constructing a graphic organizer to illustrate the interrelationships of the ideas in the text. Then before reading a new book, the teacher guides the students through prereading strategies, such as previewing the text, predicting the content, raising questions, or formulating a K-W-L chart (see Chapter 9). The students then read the text silently. Afterwards, the teacher and students engage in reciprocal teaching, that is, they take turns in assuming the role of the teacher and guide the other students through the strategies of summarizing, questioning, clarifying, and predicting. The students then complete a written response or a graphic organizer and reflect on the strategies learned and implemented during the lesson.

Total Classroom Interventions

Total classroom intervention projects include the Winston-Salem Project and a Fluency-Oriented Reading Program.

Winston-Salem Project

The Winston-Salem Project was not originally designed as an intervention program, but its success in preventing reading failure warrants its inclusion in this chapter (Cunningham, Hall, & Defee, 1991, 1998; Hall, Prevatte, & Cunningham, 1995). The focus of the project is first and second grade, but its success has prompted implementation in third grade and above (Wegner, 1996). Classroom instruction is organized into four 30-minute blocks. In the guided reading block, the teacher introduces heterogeneously grouped children to a wide array of literature selections and emphasizes comprehension instruction. The teacher models prereading strategies, guides class discussion, and supports the children in completing story maps or webs. The text is a basal anthology or multiple copies of trade books. The children read orally or silently. They read alone, with a partner, in a small group, or as an entire class.

In the self-selected reading block, students choose their own reading materials. In this block, the teacher may also read to the students. A successful self-selected reading block requires an extensive classroom library consisting of a wide variety of reading levels, genres, and topics. While most children read independently, the teacher uses the opportunity to meet with individual children.

The format of the writing block is Writer's Workshop (Routman, 1995). It consists of short minilessons in which the teacher explicitly models the writing process by thinking aloud and writing in full view of the students. The children then write independently.

The working-with-words block is divided into two activities: a Word Wall and Making Words (see Chapter 6). The Word Wall is a display of high-frequency words that are arranged in alphabetical columns. Words written on the Word Wall are reviewed each day, and new words are added. The teacher then directs the children through the activity of Making Words.

Data across approximately six years of instruction using the Four Block method has demonstrated its success. The authors report that 58 to 64% of first-grade Winston-Salem children read above grade level at the end of the year, 22 to 28% read on level, and only 10 to 17% read below (Cunningham, Hall, & Defee, 1998). At the end of second grade, results improve even further.

Fluency-Oriented Reading Program

Like the Winston-Salem Project, this program was not designed as an intervention program but as an attempt to improve second-grade reading achievement in heterogeneous classrooms (Stahl & Heubach, 1993). The instruction was modified to foster the development of reading fluency.

In the lesson structure, the teacher reads the story to the class and guides discussion. Because the story was read to students, below-level readers were able to participate in discussion. Students then reread the story up to five times before the teacher moves to another selection. These repeated readings include echo reading, reading as partners, and practicing favorite parts of the story to perform. Some selections are dramatized, with individual students or small groups taking different parts. Children also take books home and share them with parents. Every day, students also read books of their choice and keep a reading log.

At the end of the year, the average gain of students in this program was 1.88 grade levels. Students at all levels of reading made substantial advances. These results meant that students beginning on grade level were now reading almost two years above level, and students in preprimer and primer text were now close to grade-level reading. The program showed similar success during a second year with other students.

Comparing Intervention Programs

A teacher who is interested in setting up an early intervention program might seek training in one of the programs mentioned in this chapter. The teacher can also look at the common elements across all these seemingly different, but successful, programs and use them to design his or her own program. How are all these programs alike?

Emphasis on the Process of Literacy

All programs, in one way or another, emphasize the reading and writing process by teaching children the strategies of successful readers. For example, Reading Recovery™ focuses on showing the child how the semantic, syntactic, and phonological clue systems interact to aid word pronunciation. Early Steps and the Boulder Project direct the child's attention to word patterns. Success for All also emphasizes metacognitive strategies for word identification. Project Success exposes the students to the strategies of summarizing, clarifying, questioning, and predicting using a reciprocal teaching format. Consider the writing block in the Winston-Salem Project; nowhere is a process emphasis more evident than in this block, where the teacher writes in front of the children and thinks aloud as he or she models the composition process.

Clearly Defined Lesson Structure

Each intervention has a clearly defined lesson structure and a series of activities that are engaged in each day usually in the same sequence. In the past, teacher attention often focused on the structure of the lesson: what to do next and how to do it. In these programs, once the structure becomes familiar, the teacher can focus completely on the child.

Within a preplanned structure, the teacher can effectively individualize because he or she is more clearly aware of the child's reactions, successes, and confusions. The success of using volunteers in the Book Buddies program was probably intertwined with the provision of preplanned and uniform lessons. Volunteers in other programs often drop out despite initial enthusiasm because they do not know what to do or do not feel confident enough in doing it. The uniform structure may have been a factor in the high retention of volunteers in this program (Invernizzi, Juel, & Rosemary, 1996–1997).

Focus on Familiar and Easy Text

In all programs, the children read selections that they can handle successfully. If they are exposed to above-level text, as might happen in the Winston-Salem guided reading block or Fluency Oriented Reading Instruction, a variety of adaptations make this text meaningful to them. Teachers move the students to increasingly difficult selections, but only when they are able to experience success. Teacher understanding of the students' needs and ongoing teacher support are crucial components of this process. Children read a lot in these programs, as opposed to filling out work sheets and playing instructional games. The majority of instructional time is devoted to supported reading of interesting and motivating text.

Word Study

All programs emphasize some form of word study. Early Steps, the Winston-Salem Project, and the Boulder Project focus on working with word patterns. Several programs use word sorting as a means of accomplishing word recognition. Reading Recovery™, Early Intervention in Reading, Success for All, and Book Buddies emphasize phonemic awareness, the realization that words are composed of identifiable sounds. Although the format and direction of the word study segments vary somewhat, systematic attention to word recognition is a major focus in all the programs.

Focus on Fluency

All programs recognize the need for students to develop fluency, the automatic and expressive recognition of words. They all use repeated reading of easy and familiar text to develop this goal. The repeated reading takes different forms, including echo reading, group reading, and shared reading by teacher and students. Although most programs use oral repeated reading, Project Success focuses on developing silent reading fluency.

Writing

All programs include a writing component. Usually the writing is used to reinforce word recognition, although more extended and individual writing is a key component of the Winston-Salem Project and Success for All. This focus makes sense when one considers that more time is available in a classroom setting than in an intensive pull-out program.

Small Group Size

Wasik and Slavin (1993) suggest that one-to-one tutoring is the most effective form of instruction. With the exception of the classroom programs, all intervention programs provide either one-to-one or small-group instruction. The largest number in a group is seven (in Project Success). Even the classroom programs make provision for small-group and individual attention. For example, during the self-selected reading block and the writing block in the Winston-Salem Project, the teacher confers individually with students.

Application of Common Intervention Elements to Program Design

Could you design your own reading intervention program? In a small urban school, two teachers who were painfully aware that some children were not reading as well as they could did just that (Caldwell, Fromm, & O'Connor, 1997–1998). They recognized the common components of successful intervention programs: a consistent structure, an emphasis on repeated or supported oral reading or both, systematic word study, and writing. With these components in mind, they designed an intervention program for second through fifth graders who were reading well below level.

Unfortunately, meeting the children one-to-one was not feasible. Instead, the teachers decided to make the groups as small as possible. They decided that seeing two children for 30 minutes was perhaps better than seeing four or five students for 45 to 50 minutes. Accordingly, they designed the lessons to fit within a 30-minute time frame, four times per week, and limited the number of students to two for each session.

The lesson structure began with oral rereading of text that had been read during the preceding lesson. The children read the text at least two times using several formats: the teacher and the students read together, the two students read as partners, or they took turns reading individually. Following this supported oral reading, the teacher and students reviewed 10 words from the text. The words were printed on word cards, and the students took turns reading the words.

The next lesson component focused on learning key sight words and using the patterns in these words to decode unfamiliar words (Gaskins, Gaskins, Anderson, & Schommer, 1995; Gaskins, Gaskins, & Gaskins, 1991, 1992; Gaskins, Downer, et al., 1988). For example, using the key words of *am* and *her*, a student could decode *camper*. The students also played "word pickup," a form of word sort. The teacher placed word cards in front of the students and asked them to pick up words with specific characteristics, for example, words with a certain number of letters, words that began or ended with a certain letter, words that began with a certain sound, words that rhymed with another word, and words containing specific patterns.

The fourth lesson component involved the reading of new text. First the teacher read the new text while the children followed along. Then the children were supported in their oral reading attempts using shared, group, or echo reading. The teacher guided the students' response to the content of the section by calling attention to the elements of story structure and what good readers do when they read stories. They focused on identification and discussion of characters, settings, problems, and solutions. The children also discussed the selection from their own viewpoints or experiences.

Then the teacher presented 10 new word cards. Some words came from the text, and some included key words that could be used for decoding. The words often included some that had been presented previously but were still unknown. The final component involved writing. The teacher dictated a short sentence, and the students attempted to write what they heard. The teacher then guided them to correct spelling.

The teachers found that the consistent plans helped. Because they were doing the same thing every day, they did not have to worry about what to do. They made lesson-plan templates that doubled as anecdotal records of students' daily progress. The children liked knowing what came next, and this consistency contributed to a saving of time. Because they knew the structure, the children exhibited little off-task behavior as they changed from one activity to the next.

The teachers used an informal reading inventory (IRI) to measure gains in achievement. A comparison of October pretests with May posttests showed a noteworthy gain of two IRI levels for both word recognition and comprehension. These results meant that, on average, children reading at the preprimer level in October were reading at a first-grade level in May; those on a second-grade level in October were reading on a fourth-grade level in May.

Daily observations validated the effectiveness of the intervention. As the year went on, teachers noted more fluent oral reading, a rise in sight vocabulary, an increasing ability to pronounce unfamiliar words, and talk about story structure as well as what good readers should do. Children also demonstrated greater self-confidence, eagerness, and participation.

Summary

The focus of reading instruction for at-risk students has shifted from remediation to prevention. If instruction begins early enough, if it is intensive, and if it incorporates certain key components, the majority of students can learn to read successfully. Over the last decade, a variety of early intervention programs have been developed for first graders. These programs include Reading Recovery™, Early Steps, the Boulder Project, Early Intervention in Reading, and Book Buddies. Success for All focuses on kindergarten through grade three, and Project Success on grades three and above. Total classroom formats, such as the Winston-Salem Project and the Fluency-Oriented Reading Program, have also proved to be successful in preventing reading problems.

Effective programs share certain instructional components. They emphasize the process of reading as opposed to completion of instructional activities. Each has a clearly defined lesson structure, and individualization occurs through teacher and student interactions. The programs emphasize actual reading experiences with familiar and easy text. Each provides some form of systematic word study and focuses on fluency development through the use of repeated reading. Writing is a key component of all programs as is one-to-one or small-group instruction. Using these common components, a teacher can design and implement a reading intervention program that will be effective in guiding children through the developmental process of learning to read.

CHAPTER

13 Literacy in a Diverse Society

Introduction

This chapter discusses reading instruction for special populations in today's multicultural society. The chapter addresses the topics of teaching children with limited English proficiency, the role of parents in the child's developing literacy, adolescents with reading problems, and adults with reading problems.

Teaching in a Multicultural Society

The value of *cultural pluralism* and the benefits of linguistic and cultural diversity are recognized in today's society. Fellow Americans are viewed as members of unique cultural, racial, and linguistic groups that can make immeasurable contributions to society. The term *cultural pluralism* reflects this philosophy and is in contrast to an earlier view of American society, which is called the *melting pot* philosophy. The melting pot perspective expected all Americans to be integrated into a single amorphous idea of a typical American. In the melting pot view, cultural groups were expected to give up their native language and their cultural traditions; this view did not recognize or appreciate the values that stemmed from different cultures.

Today, American society is becoming increasingly pluralistic and diverse, as new immigrant groups continue to come to America with their own languages, cultures, and traditions. As new groups add their strengths and established ones maintain their heritage, American society becomes increasingly rich in cultural resources. Schools are called on to meet the challenges of increasing diversity and to respond vigorously and flexibly to these new challenges. Teachers have the responsibility to offer the best instruction they can to *all* students.

This section reviews how people from different cultures differ in their views of reading, in their perspectives of language, in their attitudes about instruction, and in their attitudes toward language differences. It also considers ways of teaching children from diverse cultures.

Views of Reading

Not all people view literacy, and literacy learning, in the same way. In fact, a student's family may view reading very differently than does a teacher. Literacy teaching in American schools is often formulated on the basis of middle-class culture, and it expects children to have the kinds of experiences that middle-class,

English-speaking parents have traditionally provided. These experiences are, in fact, much like the ones that are usually provided in school.

For example, middle-class parents frequently read stories to their children (often at bedtime) and discuss them. Through these efforts, children become aware of what a book is, how to handle it, how print and speech match, and how a story is constructed. Such experiences are also common school activities in kindergarten and first grade. Similarly, middle-class parents frequently ask their children questions for which the parents already know the answer. This practice is, again, an experience frequently repeated in school, when a teacher is questioning children about material they have read (Garcia, Pearson, & Jiménez, 1994; Heath, 1981, 1983).

However, these types of interactions are not common to all families. For example, Heath (1983) found that in one community, storybook reading was uncommon; in another community, story reading was done, but not with the adult-child interaction that fostered the ability to handle books. In both these communities, people pursued other reading activities, such as reading the Bible, mail, recipes, TV guides, word searches, and crossword puzzles. Although these activities are valuable, early experiences with books in school tend to mirror the middle-class child-parent reading interaction, and children unfamiliar with it may be unprepared for key elements of typical school instruction.

Literacy experiences that do not reflect commonly held views of schooling may, nevertheless, enrich language, cognitive skills, and reading. Moll and González (1994) describe several working-class families that shared valuable information and respected heritages in pursuing hobbies and small business projects. At times, schools were able to use this knowledge to enhance their curricula. For example, many students in one community near the Mexican border were involved in transcountry trips dealing with the sale of candy. The school used this experience to form a unit on candy, including its nutritional content, a comparison of U.S. and Mexican candy, sugar processing, and the marketing of candy. In an African American community, the school tapped the resources of a father, employed as a gardener, who possessed a wealth of knowledge about musical and theatrical performance. This man wrote and produced an original musical, which was performed by students. In addition to a focus on performing skills, the school created units on the acoustical properties of sound, construction of various instruments, and ethnomusicology (Hensley, 1994).

Teachers must remember that children come to school with different experiences. They must honor those experiences that children have already had while providing experiences the children have not had.

Views of Language

Cultural differences are also seen in styles of verbal interactions. In studies done in two countries, Cazden (1988b) found that children from some lower-class cultures were not encouraged to speak in an extended fashion until they had developed enough competence to "hold their own" on whatever topic adults were discussing.

Thus, while some parents treasure every word of a child's "baby talk" by listening to and responding to it, other parents discourage children from using it.

Because many children are not encouraged to display extended language use at home, they may not feel comfortable expressing themselves at school. Cazden (1988a,b) found that some children did not want to talk or answer questions until they were certain they were correct. Thus, they were often afraid to offer opinions or engage in conversations in class. In the children's view, a good child was a *quiet* child.

The lack of willingness to talk did not mean that children had nothing to say. Cazden (1988b) notes that both middle-class and lower-class children possessed similar amounts of information about objects presented to them. However, because of the clash of cultural styles and lack of experience in talking about objects, lower-class children needed to be prompted twice as much as middle-class children before they would verbalize what they knew. This study has important implications for teachers. As Cazden (1988a,b) found, children may not always be willing to express what they know; thus, teachers may underestimate the extent of their knowledge. In building language and reading skills, children must be encouraged to express themselves, but at the same time, teachers must realize that they may be reluctant to do so.

In addition to using language differently, students whose home experiences do not mirror school experiences may not know how to act or react in school. They may have no experience with how to behave in halls, how to play at recess, how to treat books, or how to organize themselves for instruction. Delpit (1988, 1995) calls this the "power code"—norms that are often unspoken and untaught but which children in the mainstream culture learn from their parents. Teachers sometimes need to carefully explain to children and families the types of behavior that are expected in school. They may also need to explain the curriculum they are using and why they are using it.

Views of Instruction

Different cultures see the schooling experience, and the role of teachers, differently. In some cultures, the teacher is venerated as an authority whose power is not to be challenged (Delpit, 1988, 1995). In mainstream American schools, however, a teacher is seen as a helper and guider of children. Contemporary mainstream instruction is often focused on hints and indirect teaching rather than on direct correction of errors.

Reyes (1992) noted several conflicts between the concept of a teacher for the Spanish bilingual classes she studied and the way mainstream students see teachers. These differences were a source of confusion and frustration for both bilingual students and teachers. For example, in their journal writing, bilingual students made many spelling errors (as do all children writing in journals). The teacher's method of correction was to respond to the child by writing back in the journal and using a misspelled word over again but this time spelling it correctly. To one teacher's amazement, the students never followed her spelling models. When, at the end of the year, students were asked about the teacher's corrections, they answered that they did not realize that the teacher's respellings were corrections. The students said that if their teacher wanted to correct their spelling, why not simply tell them so ("¿Porqué no me lo dijo?")? In other words they valued, and expected, direct instruction. In the same way, Reyes noted that when children were asked to choose a book and read silently, bilingual students seemed lost and simply wandered around the room. Even direction from classmates did not help them to make book choices. Instead they seemed to expect, again, direct teacher instruction in choosing and using books.

Views of Language Differences

Many children who are not in the mainstream culture talk in nonstandard ways, either because they speak a nonstandard dialect or because they speak a language other than English as their native language. Language differences are powerful in determining the way people are judged. At times, people who speak differently from the mainstream are judged harshly (Harry, 1995).

In fact, however, all dialects of English are linguistically sound ways of communicating. For example, Black English Vernacular (spoken by some African Americans) is a fully formed dialect of English with its own rules and vocabulary (Labov, Cohen, Robins, & Lewis, 1968) and is particularly rich in vocabulary. Many standard English words have originally come from this dialect. In addition, the dialect has a highly developed set of verbal games. It has been shown that proficiency in playing "The Dozens," one verbal game, predicts the ability of students to comprehend figurative language (Delain, Pearson, & Anderson, 1985). Students who speak this dialect should not be judged to have verbal problems any more than should children who speak any other form of English.

In the same way, sometimes teachers have difficulty accurately assessing students who speak a language other than English. A nine-year-old Hungarian child, recently arrived in the United States, was described as shy, unhappy, and a problem for his teacher. When someone who spoke Hungarian talked to him, she discovered an outgoing, confident child who was quite artistic and familiar with many modern artists.

Reyes (1992) claims that many instructors unconsciously feel that legitimate instruction takes place only in English and that using another language is viewed as a deficient learning experience. Such a view is, of course, contrary to United States laws and policies on bilingual education, which specify that children should, for some years, receive instruction in their strongest language.

Teaching Children from Diverse Cultures

What steps can teachers take to make schools havens where children can share their linguistic and cultural contributions and can achieve in ways that help them attain the jobs and futures they deserve? Cazden (1986) suggests that relatives, such as grandparents, and community members who work, visit, or donate time to a school can help bridge important gaps between minority and mainstream cultures. Later in this chapter, we describe several successful programs we have implemented using community volunteers. We have found that these volunteers can relate successfully to the children while helping them understand the expectations of the mainstream culture. Our volunteers were particularly helpful when misunderstandings occurred.

Teachers should fully explain their expectations and routines when working with all students. Such topics as how to choose a book, what happens during quiet time, how to take turns, and how to listen to a teacher read a story may need explicit instruction.

Books representing many cultural traditions contribute to a rich and accepting atmosphere. Pratt and Beaty (1999) outline extensive resources in a text entitled *Transcultural Children's Literature*. Table 13.1 lists multicultural children's books.

Finally, students need to make and share contributions from their own cultures. We have had several successful experiences with African American children writing raps that summarize their learning in American history and science as well as novels (Spinelli, 1998–1999).

In one school setting, each child in a fourth-grade bilingual classroom was paired with a child in an English-monolingual second grade. Each child taught five words on different topics such as sports, food, or Mexico in that child's first language to his or her partner and engaged in much animated conversation. Thus, English-speaking children learned Spanish words, and Spanish-speaking children learned English words. This activity culminated in the second-grade's participation in the annual bilingual celebration of the school as well as the communal breaking of a stubborn piñata to celebrate the holiday Cinquo de Mayo.

Families from different cultures can often share experiences and feelings in writing. The Montgomery County Public Schools (Maryland) serves many minority-language children. In one classroom, the children's older brothers and sisters were asked to write the story of how their families came to America (or to Maryland) (S. Clewell, personal communication, 1987). The response of this fifth-grade boy echoes an important promise to everyone:

My Family's Trip to America
This story all began when my family was in the war suffering. Lots of people were pushing and shoving. They pushed and shoved because they wanted to escape from the Communists. If they were caught, they would die or would be their prisoner and would be put in jail. The jail is a dark, damp dreary dungeon. Most were killed by gun shots. My family came to America. My mom and dad came from Vietnam. Freedom is what my father and mother came for. They chose the right place, America. They were glad they made it.

Limited English Proficiency

In the linguistically diverse society of the United States, more students come from homes where a language other than English is spoken. Although many of these

TABLE 13.1 Multicultural Children's Books

African and African American

Afrobets Series, S. Willis Hudson. Preschool concepts (colors, shapes, numbers) presented with African animals, artifacts, and everyday objects.

A is for Africa, I. Onyefufo. Photographs in alphabet book provide a stunning view of life in a Nigerian village.

Amazing Grace, M. Hoffman. Can an African English girl play Peter Pan in a school play? This story concerns racial awareness and self-esteem.

Mary Had a Little Lamb, S. Hale (illus. by B. McMillan). Photographs of an African American Mary offer a unique interpretation of this classic nursery rhyme.

The People Could Fly, V. Hamilton. Anthology of 24 folktales focus on the Black Experience in the southern U.S.

Pink and Say, P. Polacco. In this true story, a black Union soldier nurses a wounded Confederate soldier.

Native American

Dancing with the Indians, A. S. Medearis. African American author tells of her ancestors' participation in a Seminole Indian celebration.

Encounter, J. Yolen. Set in 1492, a Taino Indian child recounts the visit of Columbus, highlighting differences between Native Americans and Europeans.

Ikomi and the Boulder, P. Goble. Lively trickster tale explains why the Great Plains are covered with rocks and bats and have flat faces.

Knots on a Counting Rope, B. Martin, Jr., & J. Archambault. Wise grandfather helps a Native American boy to face his blindness.

Maii and Cousin Horned Toad, S. Begay. Navaho fable explains why coyotes stay away from horned toads.

Sunpainters, Baje Whitethorne. According to Navajo legend, the sun must be repainted after an eclipse.

Hispanic

Gathering the Sun, A. F. Ada. A poem for each letter of the Spanish alphabet celebrates farmworkers and their products. Poems are translated into English.

Un Cuento de Queztalcoatl, M. Parke & S. Panik. Part of the Mexican and Central American Legends series in which each of several tales is told (in separate short books) in English and Spanish. This tale tells of a game among the Aztec gods.

Diego, J. Winter. The life of the famous muralist Diego Rivera is depicted in simple bilingual text with artwork that mirrors his own.

Everybody Has Feelings, C. Abery. A bilingual (Spanish-English) exploration of people and their feelings.

First Day of School, M. Deru. Young foxes hunting for chickens make friends with them instead.

Let's Go (Vamos), E. Emberley. This book explores the four seasons in bilingual text.

Moon Rope, L. Elhert. This Peruvian folk tale (Spanish-English) about why there is a moon features a fox.

Radio Man, A. Dorros. A child of a migrant worker family (Spanish-English), sends a message to his friend via a radio. Text is bilingual.

(continued)

TABLE 13.1   Multicultural Children's Books, continued

Asian

Baseball Saved Us, K. Mochizuki. A Japanese American boy interned during World War II finds solace in baseball.

The Dragon's Robe, D. Nourse. A Chinese girl weaves a beautiful silk robe to save her father's life.

Grandmother's Path,Grandfather's Way, L. Vang & J. Lewis. Lore and legends of the Hmong Southeast Asian tribe (Hmong-English).

Jar of Dreams, Y. Uchida. Rinko, a Japanese American girl, tells about her family life in California.

The Little Weaver of Thai-Yen Village, Tran-Khanh-Yuyet. One of the Fifth World Tales Series, in Vietnamese and English. A Vietnamese girl comes to the United States for an operation. Other books in this series feature different Asian groups.

Momma Do You Love Me?, B. Joosse. An Eskimo child questions mother about "What if I . . . ?" Many Eskimo terms are explained.

This list was compiled by Susan Ali.

children come from Spanish-speaking backgrounds, many other languages are represented in our schools, including French, German, Italian, Chinese, Tagalog, Polish, Korean, Vietnamese, Portuguese, Japanese, Greek, Arabic, Hindi (Urdu), Russian, Yiddish, Thai (Laotian), Persian, French Creole, Armenian, Navaho, Hungarian, Hebrew, Dutch, Mon-Khmer (Cambodian) and Gujarathi (U.S. Bureau of the Census, 1998).

More than 15 percent of students in the United States are currently identified as Hispanic-Latino. By the year 2020, 25 percent of children in the United States will be of Hispanic descent (Ortiz, 1997; Hurdato, 1995). Because Spanish is spoken by so many students, knowing features in Spanish that contrast with English may be useful to teachers. A short list of such differences is given in Table 13.2.

Students who are truly bilingual understand and use two languages. For most students in the United States, one of these languages is English. Research shows that bilingual abilities are associated with higher levels of cognitive attainment (Ortiz, 1997; Garcia, Wilkinson, & Ortiz, 1995; Cummins, 1989). For bilingual students who are proficient in two languages, the duality of languages does not hamper overall language ability or cognitive development.

Many students, however, who speak a language other than English are not bilingual, or fluent in two languages. Instead these students have limited English proficiency (LEP), and experience difficulty in understanding and using English. Some of these children speak only in their native language; others use both English and their native language but still have considerable difficulty with English.

If a second language is perceived positively in the student's environment, learning will be enhanced. Often, however, a second language, such as English, is

TABLE 13.2 Differences Between Spanish and English Languages

Phonological

Fewer vowel sounds
no short *a* (*hat*), short *i* (*fish*)
short *u* (*up*), short double *o* (*took*)
or schwa (*sofa*)

Fewer consonant sounds
no /j/ (*jump*), /v/ (*vase*),
/z/ (*zipper*), /sh/ (*shoe*), / ŋ / (*sing*),
/hw/ (*when*), /zh/ (*beige*)

Some possible confusions

/b/	pronounced /p/	—	*cab* becomes *cap*
/j/	pronounced /y/	—	*jet* becomes *yet*
/ ŋ /	pronounced as /n/	—	*thing* becomes *thin*
/ch/	pronounced as /sh/	—	*chin* becomes *shin*
/v/	pronounced as /b/	—	*vote* becomes *boat*
/y/	pronounced as /j/	—	*yes* becomes *jes*
/sh/, /sp/, /st/	pronounced as /esk/, /esp/, /est/	—	*speak* becomes *espeak*
/a/	pronounced as /e/	—	*bat* becomes *bet*
/i/	pronounced as /ē/	—	*hit* becomes *heat*
/e/	pronounced as /i/	—	*heal* becomes *hill*
/u/	pronounced as /o/	—	*hut* becomes *hot*
/o͞o/	pronounced as /o͞o/	—	*hut* becomes *hot*

Morphological

de (of) used to show possession — *Joe's pen* becomes *the pen of Joe*
mas (more) used to show comparison — *faster* becomes *more fast*

Syntactic

use of *no* for *not*	He no do his homework
no *s* for plural	my two friend
no auxiliary verbs	She no play soccer.
adjectives after nouns	The car blue.
agreement of adjectives	the elephants bigs
no inversion of question	Anna is here?
articles with professional titles	I went to the Dr. Rodriguez.

Adapted from: C.A. O'Brien, *Teaching the Language-Different Child to Read*. Columbus, OH: Merrill, 1973.

used only in school and thus is of little value in everyday life or may be associated with people who are hostile. The more knowledge and empathy a teacher possesses toward a student's personal background and cultural heritage, the more effective English instruction will be (Jiménez, 2000; Moll & Gonzalez, 1994). Of course, exposure to English is important. If students use English frequently, they will learn it more easily. Thus, students benefit from exposure to people who communicate fluently and naturally in English.

Some children have learning or language problems in addition to their limited English proficiency. If a language disorder is present in the primary language, it will also be present in the secondary language (Ortiz, 1997; Garcia, Wilkinson, & Ortiz, 1995).

Approaches to Teaching a Second Language

This section describes widely used, current approaches to teaching LEP students: the native language approach, the sheltered English approach, English as a second language (ESL), bilingual education, dual language, and immersion.

Native Language.   In this approach, students are taught complex academic content in their native language first so that they can understand and discuss challenging material without the added demand of constantly having to translate or express ideas in a second language. Once the student learns the information in his (or her) native language, it can be transferred to English (Garcia, Wilkinson, & Ortiz, 1997; Gersten, Brengleman, & Jiménez, 1994). Underlying this view is the belief that it is not possible to read in a language one does not know. If reading involves the act of understanding complex written material, a student must have a well-developed understanding of the language of that material.

Sheltered English.   This approach introduces English more rapidly, teaching it, in large part, through reading and content-area instruction. The goal of sheltered English is for students to learn English while they develop academic and cognitive abilities in areas such as comprehension and problem solving. For this reason, schooling often takes place in English. Merging English language instruction with systematic instruction in social studies and science can accelerate academic and conceptual English language vocabulary. Reading in English is used as a method for developing English language competence. When students are given an abundance of high-interest story books in English, their progress in reading and listening comprehension increases at a rapid rate (Garcia, Wilkinson, & Ortiz, 1997; Gersten, Brengleman, & Jiménez, 1994).

English as a Second Language (ESL).   Using this approach, students learn English through carefully controlled oral repetitions of selected second-language patterns. This approach is often used in schools where children come from many different language backgrounds and providing instruction in all native languages is not feasible.

Bilingual Education.   In this method, students use their native language during part of the school day and the second language (English) during the other portion of the school day. The objective of bilingual programs is to strengthen school learning through the native language and gradually add a second language. In this way, students come to recognize and respect the importance of their native culture and language in American society. In the bilingual method, academic subjects are usually taught in the native language, and the student receives oral practice in English.

Dual Language.   When two language groups of students attend the same school, each group can learn the other's language. Children are placed together, and instruction is conducted in both languages.

Immersion.   Students are immersed in, or receive extensive exposure to, the second language. In fact, where no formal instruction is available for a person learning a second language, immersion is usually what occurs naturally. Individuals simply learn English as they live in the mainstream of an English-speaking society. Immersion is widely employed with school children in Canada, where it is used to teach French to English-speaking children by enrolling them in French-speaking schools (Genesee, 1985).

Limited research evidence is available on how different instructional methods affect students *with reading problems* whose native language is not English. However, teachers must be particularly sensitive to the needs of these students. Teachers need expertise both in teaching reading and in teaching minority language students (Ortiz, 1997).

The Bilingual Education Act

The Bilingual Education Act of 1968 is a law designed to meet the challenges faced by students who do not speak English as their native language. The primary purposes of this act are to facilitate children's learning of English in all areas of the curriculum while strengthening the development of the language and cultural skills necessary for the United States to compete effectively in a global economy (Office of Bilingual Education and Minority Languages Affairs, 1994).

The Bilingual Education Act requires that bilingual teachers be provided when 20 students in a school speak a particular language. For example, if there is a concentration of children who speak Spanish as their primary language, the school must provide bilingual Spanish teachers. In situations where the school has only a few children whose primary language is other than English or students with many different languages, English as a second language (ESL) instruction is given. The students' abilities in English and in their native language must be carefully considered so that they receive appropriate placement and instruction.

Effective Classroom Settings for LEP Students

How many sad stories have been told of past generations of immigrant children who felt lonely and lost in classrooms that did not respect their rich heritages! Many were forbidden to speak their native languages. Others were made to feel ashamed of their families. Fortunately, today's schools recognize and celebrate language and cultural differences.

The school settings in which students spend so much time should, of course, reflect their cultural backgrounds. Several strategies are presented as examples of ways to make classrooms and materials reflect the diversity of student backgrounds (Garcia & Malkin, 1993):

- Encourage minority language students to use their first language around the school even when they are not receiving instruction in it. For example, books in the classroom and library, bulletin boards, and signs can be in your students' native language. Students can also help each other. Jerzy, a child who spoke Polish, was made a helping partner to Irena, a child who had just immigrated from Warsaw. This pairing increased the self-esteem and language skills of both students.
- Display pictures that show people from various backgrounds and communities, including people from culturally diverse backgrounds at work, at home, and in leisure activities.
- Develop units for reading and language arts that use literature from a variety of linguistic and cultural backgrounds to reflect the diversity in U.S. society. Table 13.1 lists books suitable for students from many different backgrounds. Students of *all* backgrounds enjoy reading them but, of course, they are especially important for the self-esteem of students in the groups they feature.
- Be sensitive to your own speech and nonverbal communication. Because cultural norms vary, communicating biases that you do not intend is surprisingly easy.
- Use seating arrangements and class organization to encourage students to try new ways of interacting and learning. Students from different cultural groups enjoy sharing ideas and experiences. This environment is best fostered if students have a variety of opportunities in which to sit, talk, and work with others.

Instructional Practices for Teaching Reading to LEP Students

Reading is based on language. Thus, to read in English, students must understand the English words and sentence structures they meet in books. Simply pronouncing words that they do not understand is not acceptable because then students are reading without meaning. Students who are limited in English should be free to learn sophisticated information and concepts in the language they are most comfortable using. Information and abilities can be learned first in any language and then transferred to another (Hakuta, 1990).

However, because reading is connected to listening and speaking, reading done in English may be used to strengthen all language abilities in English. If students have some proficiency in English, reading English books will further all English language skills.

Following are ways that reading and language acquisition may support each other in instruction. Remember that a student's culture must always be respected.

Using English Books.   English language reading can be an excellent medium to improve general mastery of English. When students learning English are given an abundance of high-interest storybooks in English, their progress in reading and listening comprehension increases at almost twice the usual rate (Gersten, Brengleman, & Jiménez, 1994).

When using this strategy, you may need to focus on books that have repetition in language structures. For example, predictable books (see Chapters 5 and 7), which repeat refrains over and over, are excellent for learning English. Similarly, attractively illustrated books, in which pictures support the text, are excellent for students. Well-known folk tales and fairy tales with familiar plots are also useful. Allen (1994) suggests several other helpful books for students learning English. To develop concepts, use *The Toolbox* (by Rockwell); *Circles, Triangles, and Squares; Over, Under, Through, and Other Spatial Concepts*; and *Push-Pull, Empty-Full: A Book of Opposites* (by Hoban); *Bread, Bread, Bread* (by Morris); *People* (by Spier); and *Growing Vegetable Soup* (by Ehlers). Books that invite talk include *A Taste of Blackberries* (by Smith) and *The Biggest House in the World* (by Lionni); *Nana Upstairs, Nana Downstairs* (by De Paola); and *The Story of Ferdinand* (by Leaf).

Students who are more advanced in English language skills profit from using books focusing on language use, such as *Amelia Bedelia* and its sequels (by Parish), which feature common idioms in amusing situations, and *Many Luscious Lollipops* and its sequels (by Heller), which focus on parts of speech, such as adjectives, nouns, and adverbs. Finally, the increasing number of books written in two languages (see Table 13.1) allows students to match their native language patterns with corresponding English ones.

Opportunities to Use English.   Minority language students must be given many opportunities to move from learning and producing limited word translations and fragmented concepts to using longer sentences and expressing more complex ideas and feelings. As you engage students in increasingly complex reading and writing experiences, check to make sure that they understand the concepts you are teaching. Teachers should use redundant language, relatively simple sentences, and physical gestures as prompts (Gersten, Brengleman, & Jiménez, 1994). In one method, Total Physical Response (Asher & Price, 1969), nonverbal gestures foster active learning of a second language. As you work with children, be aware of the need to provide the background information that helps them to understand the concepts and language you present.

Opportunities to use more complex English vary according to the level of students. In one kindergarten class of Russian-speaking children, a game of

"Simon Says," complete with gestures, provided an active response to English. At a more advanced level, a third-grade bilingual Spanish class listened to the hilarious "twisted" fairy tale, *The True Story of the Three Little Pigs* (by Scieszka) in both English and Spanish, and then acted it out. Later that year, the class listened to *Charlotte's Web* (by White) read in English, chose their favorite words, and then matched these words in Spanish.

Using Conversation about Books to Foster Natural Language Usage.   In fostering a discussion of a story, the teacher can ask such questions as the following: "What do you think this story will be about?" "What do you think will happen next?" "Why do you think that?" "Tell me more about . . ." "What do you mean by . . . ?" Encourage students by giving them time to respond. In addition, students may respond in pairs to make the activity less threatening. Conversation about personal reactions to stories is excellent for giving meaning-based practice in using English. Students enjoy discussing their favorite characters and the best parts of a story. To aid them, the teacher may list helpful English adjectives on the board.

Using Language-Based Approaches.   Approaches based on using students' language to connect reading, writing, and speaking are excellent for teaching students English in a natural setting. Students can dictate language experience stories (see Chapters 5 and 7) that use their own experiences and language. Thus, in reading them, students are using familiar language to master English reading skills. Stories might include words both in English and in the students' native language.

Whole language methods (K. S. Goodman, 1992), which foster a natural use of all language systems together, are excellent for developing English (Chamot & O'Malley, 1994). Many activities are consistent with a whole language approach. Students may, for example, learn to read the print in their environment by using TV guides and advertisements as reading material. When reading books, authentic children's books are preferable to the tightly controlled, artificial language often found in textbooks. Role playing and drama are excellent for fostering language use. Students may also enjoy poetry, which allows them to explore rhythm and rhyming patterns in English. Finally, personal writings, especially those that reflect the children's own cultures, are valuable. Teachers may want to use the writing process to create a literate environment (see Chapter 11).

Using Cooperative Learning.   Small cooperative groups allow students to interact with peers while doing schoolwork assignments. Cooperative learning creates opportunities to use language in meaningful and nonthreatening ways. It draws on primary language skills while developing English language skills, promotes higher-order cognitive and linguistic discourse, and fosters peer modeling and peer feedback. Of course, teachers must serve as facilitators to guide these cooperative peer groups.

Fostering Home-School Collaboration.   Establishing communication with the parents and other family members such as siblings is important. More can be accomplished when the school and home work together. Parents should be contacted frequently to communicate students' successes as well as the problems their children encounter. Remember that parents often have valuable information and insights that can be useful in the teaching process. Families can also make valuable contributions to school programs. In one fourth-grade bilingual room, two mothers sewed all the costumes for 36 fifth-grade children who sang Venezuelan songs. In helping the school's celebration, parents, school staff, and students gained a sense of community involvement (Spinelli, 1998–1999; Lynn, 1999).

Collaboration in the School. Fostering the education of linguistically diverse students requires collaboration among school personnel. Classroom teachers, reading teachers, special education teachers, instructional support staff, and administrators should work together to meet the needs of children. School staff, as well as students, should share their knowledge of other languages and cultures. This sharing is a first step in fostering the understanding that adds richness to American life and education.

Role of Parents in Fostering Literacy

Parents are key to the development of a child's attitude about and preparedness for reading. When the child fails to learn to read, the parents experience feelings of frustration and anger. How can you help parents aid and encourage their children?

First, the teacher should talk regularly to parents of children with reading problems. Devoting time to understanding the needs of these families is important, for it shows your willingness to help. Parents who realize how hard the teacher is trying will often match the teacher's efforts by reading with their children at home or buying them books. Of course, in these encounters, you must be respectful of parents' perspectives. In fact, by listening to the parents' experiences with their children, you often gain information that is important to your instruction (Spinelli, 1998–1999).

In addition to communicating with parents, you may want to offer other forms of support, such as the You Read to Me—I'll Read to You Program and parent workshops.

You Read to Me—I'll Read to You Program

In this program (S. Shapiro, personal communication, 1988), a child places two books in a large bag. One is to be read by the parent to the child; the other is to be read by the child to the parent. Primary children are expected to engage in 15 minutes of personal reading and to listen to a parent read for an additional 15 minutes. For older children, the times are extended to 20 minutes. To verify that the reading has occurred, a form is provided for the parent to list the books and the number of minutes spent reading and to sign.

In this program, parents become participants in the reading process. The program also acquaints parents with a variety of reading formats. Parents may read a high-level book to their children to provide language development. Parents and children may read different books at the same time, silently, so each enjoys a private reading experience, or parents and children may read the same book and then discuss it after reading. Parents may read a book to a child, and the child can "echo read" each page that the parent has read. Parents and children can also take turns reading the same book or read a book as a play by taking the parts of different characters. Easy books and tapes can be provided to parents who are uncertain of their own reading abilities.

Parent Workshops

Being the parent of a child with a reading problem can be a frustrating and discouraging experience. Parents need to share their feelings and experiences with others and perhaps get useful ideas from them. They also need information about the best placement for their children and their rights under the law. Perhaps most important, parents need to share positive literacy experiences they have had with their children.

For a number of years, we have been conducting workshops for parents. The workshops meet once per week for about 10 sessions. Frequently they are held during the time when the children are being taught in the Reading Center. During the workshop sessions, parents share experiences and ideas with one another and often develop close relationships. Our parents have asked for information concerning laws on special education and educational placement. They have also sought ways to foster reading in their children.

What specific ideas do we use with parents? Often we ask parents to bring a favorite book that they remember reading when they were children (Jennings, Richek, Chenault, & Ali, 1993). The books they bring are easy and entertaining. This activity demonstrates that children will want to learn if the books they are encouraged to read are easy and fun. We also have asked parents to remember the affectionate experiences they and their own parents shared during reading and discuss ways to foster these happy experiences with their own children.

We share special books with parents. One semester, the parent leader showed the beautiful book *On the Day You Were Born* (by Frasier). In the following weeks, many parents read this book to their children. At the end of sessions, we had a final celebration in which parents read a description of the actual day their own individual children were born. Most descriptions were given by mothers, but two were given by fathers.

As the previous example shows, we also encourage our parents to write. This activity deepens their own understanding of literacy and helps them to understand how difficult writing can be for children. Parents come to understand the nature of the writing process and how spelling and punctuation should be a last step in writing, rather than the first step. At the end of each semester, a piece of writing from each child and participating parent is bound into a joint Reading Center book and is read at a final celebration. Each parent and child receives a copy of this joint book as a memento of a positive experience.

The leaders of the parent workshops also share strategies that parents can use with their children. Typical strategies (L. Chenault, personal communication, 1993; S. Ali, personal communication, 1994–1995) have included:

- Making family message boards to encourage literacy
- Reading a favorite book over again
- Displaying books in theme baskets (e.g., Halloween, spring)
- Suggestions on how to choose books at libraries and bookstores
- Taking field trips that support what your child is studying
- Modeling thinking about what you know about a topic before you read
- Modeling thinking about what you learned after you read
- Listing places to purchase discount children's books

Ada (1988) reports similarly successful experiences with Spanish-speaking parents in communities that included many migrant workers. Parents were delighted to record, in Spanish, their positive family experiences.

Adolescents with Reading Problems

Adolescence (the 13- to 20-year-old age range) is a well-documented period of social, emotional, and physical change. Adolescents must resolve conflicts between their desires for freedom and security as they are torn between wishing for independence and yet not ready for the responsibilities of full adulthood. They must cope with rapid physical changes in growth, appearance, and sexual drive. Peer pressure greatly affects adolescents, as they seek group acceptance and are increasingly aware of how their peers are doing. All these characteristics of adolescence present challenges that may negatively affect learning (Hammechek, 1990; Kerr, Nelson, & Lambert, 1987).

Characteristics of Adolescents with Reading Problems

Teenagers with reading problems not only have difficulty in school, but they must also cope with the normal challenges and adjustments presented by adolescence. Trying to deal with this combination creates special burdens for teenagers, such as:

1. *Passive learning.* Adolescents with reading and learning problems have often developed an attitude of *learned helplessness* and dependence (Deshler, Ellis, & Lenz, 1996). They wait for teacher direction.
2. *Poor self-concept.* Low self-esteem and other emotional problems result from years of failure and frustration (Smith, 1992).
3. *Inept social skills.* Adolescents with academic problems often have difficulty making and keeping friends during a period when friendships and peer approval are important (Bryan, 1991; Vaughn, 1991).
4. *Attention deficits.* Poor attention and concentration are common in teenagers who read poorly (Lerner, Lowenthal, & Lerner, 1995). Because long periods

of concentration are required for high school work, attention problems are quite serious.

5. *Lack of motivation.* After years of failure, many teenagers feel that they are "dumb" and that their efforts to learn are useless. Adolescents can learn only if they are motivated and can attribute success to their own efforts (Yasutake & Bryan, 1995).

Special Considerations at the Secondary Level

Schools often fail to meet the needs of adolescents with reading and learning problems. For example, only 35 percent of learning-disabled students (many of whom have reading problems) receive high school diplomas (U.S. Department of Education, 1998). Students who drop out of school often face grim futures in the streets.

Secondary students with academic problems face new challenges, as demands for excellence in education have led to increased requirements (in mathematics, foreign languages, and science) for high school graduation. Students with learning problems are no longer sheltered from the demands of the regular curriculum but are expected to meet many of the same requirements as all other students. More than three-fourths of all states now require that high school students pass minimum competency tests before receiving their diplomas.

Finally, many content-area secondary school teachers are not oriented to working with low-achieving readers. Focusing on their specializations, such teachers have not been trained to adjust their specialized curricula in mathematics, French, or physics to the student with reading problems. For this reason, a major task of the high school reading specialist is to help the content teachers understand and cope with the needs of low-achieving students.

Reading teachers can suggest many options to help disabled students. If the student has a severe reading problem, the teacher might be able to tape lessons. At times, books recorded for the blind can be made accessible to low-achieving readers through local libraries. During examinations, students might be allowed to give answers orally, to tape answers, or to dictate answers to someone else. Students who do write could be allowed additional time. Convincing high school teachers to modify their programs for special students is an essential element of a reading specialist's job and one that requires considerable skill in interpersonal relationships.

Components of Effective Secondary Programs

Zigmond (1990) identified four effective components for secondary school programs:

- *Intensive instruction in reading and mathematics.* Many students with reading problems continue to require instruction in basic skills.

- *Direct instruction in high school "survival" skills.* Training may be needed for successful functioning in a high school. "Behavior control" helps students learn how to stay out of trouble in school. "Teacher-pleasing behaviors" allow students to acquire behavior patterns (look interested, volunteer responses) that make teachers view them more positively. Strategies such as organizing time, previewing textbooks, taking notes from a lecture or text, organizing information, and taking tests are needed for academic success.
- *Successful completion of courses.* Students with problems may cut classes, come late, and not complete assignments. Empathetic, caring teachers and counselors can foster course completion. Success in the ninth grade is particularly critical for high school.
- *Planning for life after high school.* Adolescents with reading problems need to prepare for a successful transition to higher education or the world of work.

Adults with Reading Problems

For many individuals, a reading disability is a lifelong problem, one that does not disappear when schooling has been completed. This section considers the problems of adults with reading disabilities.

Adult literacy presents an ever-growing challenge. Some adults with problems in reading have dropped out of school and now find themselves blocked from employment. Others may be employed but want to advance in their jobs or enhance their personal skills. Some have been denied opportunities because they lived in countries that did not provide a free education. Yet other adult learners are concerned with learning to speak and write in English. Finally, some have continuing literacy problems that are sometimes associated with learning disabilities.

Postsecondary and College Programs

Postsecondary education includes community colleges, vocational-technical training, and colleges. Programs in a variety of settings at a growing number of colleges and other postsecondary institutions serve adult learners with reading problems.

Accommodations have been triggered by Section 504 of the Rehabilitation Act (1973), which requires educational institutions receiving federal funds to make reasonable accommodations for students who are identified as having a disability. Many such individuals suffer from reading problems.

How can you help adult students in postsecondary education cope with academic demands? Some suggestions are:

- Give course syllabi to them 4 to 6 weeks before class begins and discuss them personally.
- Begin lectures and discussions with systematic overviews of the topic.

- Use a chalkboard or overhead projector to outline lecture material and orally read what is written on the board or transparencies.
- Use a chalkboard or overhead projector to highlight key concepts, unusual terminology, or foreign words.
- Clearly identify important points, main ideas, and key concepts orally in lectures.
- Give assignments in writing and orally; be available for further clarification.
- Provide opportunities for student participation, question periods, and discussion.
- Provide time for individual discussion of assignments and questions about lectures and readings.
- Provide study guides for the text, study questions, and review sessions to prepare for exams.
- Allow oral presentations or tape-recorded assignments instead of requiring students to use a written format.
- Modify evaluation procedures: include untimed tests, wide-lined paper for tests, and alternatives to computer-scored answer sheets.

Needs of Adults with Reading Problems

Although some adults are lucky enough to get higher education, many adults with severe reading problems have great difficulty finding their niche in the world. They have trouble working, socializing, and even coping with daily tasks. Many adults with reading problems have ingenious strategies for avoiding, hiding, and dealing with their problems.

A man whose wife had died a few years before was caught in the social dating whirl. He would routinely enter a restaurant with his lady friend, put down the menu, and say, "Why don't you order for both of us, dear? Your selections are always perfect." This man hired professionals to handle all of his personal matters, including his checkbook. His friends attributed his actions to wealth and never suspected his inability to read.

Instructional Programs for Adults

Adults who seek help with their reading problems are likely to be highly motivated to learn and to demand an explanation of the goals and purposes of their programs. This commitment enables them to succeed (Gerber & Brown, 1999).

More and more adults seek help that goes beyond the basic stages of literacy. As a result, the field of adult literacy has expanded its original responsibilities from basic functional literacy to a high technical level (approximately 12th-grade reading level) (Chall, 1987, 1994).

Some instructional options for adult programs are:

- *ABE* and *GED Programs* provide adult basic education (from elementary levels through eighth grade) and a high-school-level education with a general education diploma. Both the ABE and GED are funded by the federal government and require group instruction. Approximately two-and-a-half-million adults are enrolled in these programs (Gottesman, 1994).

- *Literacy Volunteers of America*, a private organization training volunteers to work with adults, serves the needs of more than 52,000 people. Instruction is individual, and programs are aimed at the illiterate and semiliterate adult. A component for teaching English as a second language is available.
- *Laubach Literacy Action* is the U.S. division of Laubach Literacy International. Frank Laubach, a missionary, developed a program to teach literacy to people worldwide. This program uses volunteers and currently serves more than 150,000 adults. Materials, including initial instruction in a pictorial alphabet, are available through New Readers' Press.
- *ESL adult literacy programs* concentrate on English as a second language. Federal funding comes from the Adult Literacy Act. These programs currently serve more than one million limited-English-proficient adults. As more immigrants enter the United States' work force, ESL services are expected to increase (Newman, 1994).

Adults with reading problems express wishes for developing a wide variety of life skills. Needs include social skills, career counseling, developing self-esteem and confidence, overcoming dependence, survival skills, vocational training, job procurement and retention, reading, spelling, management of personal finances, and organizational skills. They often express a particular need for help in coping with jobs.

Summary

The diversity of American culture is one of its most important strengths. An increasing number of students speak English as a second language. Approaches to instruction for bilingual and limited-English-proficient students include teaching complex concepts in the student's native language; sheltered English with carefully sequenced content-area instruction; English as a second language (ESL) with controlled pattern repetition in teaching English; bilingual education, or instruction in two languages; dual language, or two groups of students learning each other's language; and immersion, or full exposure without special instruction. Effective classroom settings honor students' native cultures and do not unconsciously communicate bias. Instructional practices for teaching reading to limited-English-proficient (LEP) students include using interesting English books; a language-rich English environment; using instructional conversation about content areas; connecting reading, writing, speaking, and listening; using cooperative learning; and fostering home-school collaboration.

Families from different cultures hold views of reading, language, and instruction that may not reflect the dominant views of society. For example, some people respond to the teacher as an authority figure and are uncomfortable with informal and indirect learning. Language differences should not be interpreted as reflecting inferiority.

Parents can cooperate with the school in many ways.

Adolescents with reading problems add academic difficulties to the difficult adjustment that is typical of their age group. Instruction should reflect concern for their future. New laws have increased the number of adults in postsecondary schools and colleges. In addition, the number of adults who wish to learn English is increasing. Adults are goal-oriented in their learning.

14 Correlates of Reading Disability

Introduction

Several factors, or *correlates*, relate to difficulty in reading. The existence of a single factor in a child's life does not necessarily *cause* a reading disability. For example, many children exposed to poor environmental factors become excellent readers. Yet, with recent research showing that about the 20 percent of children encounter severe difficulty in reading (National Reading Panel, 1999), teachers should know about the nature of these correlates and their effects on reading performance. These correlates relate to reading in multiple and complex ways, and poor reading is generally the result of several of the factors, which interact with one another. As ongoing research adds to information about each of these factors, knowledge about the correlates of reading disability is expanding. This chapter shows how environmental factors, emotional factors, intelligence, language, and physical factors affect reading acquisition and performance and examines ways to assess each of these correlates.

Environmental Factors

Students live and grow in several different environments, and each environment has a strong impact on their desires and abilities to learn. Environments include the home, the school, the social group, and the cultural milieu (Figure 14.1). How do each of these environments affect a student's reading?

Home Environment

The home, a child's first environment, is the foundation for tremendous cognitive growth and development. The experiences that occur during the critical first five or six years of life are powerful influences on a child's intelligence and language.

Parents provide emotional well-being as well as intellectual stimulation. A crucial interaction known as *bonding* takes place during the early months of infancy and becomes the basis for later emotional health. Bonding depends on a successful interactive relationship between the mother (or primary parent figure) and the infant (Bowlby, 1969). The early development of the ego and self-concept are also dependent on the support and encouragement of parents. Studies that

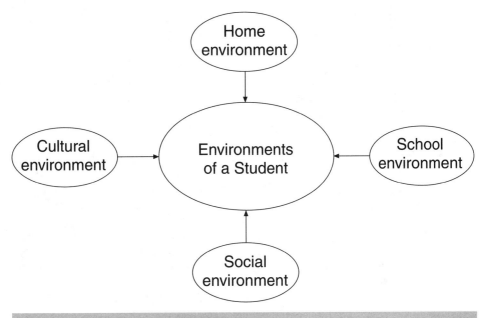

FIGURE 14.1 Environmental Factors

compare good and poor readers show that students who experience success are much more likely to have a favorable home environment (Turnbull & Turnbull, 1996; Levine & Havighurst, 1992; Whitman, 2000).

Parents are also important in stimulating a love for reading. Parents who read to children, take them to libraries, and buy books as presents teach children to value reading. Parents who read themselves provide a role model for literacy. The parent's role continues to be crucial even after the child enters school.

Youngsters who experience difficulty learning to read are in special need of satisfying family relationships. Parents can alleviate some of the psychological and emotional consequences of reading failure by what they do in the home environment. They can provide love, acceptance, and other opportunities for success (Turnbull & Turnbull, 1996).

Sadly, today's children come from increasingly difficult environments. About 27 percent of all children under age 18 live with a single parent who has never married, and about 69 percent of children born to unwed mothers will live near, or below, the poverty line (U.S. Department of Commerce, 1997). Understandably, children in such households may be under stress and so feel too burdened to cope with school demands (Whitman, 2000).

School Environment

Because youngsters spend a substantial portion of their waking hours in school, the experiences and relationships in the school environment profoundly affect their lives. For the poor reader, school experiences are often unhappy ones.

Interactions within the School. Students with reading problems often have unsatisfactory relationships with adults in the schools. Studies show that poor achievers tend to be perceived negatively by teachers, paraprofessionals, and principals. Teachers identify these students as aggressive, lacking self-discipline, and unmotivated. Low achievers receive little praise or acknowledgment from teachers, and they are more likely to be criticized (Bryan, Sullivan-Burnstein, & Mathur, 1998; Good, 1983). These findings have serious implications for students with reading problems.

Instructional Factors in Reading Problems. As emphasized in Chapters 2 and 4, instruction that does not meet a student's needs can be an important factor in a reading problem. When immature children are given formal reading instruction before they can profit from it, they may become frustrated and develop reading problems. When children do not receive sufficient instruction in critical skills, they may fail in the initial stages of learning to read. For example, research demonstrates that an important link exists between phonemic awareness and early reading. If children do not develop the critical skill of phonemic awareness by first grade, their reading in all of the following grades is affected. Finally, low-achieving students often do not read enough to become better readers (Johnson & Allington, 1991; Lyon, 1998).

Social Environment

Successful interactions with friends should provide many satisfactions and opportunities to gain confidence. Unfortunately, a sizable body of evidence shows that social unpopularity tends to accompany school failure. Poor achievers are often rejected or ignored by classmates and are uninvolved in extracurricular activities (Bryan, Sullivan-Burnstein, & Mathur, 1998).

Students with reading problems tend to have problems interacting with others, and they exhibit poor social perception skills (Bryan, 1991; Haager & Vaughn, 1995). When children develop normally, they learn social skills in a casual and informal manner. Through incidental experiences, they learn appropriate ways of acting with people: what to say, how to behave, and how to "give and take" in a human situation. However, students with reading and learning problems are sometimes not sensitive to social nuances, and they may be unaware of how others interpret their behavior.

Often students with reading problems are unable to accommodate themselves to another person's point of view. Because they fail to consider the needs of other people, their chances for successful social interaction with peers are reduced. Role-playing games, in which one person is made to adopt the viewpoint of another person, may help to improve social relationships.

In contrast to normal achievers, low-achieving students tend to overestimate their own popularity (Bryan, Sullivan-Burnstein, & Mathur, 1998). They seem unable to recognize their own social shortcomings and have difficulty relating to peers in a social setting.

Cultural Environment

The population of North America is a composite of hundreds of different ethnic and cultural traditions. In today's society, ever-changing patterns of immigration and movement occur as new groups of people add their cultural riches to the schools. A few decades ago, Americans assumed that everyone would be assimilated into the "melting pot" of the dominant culture. Since then, a new effort to value and maintain diverse cultural traditions has occurred. One of the greatest challenges schools face is providing an excellent education to students of all cultures, whatever their geographical origin, socioeconomic status, or language.

Because a significant portion of American families live below a specified poverty level, teachers need to be aware of the possible effects of poverty on students' academic performance. Although individuals with incomes below the poverty level come from diverse backgrounds, they tend to have certain similarities. Because they are necessarily concerned with basic survival needs, parents are likely to have less energy to devote to their children's development. As a consequence, children from these families often must care for themselves at a young age and may come to school with relatively limited background experiences (Carnegie Corporation, 1994; Levine & Havighurst, 1992; Ortiz, 1997).

Sometimes students reject the traditional values of the school and identify with subcultures whose values work against academic learning. This trend is particularly evident when adolescents join gangs. The reading achievement of gang members is often substantially below that of other students, despite a high degree of verbal skills, leadership qualities, and intelligence in gang members (Labov, Cohen, Robins, & Lewis, 1968). Cultural differences, particularly those arising from a culture of poverty, may lead to intense suspicion and discomfort with individuals perceived to be in the dominant culture.

These generalizations do not, of course, hold true for all low-income students. In many poor families, education is cherished, the values of the school are upheld, and family members are encouraged to read and achieve. The opportunity to progress from poverty to economic security is a fundamental promise of democratic nations.

Assessing Environmental Factors

Chapter 2 presented interviews and questionnaires as tools for gathering information about environmental factors. This chapter adds a discussion of *systematic observation*, a sophisticated tool for assessing the environment. Systematic observation is a useful method of assessing student behavior and interaction with many different environments, both social and academic. Even short observations can provide valuable information because they provide objective evidence about behavior.

The key to behavioral observation is to identify and describe clearly behaviors that are being observed. The observation should not consist of value judgments, such as "Amy caused trouble." A written observation is a careful recording of actual behaviors; for example, "Amy walked up to Mary's desk and tore up Mary's spelling paper." The cumulative records of many observations provide a basis for making diagnostic decisions and planning instruction.

Many different systems can be used for observing behavior. These systems include time sampling, event sampling, and the anecdotal record:

- *Time Sampling*. This method enables the teacher to observe the length of time a student persists in certain behaviors. Generally, one type of behavior, such as maintaining attention, is chosen for analysis. The teacher records the number of times the behavior occurs and the length of time it persists during the observation period.
- *Event Sampling*. The teacher chooses a specific type of event for recording. The observer tries to record the event in as much detail as possible each time it is observed. Event samples often last several days.
- *Anecdotal Record*. In this system, the student is observed throughout an extended period, and all incidents of particular interest are described in detail. Many different types of activities can be recorded in the anecdotal record, because it is meant to give the "flavor" of a student's activities.

Emotional Factors

Low-achieving students, particularly those with a long history of failure, often have accompanying emotional problems that impede learning. Moreover, emotional problems tend to increase as a youngster moves up through the elementary years and enters adolescence.

Sometimes teachers have a hard time determining whether a reading problem is the result of an underlying emotional disorder or if emotional problems have developed because of the reading disability. Trying to determine whether the learning failure or the emotional problem is the primary precipitating factor is of little value. A more constructive approach is to help the student experience success in reading, and this success, in turn, builds feelings of self-worth and confidence. Accomplishment in reading then becomes a kind of therapy. A therapeutic approach to the teaching of reading can build confidence, establish self-esteem, and capture the pupil's interest. However, students with severe emotional disorders may need psychotherapy or counseling (Rock, Fessler, & Church, 1997; Silver, 1998; Yasutake & Bryan, 1996) before reading improves.

Emotional Responses to Reading Problems

No one personality type describes all low-achieving students, for students react to learning problems in different ways. Some failing readers evidence no emotional problems; others display a variety of disordered psychological behaviors (Rock, Fessler & Church, 1997; Kauffman, 1997; Silver, 1998).

Learning Block.   If learning has been a painful experience, the student may simply block it. In this way, the student keeps pain and distress out of the reach of consciousness. Learning blocks can often be overcome when reading is taught in interesting and nonthreatening ways and students begin to enjoy learning.

Nine-year-old Maria developed an emotional block against books. Whenever the teacher brought out a book her response was, "I told you I can't read a book." To solve this problem, the teacher copied all the words from one picture book and taught them, one word at a time, without showing Maria the source. After all the words were mastered, the teacher presented the book to Maria who, of course, at first refused to read it. However, when the teacher demonstrated that Maria could read any word in the book, she overcame her fear and went on to read that book and others.

Hostile-Aggressive Behavior.   Pupils with reading problems may become hostile and overly aggressive to compensate for feelings of inadequacy. Students who appear to be tough, ready to fight, and even delinquent may be seeking a sense of accomplishment that they are unable to find in school. Antisocial behavior can be a manifestation of students' anger and frustration with academics and with the failure of others to understand them. Often such students display less hostility when they are taught in small groups or individually and when their problems receive earnest attention from teachers.

Learned Helplessness.   Avoiding failure can be an important goal for some disabled readers. To make sure that they do not fail, students may refuse to try. Thus, they avoid stress through withdrawal and apathetic behavior. Such students may become passive and refuse to complete assignments, participate in class discussions, or read. They need to be encouraged to take risks (such as guessing at words they are not sure of) and to learn that a certain amount of failure is an unavoidable and acceptable part of living. When instructing these students, teachers should tell them what they will be learning and why they are learning it. Encouraging and rewarding students for "guessing" may also be helpful.

In some cases poor achievers cannot accept personal responsibility for learning even when they are successful. *Attribution theory* suggests that such students attribute their success and failure to the teacher who is in charge of the learning situation and has caused the learning to occur (Yasutake & Bryan, 1995). These students need more personal involvement in the learning situation and need to take responsibility for it.

Low Self-esteem and Depression.   Understandably, students who have been subjected to continual failure develop a low opinion of themselves. They display a negative self-image, poor ego development, and a lack of confidence. The problem often deepens as students become older and realize that they are not meeting society's expectations (Brooks, 1997; Silver, 1998).

A self-defeating "what's the use" attitude may result in overall depression. Such students need to know that they are accepted as they are and that the teacher understands their problems and has confidence that they can learn. Every in-structional success must be emphasized for these students.

Anxiety.   Anxious students are never sure of their abilities and are afraid of mak-ing mistakes and being reprimanded. Stress clouds their lives and drains their en-ergy and ability to concentrate on learning. Anxious students need reassurance that they can learn.

Assessing Emotional and Behavioral Factors

Teachers who are aware of students' emotional responses are more effective in teaching them to read. Usually, an informal assessment of emotional factors is suf-ficient for the purposes of the reading diagnosis.

Occasionally, teachers may need to refer a student to mental health spe-cialists (such as psychiatrists, psychologists, or social workers) for further eval-uation and possible psychotherapy or counseling. Such referrals are needed when emotional problems are so severe that they interfere with reading pro-gress to the extent that the student achieves little growth over a long period of instruction.

One helpful informal assessment measure that can be used by a reading teacher is the *sentence completion activity*. In addition, information from inter-views (see Chapter 2) provides useful information about the student's emotional status.

The sentence completion activity is a series of beginning sentence fragments that the student completes, such as "I like _____." In finishing these sentences, students often provide insights into their thoughts and feelings. The ac-tivity can be administered orally or in writing. A sample sentence completion form is given in Figure 14.2. In interpreting results, however, bear in mind that it is only an informal measure. Although it may suggest ideas about student atti-tudes, these hypotheses should be verified through interview, observation, and perhaps the administration of formal measures.

Intelligence

The factor of intelligence provides an estimate of the student's capacity or poten-tial for learning and for reading achievement. Teachers cannot help but notice differences in their students' abilities to learn. In the process of instruction, one student grasps the lesson quickly, another student learns the lesson in an unusual or unique way, and a third student has great difficulty catching on.

Notions about the nature of intelligence and its measurement have changed over the years and are continuing to evolve. Among the questions studied by the scientific community is "What is intelligence, and how much can it be changed?"

FIGURE 14.2 **Sample Sentence Completion Form**		

1. I like_____.
2. Eating _____.
3. I am happiest when _____.
4. School is _____.
5. My greatest fear is _____.
6. I wish I could_____.
7. There are times _____.
8. My mother_____.
9. My father_____.
10. Sometimes I wish _____.
11. I sleep _____.
12. When I dream _____.
13. I want to _____.
14. One thing that bothers me is _____.
15. Sometimes I hope_____.
16. I think I will never_____.
17. Other people are _____.
18. One thing I don't like is_____.
19. I feel sorry for people who_____.
20. My mind _____.
21. Most of the time _____.
22. I try to _____.

Definitions of Intelligence

For centuries, philosophers and scholars have attempted to define intelligence, yet theories about its nature continue to be controversial. Intelligence has been defined as the capacity to understand the world and the resourcefulness to cope with its challenges (Wechsler, 1975). As generally used, however, intelligence refers to an individual's cognitive or thinking abilities or to the child's potential for acquiring school skills. In fact, most intelligence tests have been validated by comparing them with school performance.

Because a person's intelligence cannot be observed directly, what is called intelligence is inferred through responses in a test situation. These responses are used to explain intellectual differences among people in their present behavior and to predict their future behavior. The Intelligence Quotient (IQ) is a score obtained on an intelligence test, which reports performance on the test questions in relation to peers of the same age (see Chapter 16 for a discussion of IQ tests).

New Views of Intelligence

New theories about intelligence are based on the view that several different components make up the factor called intelligence. A student may exhibit a high capacity in one component, such as verbal abilities, and low aptitude in another, such as spatial abilities. For example, the *Wechsler Intelligence Scale for Children–Third Edition (WISC-III)* provides scores on two major components: verbal intelligence and performance intelligence. The *Kaufman Assessment Battery for Children* (K-ABC) divides intelligence into sequential and simultaneous processing. Another theory of intelligence is that of *multiple intelligences*, which is proposed by Gardner (1985). He suggests eight components of intelligence: linguistic, musical, logical-mathematical, spatial, bodily kinesthetic, sense of self, sense of others, and naturalistic.

Sternberg (1999) believes that intelligence tests and achievement tests actually measure similar accomplishments. Both are a form of developmental expertise. Moreover, people are constantly in the process of developing expertise as they work in a given domain. This model of intelligence has five key components:

- *Metacognitive skills:* the ability to direct and control one's learning.
- *Learning skills:* explicit learning skills, which require an effort to learn, and implicit learning skills, which are learned more casually.
- *Thinking skills:* critical or analytical thinking, creative thinking, and practical thinking.
- *Knowledge:* declarative knowledge (factual knowledge) and procedural knowledge (strategies for knowing how the system operates).
- *Motivation:* indispensable for school success; without it, the student never even tries to learn.

Evidence That a Person's Intelligence Can Be Changed

A major question concerning intelligence has been whether a persons's intelligence is determined by *heredity* (the result of one's biological makeup) or by *environment* (the result of one's personal experiences). Research shows that both heredity and environment contribute to a person's cognitive abilities. A complex sequence of interactions between heredity and environmental factors occurs during the development of an individual's intelligence. Although heredity may account for much of the variance in intelligence, the child's environment also contributes a substantial portion (Slavin, 1991).

Scientists are finding that the human brain is literally shaped by experience and develops more fully in enriched environments. The human brain grows rapidly during the first few years of life. Trillions of connections (or synapses) form to link the billions of neurons that make complex thinking possible. Neural pathways that are not used disappear forever. Eventually, the brain no longer is elastic but becomes hardwired, and the neurological structure that has been established serves the individual for life. In this way, a child's environment actually influences the number of brain cells formed and the connections that are made between them (Carnegie Corporation, 1994). Thus, the child's home and social environments, the level of health care and nutrition, and school learning experiences all can influence intelligence.

A child's mental abilities can change significantly under favorable conditions. Studies of preschool at-risk children show that intelligence test scores are highly modifiable at this level and can increase substantially when children receive early intervention (Berrueta-Clement, Schweinhart, Barnett, Epstein, & Weikart, 1985). Improvements in cognitive ability can also occur in adolescents. Feuerstein's (1980) work with mentally retarded adolescents demonstrates that intelligence can be modified at all ages and stages of cognitive development.

Basic to the teaching profession is the conviction that the ability to learn is present at all stages of development and that teachers play a vital role in the teaching-learning process. Teachers can make an important difference.

Cultural Bias in the Measurement of Intelligence

Intelligence tests have been criticized because of cultural bias. Studies show race and class differences in IQ scores: students from middle-class homes score higher than children from lower-class homes. Also, intelligence test items do not match the experiences that minority and lower-class children have in their cultural environment (Levine & Havighurst, 1992).

In the landmark legal case, *Larry P. v. Riles* (1979), the court ruled that IQ testing is racially and culturally discriminatory when used as the sole criterion for placing children in classes for the mentally retarded. However, in a later case, *PASE v. Hannon* (1980), the court ruled that it saw little evidence that the items were biased. The issue of bias in assessment through the use of intelligence tests continues to be debated in both the courtroom and academic research.

Using Intelligence Tests to Determine the Existence of a Reading Disability

Chapter 3 defined a reading problem in terms of the difference between the student's appropriate reading level (usually a student's grade placement) and the student's actual achievement. In addition, intelligence test scores are sometimes used to determine whether a student has a reading disability. Using this method teachers can determine whether a significant discrepancy exists between the student's *potential* for reading achievement (as measured by an intelligence test) and the student's *actual* reading performance. A large gap or discrepancy between reading potential and reading achievement indicates a reading disability, because the student has the potential to read much better.

In calculating a discrepancy, an intelligence test, such as the *WISC-III scale*, is used to measure potential and a standardized reading test is used to measure current reading achievement. (The *WISC-III* and other tests of intelligence are discussed in Chapter 16). In calculating a discrepancy, determine a *reading expectancy level* and compare it to *current reading achievement*.

Harris and Sipay (1985) developed a method for calculating a student's *reading expectancy age*. This method uses a mental age (MA) to calculate whether a reading problem exists. The MA is obtained by multiplying the student's IQ by his or her chronological age (CA) and dividing the product by 100, as in the following formula:

$$MA = \frac{IQ \times CA}{100}$$

Express the MA and CA in years and tenths, rather than years and months.

Once you obtain the MA, you can calculate the reading expectancy age (REA):

$$REA = \frac{2MA + CA}{3}$$

To convert the REA to a *reading expectancy grade* (REG), subtract 5.2 from the REA.

For example, Marion is 10.0 years old, and she has an IQ of 120. Her MA is 12.0 years. The REA formula indicates she has a reading expectancy age of 11.3 and a reading expectancy grade of 6.1 (11.3 - 5.2). If Marion's current level of reading is 3.0, she would have a discrepancy of 3.1 years.

$$REA = \frac{2(12.0) + 10.0}{3} = 11.3$$

$$REG = 11.3 - 5.2 = 6.1$$

Discrepancy = Reading Expectancy − Reading Achievement
$$= 6.1 - 3.0 = 3.1$$

Table 14.1, based on the Harris and Sipay formula, helps you avoid doing these calculations. If you know the IQ and CA of a student, the reading expectancy grade can then be found by noting the intersection of the CA with IQ. For students over 15 years of age, use 15.0 as the chronological age. If the CA and IQ fall between two values on a table, use the closest value. For convenience, the expectancy *grade* level, rather than *age*, is reported directly.

TABLE 14.1 Reading Expectancy Grade Levels

	IQ Score															
Chronological Age (in years and months)	70	75	80	85	90	95	100	105	110	115	120	125	130	135	140	145
6–0	—	—	—	—	—	—	—	1.0	1.2	1.4	1.6	1.8	2.0	2.2	2.4	2.6
6–3	—	—	—	—	—	—	1.0	1.2	1.5	1.7	1.9	2.1	2.3	2.5	2.7	2.9
6–6	—	—	—	—	—	1.1	1.3	1.5	1.7	2.0	2.2	2.4	2.6	2.8	3.0	3.2
6–9	—	—	—	—	1.1	1.3	1.6	1.8	2.0	2.2	2.4	2.7	2.9	3.1	3.4	3.6
7–0	—	—	—	1.1	1.3	1.6	1.8	2.0	2.3	2.5	2.7	3.0	3.2	3.4	3.7	3.9
7–3	—	—	1.1	1.3	1.6	1.8	2.0	2.3	2.5	2.8	3.0	3.2	3.5	3.7	4.0	4.2
7–6	—	1.0	1.3	1.6	1.8	2.0	2.3	2.6	2.8	3.0	3.3	3.6	3.8	4.0	4.3	4.6
7–9	1.1	1.3	1.5	1.8	2.0	2.3	2.6	2.8	3.1	3.3	3.6	3.8	4.1	4.4	4.6	4.9
8–0	1.2	1.5	1.7	2.0	2.3	2.5	2.8	3.1	3.3	3.6	3.9	4.1	4.4	4.7	4.9	5.2
8–3	1.4	1.7	2.0	2.2	2.5	2.8	3.0	3.3	3.6	3.9	4.2	4.4	4.7	5.1	5.3	5.5
8–6	1.6	1.9	2.2	2.4	2.7	3.0	3.3	3.6	3.9	4.2	4.4	4.7	5.0	5.3	5.6	5.8
8–9	1.8	2.1	2.4	2.7	3.0	3.3	3.6	3.8	4.1	4.4	4.7	5.0	5.3	5.6	5.9	6.2
9–0	2.0	2.3	2.6	2.9	3.2	3.5	3.8	4.1	4.4	4.7	5.0	5.3	5.6	5.9	6.2	6.5
9–3	2.2	2.5	2.8	3.1	3.4	3.7	4.0	4.4	4.7	5.0	5.3	5.6	5.9	6.2	6.5	6.8
9–6	2.4	2.7	3.0	3.4	3.7	4.0	4.3	4.6	4.9	5.2	5.6	5.9	6.2	6.5	6.8	7.2
9–9	2.6	2.9	3.2	3.6	3.9	4.2	4.6	4.9	5.2	5.5	5.8	6.2	6.5	6.8	7.2	7.5
10–0	2.8	3.1	3.5	3.8	4.1	4.5	4.8	5.1	5.5	5.8	6.1	6.5	6.8	7.1	7.5	7.8
10–3	3.0	3.3	3.7	4.0	4.4	4.7	5.0	5.4	5.7	6.1	6.4	6.8	7.1	7.4	7.8	8.1
10–6	3.2	3.6	3.9	4.2	4.6	5.0	5.3	5.6	6.0	6.4	6.7	7.0	7.4	7.8	8.1	8.4
10–9	3.4	3.8	4.1	4.5	4.8	5.2	5.6	5.9	6.3	6.6	7.0	7.3	7.7	8.1	8.4	8.8
11–0	3.6	4.0	4.3	4.7	5.1	5.4	5.8	6.2	6.5	6.9	7.3	7.6	8.0	8.4	8.7	9.1
11–3	3.8	4.2	4.6	4.9	5.3	5.7	6.0	6.4	6.8	7.2	7.6	7.9	8.3	8.7	9.0	9.4
11–6	4.0	4.4	4.8	5.2	5.5	5.9	6.3	6.7	7.1	7.4	7.8	8.2	8.6	9.0	9.4	9.8
11–9	4.2	4.6	5.0	5.4	5.8	6.2	6.6	7.0	7.3	7.7	8.1	8.5	8.9	9.3	9.7	10.1
12–0	4.4	4.8	5.2	5.6	6.0	6.4	6.8	7.2	7.6	8.0	8.4	8.8	9.2	9.6	10.0	10.4
12–3	4.6	5.0	5.4	5.8	6.2	6.6	7.0	7.4	7.9	8.3	8.7	9.1	9.5	9.9	10.3	10.7
12–6	4.8	5.2	5.6	6.0	6.5	6.9	7.3	7.7	8.1	8.6	9.0	9.4	9.8	10.2	10.6	11.0
12–9	5.0	5.4	5.8	6.3	6.7	7.1	7.6	8.0	8.4	8.8	9.2	9.7	10.1	10.5	11.0	11.4
13–0	5.2	5.6	6.1	6.5	6.9	7.4	7.8	8.2	8.7	9.1	9.5	10.0	10.4	10.8	11.3	11.7
13–3	5.4	5.8	6.3	6.7	7.2	7.6	8.0	8.5	8.9	9.4	9.8	10.2	10.7	11.1	11.5	12.0
13–6	5.6	6.0	6.5	7.0	7.4	7.8	8.3	8.8	9.2	9.6	10.1	10.6	11.0	11.4	11.9	12.4
13–9	5.8	6.3	6.7	7.2	7.6	8.1	8.6	9.0	9.5	9.9	10.4	10.8	11.3	11.8	12.2	12.7
14–0	6.0	6.5	6.9	7.4	7.9	8.3	8.8	9.3	9.7	10.2	10.7	11.1	11.6	12.1	12.5	13.0
14–3	6.2	6.7	7.2	7.6	8.1	8.6	9.0	9.5	10.0	10.5	11.0	11.4	11.9	12.4	12.8	13.3
14–6	6.4	6.9	7.4	7.8	8.3	8.8	9.3	9.8	10.3	10.8	11.2	11.7	12.2	12.7	13.2	13.6
14–9	6.6	7.1	7.6	8.1	8.6	9.1	9.6	10.0	10.5	11.0	11.5	12.0	12.8	13.0	13.5	14.0
15–0	6.8	7.3	7.8	8.3	8.8	9.3	9.8	10.3	10.8	11.3	11.8	12.3	12.8	13.3	13.8	14.3

This table gives reading expectancy grade level. If the intelligence score or chronological age falls between two values, use the closest one. For students over 15 years of age, use the 15.0 chronological age value.

Language Abilities

Language has been recognized as one of the greatest of human achievements—more important than all the physical tools invented in the last ten thousand years. Language permits human beings to speak of things unseen, recall the past, and verbalize hopes for the future.

Reading is an integral part of the language system of literate societies. The student's ability to express and receive thoughts through oral language provides the foundation for reading; in other words, reading is based on language development. Not surprisingly, some students with reading problems have underlying problems with language. This section describes the many different components of language.

Written and Oral Language

Language is an integrated system linking the *oral* language forms of listening and talking to the *written* language forms of reading and writing. As children mature, language plays an increasingly important part in the development of thinking and the ability to grasp abstract concepts. Words become symbols for objects, classes of objects, and ideas.

As children gain competence using language in one form, they also build knowledge and experience with the underlying language system, and this learning carries over to learning language in another form. Oral language provides a knowledge base for reading and writing. Similarly, practice in writing improves both reading and oral language. Oral language problems of one form or another are a factor related to reading disability. About 8 percent of children fail to develop speech and language at the expected age (Tallal, Miller, Jenkins, & Merzenich, 1997). Children who have delayed speech and language development often experience problems in reading.

Receptive and Expressive Language

An important distinction needs to be made between receptive language (understanding through listening or reading) and expressive language (using language in speaking and writing). Usually, people's receptive abilities exceed their expressive ones. That is, they understand more words than they use in speech and can read more words than they can write.

At times, a student may appear to have poor language abilities because he or she engages in little conversation or gives one-word replies to questions. However, oral expressive language can be influenced by a student's comfort level. Therefore, teachers must consider the student's language abilities in both receptive and expressive oral language.

Systems of Oral Language

Linguists have shown that four different systems are involved in oral language: *phonology* (the sounds of language), *morphology* (meaningful elements within words), *syntax* (the grammatical aspects of language), and *semantics* (the vocabulary of language). Students with reading problems may exhibit difficulties in one of these linguistic systems.

Phonology. *Phonology* refers to the sound system of a language. Oral language consists of a stream of sounds, one after the other. Each individual sound is called a *phoneme*. Important differences exist in the ways speakers of different languages think about phonemes. For example, in English the /*b*/ and /*v*/ sounds are two different phonemes, or sounds. In Spanish, they are simply variations on one phoneme. These differences make the mastery of English difficult for students whose native language is not English, just as Spanish or French is difficult for native English speakers.

Young children may have difficulty producing certain speech sounds, or phonemes. Typically children do not complete full articulation development until about the age of eight. Consonant sounds that are acquired later include *r, l, ch, sh, j, th* (as in *thy* and *thigh*), *s, z, v,* and *zh* (as in *pleasure*). Young children who have not mastered these sounds in speech may have difficulty distinguishing them in reading.

Phonological or *phonemic awareness,* is developed as children learn to recognize that words are made up of phonemes, or sounds. This ability is closely related to success in beginning reading (see Chapter 5). Auditory discrimination, or the ability to hear distinctions between phonemes (for example, to recognize that *big* and *pig* are different), is another problem area for some disabled readers (Wiig & Semel, 1984).

As discussed in Chapter 6, the phonics system in English, which links spoken sounds and written letters, is not completely regular. For example, the letter *c* represents two different sounds, as in the words *city* and *cat*. Although the English alphabet has only 26 letters, the average American English dialect contains 46 sounds.

Morphology. The morphological system refers to meaningful units, or *morphemes*, that form words or word parts. For example, the word *walked* contains two morphemes: *walk* and *ed*, a morpheme that signals the past tense. Other examples of morphemes are *s* (game*s*) and *re* (*re*wind). Many students with reading problems have deficits in morphological development (Torgensen, 1998). The ability to recognize different morphemes when they appear in reading is called *structural analysis* (see Chapters 6 and 10).

Syntax. *Syntax*, also known as grammar, governs the formation of sentences in a language. For example, in English a well-formed sentence has a subject and a verb (e.g., *Jane walks*). Further, sentences are combined by using conjunctions, such as *Jane walks and Jane runs.*

Children do not acquire syntactic ability passively. Rather, they construct syntactic rules for themselves. For example, a young child who says *he goed* for the past tense of *go* is using the rule that the past tense is formed by the addition of *ed*, even though the child is overgeneralizing this rule. Although most basic syntactic structures are acquired by the age of 6, some growth in syntax continues through the age of 10. Development of the ability to understand complex or difficult sentence patterns may continue even throughout the high school years. Because syntactic abilities continue to develop through the school years, teaching sentence comprehension is important to reading instruction. Table 14.2 presents examples of difficult sentence types.

Semantics.   The semantic system refers to the acquisition of vocabulary or word meanings. Compared with other languages, English has an extremely large vocabulary. The complexity and rich variety of English words makes the mastering of English vocabulary a lifelong task. Because vocabulary is highly related to reading achievement (Anderson & Freebody, 1981), limited vocabulary development can seriously hamper reading.

Factors involved in mastering English vocabulary include:

- *Size of vocabulary:* The number of words that students can use or understand.
- *Knowledge of multiple meanings of words:* Words such as *plane* and *cold* that have several meanings.

TABLE 14.2   Difficult Sentence Types

Category	Example
Passive sentences: reversible°	John was given the pen by Mary.
Out-of-order time sequences*	Move a yellow bead, *but first* move a red one. Move a yellow bead *after* you move a red one.
Relative clause construction	John, *who is in the second grade*, is learning to read. The man *standing on the corner* is nice.
Appositives	Mr. Smith, *the postman*, is very nice.
Complement structures	The fact *that Steve is silly* worries Meg. *Steve's being silly* worries Meg. *For Steve to be silly* worries Meg. Steve asked Meg *what was worrying her.*
Delayed reference in sentences†	John promised Mary to go. John asked Mary what to feed the doll.
Anophoric, or reference structures	John saw Mary and *he* said hello. John saw Mary and said hello.
Sentence connectives	*If you don't* do this, I will go. *Unless* you do this, I will go.

°The nonreversible sentence *The ball was dropped by the boy* would be easier.
*The construction *Move the yellow one and then the red* would be simpler because it occurs in time order.
†In these cases, *John* does the action of going or feeding the doll. In a sentence such as *John told Mary what to feed the doll*, *Mary* feeds the doll. The latter type of sentence is easier to comprehend.

- *Accuracy of vocabulary meaning:* Children may overextend or underextend the meanings of words. For example, in an overextension, a small child may call all four-legged animals *dogs*.
- *Accurate classification of words:* For example, *red, blue,* and *green* all belong to colors.
- *Relational categories of words:* Relational words include prepositions (*under, over, besides, to, from*); comparative terms (*good-bad, better-worse, lighter-darker*); time elements (*yesterday-today-tomorrow*); and terms of human relationship (*mother, aunt, grandmother*).

Speech Problems and Language Disorders

Because reading is an integral part of the language system, underlying problems with language can affect the ability to read. Two types of language problems are speech problems and language disorders.

Speech Problems. Children display three kinds of speech problems: *articulation problems* (the inaccurate production of sounds), *voice disorders* (improper pitch or intonation), and *stuttering* (breath or rhythm problems). Although low-achieving readers have a somewhat higher incidence of speech problems, these problems do not necessarily lead to reading problems. Nevertheless, students who exhibit speech difficulties should be referred to a speech-language specialist for further evaluation and, if needed, therapy. If a speech problem is noted, hearing acuity should be tested, for sometimes a hearing impairment is the cause of a speech problem. Students with speech problems can be embarrassed when asked to read orally, and therefore oral reading should be avoided for them.

Language Disorders. Language disorders refer to the slow or atypical development of receptive and expressive oral language. The child with a language delay is slow at talking and poor in vocabulary development and may have difficulty in learning to formulate sentences. Language delay is often a forerunner of later difficulty in reading (Torgesen, 1998). If a reading teacher suspects an underlying language disorder, a speech-language specialist can provide further evaluation and treatment.

Rapid Automatized Naming (RAN). Some children with language delays have difficulty with *rapid automatized naming* (RAN); that is, they cannot quickly and automatically name objects and are slow with word finding. For example, when given the task of naming pictures as they are shown, these children cannot rapidly produce the names of the pictures. A slowness in word finding and naming is an accurate predictor of later reading disabilities. Slowness in naming is probably due to memory retrieval problems, which make accessing verbal and phonological information difficult (German, 1994).

Problems with naming and slow word retrieval affect adolescents and adults with reading disabilities as well as children. Word finding problems can be a lifelong source of difficulty in reading, learning, and using expressive language. Tests for assessing word finding difficulty are the *Test of Word Finding, Second Edition (TWF-2)* and the *Test of Adolescent/Adult Word Finding (TAWF)*, both from Pro-Ed.

Nonstandard Dialects

Many students have a personal language that differs from the standard language of school instruction. A *nonstandard dialect* is a language pattern used by a subgroup of the speakers of a language. American English has many dialects. People from specific parts of the country may speak in different dialects. For example, people from the New England area may speak differently than people from the Southwest just as people from the Midwest may speak differently than people in the Southeast. Some students raised in certain specific cultural groups speak a dialect of English used in their environment, such as Appalachian, or a dialect referred to as Black English Vernacular (BEV). To illustrate the differences between one such dialect of English and the dialect that is generally considered to be Standard English, features of BEV are given in Table 14.3.

TABLE 14.3 Features of Black English Vernacular

Phonological or Sound Changes

Category	Examples
When two or more consonants are at the end of a word, one may be omitted.	*Test* is pronounced like *tes.*
	Bump is pronounced *bum.*
R may be omitted.	*Fort* is pronounced like *fought.*
L may be omitted.	*Toll* is pronounced like *toe.*
Short *i* and short *e* are pronounced the same before some consonants.	*Pin* is pronounced like *pen.*

Syntactic or Grammatical Changes

Category	Examples
The possessive may be omitted.	That's Molly('s) book.
The verb *to be* may be omitted.	He('s) downstairs; they('re) there.
The past-tense ending may be omitted.	He walk(ed) to the store yesterday.
The third-person-singular ending may be omitted.	She think(s) he is very nice.
Contractions signaling the future may be omitted.	He('ll) be there soon.
A *be* construction to indicate ongoing action may be inserted.	I *be* going there on Thursdays.

Source: Labou, Cohen, & Lewis (1968).

Linguists who have studied American dialects conclude that all dialects, regardless of their cultural associations, are logical, rule-based systems of English (Labov, Cohen, Robins, & Lewis, 1968; Wolfram, 1969). In fact, the BEV dialect has made many important contributions to standard English. Although dialects may differ, all English speakers share common underlying language forms. Students who speak nonstandard English can learn to read texts in standard English without changing their speech patterns.

When assessing and instructing students who speak nonstandard dialects, teachers should be aware of some pitfalls. First, constant correction of a student's oral language is damaging to a student's self-concept. A barrier between the student and teacher may form that reduces verbal output in the classroom. Students who avoid talking do not develop rich language. Second, dialect differences should not be mistaken for cognitive deficits or disorders in language development.

Bilingual and Limited English Proficiency

Chapter 13 discusses the growing number of students in the United States and Canada who speak English as a second language. These students must master English while maintaining their first language and their cultural heritage. Specific strategies are discussed in Chapter 13.

Assessing Language Development

Frequently used formal tests to assess language development are described in Chapter 16. In addition, a student's listening level provides an informal estimate of how well that student can understand language. The ability to comprehend oral language through listening is sometimes used as an informal measure of a student's receptive language abilities and reading potential. A high listening level indicates that a student understands language well and has potential to read at a high level. A low listening level indicates that a student needs language development. Chapters 3 and 10 discuss methods for determining a listening level from an informal reading inventory and a standardized test.

Physical Factors

Good health is important to learning. This section describes a variety of physical factors that can affect reading problems.

Hearing Impairment

Because the ability to acquire reading skills may be severely affected by even moderate or temporary hearing loss, pupils should be screened for *auditory acuity*, or the ability to hear sounds. Auditory acuity is different from the ability to work with or distinguish sounds.

Hearing loss has several causes: *childhood diseases*, such as scarlet fever, meningitis, mumps, or measles; *environmental conditions*, such as repeated exposure to loud noises; *congenital conditions*, such as malformation of or injury to the hearing mechanism; *temporary or fluctuating conditions*, due to allergies, colds, or even a buildup of wax in the ears; *maternal prenatal infection*, including rubella; *middle ear infection* or problems; and *certain medications*, such as amino glycosides and some diuretics.

Screening for Hearing Impairment.   *Hearing acuity* is measured in two dimensions: frequency and intensity. Frequency refers to the ability to hear different pitches, or vibrations of a specific sound wave. The pitches are actually musical tones: the higher the tone, the higher the frequency. Because different sounds of the spoken language have different frequency levels, a person may be able to hear sounds clearly at one frequency but not at another.

Intensity refers to the loudness of a sound and is measured in decibels. The louder the sound, the higher the intensity, or decibel level. How loud does a sound (or decibel level) have to be before a person should be able to hear it? A person who can hear soft sounds at 0 to 10 decibels has excellent hearing. Students who cannot hear sounds at 30 decibels are likely to encounter some difficulty in school learning.

The audiometer is an electronic instrument for measuring hearing acuity. In screening for a hearing loss, students wear headphones and sit with their backs to the examiner. The examiner produces a tone on the machine and asks the subject to raise a hand when a tone is heard. For screening, the audiometer is usually set at one frequency level, and the examiner determines how loud (or intense) the sound needs to be before the student can hear it. The right and left ears are tested separately for each frequency. The screening must take place in a quiet room.

An audiogram showing the results of an audiometric hearing test is illustrated in Figure 14.3. Students who cannot hear frequency sounds at the preset level of 30 decibels at one or more frequencies should be referred to a hearing specialist for further testing. The pupil whose audiogram appears in Figure 14.3 showed a 40 decibel loss at 2000 and 4000 frequencies in the right ear and was therefore referred to a hearing specialist.

If an auditory screening indicates a hearing problem, students should be referred to an audiologist (a nonmedical specialist in hearing) or to an otologist or an otolaryngologist (medical specialists in hearing). Although the audiometer is a good device for screening, only a specialist trained in measuring and treating hearing difficulties can make a final determination of the extent and nature of a possible hearing impairment.

Alleviating Hearing Problems.   Medical specialists can also take measures to alleviate a student's hearing problem. Sometimes, medication or tubes in a child's ear can alleviate clogged passages and improve hearing. Other children may need to be fitted with hearing aids.

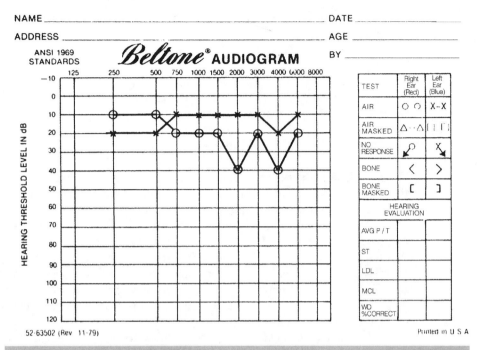

FIGURE 14.3 Sample Audiogram

Reprinted with the permission of Beltone Electronics Corporation.

Sometimes students pass the audiometric screening test yet still have hearing problems. One little girl had a sporadic hearing loss resulting from allergies, but because her visits to the pediatrician came after the allergy season, the hearing problem went undetected for years. Although the hearing problem was eventually cleared up, she had missed some important early language growth, and her difficulties in reading continued into the later grades. Thus, if a reading teacher even *suspects* a hearing loss, the student should be referred to a professional for continued monitoring.

Even moderate loss in the ability to hear may substantially affect the ability to read. A hearing loss impedes communication with teachers and peers, and so the student has difficulty functioning in class. Students may have difficulty learning phonics because they do not hear certain sounds. A low-frequency hearing loss (500–1500 Hz) may cause difficulty with vowel sounds; high-frequency losses (2000–4000 Hz) may cause difficulty with consonant sounds that continue, such as /s/, /z/, /j/, /v/, /th/, /sh/, and /ch/.

The most devastating effect of a hearing loss is that it prevents normal language development. When children cannot hear adequately, they are deprived of the communication necessary for normal language acquisition and growth. Their vocabulary, grammar, and verbal thinking processes often remain poorly developed, and their language skills may be inadequate to acquire higher-level reading skills.

Visual Impairment

The ability to see clearly is obviously critical to the reading process. However, the relationship between reading and vision is complicated. A particular visual impairment may impede reading in one individual, but another person with a similar problem may be able to read effectively.

Types of Vision Problems.   Several types of visual impairment are of concern to the reading teacher. These impairments include myopia, hyperopia, astigmatism, binocular vision problems, and color perception.

Myopia or *nearsightedness* is the inability to see objects at a distance. Myopia is caused by an elongated eyeball that focuses visual images in an improper way. Although the problem of myopia is not highly related to reading difficulty (Lerner, 2000), a student with myopia could have difficulty seeing objects such as writing on the blackboard. A substantial portion of the population is myopic; the condition often begins between the ages of nine and twelve. Myopia is usually correctable with eyeglasses.

Hyperopia or *farsightedness* is the inability to see objects clearly at nearpoint (that is, 13 inches or less). In children, it is often caused by an eyeball that is too short to permit focusing. Children are typically hyperopic until they reach the age of seven or eight; thus, primary-grade textbooks generally contain large print. If hyperopia is a continuing problem, it can be corrected with lenses. Because reading is done at nearpoint, hyperopia can affect the ability to read.

An *astigmatism* is the blurring of vision because of irregularities in the surface of the cornea. This condition is generally correctable with lenses.

Binocular difficulties refer to the inability to focus both eyes on the same object, and is one of the most complicated of visual functions. Both eyes focus together easily on an object that is far away, but as that object moves closer, the eyes must turn inward to maintain their focus. If the eyes cannot focus together, a double image may result. This condition is not tolerated well by the brain, and the image of one eye may be suppressed, possibly leading to a deterioration of that eye. In severe cases, the eyes appear to be crossed. Binocular vision problems may blur vision and also cause the reader to become easily fatigued. Thus they can interfere with reading.

Unfortunately, binocular vision is not as easily correctable as other visual problems. Three strategies used to correct binocular problems are surgery (often used to correct a cross-eyed condition), corrective lenses in eyeglasses, and visual exercises to strengthen eye muscles. Opinions differ among eye specialists about the value of visual exercises as a treatment in overcoming binocular difficulties (American Academy of Pediatrics, 1992; Wesson, 1993).

Color perception is also a part of vision. A small portion of the population, usually male, is unable to perceive color. *Color blindness*, which may be limited to a few colors, is not associated with reading problems. In addition, a set of controversial new treatments focuses on the glare that is experienced by some individuals during reading. This problem is often called *scotopic sensitivity*. To eliminate this glare, colored overlays or lenses may be provided. Although some have reported decreased problems in reading, this controversial treatment has had somewhat inconsistent results (Fletcher & Martínez, 1994; Ward, 1992). Nevertheless, it remains one treatment option for possible visual problems.

Screening for Visual Impairment. Students with reading problems should be screened for possible visual difficulties. An adequate visual screening should at least test nearsightedness, farsightedness, and binocular visual functioning. As with the hearing tests that are used by the reading teacher, visual tests given by schools or teachers are intended only for screening purposes. Students who do poorly on a visual screening test should be referred to an ophthalmologist (a physician who specializes in eye problems) or to an optometrist (a nonmedical eye specialist) for further testing. Vision tests that can easily be administered by a teacher include the *Keystone Telebinocular Vision Tests* and the *Orthorater* instruments.

Neurological Factors

All learning, including learning to read, is neurologically based. The reading process is a complex human task that requires an intact and well-functioning brain and central nervous system. A dysfunction in the central nervous system can interfere with learning to read. Knowledge about the brain and its relationship to learning is rapidly expanding. Functional magnetic resonance imaging (fMRI) is a new noninvasive MRI method for studying the human brain as it is working. Shaywitz and Shaywitz (1998) conducted research using the fMRI to image the brains of 32 nondyslexic and 29 dyslexic adults while they attempted to perform a progressively complex series of reading tasks, which included letter recognition, rhyming letters and words, and categorizing words. Figure 14.4 maps the location in the brain for phonological processing, word meaning, and letter identification. The study found measurable differences in brain activity between dyslexic and nondyslexic subjects. During reading, subjects with dyslexia show a pattern of underactivation in a larger posterior brain region, an area that connects the visual areas with the language areas. Theories about the relationship of neurological function to reading performance, current research on neurological dysfunction, and the condition of dyslexia are discussed in Chapter 15.

Gender Differences

More boys than girls are identified as having reading disabilities. In fact, about four times more boys are in special reading programs. Yet recent research sponsored by the National Institute of Child Health and Human Development (NICHD) shows that as many girls as boys may have reading disabilities, but the

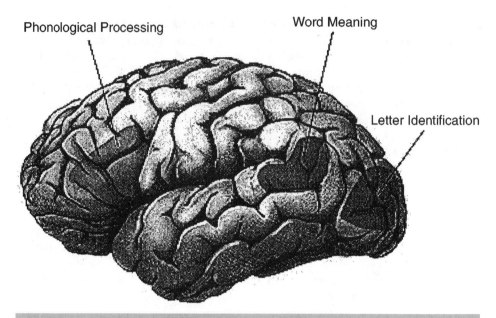

FIGURE 14.4   fMRI Brain Image

Adapted from Shaywitz, S. E., Shaywitz, B. A., Pugh, K. R., Fulbright, R. K., Constable, R. T., Mencl, W. E., Shankweiler, D. P., Liberman, A. M., Skudlarski, P., Fletcher, J. M., Katz, L., Marchione, K. E., Lacadie, C., Gatenby, C., and Gore, J. C. (1998). Functional disruption in the organization of the brain for reading in dyslexia. *Proceedings of the National Academy of Sciences, USA, 95,* 2636–2641. Used with permission.

girls are not being identified. Girls with reading disability are considered an underserved population (National Reading Panel, 1999).

Several reasons have been suggested for more boys than girls being identified with reading disabilities:

- Boys mature physically later than girls. At the age of beginning reading instruction, boys may not have developed certain skills that aid in reading, such as the ability to pay attention and the ability to manage pencils and books.
- The school environment may affect boys and girls differently. Most primary-grade classrooms in the United States are taught by female teachers, and boys may have more difficulty relating to them. In addition, rewards tend to be given for being neat and quiet in the primary grades, and these qualities are more characteristic of girls than boys.

The fact is that more boys are in special reading classes. Teachers must make these students feel welcome and happy in the reading environment.

Other Physical Problems

Good physical health is an important basic condition for learning. The pupil who is listless, tires easily, and cannot maintain attention may have an underlying medical problem. Prolonged illness, especially if accompanied by high fevers and long periods of absence from school, can also contribute to a reading problem.

General Health and Nutrition. Nutrient deficiency in infancy or early childhood has been shown to result in anatomical and biochemical changes in the brain. Early malnutrition impairs growth, both of the body in general and of the central nervous system in particular (Fishbein & Meduski, 1987). Other health concerns include nutrition problems, rheumatic fever, asthma, lack of sleep, biochemical imbalances, and endocrine problems. A general physical examination is often recommended as part of a complete assessment for reading problems.

Injuries and Illnesses That Affect the Brain. Concussions, or swelling of the brain, can affect cognitive functioning. Concussions are often caused by injuries. If a brain injury results in unconsciousness, a student has experienced a concussion. In addition, some illnesses, such as spinal meningitis and brain tumors, can destroy cognitive functioning.

Controversial Medical Conditions. Some students with reading problems receive medical or medically related treatments that are purported to alleviate their educational problems. Because teachers may be asked to provide feedback to physicians or parents about students, they must be aware of both the underlying conditions and the therapies. Some common conditions are:

- *Hypoglycemia.* This condition, a deficiency in the level of blood sugar, is thought by some to cause learning problems. Treatment consists of controlling various elements in the student's diet (Runion, 1980).
- *Allergies.* Other authorities feel that allergies, which are caused by both the diet and the environment, can cause learning difficulties. Treatment consists of the removal of the element causing the allergy (Crook, 1977; Rapp, 1979). The precise relationship of allergies to the learning process is yet to be determined.
- *Medication therapy.* Many students with learning problems, particularly those with attention deficit disorder (ADD), are prescribed medication intended to control hyperactivity, increase attention span, and reduce impulsive behavior. Psychostimulant medications include Ritalin®, Dexedrine®, Adderall®, Cylert®, and Concerta™. These medications are effective in more than 75 to 80 percent of cases (Lerner, 2000). Monitoring the effects of medication is important. Teachers are an important resource for providing feedback to physicians.

■ *Food additives*. One of the most widely discussed and controversial theories on the negative effects of food additives is that of Feingold (1975), who points out that artificial flavors, colors, and preservatives are used increasingly in the American diet. Feingold's treatment consists of the removal of foods that contain additives and the inclusion of certain natural foods. However, a panel of experts at the National Institutes of Health concluded that the evidence to recommend this diet for treating childhood hyperactivity was insufficient (Silver, 1998).

Reviewing many of the medical and biomedical treatments for learning problems, Silver found their effectiveness to be unproven. He concluded that the treatment of choice for reading problems is the best educational instruction available taught by a well-qualified and sensitive teacher.

Summary

A number of correlates, or factors, may be related to a student's reading disability. Environmental factors include the home, school, cultural, and social environments.

The home is the child's first environment, where the critical learning of the early years occurs. The school environment is another important system for the student, one that is often difficult for students with reading problems. Students with reading disabilities tend to have difficulty in their social environments.The cultural environment is another system that affects attitudes and interest in reading. Methods of assessing environmental systems include several systems of observation.

Factors within the individual that are related to reading include emotional factors, intelligence, language, and physical factors.

Emotional problems influence reading achievement. Opinions differ about the need to treat emotional problems prior to the treatment of reading problems. Among the emotional problems exhibited by poor readers are emotional blocks, hostility, aggressiveness, learned helplessness, low self-esteem, depression, and anxiety. Emotional factors may be informally assessed using the sentence-completion activity.

Intelligence refers to the potential for learning. New views of intelligence divide intelligence into several components. Intelligence tests measure scholastic aptitude. Although much of what is called intelligence is inherited, a child's intelligence can be dramatically influenced by environmental conditions. In general, the child's experiences and environment, including teaching, can make a significant difference.

Separate components or abilities make up intelligence. The *WISC-III* has subtests that are useful for gathering information about different substandard abilities. This test yields scores for verbal and performance intelligence. The *K-ABC* measures simultaneous and sequential processing. A discrepancy between estimated potential for reading based on intelligence and actual reading level can be used to determine if a reading disability exists.

The child's language is an important factor related to reading performance. Language includes oral language (listening and speaking) and written language (reading and written).

The four oral language systems are phonology, morphology, syntax, and semantics or vocabulary. Studies show that some students with reading disabilities have difficulty with one or more of these linguistic systems. Speech problems and language disorders can affect the learning of reading. Some children with reading disabilities have an underlying language disorder. Nonstandard English should not be interpreted as language inferiority.

Physical factors are also related to reading disability. Hearing impairment, including a mild or temporary hearing loss, can affect language learning and learning to read. The audiometer is used to screen for a hearing loss. Visual impairment is also related to reading disability. Visual problems include myopia, hyperopia, astigmatism, poor binocular vision, and perhaps color sensitivity. Teachers can screen for visual impairment.

Other physical factors, such as general health and nutrition or neurological conditions, are related to reading disabilities. Many disabled readers receive medication and other treatments, including control of food additives, for hypoglycemia and allergies. Teachers should be aware of such conditions and the students who are receiving such treatment. Neurological conditions may be a factor for some severely disabled readers. Research suggests that these students have central nervous system dysfunctions. Reading difficulties are identified more frequently in boys than girls. However, research shows that girls may have as many reading difficulties but are just not identified.

15 Severe Reading Disabilities

Introduction

This chapter examines the issue of students who have extreme difficulty in learning to read and describes methods for teaching these readers. Individuals with severe reading disabilities have difficulty acquiring the most basic reading skills and often struggle for years with first-grade books. The first part of the chapter discusses the characteristics of individuals with severe reading disabilities. The second part presents an overview of special strategies that are used to teach students with severe reading disabilities.

Characteristics of Students with Severe Reading Disabilities

Severe reading disabilities have a number of different causes. This section discusses students with dyslexia, students who are considered at risk, students with learning disabilities, and students with attention deficit disorder.

Dyslexia: The Baffling Reading Disorder

Severe, persistent, and baffling problems in learning to read are often called *dyslexia*. Such conditions have puzzled the educational and medical communities for many years. Individuals with these severe inborn reading disorders are often intelligent in other ways and even excel in areas such as mathematics and art. People with these problems find recognizing letters and words and interpreting information that is presented in print form extremely difficult. Dyslexic adults can recall the anguish of trying to cope with this mysterious condition in a world that requires people to read. Even though many become successful, their reading problem often continues throughout their lives. A follow-up study of children who were identified with dyslexia in the early grades showed that they continued to display symptoms of dyslexia as adolescents (Shaywitz, et al., 1999). Charles Schwab, the founder of the successful and innovative stock brokerage firm, struggled with severe reading problems throughout his life. Schwab coped by developing other abilities, such as the ability to envision, to anticipate where things are going, and to conceive a solution to a business problem. He felt his reading problem forced him to develop these skills at a higher level than people for whom reading came easily (Kantrowitz & Underwood, 1999; West, 1997).

Reading experts have a number of different definitions and explanations of dyslexia. Some reading experts have even questioned whether the term is even needed. Yet Hynd (1992) finds that the many definitions of dyslexia agree on four points:

- Dyslexia has a biological basis and is due to a congenital neurological condition.

- Symptoms of dyslexia persist into adolescence and adulthood.
- Dyslexia has perceptual, cognitive, and language dimensions.
- The condition of dyslexia leads to difficulties in many areas of life as the individual matures.

Neurological Basis of Dyslexia.   For many years, scholars strongly suspected that dyslexia had a neurobiological basis, but until recently they lacked the scientific evidence to support this belief. Now evidence strongly indicates that dyslexia is caused by an abnormality in brain structure, a difference in brain function, and genetic factors (Shaywitz & Shaywitz, 1998). Current research in the neurosciences demonstrates that the cognitive deficit in dyslexia is related to a pattern of brain organization different from that seen in nonimpaired readers. Specifically, this neural signature of dyslexia is characterized by underactivation in posterior brain regions (particularly the angular gyrus) and overactivation in anterior brain regions as dyslexic readers engage in phonological analysis (Shaywitz, et al., 1999).

One of the major tools for this brain research is functional magnetic resonance imaging (fMRI). This new, noninvasive MRI method studies the human brain as it is working. Shaywitz and Shaywitz (1998) used the fMRI to image the brains of nondyslexic and dyslexic adults attempting to perform a progressively complex series of reading tasks, including letter recognition, rhyming letters and words, and categorizing words. The research showed measurable differences in brain activity between dyslexic and nondyslexic subjects (see Chapter 14, p 349).

Accumulating research shows that students with dyslexia have a deficit in identifying the sound structure of words. They encounter difficulty with *phonological awareness*, which is the inability to notice, think about, or manipulate individual sounds (Blachman, 1997; Shaywitz, et al., 1999). These students cannot identify the component sounds in a whole word, cannot take words apart or blend sounds together to form spoken words, cannot identify the first (or last) sound in a spoken word, and cannot understand rhyming patterns. Suggestions for assessing and developing phonological awareness are given in Chapter 5.

Genetics of Dyslexia.   Knowledge about the genetics and inheritability of dyslexia has increased significantly in recent years (Pennington, 1995). Two types of genetic studies of dyslexia are the family studies and the twin studies. Family studies present strong evidence that the tendency for dyslexia is inherited and appears to have a genetic basis (Pennington, 1995). The twin study research provides further evidence that genetics play a significant role in dyslexia (DeFries, Stevenson, Gillis, & Wadsworth, 1991; Pennington, 1995). Research shows that twins have similar characteristics in terms of reading disabilities even when they are reared apart.

Students Who Are at Risk

Many of the nation's students are considered at risk for learning and learning to read. These students often live in poverty, are born into single-parent homes, and have other types of risk factors that lead to reading disabilities. These factors include fetal alcohol syndrome, drug dependence at birth, exposure to malnutrition and smoking during mother's pregnancy, lead exposure, premature birth, child abuse, and lack of early cognitive and language stimulation. An estimated one-third of the nation's children are at risk for school failure before they enter kindergarten.

A wide-ranging study of the Carnegie Corporation of New York (Chira, 1994) indicates that millions of infants and toddlers are so deprived of medical care, loving supervision, and intellectual stimulation that their growth into healthy and responsible adults is threatened. Such students often have problems in the early childhood years, from birth through age three, which are critical in the development of the brain. Research on brain development suggests that any attempt to maximize intellectual growth must begin during the first three years of life. Research summarized by the Carnegie Corporation (1994) shows that:

- Brain development before age one is more rapid and extensive than previously realized.
- Brain development is much more vulnerable to environmental influence than suspected.
- The influence of early environment on brain development is long lasting.
- Environment affects the number of brain cells, connections among them, and the way connections are wired.
- Early stress has a negative impact on brain function.

In other words, a healthy, nurturing, stress-free environment actually nurtures intelligence. Sadly, many at-risk students lack this environment and hence are especially prone to developing severe reading disabilities.

Many at-risk students receive instruction through supplementary instructional programs supported through Title I of the Elementary and Secondary Education Act, which was reauthorized by the U.S. Congress in 1997 (U.S. Department of Education, 1997). The purpose of Title I legislation is to provide education to at-risk students from low-income homes.

Title I grants, which are distributed through school districts, serve students whose academic performance is below grade-level criteria (as determined by the state or local education agency) and who attend a school that has enough low-income children to warrant funding. Schools that are eligible for Title I funds provide supplementary instruction oriented to achieving high standards. As of a 1994 report, more than 75 percent of the students in Title I programs received reading instruction (Garcia, Pearson, & Jiménez, 1994).

In many low-income area schools, programs for students with learning problems are supported predominantly through Title I funds. As of 1994, the program served 7 million students. Recent revisions of Title I rules encourage programs that serve all students in a low-achieving school, urge professionals to help students within the regular classroom setting (rather than in a pull-out situation), and require that schools develop written policies to include parents in the programs.

Learning Disabilities

A learning disability is one type of special education classification that receives funds under the provision of IDEA (Individuals with Disabilities Education Act, 1997); the IDEA is a federal special education law. More than one-half of the students served under IDEA, a figure comprising 5 percent of U.S. schoolchildren, are identified as learning disabled (Lerner, 2000). The legal definition of specific learning disabilities in this law is:

> a disorder in one or more of basic psychological processes involved in using language, spoken or written, which may manifest itself in an imperfect ability to listen, think, speak, read, write, spell, or to do mathematical calculations. The term includes such conditions as perceptual handicaps, brain injury, minimum brain dysfunction, dyslexia, and developmental aphasia. The term does not include children who have learning problems that are primarily the result of visual, hearing, or motor handicaps, of mental retardation or emotional disturbance, or of environmental, cultural, or economic disadvantage.

The IDEA also requires that students with learning disabilities exhibit a discrepancy between potential and academic achievement.

In the 1997 IDEA definition, a learning disability is explained as a problem in using language. Because reading is one aspect of language, it is not surprising that 80 percent of students with learning disabilities exhibit reading problems (Lerner, 2000). Furthermore, many severely disabled readers are classified as learning disabled.

The IDEA-1997 is federal legislation, mandating that individuals with disabilities, ages 3 to 21, have the right to a free, appropriate, public education (FAPE). Under this act, students with disabilities, including those with learning disabilities, are entitled to an individual educational program (IEP). Specific provisions of IDEA and the IEP process are found in Figure 15.1.

Increasingly, students with learning disabilities, as well as other categories of special education students, are served in regular classrooms. In fact, many schools are using an *inclusion* policy, which means that *all* children, including those with disabilities, should be instructed in regular classrooms. Thus, students with all types of disabilities, both severe and mild, are being placed in regular classrooms for instruction. Inclusion supporters feel that students with disabilities are best served through experiencing mainstream society and having integrated social opportunities. Inclusion receives support in the *least restrictive environment* provision of the IDEA law. At times, however, accommodating children with severe disabilities in the regular classroom setting may be difficult. As a result, inclusion has become one of the most controversial issues in education (Lerner, 2000).

Attention Deficit Disorder

Attention deficit disorder (ADD) constitutes a neurological condition characterized by developmentally inappropriate attention skills, impulsivity, and in some

> **FIGURE 15.1   Some Key Provisions of the 1997 Individuals with Disabilities Education Act (IDEA-1997)**
>
> **Categories of Disabilities in the Law:** specific learning disabilities, seriously emotionally disturbed, mental retardation, hard of hearing, deaf, speech or language impaired, visually impaired, seriously emotionally disturbed, orthopedically impaired, other health impaired, autistic, deaf–blind, multihandicapped, and traumatic brain injured.
>
> **IEP Process and Provisions:** Each student must have a written *individualized education program* (IEP), developed as follows:
>   (1) *Referral* for those potentially in need of special educational services.
>   (2) *Assessment*. A multidisciplinary team gathers information and develops an IEP within 30 days of initial referral. The IEP indicates long-range goals, short-term goals, objectives, and suitable instructional placements. It states dates for initiation, anticipated duration of services, and evaluation. Related services (e.g., speech therapy, social work services) may also be specified.
>   Participants in the IEP meeting must include a school representative, the student's teacher, parents, the student (when appropriate), and other professionals (e.g., social workers, advocates, lawyers). The parents and school personnel must sign an agreement to the IEP before it can be put into effect.
>   (3) *Implementation and evaluation*. The plan is implemented. Goals are evaluated annually, and a complete evaluation is done every 3 years.
>
> **Procedural safeguards.** Parents must give written consent to evaluation and IEP provisions. They have a right to all information collected. Assessment must be conducted in the student's native language, and findings must be reported in the parents' native language. Evaluation procedures must be free of racial or cultural bias; the student's confidentiality must be respected.
>   Parents and students can challenge decisions with a "due process" hearing. If parents (or the school) disagree with the findings of this hearing, they are entitled to a higher-level hearing. Further challenges require a civil action law suit.
>
> **Placement for Instruction.** *Continuum of alternative placements* states that schools are to establish an array of educational placements (regular classes, resource rooms, special schools) to meet the varied needs of students with disabilities. *Least restrictive environment* (LRE) states that the IEP team must foster, to the extent appropriate, the education of disabled students with nondisabled students.

cases, hyperactivity. Attention deficit disorder is thought to be caused by a brain-based neurological dysfunction. As the most commonly diagnosed disorder of childhood, ADD accounts for one-half of all child referrals to outpatient mental health clinics (Barkely, 1998; Lerner, 2000). Although more boys than girls are *identified* with ADD, the research shows that as many girls as boys have ADD (Shaywitz, et al., 1999).

Many students with ADD encounter reading problems. These students cannot concentrate and pay attention, may have social problems, may fight with classmates, and may suffer from depression. Such problems distract the child from learning. However, some students with ADD are good readers.

Different terms are used to refer to this condition. The American Psychiatric Association refers to attention deficit hyperactivity disorder (ADHD), and the U.S. Department of Education uses attention deficit disorder (ADD) (American Psychiatric Association, 1994; U.S. Department of Education, 1999). Both terms refer to the same condition.

The major characteristics of ADD are inattention, impulsivity, and sometimes hyperactivity. *Inattention* is the inability to concentrate on a task. *Impulsivity* is the tendency to respond quickly without thinking through the consequences of an action. *Hyperactivity* refers to behavior that has a constant, driving motor activity in which the child races from one endeavor or interest to another. To identify an individual with ADD, according to the *Diagnostic and Statistical Manual of Mental Disabilities*, 4th Edition (American Psychiatric Association, 1994), the individual must meet several criteria:

- *Severity*. The symptoms must be more frequent and severe than is typical of other children at similar developmental levels.
- *Early onset*. At least some of the symptoms must have appeared before the child is seven years of age.
- *Duration*. The child's symptoms must have persisted for at least six months prior to the diagnosis.

Eligibility of Children with ADD for Services.   The 1999 Regulations for the IDEA-1997 state that children with ADD or ADHD are eligible for special education services in the schools and can be identified under the IDEA-1997 special education category: *other health impaired*. Children with ADD or ADHD are also eligible for services under Section 504 of the Rehabilitation Act of 1973. In this case, reasonable accommodations must be made in the general education classroom for these students.

Medication for Students with ADD.   Many students with ADD receive medication to improve their attention and to control their hyperactive behavior. The most commonly used types of medication for treating ADD are psychostimulant medications, and about 75 to 85 percent of students with ADD or ADHD show general improvement with psychostimulant medication. The most widely used psychostimulant medications for ADD are Ritalin®, Dexedrine®, Cylert®, Adderall®, and Concerta™.

Behavioral Problems.   The characteristics of ADD often lead to behavioral problems. Teachers should understand that although the behavior of students is at times annoying, this behavior is not an intentional ploy to defy educational authority. The activity level of students with ADD is not usually under their voluntary control.

Instructional Methods for Teaching Students with Severe Reading Disabilities

This section outlines ways to teach students with severe reading disabilities. As noted, researchers have begun to identify specific causes for extreme, or "hard core," reading disability. However, professionals find that many of the same teaching strategies that are successful with all low-achieving students are also successful with severely disabled students. When working with severely disabled readers, strategies must be used more intensively and more slowly, for severely disabled students need much direct, explicit instruction and frequent monitoring of progress (Roswell & Chall, 1994a).

This section provides additional methods for dealing with severely disabled students. These methods deal with teaching prerequisite (or psychological processing) abilities, adapting a standard method, special remedial approaches, teaching to different learning styles, and direct instruction.

Building Auditory and Visual Prerequisite Abilities

Most students, even severely disabled ones, have auditory and visual abilities that are well enough developed to enable them to read. If further work in developing these abilities is needed, first use an emergent literacy approach, which combines reading and writing with teaching underlying abilities.

Some published tests, such as the *Detroit Test of Learning Aptitudes*, which stem from a learning disabilities perspective, are available for assessing auditory and visual perception. However, a number of studies have found that training in auditory and visual skills is unproductive (Allington, 1982; Kavale & Forness, 1987; Vellutino, 1987). Therefore, we do not recommend such training.

Adapting Standard Reading Methods to Severe Disabilities

Methods or materials designed for teaching reading in the regular classroom often can be modified for use with severely disabled readers. This approach requires few specialized materials and allows much flexibility in instruction. Effective adaptations of standard reading methods can be made for sight word strategies and phonics methods. In using a standard reading approach, avoiding situations in which the student learns one method in the regular classroom and a different method from a reading teacher is especially important.

Your student may acquire skills at a slow pace, particularly at the beginning phases of instruction. Ronnie, a boy in the Reading Center, spent 10 weeks learning eight sight words. Although this progress seems very slow, it was a remarkable achievement for Ronnie. In fact, these words were the first that he had been able to learn and retain. Because progress may be painstaking, highlighting every success by charting or graphing progress on the road to reading is especially important.

Selecting a Method. To select the most appropriate method for an individual student, Roswell and Chall (1994a) advise that the teacher administer informal and formal diagnostic tests and give informal trial teaching sessions. The diagnostic tests provide an estimate of strengths and weaknesses in various components of reading. The informal trial lessons help to find methods and materials that are appropriate for teaching the student.

Roswell and Chall (1994b) have developed a complete assessment instrument, *Diagnostic Assessments of Teaching with Trial Teaching Strategies (DARTTS),* which measures reading potential, determines reading strengths and weaknesses, and provides informal trial teaching sessions. This battery is further described in Appendix B.

In addition, a diagnostic word-learning lesson can help determine the student's comparative abilities in learning through sight or phonics. In this task a student learns two sets of words: five words are presented as sight words, and five words are presented as phonics words. By comparing performance on these two tasks, the teacher can judge the student's learning strengths. A sample word learning task with directions is presented in Figure 15.2. A student who learns better through the sight word task might be instructed using a sight or language experience method. For a student who does better on the phonics test, employ a phonics teaching strategy first. In addition to learning about achievement on the two tasks, the process of watching students learn by different methods provides many diagnostic insights.

Adapting a Sight Word Method. The sight word method involves teaching students to recognize the visual forms of words instantly, without further analysis. In using this approach with severely disabled students, words should be selected with care. In general, long words are harder to learn than short words, although an occasional long word adds interest. Concrete words are easier to learn than abstract words. For example, the student's name, parts of the body, the name of the school, and so on are far easier to learn than function words, such as *the, when,* or *to.*

The words selected for instruction should also be varied in shape or configuration and in length to avoid visual confusion. Move carefully from words to sentences to books. Words should also be reviewed many times to firmly establish them in the student's memory. Be careful to use standard manuscript writing for all teacher-made materials. Because severely disabled readers may focus on small differences, they may be confused by a letter *d* with a "tail" attached.

Adapting a Phonics Method. Adaptations for phonics methods that are suitable for severely disabled readers can be classified into two groups: *synthetic phonics* and *analytic (or linguistic)* approaches.

In the *synthetic* method, the student first learns individual letter sounds and then how to blend letter sounds or groups of letter sounds into a whole word. For example, the student learns the individual sounds for *r, a,* and *t.* Then the student learns to blend these sounds into the word *rat.* The synthetic method requires that

> **FIGURE 15.2   Example of a Diagnostic Word Learning Task**
>
> 1. *Sight word task:* Words are *house, children, boy, farm, wagon.*
>   a.   Print the words carefully on cards.
>   b.   Go through each word. Read it to the student, use it in a sentence, point out visual features of the word (*children* is long; *boy* is short, etc.).
>   c.   Mix up cards. Present five trials of the word, mixing the words after each trial.
>   (1)   For the first three trials, pronounce incorrect words for the student and use them in a sentence.
>   (2)   For the last two trials, do not correct incorrect responses.
>   d.   Mark results of all trials on the form below.
> 2. *Phonics word task:* Words are *at, bat, cat, rat, fat.*
>   a.   Print the words carefully on cards.
>   b.   Present the *at* card first; pronounce this word for the student.
>   c.   Mix up cards. Present five trials of the word, mixing the words after each trial.
>   (1)   For the first three trials, pronounce incorrect words after each trial.
>   (2)   For the last two trials, do not correct incorrect responses.
>   d.   *Response form:* Mark correct or incorrect.
>
> | **Sight Word Task Trial** | | | | | | **Phonics Task Trial** | | | | |
> |---|---|---|---|---|---|---|---|---|---|---|
> | | 1 | 2 | 3 | 4 | 5 | | 1 | 2 | 3 | 4 | 5 |
> | house | | | | | | at | | | | | |
> | children | | | | | | bat | | | | | |
> | boy | | | | | | cat | | | | | |
> | farm | | | | | | rat | | | | | |
> | wagon | | | | | | fat | | | | | |
>
> Adapted from Barr, 1970.

students learn certain phonics rules, such as the rule that would guide the reader to pronounce *rat* and *rate* differently.

The concept of synthetic phonics is often difficult for the severely disabled reader to grasp at first. Before instructing through a synthetic approach, teachers should make sure the student possesses needed skills, such as phonemic awareness. However, once basic phonics concepts are mastered, the student often gains rapidly in reading performance. Sample materials that use this approach include the *Key Text* reading series (Economy Company).

Although intense effort is required, this method works for some severely disabled readers. Betty, an intelligent 13-year-old, had a long history of reading failure, but she was anxious to learn. Her teacher taught her the sounds of the consonants followed by the sounds of *long* and *short a* and rules for using them in a tedious process that took several months. Once these initial steps were mastered, however, progress was much faster. In fact, she learned the other vowels quite easily, and in her second six months of instruction, Betty demonstrated gains of more than two years.

In the *analytic* method, students learn whole words that contain regular phonics patterns. By presenting the words over and over again in patterns (or word families), such as *at, bat, cat,* or *run, sun, fun,* the student begins to form generalizations about sound regularities. This method is similar to the *analogy* method presented in Chapter 6. Books using the linguistic approach are based on patterns of word families; thus text may look like the following:

- Dan ran the fan.
- Can Dan fan Nan?
- The pet is wet.
- Is the pet wet?

An important prerequisite skill for learning analytic phonics is the skill of *rhyming*. Often older severely disabled readers prefer analytic phonics because it gives them considerable independence. Materials that have featured this approach have included the *Sullivan Program*, the *Merrill Linguistic Readers*, the *SRA Reading Program* and the *Phonic Remedial Reading Lessons* (Kirk, Kirk, & Minskoff, 1985). Although the first three programs present words in context, the *Phonic Remedial Reading Lessons* present organized word drills.

Ten-year-old Billy was a nonreader who was taught analytic phonics for several months. His initial learning rate was one word family per week for four weeks and two families a week thereafter. Billy's teacher controlled the word families carefully so that they would not be too similar. After each word family was learned, it was presented in a story. The words from the word family were at first color coded (for example, one family was written in yellow and another in red). Billy's independent reading was done with books containing rhyming words, such as Dr. Seuss's *Hop on Pop* and *Green Eggs and Ham*. He also created his own book of word families that featured one word family (e.g., *ight, ake*) with many example words on each page.

Differences in Learning Styles

Not all people learn in the same way. Differences in temperamental styles have even been observed in infants and young children (Thomas & Chess, 1977). Some babies are alert and responsive; others are irritable or passive. Some researchers and practitioners have suggested that teachers adjust instruction to the learning styles of students (Carbo, Dunn, & Dunn, 1986). They believe that if the learning style of the student is at odds with the style required to succeed in the classroom, serious learning problems can occur. This section reviews possible options for matching instruction and learning style.

One view of learning styles involves psychological processes. For example, some students might learn best by listening (an auditory style), some by looking (a visual style), some by touching (a tactile style), and some by performing an action (a kinesthetic style). Adults, too have preferred ways of learning. Some adults learn best by listening to an explanation, others know that to learn something they must read about it or watch it being done, and still others learn best by writing or going through the actions themselves.

Reflecting these differences in prerequisite abilities, the suggestion that there are "auditory" and "visual" learners was made several years ago by researchers in learning disabilities, and has received some renewed support (Beattie, 1994). Some have put forth the theory that students with stronger visual processing skills will learn better through sight word or language experience methods and that students with stronger auditory processing skills learn best through phonics methods (Johnson & Myklebust, 1967). This theory is often called the aptitude-treatment interaction.

Researchers have not found that differences in modes of processing, although appealing from a commonsense viewpoint, predict reading success (Allington, 1982; Robinson, 1972). In fact, Caldwell (1991) found that the amount of reading done by disabled students rather than their auditory or visual aptitude determined reading progress. For this reason, you should use trial teaching rather than prerequisite skills to determine instructional methods for severely disabled students.

Carbo, Dunn, & Dunn (1986) have postulated eight different learning styles for students and have unique instructional suggestions for each. Although many of the teaching suggestions they give are valuable, the research establishing learning styles has received serious challenges (Stahl, 1988).

Styles of learning may also be *active* or *passive*. Efficient learning requires an active and dynamic involvement in the learning process. Active learners organize information, ask themselves questions about the material, and compare new information to what they already know. They are motivated and have a desire to learn (Brown & Campione, 1986).

Students with passive learning styles lack interest in learning, possibly because of frustrating past experiences. Believing that they can not learn, these students become passive and dependent, a style that is often called *learned helplessness*. Passive learners wait for the teacher to do something to lead them to the learning instead of taking the initiative. In effect, they expect to be "spoon fed," step-by-step.

Until research issues can be further clarified, teachers may consider learning styles one option that may be related to some severe reading disabilities, but they should not rule out other options.

Characteristics of Multisensory Methods

Multisensory methods are built on the premise that stimulation of several sensory avenues reinforces learning. The multisensory concept is indicated in the abbreviation *VAKT* (visual, auditory, kinesthetic, tactile). To simulate all of these senses, children might *hear* the teacher say a word, *say* the word to themselves, *hear* themselves say the word, *feel* the muscle movement as they *trace* the word, *feel* the tactile surface under their finger tips, *see* their hands move as they *trace* the word, and *hear* themselves say the word as they *trace* it.

The VAKT method emphasizes the tracing process. Children may trace the word by having their fingers in contact with the paper. To increase the tactile and kinesthetic sensation, sandpaper letters, sand or clay trays, and finger paints are sometimes used.

A number of reading programs are built on the multisensory approach to reading instruction (Birsh, 1999), including the Orton-Gillingham Method, Project Read, the Wilson Method, Alphabetic Phonics, the Herman Method, and the Spalding Method. The Orton-Gillingham method (described later in this chapter) was the first multisensory program and is considered the basis for the other programs (Birsh, 1999; Henry, 1998). The multisensory methods have the following similar characteristics (Lerner, 2000):

- They help anchor verbal information by providing linkages with the visual, auditory, tactile, and kinesthetic pathways for learning.
- They use highly structured phonics instruction with an emphasis on the alphabetic system.
- They include abundant drill, practice, and repetition.
- They have carefully planned sequential lessons.
- They emphasize explicit instruction in the language rule system to guide reading and spelling.

Orton-Gillingham Method

The Orton-Gillingham Method, a multisensory approach for teaching reading, is an outgrowth of Samuel Orton's neurological theory of language disorders (Orton, 1937). More than 50 years ago, Orton, a physician who specialized in children with language disorders, worked with a teacher, Anna Gillingham, to develop a multisensory, synthetic phonics approach using direct instruction. The approach is associated with the International Dyslexia Society, which is dedicated to finding causes and treatments for dyslexia.

The original Orton-Gillingham (Gillingham & Stillman, 1970) Method is a highly structured approach requiring five lessons a week for a minimum of two years. The initial activities include learning letters and sounds, learning words, and using words in sentences.

Letter names and sounds are learned through six sensory associations. These are visual-auditory (V-A), auditory-visual (A-V), auditory-kinesthetic (A-K), kinesthetic-auditory (K-A), visual-kinesthetic (V-K), and kinesthetic-visual (K-V). Instruction takes place in three phases:

- *In Phase I*:
  1. A V-A association with the letter name is established. The teacher shows

a card with a letter on it and says the letter name, which the student repeats. In saying the letter, an A-K association is made. This step is the foundation for oral reading.

2. When mastery of the letter name has occurred, a V-A association with the sound is developed. The teacher says the sound while exposing the card, and the pupil repeats the sound. Thus, both V-A and A-K associations are being used.

- *In Phase II*: The student develops the ability to relate the sound to the letter name. The teacher, without showing the card, makes the letter sound, and the pupil tells the name of the letter. This step is the basis for oral spelling.
- *In Phase III*:
  1. The letter is printed by the teacher and its construction explained. The student then traces over the original, copies it, and finally writes the letter from memory while averting eyes from the paper. This association is V-K and K-V.
  2. The teacher says the sound and the pupil writes the letter that has that sound, thereby developing the A-K association.

After learning letter-sound associations, the student learns to *read words*. This learning starts by blending letter sounds and spelling the words. The initial words taught contain two vowels, *a* and *i*, and eight consonants, *b, g, h, j, k, m, p,* and *t*. The blended words follow a consonant-vowel-consonant (CVC) pattern, and blending occurs by pronouncing the first consonant and vowel together (*ra*) and then adding the final consonant (*rat*). These words are written on colored cards, which are called the student's "jewel case." Sample jewel case words are *bat, hip, bib,* and *job*. After these words are mastered, words containing other letters are added.

After a basic set of words has been learned, the words are *combined into sentences* and stories, and the student learns to read these. Reading continues to be taught by a phonics method and combines spelling and dictation exercises.

Fernald Method

More than 50 years ago, Fernald (1943/1998) developed a multisensory approach for extremely poor readers that simultaneously involves four sensory avenues—visual, auditory, kinesthetic, and tactile—as well as the language experience approach. Because progress with this method may be slow, it is generally used only when other methods have failed. The student learns a word as a total pattern by tracing the entire word and thereby strengthening the memory and visualization of the entire word. The words to be learned are selected by the student. The method consists of four stages.

Lindamood Phoneme Sequencing Program (LIPS)

This program is a phonemic awareness and phonics program for children with severe reading problems. It focuses on the conscious processing of sensory information, particularly involving the mouth and speech mechanism. The program enables metacognitive phoneme awareness of the lip, the tongue, and mouth actions that produce the sounds students hear in words. It strives to teach students to use sensory information from feeling, seeing, and hearing to develop a feedback system that promotes self-correction in speech, reading, and spelling (Lindamood & Lindamood, 1998).

Direct Instruction Reading Program

Direct instruction has been shown to be highly effective with children who are considered at risk because of poverty (Carnine, Silbert, & Kameenui, 1990). A collection of *Direct Instruction Programs* includes a *Direct Instruction Reading Program* (Engelmann & Bruner, 1995), which is a revision of the former DISTAR reading program (Engelmann & Bruner, 1974). The Direct Instruction Reading Program consists of six levels, roughly corresponding to Grades 1 through 6. A sample page from this program is shown in Figure 15.3.

This highly structured reading program consists of lessons based on carefully sequenced skill hierarchies. Based on principles of behavioral psychology,

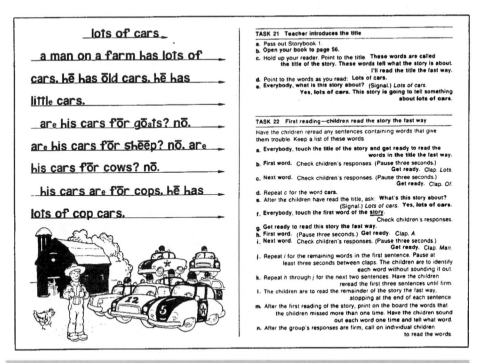

FIGURE 15.3   Sample Page from Direct Instruction Reading Program

Source: Reading Mastery Series Guide Rainbow Edition: SRA Macmillian/McGraw Hill. 250 Old Wilson Bridge Road, Suite 310; Worthington, Ohio 43085.

the program contains drills and instructional reading, as well as repetition and practice. Students progress in small planned steps, and teacher praise is used as reinforcement. Teachers are guided in specific procedures and oral instructions through each step of the program. The program uses a synthetic phonics approach, and students are first taught the prerequisite skill of auditory blending to help them combine isolated sounds into words. In addition, the shapes of some alphabet letters are modified to provide clues to the letter sounds. The special alphabet is gradually phased out as children progress.

In this program, the teacher presents fully scripted lessons. The Direct Instruction program prescribes what the teacher says and does. The students (individually and in unison as a group) provide the anticipated response. The teacher evaluates the degree of mastery of individuals and of the group on criterion-referenced tasks and tests.

The *Corrective Reading Program* (Engelmann, Becker, Hanner, & Johnson, 1988) is designed for the older student (Grades 4 through 12). It consists of two strands: decoding, which follows the regular Direct Instruction format, and comprehension, which uses text materials of interest to the older student. The web address for *Direct Instruction Programs* is http://www.sra-4kids.com.

Fast ForWord

Fast ForWord is an Internet- and CD-ROM-based training program for children with language and reading problems. It is designed for children who have trouble processing sounds quickly enough to distinguish rapid acoustical change in speech. This program alters the acoustics of speech by drawing out sounds and then gradually speeding them up, that is, stretching out certain speech sounds and emphasizing rapidly changing speech components by making them slower and louder. In an intensive series of adaptive interactive exercises using acoustically modified speech sounds, the Fast ForWord program stimulates rapid language skill development as children learn to distinguish the various components of speech (Miller, et al., 1998).

Fast ForWord Two is an advanced program that uses the Internet and a CD-ROM training program to help students develop the language and reading skills critical for reading or becoming a better reader using adaptive technology. The program uses interactive exercises to cross-train the brain on a number of skills that improve listening, thinking, and reading skills. The Fast ForWord program is used with children ages 5–12 (Miller, et al., 1998). The web site for *Fast ForWord* is http://www.scientificlearning.com.

Summary

Students have severe difficulties in learning to read for a variety of reasons. The condition known as dyslexia is a rare type of severe reading disorder that has baffled and intrigued the professional community for many years. People with dyslexia have extreme difficulty recognizing letters and words and interpreting printed language. Recent brain research has shed much light on this condition by showing that individuals with dyslexia have differences in brain structure and function.

Many students in our culturally diverse society are at risk for reading failure because of environmental conditions, extreme poverty, or lack of a stimulating home environment. Research on brain development shows that the most important brain growth occurs from birth to three years old. Many at-risk students are served by federal Title I programs.

About 80 percent of students with learning disabilities display reading problems. Students with learning disabilities are covered by the IDEA-1997 law and may receive services through special education.

Many students with attention deficit disorder (ADD) or attention deficit hyperactivity disorder (ADHD) have reading problems. Services in the schools for these children are covered under the IDEA-1997 category *other health impaired* or by Section 504 of the Rehabilitation Act of 1973.

A number of instructional methods are used to teach reading to students with severe reading problems. Standard reading methods can be adapted for use with students who have severe reading disabilities. Both sight word and phonics methods can be used if they are adapted to meet the needs of the students. The child's learning style should also be considered.

Multisensory methods use the visual, auditory, tactile, and kinesthetic sensory pathways to reinforce learning.

Among the methods that are used to teach students with severe reading problems are the Fernald Method, the Orton-Gillingham Method, *Lindamood Phoneme Sequencing Program, Direct Instruction Reading Program*, and *Fast ForWord.*

Assessing Reading Achievement: Formal Measures

Introduction

This chapter discusses formal tests and their use in assessing students with reading problems. Earlier, this text described a number of *informal measures* for evaluating a student's reading. Teachers find that informal and authentic assessment methods provide immediate, usable, and practical information about students. Informal measures, such as informal reading inventories, trial lessons, curriculum-based assessment, and structured observations, are described in Chapter 3. However, for a comprehensive evaluation of a student with reading problems, formal tests offer additional usable information. Formal tests serve several purposes:

- They allow teachers to compare a student to others of the same age or grade level.
- They provide scores that are more familiar to parents and other professionals, such as psychologists and physicians.
- They help teachers make objective decisions about a student's performance.
- They fulfill the legal requirements for certain local, state, school, and federal policies.

This chapter first presents an overview of formal tests. Then, several different types of tests, including tests of general reading assessment, tests of diagnostic reading assessment, and tests of intelligence are discussed. Many additional tests are listed and described in Appendix B.

The information in this chapter serves as a guide to help you choose, administer, and interpret formal tests. For additional information, you can refer to *Tests in Print V* (Murphy, Impara, & Plake, 1999), a resource that contains extensive reviews of many different tests.

One of the criticisms of formal tests has been that they lack authenticity, which means that formal tests tend to assess the reader's proficiency with short passages and isolated words rather than using the types of reading students do in school. However, some formal test publishers are now creating longer, more authentic passages for students to read. One example is the *Iowa Test of Basic Skills* published by Houghton Mifflin. New assessment tools also provide ways to combine formal and informal assessment. The Psychological Corporation has published an *Integrated Assessment System*, which provides formal assessment of a collection of student work (portfolio) and authentic tasks.

Overview of Formal Tests

Formal tests include a broad class of instruments that are commercially produced, formally printed, and published. They also have specific procedures for administration and scoring. Two types of formal tests are norm-referenced and criterion-referenced tests.

Norm-Referenced Tests

Most formal tests are *norm-referenced* (also called *standardized*), which means that they have statistics (or *norms*) for comparing the performance of a student to a large sample of similar students (the *norm sample*). Norm-referenced tests are developed carefully using a norm sample, which is a large number of students who are representative of the general population. The test is given to each student in the norm sample, and norms are established to determine, for example, how well the average fourth grader does on the test. These norms permit you, as a teacher, to compare the fourth grader you are testing with the fourth graders in the norm sample. To ensure that your student's scores can be compared with the norm sample, you must strictly follow the procedures for test administration, scoring, and interpretation.

Criterion-Referenced Tests

Some formal tests are *criterion-referenced*. In this type of test, a student's performance is compared to a specific *standard* or *criterion* (rather than to the norm sample). This test determines whether a student has mastered certain competencies or skills. For example, can the student recognize *ing* endings or find the main idea in a paragraph? Criterion-referenced tests are useful because they provide a means of accountability that can be related to the curriculum. For example, a teacher can determine whether a student has mastered the concept of the main idea after it has been taught.

To understand the difference between a normed and a criterion-referenced test, look at an analogy to another area of learning: swimming. In norm-referenced terms, a child can be tested in swimming and judged to swim as well as the average nine-year-old. In criterion-referenced terms, a child is judged on the basis of certain accomplishments, such as putting his or her face in the water, floating on his or her back, and doing the crawl stroke. In other words, criterion-referenced tests measure mastery rather than grade level, or they *describe* rather than *compare* performance.

Bias in Testing

Tests should be fair in representing student performance and should be free of racial or cultural bias. The content of the test should represent the experiences and values of all groups taking the test. For example, a reading test should not contain vocabulary, pictures, or stories that are unfamiliar to certain populations taking the test. As discussed in Chapter 14, formal intelligence tests, in particular, have been subjected to the criticism of cultural bias.

Ethical Considerations

In using formal tests for assessment, professionals must comply with basic professional standards. If professionals from different disciplines are involved in assessment (i.e., educators, psychologists, counselors, social workers, medical specialists), each must abide by the standards of his or her own profession. All must maintain the confidentiality of the student, keep complete records, and follow standard testing criteria. The International Reading Association has published guidelines for the administration of tests in reading.

Scores on Norm-Referenced Tests

The scores on norm-referenced tests indicate how an individual student has performed compared to students of the same grade or age level who are in the norm sample. After a teacher gives a test, the teacher determines a *raw score*, which is usually the number correct on the test. Raw scores are then converted into *derived scores*, which can be used for interpreting the student's performance. Derived scores on norm-referenced reading tests can be reported as standard scores, reading grade equivalents, percentiles, normal curve equivalents (NCEs), and stanines.

Many scores on reading and other academic tests are based on a *normal distribution curve* of scores. Most scores in a normal distribution fall in the middle, creating a "humped curve." However, some high and low scores fall at the upper and lower ends of the curve. In other words, most scores are average, but some are very high or low. The more extreme (high or low) the score, the less frequent it is.

The highest point on the curve is the *mean* (or average) point. The "area" within each vertical division represents the percent of people in it. The closer to the mean a division is, the more individuals are in it.

Standardized tests are statistically designed so that one-half of the students are below the mean (or average) and one-half are above. Of course, communities want all of their children to score above average. The humorist Garrison Keillor lampoons this notion in his tales of the mythical town of Lake Wobegon, where "all the children are above average."

Standard Scores.   Some formal tests report *standard scores*, which refer to scores in which the mean and the standard deviation (which is a measure of variation) have been assigned preset values. For example, in the *Weschler Intelligence Scale for Children, Third Edition (WISC-III)*, the mean is set at 100, and the standard deviation at 15.

Grade Equivalent (GE).   The reading grade equivalent indicates how well a student reads in terms of grade level. For example, a score of 4.5 (the fifth month of the fourth grade) indicates that the student correctly answered the same number of questions on this particular test as the average pupil in the fifth month of the fourth grade. Reading grade equivalents do not indicate absolute performance; they indicate how the student performed in relation to the students in the norm sample population.

Percentiles (PR). Percentiles describe the student's performance in relation to others in the same age group or grade. Percentiles can be understood as a rank within 100, expressed in numbers from 1 to 99. A percentile rank is the percentage of students that scored lower than the student being tested. For example, a percentile score of 57 indicates that this student scored higher than 57 percent of the comparison group and lower than 42 percent. The 50th percentile indicates the median (or middle) score. The highest percentile is 99 and the lowest is 1. The higher the percentile, the better the student's performance.

Equal distances in percentiles, however, do not indicate equal differences in raw score points. Because many scores center near the mean, the difference between the 50th and 60th percentiles may be only a few raw score points, whereas the distance between the 18th and 19th percentiles often represents a great many raw score points on the test (Figure 16.1).

Normal Curve Equivalent (NCE) Scores. The NCE scores are similar to percentiles in that they have a range from 1 to 99 and a mean of 50. They differ

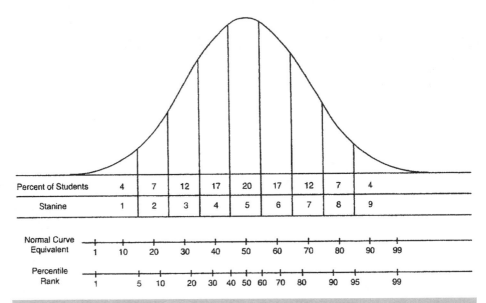

Percent of Students	4	7	12	17	20	17	12	7	4
Stanine	1	2	3	4	5	6	7	8	9

Normal Curve Equivalent: 1 10 20 30 40 50 60 70 80 90 99

Percentile Rank: 1 5 10 20 30 40 50 60 70 80 90 95 99

FIGURE 16.1 Relation among Stanines, NCEs, and Percentiles

from percentile scores because they have been transformed into equal units of reading achievement. For example, the difference between the 50th and 60th NCE and the 18th and 19th NCE is the same in raw point scores. Figure 16.1 shows the distribution of NCE scores in comparison to percentiles.

Stanines.   The stanine score ranks pupils from 1 to 9. The lowest stanine score is 1, the median stanine is 5, and the highest is 9. Stanine scores are assigned so that the results represent a normal distribution. Thus, in an average class, most students will receive stanine scores of 4, 5, or 6; and a few will receive stanine scores of 1 or 9.

The name *stanine* is a contraction of "standard nine" and is based on the fact that the score runs from 1 to 9. Stanines are normalized standard scores with a mean of 5 and a standard deviation of 2. Figure 16.1 shows the percentage of students in each stanine and in each 10 NCE units and compares these with percentiles.

Standardization, Validity, and Reliability

Which norm-referenced tests are the best? In judging the value of a norm-referenced test, teachers should consider the test's standardization, validity, and reliability.

Standardization.   To standardize a test, it is given to a large representative group of students (the norm sample). Based on data derived from this norm sample, inferences are made about other students who take the test. When selecting a test, teachers should consider whether the norm sample was large enough to establish stable performance norms. In addition, the characteristics of the individuals who comprise the norm sample are important. Did the norm sample include representatives of the students who are being tested? If the norm sample group is not considered representative, some school districts develop their own local norms.

Validity.   Validity refers to whether a test measures what it is supposed to measure. Two types of validity are content validity and criterion validity. Content validity involves inspecting the test to see whether the items are valid for testing purposes. For example, a valid reading comprehension test would probably contain passages with questions. In contrast, a comprehension test that required the student to match words would have questionable content validity.

Criterion validity refers to how the test compares with some other aspects of achievement. Most norm-referenced reading tests provide information about the comparison of performance on the reading test with some aspect of school achievement (for example, grade-point average). The comparison is usually done in the form of a statistical correlation. This correlation may range from +1.0 (a high positive correlation) to –1.0 (a very negative correlation). For acceptable criterion validity, the correlation should be *positive* and *high* (generally at least 0.70).

Reliability.   Reliability refers to the stability of test scores. If a test is reliable, the person will receive the same score on repeated testings. To be useful for making decisions about an individual, a test must have high reliability. Salvia and Ysseldyke (1998) believe that acceptable reliability for a test depends on the situation. If test scores are reported for groups of students for general administration purposes or screening, a reliability score of about 0.80 is acceptable. For individual decisions about students, such as placement in a Title I class or in special education, the reliability of the test should be 0.90.

Two forms of reliability are test-retest reliability and internal consistency reliability. In test-retest reliability, the test is given to a group of students two times. Then the scores are correlated to determine whether individual students perform about the same on the first and second administrations. In internal reliability, items within a test are compared with one another. In one form of internal reliability, split-half reliability, a group of students' scores on one-half of the test items is correlated with performance on the items from the other half.

Tests of General Reading Assessment

Tests of general reading assessment are used to evaluate a student's general level of achievement as well as to determine the general areas of reading strengths and weaknesses. Types of tests that are used in the general reading assessment phase include group survey tests, individual survey tests, normed oral reading tests, and literacy tests.

Group Survey Tests

Survey tests are norm-referenced tests that are used to assess the student's reading level. Both group survey tests and individual survey tests are used for this purpose.

Group survey tests are the most commonly used tests in schools. They are generally used once per year to assess student progress in reading and other academic subjects, to identify those who may have problems, or to evaluate the success of a program. Examples of group survey tests for reading are the *Stanford Achievement Test*, the *Iowa Tests of Basic Skills* (*ITBS*), the *California Reading Test*, and the *Gates–MacGinitie Reading Tests,* ™*Fourth Edition*. These tests are designed for use with a group of students in a class, but they are also useful for testing individual students. All standardized group reading tests permit teachers to compare a student's score to scores in large norm samples.

A group survey test is actually a series of tests at different levels. The different levels are suitable for students at different grade levels. In addition, each level usually has a few equivalent forms (for example, Form A and Form B). Because the two forms are normed similarly, the scores on the two forms can be compared. If Form A is given during an initial assessment and Form B is given after a period of instruction is completed, the student's progress can be evaluated easily.

Despite their excellent statistical properties, group survey tests have some limitations for use with students with reading problems:

- *Out-of-level tests.* Students with reading problems must be given test levels that are appropriate for their reading level but not for their age level. For example, an eighth grader reading at a second-grade level will find the eighth-grade test to be too hard but the second-grade test too "babyish."
- *Inability to measure school-related tasks.* Over a period of years, many strides have been made in making these tests better reflect the actual types of reading students do in school. However, the tests continue to measure more discrete tasks, such as reading single words and relatively short passages. For this reason, the teacher must supplement information from standardized tests with informal measures that assess such abilities as reading whole stories and taking notes.
- *Limits of a formal situation.* Some students "freeze" on standardized tests. In addition, because they require a standard procedure, formal tests do not allow teachers to observe student performance closely and to probe a student's responses. Informal assessment, with its ability to adjust situations to a student's needs, may give far more information.

A description of a few tests that are widely used for students with reading problems gives examples of group survey tests that the reading teacher is likely to encounter.

The *Stanford Diagnostic Reading Test, Fourth Edition (SDRT4)* is intended for use with lower achievers and contains more easy items than most survey tests at the same levels. The four levels of the test are red, green, brown, and blue; at each level, the test contains two forms. Phonics abilities are tested at all levels of the test. The red level, for Grades 1–2, tests auditory discrimination, basic phonics skills, auditory vocabulary, word recognition, and comprehension. The green level, for Grades 3–4, tests auditory discrimination, phonetic analysis, structural analysis, auditory vocabulary, comprehension, and reading rate. The brown level, for Grades 5–6, tests phonetic analysis, structural analysis, auditory vocabulary, comprehension, and reading rate. Finally, the blue level, for Grades 9–12 and community colleges, tests phonetic analysis, structural analysis, word meaning, word parts, comprehension, reading rate, and scanning and skimming. The test is well standardized and reports many different types of norms for students.

In addition, the *SDRT* contains a criterion-referenced section called Progress Indicators. All of the test items measuring a certain skill are added together, and a criterion is given for mastery of that skill.

The *Gates–MacGinitie Reading Tests™ (GMRT™), Fourth Edition*, is another standardized reading test often used with low-achieving students. The test comes in five reading levels: prereading level, beginning reading level (Grade 1), Levels 1 and 2 (primary-level developmental reading skills), Levels 3–12 (two tests: vocabulary and comprehension), and adult reading level (two tests: vocabulary and comprehension).

In the vocabulary test, which has a 20-minute time limit, students match isolated words to one of four pictures (at low levels) or one of four synonyms (at higher levels). In the comprehension tests, students read short passages and either match them to one of four pictures (at lower levels) or answer multiple-choice questions (at higher levels). This well-standardized test is used widely in Title I programs.

Individual Survey Tests

Individual survey tests, which are used widely in assessing students with reading problems, are designed to be administered to a single student. As survey tests, they give general information about reading scores rather than a detailed analysis of reading. In fact, many of these tests also include information about areas such as mathematics and spelling.

Individual survey tests usually consist of one level that is suitable for a wide range of reading abilities. Because an individual survey test might cover Grades 1 through 9, it would be suitable for an older reader who is reading at a primary-grade level. Individual survey tests are usually standardized, so they permit valid comparison with a norm sample.

Through careful observation, the teacher can obtain diagnostic information during the process of giving a survey test. For example, the teacher can note whether the student hesitates or recognizes words instantly and whether the student uses decoding methods.

The actual reading tasks that students perform vary greatly from test to test. Many of the test authors use considerable ingenuity to make their tests brief or to use a multiple-choice format. Unfortunately, such methods may lead to tests that do not measure the authentic ability to read. Before using a test, the teacher should inspect the actual items to determine exactly what they require the student to do. The name of the test, or of its subtests, may not reflect the content.

Widely used individual survey tests include the *Wide Range Achievement Test, 3rd Edition (WRAT3)*, the *Slosson Oral Reading Test (SORT)*, the *Peabody Individual Achievement Test–Revised (PIAT-R)*, and the *Kaufman Test of Educational Achievement (KTEA)*.

The *Wide Range Achievement Test, 3rd (WRAT3)*, comes in two forms and has three subtests: reading, spelling, and arithmetic. The reading subtest assesses skills in letter recognition, letter naming, and pronunciation of words in isolation. A grade level is obtained by having students read individual words orally. The *WRAT3* is widely used because it is short and convenient. However, isolated word reading does not provide a comprehensive assessment of a person's reading abilities (McCormick, 1995; Salvia & Ysseldyke, 1998). The *WRAT3* should be used only for an initial assessment.

The *Slosson Oral Reading Test (SORT)* is another test of reading based solely on word lists. Similarly, it should not be used as a reliable measure of reading level but only as an initial reading screening device. Because both the *WRAT3* and the *SORT* are short, usually taking less than 10 minutes, they are perhaps overused. Both should be supplemented by other measures.

The *Peabody Individual Achievement Test–Revised (PIAT-R)* is a norm-referenced, individually administered test designed to provide a wide-range screening measure of academic achievement in six content areas: mathematics, reading recognition, reading comprehension, spelling, general information, and written expression. Two subtests assess reading, and a total reading score on the *PIAT-R* is obtained by combining scores of the reading recognition and reading comprehension subtests.

Reading recognition is measured through oral reading of words in isolation and, for beginning items, matching letters and naming capital and lowercase letters. The reading comprehension subtest contains 81 multiple-choice items assessing skill development in understanding what is read. After reading a sentence, the student must indicate comprehension by choosing the correct picture out of a group of four. The reading recognition and reading comprehension subtests are interrelated, and a student cannot take the comprehension subtest unless a score of 18 or above is achieved on the reading recognition subtest.

The *PIAT-R* also has subtests for mathematics, general information, and written expression. The standardization of the *PIAT-R* is considered good, and its reliability and validity are considered adequate for making important educational decisions about students (Salvia & Ysseldyke, 1998).

The *Kaufman Test of Educational Achievement (KTEA)* is an individually administered, norm-referenced, multiple-skill achievement test that can be used with students in Grades 1 through 12. It comes in two quite different versions: the Comprehensive Form and the Brief Form. The Comprehensive Form contains five subtests, two of which are reading decoding and reading comprehension. The other subtests are mathematics applications, mathematics computation, and spelling. In the reading decoding subtest, students identify letters and then read phonetic and nonphonetic words. In the reading comprehension subtest, the student must first respond through gestures or oral statements to directions in printed sentences. For the rest of the test, the student reads passages and answers questions. The Brief Form contains reading, mathematics, and spelling subtests. The reading subtest of the brief form has features of both the reading decoding and reading comprehension subtests described above.

The *KTEA* is considered acceptable in terms of standardization and reliability. Teachers need to check the curriculum they are teaching to determine whether the *KTEA* meets their needs (Salvia & Ysseldyke, 1998).

Normed Oral Reading Tests

Normed oral reading tests, like informal reading inventories (see Chapter 3), contain graded passages for oral reading. However, unlike informal reading inventories, these tests include statistical norms. Thus, you have another way to obtain a general reading assessment that compares your student to others in a normed sample.

Several normed tests of oral reading are available through commercial publishers—for example, the *Gilmore Oral Reading Test* and the *Formal Reading Inventory*. Chapter 3 discusses oral reading assessment and the rich diagnostic opportunities oral reading tests provide. The *Qualitative Reading Inventory–3* has been particularly highly rated (Taylor, Harris, Pearson, & Garcia, 1995). The test inventory in Appendix B includes descriptions of several tests of oral reading.

Diagnostic Reading Tests

Diagnostic reading tests yield more specific information than general survey reading tests. These diagnostic tests provide a more detailed analysis of specific reading strengths and weaknesses. Two kinds of tests are described in this section: diagnostic reading batteries and diagnostic tests of specific areas of reading. Both are listed in Appendix B.

Diagnostic Reading Batteries

A diagnostic reading battery consists of a group of subtests, each of which assesses a different component of reading. It offers useful information for obtaining a profile of the student's reading in several areas, such as oral reading, phonics, sight vocabulary, and comprehension. As with all tests, teachers should examine the subtests to make sure that they actually test the skills they describe.

Typically, diagnostic batteries are more suitable for beginning readers. Although they sample several components of reading, they tend to emphasize emergent literacy and word recognition rather than comprehension or word meaning.

Because diagnostic batteries often do not contain extensive reading passages, they should be used in conjunction with other tests of actual reading and comprehension. Sometimes teachers may administer only the sections of these batteries that are relevant to a particular student, rather than the entire battery. Four widely given diagnostic batteries are the *Woodcock Reading Mastery Test–Revised (WRMT-R)*, the *Woodcock Diagnostic Reading Battery (WDRB)*, the *BRIGANCE® Comprehensive Inventory of Basic Skills–Revised, (CIBS-R™)*, and the *Gates-McKillop-Horowitz Reading Diagnostic Test–Revised*. Each of these tests is briefly described in the following sections.

Woodcock Reading Mastery Test–Revised (WRMT-R). The *Woodcock Reading Mastery Test–Revised (WRMT-R)* is a widely used reading diagnostic test that measures individuals from a beginning reading level through that of an advanced adult. It is available in two forms (Form G and Form H), both of which are accompanied by a comprehensive and well-organized test manual. Form G contains all six subtests, and Form H contains the four reading achievement tests. The test was renormed in 1998.

In Form H, the four basic reading achievement subtests of the *WRMT-R* are word identification, word attack, word comprehension, and passage comprehension. These four subtests may be combined to obtain a full-score reading performance assessment (Figure 16.2).

WRMT-R
Clusters:

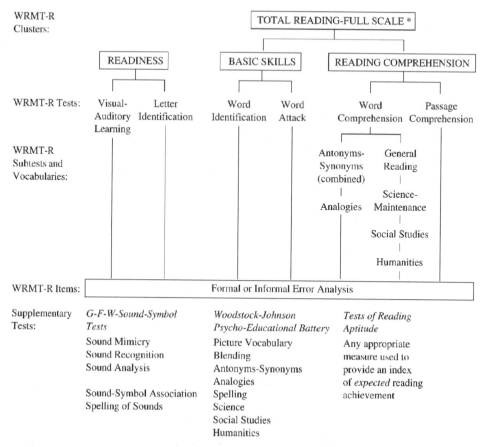

FIGURE 16.2 **Structure of Information Included in the Total Interpretation Plan of the *Woodcock Reading Mastery Test–Revised* (Renormed in 1998)**

In the word identification subtest, the student reads single words aloud. In the word attack subtest, the student sounds out nonsense words. The word comprehension subtest requires the student to perform three separate tasks with vocabulary: providing antonyms, providing synonyms, and completion of analogies for a word (e.g., day is to night as up is to _____). The words used in the word comprehension subtest are divided into general reading, science and mathematics, social studies, and humanities. In the passage comprehension subtest, the student orally fills in a missing word in a paragraph.

Form G also contains two subtests for beginning readers: a visual-auditory test in which children are assessed on their ability to associate words to picture-like symbols and a test of letter identification.

The *WRMT-R* contains many useful features and teacher aids. However, the ability to read in context is measured only in the reading comprehension subtest. Furthermore, this subtest requires only oral reading and, as a response, asks the student to fill in a word. This task is somewhat different from the silent reading and responses to questions that most students are required to do in school.

Figure 16.2 details the structure of the test. The *WRMT-R* is considered appropriately and adequately normed, and evidence for reliability and validity is good (Salvia & Ysseldyke, 1998).

Woodcock Diagnostic Reading Battery (WDRB). The *Woodcock Diagnostic Reading Battery (WDRB)* assesses reading achievement and reading-related abilities to help determine why a reading problem exists. It is individually administered and norm-referenced and is designed for individuals between the ages of 4 and over 90. This battery uses subtests from the *Woodcock-Johnson Psycho-Educational Battery–Revised:* six subtests from the *Tests of Cognitive Ability–Revised* and four tests from the *Tests of Achievement–Revised*.

The *WDRB* has 10 subtests, which can be organized into seven clusters for interpretation. The clusters are total reading, broad reading, basic reading skills, reading comprehension, phonological awareness, oral comprehension, and reading aptitude. Each subtest fits into one or more cluster(s).

The Profile page for the *WDRB* is shown in Figure 16.3.

BRIGANCE® Comprehensive Inventory of Basic Skills–Revised (CIBS-R™). The *BRIGANCE® Comprehensive Inventory of Basic Skills–Revised (CIBS-R™)* is another widely used set of diagnostic batteries. The test was revised in 1999 and covers prekindergarten to Grade 9. It is a criterion-referenced test that also provides normed (standardized) information.

The *CIBS-R* has 10 criterion-referenced grade-placement tests. They are listening vocabulary comprehension, listening comprehension, word recognition, oral reading, reading vocabulary comprehension, reading comprehension, spelling, sentence writing, math comprehension skills, and math problem solving.

In addition, the standardized portions of *CIBS-R* are designed to meet state and federal assessment requirements. This portion produces grade and age equivalents, percentiles, and quotients in six areas of achievement: basic reading, reading comprehension, written expression, listening comprehension, and math.

Gates-McKillop-Horowitz Reading Diagnostic Tests. The *Gates-McKillop-Horowitz Reading Diagnostic Tests* is a battery with eight distinct parts. The battery contains an oral reading inventory with an analysis of oral reading, a test of reading sentences, flashed (automatic) words, untimed words, word attack, recognition of vowels, two auditory perception tests (blending and discrimination), and written expression. The oral reading test consists of one continuous passage that

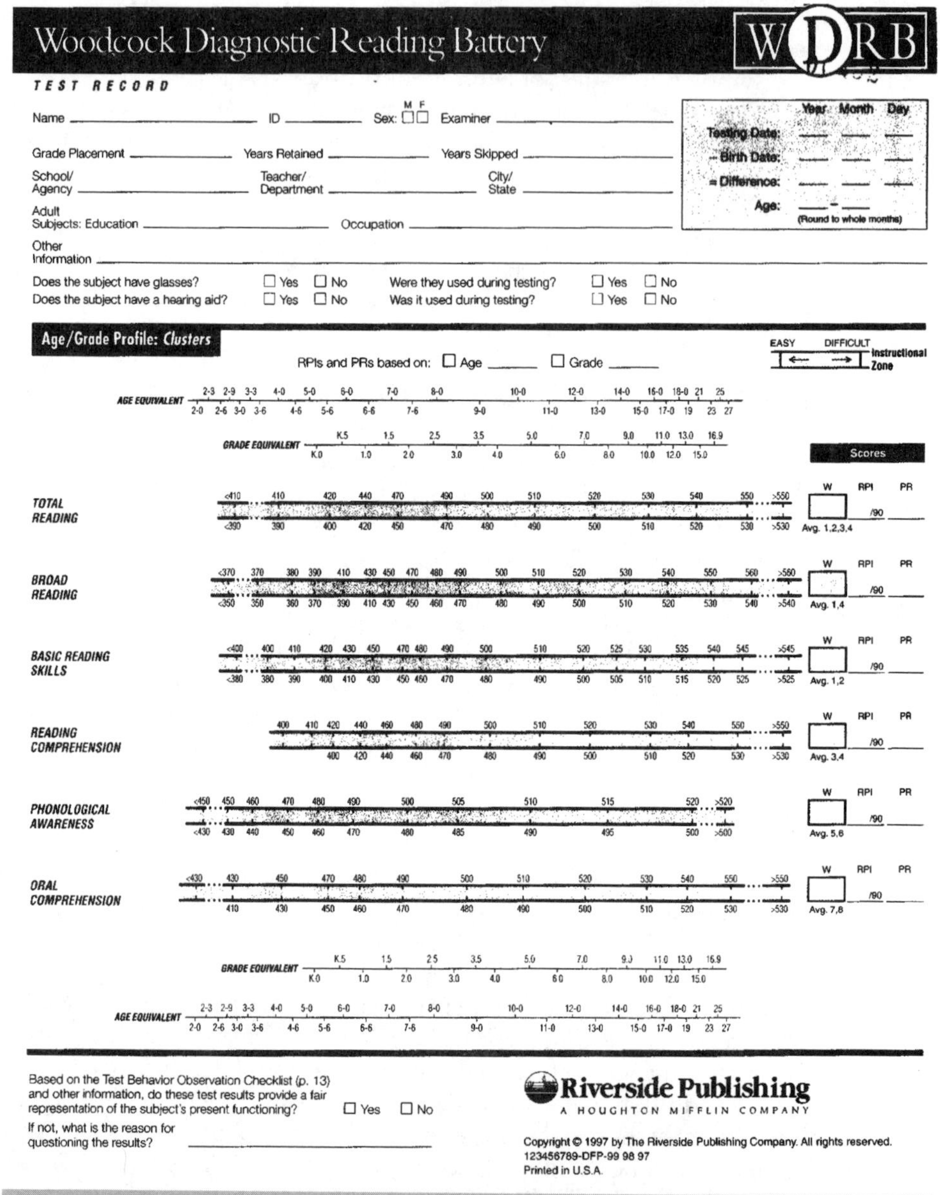

FIGURE 16.3 Profile Page for the *Woodcock Diagnostic Reading Battery* (WDRB)

Copyright © 1997 by The Riverside Publishing Company. All rights reserved. From the *Woodcock Diagnostic Reading Battery* by Richard W. Woodcock, with permission of the publisher.

increases in difficulty and has only 30 words on any specific grade level. The grade-placement score is based solely on oral reading because no comprehension questions are asked. In addition, auditory perception, emergent literacy abilities, and word recognition are emphasized. The inclusion of spelling and writing sub-tests reflects an integrated language philosophy.

Diagnostic Tests of Specific Areas

Tests of specific areas concentrate on an in-depth evaluation of a specific area of reading. These tests are particularly useful in gathering detailed information about one area of reading, such as the student's abilities in phonics.

One example of such a test is the *Test of Reading Comprehension, Third Edition (TORC-3)*, which analyzes the student's skills in reading comprehension. Another is the *Diagnostic Assessments of Reading with Trial Teaching Strategies (DARTTS)*. This test assesses strengths and weaknesses in reading through six areas: word recognition, word analysis, oral reading, silent reading comprehension, spelling, and word meaning.

Measuring Intelligence

Perhaps no concept has provided more controversy in education than the measure of intelligence. Heated public debate periodically erupts on the nature of intelligence, its role in achievement, and the role of culture in intelligence. This important measure is used in making decisions about who is entitled to special education services and, in some instances, who should be classified as reading disabled (see Chapter 14). For this reason, a special section is devoted to the measurement of intelligence.

The full concept of intelligence is much richer than what is actually measured by intelligence tests. Intelligence includes mechanical ability, street knowledge, creativity, and social skills. However, most intelligence (IQ) tests simply predict whether an individual is likely to do well in schoolwork, especially in learning tasks with highly verbal content (Salvia & Ysseldyke, 1998). Therefore, intelligence tests can be best regarded as measures of scholastic aptitude.

An IQ score, in part, reflects a student's background. Intelligence scores are also affected by a student's comfort with the testing situation. Thus, intelligence cannot be measured with absolute accuracy. Nor can teachers learn how much a particular student might ultimately achieve. Intelligence tests measure only the current potential for learning; future potential is unknown. In summary, intelligence must be interpreted in a judicious manner.

Teachers should remember that the content of these tests and the validity of their scores have come under serious criticism. An IQ test cannot give a de-finitive or permanent rating of a student's mental ability. Thus, teachers should be alert to the many other sources of information about students, including be-

havior in class, independence in living, and interests and accomplishments outside the school setting.

Using Intelligence Test Information in Reading Assessment

The purpose of obtaining information on a student's cognitive abilities and aptitude for learning is to help the teacher better understand the reading problem. The
intelligence test information can be used to assess a student's current potential,
analyze a student's component cognitive abilities, and observe the student's behavior during the testing situation. Each of these uses is discussed below.

Assessing a Student's Potential.   As described in Chapter 14, information from
an intelligence test can help the teacher determine whether a student has the potential to read better than he or she does at present. To illustrate this use in the case
of Ellen, her intelligence test score indicated a potential for reading that is much
higher than her present reading achievement level. This discrepancy between potential and performance shows she has the cognitive ability to read much better
than she does at present. In contrast, Mark's evaluation indicated that although he
is reading poorly, he is actually doing fairly well in relation to his potential for
learning. Mark, however, will still benefit from reading instruction suited to his
individual needs.

When evaluating a student with suspected learning disabilities, federal law
(Individuals with Disabilities in Education Act-IDEA-1997) requires the evaluation team to consider whether the student has a severe discrepancy between the
potential for learning and the current level of performance. Methods for determining the discrepancy are described in Chapter 14.

Most states use discrepancy scores to identify students with learning disabilities. However, the policy of using discrepancy scores is being questioned for
several reasons (Lerner, 2000; Fletcher, 1998; Fletcher, Francis, et al., 1998):

- *How useful is the IQ score in establishing a child's potential?* The IQ score may
  not accurately reflect the child's potential for learning. It may be more of an
  achievement score, and a child's IQ can be adversely affected by culture and
  personal experiences.
- *Discrepancy formulas vary from state to state.* Different states, as well as different school districts, use different discrepancy formulas. Thus, a child identified as having learning disabilities in one state may not be eligible for services in another. However, the learning disabilities do not disappear when
  the child moves to another state.
- *A discrepancy formula does not identify learning disabilities in young children.*
  Because the aptitude-achievement discrepancy is based on school failure in
  academic skills, young children who have not yet been exposed to academic
  skills are not identified. Thus, young children are not given services when it
  is most effective. This approach is called *wait and fail.*

Analyzing a Student's Component Cognitive Abilities. Intelligence is more than a single general factor. The current theory of intelligence is that intelligence comprises many separate abilities (Sternberg, 1985, 1999). In addition to providing an overall general score (IQ score), many tests of intelligence contain subtests and subscales that measure different (or component) cognitive functions. These tests help teachers analyze the student's strengths and weaknesses in learning aptitude. Several methods are used in determining cognitive patterns in students with reading and learning problems (Salvia & Ysseldyke, 1998):

- *Comparison of subscales.* The subscales contained in some intelligence tests allow comparisons of cognitive abilities. The widely used *Wechsler Intelligence Scales*, including the *Wechsler Intelligence Scale for Children, Third Edition (WISC-III)*, the *Wechsler Preschool and Primary Scale of Intelligence–Revised (WPPSI-R)*, and the *Wechsler Adult Intelligence Scale–Third Edition (WAIS-III)*, classify subtests as either verbal tests or performance tests. The *Kaufman Assessment Battery for Children* identifies sequential and simultaneous processing.
- *Evidence of subtest scatter and variability.* Some intelligence tests, such as the *Wechsler Intelligence Scale for Children, Third Edition (WISC-III)* and the *Woodcock-Johnson Psycho-Educational Battery–Revised–Test of Cognitive Abilities*, and the *Kaufman Assessment Battery for Children* contain subtests that tap differing abilities. A significant scatter among subtest scores, with a student doing well in some subtests and poorly in others, suggests variability in cognitive functioning.
- *Clustering of subtest scores to ascertain unique cognitive patterns.* Another approach is to regroup or cluster subtest scores to provide a better understanding of the student's strengths or weaknesses in cognitive functioning. Bannatyne (1974) suggests regrouping the subtests of the *WISC-III* into four areas: spatial ability, sequencing ability, verbal conceptualization ability, and acquired knowledge. Kaufman (1981) uses factor analysis to regroup *Wechsler Intelligence Scale for Children, Third Edition (WISC-III)* subtests into clusters of verbal comprehension, perceptual organization, and freedom from distractibility. The scoring system of the *Woodcock-Johnson Psycho-Educational Battery–Revised–Tests of Cognitive Ability* enables the tester to group individual subtests to obtain general clusters of cognitive factors, including verbal ability, reasoning, perceptual speed, and memory (Lerner, 2000).

Observing a Student's Behavior. According to Yogi Berra, "Sometimes you can observe a lot just by watching." Testers have the opportunity to observe students as they take intelligence tests. The tester can observe which activities the student enjoys, which activities are frustrating, and how the student goes about doing tasks. For this reason, examiners watch carefully as students use problem-solving strategies to perform the many different tasks on an intelligence test.

Types of Intelligence Tests

Instruments that assess intellectual ability can be divided into two types: group tests and individual tests. Group tests are designed to be given to several students at a time, and they are sometimes routinely administered as screening devices to identify those pupils who are different enough from average to warrant a more thorough examination. A drawback of group intelligence tests is that they often require students to read, thus making the IQ score dependent on reading ability. In addition, they do not provide in-depth information (Salvia & Ysseldyke, 1998). In general, then, more credence is given to individual intelligence tests than to group tests.

Individual tests must be given to an individual student. Some individual intelligence tests must be given by a trained examiner, and often this person is the school psychologist. Although other individual tests can be given by a reading teacher, these tests also require training in administration and scoring.

A listing and brief description of tests of intelligence and potential are presented in the test inventory in Appendix B. Some individual intelligence tests that are frequently used in a reading diagnosis are discussed below.

The *Wechsler Intelligence Scale for Children, Third Edition (WISC-III)* is one of the most frequently administered individual intelligence tests. It must be administered by a trained examiner, usually the school psychologist. However, in diagnosing a student's reading problem, teachers can make good use of the information obtained in the *WISC-III* by examining subtest scores as well as the scores of the full IQ, verbal IQ, and performance IQ. The test covers ages 6 to 16 (other Wechsler tests cover younger and older individuals; see Appendix B).

The *WISC-III* is particularly useful for measuring component subskills of intelligence. The test yields a verbal IQ score, a performance IQ score, and a full IQ score; of the 13 subtests, 6 are verbal, and 7 are performance. A full score is obtained by giving five verbal subtests and five performance subtests.

Verbal Scale
- *Information:* answering information questions.
- *Similarities:* noting how two things are alike.
- *Arithmetic:* solving timed problems.
- *Vocabulary:* defining words.
- *Comprehension:* dealing with everyday situations and abstract issues.
- Alternate Test: *Digit Span:* repeating digits forward and backward.

Performance Scale
- *Picture Completion:* determining missing items.
- *Coding:* matching and writing symbols and numbers.
- *Picture Arrangements:* sequencing pictures to tell a story.
- *Block Design:* duplicating a pictorial design with red and white blocks.
- *Object Assembly:* fitting puzzle pieces together.
- Alternate Test: *Mazes:* finding the way through a maze.
- Alternate test for coding only: *Symbol Search:* searching to see if a target symbol appears in a "search" group.

The examiner converts the raw score on each subtest to a standard (or scaled) score. The average standard score is 10. By comparing the various subtest scores, the patterns in the components of mental functioning may be revealed. Students with learning problems exhibit somewhat more "scatter," or differences among subscales, than normal learners. In addition, students with reading problems tend to have higher scores in performance IQ than verbal IQ (Lerner, 2000).

The *Woodcock-Johnson Psycho-Educational Battery–Revised* is an individual test that can be used for a wide range of ages. There are two parts: Tests of Cognitive Ability and Tests of Achievement (mentioned earlier in this chapter). The test can be administered by teachers and is designed so that a discrepancy analysis can be developed by comparing aptitude and achievement scores. It uses subtest clusters for interpretation, and a computer program is available to assist the scorer.

Of most interest to the reading teacher is with the first part: the *Tests of Cognitive Ability*. The Standard Battery of the cognitive subtests consists of seven tests:

- *Memory for Names:* auditory-visual tasks in which the individual learns the names of nine pictures of space creatures.
- *Memory for Sentences:* ability to repeat orally presented sentences.
- *Visual Matching:* timed assessment of skill in identifying two identical numbers in a row of six numbers.
- *Incomplete Words:* words with one or more missing phonemes that the student is to identify.
- *Visual Closure:* identification of visual stimuli in distorted or incomplete pictures.
- *Picture Vocabulary:* ability to identify pictured objects or actions.
- *Analysis-Synthesis:* ability to analyze the parts of an equivalency statement and create a new one.

The supplementary battery of the cognitive tests consists of another 14 subtests.

The achievement part of the *Woodcock-Johnson Psycho-Educational Battery–Revised* consists of 14 achievement subtests, which test four academic areas (reading, mathematics, written language, and knowledge). Two subtests are the same as those in the *Woodcock Reading Mastery Test–Revised (WRMT-R)*. The scores of the *Woodcock-Johnson-Revised* can be combined into seven cognitive factor clusters, four scholastic aptitude clusters, two oral language clusters, and three total scores.

The *Slosson Intelligence Test-Revised (SIT-R)* is an individual test and can be administered by teachers. This relatively short screening test includes many items that appear in the Stanford-Binet Intelligence Scale (see the test inventory in Appendix B). The test yields a single IQ score. It covers a wide range of ages, but norms are based on a relatively small sample.

The *Kaufman Assessment Battery for Children (K-ABC)* contains two processing scales that can be combined into a Mental Processing Scale. A nonverbal scale can also be included in assessing intelligence. In addition to these scales, which measure cognitive functioning, an Achievement Scale measures school achievement. Two of the subtests in the achievement test measure reading.

The subtests of the basic cognitive battery relevant to school-aged children include:

Sequential Processing Scale
- *Hand Movements:* recreating a sequence of taps the examiner makes.
- *Number Recall:* repeating digits.
- *Word Order:* pointing to silhouettes of common objects in the order that was named.

Simultaneous Processing Scale
- *Gestalt Closure:* completing and describing an inkblot drawing.
- *Triangles:* assembling triangles to match a design.
- *Matrix Analogies:* selecting a picture or design to complete a visual analogy.
- *Spatial Memory:* remembering where pictures were arranged on a page.
- *Photo Series:* organizing and sequencing photos that illustrate an event.

The test is also available in a shortened form, called the *Kaufman Brief Intelligence Test (K-BIT)*. The Kaufman scales are considered adequate in reliability and validity.

Interpreting Intelligence Test Scores

Modern intelligence scores are reported as deviation scores, as a student's score is compared with the scores of a norm group. The IQ score is based on the concept of a normal curve, as shown in Figure 16.4. An IQ of 100 is designated as the mean for each age group. As shown in Figure 16.4, approximately 34 percent of the population will fall within one standard deviation below the mean, and 34 percent of the population will fall within one standard deviation above the mean.

To illustrate (Figure 16.4) one standard deviation on the *Wechsler Intelligence Scale for Children, Third Edition (WISC-III)* is 15 points. Therefore, 34 percent of the population will score between 85 and 100, and 34 percent of the population will score between 100 and 115.

Intelligence ranges for the *WISC-III* can be interpreted as follows:

130 and above	Very superior
120–129	Superior
110–119	High average (bright)
90–109	Average
80–89	Low average (dull)
70–79	Borderline
69 and below	Mentally deficient

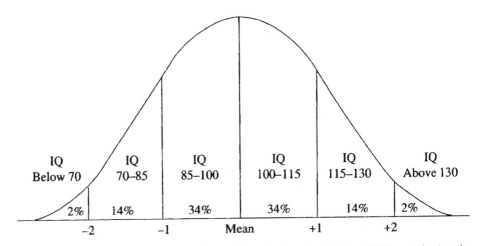

•Scores are clustered around the mean, which is the tallest point. A standard deviation (SD) is a number (e.g., in the WISC-R it is 15). A child scoring one standard deviation above the mean, if the mean is 100 and the standard deviation is 15, would score 115. A child scoring two standard deviations above the mean would score 130. The percentages show what percent of the population is included in any standard deviation. For example, 34 percent of the people score between zero and one standard deviation below (or above) the mean. Two percent of the population scores between two and three standard deviations below (or above) the mean.

FIGURE 16.4   Distribution of WISC-III IQ Scores on a Normal Curve

Teachers will find these interpretations useful for reporting the results of this IQ test to parents. If tests other than the *WISC-III* are used, the test manual should be consulted for the IQ range for those tests. Although almost all IQs have means of 100, some variations in the standard deviations are reported.

Summary

Formal tests are published tests meant to be administered according to prescribed procedures. Some are norm-referenced and compare students to a norm sample. Others are criterion-referenced and determine whether a student has achieved mastery. Formal tests that compare students to others of the same grade and age are familiar to professionals, permit objective decision making, and are required by some laws.

Scores on norm-referenced tests derive standard scores from raw scores generally by using means and standard deviations. Scores include reading grade scores, percentiles, normal curve equivalents (NCEs), and stanines. Normed tests should have an adequate standardization sample, good validity (testing what is supposed to be tested), and reliability (stability of scores).

Tests of general reading assessment include survey tests (both group and individual), normed oral reading tests, and literacy tests. Diagnostic reading tests include batteries of specific skills and tests of individual areas.

Intelligence tests can be used to estimate a student's potential for school achievement, although the results can change with appropriate conditions. Patterns of scores and behavior during testing also give insight into learning. Widely used intelligence tests include the *Wechsler Intelligence Scale for Children, Third Edition, Woodcock-Johnson Psycho-Educational Battery–Revised, Kaufman Assessment Battery for Children* (and short form), and the *Slosson Intelligence Test.* Scores on an IQ test are distributed on a normal curve distribution.

APPENDIX A

Instructional Materials for Students with Reading Problems

Abbreviations Used in This Appendix

RL denotes Reading Level
IL denotes Interest Level
ABE denotes Adult Basic Education
ESL denotes English as Second Language

Both interest and reading levels are given in grades throughout this table. Interest Levels are only listed when they differ from Reading Levels.

High-Interest Books

A New True Book (Children's Press)   RL 1
    Informational books on lots of topics.
Achievers (Lerner Publications)   RL 4+, IL reluctant reader, adult
    Composed of 10 biographies.
Adventures in Reading (Dominie Press)   RL K–1
    Seven titles recommended for reluctant readers, early literacy intervention programs, and Chapter I programs.
All Aboard Reading Books. (Grosset & Dunlap)   RL K–3
    About 80 fiction and nonfiction titles designed to be appealing to children.

Amazing Adventures (Globe Fearon)   RL 3, IL 6–adult
> Eight short novels.

Beginner Books® (Random House)   RL 1–2
> Begun by Dr. Seuss, hardcover books have large print, easy vocabulary, and large illustrations.

BesTellers® (Globe Fearon)   RL 2–4, IL 6–12, ABE
> Four sets of easy-to-read novels on topics of mystery, science fiction, suspense, and adventure.

Bright & Early Books® (Random House)   RL preschool–1
> Features imaginative stories and colorful pictures in hardcover format. Contributors include Dr. Seuss.

Carousel Readers (Dominie Press)   RL K–1
> Recommended for reluctant readers, early literacy intervention programs, and Chapter I programs. Big books and eight sets of books, 11 titles in each set.

Creative Minds Biographies (Lerner Publications)   RL 3+, IL reluctant readers and adults
> Forty-five stories of courageous individuals with text suitable for "older reluctant readers."

Dolch First Reading Books (SRA)   RL 1–3
Dolch Basic Vocabulary   RL 2
Dolch Classic Folklore of the World Books   RL 3
Dolch Classic Pleasure Books   RL 3–6
> Stories with vocabulary based on the Dolch Basic Sight Words, the Dolch list of Storyteller's Vocabulary Words, and the Dolch list of First One Thousand Words.

Double Fastbacks® Books, Fastbacks® Books (Globe Fearon)   RL 4–5, IL 6–12, ABE
> Six series (mystery, romance, horror, spy, strange occurrences, sports) in Double Fastbacks Books. Seven sets (spy, crime and detectives, science fiction, mystery, romance, horror, sports) in Fastbooks Books.

Drama for Reading & Performance (Perfection Learning Corporation)   RL 6–8+, IL 6–12
> Two collections of one- and two-act plays by award-winning contemporary playwrights. Includes teaching and performance suggestions.

Freedom Fighters (Globe Fearon)   RL 3–4, IL 6–12, ABE, ESL
> Five short readable biographies.

Great Series (Steck-Vaughn)   RL 2–4, IL 6–Adult
> Nine series with short (4–6 pages) selections on past and present events. Exercises follow each selection.

Hello USA (Lerner Publications)   RL 3+, IL reluctant reader, adult
> Fifty-two books addressing the richness and diversity of our country.

Holidays and Heroes (Phoenix Learning Resources)   RL 2–3, IL 1–5
> Selections based on a variety of holidays and well-known heroes.

Hopes and Dreams (Globe Fearon)   RL 3, IL 6–12, adult, ESL, ABE Selections on the immigrant experience.

I Can Read Books® (HarperCollins)   RL preschool–4
Large type, simple vocabulary, and chapter-like divisions. Has three levels: Level 1 (preschool–1), Level 2 (1–3), Level 3 (2–4).

Jamestown Classics (Jamestown)   RL 4–5, IL 6–12
Short stories adapted from Poe, Stevenson, London, Harte, O. Henry, Sir Arthur Conan Doyle. Questions and activities accompany each story.

Laugh Aloud Puffins (Penguin Puffin)   RL 1–5
Designed to entice reluctant readers.

Multicultural Biographies Collection (Globe Fearon)   RL 6, IL 6–12, ABE, ESL
Four sets: Asian American, Native American, African American, and American biographies.

Nature Watch (Lerner Publications)   RL 2+, IL reluctant reader, adult
Thirty-five books about animals.

Nature Science Books (Lerner Publications)   RL 4+, IL reluctant reader, adult
Thirty-five books on a variety of nature topics: ants, apple trees, bats, beetles, etc.

One Act (Perfection Learning Corporation)   RL 3–8
Designed for oral reading in a class period for entire class or small group. From 7–19 reading parts in each play. Background knowledge and teacher's guide included.

On My Own Books (Lerner Publications)   RLK+, IL reluctant reader and adult
Twelve nonfiction books.

Our Century Magazines (Globe Fearon)   RL 3–4, IL 6–12, ABE, ESL
Nine 64-page magazines each focusing on events of a single decade.

Pacemaker Classics and Plays (Globe Fearon)   RL 3–4, IL 5–12, ABE, ESL
Cassette tapes and teacher's study guides accompany 32 classics.

Phoenix Everyreader (Phoenix Learning Resources)   RL 4, IL 4–adult, ESL
Easy paperback adaptations of famous adventures.

Puffin Speedsters (Penguin Puffin)   RL 3–9
Suitable for "reluctant readers and children who have just learned to enjoy independent reading."

Read More Books (Dominie Press)   RL K–1
A collection of 16 nonfiction books based on real-life situations for the emergent reader.

Reading About Science (Phoenix Learning Resources)   RL 2–6, IL 2–adult, ESL
High-interest science articles.

Reading Corners (Dominie Press)   RL K–1
Recommended for reluctant readers. Four sets cover Grades K–4.

Reading for Today (Steck-Vaughn)   RL K–6, IL adult
Six books in magazine format stress contemporary adult themes. Controlled vocabulary.

Reading Milestones®, Second Edition (Pro-Ed)   RL Preprimer–5
> Includes 60 stories for each of six reading levels and two reading bridge levels that provide a bridge to general reading materials at the fourth- and fifth-grade levels. Also five fairy tales for Grades 1.9–2.3, eight simple English classics for Grades 2.5–4, four most-loved classics for Grades 2.5–3.5 and the *Dormac Easy English Dictionary*.

Retold Classics Anthologies™ (Perfection Learning Corporation)   RL 6, IL 6–8+
> Eight anthologies of adapted fiction and nonfiction for reluctant readers. Each anthology contains eight selections, author information, footnotes, and illustrations. Also six **Retold Classic Novels™** with activities.

Science and Nature (Troll Communications)   RL 1–6
> Nonfiction about nature. Some big books available for some of the primary books. Word-for-word cassettes available for some titles.

Short Classics (Steck-Vaughn)   RL 4–6, IL 4–adult
> Twenty-eight shortened versions of classical literature with controlled vocabulary. Teacher guides available.

Silver Screen (Lerner Publication Co.)   RL 5+, IL Reluctant reader, adult
> Seven books for readers interested in movies.

Smithsonian Wild Heritage Collection (Soundprints)   RL K–3
> Nature/environmental themes with audiocassettes available.

Sports Achievers (Lerner Publications)   RL 4+, IL Reluctant reader, adult
> Fifty-five highly readable biographies of popular sports figures.

Spotlight on Literature (SRA)   RL 3–6
> Eight anthologies feature more than 60 authors. A teacher's guide is available.

Spotlight on Readers Theatre (Phoenix Learning Resources)   RL 2–4, IL 1–5
> Content-based plays with a social studies emphasis.

Sports, Sports, Sports (Troll Communications)   RL 4–9
> Sixteen nonfiction titles about sports.

Talk About Books (Dominie Press)   RL K–1
> Eight titles recommended for reluctant readers, early literacy intervention programs, and Title I programs.

Troll First-Start Easy Readers (Troll Communications)   RL K–3
> Ten stories featuring simple sentences and carefully controlled vocabulary. A word list in each book identifies the basic words used.

Tune in for Reading (Continental Press)   RL 4–8, ABE, Pre-GED, Literacy, ESL
> Recreational and informational reading from contemporary magazines with audiocassette support.

Zoobooks. (Wildlife Education)   RL 4–8
> Expository selections with many titles available in Spanish as well as English.

Predictable Books

City Kids (Rigby)   RL 2–3, IL 3–6
> Set of 54 short comic paperbacks about irreverent kids who get into trouble. Good for older students at beginning levels.

Infomazing (Rigby)   RL 1–2
Beginning books of expository information on several levels.

Literacy 2000 (Rigby)   RL K–5 & beyond
Hundreds of titles include **Traditional Tales** and **Infomazing Science** as well as many other series by this company. Eight levels.

Pebble Books (Children's Press/Franklin Watts)   RL emergent, IL K–2
Classroom set of 104 books. Arranged in themed sets of four. Topics include animals, plants, family, seasons, health, and transportation.

Rookie Readers (Children's Press/Franklin Watts)   RL beginning readers
Classroom set of 55 titles approved for use in Reading Recovery.

SUNSHINE™ Books (Wright Group)   RL K–3, IL K–2
Short predictable books. Contains eleven levels. Plays are also included.

The Story Box (Wright Group)   RL K–3, IL K–4
Short enchanting predictable books. Big books and audiocassettes available.

Traditional Tales (Rigby)   RL 1–8
A variety of excellent and colorful books in eight stages. Audiocassettes for all titles. Some in Spanish.

Materials for Focused Instruction

Multiarea Development

Biographies from American History (Globe Fearon)   RL 2, IL 6–12
Thirty short biographies with pre- and post-reading exercises included.

Conquests in Reading, 2nd edition (Phoenix Learning Resources)   RL 1–8, IL 4–adult, ESL
Text and workbooks that focus on basic word attack and comprehension.

The Final Chapter (SRA)   RL 3–6
Stories about real people from diverse cultures. Each story has a surprise ending and is accompanied by vocabulary, comprehension, and writing activities.

Focus on Reading (SRA)   RL 1–3, 2–6
High-interest reading experiences. Plentiful vocabulary exercises and a focus on literal and inferential comprehension.

The Globe Reader's Collection (Globe Fearon)   RL 3–8, IL 6–12, ABE, ESL
Fifteen anthologies containing short high-interest selections followed by reading improvement exercises.

Hello Math Reader™ (Scholastic-Cartwheel)   RL preschool–3
Combines simple math concepts in easy-to-read story. Includes six pages of math activities for families.

Insights: Reading as Thinking (Charlesbridge Publishing)   RL K–8
Develops strategies for comprehension, such as comparing and contrasting, analyzing, summarizing, and interpreting.

Interactive Reading Program (SRA)   RL 1.5–5.0
Contemporary stories each accompanied by audiocassette tapes. Workbook exercises develop problem solving, predicting, and critical thinking skills.

Merrill Reading Skilltext® Series (SRA)   RL 1–6
> Appealing story content and easy-to-understand directions. Diagnostic tests determine problem areas and progress tests monitor growth.

Passages to Reading Program (Perfection Learning Corporation)   RL 3–6, IL 6–12
> Thirty-seven novels with reading levels at least two grade levels below interest levels. Matching workbook for each novel.

Reading Booster (Phoenix Learning Resources)   RL 1–4.5, IL 1–6, ESL
> Program designed to bring poor readers up to and beyond grade level quickly and effectively.

SRA Reading Laboratory Series (SRA)   RL 2–9
> Selections grouped according to colors. Reading selections with accompanying skill exercises boxed according to levels.

Sprint Plus (Scholastic)   RL 3–6
> Six levels. Each includes three skills books, a short story, a play book, and a teaching guide.

Turning Point (Phoenix Learning Resources)   RL 1.8–4, IL 7–adult, ESL
> High-interest program for older students with marginal reading skills.

Word Recognition

Basic Reading Series (SRA)   RL K–2
> Systematic organization of vocabulary so students are not asked to read any phonetic element not specifically taught and practiced.

Bob Books® (Scholastic)   RL preschool–1
> Each book focuses on a few vowel or consonant sounds and limits the story to a few words. Humorous line drawings to color. Includes finger puppets.

BRIGANCE® Prescriptive Word Analysis: Strategies and Practices (Curriculum Associates)   RL 1–6, IL 1–adult
> Two volumes of activities, strategies and reference materials for teaching phonetic and structural word analysis.

Hello Reader® (Scholastic-Cartwheel)   RL preschool–4
> Uses basic words. Has punch-out flash cards and skill-building activities. Five levels: **My First Hello Reader™** and Levels 1–4.

Merrill Phonics Skilltext® Series (SRA)   RL K–6
> Builds skills in four areas: phonics, structural analysis, vocabulary, and dictionary skills.

MCP "Plaid" Phonics Program (Modern Curriculum Press)   RL 1–6
> Series of workbooks presenting phonics skills.

Merrill Linguistics (SRA)   RL K–3
> Organized around the basic spelling patterns of the English language. Includes readers, skills books, and tests.

Phonics: A Sound Approach (Curriculum Associates)   RL 1–4, IL 4–adult, ESL
> Five levels of workbooks on word-attack skills. Features listening, speaking, writing activities.

Phonics for Reading (Curriculum Associates, Inc.)   RL 1–4, IL 1–adult
   A five-level series to develop word attack skills.
Phonics Practice Readers (Modern Curriculum Press)   RL 1–3, IL 1–4
   Each eight-page book tells a short story, using words focusing on one phonics element.
Puffin Easy-To-Read (Penguin Puffin)   RL preschool–4
   Three levels of easy-to-read books: Level 1 (Just Getting Started), Level 2 (Beginning to Read) and Level 3 (Reading Alone).
Step into Reading™ (Random House)   RL preschool–4
   Paperbacks covering a variety of fiction and nonfiction.
SRA Phonics (SRA)   RL K–1
   Readers accompanied by skills activities. Big books available for some selections.

Vocabulary Development

Lessons in Vocabulary Development (Curriculum Associates)   RL 4–6
   Words in student skillbook are introduced thematically. Pre- and post-tests and writing activities are included.
Lessons for Vocabulary Power (Curriculum Associates)   RL 6–10, adult
   Twenty thematic lessons promoting the transfer of vocabulary to speaking and writing.
Stanford Vocabulary (Phoenix Learning Resources)   RL 4–8, IL 7–adult, ESL
   A self instructional program for building vocabulary for secondary students.
Survival Vocabularies (Globe Fearon)   RL 1–3, IL 6–12, ABE, ESL
   Fifteen texts each teaching 80 words or phrases associated with common settings such as banking, clothing, medical, restaurant, etc.
Vocabulary Booster (Phoenix Learning Resources)   RL 4–5, IL 4–6
   A vocabulary development program in 60 story lessons.
Vocabulary Drills (Jamestown)   RL 2–6
   Twenty selections present words that students encounter regularly. A variety of activities follow each selection: composing definitions, using context, completing analogies, and connecting words to synonyms and antonyms.
Vocabulary for the Twenty-First Century (Curriculum Associates)   RL 3–8, IL 2–adult
   Four books, each containing 12 regular and 3 review lessons. Writing activities are part of the program.
Vocabulary: Meaning and Message (Globe Fearon)   RL 2–4, IL 5–12
   Four texts each present essential vocabulary in history, math, science, life skills, survival skills, jobs, sports, entertainment, and the world today.
World of Vocabulary (Globe Fearon)   RL 3–10, IL 6–12, ABE, ESL
   Eight-volume series of contemporary short nonfiction articles. Short skills exercises follow the articles.

Comprehension

Building Basic Reading Skills (Continental Press)   RL 1–8
Three workbooks on main ideas, inferencing, and sequencing using high-interest, real-world reading selections.

Caught Reading Program (Globe Fearon)   RL 1–4, IL 6–12, ABE
Seven novels incorporating a planned cycle of instruction: prereading, review, reading, and comprehension.

CLUES for Better Reading (Curriculum Associates)   RL K–5
Focuses on finding main idea and details, sequencing, and following directions. Can be paired with **CLUES for Better Writing.**

Comprehension Skills Series, 2nd Edition (Jamestown)   RL 3–6, 4–8, 8–12
Provides concentrated help in 10 reading comprehension categories, including recognizing main idea, making judgments, and understanding characters.

Critical Reading Skills Series (Jamestown)   RL 6–8, IL 6–12
High-interest nonfiction to motivate "tentative readers." Each selection is followed by four exercises: finding the main idea, recalling facts, making inferences, and using words precisely.

Essential Skills Series (Jamestown)   RL 3–12, IL 6–12
Develops comprehension in six key areas: subject matter, supporting details, conclusions, clarifying devices, vocabulary in context, and main idea.

Matchbook Five-Minute Thrillers (Globe Fearon)   RL 3, IL 6–12, ABE, ESL
Twenty short tales with comprehension and vocabulary exercises and audiotapes.

Multiple Skills Series (SRA)   RL K–9
Develops four key comprehension skills: getting the main idea, making inferences and drawing conclusions, interpreting context clues, and grasping significant facts.

New Practice Readers (Phoenix Learning Resources)   RL 2–6.8, IL 2–Adult, ESL
Developmental and remedial comprehension program containing graded articles and books to teach comprehension.

Reading Comprehension Series (Steck-Vaughn)   RL 1–6, IL 1–9
Eight workbooks of stories containing controlled vocabulary followed by varied exercises. Review lessons.

Reading for Comprehension–2000 (Continental Press)   RL 1–8
Readability below target level to ensure success for reluctant readers. Nonfiction selections with teacher's guide and audiocassette tapes available.

Reading for Concepts, 3rd Edition (Phoenix Learning Resources)   RL 1.6–6.7, IL 2–adult, ESL
Developmental and remedial program with articles unified by themes to teach comprehension and critical thinking.

Reading for Today (Steck-Vaughn)   RL K–6, IL adult
Five books in magazine format stress contemporary adult themes.

Reading for Understanding (Scholastic)   RL 3–6
   Workbook and teaching guide for nonfiction comprehension.
Reading Reinforcement Skilltext® Series (SRA)   RL 1–5
   Theme-based stories followed by exercise that develop comprehension and
   vocabulary skills. Controlled vocabulary.
Reading Strategies Units (Charlesbridge)   RL 3–adult
   Covers nine comprehension strategy areas, such as main idea and details,
   making inferences, and context clues.
Reading-Thinking Skills (Continental Press)   RL 1–6, IL 3–8
   Six leveled workbooks for comprehension and critical thinking.
Single Skills Series (Jamestown)   RL 3–12, IL 6–12
   Ten levels for each skill: subject matter, main idea, supporting details, con-
   clusions, clarifying devices, and vocabulary in context. Placement test places
   the student in the appropriate skill. Factual and high-interest selections.
Six-Way Paragraphs (Jamestown)   RL 4–8, IL 8–12
   High-interest passages and questions focus on six essential comprehension
   skills: main idea, subject matter, supporting details, conclusions, clarifying
   devices, and vocabulary in context. Each book begins with a lesson followed
   by 100 passages, each with its own set of comprehension questions.
Tales for Thinking (Curriculum Associates)   RL 1–4, IL 2–8, ESL
   Multicultural fairy tales. The program employs the Directed Reading-
   Thinking Activity.

Content Areas

Cloze in the Content Areas: Science and Social Studies (Continental Press)   RL
   2–6
   High-interest nonfiction articles correlated to the science and social studies
   curricula. Teacher guides available.
Connections (Steck-Vaughn)   RL 6–8, IL 9–12
   Practice in content area reading skills: writing, literature, mathematics,
   science, and social studies.

Rate Development

Reading Drills, 2nd Edition (Jamestown)   RL 4–6, 6–8, 7–10
   Each volume contains 30 timed passages taken from fiction and nonfiction
   selections. Comprehension activities after each selection include questions,
   cloze test, and vocabulary questions.
Timed Readings and Timed Readings in Literature (Jamestown)   RL 4–13+, IL
   7+
   Fifty 400-word passages in each of ten books for lasting rate improvement. Ten questions following each passage maintain a focus on comprehension.

Life Skills

LifeTimes (Globe Fearon)   RL 3, IL 9–12, ABE
> Two seven-book sets about realistic situations such as returning to school, dealing with alcoholism and choosing between family and career.

LifeSchool 2000 (Globe Fearon)   RL 1–4, IL 9–12, ABE, ESL
> Six binders containing 60 learning modules in a variety of areas: consumer economics, occupational knowledge, health, community resources, government and law, interpersonal relations.

Today's Reading . . . for Tomorrow (Continental Press)   RL 3–4, ABE, ESL
> Four units relating to different aspects of topics such as consumer affairs, health, basic community services, safety, adult education, and citizenship.

WorkTales (Globe Fearon)   RL 2–3, IL 9–12, ABE, ESL
> Ten novels dramatize workplace issues, such as job stress, retraining, safety, substance abuse, and personal conflicts.

APPENDIX B

Frequently Used Tests

The following table presents tests frequently used in reading diagnoses. Many of these tests are described in the text of this book. This table includes tests of physical factors, intelligence and cognitive processing, language development, overall academic achievement, reading tests, survey and diagnostic, and informal reading inventories. For each test, we have included the name of the test, its publisher, the ages or grades for which it may be used, levels included, a description of its contents, the scores yielded by the test, the estimated time needed for administration, and whether special training is needed to administer the test.

Tests of Physical Factors

Audiometer

Beltone Electronic Corporation
Maico Hearing Instruments
Used as a screening test to determine students' hearing threshold for series of tones at various frequencies and decibels. Results are graphed on an audiogram.
Individual administration: 10–20 min.

Keystone Vision Screening for Schools

Keystone View Company
Comprised of two parts. Four-part rapid screening measure includes near-point and far-point items. Comprehensive measure includes 14 subtests, which test eye posture, binocular imbalance, binocular depth perception, color discrimination, usable binocular vision, and near-point and far-point acuity. Eyes tested separa-

tely and in coordination. Yields ratings of unsatisfactory, retest, and satisfactory. Provides analytical summary for reporting results. *Individual administration:* 10–15 min.

Orthorater

Bausch and Lomb
Contains 12 subtests that screen for binocular action of the eyes, near-point and far-point vision, depth perception, and color discrimination. Norms are available for job-related activity. An adapted version may be used with children. *Individual administration:* 15–20 min.

Snellen Chart

American Optical Company
Consists of a wall chart containing rows of letters gradually decreasing in size in each descending row. The letters are read at a distance of 20 feet, testing only far-point vision. *Individual administration:* 2–3 min.

Tests of Intelligence and Cognitive Processing

Detroit Test of Learning Aptitude–4th Edition (DTLA–4)

Ages 6–17
Pro-Ed
Provides detailed profiles of students' abilities and weaknesses. Used to diagnose learning disabilities. Includes 10 subtests: word opposites, design sequences to measure visual discrimination and memory, sentence imitation, reversed letters, story construction, design reproduction from memory, basic information, symbolic relations, word sequences, and story sequences. Provides an overall composite score and six domain composites: verbal, nonverbal, attention-enhanced, attention-reduced, motor-enhanced, and motor-reduced. Provides standard scores, percentiles, and age equivalents for subtests and composites. *Individual administration:* 40–120 min.

Kaufman Intelligence Tests

American Guidance Service

Kaufman Assessment Battery for Children (K–ABC)
Ages 2.5–12.5
Includes 16 subtests. Sequential processing scale includes hand movements, number recall, and word order; child must arrange stimuli in sequential or serial order. Simultaneous processing scale includes magic windows, face recognition,

Gestalt closure, triangles, matrix analogies, spatial memory, and photo series; requires integration and synthesis of information. Achievement scale includes expressive vocabulary, faces and places, arithmetic, riddles, reading/decoding, and reading/understanding; measures child's ability to apply mental processing skills to various learning situations. Provides standard scores and percentile ranks; grade equivalents provided for arithmetic and reading subtests. *Individual administration:* 35–85 min. Special training needed for administration.

Kaufman Brief Intelligence Test (K–BIT)
Ages 4–90
Includes verbal and nonverbal subtests. Verbal subtests include expressive vocabulary and definitions. Nonverbal subtest requires students to solve problems using pictures and abstract designs. Provides verbal, performance, and composite IQ scores. *Individual administration:* 15–30 min. Requires graduate training in measurement to administer.

Kaufman Adolescent & Adult Intelligence Test (KAIT)
Ages 11–85+
Includes core and expanded batteries. Core battery consists of two scales: crystallized and fluid. Crystallized scale includes auditory comprehension, multiple word meanings, and definitions when given a clue. Fluid scale includes rebus learning, using codes, and using logic to solve problems. The expanded battery includes design memory, identifying famous people, using previously learned rebuses to "read," and auditory recall. Provides fluid, crystallized, and composite IQ scores. *Individual administration:* core battery, 60 min.; extended battery, 90 min. Special training needed for administration.

Slosson Intelligence Test–Revised (SIT–R)

Ages 4–65
Slosson Educational Publications, Inc.
Designed to measure verbal intelligence in six areas: vocabulary, general information, similarities and differences of objects or concepts, comprehension of common sayings, quantitative skills, and auditory memory for repeating sequences forward and backward. Yields a single quantitative index of intelligence. Norming samples and descriptions of norming procedures considered inadequate. Useful only as a screening device. *Individual administration:* 10–20 min.

Stanford-Binet Intelligence Scale, Fourth Edition

Ages 2–Adult
Riverside Publishing
Consists of 15 subtests grouped in four cognitive areas: verbal reasoning, quantitative reasoning, abstract/visual reasoning, and short-term memory. Verbal reasoning includes vocabulary, comprehension absurdities, and verbal relations. Quantitative reasoning includes quantitative number series and equation building.

Abstract/visual reasoning includes pattern analysis, copying, matrices, and paper folding and cutting. Short-term memory includes bead memory, memory for sentences, memory for digits, and memory for objects. Yields standard age scores for each area, composite IQ score, percentile rank, and scaled and raw scores. *Individual administration:* time varies. Special training needed for administration.

Wechsler Intelligence Scales

The Psychological Corporation

Wechsler Intelligence Scale for Children®, Third Edition (WISC–III®)
Ages 6–16.11

A widely used individual measure of children's intellectual ability. Includes 10 core subtests and 3 supplemental subtests. Verbal subtests include information, similarities, arithmetic, vocabulary, comprehension, and digit span (supplementary). Performance subtests include picture completion, coding, picture arrangement, block design, object assembly, and symbol search and mazes (both supplementary). Yields performance, verbal, and full-scale IQ scores. *Individual administration:* 50–70 min. for core subtests; 10–15 min. for supplemental subtests. Special training needed for administration.

Wechsler Preschool and Primary Scale of Intelligence®–Revised (WPPSI–R®)
Ages 3–7.3

Includes 12 subtests. Verbal subtests include information, comprehension, similarities, arithmetic, vocabulary, and sentences (supplementary). Performance subtests include picture completion, block design, object assembly, coding, mazes, object assembly, and geometric design (visual recognition and discrimination for younger children and drawing of figures for older children). Yields verbal, performance, and full-scale IQ scores. *Individual administration:* 75 min. Special training needed for administration.

Wechsler Adult Intelligence Scale®–Third Edition (WAIS–III®)
Ages 16–89

Includes 11 subtests. Verbal subtests include information, comprehension, similarities, arithmetic, vocabulary, digit span, and letter-number sequencing (supplementary). Performance subtests include picture arrangement, block design, digit symbol, picture completion, matrix reasoning, symbol search (supplementary), and object assembly (optional). Yields IQ scores. *Individual administration:* 60–90 min. Special training needed for administration.

Woodcock-Johnson® Psycho-Educational Battery–Revised

Ages 2–90+
Riverside Publishing

Includes *Tests of Cognitive Ability* and *Tests of Achievement.*

Woodcock-Johnson® Tests of Cognitive Ability–Revised

Cognitive battery comprised of a standard battery and a supplemental battery. Standard battery consists of seven subtests: memory for names, memory for sentences, visual matching, incomplete words, visual closure, picture vocabulary, and analysis-synthesis. The early development battery consists of memory for names, memory for sentences, incomplete words, visual closure, and picture vocabulary. The supplementary battery consists of visual-auditory learning, memory for words, cross out, sound blending, picture recognition, oral vocabulary, concept formation, delayed recall to test memory for names, delayed recall to test visual-auditory learning, reversed numbers, sound patterns, spatial relations, listening comprehension, and verbal analogies. *Individual administration:* early development battery, 30 min. or less.

Woodcock-Johnson® Tests of Achievement–Revised

Standard battery includes letter-word identification, passage comprehension, calculation, applied problems, dictation, writing samples, science, social studies, and humanities. Supplemental battery includes five subtests: word attack, reading vocabulary, quantitative concepts, proofing, and writing fluency. Provides individual test scores and cluster scores, percentile ranks, standard scores, and age and grade equivalents for K–16.9. *Individual administration:* 30–40 min.

Tests of Language Development

Comprehensive Receptive and Expressive Vocabulary Test (CREVT)

Ages 4–17
Pro-Ed

Consists of two subtests. In the expressive vocabulary subtest, students provide definitions of words pronounced by examiners. In the receptive vocabulary subtest, students point to pictures of words pronounced by examiners. Pictures are color photographs rather than line drawings. Two equivalent forms. Provides standard scores, percentiles, and age equivalents. *Individual administration:* 20–30 min.

Goldman-Fristoe Test of Articulation

Ages 2–16+
American Guidance Service

Measures students' ability to articulate consonant sounds in initial, medial, and final positions. Includes three subtests: sounds-in-words, which requires students to identify pictures; sounds-in-sentences, which measures sound production as students engage in connected speech; stimulability, in which examiners pronounce words previously mispronounced by students to determine if they can correctly produce modeled sounds. Sounds-in-words and stimulability subtests yield percentile ranks by age. *Individual administration:* 30–60 min.

Peabody Picture Vocabulary Test–Third Edition (PPVT–III)

Ages 2.6–90+
American Guidance Service
Measures receptive vocabulary. Each item consists of four pictures; administrator pronounces a stimulus word, and student points to corresponding picture. Consists of two equivalent forms. Yields standard scores, percentile ranks, stanines, and age equivalents. *Individual administration:* 10–15 min.

Test de Vocabulario en Imágenes Peabody (TVIP)

Ages 2.6–17.11
American Guidance Service
Based on the *PPVT-III* for Spanish-speaking and bilingual students. Manual available in English and Spanish. Provides standard scores, percentile ranks, and age equivalents. *Individual administration:* 10–15 min.

Test of Adolescent and Adult Language–Third Edition (TOAL–3)

Ages 12–24
Pro-Ed
Comprehensive evaluation for adolescents and adults. Consists of ten subtests to measure listening, speaking, reading, writing, spoken language, written language, vocabulary, grammar, receptive language, and expressive language. Yields percentiles and composite and standard scores. *Individual or group administration:* 60–180 min.

Tests of Language Development, Primary and Intermediate (TOLD–3)

Pro-Ed
Assesses understanding and use of spoken words, grammar, pronunciation, and ability to distinguish between similar-sounding words. *Individual administration.*

TOLD–P:3, Primary
Ages 4–8.11
Has nine subtests. In the picture vocabulary subtest, students point to pictures of words pronounced by examiners. In oral vocabulary, students provide definitions of stimulus words. Grammatic understanding measures ability to understand syntactic structures. Sentence imitation requires repetition of complex sentences. In grammatic completion, students provide the last words in sentences. In word discrimination, students identify pairs of similar words as the same or different. Word articulation measures ability to pronounce individual words. Relational vocabulary and phonemic analysis subtests are also included. Provides standard

scores, percentile ranks, and age equivalents for subtests as well as listening, speaking, semantics, syntax, and phonology. *Individual administration:* 60 min.

TOLD–I:3, Intermediate
Ages 8.0–12.11
Subtests cover generals, malapropisms, picture vocabulary sentence combining, word ordering, and grammatic comprehension. Yields standard scores and percentile ranks. *Individual administration:* 30–60 min.

Test of Phonological Awareness (TOPA)

Levels: Kindergarten–2
Joseph K. Torgesen and Brian R. Bryant
Pro-Ed
Identifies children who may profit from instructional activities to enhance their phonemic awareness in preparation for reading instruction. Two versions: one suitable for kindergarten and one for first- and second-grade children. Can be *administered individually or to groups* (group administration takes about 20 min.). Complete kit contains examiner's manual, 25 student booklets for each version, and 25 records each for each version.

Tests of Word Finding

Pro-Ed

Test of Word Finding, Second Edition (TWF-2)
Ages 6.6–12.11
Includes five sections: picture naming of nouns, picture naming of verbs, sentence completion naming, description naming, and category naming. Measures both speed and accuracy. Yields standard scores, percentile ranks, and grade standards for item-response time. Includes grade norms for Grades 1–6. Provides suggestions for analyzing gestures, extra verbalizations, and substitution types. *Individual administration:* 20–30 min.

Test of Adolescent/Adult Word Finding (TAWF)
Ages 12–80
Similar test to TWF-2, with similar subtests. TAWF includes a 40-item brief test. Yields standard scores, percentile ranks, and grade norms included for Grades 7–12. *Individual administration:* 20–30 min.

Test of Word Knowledge (TOWK)

The Psychological Corporation
Assesses knowledge of figurative language, multiple meanings, conjunctions and transition words, and receptive and expressive vocabularies. Core battery consists of two receptive language and two expressive language subtests. Includes sup-

plementary subtests. Provides raw scores, standard scores, receptive and expressive composite scores, age equivalents, percentile ranks, stanines, and means.

Level 1
Ages 5–8
Subtests include expressive vocabulary, word definitions, receptive vocabulary, and word opposites. Supplementary subtest, Synonyms, included for 6- to 8-year-olds. *Individual administration:* 25 min. for core battery; 6 min. for supplemental test.

Level 2
Ages 8–17
Subtests include word definitions, multiple contexts, synonyms, and figurative use. Supplementary subtests include word opposites, receptive vocabulary, expressive vocabulary, conjunctions, and transition words. *Individual administration:* 40 min. for core battery; 25 min. for supplemental test.

Tests of Overall Academic Achievement

BRIGANCE® Inventories

Curriculum Associates
Provides assessment in readiness, speech, word recognition and placement, oral reading, reading comprehension, listening, word analysis, reference skills, graph and maps, spelling, writing, and mathematics. Criterion referenced; helpful in developing IEPs. Software for writing IEPs and monitoring student progress available for both IBM and Macintosh. *Individual administration:* 15–90 min.

BRIGANCE® Diagnostic Inventory of Early Development, Revised
Ages Birth–7
Includes 11 skill areas: preambulatory motor, gross motor, fine motor, self-help, speech and language, general knowledge and comprehension, social and emotional development, readiness, basic reading, manuscript writing, and basic math.

BRIGANCE® Diagnostic Comprehensive Inventory of Basic
Skills, Revised
Grades Pre-K–9
Includes assessment in 26 skill areas, including readiness, speech, word recognition, oral reading, reading comprehension, listening, word analysis, reference skills, graphs and maps, spelling, writing, and math.

BRIGANCE® Comprehensive Inventory of Basic Skills–Revised (CIBS–R™)
Grades Pre-K–9
Has 10 criterion-referenced grade-placement tests: listening vocabulary comprehension, listening comprehension, word recognition, oral reading, reading vocab-

ulary comprehension, reading comprehension, spelling, sentence writing, math comprehension skills, and math problem solving.

BRIGANCE® Diagnostic Assessment of Basic Skills, Spanish Edition
Grades K–8
Includes 10 major areas: readiness, speech, functional word recognition, oral reading, reading comprehension, word analysis, listening, writing and alphabetizing, numbers and computation, and measurement.

BRIGANCE® Diagnostic Inventory of Essential Skills (IES)
Grades 6–Adult Ed.
Assesses strengths and weakness of secondary students in three academic areas. Reading and language arts covers word recognition, oral reading, reading comprehension, word analysis, writing, and spelling. Math includes numbers, number facts, computation, measurement, metrics, and math vocabulary. Study skills covers reference skills, schedules and graphs, and forms. Life skills assessments include food and clothing, money and finance, travel and transportation, and communication and telephone skills. Measures applied skills, such as health and attitude, responsibility and self-discipline, job interview preparation, communication, and auto safety.

California Achievement Tests, Sixth Edition

Grades K–12
CTB/McGraw-Hill
Organized into five broad areas: reading/language arts, mathematics, social studies, and science. Each level includes two equivalent forms. Also provides a locator test to determine appropriate levels for administration so examiners can test students on performance levels rather than grade placement levels. Yields percentile ranks, stanines, grade equivalents, normal curve equivalents, and scale scores. Also provides curriculum referenced scores. *Group administration:* time varies.

Iowa Tests of Basic Skills and Tests of Achievement and Proficiency

Riverside Publishing

Iowa Tests of Basic Skills® (ITBS®), Form M
Grades K–9, Levels 5–14
Basic battery measures vocabulary, reading, language arts, mathematics, and study skills. Supplementary subtests measure science, social studies, sources of information, and listening (optional). Two forms available at each level. Yields raw scores, standard scores, grade equivalents, national percentile ranks, stanines, and normal curve equivalents. Both norm- and criterion-referenced.

Iowa Tests of Achievement and Proficiency™ (TAP™)
Grades 9–12, Levels 15–18
Subtests include vocabulary, reading comprehension, written expression, math concepts and problem solving, math computational (optional), science, social studies, and information processing. *Group administration:* time varies.

Kaufman Test of Educational Achievement (KTEA)

Grades 1–12, Ages 6–22
American Guidance Service
Provides age- and grade-based standard scores, grade equivalents, percentile ranks, normal curve distributions, and stanines. Requires special training for administration.

Comprehensive Form
Consists of five subtests: reading decoding, reading comprehension, mathematics applications, mathematics computation, and spelling. Provides individual subtest scores and composite scores by grade or age, percentile ranks, stanines, normal curve equivalents, and age and grade equivalents. *Individual administration:* 30–75 min.

Brief Form
Consists of three subtests: mathematics, reading, and spelling. Provides norm-referenced subtest scores and a battery composite. *Individual administration:* 20–30 min.

Peabody Individual Achievement Test–Revised (PIAT–R)

Ages 5–22.11
American Guidance Service
Consists of six subtests: general information, reading recognition, reading comprehension, spelling, mathematics, and written expression. Written expression consists of two levels: Level I for K–1 and Level II for Grades 2–12. Provides standard scores, age and grade equivalents, percentile ranks, normal curve equivalents, and stanines. *Individual administration:* 60 min. Requires special training for administration.

Stanford Achievement Test Series, Ninth Edition

Grades K–Community College
The Psychological Corporation
Consists of three measures: the Stanford Early School Achievement Test (SESAT), the Stanford Achievement Test (SAT), and the Test of Academic Skills (TASK).

Basic battery can be used to assess reading, mathematics, and/or listening comprehension. Norm- and criterion-referenced. *Group administration:* Times vary.

TerraNova®

Grades K–12
CTB/McGraw-Hill
Assesses academic achievement in reading/language arts (reading comprehension, language expression, vocabulary, and reference skills); mathematics (estimation and mental computation); science (life science, physical science, earth and space science, and science inquiry); and social studies (interrelationships of history, geography, government, and economics). Has 12 levels with two forms (A and B) for each level. Supplemental tests available in word analysis, vocabulary, language mechanics, spelling, and mathematics computation. SUPRA® is the Spanish language edition. *Group administration:* 45–115 min. (varies by test and grade level).

Wechsler Individual Achievement Test® (WIAT®)

Ages 5–19
The Psychological Corporation

Comprehensive Form
Consists of eight subtests: basic reading, mathematics reasoning, spelling, reading comprehension, numerical operations, listening comprehension, oral expression, and written expression. Provides age- and grade-based standard composite scores, percentile ranks, stanines, normal curve equivalents, and age and grade equivalents. *Individual administration:* 30–50 min. for young children; 50–75 min. for adolescents. Special training required for administration.

Screener Form
Consists of three subtests: basic reading, mathematics reasoning, and spelling. Provides scores comparable to comprehensive form. *Individual administration:* 10–18 min., depending on age.

Wide Range Achievement Test 3 (WRAT3™)

Ages 5–75
The Psychological Corporation
Consists of three subtests: reading (recognizing and naming letters and pronouncing printed words); spelling (writing name and writing letters and words from dictation); and arithmetic (counting, reading numerals, and oral and written computation). Two equivalent forms. Provides raw scores, standard scores, percentile ranks, and grade equivalents. *Individual administration for reading; small group administration for spelling and arithmetic:* 15–30 min.

Reading Tests: Survey and Diagnostic

Diagnostic Assessments of Reading with Trial Teaching Strategies™ (DARTTS®)

Grades 1–12, Adult
Riverside Publishing

Diagnostic Assessments of Reading

Identifies strengths and weaknesses in reading through six areas: word recognition, word analysis, oral reading, silent reading comprehension, spelling, and word meaning. Identifies students' reading levels. *Individual administration:* 20–30 min.

Trial Teaching Strategies

Teaching sessions to identify most effective teaching methods and instructional materials for individual students. Provides three reading levels: potential, instructional, and independent. Criterion-referenced. *Individual administration:* 30 min.

Formal Reading Inventory

Grades 1–12
Pro-Ed

Consists of four forms: Students read Forms A and C silently and Forms B and D orally. Each form contains 13 graded passages. After reading each passage, students answer five multiple-choice questions. Miscues in the oral reading passages are categorized according to their similarity to the target words by meaning, function, or graphic/phonemic. If miscues fit more than one category, they are scored as multiple sources: self-corrections are also recorded. Scores include a silent reading comprehension quotient, percentiles for silent reading comprehension, and oral reading miscue classification. Examiners may use the manual from this test to determine an oral reading comprehension score. *Individual administration:* 15 min.

Gates-MacGinitie Reading Test™ (GMRT™), Fourth Edition

Grades K–12, Adult
Riverside Publishing

Measures vocabulary and reading comprehension at 11 levels. Yields standard scores, grade equivalents, stanines, percentile ranks, and norm curve equivalents. *Group administration:* 75–100 min. for Levels PR and BR, 75 min for Level 2, and 55 min. for all other levels.

Level PR: Prereading Evaluation
Grades K.7–1.4
Subtests on literacy concepts, phonemic awareness, letters and letter-sound correspondences, and listening comprehension.

Level BR: Beginning Reading
Grades 1.0–1.9
Subtests on initial consonants and consonant clusters, final consonants and consonant clusters, vowels, and basic story words.

Level 1
Grades 1.5–1.9
Subtests on word decoding and comprehension.

Level 2
Grades 1.1–3.9
Subtests on word decoding, word knowledge, and comprehension.

Levels 3, 4, 5, 6, 7/9, 10/12, Adult
Grades 2.1–12.9, Post High School
Subtests on vocabulary and comprehension.

Gates-McKillop-Horowitz Reading Diagnostic Tests

Grades 1–6
Teachers College Press
Tests oral reading, sight knowledge, phonics, spelling, and writing. Subtests include sets of graded short oral reading paragraphs; four reading sentences with regular words; flashwords presented with tachistoscope; untimed word list for sight recognition and analysis; word attack test using nonsense words to test syllabication, recognizing and blending word parts, reading words, identifying letter sounds, and naming capital and lowercase letters; identifying spoken vowel sounds; auditory blending and discrimination; spelling test; informal writing sample. Provides grade equivalent scores and informal ratings. Also provides analysis of oral reading errors and phonics skills. *Individual administration:* 60–90 min.

Stanford Diagnostic Reading Test, Fourth Edition (SDRT 4)

Grades 1.5–13
The Psychological Corporation
Six levels with two equivalent forms at each level. Norm- and criterion-referenced. Provides raw scores for each subtest, percentile ranks, stanines, grade equivalents, and scaled scores.

Red Level
Grades 1.5–2.5
Subtests on auditory vocabulary, auditory discrimination, phonetic analysis with consonants and vowels, word reading, and reading comprehension in sentences and paragraphs. *Group administration:* 105 min.

Orange Level
Grades 2.5–3.5
Subtests on phonetic analysis, auditory vocabulary, and comprehension using cloze and paragraphs. *Group administration:* 100 min.

Green Level
Grades 3.5–4.5
Subtests on reading vocabulary, phonetic analysis, and reading comprehension in paragraphs. *Group administration:* 114 min.

Purple Level
Grades 4.5–6.5
Subtests on reading vocabulary, comprehension of different kinds of text, and scanning. *Group administration:* 85 min.

Brown Level
Grades 6.5–8.9
Subtests on vocabulary, comprehension, and scanning. *Group administration:* 85 min.

Blue Level
Grades 9.0–13
Subtests on comprehension, vocabulary, and scanning. *Group administration:* 85 min.

Test of Early Reading Ability, Second Edition (TERA-2)

Ages: 3.0–9.11
Pro-Ed
Measures actual reading ability of young children by measuring contextual meaning, alphabet, and conventions. Has two alternate, equivalent forms so examiners can test with one form, initiate intervention program, and retest with alternate form. Easy-to-use easel-back format. Uses picture book. *Individual administration:* 15–30 min.

Test of Reading Comprehension, Third Edition (TORC-3)

Ages 7–17
Pro-Ed
Measures silent reading. Four subtests include general vocabulary, syntactic similarities, paragraph reading, and sentence sequencing. Supplementary subtests include reading vocabulary in math, science, social studies, and directions. Provides standard scores. *Group administration:* 30 min.

Test of Word Reading Efficiency (TOWRE)

Ages: 6.0–24.11
Pro-Ed
Nationally normed measure of word reading accuracy and fluency. Contains two subtests: Sight Word Efficiency (SWE) assesses number of words that can be accurately identified in 45 seconds; Phonetic Decoding Efficiency (PDE) measures number of pronounceable printed nonwords accurately decoded in 45 seconds. Each subtest has two forms of equivalent difficulty. Gives percentiles, standard scores, and age and grade equivalents. *Individual administration:* 5–10 min.

Woodcock Reading Mastery Tests–Revised (WRMT–R)

Ages 5–75+
American Guidance Service
Consists of two forms. Form G includes two readiness tests and four achievement tests: visual-auditory learning, letter identification, word identification, word attack, word comprehension, and passage comprehension. Form H includes four achievement tests: word identification, word attack, word comprehension (measures reading vocabulary in reading, science/mathematics, social studies, and humanities), and passage comprehension. Provides percentile ranks, standard scores, normal curve equivalents, and age and grade equivalents. Norms updated in 1998. *Individual administration:* 10–30 min. for each test cluster.

Gray Oral Reading Test, Third Edition (GORT–3)

Ages 7–18.11
Pro-Ed
Two equivalent forms containing 13 sequenced passages. Each passage is followed by five comprehension questions. Provides standard scores, percentile ranks, and grade equivalents. Provides a system to analyze miscues by meaning similarity, function similarity, graphic/phonemic similarity, and self-correction. Norm referenced. *Individual administration:* 15–30 min.

Gray Oral Reading Test–Diagnostic (GORT–D)

Ages 5.6–12.11
Pro-Ed

Used as a supplement to GORT–3. Two equivalent forms to use with beginning readers. Subtest on paragraph reading administered first. Other subtests, administered to students who perform poorly on paragraph reading, include decoding, word identification, word attack, morphemic analysis, contextual analysis, and word ordering. Provides grade equivalents, standard scores for subtests and composites, and percentile ranks. *Individual administration:* 45 min.

Observational Survey

An Observation Survey of Early Literacy Achievement

Marie M. Clay
Heinemann, Inc.

Systematic observational procedures for teachers to be used with *Sand* and *Stones* and *Reading Recovery: A Guidebook for Teachers in Training,* also by Marie M. Clay. *Introduction* provides techniques for observing progress in oral language and emergent literacy, detecting difficulties, and early intervention. *The Observation Survey: Part One* includes directions for taking running records, procedures for observing text reading, a sample running record sheet, and directions for analyzing reading behaviors. *The Observation Survey: Part Two* includes letter identification; the Concepts about Print test and a sample score sheet; Word Tests and score sheets; Writing Samples, a sample writing vocabulary observation sheet, and a Weekly Record Sheet; a Dictation Task; and an observation sheet. Directions for administration and scoring and guidelines for interpretation of results included for each task. Also includes suggestions for summarizing results of the Observation Survey and a Survey Summary Sheet. *Individual administration:* 30–60 min.

Informal Reading Inventories

Analytical Reading Inventory (ARI), Sixth Edition

Levels: Primer–9
Mary Lynn Woods and Alden J. Moe
Merrill

Forms A, B, and C consist of word lists of 20 words for Levels 1–6 and narrative passages for Primer–Level 9. Each level has word lists for initial placement and assesses prediction, prior knowledge, miscues, fluency and retelling, comprehension, emotional status of reader, and reading and listening levels. Most administered orally; however, alternate forms can be used to test silent reading. Form S has expository science passages for Levels 1–9, and Form SS has expository social science passages for Levels 1–9. *Individual administration:* 30–60 min.

Basic Reading Inventory, Seventh Edition

Levels: Preprimer–Grade 12, Early Literacy Assessments
Jerry L. Johns
Kendall/Hunt Publishing Company

Has five forms: A, B, and C have word lists from Preprimer–Grade 12 and passages from Preprimer–Grade 8. Form A is for silent reading; Form B for silent reading uses expository passages at higher grade levels; and Form C assesses listening or can be used as a posttest. Form LN has 10 longer (250-word) narrative passages, and Form LE has 10 longer expository passages for Grades 3–12. Determines independent, instructional, and frustrational reading levels for word recognition and comprehension. Appendix A has early literacy assessments; Appendix B details eliciting and evaluating passage retellings; Appendix C has extra passages; and Appendix E provides forms. *Individual administration:* 30–90 min.

Burns Roe Informal Reading Inventory: Preprimer to Twelfth Grade, 5th Edition

Grades: Preprimer–12
Revised by Betty D. Roe
Riverside Publishing

Two equivalent sets of graded word lists and four equivalent sets of passages at each level. Comprehension questions on main idea, details, inference, sequence, cause and effect, and vocabulary for each passage. Passages for upper grades include articles about science and social sciences. Yields independent, instructional, and frustrational reading levels and listening comprehension level. Provides guidelines to analyze word recognition miscues, comprehension questions, and retellings. *Individual administration:* 20–50 min.

Classroom Assessment of Reading Processes (CARP)

Levels: 1–6
Rebecca Swearingen and Diane Allen
Houghton Mifflin Company

While not a traditional IRI, CARP assists teachers in measuring the thinking processes related to reading and assesses obtaining meaning from text by using retellings and think-alouds. Forms A and B have narrative and expository passages. For narrative passages, assesses level of comprehension (independent, instructional, and frustrational), knowledge of story structure, miscue analysis, inferencing, and sequencing. For expository passages (developed around a modified K-W-L format), assesses level of comprehension, prior knowledge, recall, inferencing, and main idea. Contains word lists. Has annotated bibliography of graded children's literature. *Individual administration:* about 12 min.

Classroom Reading Inventory (CRI), Eighth Edition

Levels: Preprimer–8
Nicholas J. Silvaroli
McGraw Hill
Consists of subskills (Form A) and reader-response (Form B) formats. Subskills format has graded word lists and paragraphs. Student's background knowledge and responses to factual, literal, inferential, and vocabulary questions are assessed. Reader-response format has graded paragraphs to assess inferential and critical reading and thinking abilities. Student predicts story from title and answers questions about characters, problem, and resolution. Both formats have pretests and posttests. Comprehension assessed as excellent, needs assistance, or inadequate; and reading level assessed as above, average, or below. Customized format for high school students and adults available from Brown and Benchmark Publishers. *Individual administration:* 15 min. for each form of CRI.

Developmental Reading Assessment (DRA)

Levels: Kindergarten–Fifth Grade
Joetta Beaver
Celebration Press
Levels A–2 (kindergarten) have repeated word patterns and simple illustrations. Levels 2–16 are read orally. Stories in Levels 3–8 use predictable text with pictures. Stories in 10–14 have problems, solutions, and moderate picture support. Levels 16–44 are read orally and silently. Stories in 16–28 have beginnings, middles, ends, and resolutions. Levels 30–44 describe setting, characters, problems, and resolutions in more detail.

Ekwall/Shanker Reading Inventory (ESRI), Fourth Edition

Levels: Preprimer–9
James L. Shanker and Eldon E. Ekwall
Allyn and Bacon
Graded word lists check word recognition and analysis skills and determine independent, instructional, and frustrational levels. Four equivalent reading passages: A (oral reading), B (silent reading), and C and D (supplemental passages). Other tests assess emergent literacy (phonemic awareness, concepts about print, letter knowledge), basic sight vocabulary, phonics, structural analysis, and contractions. Includes reading interests surveys. *Individual administration:* about 10–30 min. for oral and silent reading passages.

Flynt-Cooter Reading Inventory for the Classroom (RIC), Third Edition

Levels: Preprimer–12
E. Sutton Flynt and Robert B. Cooter, Jr.
Merrill
Forms A, B, C, and D each have three sections: sentences to determine initial passage selection, passages, and assessment protocols. A and B have narrative

passages for preprimer–9. Students read silently, retell, and answer comprehension questions. Then students read aloud while examiner records miscues. Reading performance categorized as easy, adequate, or too hard. Form C assesses expository passages for Levels 1–9. Form D has expository passages for Levels 10–12. Interest-attitude interviews included. An *English-Español Reading Inventory for the Classroom* is also available. *Individual administration: 30–60 min.*

Qualitative Reading Inventory–3

Levels: Preprimer–High School
Lauren Leslie and JoAnne Caldwell
Longmans
Includes 20-item word lists for each level, passages with and without pictures for preprimer through Level 2, and 6 passages at each of Levels 3–6. Upper middle school levels have two passages each of literature, social studies, and science. High school level has lengthy passages of literature, social science, and science. Includes both fiction and nonfiction at all levels. Questions tap students' prior knowledge. Includes retellings and explicit and implicit comprehension questions. Uses look-backs for Levels 3 through high school and think-alouds for high school. Yields independent, instructional, and frustrational levels. Includes a miscue analysis worksheet and retelling scoring guides.

Spanish Reading Inventory

Grades K–4
Jerry L. Johns
Kendall/Hunt Publishing Company
Assesses ability to read Spanish. Has two versions (A and B) of graded word lists and passages with comprehension questions on topic, fact, inference, evaluation, and vocabulary. Patterned after *Basic Reading Inventory* by Jerry L. Johns. *Individual administration.*

Standardized Reading Inventory–Second Edition (SRI–2)

Grades Preprimer–8; Ages 6.0–14.6
Phyllis Newcomer
Pro-Ed
Each of two forms consists of 10 graded passages that incorporate key words extracted from five popular basal reading series. Oral and silent reading and predictive comprehension are assessed before students answer comprehension questions. Scores in word recognition and comprehension on each passage reveal independent, instructional, and frustrational levels. Includes two alternative forms of vocabulary-in-context subtest and reading passages. *Individual administration: 20–90 min.* Vocabulary-in-context subtest can be administered to individuals or groups.

APPENDIX C

Publishers

American Guidance Service, 4201 Woodland Road, Circle Pines, MN 55014-1796, 900-328-2560, www.agsnet.com

Charlesbridge Publishing, 85 Main Street, Watertown, MA 02472, 800-225-3214, www.charlesbridge.com

Children's Press/Franklin Watts, 90 Sherman Turnpike, Danbury, CT 06816, 800-621-1115, www.publishing.grolier.com

Continental Press, 520 East Bainbridge Street, Elizabethtown, PA 17022, 800-233-0759, 800-233-0759, www.continentalpress.com

Crestwood House, Highway 66, Box 3427, Mankato, MN 56002-3427, 507-373-0188

CTB/McGraw-Hill, 20 Ryan Ranch Road, Monterey, CA 93940, 800-538-9547, www.ctb.com

Curriculum Associates, 153 Rangeway Road, P.O. Box 2001, North Billerica, MA 01862-2021, 800-225-0248, www.curriculumassociates.com

Dominie Press, Inc., 1949 Kellogg Avenue, Carlsbad, CA 92008, 800-232-4570, www.dominie.com

Globe Fearon, 4350 Equity Drive, P.O. Box 2649, Columbus, OH 43216-2649, 800-848-9500, www.globefearon.com

Grossett & Dunlap, 345 Hudson Street, New York, NY 10014, 800-253-2304, www.penguinputnam.com

HarperCollins, Publishers, Inc. 10 East 53rd Street, New York, NY 10022, 800-242-7737, www.harpercollins.com

Heinemann, 88 Post Road West, P.O. Box 5007, Westport, CT 06881, 800-793-2154, www.heinemann.com

Houghton Mifflin, 222 Berkeley Street, Boston, MA 02116, 617-351-5000, www.houghtonmifflin.com

Jamestown Publishers, 4255 West Touhy Avenue, Lincolnwood 60646-1975, 800-872-7323, www.jamestownpublishers.com

Kendall/Hunt Publishing Company, 4050 Westmark Drive, P.O. Box 1840, Dubuque, IA 52004-1840, 800-228-0810, www.kendallhunt.com

Lerner Publications, 1251 Washington Avenue North, Minneapolis, MN 55401, 800-328-4929, www.lernerbooks.com

Macmillan Publishers Ltd., 25 Eccleston Place, London, SW/W 9NF, England, www.macmillan.com

Modern Curriculum Press, 4350 Equity Drive, P.O. Box 2649, Columbus, OH 43216-2649, 800-526-9907, www.mcschool.com

Penguin Puffin, 405 Murray Hill Parkway, East Rutherford, NJ 07073, 800-788-6262, www.penguinpuffin.com

Perfection Learning Corporation, 1000 North Second Avenue, P.O. Box 500, Logan, IA 51546-0500, 800-831-4190, www.perfectionlearning.com

Phoenix Learning Resources, 2349 Chaffee Drive, St. Louis, MO 63146-9675, 800-221-1274, www.phoenixlr.com

Pro-Ed, 8700 Shoal Creek Boulevard, Austin, TX 78757, 512-451-3246, 800-897-3202, www.proedinc.com

The Psychological Corporation, 555 Academic Court, San Antonio, TX 78204, 800-211-8378, www.psychcorp.com

Random House, 1540 Broadway, New York, NY 10036, 800-323-9872 or 800-733-3000, www.randomhouse.com

Rigby, 500 Coventry Lane, Crystal Lake, IL 60014, 800-822-8661, 800-822-8661, www.rigby.com

Riverside Publishers, 425 Spring Lake Drive, Itasca, IL 60143, 800-323-9540, www.riverpub.com

Scholastic Inc., 555 Broadway, New York, NY 10012, 800-724-6527, www.scholastic.com

Slosson Educational Publications, Inc., 538 Buffalo Road, P.O. Box 280, East Aurora, NY 14052-0280, 888-756-7766, www.slosson.com

Soundprints, c/o Trudy Corporation, 353 Main Avenue, Norwalk, CT 06851, 800-577-2413, www.soundprints.com

SRA, division of McGraw-Hill, 1221 Avenue of the Americas, New York, NY 10020, 800-352-3566, 888-772-4543, www.sra.4kids.com

Steck-Vaughn, P.O. Box 690-789, Orlando, FL 32819-0789, 800-531-5015, www.steck-vaughn.com

Teachers College Press, 1234 Amsterdam Avenue, New York, NY 10027, 800-575-6566

Troll Communications, 100 Corporate Drive, Mahwah, NJ 07430, 800-526-5289, www.troll.com

Wildlife Education Ltd., 888-513-7600. 12233 Thatcher Court, Poway, Ca 92064-6880, 800-992-5034, www.zoobooks.com

Wright Group, 19201 120th Avenue NE, Bothell, WA 98011, 800-648-2970, www.wrightgroup.com

APPENDIX D

Jennings Informal Reading Assessment

The *Jennings Informal Reading Assessment*, an informal reading inventory (IRI), was developed by Dr. Joyce Jennings. It was field-tested in the Reading Center of Northeastern Illinois University and in several schools in the Chicago metropolitan area with the help of graduate students in the Departments of Reading and Special Education at Northeastern Illinois University.

The word lists consist of 25 words each. They were developed using *Basic Reading Vocabularies* (Harris & Jacobson, 1982). Each word presented in the word lists is included in the passages read by the students. For those words appearing in the oral reading passages, you can compare students' ability to recognize words in isolation and in context.

The reading passages consist of two passages per level: Preprimer through Grade 8. One set of these graded passages can be used to assess students' oral reading, and the other can be used to assess silent reading. You may also wish to use the silent reading passages to assess students' listening comprehension.

Abbreviations used in this instrument include:

Lit. = Literal   Ind. = Independent Level
Inf. = Inferential   Inst. = Instructional Level
Comp. = Comprehension   Frust. = Frustrational Level

When you have completed the IRI, use the Summary Record Sheet to record your results. Then determine the oral, silent, and estimated overall reading levels as described in Chapter 3.

Informal Reading Inventory
Summary Record Sheet

| Level | Oral Passages | | | Silent Passages | Total Reading | Listening |
	Word Recognition Accuracy Level	Comp. Level	Passage Level	Comp. and Passage Level	Passage Level	Passage Level
Preprimer						
Primer						
1						
2						
3						
4						
5						
6						
7						
8						

Word Lists

Preprimer Level	Primer Level	Level 1	Level 2	Level 3
play	his	other	camp	miserable
with	dad	children	year	chosen
they	animals	stay	spend	parents
like	went	grandma	whole	study
to	lake	coming	week	harbor
run	sat	family	packed	discovered
and	next	clean	clothes	unusual
jump	still	chairs	dressed	seaweed
ride	then	watch	brushed	dusk
day	saw	brother	teeth	underwater
make	duck	baked	kitchen	camera
in	swim	cake	eggs	capture
said	rock	heard	toast	film
she	made	noise	seemed	accident
yes	fast	sounded	forever	maple
it	why	bark	hundreds	excitement
good	over	stuck	shorts	dangerous
a	green	best	shirts	underneath
pet	frog	doctor	tent	screeched
he	tree	tiger	knew	rescue
dog	house	zoo	teacher	arrived
this	mother	hurt	world	bandage
is	got	leg	playground	reporters
home	bed	soon	classroom	information
the	box	again	card	passengers

Level 4	Level 5	Level 6	Level 7	Level 8
champion	placid	sunup	algebra	excelled
skater	surroundings	perspiration	comical	biological
instruction	spectacular	embarrassment	bifocals	dissecting
ladybug	adventurous	frustration	desperation	agonizing
approval	refreshing	drainage	computation	envision
performance	nightfall	parallel	bolstered	overpowering
junior	rainfall	effective	mistrust	hysteria
competes	belongings	downpour	expectation	preserved
article	continuous	alternate	quizzical	contemplation
brilliant	tensions	rainwater	cartoonist	dismantled
athlete	cramped	acknowledged	appreciative	corrugated
confidence	rampaging	midafternoon	perceived	innermost
countless	roused	inspection	confront	administrator
represent	thrashed	enterprising	ample	disheartened
national	thunderbolts	declined	alternative	extensive
permit	destruction	veterinarian	tolerated	journalist
slopes	woodpile	biology	coordination	correspondent
convince	restore	recommended	acrobatic	southeastern
daybreak	ranger	zookeeper	inseparable	eroded
icicles	camper	placement	enthusiastically	seacoasts
mountainside	injured	observation	contempt	devastated
challenger	mechanic	orangutan	gymnastics	phenomenal
gear	frontier	specialize	cartwheel	inclination
sunrise	reassured	equipped	unison	prestigious
disappointment	civilization	surgery	elegance	ambassadors

Preprimer Level, Oral Passage   **86 Words**

Background Question *Do you have a special friend? What do we mean when we say that someone is a special friend?*

Prompt: *In this story, Jill and Sue are friends. Read this story to find out what they like to do together.*

Jill and Sue Make a Cake

Jill likes to play with Sue. They like to run and jump. They like to ride bikes, too.

One day, they wanted to make a cake. Jill asked her mom if they could make a cake in her house. Jill's mom said no. She did not have time to help.

Jill and Sue went to Sue's house. Sue asked her mom if they could make a cake in her house. Sue's mom said yes.

Jill and Sue made a cake. Sue's mom helped. It was good.

Comprehension Questions

Inf-1 *Who is Jill's friend?*
        Sue

Lit-2 *What are two things they like to do together?*
        Name two: play, run, jump, play games, ride bikes, bake

Lit-3 *What did they ask Jill's mother?*
        If they could bake a cake

Inf-4 *Why couldn't they make the cake at Jill's house?*
        Accept either: Jill's mom didn't have time to help them or Jill's mom said no

Lit-5 *What did Sue's mother say when they asked to make the cake at Sue's house?*
        Yes

Inf-6 *What was said in the story that made you know that Jill and Sue liked the cake?*
        It was good

Background	Word Recognition Accuracy			Comprehension			Rate/Fluency	
Check + or −	# of errors			# correct	Check IND, INST, or FRUS		Adequate/Inadequate + or −	
+	−	0–2	Independent		5½–6	Independent		# of seconds =	
		3–4	Instructional		4½–5	Instructional		# secs/60 =__min/_secs	
		5 or more	Frustrational		4 or less	Frustrational		≤ 6 min, 37 sec?	

Primer Level, Oral Passage   **96 Words**

Background Question: *What kinds of animals do you know that live in or near water?*
Prompt: *In this story, Nick and his dad are watching animals that live in and near a lake. Read it to find out what happens.*

Nick's Trip to the Lake

Nick and his dad like animals. One day, Nick and his dad went to the lake. They went to see the animals. They sat next to the lake. They were very still.

Then Nick saw a big duck. He saw the duck swim to a big rock in the lake. Something made the duck fly away fast.

Nick asked his dad, "Why did the duck fly away?"

Nick's dad said, "Look over there." He showed Nick something in the lake. Nick thought he would see something big.

What a surprise to see a little green frog!

Comprehension Questions

Lit-1   *Where did Nick and his dad go?*
          To the lake

Inf-2   *Why do you think Nick and his dad were trying to be still?*
          Accept either: so the animals would come close to them or so they wouldn't frighten the animals

Lit-3   *What two animals did Nick and his dad see?*
          Duck, frog

Lit-4   *What did the duck do?*
          Accept either: swam to the rock or flew away

Inf-5   *What made the duck fly away?*
          Accept either: the frog or the noise the frog made

Inf-6   *Why was Nick surprised to see a frog?*
          Accept either: he thought he would see something big, and the frog was little or the duck was big and the frog was little, but the frog scared the duck

Background	Word Recognition Accuracy			Comprehension			Rate/Fluency	
Check + or −	# of errors			# correct	Check IND, INST, or FRUS		Adequate/Inadequate + or −	
+	−	0–2	Independent	5½–6	Independent		# of seconds =	
		3–4	Instructional	4½–5	Instructional		# secs/60 =__min/_secs	
		6 or more	Frustrational	4 or less	Frustrational		≤ 3 min, 26 sec?	

Level 1, Oral Passage   **109 Words**

Background Question: *Do you ever help your mom or dad clean up the house? How do you feel when you want to do something fun and your mom or dad want you to work?*

Prompt: *Read this story about how Ben helped his mom.*

Ben Helps his Mom

Ben was sad. He wanted to go to the park with the other children. But his mom said he had to stay home.

Ben's grandma was coming to see his family. He had to help clean the house.

Ben had to put away his toys. He had to make his bed. He had to move the chairs. Then Mom cleaned the floor.

Then he had to watch his baby brother while Mom baked a cake.

At last, Grandma's car was coming down the road! She got out of the car. She had a big box. Ben heard a noise. It came from the box. It sounded like a bark!

Comprehension Questions

Lit-1   What did Ben want to do?
   Accept either: he wanted to go to the park or he wanted to play with other children

Lit-2   What did Ben's mom want him to do?
   Accept either: help her clean the house or a list of specific jobs

Inf-3   Why did Ben's mom want him to move the chairs?
   So she could clean the floor

Inf-4   Why did Ben's mom want the house to be clean?
   Ben's grandma was coming to visit

Lit-5   What were two jobs that Ben's mom wanted him to do?
   Accept any two: put away his toys, move chairs, watch his brother or make his bed

Inf-6   What do you think was in the box that Ben's grandma had?
   A dog

Background		Word Recognition Accuracy			Comprehension			Rate/Fluency	
Check + or −		# of errors			# correct	Check IND, INST, or FRUS		Adequate/Inadequate + or −	
+	−	0–2	Independent		5½–6	Independent		# of seconds =	
		3–6	Instructional		4½–6	Instructional		# secs/60 =__min/_secs	
		7 or more	Frustrational		4 or less	Frustrational		≤ 3 min, 31 sec?	

Level 2, Oral Passage   **140 Words**

Background Question: *Have you ever been to camp? What is a camp like?*
Prompt: *Read this story to find out why Danny is so excited about going to camp this year.*

Danny Goes to Camp

Danny is very happy this morning! This is the first day of camp. Last year, Danny went to day camp. This year, he can spend nights at camp. He is going to stay a whole week, just like his brother.

Last night, Danny packed his clothes. This morning, he dressed and brushed his teeth. Then he went to the kitchen. Danny's dad gave him some eggs and toast. But Danny was too happy to eat!

Danny's dad drove him to camp. The trip seemed like it would take forever. Finally, they came to the camp. There were hundreds of boys and girls all dressed in blue shorts and yellow shirts. As soon as the car stopped, Danny saw his friend Joe. Joe told him they would be sleeping in the same tent. Danny knew this would be a great week!

Comprehension Questions

Lit-1   *Where was Danny going?*
          To camp

Inf-2   *What is different between this camp and last year's?*
          Last year Danny couldn't stay overnight, but this year he can

Lit-3   *How long will Danny be at camp?*
          A week

Lit-4   *Why couldn't Danny eat?*
          He was too excited

Lit-5   *How did Danny get to camp?*
          His dad drove him

Inf-6   *How do you know this was a big camp?*
          There were hundreds of boys and girls

Inf-7   *How did Danny feel about sleeping in the tent with Joe?*
          He was happy that he would be with Joe

Inf-8   *Why does Danny think this will be a great week?*
          Accept either: he wanted to go to camp or now he will be with his friend

Background		Word Recognition Accuracy				Comprehension		Rate/Fluency	
Check + or −		# of errors			# correct	Check IND, INST, or FRUS		Adequate/Inadequate + or −	
+	−	0–3	Independent		7–8	Independent		# of seconds =	
		4–7	Instructional		5½–6½	Instructional		# secs/60 =__min/_secs	
		8 or more	Frustrational		5 or less	Frustrational		≤ 2 min, 41 sec?	

Level 3, Oral Passage   **187 Words**

Background Question: *What is an island? What would it be like to live on an island?*
Prompt: *In this story, Kay lives on an island. Read to find out what it is like for Kay.*

Kay's Island Home

Kay lives on an island far out in the ocean. You may think that it would be fun to live on an island. But Kay is miserable. Kay hasn't seen her friends in a year. There is no one to play with or talk to. There isn't even a school!

Why has Kay's family chosen such a lonely life? Kay's parents study animals that only live in the harbor of this island. But Kay's dad knows how unhappy Kay is. He wants to do something to make her happy.

Kay's dad discovered a new kind of fish. It has bright orange fins and a blue tail. Dad named this unusual fish after Kay. He calls it the Kayfish. It hides in the seaweed. It only comes out in the morning and at dusk.

Kay's dad takes his underwater camera to the harbor every day. He hopes to capture the Kayfish on film. Maybe someday her dad will learn enough about the Kayfish. Then Kay can go back to her old school. Then she can see all her old friends again. Kay hopes that day will come soon.

Comprehension Questions

Lit-1 *Where does Kay live?*
On an island

Lit-2 *Why is Kay unhappy?*
Accept either: she doesn't have any friends or she is lonely

Inf-3 *How long has Kay's family lived on the island?*
A year

Lit-4 *Why do Kay's parents want to live on the island?*
Accept any of the following: they are studying the animals, they are discovering new animals, or they are photographing animals

Inf-5 *Why do you think Kay's father plans to name his discovery after her?*
Accept either: he knows she is unhappy or he wants to make her feel better

Lit-6 *What colors is the fish that Kay's father discovered?*
Accept either: orange fins or blue tail

Inf-7 *Why is it so hard for Kay's father to take a picture of the Kayfish?*
Accept either: it only comes out in the morning and just before night or it hidesin the seaweed

Inf-8 *Why does Kay want to go back to her old home?*
Accept either: to go to her old school or to see her friends

Background		Word Recognition Accuracy			Comprehension			Rate/Fluency	
Check + or −		# of errors			# correct	Check IND, INST, or FRUS		Adequate/Inadequate + or −	
+	−	0–4	Independent		7–8	Independent		# of seconds =	
		5–10	Instructional		5½–6½	Instructional		# secs/60 =__min/_secs	
		11 or more	Frustrational		5 or less	Frustrational		≤ 2 min, 12 sec?	

Background Question: *What is ice skating?*
Prompt: *Read this story to find out about an ice skater named Jessie.*

Jessie, Champion Skater

More than anything, Jessie wants to be a champion skater! She can't remember a time she didn't want to skate or a time she didn't want to be the best.

Jessie began skating instruction when she was three years old. In her first ice show, she played the part of a ladybug. She still remembers her red and black spotted costume. Most of all, Jessie remembers the audience clapping their approval of her first performance.

Jessie doesn't have much time for ice shows anymore. Now she must practice jumps and turns. When Jessie was six, she started skating in contests for ages six to twelve. By the time she was eight, Jessie was the junior state champion. Now that she is thirteen, Jessie competes with adults. She is the state champion in ice skating.

Last week, a sports writer wrote an article about Jessie's performance. It said she was a "brilliant young athlete." It said her skating showed "confidence and grace." Jessie thought about the countless falls she had taken to make each jump look perfect. She didn't feel very graceful or confident!

Next week, Jessie will represent her state in a national meet. This will be the first time she has skated at this level. She hopes all her practice and hard work will pay off. Jessie hopes that her confidence and grace will help her win.

Comprehension Questions

Lit-1 *What does Jessie want to be?*
         A champion ice skater

Inf-2 *Why doesn't Jessie have time to be in ice shows any more?*
         Accept either: she's too busy competing or she has to practice

Lit-3 *When did Jessie start taking skating lessons?*
         When she was three

Inf-4 *How did Jessie know the audience liked her first performance?*
         They applauded

Lit-5 *How old is Jessie now?*
         Thirteen

Inf-6 *Why doesn't Jessie feel graceful?*
         She falls so many times in practice

Inf-7 *Why did the sports writer describe Jessie as "brilliant"?*
         Accept either: she is competing with adults although she is so young or she can skate better than other people

Lit-8 *What kind of competition will Jessie be in next week?*
         National

Background		Word Recognition Accuracy			Comprehension			Rate/Fluency	
Check + or −		# of errors			# correct	Check IND, INST, or FRUS		Adequate/Inadequate + or −	
+	−	0–4	Independent		7–8	Independent		# of seconds =	
		5–9	Instructional		5½–6½	Instructional		# secs/60 =__min/_secs	
		10 or more	Frustrational		5 or less	Frustrational		≤ 3 min?	

Level 5, Oral Passage   **289 Words**

Background Question: *What is it like to go camping? What kinds of things do people do when they go camping?*

Prompt: *Read this story to find out what happened when Ted and his family went camping.*

Ted's Camping Trip

Ted's family was taking one last camping trip before school started. They found the perfect campsite! It was just where a clear stream trickled into placid Green Lake. The surroundings were ideal. Ted and his brothers could swim to their hearts' content. They could row into hidden coves along the shore. It was a perfect place to fish or relax.

The first two days were great, with spectacular sunrises and adventurous days. The nights were cool and refreshing. Just before nightfall on the third day, a rainfall began. Everyone joked and laughed as they packed their belongings. But, by the second day of continuous rain, tensions rose. The four boys grew tired of sharing their cramped tent. Late that night, Ted was awakened by a loud crash. He realized he was floating! Their quiet stream had become a rampaging river and their tent had been washed into it! Ted roused his brothers and they thrashed about in the darkness as they struggled to pull themselves onto the riverbank. Streaks of lightning flashed across the sky. Thunderbolts shook the earth. The storm raged through the night.

Near daybreak, the lightning and thunder ceased. The brothers could see the path of destruction left by the storm. The huge oak across the stream had been struck down. Now it was no more than a jumbled woodpile. Their canoes had been tossed about the shore like toys. They worked hard all morning to restore their campsite. During lunch, a park ranger came by to see if they were okay. He told them a camper had been injured when a tree was hit by lightning and fell on his tent. Ted and his brothers were lucky to have escaped with only scratches and bruises.

Comprehension Questions

Inf-1   Why did Ted and his family think the campsite was perfect?
           Accept any of the following: They could do all the things they liked, it was quiet, or it was near a lake

Lit-2   What were some of the things that Ted and his brothers liked to do?
           Accept any two: swim, fish, row

Inf-3   What was the loud crash that Ted heard?
           Accept either: lightning and thunder or the oak tree falling

Lit-4   What awoke Ted?
           Accept any of the following: a loud noise, thunder or the tree falling

Inf-5   How did the stream become a dangerous river?
           All the rain made it bigger and faster

Lit-6   What did the brothers see when the storm was over?
           Accept either: How much of the area had been destroyed or specific items, damaged canoes or tree

Lit-7   Why did the park ranger come to the campsite?
           To see if they were okay

Inf-8   Why did Ted and his brothers have to work so hard to restore the campsite?
           Because the storm had done so much damage

Background		Word Recognition Accuracy			Comprehension			Rate/Fluency	
Check + or −		# of errors			# correct	Check IND, INST, or FRUS		Adequate/Inadequate + or −	
+	−	0–7	Independent		7–8	Independent		# of seconds =	
		8–15	Instructional		5½–6½	Instructional		# secs/60 =__min/_secs	
		16 or more	Frustrational		5 or less	Frustrational		≤ 3 min, 42 sec?	

Level 6, Oral Passage   328 Words

Background Question: *What do you have to do if you don't have enough money to buy something special?*

Prompt: *Read this story to find out how Mike worked to earn money for something he wanted very badly.*

Mike's New Bike

Mike squinted at the midday sky. He had been working since sunup and needed a break. Wiping the perspiration from his face, he continued his exhausting work.

Mike had been working all summer to earn enough money for a new bike. His ancient, beaten up bike was a total embarrassment. But his mom said they couldn't afford a new one. Even though Mike knew she was right, in his frustration, he shouted back at her, "You never give me anything!"

He only needed fifty more dollars. Mr. Painter had offered him forty dollars to dig a new drainage ditch. He wanted to stop the flooding in his rose garden. Mr. Painter wanted the new ditch to run parallel to the old one. Mike didn't think that would be effective in a downpour. So he suggested an alternate plan to direct the rainwater away from the house.

Mike noticed Mr. Painter watching him from behind a curtain. Knowing the old grouch, he'd deduct that little brow-wiping break from his pay. As he returned to his work, Mike waved. Mr. Painter acknowledged the wave and disappeared.

Mike worked steadily until midafternoon. Then Mr. Painter came out for an inspection. "Why don't you lay off for today and get a fresh start tomorrow?"

"I'd rather finish up," replied Mike. "It's supposed to rain tonight, and I'd like to have this operational before the next storm."

About six-thirty, Mike laid the last pipe in place. As he was returning the tools to the shed, Mr. Painter walked up, "Mike, you're an enterprising young man. You don't see many young people these days who care about their work." He handed Mike an envelope and went to inspect his roses.

When Mike opened the envelope, he counted three twenty-dollar bills. He ran to catch Mr. Painter and started to hand one back to him. Mr. Painter declined the offer, "Take it as thanks for keeping an old man from making the same mistake twice."

Comprehension Questions

Lit-1   *Why was Mike trying to earn money?*
          To buy a bike

Lit-2   *What was Mike doing to earn money?*
          Digging a ditch

Inf-3   *What was wrong with Mike's old bike?*
          Accept either: it was an embarrassment or it was old and beaten up

Inf-4   *Why did Mike yell at his mom?*
          Accept either: He was frustrated or angry that she said she couldn't buy him a bike

Inf-5   *Why didn't Mike think Mr. Painter's plan for the drainage ditch would be effective?*
          It was in the same direction as the old ditch

Inf-6   *How do you think Mike felt about Mr. Painter as he was working?*
          He didn't like him

Lit-7   *How much more money did Mike need to buy the bike he wanted?*
          Fifty dollars

Lit-8   *Why didn't Mike want to stop when Mr. Painter suggested he quit for the day?*
          He wanted to finish before it rained

Lit-9   *How much did Mr. Painter promise to pay Mike for digging the ditch?*
          Forty dollars

Inf-10 *Why do you think Mr. Painter paid Mike more than he had promised?*
          Accept any of these: Mike suggested how to dig the ditch, he wanted to stay and finish, or he cleaned the tools

Background		Word Recognition Accuracy			Comprehension			Rate/Fluency	
Check + or −		# of errors			# correct	Check IND, INST, or FRUS		Adequate/Inadequate + or −	
+	−	0–7	Independent		9–10	Independent		# of seconds =	
		8–18	Instructional		7–8½	Instructional		# secs/60 =__min/_secs	
		19 or more	Frustrational		6½ or less	Frustrational		≤ 2 min, 54 sec?	

Level 7, Oral Passage   **350 Words**

Background Question: *What happens when someone gets in trouble in your class?*
Prompt: *In this passage, Peter gets in trouble with Mr. Galvin. Read it to find out what happens.*

In Trouble Again

I knew I shouldn't be drawing in algebra class, but I just couldn't resist. Mr. Galvin had such a comical look as he peered over his bifocals at Jamie's futile attempt to solve the problem on the board. Maybe I could call this brilliant work of art "Galvin-eyes" or something equally insulting.

I suddenly realized Mr. Galvin was calling my name, "Peter, what is your solution to this problem?" Oh no, Mr. Galvin was walking in my direction! If I got in trouble again, I could be suspended. In desperation, I tried to adjust my book to cover the drawing, but it was too late. "Peter, have you completed the computation for problem number seven?"

Even though I hadn't even started the problem, I replied in my most respectful tone, "Not quite, sir." When he stopped at the front of the row, it bolstered my confidence. "I'll have it done in just a couple of minutes." Why did I always have to open my big mouth, instead of leaving well-enough alone? Now he was coming directly toward my desk.

Mr. Galvin, in a tone of total mistrust, suggested, "Why don't you come to the board and show us how far you've gotten, and perhaps your classmates can help you complete the problem?"

As I fumbled for an answer, Mr. Galvin reached my desk. He lifted my book with the expectation of finding a partially solved algebra problem. Instead, he found a drawing of himself, bifocals and all, glaring at Jamie with a quizzical look on his face. At least I hadn't had time to write the caption!

"Peter!" boomed Mr. Galvin, "just what do you expect to make of yourself with this kind of behavior?"

Without thinking how it might be taken, I replied, "A cartoonist."

Wrong answer! The class gave an appreciative round of applause. But Mr. Galvin perceived this as yet another attempt on my part to confront him. Once again, I had tried to undermine his authority with the class.

I had ample opportunity to think of alternative replies while I waited in the assistant principal's office.

Comprehension Questions

Lit-1   *What was Peter doing instead of his algebra problem?*
He was drawing a cartoon of Mr. Galvin

Inf-2   *Why was Peter drawing a picture of Mr. Galvin?*
Accept any of these: Because he thought he looked so funny, he didn't like him or he wanted to be a cartoonist

Inf-3   *Why did Peter lie when Mr. Galvin asked him if he had finished the problem?*
If he got in trouble any more, he could be suspended

Lit-4   *Who did Mr. Galvin say could help Peter finish the problem?*
His classmates

Lit-5   *What did Mr. Galvin expect to find under Peter's algebra book?*
His algebra problem

Lit-6   *What did Mr. Galvin really find under the algebra book?*
Accept either: Peter's drawing or a picture of himself

Inf-7   *Why do you think Peter was glad he hadn't written a caption?*
It would have been even more insulting to his teacher than the drawing

Lit-8   *What does Peter want to be when he grows up?*
A cartoonist

Inf-9   *Why did Peter's answer make Mr. Galvin so angry?*
Accept any of the following: He thought Peter was making fun of him, he thought Peter was confronting him, or he thought Peter was trying to undermine his authority

Inf-10 *How do you know this isn't the first time Peter has gotten in trouble in algebra class?*
Accept either: Mr. Galvin thinks this was another attempt by Peter to disrupt the class or Peter thinks if he gets in trouble again, he will be suspended

Background	Word Recognition Accuracy			Comprehension			Rate/Fluency	
Check + or −	# of errors			# correct	Check IND, INST, or FRUS		Adequate/Inadequate + or −	
+	−	0–8	Independent	9–10	Independent		# of seconds =	
		9–19	Instructional	7–8½	Instructional		# secs/60 =__min/_secs	
		20 or more	Frustrational	6½ or less	Frustrational		≤ 3 min, 6 sec?	

Level 8, Oral Passage   336 Words

Background Question: *What is biology? What does dissecting mean?*
Prompt: *In this passage, James is about to take biology. Read it to find out what happens.*

Biology Woes

James had always excelled in science, winning every science fair and making straight A's. But this year, he would be taking Biological Studies, and he knew that meant dissecting animals. He was agonizing over the thought of cutting up a creature that had been alive. He couldn't even envision cutting into a cockroach—and he hated those! James started the summer with an overpowering fear of embarrassing himself. By July, he had worked himself into a state of near hysteria.

To solve his problem, James bought a dissecting kit to practice. Inside the kit, he found an address to order preserved animals. After some contemplation, James chose an earthworm, a crawfish, a frog, and a snake.

When the animals arrived, James carefully dismantled the corrugated box so he wouldn't damage the contents. When he reached the innermost container, he was shocked beyond words! There must have been a mistake. Not only were these animals not preserved, they weren't even dead! James looked at the order form and discovered his mistake. He had marked the wrong code!

Suddenly, James was the proud owner of four creatures who were very much alive. He had no idea what to feed any of these animals, nor any desire to find out. Deciding to dispose of them as quickly as possible, he biked to the nearest pet shop to sell the animals. The manager told him they only bought from licensed dealers. He tried the administrator of the zoo, but she didn't have room for any more animals just now. James was disheartened. He realized he would have to accept responsibility for the animals himself.

First, James went to the library. There he learned that the animals would have to be housed in separate containers. He went back to the pet store and bought four small aquariums. By the end of the summer, James had learned an extensive amount of information about his new pets. What had started as a dissection project had turned into a valuable study of live animals.

Comprehension Questions

Lit-1   *What school subject was James best at?*
Science

Inf-2   *Why was James worried about taking biology?*
Accept either: he was afraid he would embarrass himself or he didn't want to cut up animals

Lit-3   *How did James decide to solve his problem?*
He bought a dissecting kit to practice

Lit-4   *What is one kind of animal that James thought he would need?*
Accept any: Earthworm, crawfish, snake, frog

Inf-5   *Why was James surprised when he opened the boxes?*
The animals were alive

Lit-6   *Why wouldn't the pet shop take the animals?*
They could only buy from licensed dealers

Lit-7   *Why wouldn't the children's zoo take the animals?*
They didn't have room

Inf-8   *How do we know that James cared about animals?*
Accept any of these: he tried to find a home for them, he fed them, he took care of them, or he didn't want to dissect them

Inf-9   *What did James finally do with the animals?*
Accept either: he kept them or he took care of them

Inf-10 *How did James' mistake become a positive experience?*
Accept either: he learned a lot about the animals or he got four new pets

Background	Word Recognition Accuracy			Comprehension			Rate/Fluency
Check + or −	# of errors			# correct	Check IND, INST, or FRUS		Adequate/Inadequate + or −
+ −	0–8	Independent		9–10	Independent		# of seconds =
	9–18	Instructional		7–8½	Instructional		# secs/60 =__min/_secs
	19 or more	Frustrational		6½ or less	Frustrational		≤ 2 min, 58 sec?

Preprimer Level, Silent Passage   **62 Words**

Background Question: *What is a pet?*
Prompt: *Read this story to find out what happened when Bill wanted a pet.*

Bill Wants a Pet

Bill wanted a pet. He asked his mom for a pet. She said he had to wait.

One day, Bill saw a little dog. The dog was crying.

Bill said, "This dog is lost." Bill took the dog home.

Bill's mom saw the dog. Bill asked, "May I keep it?"

Bill's mom said he could keep the dog.

Bill had a pet!

Comprehension Questions

Lit-1   *What did Bill want in this story?*
         Accept either: a pet or a dog

Lit-2   *In the beginning of the story, what did Bill's mother say when he asked for a pet?*
         Accept either: he had to wait or no

Inf-3   *Why did Bill think the dog was lost?*
         It was crying

Lit-4   *Where did Bill and the dog go?*
         Home

Inf-5   *Why did Bill take the dog home?*
         Accept any: he wanted to keep it, it was crying, or it was lost

Inf-6   *How did Bill finally get a pet?*
         Accept either: he took a lost dog home to show his mother or his mother let him keep it

Background		Comprehension			Rate/Fluency	
Check + or −		# correct	Check IND, INST, or FRUS		Adequate/Inadequate + or −	
+	−	5½–6	Independent		# of seconds	
		4½–5	Instructional		# sec/60 = ___ min/___ secs	
		4 or less	Frustrational		≤ 4 min, 46 sec?	

Retelling Protocol

Story Element	Student's Response	1	½	0
Characters	Includes Bill, mom, and dog			
Problem/Issue	Bill wants a pet, but his mom says he has to wait			
Events	Bill asked his mom for a pet			
	She said he had to wait			
	Bill found a dog			
	The dog was lost or crying			
	Bill took the dog home			
	Bill asked if he could keep the dog			
	Bill's mom said he could keep the dog			
Resolution	The dog became Bill's pet			
Total				
Check IND/INST/FRUS	IND = 9–10	INST = 7–8		FRUS = ≤ 6½

Other information included in retelling:

Background Question: *Have you ever made a pretend house to play in with your friends? What kinds of things could you use to make a pretend house?*

Prompt: *Read this story to find out how Jane and Meg made a house to play in.*

Jane and Meg's House

Jane and Meg are friends. One day, Meg went to Jane's house to play.

They went outside. Jane showed Meg a big tree. Jane said, "I want to make a house next to this tree."

Meg said, "I know! Come to my house! My mother just got a new bed. It came in a very big box. Maybe we can have the box for our house."

Meg and Jane went to Meg's house. They asked Meg's mother if they could have the box. Meg's mother said yes.

Jane and Meg took the box to make a house. They had fun.

Comprehension Questions

Lit-1 Where were Meg and Jane playing?
Accept either: at Jane's house or in the yard

Lit-2 What did Jane want to make?
A house

Lit-3 Where did Jane want to make the house?
Next to the tree

Inf-4 How did Meg's mother help the girls?
She said they could use the box from her mom's new bed

Inf-5 Why did Meg's mother have a box?
Her new bed came in it

Inf-6 Why did Meg think the box will be good for a house?
It is big

Background		Comprehension			Rate/Fluency	
Check + or −		# correct	Check IND, INST, or FRUS		Adequate/Inadequate + or −	
+	−	5½–6	Independent		# of seconds	
		4½–5	Instructional		# sec/60 = ___ min/___ secs	
		4 or less	Frustrational		≤ 3 min, 34 sec?	

Retelling Protocol

Story Element	Student's Response	1	½	0
Characters	Includes Jane, Meg (may include Meg's mother)			
Problem/Issue	Jane and Meg want to make a house			
Events	Jane and Meg are friends			
	They went to Jane's house to play			
	They wanted to make a house (next to a tree)			
	Meg invites Jane to her house (because Meg's mom has a big box)			
	Meg's mother just got a new bed, which came in a big box			
	They asked Meg's mother if they could have the box			
	Meg's mother gave them the box			
Resolution	They used the box to make a house			
Total				
Check IND/INST/FRUS	IND = 9–10	INST = 7–8	FRUS = ≤ 6½	

Other information included in retelling:

Level 1, Silent Passage   **101 Words**

Background Question: *What kinds of books do you like to read?*
Prompt: *Read this story about Jan and her favorite kind of book.*

Jan's Favorite Book

Jan loves to read books. Most of all, Jan loves books about animals. She likes books about dogs that help put out fires. She likes books about cats that get stuck in trees.

The best book is about a doctor. The doctor in the book takes care of animals. Jan loves to read about him.

In the book, a tiger at the zoo was hurt. The doctor came to the zoo. He put something on the tiger's leg. Soon the tiger was well again. When Jan grows up, she wants to be a doctor. She will take care of animals, too.

Comprehension Questions

Lit-1 What does Jan like to do?
         Read books

Lit-2 What does Jan like to read about?
         Accept either: animals or animal doctors

Inf-3 Why do you think Jan likes to read about animals so much?
         Accept any of these: she wants to take care of them, she likes to read about them, or she wants to be a vet

Lit-4 What are two animals that Jan likes to read about?
         Accept any two: dogs, cats, tiger

Lit-5 What is Jan's favorite book about?
         Accept either: A doctor that takes care of animals or animals

Inf-6 Why did the doctor in the book have to go to the zoo?
         To take care of the tiger

Inf-7 What kind of doctor does Jan want to be?
         One that takes care of animals

Inf-8 How do you know Jan likes animals?
         Accept either: she likes to read about them or she wants to be a doctor who takes care of animals

Background		Comprehension			Rate/Fluency	
Check + or −		# correct	Check IND, INST, or FRUS		Adequate/Inadequate + or −	
+	−	7–8	Independent		# of seconds	
		5½–6½	Instructional		# sec/60 = ___ min/___ secs	
		5 or less	Frustrational		≤ 3 min, 10 sec?	

Retelling Protocol

Story Element	Student's Response	1	½	0
Characters	Jan			
Problem/Issue	Jan likes to read books			
Events	Jan loves to read books			
	She especially likes books about animals (cats, dogs)			
	Jan's favorite book is about a doctor			
	In the book, a tiger at the zoo was hurt			
	The doctor came to the zoo			
	The doctor put something on the tiger's leg to make it well			
Resolution	When Jan grows up she wants to be an animal doctor			
Total				
Check IND/INST/FRUS	IND = 9–10	INST = 7–8	FRUS = ≤ 6½	

Other information included in retelling:

Level 2, Silent Passage   **184 Words**

Background Question: *What is it like to go back to school when you don't know your teacher? What would it be like to think you were going to have one teacher and then to find out that teacher wouldn't be there and you would have a new teacher?*

Prompt: *Read this story to find out why Sarah is so worried about having a new teacher that she doesn't want to go to school.*

Sarah's New Teacher

Today is the first day of school. But Sarah doesn't want to go. This year, Sarah was supposed to have Mrs. Black for her teacher. But last June, Mrs. Black told the class she wouldn't be back this year. She told them their new teacher would be very nice.

Mrs. Black is the best teacher in the world! Last year, sometimes the big girls on the playground wouldn't let Sarah and her friends jump rope. Then Mrs. Black would come out to turn the rope just for them. Sarah doesn't think a new teacher will do that.

Sarah was surprised when she got to her classroom. The new teacher's name was Mr. Black. He said, "Good morning, boys and girls. My name is Mr. Black. I am married to Mrs. Black. I will be your new teacher. Mrs. Black asked me to tell you that she had a baby on Friday. I brought a picture of Mrs. Black and the baby."

Sarah and her friends made a card for Mrs. Black and the baby. Maybe the new teacher wouldn't be so bad after all.

Comprehension Questions

Inf-1   Why didn't Sarah want to go to school?
Accept either: Mrs. Black wouldn't be there or she was going to have a new teacher

Lit-2   What did Mrs. Black tell the class about the new teacher?
She said the new teacher would be nice

Inf-3   Why did Sarah think Mrs. Black was so nice?
She turned the jump rope for Sarah and her friends

Inf-4   Why wasn't Mrs. Black coming back this year?
She was going to have a baby

Inf-5   What did Sarah find out when she got to her classroom?
Accept either: the new teacher was Mr. Black or Mrs. Black had had a baby

Lit-6   Who is the new teacher?
Accept either: Mr. Black or Mrs. Black's husband

Lit-7   What did Sarah and her friends do for Mrs. Black?
Made cards for her and the baby

Lit-8   What does Sarah think of the new teacher at the end of the story?
Accept either: she thinks he won't be so bad or she thinks he is nice

Background		Comprehension		Rate/Fluency	
Check + or −		# correct	Check IND, INST, or FRUS	Adequate/Inadequate + or −	
+	−	7–8	Independent	# of seconds	
		5½–6½	Instructional	# sec/60 = ___ min/___ secs	
		5 or less	Frustrational	≤ 3 min, 32 sec?	

Retelling Protocol

Story Element	Student's Response	1	½	0
Characters	Sarah, friends, Mr. and Mrs. Black			
Problem/Issue	Sarah doesn't want to go to school because she isn't going to have Mrs. Black for her teacher			
Events	Today is the first day of school			
	Sarah doesn't want to go			
	She was supposed to have Mrs. Black			
	Mrs. Black told them (last June) that she wouldn't be back this year			
	Mrs. Black told them their new teacher would be very nice			
	Mrs. Black is a good teacher because she turned the jump rope for Sarah and her friends			
	The new teacher is Mr. Black or Mrs. Black's husband			
	Mr. Black told the children Mrs. Black had a baby on Friday			
	Mr. Black brought a picture of Mrs. Black and the baby			
	The children made a card for Mrs. Black and the baby			
Resolution	Sarah decided the new teacher would be OK			
Total				
Check **IND/INST/FRUS**	IND = 11½–13	INST = 9–11	FRUS = ≤ 8½	

Other information included in retelling:

Level 3, Silent Passage   **224 Words**

Background Question: *What does a person have to do to be a hero?*
Prompt: *Read this story to find out how Bill's dad became a hero.*

The Accident

Yesterday, Bill's dad ran into the kitchen, shouting, "There has been an accident!" He told Bill to call the police. He said to tell them a bus had hit a car at the corner of Oak and Maple streets.

Bill wanted to go back to the corner with his dad. He wanted to join the excitement. But his dad said it was too dangerous. Bill watched out the window as his dad ran back out to the street. He hoped his dad wouldn't go on the bus. It was leaning against a wall. The car was underneath the bus, and gas was all over the ground.

But his dad did go back on the bus. Bill watched as his dad carried people from the bus to the grass. Bill saw his dad carry a little girl from the bus. She was clinging to a teddy bear. He said, "Thank goodness, that's the last one!" Just then, a truck screeched to a stop as the rescue workers arrived. The rescue workers rushed to care for the people who were hurt. They even put a bandage on the little girl's bear!

Then the news reporters arrived. They wanted information about Bill's dad. This morning there was a picture of Bill's dad in the paper. Under the picture, in big print, it said, "LOCAL HERO SAVES PASSENGERS."

Comprehension Questions

Inf-1   *How did Bill find out about the accident?*
Accept either: his dad told him or his dad ran into the kitchen shouting about it

Lit-2   *What did Bill's dad tell him to do?*
Accept either: to call the police or to tell the police there had been an accident

Lit-3   *Why didn't Bill's dad let him go to the corner?*
He said it was too dangerous

Inf-4   *Why didn't Bill want his dad to go on the bus?*
Accept either: he was afraid it would fall over or he thought it was too dangerous

Lit-5   *How did Bill's dad help the people on the bus?*
He carried them off the bus

Lit-6   *What did the rescue workers do?*
Accept either: they cared for the people who were hurt or they put a bandage on the little girl's bear

Inf-7   *Why did the news reporters come to the accident?*
Accept either: they wanted to find out about Bill's dad or they wanted to put the accident on the news

Inf-8   *Why did reporters want information about Bill's dad?*
He was a hero or they wanted to write an article about him

Background		Comprehension			Rate/Fluency	
Check + or −		# correct	Check IND, INST, or FRUS		Adequate/Inadequate + or −	
+	−	7–8	Independent		# of seconds	
		5½–6½	Instructional		# sec/60 = ___ min/___ secs	
		5 or less	Frustrational		≤ 2 min, 38 sec?	

Retelling Protocol

Story Element	Student's Response	1	½	0
Characters	Bill, Dad, may include little girl, rescue workers, and reporters			
Problem/Issue	There has been an accident between a bus and a car			
Events	Bill's dad came into the kitchen and told him there had been an accident			
	Bill's dad asked him to call the police			
	Bill wanted to go to the corner with his dad			
	His dad said he couldn't go because it was too dangerous			
	Bill doesn't want his dad to go on the bus because there was gas leaking			
	Bill's dad went back on the bus			
	Bill watched as his dad carried people from the bus to the grass			
	Bill saw his dad carry a little girl from the bus (little girl had a teddy bear)			
	Rescue workers arrive			
	Rescue workers cared for people who were hurt			
	News reporters arrived to get information about Bill's dad			
Resolution	A picture of Bill's dad was in the paper and he was called a hero			
Total				
Check IND/INST/FRUS	IND = 12½–14	INST = 10–12	FRUS = ≤ 9½	

Other information included in retelling:

Level 4, Silent Passage   **236 Words**

Background Question: *What is skiing? What do you have to have to ski? What do you think it would be like to ski down a mountain?*

Prompt: *Read this story about Josh's ski trip.*

Josh's Ski Trip

At daybreak, Josh looked out the window of the cabin. He looked through the icicles to the snow-covered mountainside. He couldn't wait to get out on the slopes! This year he would get to go on the Challenger Slope. He wanted to feel the wind rushing past his face as he raced down the hill.

When Josh's family came to Bear Mountain last year, Josh was the best skier in his class. But he was too short, and the ski patrol wouldn't permit him on the more difficult slopes. He tried to convince the captains of the ski patrol. He knew he was good enough to go on the tougher slopes, but they wouldn't bend the rules for anyone.

But during the long summer months, Josh had grown to five feet, seven inches, and nobody could stop him now! It was the first ski trip of the new season. The mountain was just outside the window, but everyone else was still sleeping peacefully. Josh couldn't stand it any longer! In silence, he picked up his boots and goggles and crept downstairs. He quietly lifted his gear down from the rack and slipped out the door.

The morning was perfect! The air was crisp, and the snow sparkled like silver in the sunrise as Josh made his way to the ski lift. He was anxious to feel the wind in his face. What a disappointment when he saw the new sign: "No Children under Fifteen without an Adult!"

Comprehension Questions

Lit-1   *Where is Josh in this story?*
          Accept any of these: on a ski trip at Bear Mountain or in a cabin

Lit-2   *What does Josh want to do?*
          Accept any of these: go out on the mountain, ski, or go on the Challenger slope

Lit-3   *Why couldn't Josh ski on the Challenger slopes last year?*
          He was too short

Inf-4   *How do you know Josh is a good skier?*
          Accept any of these: He was the best in his class, he could handle more difficult slopes, or he liked skiing

Inf-5   *Why did Josh decide to sneak out of the house?*
          Everyone else was sleeping and he didn't want to wait

Inf-6   *How far away is the ski slope?*
          On the mountain, just outside the window

Inf-7   *Why did Josh creep downstairs?*
          He was trying to sneak out of the house

Inf-8   *Why can't Josh go on the "Challenger" slope now?*
          He is too young

Background		Comprehension		Rate/Fluency	
Check + or −			Check IND, INST, or FRUS	Adequate/Inadequate + or −	
+	−	# correct		# of seconds	
		7–8	Independent	# of seconds	
		5½–6½	Instructional	# sec/60 = ___ min/___ secs	
		5 or less	Frustrational	≤ 3 min, 10 sec?	

Retelling Protocol

Story Element	Student's Response	1	½	0
Characters	Josh			
Problem/Issue	Josh wants to get out on the slopes to ski but his family is still asleep			
Events	Josh is looking out the window, wanting to get out on the slopes to ski			
	He wants to ski on the Challenger slope			
	Last year, Josh was the best skier in his class			
	Last year, Josh was too short to ski on the difficult slopes			
	Josh tried to convince the ski patrol to let him go on the difficult slopes, but they wouldn't bend the rules			
	Josh had grown (during the summer)			
	Josh quietly left the cabin (where everyone was sleeping)			
	Now he found a sign that said "No children under 15 without an adult"			
Resolution	Josh still can't go on the Challenger slope			
Total				

Check IND/INST/FRUS	IND = 9–11	INST = 7½–8½	FRUS = ≤ 7		

Other information included in retelling:

Level 5, Silent Passage   **244 Words**

Background Question: *What do you think it would be like to live on a farm?*
Prompt: *Read story to find out why Beth wishes she could live in the country.*

Grandpa's Farm

Sometimes Beth hated towns and cities! They were taking over, and the farms and open land were disappearing. Beth wished she could live on a farm, but her dad was a mechanic. He repaired machinery for a mill in town.

Beth's favorite times were spent with Grandpa on his farm. Beth spent almost all her weekends with Grandpa. On cool evenings, Grandpa would light a fire. Beth loved to read by the firelight, just like girls did when this was the frontier.

On Saturday mornings, Grandpa was always up early, ready for his long day of chores. First, the pigs had to be fed, and the chicken coop had to be cleaned. Then the stallion had to be brushed. When Beth was little, Grandpa let her help milk the cows, but now he used milking machines.

In the afternoon, Beth and Grandpa walked the horses. This was Beth's favorite chore. Grandpa's favorite place to walk the horses was Bear Mountain. It took most of the afternoon to ride all the way out to the mountain and back. Grandpa and Beth always packed a snack to eat on the mountaintop. As they shared their fruit and milk, they talked. Grandpa told her how much he liked to look out over the farms and towns for miles. These trips to the mountain reassured Beth. They showed her that there was still enough land and open spaces. They helped her to feel less closed in by civilization.

Comprehension Questions

Inf-1 *Why didn't Beth like where she lived?*
Accept any of these: she had to live in town, it was too crowded for her, or the town had no open land or farms

Lit-2 *Where did Beth like to spend her weekends?*
On Grandpa's farm

Lit-3 *Why did Beth's family live in town?*
Because her dad was a mechanic

Inf-4 *Why did Beth like going to her grandfather's farm?*
Accept any of these: she liked to do chores, to read by firelight, to go to the mountain, or she liked lots of space

Lit-5 *What were some of the chores that Beth and her grandfather did?*
Name two: feed the pigs, clean the chicken coop, brush the stallion, walk the horses

Inf-6 *Why do you think Beth's favorite chore was walking the horses?*
Accept either: because she likes to go to the mountain or she likes horses

Lit-7 *What did Beth and Grandpa take with them to the mountain?*
Snack

Inf-8 *Why did Beth like to go to the mountain?*
It made her feel there was enough space for people like her

Background		Comprehension			Rate/Fluency	
Check + or −		# correct	Check IND, INST, or FRUS		Adequate/Inadequate + or −	
+	−	7–8	Independent		# of seconds	
		5½–6½	Instructional		# sec/60 = ___ min/___ secs	
		5 or less	Frustrational		≤ 3 min, 8 sec?	

Retelling Protocol

Story Element	Student's Response	1	½	0
Characters	Beth and Grandpa			
Problem/Issue	Beth hated towns and cities, but her family lived in town because of her dad's job			
Events	Beth wished she could live on a farm because she hated cities			
	Beth couldn't live on a farm because her dad is a mechanic for a mill in town			
	Beth liked to spend time with her grandpa on his farm (she spent most weekends there)			
	Beth liked to read by firelight (just like frontier girls)			
	Beth did chores with grandpa			
	Beth's favorite chore was walking horses			
	Beth liked to walk the horses to the mountain (snack on mountain, all afternoon)			
Resolution	Beth liked the trips to the mountain because they made her feel there was enough room for people like her			
Total				
Check IND/INST/FRUS	IND = 9–10	INST = 7–8½		FRUS = ≤ 6½

Other information included in retelling:

Level 6, Silent Passage   333 Words

Background Question: *What is a veterinarian?*
Prompt: *Read this passage to find out about a girl named Pam, who wants to be a veterinarian.*

Pam's New Job

More than anything, Pam wanted to be a veterinarian. She was great with animals. For the last two years, Pam had volunteered at the zoo. But this summer, she was going to be paid. Pam's biology teacher had recommended her to work in a special science program.

Pam was disappointed when she found out she was assigned to the zoo nursery. Pam didn't want to feed a bunch of baby animals. She had hoped for something more exciting, like reptiles. Pam decided to talk to the zoo's vet, Dr. Mack. Maybe she would understand how Pam felt, and Pam could ask her to convince the zookeeper to change her placement.

When Pam arrived at the zoo, Dr. Mack was in the nursery. There had been an emergency, and Dr. Mack had been called to help. The nurse asked Pam to wait for Dr. Mack in the observation room. She was surprised to find that the observation room overlooked a small operating room. There she saw Dr. Mack, working frantically to save a baby orangutan. After several minutes, the tiny ape started to breathe on its own, and Dr. Mack came out to greet Pam, "I thought we were going to lose her! Since we rescued her from a fire, we've been trying to bottle-feed her, but suddenly she stopped breathing. The nurse called me because I specialize in great apes. Now that I'm sure she'll be all right, how can I help you?"

"I'm glad she's going to be okay," replied Pam, "I didn't know you were equipped for surgery."

"That's why we need someone like you. We just added the hospital last winter. We had it built in the nursery because it had separate rooms to house sick or injured animals. We need someone who can handle frightened animals and comfort them while they wait for surgery and while they recover. Now, what was it you wanted to discuss?"

Pam replied, "I think you've answered all my questions. When can I start?"

Comprehension Questions

Inf-1   Who helped Pam get the job at the zoo?
Her biology teacher

Lit-2   Where did the zookeeper want Pam to work?
In the children's zoo

Inf-3   Why didn't Pam want to work in the baby animal zoo?
She didn't think it was an important job

Inf-4   What did Pam think would happen if she talked to the zoo's veterinarian?
She thought the veterinarian would convince the zookeeper to let her work with other animals

Lit-5   Why wasn't Dr. Mack in her office when Pam arrived at the zoo?
She had been called to help with an emergency

Lit-6   Where did the nurse ask Pam to wait for Dr. Mack?
In an observation room

Lit-7   What was wrong with the baby orangutan?
Accept either: she had stopped breathing or she had been in a fire

Lit-8   How did the zoo get the baby orangutan?
They rescued her from a fire

Lit-9   What was the job that Dr. Mack wanted Pam to do?
Handle the frightened animals and take care of them while they recovered from surgery

Inf-10   Why didn't Pam ever ask Dr. Mack to talk to the zookeeper?
After she learned about the job Dr. Mack wanted her to do, she realized it was important

Background		Comprehension			Rate/Fluency	
Check + or −		# correct	Check IND, INST, or FRUS		Adequate/Inadequate + or −	
+	−	9–10	Independent		# of seconds	
		7–8½	Instructional		# sec/60 = ___ min/___ secs	
		6½ or less	Frustrational		≤ 3 min?	

Retelling Protocol

Story Element	Student's Response	1	½	0
Characters	Pam, Dr. Mack			
Problem/Issue	Pam doesn't want to work in the nursery at the zoo because she thinks it will not be exciting enough			
Events	Pam wants to be a veterinarian (she is great with animals)			
	Pam had been doing volunteer work at the zoo			
	This year Pam was going to work at the zoo for pay			
	Pam was supposed to work in the nursery at the zoo			
	Pam wanted to work somewhere more exciting (such as with the reptiles)			
	Pam went to the zoo to ask the zoo's vet to change her assignment			
	Dr. Mack (zoo's vet) was in the nursery			
	Pam watch Dr. Mack operating on a baby orangutan			
	Dr. Mack explained that they had put the hospital in the nursery because it had separate rooms for sick or injured animals			
Resolution	Pam decided not to ask for a different placement			
Total				
Check IND/INST/FRUS	IND = 11 ½–13	INST = 9–11	FRUS = ≤ 8½	

Other information included in retelling:

Level 7, Silent Passage   360 Words

Background Question: *What do people do in gymnastics?*
Prompt: *Read this passage to find out about what happens when Debbie and Kim do gymnastics in gym class.*

Gym Class

Sometimes, Debbie wondered how she and Kim even tolerated each other, much less remained best friends. While Debbie was outgoing, Kim was quiet and shy. While Debbie was famous for her total lack of coordination, Kim was the most acrobatic person in the entire school. Yet the girls were inseparable, best friends since kindergarten. They were thrilled to find out they would be in gym class together. But as usual, they had opposite opinions about actually taking gym. Kim greeted the class enthusiastically, and Debbie had nothing but contempt for it.

Today, they began the gymnastics unit, and Debbie wished she could crawl into a deep hole and disappear. Down the hall came the new gymnastics teacher, Ms. Bain. She announced that today they would be tumbling. Then Ms. Bain described some of the moves the girls would be doing, the forward roll, the backward roll, and the cartwheel.

Ms. Bain asked if anyone could demonstrate any of the moves for the class. The whole class sang out in unison, "Kim!" Then Ms. Bain asked Kim if she had taken lessons, and she nodded shyly. When Ms. Bain asked if Kim had gotten far enough along to demonstrate any of these moves, the class giggled. Debbie realized that Kim was too modest to tell Ms. Bain the truth, so she spoke up proudly, "Ms. Bain, Kim is the state champion in gymnastics. She's a competitor at the national level."

Ms. Bain smiled at Kim and said, "Maybe you could give us a demonstration of the routine you performed at the state meet." With some encouragement from her classmates, Kim agreed to show the class part of her tumbling routine.

As Debbie watched in admiration, Kim stepped onto the floor mat. As soon as she started to perform, her whole personality changed. Usually Kim was awkward in front of people, but when she stepped onto the gym floor, her body became elegance in motion. Kim's normal shyness disappeared, and she seemed to be an actress playing the part of a gymnast. Even Ms. Bain was taken aback! She applauded approvingly and said she hoped Kim would invite her to her next meet.

Comprehension Questions

Inf-1   *Why didn't Debbie like gym class?*
       She is clumsy

Inf-2   *Why did Kim like gym class?*
       Accept either: she is acrobatic or she likes gymnastics

Lit-3   *When did Debbie and Kim become friends?*
       In kindergarten

Lit-4   *What tumbling moves did the teacher want the girls to do?*
       Accept any: forward roll, backward roll, or cartwheel

Inf-5   *Why did the girls in the gym class suggest that Kim demonstrate the tumbling moves?*
       Accept either: they knew she was good at gymnastics or she was state champion

Inf-6   *Why did the girls giggle when Ms. Bain asked if Kim had enough experience to demonstrate for the class?*
       Accept either: they all knew that Kim was state champion or they knew that Kim had been taking gymnastics a long time

Lit-7   *Why didn't Kim tell the teacher about her experience in gymnastics?*
       Accept either: she was too modest or she was too shy

Inf-8   *Why did Kim need encouragement from her classmates before she would perform?*
       Accept any one: she was shy, she felt awkward in front of people, or she was modest

Inf-9   *Why did Debbie admire Kim?*
       Accept any: she was coordinated, she was state champion, or she was good at gymnastics

Lit-10   *What did Ms. Bain do when Kim finished her performance?*
       Accept either: she applauded, or she said she would like to go to Kim's next meet

Background	Comprehension		Rate/Fluency	
Check + or −	# correct	Check IND, INST, or FRUS	Adequate/Inadequate + or −	
+	−	9–10	Independent	# of seconds	
		7–8½	Instructional	# sec/60 = ___ min/___ secs	
		6½ or less	Frustrational	≤ 2 min, 40 sec?	

Retelling Protocol

Story Element	Student's Response	1	½	0
Characters	Debbie, Kim, Ms. Bain (and classmates)			
Problem/Issue	Debbie and Kim are best friends in spite of their opposite personalities			
Events	Debbie and Kim have opposite personalities			
	Debbie was outgoing and Kim shy or Kim was athletic and Debbie was not			
	Girls have been best friends (since kindergarten)			
	Today was the beginning of the gymnastics unit (they would be tumbling)			
	Teacher asked someone to demonstrate			
	Class suggested Kim			
	Kim was too shy to admit her abilities in gymnastics			
	Debbie announced Kim was state champion			
	When Kim performed, her personality changed			
Resolution	Teacher was impressed, asked to come to Kim's next meet			
Total				
Check IND/INST/FRUS	IND = 11–12	INST = 8½–10½	FRUS = ≤ 8	

Other information included in retelling:

Level 8, Silent Passage   298 Words

Background Question: *What does a journalist do?*
Prompt: *Read this passage to find out how Kate becomes a special kind of journalist.*

Kate Becomes a Journalist

Kate's greatest ambition is to be a journalist. Throughout her high school years, she has been a photographer on the school newspaper. Now she is the senior editor of the school paper, but her goal is to be a foreign correspondent. Kate is taking a class in photography and learning how to use pictures to tell a story. Kate would like to find a way to combine writing about international relations and photography, perhaps writing for a news magazine or for a TV news show but using her own photographs.

Two years ago, Kate's history class took a trip to the southeastern states. She took her camera and photographed the eroded seacoasts. When Kate's pictures were published in the local newspaper, there were many letters to the editor, praising her work.

Last year, when Kate was a junior, her class went to Mexico. Kate took pictures of how the recent earthquake had devastated the entire region. When Kate showed her pictures to the editor of the town newspaper, he asked her to write an article to go with her pictures. He told Kate that she had a unique talent for capturing people's attention with a profound photograph. He said if she wrote an article go with the pictures, people would understand the message in the photographs better. This time, public reaction was phenomenal! Kate could finally see a way to combine her ability to write with her interest in photography.

Now in her senior year, Kate is deciding where to go to college. Kate's inclination is to go to a prestigious college in Washington, DC or New York. She wants to be near the ambassadors and diplomats. Kate has never abandoned her goal to be a foreign correspondent. She keeps that in mind through all her decisions.

Comprehension Questions

Lit-1   What does Kate want to be?
Accept either: a journalist or a foreign correspondent

Lit-2   How did Kate get started in journalism?
She is on the staff of the high school newspaper

Inf-3   How will Kate's experiences in high school help her accomplish her goals?
Accept any of these: she is the editor of the high school newspaper, she is the photographer for the high school paper or she is taking a class to learn about photography

Inf-4   Why did Kate take her camera with her to Mexico?
So she could take pictures of earthquake damage

Lit-5   How did Kate get her pictures published the first time?
The local newspaper published them

Inf-6   How did the newspaper readers respond to Kate's pictures of the eroded seacoast?
They liked her work

Lit-7   Who first helped Kate get her work published?
The local newspaper editor

Inf-8   How did the local newspaper editor help Kate accomplish her goal?
He asked her to write about her pictures

Lit-9   Why did the newspaper editor suggest that Kate write an article to go with her pictures about the earthquake?
To help people understand the message of the photographs better

Inf-10   How will Kate decide which college to attend?
She will go where she can be near people who make political decisions

Background		Comprehension			Rate/Fluency	
Check + or −		# correct	Check IND, INST, or FRUS		Adequate/Inadequate + or −	
+	−	9–10	Independent		# of seconds	
		7–8½	Instructional		# sec/60 = ___ min/___ secs	
		6½ or less	Frustrational		≤ 3 min, 13 sec?	

Retelling Protocol

Story Element	Student's Response	1	½	0
Characters	Kate, (newspaper editor)			
Problem/Issue	Kate wants to be a foreign correspondent, combining writing and photography			
Events	Kate wants to be a journalist			
	She wants to be a foreign correspondent and use her own photographs			
	She has been a photographer for her high school newspaper (now senior editor)			
	When Kate's class went to the southeastern states, she took her camera and photographed erosion of seacoasts or her work was published in the local newspaper and was praised			
	When Kate's class went to Mexico, Kate took pictures of earth-quake damage or the local newspaper editor asked Kate to write an article to go with her pictures and the public liked her work			
Resolution	Kate will go to her college where she can be near ambassadors and diplomats to help her reach her goal of becoming a foreign correspondent			
Total				
Check ND/INST/FRUS	IND = 7–8	INST = 5½–6½	FRUS = ≤ 5	

Other information included in retelling:

REFERENCES

Abramson, L. Y., Garber, J., & Seligman, M. E. (1980). Learned helplessness in humans: An attributional analysis. In J. Garber & M. E. Seligman, *Human helplessness: Theory and applications* (pp. 3–34). New York: Academic Press.

Ada, A. F. (1988). The Pajaro Valley experience: Working with Spanish-speaking parents to develop children's reading and writing skills in the home through the use of children's literature. In T. Skutnabb-Kangas & J. Cunnins (Eds.), *Minority education: From shame to struggle* (pp. 223–238). Clevedon, UK: Multilingual Matters.

Adams, A. (1991). The oral reading of learning-disabled readers: Variations produced within the instructional and frustration ranges. *Remedial and Special Education, 12,* 48–52, 62.

Adams, M. J. (1990). *Beginning to read: Thinking and learning about print.* Boston: MIT Press.

Afflerbach, P. P. (1987). How are main idea statements constructed? Watch the experts. *Journal of Reading Behavior, 30,* 512–518.

Alexander, D. (1999). *Keys to successful learning: A national summit of research on learning disabilities.* New York: National Center for Learning Disabilities.

Alexander, P. A., & Jetton, T. L. Learning from text: A multidimensional and developmental perspective. In R. Barr, M. L. Kamil, P. Mosenthal, & P. D. Pearson (Eds.), *Handbook of reading research* (Vol. II, pp. 285–310). New York: Longman.

Allen, R. V. (1976). *Language experiences in communication.* Boston, MA: Houghton Mifflin.

Allen, V. G. (1994). English books that foster concepts in limited-English students. In K. Spangenberg-Urschat & R. Pritchard, *Kids come in all languages* (pp. 108–131). Newark, DE: International Reading Association.

Allington, R. L. (1977). If they don't read much, how they ever gonna get good? *Journal of Reading, 21,* 57–61.

Allington, R. L. (1980). Poor readers don't get to read much in reading groups. *Language Arts, 57,* 872–877.

Allington, R. L. (1980). Teacher interruption behaviors during primary grade oral reading. *Journal of Educational Psychology, 72,* 371–377.

Allington, R. L. (1982). The persistence of teacher beliefs in the perceptual deficit hypothesis. *Elementary School Journal, 82,* 351–359.

Allington, R. L. (1983). The reading instruction provided readers of differing abilities. *The Elementary School Journal, 83,* 548–559.

Allington, R. L. (1984). Content coverage and contextual reading in reading groups. *Journal of Reading Behavior, 16,* 85–97.

Allington, R. L. (1986). Policy constraints and effective compensatory reading instruction: A review. In J. B. Hoffman (Ed.), *Effective teaching of reading: Research and practice* (pp. 261–289). Newark, DE: International Reading Association.

Allington, R. L., & McGill-Frazen, A. (1989). School response to reading failure: Instruction for Chapter I and special education students in grades 2, 4, and 8. *Elementary School Journal, 89,* 529–543.

Allington, R. L. (1993). Michael doesn't go down the hall anymore (literacy for all children). *The Reading Teacher, 46,* 602–604.

Allington, R. L. (1994). What's special about special programs for children who find learning to read difficult? *Journal of Reading, 26,* 95–115.

Allington, R. L., & Walmsley, S. A. (1995). Redefining and reforming instructional support programs for at-risk students. In R. L. Allington & S. A. Walmsley, *No quick fix: Rethinking literacy in America's elementary schools* (pp. 19–41). New York: Teachers College Press, and Newark DE: International Reading Association.

Alvermann, D. E. (2000). Classroom talk about texts: Is it dear, cheap, or a bargain at any price? In B. M. Taylor, M. F. Graves, & P. Van Der Brock (Eds.), *Reading for Meaning* (pp. 136–151). Newark, DE: International Reading Association, and New York: Teachers College Press.

American Academy of Pediatrics (1992). Learning disabilities, dyslexia, and vision. *American Academy of Pediatrics,* volume 90, 124–126.

American Psychiatric Association (1994). *Diagnostic and statistical manual of mental disorders (DSM-IV)* (4th ed.). Washington, DC: American Psychiatric Association.

Anderson, B. (1981). The missing ingredient: Fluent oral reading. *Elementary School Journal, 81,* 173–177.

Anderson, R. C. (1984). Role of the reader's schema in comprehension, learning, and memory. In R. C. Anderson, J. Osborn, & R. J. Tierney (Eds.), *Learning to read in American schools* (pp. 243–258). Hillsdale, NJ: Erlbaum.

Anderson, R. C., & Freebody, P. (1981). Vocabulary knowledge. In J. Guthrie (Ed.), *Comprehension and teaching: Research views* (pp. 77–117). Newark, DE: International Reading Association.

Anderson, R. C., Hiebert, E. H., Scott, J. A., & Wilkinson, I. A. G. (1985). *Becoming a nation of readers.* Washington, DC: National Institute of Education.

Anderson, R. C., & Nagy, W. E. (1991). Word meanings. In R. Barr, M. L. Kamil, P. Mosenthal, & P. D. Pearson (Eds.), *Handbook of reading research* (Vol. II, pp. 690–724). White Plains, NY: Longman.

Anderson, R. C., & Pearson P. D. (1984). A schematheoretic view of basic processes in reading comprehension. In P. D. Pearson, R. Barr, M. L. Kamil, & P. Mosenthal (Eds.), *Handbook of reading research* (Vol. I, pp. 255–291). White Plains, NY: Longman.

Anderson, R. C., Wilson, P., & Fielding, L. (1988). Growth in reading and how children spend their time outside of school. *Reading Research Quarterly, 23,* 285–303.

Anderson, S. (1984). *A whole-language approach to reading.* Landham, MD: University Press of America.

Anderson, T. H., & Armbruster, B. B. (1984). Content area textbooks. In R. C. Anderson, J. Osborn, & R. J. Tierney (Eds.), *Learning to read in American schools: Basal readers and content texts* (pp. 193–226). Hillsdale, NJ: Erlbaum.

Appleby, A. N. (1978). *The child's concept of story: Ages 2–17.* Chicago: University of Chicago.

Armbruster, B. B. (1986). Using frames to organize expository text. Paper presented at National Reading Conference, Austin, TX.

Armbruster, B. B., & Anderson, T. H. (1982). *Idea-mapping: The technique and its use in the classroom* (Reading Education Report No. 36). Champaign, IL: Center for the Study of Reading, University of Illinois.

Asher, J., & Price, B. (1969). The learning strategy of total physical response: Some age differences. *Child Development, 38,* 1219–1227.

Askew, B. J., & Fountas, I. C. (1998). Building an early reading process: Active from the start! *The Reading Teacher, 52,* 126–134.

Aulls, M. (1986). Actively teaching main idea skills. In J. F. Baumann (Ed.), *Teaching main idea comprehension* (pp. 96–132). Newark, DE: International Reading Association.

Baker, K. (1993, December). *At-risk students and literature-based instruction, low-achieving students and self-selected reading.* Presentation at the National Reading Conference, Charleston, SC.

Balajthy, E. (1995). Using computer technology to aid the disabled reader. Paper presented at the annual meeting of the International Reading Association 40th Annual Convention, Anaheim CA.

Ball, E. W., & Blachman, B. A. (1991). Does phoneme awareness training in kindergarten make a difference in early word recognition and spelling? *Reading Research Quarterly, 26(1),* 49–66.

Bannatyne, A. D. (1974). Diagnosis: A note on recategorization of the WISC scaled scores. *Journal of Learning Disabilities, 7,* 272–273.

Barkley, R. (1998). *Attention deficit hyperactivity disorder.* New York: Guilford.

Barr, R. (1971). Development of a word learning task to predict success and identify methods by which kindergarten children learn to read. Final report to the U.S. Department of Health, Education, and Welfare. Office of Education, Contract 9E125.

Baumann, J. F. (1986). The direct instruction of main idea comprehension ability. In J. F. Baumann (Ed.), *Teaching main idea comprehension* (pp. 133–178). Newark, DE: International Reading Association.

Baumann, J. F., & Serra, K. K. (1984). The frequency and placement of main ideas in children's social studies textbooks: A modified replication of Braddock's research on topic sentences. *Journal of Reading Behavior, 16,* 27–40.

Beach, R., & Hynds, S. (1991). Research on response to literature. In R. Barr, M. L. Kamil, P. Mosenthal, & P. D. Pearson (Eds.), *Handbook of reading research* (Vol. 2, pp. 453–489). White Plains, NY: Longman.

Bear, D. (1994). *Word sort: An alternative to phonics, spelling, and vocabulary.* Paper presented at the National Reading Conference, San Diego, CA.

Beattie, J. (1994). Characteristic of students with disabilities and how teachers can help. In K. Wood & B. Algozzine (Eds.), *Teaching reading to high-risk learners: A unified perspective* (pp. 99–122). Needham Heights, MA: Allyn and Bacon.

Beck, I. L., & Juel, C. (1995). The role of decoding in learning to read. *American Educator, 19,* 21–25, 39–42.

Beck, I. L., Omanson, R. C., & McKeown, M. G. (1982). An instructional redesign of reading lessons: Effects on comprehension. *Reading Research Quarterly, 17,* 462–481.

Beck, I. L., Perfetti, C. A., & McKeown, M. G. (1982). The effects of long-term vocabulary instruction on lexical access and reading comprehension. *Journal of Educational Psychology, 74,* 506–521.

Bender, W. N. (1999). Learning disabilities in the classroom. In W. N. Bender (Ed.), *Professional issues in learning disabilities: Practical strategies and relevant research findings.* Austin, TX: Pro-Ed.

Bereiter, C., & Bird, M. (1985). Use of thinking aloud in identification and teaching of reading comprehension strategies. *Cognition and Instruction, 2,* 131–156.

Berliner, D. C. (1981). Academic learning time and reading achievement. In J. T. Guthrie (Ed.), *Comprehension and teaching: Research views* (pp. 203–226). Newark, DE: International Reading Association.

Berrueta-Clement, J. R., Schweinhart, L. J., Barnett, W. S., Epstein, A. S., & Weikart, D. P. (1985). *Changed lives: The effects of the Perry pre-school program on youths through age 19.* Ypsalanti, MI: Monographs of the High/Scope Educational Research Foundation, 8.

Biemiller, A. (1994). Some observations on acquiring and using reading skills in elementary schools. In C. K. Kinzer & D. J. Leu (Eds.), *Multidimensional aspects of literacy research, theory, and practice: Forty-third yearbook of the National Reading Conference* (pp. 209–216). Chicago, IL: National Reading Conference.

Birman, B. F., Orland, M. E., Jung, R. K., Anson, R. J., Garcia, G. N., Moore, M. T., Funkhouser, J. E., Morrison, D. R., Turnbull, B. J., & Reisner, E. R. (1987). *The current operation of the Chapter I program: Final report from the National Assessment of Chapter I.* Washington, DC: U.S. Government Printing Office.

Birsh, J. (1999). *Multisensory teaching of basic language skills.* Baltimore: Paul H. Brookes.

Blachman, B. (Ed.). (1997). *Foundations of reading acquisition and dyslexia: Implications for early instruction.* Mahwah, NJ: Lawrence Erlbaum.

Blachowicz, C. L. Z. (1986). Making connections: Alternatives to the vocabulary notebook. *Journal of Reading, 29,* 643–649.

Blachowicz, C. L. Z., & Fisher, P. (2000). Vocabulary instruction. In R. Barr, M. L. Kamil, P. Mosenthal, & P. D. Pearson (Eds.), *Handbook of reading research* (Vol. III, pp. 503–523). Mahwah, NJ: Lawrence Erlbaum Associates.

Blackorby, J., & Wagner, M. (1997). The employment outcome of youth with learning disabilities: A review of findings from the NLTS. In P. Gerber & D. Brown (Eds.), *Learning and employment* (pp. 57–76). Austin, TX: Pro-Ed.

Bowlby, J. (1969). *Attachment.* New York: Basic Books.

Breen, M. J. (1986). Cognitive patterns of learning disability subtypes as measured by the *Woodcock-Johnson Psycho-Educational Battery. Journal of Learning Disabilities, 19,* 86–90.

Bridge, C. A., & Tierney, R. J. (1981). The inferential operations of children across text with narrative and expository tendencies. *Journal of Reading Behavior, 31,* 210–214.

Brooks, R. B. (1997). *The self-esteem teacher.* Circle Pines, MN: American Guidance Services.

Brown, A., & Campione, J. (1986). Psychological theory and the study of learning disabilities. *American Psychologist, 41,* 1059–1068.

Brown, A. L., & Day, J. D. (1983). Macrorules for summarizing text: The development of expertise. *Technical Report No. 270.* Champaign, IL: Center for the Study of Reading, University of Illinois.

Brown, A. L., & Palincsar, A. S. (1982). Inducing strategic learning from texts by means of informed, self-control training. *Technical Report No. 262.* Champaign, IL: Center for the Study of Reading, University of Illinois.

Bryan, T. (1991). Social problems and learning disabilities. In B. Wong (Ed.), *Learning about learning disabilities* (pp. 195–231). San Diego: Academic Press.

Bryan, T., Sullivan-Burnstein, K., & Mathur, S. (1998). The influence of affect on social information processing. *Journal of Learning Disabilities, 31,* 418–426.

Busin, R. (1997). Reading and phonological awareness: What we have learned and how we can use it. *Reading Research and Instruction, 36* 199–215.

Button, K., & Johnson, M. (1997). The role of shared reading in developing effective early reading strategies. *Reading Horizons, 37,* 262–273.

Button, K., & Welton, D. (1997). Integrating literacy activities and social studies in the primary grades. *Social Studies and the Young Learner, 9,* 15–18.

Byrne, B., & Fielding-Barnsley, R. (1991). Evaluation of a program to teach phonemic awareness to young children. *Journal of Educational Psychology, 83(4),* 451–455.

Caldwell, J. (1985). A new look at the old informal reading inventory. *The Reading Teacher, 39,* 168–173.

Caldwell, J. (1990). Using think cards to develop independent and strategic readers. *Academic Therapy, 25,* 561–566.

Caldwell, J. (1991, April). *Subtypes of reading/learning disabilities: Do they have instructional relevance?* Paper presented at the Learning Disabilities Association of America.

Caldwell, J. (1993a). *Developing a metacognitive strategy for comprehension monitoring for narrative text.* Milwaukee, WI: Cardinal Stritch College. Unpublished strategy.

Caldwell, J. (1993b). *Developing an expectation grid for understanding expository text.* Milwaukee, WI: Cardinal Stritch College. Unpublished strategy.

Caldwell, J. (1993c). *Developing a text coding strategy for understanding expository text.* Milwaukee, WI: Cardinal Stritch College. Unpublished strategy.

Caldwell, J., Fromm, M., & O'Connor, V. (1997–1998). Designing an intervention for poor readers: Incorporating the best of all worlds. *Wisconsin State Reading Association Journal, 41,* 7–14.

Carbo, M., Dunn, R., & Dunn, K. (1986). *Teaching students to read through their individual learning styles.* Reston, VA: Reston Publishing Co.

Carnegie Corporation (1994). *Starting points: Meeting the needs of our youngest children.* New York: Carnegie Corporation.

Carnine, D., Silbert, J., & Kameenui, E. J. (1990). *Direct instruction in reading.* Columbus, OH: Merrill.

Carver, R. B. (1990). *Reading rate: A review of research and theory.* San Diego, CA: Academic.

Castle, J. M., Riach, J., & Nicholson, T. (1994). Getting off to a better start in reading and spelling: The effects of phonemic awareness instruction within a whole language program. *Journal of Educational Psychology, 86,* 350–359.

Cazden, C. B. (1986). Classroom discourse. In M. C. Wittrock (Ed.), *Handbook of research on teaching* (3rd ed., pp. 432–462). New York: Macmillan.

Cazden, C. B. (1988a). *Classroom discourse: The language of teaching and learning.* Portsmouth, NH: Heinemann.

Cazden, C. B. (1988b). *Interactions between Maori children and Pakeha teachers.* Aukland NZ: Aukland Reading Association. Quoted in Johnston, P., & Allington, R. L. (1991), *Remediation.* In R. Barr, M. L. Kamil, P. Mosenthal, & P. D. Pearson (Eds.), *Handbook of reading research* (Vol. II, pp. 984–1012). White Plains, NY: Longman.

Chall, J. S. (1967). *Learning to read: The great debate.* New York: McGraw-Hill.

Chall, J. S. (1979). The great debate: Ten years later with a modest proposal for reading stages. In L. B. Resnick & P. A. Weaver (Eds.), *Theory and practice of early reading* (Vol. 1, pp. 29–55). Hillsdale, NJ: Erlbaum.

Chall, J. S. (1983a). *Learning to read: The great debate* (updated version). New York: McGraw-Hill.

Chall, J. S. (1983b). *Stages of reading development.* New York: McGraw-Hill.

Chall, J. S. (1987). Reading development in adults. *Annals of Dyslexia, 37,* 252–263.

Chall, J. S. (1994). Patterns of adult reading. *Learning Disabilities: A Multidisciplinary Journal, 5(1),* 1–33.

Chamot, A. U., & O'Malley, J. M. (1994). Instructional approaches and teaching procedures. In K. Spangenberg-Urbschat & R. Pritchard (Eds.), *Kids come in all languages* (pp. 82–107). Newark DE, International Reading Association.

Chira, S. (1994, April 12). Study confirms worst fears on U.S. children. *New York Times,* p. A1, A11.

Chomsky, C. (1978). When you still can't read in third grade. After decoding, what? In S. J. Samuels (Ed.), *What research has to say about reading instruction.* Newark, DE: International Reading Association.

Clay, M. M. (1993). *An observation survey of early literacy achievement*. Portsmouth, NH: Heinemann Educational Books.

Clay, M. M. (1998). *By different paths to common outcomes*. York, ME: Stenhouse Publishers.

Clay, M. M. (1998). *Reading Recovery: A guidebook for teachers in training*. Portsmouth, NH: Heinemann Educational Books.

Clymer, T. (1963). The utility of phonic generalizations in the primary grades. *The Reading Teacher, 16*, 252–258.

Cohen, J. (1986). Learning disabilities and psychological development in childhood and adolescence. *Annals of Dyslexia, 36*, 287–300.

Cooper, H. (1979). Pygmalion grows up: A model for teacher expectation, communication, and performance influence. *Review of Educational Research, 49*, 389–410.

Cooper, J. D. (1997). *Project success: Literacy intervention for grades 3–6.* Paper presented at International Reading Association 42nd Annual Convention, Atlanta, GA.

Crain-Thoreson, C., Lippman, M. Z., & McClendon-Magnuson, D. (1997). Windows of comprehension: Reading comprehension processes as revealed by two think-aloud procedures. *Journal of Educational Psychology, 89*, 579–591.

Crawford, J. (1989). Instructional activities related to achievement gains in Chapter I classes. In R. E. Slavin, N. L. Karweit, & N. A. Madden (Eds.), *Effective programs for students at risk* (pp. 264–290). Needham Heights, MA: Allyn and Bacon/Simon and Schuster.

Critchley, M. (1970). *The dyslexic child*. Springfield, IL: Charles C. Thomas.

Crook, W. (1977). *Can your child read? Is he hyperactive?* Jacobson, TN: Professional Books.

Cummins, R. (1989). A theoretical framework for bilingual special education. *Exceptional Children, 56*, 111–120.

Cunningham, A., & Stanovich, K. (1998). What reading does for the mind. *American Educator, 22*, 8–17.

Cunningham, A. E., & Stanovich, K. E. (1993). Children's literacy environments and early recognition subskills. *Reading and Writing: An Interdisciplinary Journal, 5*, 193–204.

Cunningham, P. M. (2000). *Phonics they use: Words for reading and writing* (3rd ed.). New York: Longman.

Cunningham, P. M., & Allington, R. L. (1999). *Classrooms that work: They can all read and write* (2nd ed.). New York: Longman.

Cunningham, P. M., & Cunningham, J. W. (1992). Making words: Enhancing the invented spelling-decoding connection. *The Reading Teacher, 46*, 106–115.

Cunningham, P. M., & Hall, D. P. (1994a). *Making words*. Carthage, IL: Good Apple.

Cunningham, P. M., & Hall, D. P. (1994b). *Making big words*. Carthage, IL: Good Apple.

Cunningham, P. M., Hall, D. P., & Defee, M. (1991). Nonability grouped, multilevel instruction: A year in a first grade classroom. *The Reading Teacher, 44*, 566–571.

Cunningham, P. M., Hall, D. P., & Defee, M. (1998). Nonability-grouped, multilevel instruction: Eight years later. *The Reading Teacher, 51*, 652–654.

Dale, E. (1965). Vocabulary measurement: Techniques and major findings. *Elementary English, 42*, 895–901, 948.

Daneman, M. (1991). Individual differences in reading skills. In R. Barr, M. L. Kamil, P. Mosenthal, & P. D. Pearson (Eds.), *Handbook of reading research* (Vol. II, pp. 512–538). White Plains, NY: Longman.

Davey, B. (1983). Think aloud: Modeling the cognitive processes of reading comprehension. *Journal of Reading, 27*, 44–47.

Davis, F. B. (1968). Research in comprehension in reading. *Reading Research Quarterly, 3*, 499–545.

DeFries, J., Stevenson, J., Gillis, J., & Wadsworth, S. (1991). Genetic etiology of spelling deficits in the Colorado and London twin studies of reading disability. *Reading and Writing: An Interdisciplinary Journal, 3,* 271–283.

Delain, M. T., Pearson, P. D., & Anderson, R. C. (1985). Reading comprehension and creativity in black language use: You stand to gain by playing the sounding game. *American Educational Research Journal, 22,* 155–173.

Delpit, L. (1995). *Other people's children: Cultural conflict in the classroom.* New York: W. W. Norton & Co.

Delpit, L. D. (1988). The silenced dialogue: Power and pedagogy in educating other people's children. *Harvard Educational Review, 58,* 280–298.

Deshler, D., Ellis, E., & Lenz, B. (1996). Teaching adolescents with learning disabilities: Strategies and methods. Denver: Love Publishing.

Diener, C. I., & Dweck, C. (1978). An analysis of learned helplessness: II. The processing of success. *Journal of Personality and Social Psychology, 39,* 940–952.

Doctorow, M., Wittrock, M. C., & Marks, C. (1978). Generative processes in reading comprehension. *Journal of Educational Psychology, 70,* 109–118.

Donahue, P. L., Voelkl, K. E., Campbell, J. R., & Mazzeo, U. (1999). The NAEP 1998 reading report card for the nation and the states. *Education Statistics Quarterly, 1,* 21–27.

Dowhower, S. L. (1987). Effects of repreated readings on second-grade transitional readers' fluency and comprehension. *Reading Research Quarterly, 22,* 389–406.

Dowhower, S. L. (1994). Repeated reading revisited: Research into practice. *Reading & Writing Quarterly: Overcoming Learning Difficulties, 10,* 343–358.

Dreher, M. J., & Zenge, S. D. (1990). Using metalinguistic awareness in first grade to predict reading achievement in third and fifth grades. *Journal of Educational Research, 84,* 13–21.

Durkin, D. (1978–1979). What classroom observations reveal about reading comprehension instruction. *Reading Research Quarterly, 14(4),* 481–533.

Dymock, S. (1993). Reading but not understanding. *Journal of Reading, 37,* 86–91.

Ehri, L. C. (1991). Development of the ability to read words. In R. Barr, M. L. Kamil, P. Mosenthal, & P. D. Pearson (Eds.), *Handbook of reading research* (2nd ed.). New York: Longman.

Ehri, L. C. (1994). Development of the ability to read words: Update. In R. Ruddell & H. Singer (Eds.), *Theoretical models and processes of reading* (4th ed.). Newark, DE: International Reading Association.

Ehri, L. (1995). Phases of development in learning to read words by sight. *Journal of Research in Reading, 18,* 116–125.

Ehri, L. C. (1997). *Five ways to read words.* Symposium presented at International Reading Association 42nd Annual Convention, Atlanta, GA.

Eldridge, O. H. (1998). The quickbook share. *Journal of Adolescent & Adult Literacy, 41,* 483–474.

Elish-Piper, L., & Stahl, S. A. (1997). What's on the Web? Internet resources for literacy educators. *Illinois Reading Council Journal, 25,* 42–52.

Ellis, E. S., (1998). Watering up curriculum for adolescents with learning disabilities—Part II: Goals of the affective dimension. *Remedial and Special Education, 19,* 91–105.

Engelmann, S., Becker, W. C., Hanner, S., & Johnson, G. (1988). *Corrective Reading series guide.* Chicago: Science Research Associates.

Engelmann, S., & Bruner, E. (1995). *Direct instruction: Reading.* Worthington, OH: SRA Macmillan/McGraw-Hill.

Elley, W., & Mangubhai, F. (1983). The impact of reading on second language learning. *Reading Research Quarterly, 19,* 53–67.

Englert, C. S., & Hiebert, E. (1984). Children's developing awareness of text structure in expository material. *Journal of Educational Psychology, 26*, 65–74.

Farr, R., Lewis, M., Fasholz, J., Pinsky, E., Towle, S., Lipschutz, J., & Faulds, B. P. (1990). Writing in response to reading. *Educational Leadership, 47(6)*, 66–69.

Feingold, B. (1975). *Why your child is hyperactive.* New York: Random House.

Fernald, G. (1943/1988). *Remedial techniques in basic school subjects.* Austin, TX: Pro-Ed. (Original work published in 1943.)

Feuerstein, R. (1980). Instrumental Enrichment: An intervention program for cognitive modifiability. Baltimore: University Press.

Fishbein D., & Meduski, J. (1987). Nutritional biochemistry and behavioral disabilities. *Journal of Learning Disabilities, 20*, 505–512.

Fisher, C. W., Filby, N. W., Marliave, R., Cahen, L. S., Dishaw, M. M., & Moore, J. E. (1978a). *Teaching and learning in the elementary school: A summary of the beginning teacher evaluation study* (Beginning Teacher Evaluation Study [BTES] Report VII-I). San Francisco: Far West Laboratory for Educational Research and Development.

Fisher, C. W., Filby, N. W., Marliave, R., Cahen, L. S., Dishaw, M. M., Moore, J. E., & Berliner, D. C. (1978b). *Teaching behaviors, academic learning time and student achievement* (Final report of Phase III-B BTES). San Francisco: Far West Laboratory for Educational Research and Development.

Fisher, P. J. (1998). Teaching vocabulary in linguistically diverse classrooms. *Illinois Reading Council Journal, 26*, 16–21.

Fletcher, J. (1998). IQ discrepancy: An inadequate and iatrogenic conceptual model of learning disabilities. *Perspectives: The International Dyslexia Association, 24*, 10–11.

Fletcher, J., Francis, D., Shaywitz, S., Lyon, G., Foorman, B., Stubbing, K., & Shaywitz, B. (1998). Intelligence testing and the discrepancy model for children with learning disabilities. *Learning Disabilities Research and Practice, 13*, 186–203.

Fletcher, J., & Martínez, G. (1994). An eye-movement analysis of the effects of scotopic sensitivity correction on parsing and comprehension. *Journal of Learning Disabilities, 27*, 67–70.

Foorman, B., Francis, D., Fletcher, J., Schat-Schneider, C., & Mehta, P. (1998). The role of instruction in learning to read: Preventing reading failure in at-risk children. *Journal of Educational Psychology, 90*, 1–15.

Foorman, B. R., Francis, D. J., Novy, D. M., & Liberman, D. (1991). How letter-sound instruction mediates progress in first-grade reading and spelling. *Journal of Educational Psychology, 83(4)*, 456–469.

Fountas, I. C., & Pinnell, G. S. (1996). *Guided reading: Good first teaching for all children.* Portsmouth, NH: Heinemann.

Fry, E. (1998). The most common phonograms. *The Reading Teacher, 51*, 620–622.

Funnick, R. G., & Glopper, K. (1998). Effects of instruction in deriving word meanings from context: A meta-analysis. *Review of Educational Research, 68*, 450–469.

Fuchs, D., Fuchs, L. S., Mathes, P. G., & Simmons, D. C. (1997). Peer-assisted learning strategies: Making classroom more responsive to diversity. *American Educational Research Journal, 34*, 174–206.

Galda, L., Cullinan, B. E., & Strickland, D. S. (1997). *Language, literacy and the child* (2nd ed.). Fort Worth, TX: Harcourt Brace College Publishers.

Gambrell, L. B. (1986, December 3). *Functions of children's oral language during reading instruction.* Paper presented at the 36th annual meeting of the National Reading Conference, Austin, TX.

Gambrell, L. B., & Bales, R. J. (1986). Mental imagery and the comprehension-monitoring performance of fourth- and fifth-grade poor readers. *Reading Research Quarterly, 21*, 454–464.

Gambrell, L. B., Pfeiffer, W., & Wilson, R. (1985). The effects of retelling upon reading comprehension and recall of text information. *Journal of Educational Research, 78,* 216–220.

Garcia, G. E., Pearson, R. D., & Jiménez, R. T. (1994). *The at-risk dilemma: A synthesis of reading research.* Champaign IL: Center for the Study of Reading, University of Illinois.

Garcia, S. B., & Malkin, D. H. (1993). Toward defining programs and services for culturally and linguistically diverse learners in special education. *Teaching Exceptional Children, 26(1),* 52–58.

Garcia, S., Wilkinson, C., & Ortiz, A. (1997). Enhancing achievement for language minority students: Classroom, school, and family contexts. *Education and Urban Society, 27,* 441–462.

Gardner, H. (1985). *Frames of mind: The theory of multiple intelligences.* New York: Basic Books.

Gaskins, I. W. (1998). There's more to teaching at-risk and delayed readers than good reading instruction. *The Reading Teacher, 51,* 534–547.

Gaskins, I., Downer, M., Anderson, R., Cunningham, P., Gaskins, R., Schommer, M., & the Teachers of Benchmark School. (1988). A metacognitive approach to phonics: Using what you know to decode what you don't know. *Remedial and Special Education, 9,* 36–41.

Gaskins, I. W., & Downer, M. (1986). *Benchmark word identification/vocabulary development program: Beginning level.* Media, PA: Benchmark Press.

Gaskins, I. W., Guthrie, J. T., Satlow, E., Ostertag, J., Six, L., Byrne, J., & Conner, B. (1994). Integrating instruction of science, reading and writing: Goals, teacher development, and assessment. *Journal of Research in Science Teaching, 31,* 1039–1056.

Gaskins, I. W., Ehri, L. C., Cress, C., O'Hara, C., & Donnelly, K. (1996–1997). Procedures for word learning: Making discoveries about words. *The Reading Teacher, 50,* 312–327.

Gaskins, R. W. (1988). The missing ingredients: Time on task, direct instruction, and writing. *The Reading Teacher, 41,* 750–756.

Gaskins, R. W., Gaskins, I. W., Anderson, R. C., & Schommer, M. (1995). The reciprocal relationship between research and development: An example involving a decoding strand for poor readers. *Journal of Reading Behavior, 27,* 337–377.

Gaskins, R. W., Gaskins, J. C., & Gaskins, I. W. (1991). A decoding program for poor readers—and the rest of the class too! *Language Arts, 68,* 213–225.

Gaskins, R. W., Gaskins, J. C., & Gaskins, I. W. (1992). Using what you know to figure out what you don't know: An analogy approach to decoding. *Reading and Writing Quarterly, 8,* 197–221.

Gaskins, R. W., Soja, S., Indrisano, A., Lawrence, H., Elliot, T., Rouch, S., O'Donnell, D., Young, J., Audley, S., Bruinsma, S., MacDonald, E., Barus, B., Gutman, A., & Theilacker, S. (1989). *Benchmark work identification/vocabulary development program: Intermediate level.* Media, PA: Benchmark Press.

Genesee, F. (1985). Second-language learning through immersion: A review of U.S. programs. *Review of Educational Research, 55(4),* 541–561.

Gentry, J. R., & Gillet, J. W. (1993). *Teaching kids to spell.* Portsmouth, NH: Heinemann.

Gerber, P. (1997). Life, after School: Challenges in the workplace. In P. Gerber and D. Brown (Eds.), *Learning disabilities and employment* (pp. 3–18). Austin, TX: Pro-Ed.

Gerber, R., & Brown, D. (Eds.). (1997). *Learning disabilities and employment.* Austin, TX: Pro-Ed.

German, D. (1994). Word-finding difficulties in children and adolescents. In G. F. Wallach & K. G. Butler (Eds.), *Language learning abilities in school-age children and adolescents.* (pp. 343–347). Needham Heights, MA: Allyn & Bacon.

Gersten, R., Brengleman, S., & Jiménez, R. (1994). Effective instruction for culturally and linguistically diverse students: A reconceptualization. *Focus on Exceptional Children, 27(1),* 1–16.

Giacobbe, M. E. (1986). Learning to write and writing to learn in the elementary school. In A. R. Petrosky & D. Bartholomae (Eds.), *The teaching of writing: Eighty-fifth yearbook of the National Society for the Study of Education* (pp. 131–147). Chicago, IL: University of Chicago.

Gillet, J. W., & Temple, C. (2000). *Understanding reading problems: Assessment and instruction* (56th ed.). NY: Longman.

Gillingham, A., & Stillman, B. (1970). *Remedial training for children with specific disability in reading, spelling and penmanship.* Cambridge, MA: Educators Publishing Service.

Gipe, J. P. (1980). Use of relevant context helps kids learn new word meanings. *The Reading Teacher, 33,* 398–402.

Golden, J., & Guthrie, J. (1986). Convergence and divergence in reader response to literature. *Reading Research Quarterly, 21,* 408–421.

Goldman, S. R. (1997). Learning from text: Reflections on the past and suggestions for the future. *Discourse Processes, 23,* 357–398.

Goldman, S. R., & Pellegrino, J. W. (1987). Information processing and educational microcomputer technology: Where do we go from here? *Journal of Learning Disabilities, 20,* 144–154.

Goldman, S. R., & Rakestraw, J. A., Jr. (2000). Structural aspects of constructing meaning from text. In R. Barr, M. L. Kamil, P. Mosenthal, & P. D. Pearson (Eds.), *Handbook of reading research,* (Vol. III, pp. 311–335). Mahwah, NJ: Lawrence Erlbaum Associates.

Goldstein, R. (1969). *The poetry of rock.* New York: Bantam.

Good, T. (1983). Research on classroom teaching. In L. S. Schulman & G. Sykes (Eds.), *Handbook on teaching and policy.* White Plains, NY: Longman.

Goodman, K. S. (1965). A linguistic study of cues and miscues in reading. *Elementary English, 42,* 639–643.

Goodman, K. S. (1969). Analysis of oral reading miscues. *Reading Research Quarterly, 5,* 9–30.

Goodman, K. S. (1992). Why whole language is today's agenda in today's education. *Language Arts, 69,* 353–363.

Goodman, K. S., & Gollasch, F. V. (1980–1981). Word omissions: Deliberate and nondeliberate. *Reading Research Quarterly, 14,* 6–31.

Goodman, K. S., & Goodman, Y. (1983). Reading and writing relationships: Pragmatic functions. *Language Arts, 60,* 590–599.

Goodman, Y. M. (1976). Miscues, errors and reading comprehension. In J. Merritt (Ed.), *New horizons in reading.* Newark, DE: International Reading Association.

Goswami, U., & Bryant, P. (1990). *Phonological skills in learning to read.* Mahwah, NJ: Erlbaum.

Goswami, U., & Mead, F. (1992). Onset and rime awareness and analogies in reading. *Reading Research Quarterly, 27,* 150–162.

Gottesman, R. (1994). The adult with learning disabilities: An overview. *Learning Disabilities: A Multidisciplinary Journal, 5(1),* 1–13.

Gough, P. B., & Hillinger, M. L. (1980). Learning to read: An unnatural act. *Bulletin of the Orton Society, 30,* 171–176.

Gough, P. B., & Juel, C. (1991). The first stages in word recognition. In L. Rieben & C. A. Perfetti (Eds.), *Learning to read: Basic research and its implications.* Hillsdale, NJ: Erlbaum.

Graesser, A., Golding, J. M., & Long, D. L. (1991). Narrative representation and comprehension. In R. Barr, M. L. Kamil, P. Mosenthal, & P. D. Pearson (Eds.), *Handbook of reading research* (Vol. 2, pp. 171–205). White Plains, NY: Longman.

Graves, D. H. (1994). *A fresh look at writing.* Portsmouth, NH: Heinemann.

Graves, M. (2000). A vocabulary program to complement and bolster a middle-grade comprehension program. In B. M. Taylor, M. F. Graves, & P. Van Der Brock (Eds.), *Reading for meaning* (pp. 116–135). Newark, DE: International Reading Association, and New York: Teachers College Press.

Greene, B. G. (1995). Exploring the reading-writing relationship. *Reading Psychology: An International Quarterly, 16,* 261–268.

Guthrie, J. T., & Greaney, V. (1991). Literacy acts. In R. Barr, M. L. Kamil, P. Mosenthal, & P. D. Pearson (Eds.), *Handbook of reading research* (Vol. 2, pp. 68–96). White Plains, NY: Longman.

Haager, D., & Vaughn, S. (1995). Parent, teacher, peer and self-reports of the social competence of students with learning disabilities. *Journal of Learning Disabilities, 28,* 205–215, 231.

Hakuta, K. (1990). Language and cognition in bilingual children. In A. M. Padilla, H. H. Fairchild, & C. Valadez (Eds.), *Bilingual education: Issues and strategies* (pp. 47–59). Newbury Park, CA: Sage.

Hakuta, K., & Garcia, E. (1989). Bilingualism and education. *American Psychologist 44,* 234–239.

Hall, D. P., Prevatte C., & Cunningham, P. M. (1995). Eliminating ability grouping and reducing failure in the primary grades. In R. Allington & S. Walmsley (Eds.), *No quick fix* (pp. 137–159). New York: Teachers College Press.

Hammechek, D. (1990). *Psychology in teaching, learning, and growth.* Boston, MA: Allyn and Bacon.

Hansen, J. (1981). The effects of inference training and practice on young children's reading comprehension. *Reading Research Quarterly, 16,* 391–417.

Harp, B. (1989). What do you do when the principal asks: "Why aren't you using phonics workbooks?" *The Reading Teacher, 42,* 326–327.

Harris, A., & Sipay, E. R. (1985). *How to increase reading ability* (8th ed.). White Plains, NY: Longman.

Harry, B. (1995). African American families. In B. A. Ford, F. E. Obiakor, & M. M. Patton (Eds.), *Effective instruction for African American exceptional learners* (pp. 211–334). Austin, TX: Pro-Ed.

Heath, S. B. (1981). Questioning at home and at school: A comparative study. In G. Spindler (Ed.), *Doing ethnography: Educational anthropology in action* (pp. 102–131). New York: Holt, Rinehart, and Winston.

Heath, S. B. (1983). *Ways with words: Language, life, and work in communities and classrooms.* Cambridge, MA: Harvard University Press.

Heckelman, R. G. (1969). The neurological impress method of remedial reading instruction. *Academic Therapy, 4,* 277–282.

Henderson, E. H. (1981). *Learning to read and spell: The child's knowledge of words.* DeKalb, IL: Northern Illinois University.

Henderson, E. H. (1985). *Teaching spelling.* Geneva, IL: Houghton Mifflin.

Henry, M. (1998). Structured, sequential multisensory teaching: The Orton legacy. *Annals of Dyslexia, 48,* 3–26.

Hensley, M. (1994). *From untapped potential to creative realization: Empowering parents of multicultural backgrounds.* Paper presented at the meeting of the Society of

Applied Anthropology. Cancun, Mexico. Cited in L. C. Moll & N. González, (1994), Lessons from research with language-minority children. *Journal of Reading Behavior, 26*, 439–456.

Herman, P. A. (1985). The effect of repeated readings on reading rate, speech pauses, and word recognition accuracy. *Reading Research Quarterly, 20*, 553–564.

Herrmann, B. A. (1988). Two approaches for helping poor readers become more strategic. *The Reading Teacher, 42*, 24–28.

Hiebert, E. F., Colt, J. M., Catto, S. L., & Gury, E. C. (1992). Reading and writing of first-grade students in a restructured Chapter I program. *American Educational Research Journal, 29*, 545–572.

Hiebert, E. H. (1994). A small-group literacy intervention with Chapter I students. In E. H. Hiebert & B. Taylor (Eds.), *Getting reading right from the start: Effective early literacy interventions* (pp. 85–106). Needham Heights, MA: Allyn & Bacon.

Hirsch, E. D., Jr. (1987). *Cultural literacy*. Boston: Houghton Mifflin.

Hodgkinson, H. (1991). Reform versus reality. *Phi Delta Kappan, 73*, 9–16.

Hoffman, J. V. (1985). *The oral recitation lesson: A teacher's guide*. Austin, TX: Academic Resource Consultants.

Hoffman, J. V., McCarthey, S. J., Abbott, J., Christain, C., Corman, L., Curry, C., Dressman, M., Elliot, B., Matherne, D., Stahle, D. (1994). So what's new in the basals? A focus on first grade. *Journal of Reading Behavior, 26*, 47–73.

Hoffman, J. V., O'Neal, S. V., Kastler, L. A., Clements, R. D., Segel, K. W., & Nash, M. F. (1984). Guided oral reading and miscue focused verbal feedback in second grade classrooms. *Reading Research Quarterly, 14*, 367–384.

Holdaway, D. (1979). *The foundations of literacy*. Portsmouth, NH: Heinemann.

Holt-Ochsner, L. K. (1992). Automaticity training for dyslexics: An experimental study. *Annals of Dyslexia, 42*, 222–241.

Holt-Ochsner, L. K., & Manis, F. R. (1992). Automaticity training for dyslexics: An experimental study. *Annals of Dyslexia, 42*, 222–241.

Horowitz, R. (1985). Text patterns: Part I. *Journal of Reading Research, 28*, 448–454.

Hurdato, A. (1995). Variations, combinations, and evolutions: Latino families in the United States. In R. Zambrana (Ed.), *Understanding Latino families: scholarship, policy and practice* (p. 4061). Thousand Oaks, CA: Sage.

Hynd, G. (1992). Neurological aspects of dyslexia: Comments on the balance model. *Journal of Learning Disabilities, 25*, 110–113.

Idol, L., & Rutledge, M. (1993). Teaching phonics to poor readers: Direct instruction using sound sheets. *Teaching Exceptional Children, 25*, 58–61.

Individuals with Disabilities Education Act (1990). PL 101–476. U.S. Congress.

Ingham, J. (1982). *Books and reading development: The Bradford book flood experiment* (2nd ed.). Exeter, NH: Heinemann.

Invernizzi, M., Juel, C., & Rosemary, C. A. (1996–1997). A community volunteer tutorial that works. *The Reading Teacher, 50*, 304–311.

Invernizzi, M., Rosemary, C. A., Juel, C., & Richards H. C. (1997). At-risk readers and community volunteers: A three year perspective. *Journal of the Scientific Studies of Reading, 3*, 277–300.

Iversen, S., & Tunmer, W. E. (1993). Phonological processing skills and the reading recovery program. *Journal of Educational Psychology, 85*, 112–126.

Jenkins, J. R., Heliotis, J., Haynes, M., & Bweck, K. (1986). Does passive learning account for readers' comprehension deficits in ordinary reading situations? *Learning Disability Quarterly, 9*, 60–76.

Jenkins, J. R., Pious, C., & Peterson D. (1988). Categorical programs for remedial and handicapped students: Issues of validity. *Exceptional Children, 55*, 147–158.

Jennings, J. H. (1991). A comparison of summary and journal writing as components of an interactive comprehension model in social studies. In *The fortieth yearbook of the National Reading Conference* (pp. 67–82). Chicago, IL: National Reading Conference.

Jennings, J. H. (2001). Jennings Informal Reading Assessment. In M. A. Richek, J. S. Caldwell, J. H. Jennings, & J. W. Lerner, *Reading problems: Assessment and teaching strategies* (4th ed.). Boston: Allyn and Bacon.

Jennings, J. H., Richek, M. A., Chenault, L. R., & Ali, S. L. (1993, December). *A parental literacy support program: Helping parents to help at-risk children.* Paper presented at the National Reading Conference, Charleston, SC.

Jiménez, R. T. (2000). Literacy lessons derived from the instruction of six Latina/Latino teachers. In B. Taylor, M. Graves, & P. Van Der Brock (Eds.), *Reading for meaning* (pp. 152–160). New York: Teachers College Press.

Johns, J. L. (1993). *Informal reading inventories: An annotated reference guide.* DeKalb, IL: Communitech.

Johnson, D. D. (1971). The Dolch list reexamined. *The Reading Teacher, 24*, 449–457.

Johnson, D. D., & Baumann, J. F. (1984). Word identification. In P. D. Pearson (Ed.), *Handbook of reading research* (pp. 583–608). White Plains, NY: Longman.

Johnson, D., & Myklebust, H. (1967). *Learning disabilities.* New York: Grune and Stratton.

Johnson, M. J., Kress, R. A., & Pikulski, J. L. (1987). *Informal reading inventories* (2nd ed.). Newark, DE: International Reading Association.

Johnston, F. R. (1998). The reader, the text, and the task: Learning words in first grade. *The Reading Teacher, 51*, 666–675.

Johnston, F. R. (1999a). The timing and teaching of word families. *The Reading Teacher, 53*, 64–75.

Johnston, F. R. (1999b). *The utility of phonic generalizations: Let's take another look at Clymer's conclusions.* Paper presented at National Reading Conference, Orlando, FL.

Johnston, P. H. (1984). Instruction and student independence. *Elementary School Journal, 84*, 338–344.

Johnston, P. H. (1997). *Knowing literacy: Constructive literacy assessment.* York, ME: Stenhouse Publishers.

Johnston, P. H., & Allington, R. (1991). Remediation. In R. Barr, M. L. Kamil, P. Mosenthal, & P. D. Pearson (Eds.), *Handbook of reading research* (Vol. II, pp. 984–1012). White Plains, NY: Longman.

Johnston, P. H., Allington, R. L., & Afflerbach, P. (1985). Congruence of classroom and remedial reading instruction. *Elementary School Journal, 85*, 465–478.

Josel, C. A. (1986). A silent DRTA for remedial eighth graders. *Journal of Reading, 29*, 434–439.

Josel, C. A. (1988). In a different context. *Journal of Reading, 31*, 374–377.

Jouzaitis, C. (1994, July 13). Unwed mother a common target in welfare debates. *Chicago Tribune*, Section 1, p. 3.

Juel, C. (1983). The development and use of mediated word identification. *Reading Research Quarterly, 18*, 306–327.

Juel, C. (1988). Learning to read and write: A longitudinal study of fifty-four children from first through fourth grades. *Journal of Educational Psychology, 80*, 437–447.

Juel, C. (1994). *Learning to read and write in one elementary school.* New York: Springer-Verlag.

Juel, C., Griffith, P. L., & Gough, P. B. (1986). Acquisition of literacy: A longitudinal study of children in first and second grade. *Journal of Educational Psychology, 78*, 243–255.

Kameenui, E. J. (1993). Diverse learners and the tyranny of time: Don't fix blame; fix the leaky roof. *The Reading Teacher, 46,* 376–393.

Kamhi, A. G. (1992). Response to historical perspective: A developmental language perspective. *Journal of Learning Disabilities, 25,* 48–52.

Kantrowitz, B., & Underwood, A. (1999 November 2). Dyslexia and the new science of reading. *Newsweek, 134,* 72–80.

Kaufman, A. S. (1981). The WISC and learning disabilities assessment: State of the art. *Journal of Learning Disabilities, 14,* 520–526.

Kaufman, J. M. (1997). *Characteristics of emotional and behavioral disorders of children and youth.* Upper Saddle River, NJ: Merrill.

Kavale, K. A., & Forness, S. R. (1987). The far side of heterogeniety: A critical analysis of empirical subtyping research in learning disabilities. *Journal of Learning Disabilities, 6,* 374–382.

Kerr, M., Nelson, C., & Lambert, D. (1987). *Helping adolescents with learning and behavior problems.* Columbus, OH: Merrill.

Kibby, M. (1995). *Practical steps for informing literacy instruction: A diagnostic decision making model.* Newark, DE: International Reading Association.

Kirk, S., Kirk, W., & Minskoff, E. (1985). *Phonic remedial reading lessons.* Novato, CA: Academic Therapy.

Koskinen, P. S., Gambrell, L. B., Kapinus, B. A., & Heathington, B. S. (1988). Retelling: A strategy for enhancing students' reading comprehension. *The Reading Teacher, 41,* 892–896.

Krueger, E., & Braun, B. (1998–1999). Books and buddies: Peers tutoring peers. *The Reading Teacher, 52,* 410–414.

Kutiper, K., & Wilson, P. (1993). Updating poetry preferences: A look at the poetry children really like. *The Reading Teacher, 47,* 28–34.

LaBerge, D., & Samuels, S. M. (1974). Toward a theory of automatic information processing in reading. *Cognitive Psychology, 6,* 293–323.

Labov, W. (1967). Some sources of reading problems for Negro speakers of nonstandard English. In A. Frasier (Ed.), *New directions in elementary English* (pp. 293–323). Champaign, IL: National Council of Teachers of English.

Labov, W., Cohen, P., Robins, C., & Lewis, J. (1968). *A study of the nonstandard English of Negro and Puerto Rican speakers in New York City: Final report* (Cooperative Research Project, 3288). Washington, DC: Office of Education.

Lancia, P. J. (1997). Literary borrowing: The effects of literature on children's writing. *The Reading Teacher, 50,* 470–475.

Lansdown, S. (1991). Increasing vocabulary knowledge using direct instruction, cooperative grouping, and reading in junior high school. *Illinois Reading Council Journal, 19,* 15–21.

Larkin, M. J., & Ellis, E. S. (1995). *How do we teach? How will we teach?: Assessing teachers' perspectives of traditional and potentially emerging instructional practices for students who are learning disabled.* Paper presented at the Annual Meeting of the Mid-South Educational Research Association, Biloxi, MS.

Larry P. v. Riles, 495. Supp. 96 (N. D. Cal, 1979). *affd,* 1988–84. E.H.I.R.D.E.C. 555;304 (9th Cir. 1984).

Lerner, J. W. (2000). *Learning disabilities: Theories, diagnosis, and teaching strategies* (8th ed.). Boston: Houghton Mifflin.

Lerner, J. W., Lowenthal, B., & Lerner, S. (1995). *Attention deficit disorders: Assessment and teaching.* Pacific Grove, CA: Brooks/Cole.

Leslie, L. (1993). A developmental-interactive approach to reading assessment. *Reading and Writing Quarterly, 9,* 5–30.

Leslie, L., & Allen, L. (1999). Factors that predict success in an early literacy intervention project. *Reading Research Quarterly, 34,* 404–425.

Leslie, L., & Caldwell, J. (2001). *The Qualitative Reading Inventory III,* New York: Longman.

Levine, D. U., & Havighurst, A. J. (1992). *Society and education.* Boston: Allyn and Bacon.

Liebert, R. E. (1970–1). Ten minutes as a retarded reader. *Journal of Reading Behavior, 3,* 74–76.

Lindamood, P., and Lindamood, P. (1998). *The Lindamood Phoneme Sequencing Program for reading, spelling, and speech (LIPS).* Austin, TX: Pro-Ed.

Lipson, M. Y., Cox, C. H., Iwankowski, S., & Simon, M. (1984). Exploration of the interactive nature of reading: Using commercial IRI's to gain insights. *Reading Psychology: An International Quarterly, 5,* 209–218.

Lynch-Brown, C., & Tomlinson, C. M. (1999). *Essentials of children's literature* (3rd ed.). Boston, MA: Allyn and Bacon.

Lynn, L. (1997 September/October). Family involvement in schools: It makes a big difference but remains rare. Harvard University Newsletter, 13.

Lyon, G. R. (1998). Why reading is not a natural process. *Educational Leadership, 55,* 14–18.

Lyon, G. R. (1997). Progress and promise in research: Learning disabilities. *Learning Disabilities: A Multidisciplinary Journal, 8,* 1–6.

Lyon, G. R., & Moats, L. (1997). Critical conceptual and methodological considerations in reading intervention research. *Journal of Learning Disabilities, 30,* 578–588.

Lyons, C. A., & Beaver, J. (1995). Reducing retention and learning disability placement through Reading Recovery: An educationally sound cost-effective choice. In R. L. Allington & S. A. Walmsley, *No quick fix: Rethinking literacy in America's elementary schools* (pp. 116–136). New York: Teachers College Press, and Newark DE: International Reading Association.

MacArthur, C., Schwartz, S., & Graham, S. (1991). Effects of a receptor peer revision strategy in special education classrooms. *Learning Disabilities: Research and Practice, 6,* 201–210.

Mathes, P. G., Grek, M. L., Howard, J. K., Babyak, A. E., & Allen, S. H. (1999). Peer-assisted learning strategies for first-grade readers: A tool for preventing early reading failure. *Learning Disabilities Research and Practice, 14,* 50–60.

Mayher, J. S., Lester, N. B., & Pradl, G. M. (1983). *Learning to write/writing to learn.* Upper Montclair, NJ: Boynton/Cook.

McCormack, R. L., & Paratore, J. R. (1999) *"What do you do down there anyway,"* teachers ask: *A reading teacher's intervention using grade-level text with struggling third-grade readers.* Paper presented at National Reading Conference, Orlando, FL.

McCormick, S. (1999). *Instructing students who have literacy problems.* Upper Saddle River, NJ: Merrill.

McCormick, S. (1995). *Instructing students who have literacy problems* (2nd ed.). Englewood Cliffs, NJ: Merrill/Prentice Hall.

McCormick, S. (1994). A nonreader becomes a reader: A case study of literacy acquisition by a severely disabled reader. *Reading Research Quarterly, 29,* 156–177.

McDermott, R. P. (1978). Pirandello in the classroom: On the possibility of equal educational opportunity in American culture. In M. C. Reynolds (Ed.), *Futures of exceptional children: Emerging structures* (pp. 41–64). Reston, VA: Council for Exceptional Children.

McGill-Franzen, A., & Allington, R. L. (1991). The gridlock of low reading achievement: Perspectives on practice and policy. *Remedial and Special Education, 12,* 20–30.

McGinley, W. J., & Denner, P. R. (1987). Story impressions: A prereading/writing activity. *Journal of Reading, 31,* 248–253.

McKenna, M. C. (1983). Informal reading inventories: A review of the issues. *The Reading Teacher, 36*, 670–679.

McKeown, M. G. (1993). Creating effective definitions for young word learners. *Reading Research Quarterly, 28*, 16–31.

Mead, M. (1995). Enriching the reading process with software. *Closing the Gap, 13(5)*, 1, 11.

Meyer, B. S. F., & Freedle, R. O. (1984). Effectiveness of discourse type on recall. *American Educational Research Journal, 21*, 121–143.

Miller, G. A., & Gildea, P. (1987). How children learn words. *Scientific American, 257*, 94–99.

Miller, S., DeVivo, K., LaRossa, A., Pycha, A., Peterson, B., Tallal, P., Merzenich, M., & Jenkins, W. (1998). Acoustically modified speech and language training reduces risk for academic difficulties. *Society for Neuroscience, 24*.

Miller, S. D., & Yochum, N. (1991). Asking students about the nature of their reading difficulties. *Journal of Reading Behavior, 23*, 465–485.

Moats, L. (1998). Teaching decoding. *American Educator, 22*, 42–65.

Moffett, J. M., & Wagner, B. J. (1983). *Student-centered language arts and reading, K-13: A handbook for teachers* (3rd ed.). Boston: Houghton Mifflin.

Moll, L. C., & González, N. (1994). Lessons from research with language-minority children. *Journal of Reading Behavior, 26*, 439–456.

Moore, D., & Arthur, S. V. (1981). Possible sentences. In E. D. Dishner, T. W. Bean, & J. E. Readence (Eds.), *Reading in the content areas: Improving classroom instruction* (pp. 138–142). Dubuque IA: Kendall/Hunt.

Morris, D. (1998). Assessing printed word knowledge in beginning readers: The Early Reading Screening Instrument (ERSI). *Illinois Reading Council Journal, 26*, 30–41.

Morris, D., & Nelson, L. (1992). Supported oral reading with low-achieving second graders. *Reading Research and Instruction, 31*, 49–63.

Morris, D., Shaw, B., & Perney, J. (1990). Helping low readers in grades 2 and 3: An after school volunteer tutoring program. *Elementary School Journal, 91*, 133–150.

Morrow, L. M., Gambrell, L., Kapinus, B., Koskinen, P., Marshall, N., & Mitchell, J. N. (1986). Retelling: A strategy for reading instruction and assessment. In J. A. Niles & R. Lalik (Eds.), *Solving problems in literacy: Learners, teachers, and researchers: Thirty-fifth yearbook of the National Reading Conference* (pp. 73–80). Rochester, NY: National Reading Conference.

Morrow, L. M., & Weinstein, C. S. (1986). Encouraging voluntary reading: The impact of a literature program on children's use of library corners. *Reading Research Quarterly, 21*, 330–346.

Mossburg, J. (1989). A new approach to an old problem: Remediation not just another pull-out. *The Reading Teacher, 42*, 342–343.

Moustafa, M. (1993). Recoding in whole language reading instruction. *Language Arts, 70*, 483–487.

Moustafa, M. (1995). Children's productive phonological recoding. *Reading Research Quarterly, 30*, 464–476.

Moustafa, M., & Maldonado-Colon, E. (1998). Whole-to-part phonics instruction: Building on what children know to help them know more. *The Reading Teacher, 52*, 448–461.

Murphy, L., Impara, J., & Plake, B. (Eds.). (1999). *Tests in Print V: An index to tests, test reviews, and the literature on special tests*. Lincoln, NB: Buros Institute of Mental Measurements, University of Nebraska-Lincoln.

Muter, V., Hulme, C., & Taylor, S. (1998). Segmentation, not rhyming, predicts early progress in learning to read. *Journal of Experimental Child Psychology, 71*, 3–27.

Myers, J., & Lytle, S. (1986). Assessment of the learning process. *Exceptional Children, 53,* 138–144.

Nagy, W., Anderson R., & Herman, P. (1987). Learning word meanings from context during normal reading. *American Educational Research Journal, 24,* 237–270.

Nagy, W. E., & Scott, J. A. (2000). Vocabulary processes. In R. Barr, M. L. Kamil, P. Mosenthal, & P. D. Pearson (Eds.), *Handbook of reading research* (Vol. III, pp. 269–284), Mahwah, NJ: Lawrence Erlbaum Associates.

Nasland, J. C., & Schneider, W. (1996). Kindergarten letter knowledge, phonological skills, and memory processes: Relative effects on early literacy. *Journal of Experimental Child Psychology, 62,* 30–59.

National Assessment of Educational Progress. (1999). *NAEP 1998 reading report card: National and state highlights.* Washington, DC: National Center for Educational Statistics, Office of Educational Research and Improvement, U.S. Department of Education.

National Institute of Child Health and Human Development. (1999). *Keys to successful learning* (pp. 1–3). Washington, DC: National Institute for Child Health and Development.

National Reading Panel. (1999 February 22). *Progress report.* Washington, DC: National Institute of Child Health and Human Development.

National Research Council. (1998). *Preventing reading difficulties in young children.* Washington, DC: National Academy of Sciences.

Newman, A. P. (1994). Adult literacy programs: An overview. *Learning Disabilities: A Multidisciplinary Journal, 5(1),* 51–61.

Nist, S. L., & Kirby, K. (1986). Teaching comprehension and study strategies through modeling and thinking aloud. *Reading Research and Instruction, 25,* 254–264.

O'Brien, C. A. (1973). *Teaching the language-different child to read.* Columbus, OH: Merrill.

Office of Bilingual Education and Minority Languages Affairs (1994, November 1). *NABE News,* pp. 5–6.

Ogle, D. (1986). KWL: A teaching model that develops active reading of expository text. *The Reading Teacher, 39,* 564–570.

Ortiz, A. (1997). Learning disabilities occurring concomitantly with linguistic differences. *Journal of Learning Disabilities, 30,* 221–232.

Orton, S. (1937). *Reading, writing, and speech problems of children.* New York: Norton.

Pace, A. J., Marshall, N., Horowitz, R., Lipson, M. Y., & Lucido, P. (1989). When prior knowledge doesn't facilitate some text comprehension: An examination of some of the issues. In S. McCormick & J. Autell (Eds.), *Cognitive and social perspectives for literacy research and instruction: Thirty-eighth yearbook of the National Reading Conference* (pp. 213–224). Chicago, IL: National Reading Conference.

Palincsar, A., & Brown, A. L. (1984). Reciprocal teaching of comprehension: Fostering and comprehension-monitoring activities. *Cognition and Instruction, 1,* 117–175.

Paris, S. G., Wasik, B. A., & Turner, J. C. (1991). The development of strategic readers. In R. Barr, M. L. Kamil, P. Mosenthal, & P. D. Pearson (Eds.), *Handbook of reading research* (Vol. II, pp. 609–640). White Plains, NY: Longman.

PASE v. *Hannon,* 506 F. Supp 832 (N. D. Ill, 1980).

Pearl, R., Donahue, M., & Bryan, T. (1986). Social relationships of learning disabled children. In J. Toregeson & B. Wong (Eds.), *Psychological and educational perspectives on learning disabilities* (pp. 257–296). Orlando, FL: Academic Press.

Pearson, P. D., & Fielding L. (1991). Comprehension instruction. In R. Barr, M. L. Kamil, P. Mosenthal, & P. D. Pearson, *Handbook of reading research* (Vol. II, pp. 815–860). White Plains, NY: Longman.

Pennington, B. (1995). Genetics of learning disabilities. *Journal of Child Neurology, 10*, 9–577.

Perfetti, C. A. (1983). Discourse context, word identification, and reading ability. In J. F. Le Ny & W. Kintsch (Eds.), *Language and comprehension.* New York: North-Holland Publishing Company.

Perfetti, C. A. (1985). *Reading ability.* New York: Oxford University Press.

Perfetti, C. A. (1988). Verbal efficiency in reading ability. In M. Daneman, G. E. MacKinnon, & T. G. Waller (Eds.), *Reading research: Advances in theory and practice* (Vol. 6, pp. 109–143). New York: Academic.

Perfetti, C. A. (1991). Representations and awareness of the acquisition of reading competence. In L. Rieben & C. A. Perfetti (Eds.), *Learning to read: Basic research and its implications* (pp. 33–44). Hillsdale, NJ: Erlbaum.

Pflaum, S. W., Walberg, H. J., Karegianes, M. L., & Rasher, S. W. (1980). Reading instruction: A quantitative analysis. *Educational Researcher, 9*, 12–18.

Phillips, M. (1990, December 2). Ephemeral ixia plant kept off federal endangered list. *Miami Herald,* p. 6B.

Pikulski, J. J. (1994). Preventing reading failure: A review of five effective programs. *The Reading Teacher, 48*, 30–39.

Pikulski, J. J., & Shanahan, T. (1982). Informal reading inventories: A critical analysis. In J. J. Pikulski & T. Shanahan (Eds.), *Approaches to the informal evaluation of reading* (pp. 94–116). Newark, DE: International Reading Association.

Pinnell, G. S. (1989). Reading Recovery: Helping at-risk children learn to read. *The Elementary School Journal, 90*, 161–183.

Pinnell, G. S., Deford, D. E., & Lyons, C. A. (1988). *Reading Recovery: Early intervention for at-risk first graders.* Arlington, VA: Educational Research Service.

Pinnell, G. S., Fried, M. D., & Estice, R. M. (1990). Reading Recovery: Learning to make a difference. *The Reading Teacher, 43*, 282–295.

Pinnell, G. S., Lyons, C. A., Deford, D. E., Bryk, A. S., & Seltzer, M. (1994). Comparing instructional models for the literacy education of high-risk first graders. *Reading Research Quarterly, 29*, 9–39.

Pratt, L., & Beaty, J. J. (1999). *Transcultural children's literature.* Columbus OH: Merrill.

Pressley, M. (2000). Comprehension instruction in elementary schools: A quarter-century of progress. In B. M. Taylor, M. F. Graves & P. Van Der Brock (Eds.), *Reading for Meaning* (pp. 32–51). Newark, DE: International Reading Association, and New York: Teachers College Press.

Pressley, M. (2000). What should comprehension instruction be the instruction of. In R. Barr, M. L. Kamil, P. Mosenthal, & P. D. Pearson (Eds.), *Handbook of reading research* (Vol. III, pp. 545–561). Mahwah, NJ: Lawrence Erlbaum Associates.

Pressley, M., & Afflerbach, P. (1995). *Verbal protocols of reading: The nature of constructively responsive reading.* Hillsdale, NJ: Erlbaum.

Purcell-Gates, V. (1986). Lexical and syntactic knowledge of written narrative held by well-read-to kindergarteners and second graders. *Research in the Teaching of English, 22*, 128–157.

Purves, A. C., Rogers, T., & Soter, A. O. (1995). *How porcupines make love III: Readers, texts, cultures in the response-based literature classroom.* White Plains, NY: Longman.

Quirk, T. J., Tristman, D. A., Nailn, K., & Weinberg, S. (1975). Classroom behavior of teachers during compensatory reading instruction. *Journal of Educational Research, 68*, 185–192.

Rabinovitch, R. (1989). Dyslexia: Psychiatric considerations. In J. Money (Ed.), *Reading disability: Progress and research needs in dyslexia.* Baltimore, MD: Johns Hopkins University Press.

Rapp, D. (1979). Food allergy treatment for hyperkinesis. *Journal of Learning Disabilities, 12,* 608–616.

Rashotte, C. A., & Torgesen, J. K. (1985). Repeated reading and reading fluency. *Reading Research Quarterly, 20,* 180–188.

Rasinski, T. V., & Padek, N. D. (1996). *Holistic reading strategies: Teaching children who find reading difficult.* Columbus, OH: Merrill.

Rasinski, T. V., Padak, N. D., Linek, W. L., & Sturdevant, E. (1994). Effects of fluency development on urban second graders. *Journal of Educational Research, 87,* 158–165.

Read, C. (1971). Preschool children's knowledge of English phonology. *Harvard Educational Review, 41,* 1–34.

Read, C. (1975). *Children's categorization of speech sounds in English* (NCTE Research Reports, No. 17). Urbana, IL: National Council of Teachers of English.

Rehabilitation Act of 1993, Pub. L. No. 93–112, §504 (1973).

Reyes, M. D. (1992). Challenging venerable assumptions: Literacy instruction for linguistically different students. *Harvard Education Review, 62,* 427–446.

Richek, M. A. (1969). *A study of the affix structure of English: Affix frequency and teaching methods.* Unpublished paper, University of Chicago.

Richek, M. A. (1987). DRTA: 5 variations that facilitate independence in reading narratives. *Journal of Reading, 30,* 632–636.

Richek, M. A. (1989). *Increasing the achievement of your remedial reading students.* Paso Robles, CA: Bureau of Education and Research.

Richek, M. A. (1994). Field project at the Piccolo Elementary School, Chicago, IL.

Richek, M. A. (1999). *Reading success for at-risk children: Ideas that work.* Bellevue, WA: Bureau of Education and Research.

Richek, M. A., & Glick, L. C. (1991). Coordinating a literacy-support program with classroom instruction. *The Reading Teacher, 45,* 474–479.

Richek, M. A., & McTague, B. (1988). The "Curious George" strategy for students with reading problems. *The Reading Teacher, 42,* 220–225.

Richek, M. A., McTague, B. K., Anderson, C. A., Baker, K. S., Luchitz, M. M., Hendler, L. W., Hatchett, M. B., McGuier, D., & Nevel, M. (1989). The "Curious George" strategy: Experiences of nine teachers. *Reading: Issues and Practices, Maryland Reading Journal of the International Reading Association, 6,* 36–44.

Roberts, B. (1996). Spelling and the growth of concept of word as first graders write. *Reading Psychology: An International Quarterly, 17,* 229–252.

Robinson, H. M. (1972). Visual and auditory modalities related to methods for beginning reading. *Reading Research Quarterly, 8,* 7–41.

Rock, E., Fessler, M., & Church, R. (1997). The concomitance of learning disabilities and emotional/behavioral disorders: A conceptual model. *Journal of Learning Disabilities, 30,* 245–263.

Rosenblatt, L. (1983). *Literature as exploration* (4th ed.). New York: Modern Language Association.

Rosenthal, R., & Jacobson, L. (1968). *Pygmalion in the classroom.* New York: Holt, Reinhart, and Winston.

Roswell, F., & Chall, J. (1994a). *Creating successful readers: A practical guide to testing and teaching at all levels.* Chicago: Riverside.

Roswell, F., & Chall, J. (1994b). *Diagnostic assessments of reading with trial teaching strategies (DARTTS).* Chicago: Riverside.

Routman, R. (1995). *Invitations.* Portsmouth, NH: Heinemann.

Rowan, B., & Guthrie, L. T. (1989). The quality of Chapter I instruction: Results from a study of twenty-four schools. In R. E. Slavin, N. L. Karweit, & N. A. Madden (Eds.),

Effective programs for students at risk (pp. 195–219). Needham Heights, MA: Allyn and Bacon.

Rumelhart, D. E. (1985). Toward an interactive model of reading. In H. Singer & R. B. Ruddell (Eds.), *Theoretical models and processes of reading* (3rd ed.). Newark, DE: International Reading Association.

Runion, H. J. (1980). Hypoglycemia—fact or fiction? In W. Cruckshank (Ed.), *Approaches to learning disabilities: Vol. 1. The best of ACLD.* Syracuse, NY: Syracuse University Press.

Sadowski, M. (1985). The natural use of imagery in story comprehension and recall. *Reading Research Quarterly, 20,* 658–667.

Salvia, J., & Ysseldyke, J. (1998). *Assessment* (8th ed.). Boston: Houghton Mifflin.

Samuels, S. J. (1979). The method of repeated readings. *The Reading Teacher, 32,* 403–408.

Samuels, S. J. (1988). Decoding and automaticity: Helping poor readers become automatic at word recognition. *The Reading Teacher, 41,* 756–761.

Samuels, S. J. (1997). The method of repeated readings. *The Reading Teacher, 50,* 376–381.

Santa, C., Havens, L., & Harrison, S. (1989). Teaching secondary science through reading, writing, studying, and problem solving. In D. Lapp, J. Flood, & N. Farnan (Eds.), *Content area reading and learning: Instructional strategies.* Englewood Cliffs, NJ: Prentice Hall.

Santa, C. M., & Hoien, T. (1999). An assessment of Early Steps: A program for early intervention. *Reading Research Quarterly, 34,* 54–79.

Santa, C. M., Ford, A., Mickley, A., & Parker, D. (1997). *Reading intervention for primary students: First steps.* Paper presented at International Reading Association 42nd Annual Convention, Atlanta, GA.

Schlagal, R. C. (1989). Constancy and change in spelling development. *Reading Psychology: An International Quarterly, 10,* 207–232.

Sebesta, S. (1993). Creative drama and language arts. In B. E. Cullinan (Ed.), *Children's voices: Talk in the classroom* (pp. 33–46). Newark, DE: International Reading Association.

Segalowitz, N., & Gatbonton, E. (1995). Automaticity and lexical skills in second language fluency: Implications for computer assisted language learning. *Computer Assisted Language Learning, 8,* 129–149.

Shanahan, T., & Shanahan, S. (1997). Character perspective charting: Helping children to develop a more complete conception of story. *The Reading Teacher, 50,* 668–677.

Shapiro, S. (1994). From reading poetry to poetry reading in the classroom. *Illinois Reading Council Journal, 21,* 67–71.

Shapiro, S., & Welch, M. (1991). Using poetry with adolescents in a remedial reading program: A case study. *Reading Horizons, 31,* 318–331.

Shaywitz, B., & Shaywitz, S. (1998). Biological basis for reading disability: Functional disruption in the organization of the brain for reading disability. *Proceedings of the National Academy of Sciences, 95,* 1–3.

Shaywitz, S., Fletcher, J., Holahan, J., Shneider, A., Marchione, K., Steubing, K., Francis, D., Pugh, K., & Shaywitz, B. (1999). Persistence of dyslexia: The Connecticut longitudinal study at adolescence. *Pediatrics, 104,* 1351–1360.

Shelfelbine, J. (1991). *A syllabic-unit approach to teaching syllabication strategies.* New York: Teachers College, Columbia University.

Silver, L. (1998). *The misunderstood child.* New York: Times Books.

Sitler, H. C. (1995). Letters from Emily: Writing-reading connections. *Language Arts, 72,* 360–365.

Slavin, R. (1991). *Educational psychology.* Englewood Cliffs, NJ: Prentice Hall.

Slavin, R. E. (1984). Students motivating students to excel: Cooperative incentives, cooperative tasks, and student achievement. *Elementary School Journal, 85,* 53–64.

Slavin, R. E., Madden, N. A., Karweit, N. L., Dolan, L., & Wasik, B. A. (1992). *Success for All: A relentless approach to prevention and early intervention in elementary schools.* Arlington, VA: Educational Research Service.

Slavin, R. E., Madden, N. A., Karweit, N. L., Livermon, B. J., & Dolan, L. (1990). Success for All: First year outcomes of a comprehensive plan for reforming urban education. *American Educational Research Journal, 27,* 255–278.

Smith, S. (1992). Familial patterns of learning disabilities. *Annals of Dyslexia, 42,* 143–158.

Snider, V. E., & Tarver, S. G. (1987). The effect of early reading failure on acquisition of knowledge among students with reading disabilities. *Journal of Learning Disabilities, 20,* 351–356.

Snow, C. E., Burns, M. S., & Griffin, P. (1998). *Preventing reading difficulties in young children.* Washington, DC: National Academy Press.

Spache, G. D. (1981). *Diagnosing and correcting reading disabilities.* Boston: Allyn and Bacon.

Spear-Swerling, L., & Sternberg, R. J. (1996). *Off track: When poor readers become "learning disabled."* Boulder, CO: Westview Press.

Spiegel, D. L. (1988). Silver bullets, babies, and bath water: Literature response groups in a balanced literary program. *The Reading Teacher, 52,* 114–124.

Spinelli, C. G. (1998–1999). Breaking down barriers—building strong foundations: Parents and teachers of exceptional students working together. *Learning Disabilities: A Multidisciplinary Journal, 9,* 123–130.

Spiro, R. J., Bruce, B. C., & Brewer, W. F. (Eds.). (1980). *Theoretical issues in reading comprehension.* Hillsdale, NJ: Erlbaum.

Stahl, S. A. (1988). Is there evidence to support matching reading styles and initial reading methods? A reply to Carbo. *Phi Delta Kappan, 70,* 317–322.

Stahl, S. A. (1992). Saying the "p" word: Nine guidelines for exemplary phonics instruction. *The Reading Teacher, 45,* 618–625.

Stahl, S. A., & Fairbanks, M. (1986). The effects of vocabulary instruction: A model-based meta-analysis. *Review of Educational Research, 56,* 72–110.

Stahl, S. A., & Heubach, K. (1993). *Changing reading instruction in second grade: A fluency-oriented program.* University of Georgia: National Reading Research Center.

Stahl, S. A., & Murray, B. A. (1994). Defining phonological awareness and its relationship to early reading. *Journal of Educational Psychology, 86,* 221–234.

Stahl, S. A., Richek, M. A., & Vandiver, R. J. (1991). Learning meaning through listening: A sixth-grade replication. In J. Zutell & S. McCormick (Eds.), *Learner factors/teacher factors: Issues in literacy research and instruction* (pp. 185–192). Chicago, IL: National Reading Conference.

Stahl, S., Heubach, K., & Cramond, B. (1997). *Fluency-oriented reading instruction.* Reading Research Report No. 79. Athens, GA, and College Park, MD: National Reading Research Center of the University of Georgia and the University of Maryland.

Stanovich, K. E. (1980). Toward an interactive-compensatory model of individual differences in the development of reading fluency. *Reading Research Quarterly, 16,* 32–71.

Stanovich, K. E. (1982a). Individual differences in the cognitive processes of reading: I. Word decoding *Journal of Learning Disabilities, 15,* 485–493.

Stanovich, K. E. (1982b). Individual differences in the cognitive processes of reading: II. Text level processes. *Journal of Learning Disabilities, 15,* 549–554.

Stanovich, K. E. (1986). Matthew effects in reading: Some consequences of individual differences in the acquisition of literacy. *Reading Research Quarterly, 21,* 360–406.

Stanovich, K. E. (1988a). *Children's reading and the development of phonological awareness.* Detroit: Wayne State University Press.

Stanovich, K. E. (1988b). The right and wrong places to look for the cognitive locus of reading disability. *Annals of Dyslexia, 38,* 154–177.

Stanovich, K. E. (1991). Word recognition: Changing perspectives. In R. Barr, M. L. Kamil, P. Mosenthal, & P. D. Pearson (Eds.), *Handbook of reading research* (Vol. 2, pp. 418–452). New York: Longman.

Stanovich, K. E. (1993–1994). Romance and reality. Distinguished educator series. *The Reading Teacher, 47,* 280–291.

Stanovich, K. E., & Cunningham, A. E. (1993). Where does knowledge come from? Specific associations between print exposure and information acquisition. *Journal of Educational Psychology, 85,* 211–229.

Stanovich, K. E., & Siegel, L. S. (1994). Phenotypic performance profile of children with reading disabilities: A regression-based test of the phonological-core variable difference model. *Journal of Educational Psychology, 86,* 24–58.

Stauffer, R. G. (1975). *Directing the reading-thinking process.* New York: Harper and Row.

Stauffer, R. G. (1980). *The language experience approach to the teaching of reading* (2nd ed.). New York: Harper and Row.

Sternberg, R. J. (1985). *Beyond IQ: A triarchic theory of human intelligence.* New York: Cambridge University Press.

Sternberg, R. J. (1987). Most vocabulary is learned from context. In M. G. McKeown & M. E. Curtis (Eds.), *The nature of vocabulary acquisition* (pp. 89–105). Hillsdale, NJ: Erlbaum.

Sternberg, R. J. (1999). Ability and expertise: It's time to replace the current model of intelligence. *American Educator 23,* 1–30, 50.

Sundbye, N. (1987). Text explicitness and inferential questioning: Effects on story understanding and recall. *Reading Research Quarterly, 22,* 82–98.

Superkids Educational Software (1999). *www.superkids.com/aweb/pages/reviews/typing1/sw_suml.shtml.*

Tallal, P., Miller, S. L., Jenkins, W., & Merzenich, M. M. (1997). The role of temporal processing in developmental language-based learning disorders: Research and Clinical implications. In B. Blachman (Ed.), *Foundations of reading acquisition and dyslexia* (pp. 49–66). Mahwah, NJ: Lawrence Erlbaum.

Taylor, B. M. (1992): Text structure, comprehension, and recall. In S. J. Samuels & A. E. Farstrup (Eds.), *What research has to say about reading comprehension* (pp. 220–235). Newark, DE: International Reading Association.

Taylor, B. M., Frye, B. J., Short, R., & Shearer, B. (1992). Classroom teachers prevent reading failure among low-achieving first-grade students. *The Reading Teacher, 45,* 592–597.

Taylor, B. M., Strait, J., & Medo, M. A. (1994). Early intervention is reading: Supplemental instruction for groups of low-achieving students provided by first grade teachers. In E. H. Hiebert and B. M. Taylor (Eds.), *Getting reading right from the start: Effective early literacy interventions.* New York: Allyn & Bacon.

Thomas, A., & Chess, S. (1977). *Temperament and development.* New York: Bruner/Mazel.

Thomson, N. (1987). *Understanding teenagers' reading.* New York: Nichols.

Thorndike, R. L. (1973). *Reading comprehension education in fifteen countries.* New York: Wiley.

Tierney, R. J. (1990). Redefining reading comprehension. *Educational Leadership, 47,* 37–42.

Trachtenburg, P. (1990). Using children's literature to enhance phonics instruction. *The Reading Teacher, 43,* 648–654.

Torgesen, J. (1998). Catch them before they fall. *American Educator, 22,* 32–51.

Torgeson, J. K. (1998). Learning disabilities: An historical and conceptual overview. In B. Y. L. Wong (Ed.), *Learning about learning disabilities*. (2nd ed., pp. 3–34). San Diego, CA: Academic Press.

Treiman, R. (1985). Onsets and rimes as units of spoken syllables: Evidence from children. *Journal of Experimental Child Psychology, 39,* 161–181.

Trieman, R., Tincoff, R., & Richmond-Welty, E. D. (1996). Letter names help children to connect print and speech. *Developmental Psychology, 32,* 505–514.

Turnbull, A., and Turnbull, H. (1996). Families, professionals, and exceptionality. Upper Saddle River, NJ: Merrill.

U.S. Census Bureau. (1998). Washington, DC. Website: *http://pbs.or/manyfaces/statistics/language_table.html.*

U.S. Department of Commerce, Economics and Statistics Administration, Bureau of the Census. (1977). *Census brief: Children with single parents—how they fare.* Washington, DC: U.S. Department of Commerce; Bureau of the Census.

U.S. Department of Education. (1994). *The national adult literacy survey.* Washington, DC: U.S. Department of Education.

U.S. Department of Education. (1997). *Reauthorization of the Elementary and Secondary Education Act.* Washington, DC: U.S. Department of Education.

U.S. Department of Education (1998). *To assure the free appropriate public education of all children with disabilities. Twentieth annual report to Congress on the implementation of Individuals with Disabilities Education Act.* Washington, DC: U.S. Government Printing Office.

U.S. Department of Education. (1999). *Final regulations for the 1997 Individuals with Disabilities Education Act (IDEA-1997).* Washington, DC: U.S. Government Printing Office.

Vacca, J., Vacca, R., and Gove, M. (2000). *Reading and learning to read.* New York: Longman.

van den Bosch, K., van Bon, W. H. J., & Schreuder, R. (1995). Poor readers' decoding skills: Effects of training with limited exposure duration. *Reading Research Quarterly, 30,* 110–125.

Van Der Brock, P., & Kremer, K. E. (2000). The mind in action: What it means to comprehend during reading. In B. M. Taylor, M. F. Graves, & P. Van Der Brock (Eds.), *Reading for meaning: Fostering comprehension in the middle grades* (pp. 1–31). Newark, DE: International Reading Association, and New York: Teachers College Press.

van Dijk, T. A., & Kintsch, W. (1983). *Strategies of discourse comprehension.* San Diego, CA: Academic.

van Ijzendoorn, M. H., & Bus, A. G. (1994). Meta-analytic confirmation of the nonword reading deficit in developmental dyslexia. *Reading Research Quarterly, 29(3),* 250–264.

Vaughn, S. (1991). Social skills enhancement in students with learning disabilities. In B. Wong (Ed.), *Learning about learning disabilities* (pp. 408–440). San Diego, CA: Academic Press.

Vellutino, F. R. (1987). Dyslexia. *Scientific American, 256,* 34–41.

Vellutino, F. R., Scanlon, D. M., Sipay, E. R., Small, S. G., Chen, R., Pratt, A., & Denckla, M. B. (1996). Cognitive profiles of difficult-to-remediate and readily remediated poor readers: Early intervention as a vehicle for distinguishing between cognitive and experiential deficits as basic causes of specific reading disability. *Journal of Educational Psychology, 88,* 601–638.

Wade, S. E. (1990). Using think-alouds to assess comprehension. *The Reading Teacher, 43,* 442–451.

Walmsley, S., & Allington, R. (1995). Redefining and reforming instructional support programs for at-risk readers. In R. Allington & S. Walmsley (Eds.), *No quick fix: Rethinking literacy programs in America's elementary schools* (pp. 19–44). Newark, DE: International Reading Association.

Walsh, D. J., Price, G. G., & Gillingham, M. G. (1988). The critical but transitory importance of letter naming. *Reading Research Quarterly, 23(2),* 108–122.

Ward, B. J. (1992). [Letter to the editor]. *Journal of Learning Disabilities, 25,* 274–275.

Ware, C. (1995). *www.kentuckyconnect.com/heraldleader/software/1995/0712/f0916ware.html.*

Warner, S. A. (1963). *Teacher.* New York: Simon and Schuster.

Wasik, B. A., & Slavin, R. E. (1993). Preventing early reading failure with one-to-one tutoring: A review of five programs. *Reading Research Quarterly, 28,* 179–200.

Wechsler, D. (1975). *The measurement and appraisal of adult intelligence.* Baltimore, MD: Williams & Wilkins.

Weech, J. (1994). Writing the story before reading it. *Journal of Reading, 37,* 364–367.

Wegner, P. (1996). All school implementation of a new grouping format. In J. Caldwell and M. Ford (Eds.), *Where have all the bluebirds gone: Transforming ability-based reading classrooms* (pp. 110–117). Schofield, WI: Wisconsin State Reading Association.

Wells, M. C. (1992–1993). At the junction of reading and writing: How dialogue journals contribute to students' reading development. *Journal of Reading, 36,* 294–302.

Wesson, M. D. (1993). Diagnosis and management of reading dysfunction for the primary care optometrist (symposium). *Optometry and Vision Science, 70,* 357–368.

West, R. F., Stanovich, K. E., & Mitchell, H. R. (1993). Reading in the real world and its correlates. *Reading Research Quarterly, 28,* 35–50.

West T. (1997). Slow words, quick images—Dyslexia as an advantage in tomorrow's workplace. In P. Gerber & D. Brown (Eds.), *Learning Disabilities and Employment.* Austin, TX: Pro-Ed.

White, B. F. (1995). Effects of autobiographical writing before reading on students' responses to short stories. *Journal of Educational Research, 88,* 173–184.

Whitman, B. Y. (2000). Living with a child with ADHD: Principles of family living, behavior management, and family support. In P. Accardo, T. Blondis, B. Whitman, & M. Stein (Eds.), *Attention deficits and hyperactivity in children and adults* (pp. 441–460). New York: Marcel Dekker, Inc.

Williams, J. P. (1993). Comprehension of students with and without learning disabilities: Identification of narrative themes and idiosyncratic text representations. *Journal of Educational Psychology, 93,* 631–641.

Wilson, P. T. (1988). *Let's think about reading and reading instruction: A primer for tutors and teachers.* Dubuque, IA: Kendall/Hunt.

Wittrock, M. C. (1984). Writing and the teaching of reading. In J. M. Jensen (Ed.), *Composing and comprehending* (pp. 77–83). Urbana, IL: ERIC Clearinghouse on Reading and Communication Skills.

Wixson, K. (1983). Questions about a text: What you ask about is what children learn. *The Reading Teacher, 37,* 287–293.

Wixson, K., Peters, C., Wever, E., & Roeber, E. (1987). New directions in statewide reading assessment. *The Reading Teacher, 40,* 749–755.

Wolf, S. A. (1998). The flight of reading: Shifts in instruction, orchestration, and attitudes through classroom theater. *Reading Research Quarterly, 33,* 382–415.

Wolfram, W. (1969). *A sociolinguistic description of Detroit Negro speech.* Washington, DC: Center for Applied Linguistics.

Wollman-Bonilla, J. E., & Werchadlo, B. (1995). Literature response journals in a first-grade classroom. *Language Arts, 72,* 562–570.

Wong, B. Y. (1986). A cognitive approach to teaching spelling. *Exceptional Children, 53,* 169–172.

Yopp, H. K. (1992). Developing phonemic awareness in young children. *The Reading Teacher, 45,* 696–703.

Yasutake, D., & Bryan, T. (1995). The influence of affect on the achievement and behavior of students with learning disabilities. *Journal of Learning Disabilities, 28,* 329–334.

Yasutake, D., & Bryan, T. (1996). The influence of induced positive affect on middle school children with and without learning disabilities. *Learning Disabilities Research and Practice, 10,* 38–45.

Zigmond, N. (1990). Rethinking secondary programs for students with learning disabilities. *Focus on Exceptional Children, 23,* 1–23.

Zigmond, N., Vallecorsa, A., & Leinhardt, G. (1980). Reading instruction for students with learning disabilities. *Topics in Language Disorders, 1,* 89–98.

NAME INDEX

SUBJECT INDEX

TEST INDEX